ELDRIDGE
TIDE AND PILOT
2019

Our One Hundred Forty-Fifth Year of Continuous Publication

CONTENTS

☛ **NOTE:** The information in this volume has been compiled from U. S. Government sources and others, and carefully checked. The Publishers cannot assume any liability for errors, omissions, or changes.

Printed in U.S.A.   Copyright 2018 by Eldridge Maritime LLC   ISBN 978-1-883465-25-4

The History of ELDRIDGE

In 1854 George Eldridge of Chatham, a celebrated cartographer, published "Eldridge's Pilot for Vineyard Sound and Monomoy Shoals." Its 32 pages were devoted to "Dangers," embellished with his personal observations, and to Compass Courses and Distances, etc. This volume was the precursor of the Tide and Pilot Book, which followed 21 years later. In 1870 George Eldridge published another small book, called the "Compass Test," and asked his son, George W. Eldridge, to go to Vineyard Haven and sell it for him, along with the charts he produced.

Son George W. Eldridge was dynamic, restless, and inventive. He was glad to move to the Vineyard, for Vineyard Haven was at that time an important harbor for large vessels. Frequently as many as 100 schooners would anchor to await a fair current and George W. would go out to them in his catboat to sell his father's publications. He was constantly asked by mariners what time the current turned to run East or West in the Sound, so he began making observations. One day, while in the ship chandlery of Charles Holmes, he made the first draft of a current table. Shortly after, with the help of his father, he worked out the tables for places other than Vineyard Sound, and in 1875 the first Tide Book was published. It did not take long for mariners to realize the value of this information, and it soon became an indispensable book to all who sailed the Atlantic Coast from New York east. Gradually George W. added more important information, such as his explanation of the unusual currents which caused so many vessels to founder in the "Graveyard."

Captain George W. Eldridge based the tables on his own observations. In later years, knowing that the government's scientific calculations are the most accurate obtainable, the publishers have made use of them; some tables are directly taken from government figures and others, which the government does not give in daily schedules, are computed by the publishers from government predictions. Since the Captain's day there have been many changes and additions in the book to keep abreast of modern navigational aids.

In 1910 Captain George W. Eldridge transferred the management of the book to the next generation of his family, as he was interested in developing his chart business and inventing aids to navigation. On his death in 1914, his son-in-law, Wilfrid O. White became Publisher. An expert in marine navigation and President of Wilfrid O. White & Sons Co., compass manufacturers, Wilfrid served as Publisher until his death in 1955. Wilfrid's son Robert (Bob) Eldridge White and Bob's wife Molly then became publishers and expanded the coverage of the book and significantly increased its readership. On Bob's death in 1990, Molly continued as Publisher with valuable assistance from her son Ridge and daughter-in-law Linda. On Molly's passing in 2004 the book moved once again into the hands of the next (fifth) generation. Ridge and Linda continued the book's traditions while modernizing its production. With Linda's passing in 2015, daughter Jenny and her husband Peter joined Ridge as publishers, becoming the sixth generation of family members to hold the title.

Whether new to ELDRIDGE or a longtime reader, we welcome you aboard! Please continue to offer your suggestions and, where necessary, corrections. Your sharp eyes keep us on course. We hope, as did Captain George W. Eldridge, that this book might ensure for you a "Fair Tide" and the safety of your ship.

The Publishers

Yours for a fair tide
Geo. W. Eldridge

Contact Us

Publishers: Jenny White Kuliesis, Peter Kuliesis, and Robert Eldridge White, Jr.

18 Overlook Road   pilot@eldridgetide.com   (617) 449-7393
Arlington, MA 02474

Free Supplement
Available June 1 — Changes and updates through May 15, 2019

Download or sign up to receive a copy via email at http://eldridgetide.com/up-dates/, or mail a self-addressed, stamped envelope to the address above.

Story Contest 2020: What has the sea given you?

"Neptune giveth!"—In our family, mostly exclaimed when a tennis ball unexpect-edly washes ashore, much to our dogs' delight. Perhaps you have a tale of greater significance.

> Did the perfect pair of ash oars with neatly sewn leathers wash up on your stretch of marsh?
> Perhaps you met your soulmate while plucking mussels from the jetty?
> Did time aboard shape who you are?

For the 2020 edition, we want to hear your true story about a gift, material or otherwise, that came to you from the sea.

Deadline: August 17, 2019
Length: 600 words, give or take a few
How to submit: Email (preferred) or mail submissions to the address above. Submitted materials will not be returned.

The winning entry will be published in the 2020 edition and the author will receive a copy of the book, an Eldridge tote bag and $200. Submissions must be original, previously unpublished works and grant the publisher nonexclusive rights to publish winning entries in the book and on our website.

Be sure to read the winning 2019 submission on p. 260.

A Note From the Publishers

Dear Readers:

Your continued enthusiasm for this little yellow book, your feedback and engagement, makes this unique publication what it is. Know that, as in years past, ELDRIDGE is the work of many. Our thanks to the topic experts, article editors, authors, and advisors who contributed to this edition. We also want to acknowledge the committed advertisers whose support is essential to this book.

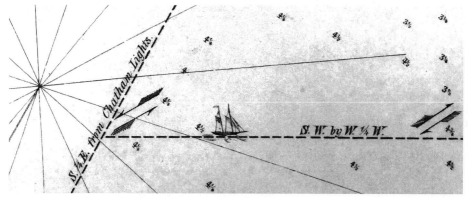

Detail from the 1852 Eldridge chart *Chatham Lights to South West Part of Handkerchief*

While plotting your course up the coast or waiting for the clam flats to emerge from the retreating tide, we trust you'll find a moment to enjoy some of the additions for 2019:

- ☞ Jan Adkins, prolific author and expert in many fields, provides an illustrated how-to on line work (p. 262) as well as a treatise on how to be a top-notch guest aboard (p. 216)
- ☞ Jennifer Francis, Research Professor in Marine & Coastal Sciences, explores why coastal flooding events have increased six-fold along the east coast since the 1970s (p. 174)
- ☞ Rusty Kransky, our 2019 Eldridge Story Contest Winner, shares his tale (p. 260)
- ☞ Jay MacLaughlin, fisherman and boater, extols the value of immersion (p. 252)
- ☞ Pete Malinowski of Billion Oyster Project shares its history and mission (p. 237)
- ☞ Peter Spectre, freelance writer, takes a look at the perils of progress when a bridge is built to Deer Island (p. 211)
- ☞ Erica M. Szuplat, a Cape Cod-based artist, has penned sketches found throughout the book (pp. 175, 203, 260, 271)
- ☞ Lou Tabory, a pioneer of East Coast fly fishing, highlights the thrill of fishing fast water—and the skill required to do it well (p. 270)

Yours for a fair tide,

Jenny White Kuliesis, Peter Kuliesis, and Robert Eldridge White, Jr.

INLAND NAVIGATION RULES

Good Seamanship Rule (Rule 7): Every vessel shall use all available means appropriate to the prevailing circumstances and conditions to determine if risk of collision exists. If there is any doubt, such risk shall be deemed to exist.

General right-of-way (Rule 18): Vessel categories are listed in <u>decreasing</u> order of having the right-of-way:

- Vessel not under command (most right of way)
- Vessel restricted in ability to maneuver, in a narrow fairway or channel
- Vessel engaged in fishing with nets, lines, or trawls (but not trolling lines)
- Sailing vessel (sails only)
- Power-driven vessel (least right of way)

Vessels Under Power

Overtaking (Rule 13): A vessel overtaking another is the "give-way" vessel and must stay clear of the overtaken or "stand-on" vessel. The overtaking vessel is to sound one short blast if it intends to pass on the other vessel's starboard side, and two short blasts if it intends to pass on the other's port side. The overtaken vessel must respond with the identical sound signal if it agrees, and must maintain course and speed during the passing situation.

Meeting head-on (Rule 14): When two vessels are meeting approximately head-on, neither has right-of-way. Unless it is otherwise agreed, each vessel should turn to starboard and pass port to port.

Memorized for generations by mariners, the verse below tells what to do when power vessels meet at night.

The Rule of the Road

When all three lights I see ahead,
I turn to **Starboard** and show my **Red:**
Green to Green, Red to Red,
Perfect Safety – Go Ahead.

But if to **Starboard Red appear,**
It is my duty to keep clear –
To act as judgment says is proper:
To **Port** or **Starboard, Back** or **Stop** her.

And if upon my **Port** is seen
A Steamer's **Starboard** light of **Green,**
I hold my course and watch to see
That **Green** to **Port** keeps Clear of me.

Both in safety and in doubt
Always keep a good look out.
In danger, with no room to turn,
Ease her, **Stop** her, **Go Astern.**

Crossing (Rule 15): When two vessels approaching each other are neither in an overtaking or meeting situation, they are deemed to be crossing. The power vessel which has the other on its starboard side is the give-way vessel and must change course, slow down, or stop. The vessel which is on the right, is in the right.

Vessels Under Sail

Port-Starboard (Rule 12): A vessel on the port tack shall keep clear of one on the starboard tack.

Windward-Leeward (Rule 12): When both vessels are on the same tack, the vessel to windward shall keep clear of a vessel to leeward.

Sail vs. Power (Rule 18): Generally, a sailboat has right of way over a powerboat. However: (1) a sailboat overtaking a powerboat must keep clear; (2) sailboats operating in a narrow channel shall keep clear of a power vessel which can safely navigate only within a narrow channel; (3) sailboats must give way to a vessel which is fishing, a vessel restricted in its ability to maneuver, and a vessel not under command.

FEDERAL SAFETY EQUIPMENT REQUIREMENTS
(These are minimum requirements. Some states require additional equipment.)

Sound Signaling Devices

Under 39.4' or 12 meters:
> Must have some means of making an efficient sound signal

Over 39.4' or 12 meters to 65' or 20 meters:
> Must have a whistle or horn

Over 65' or 20 meters:
> Must have a whistle or horn and a bell

Visual Distress Signals

Under 16' or 5 meters:
> Night: 1 electric SOS flashlight or 3 day/night red flares

Over 16' or 5 meters:
> Day only: 1 orange flag, 3 floating or hand-held orange smoke signals
> Day and night: 3 hand-held, or 3 pistol, or 3 hand-held rocket, or 3 red flares

The following signals indicate distress or need of assistance:
see p. 243, Marine Emergency and Distress Calls

- A gun or other explosive signal fired at intervals of about 1 minute
- A continuous sounding with any fog-signaling apparatus
- Rockets or shells, fired one at a time or at short intervals
- SOS transmitted by any signaling method
- "Mayday" on the radiotelephone (channel 16)
- International Code Signal flags "NC"
- An orange square flag with a black square over a black ball
- Flames on the vessel
- Rocket parachute flare or hand-held flare
- Orange colored smoke
- Slowly and repeatedly raising and lowering outstretched arms
- Signals transmitted by EPIRB
- High intensity white light flashing 50-70 times per minute

Personal Flotation Devices (must be USCG approved)

Under 16' or 5 meters:
> 1 Type I, II, III, or V per person, USCG approved

Over 16' or 5 meters:
> 1 Type I, II, III, or V per person, and 1 Type IV per boat, USCG approved

Portable Fire Extinguishers (approved)

Under 26' 1 B-I, if no fixed extinguisher system in machinery space.
> (Not required on out-boards built so that vapor entrapment cannot occur.)

26-39' 2 B-I or 1 B-II if no fixed exting. system; 1 B-I, with a fixed exting. system.

40-65' 3 B-I or 1 B-II & 1 B-I, if no fixed exting. system; 2 B-I or 1 B-II with a fixed exting. system.

Back-Fire Flame Arrestor

One approved device per carburetor of all inboard gasoline engines.

At least 2 ventilator ducts fitted with cowls or their equivalent to ventilate efficiently the bilges of every engine and fuel tank compartment of boats using gasoline or other fuel with a flashpoint less than 110°F.

NAVIGATION LIGHTS

Definition of Lights

Masthead Light — a white light fixed over the centerline showing an unbroken light over an arc of 225°, from dead ahead to 22.5° abaft the beam on either side.

Sidelights — a green light on the starboard side and a red light on the port side showing an unbroken light over an arc of the horizon of 112.5°, from dead ahead to 22.5° abaft the beam on either side.

Sternlight — a white light placed as nearly as practicable at the stern showing an unbroken light over an arc of the horizon of 135°, 67.5° from dead aft to each side of the vessel.

All-round Light — an unbroken light over an arc of the horizon of 360°.

Towing Light — a yellow light with same characteristics as the sternlight.

Note: R. and Y. Flashing Lights are now authorized for vessels assigned to Traffic Control, Medical Emergencies, Search and Rescue, Fire-Fighting, Salvage, and Disabled Vessels.

When under way, in all weathers from sunset to sunrise, every vessel shall carry and exhibit the following lights

When Under Power Alone or When Under Power and Sail Combined

Under 39.4' or 12 meters:
 Masthead light visible 2 miles
 Sidelights visible 1 mile
 Stern light visible 2 miles (or in lieu of separate masthead and stern lights, an all-round white light visible 2 miles)

Over 39.4' or 12 meters to 65' or 20 meters::
 Masthead light visible 3 miles
 Sidelights visible 2 miles
 Stern light visible 2 miles

Sailing Vessels Under Way (Sail Only)

Under 22' or 7 meters:
 Either the lights listed below for sailing vessels under 65'; or a white light to be exhibited (for example, by shining it on the sail) in sufficient time to prevent collision
Under 65' or 20 meters: *may be combined in one tricolor lantern carried near top of mast*
 Sidelights visible 2 miles
 Stern light visible 2 miles

At Anchor

Vessels under 50 meters (165') must show an all-round white light visible 2 miles.

Vessels under 7 meters (22') need no light unless they are near a channel, a fairway, an anchorage or area where other vessels navigate.

Fishing

Vessels Trawling shall show, in addition to the appropriate lights above, 2 all-round lights in a vertical line, the upper green and the lower white.

Vessels Fishing (other than trawling) shall show, in addition to the appropriate lights above, 2 all-round lights, the upper red and the lower white.

When Towing or Being Towed

Towing Vessel: 2 masthead lights (if tow is less than 200 meters); 3 masthead lights in a vertical line forward (if tow exceeds 200 meters); sidelights; sternlight; a yellow tow light in vertical line above sternlight; a diamond shape where it can best be seen (if tow exceeds 200 meters).

Vessel Being Towed: sidelights; sternlight; a diamond shape where it can best be seen (if tow exceeds 200 meters).

SOUND SIGNALS FOR FOG

Ask your Chart Dealer for the latest Navigation Rules—Inland/International

Frequently, in fog, small sail or power boats cannot be heard or picked up by other vessels' radar. The Coast Guard strongly recommends that, to avoid collisions, all vessels carry Radar Reflectors mounted as high as possible.

All signals prescribed by this article for vessels under way shall be given:

> **First:** By Power-driven Vessels – On the Whistle or Horn.
> **Second:** By Sailing Vessels or Vessels being Towed – On the Fog Horn.

A prolonged blast shall mean a blast of 4 to 6 seconds' duration.
A short blast shall mean a blast of about one second's duration.

A power-driven vessel making way through the water shall sound at intervals of no more than 2 minutes a prolonged blast.

A power-driven vessel under way, but stopped and making no way through the water, shall sound at intervals of no more than 2 minutes 2 prolonged blasts with about 2 seconds between them.

A sailing vessel under way shall sound at intervals of not more than 2 minutes 1 prolonged blast followed by 2 short blasts regardless of tack.

A fishing vessel or a power-driven vessel towing or pushing another vessel shall sound every 2 minutes 1 prolonged blast followed by 2 short blasts. A vessel being towed shall sound 1 prolonged blast followed by 3 short blasts.

A vessel at anchor shall ring a bell rapidly for about 5 seconds at intervals of not more than 1 minute and may in addition sound 3 blasts — 1 short, 1 prolonged, 1 short — to give warning of her position to an approaching vessel. Vessels under 20 meters (65') shall not be required to sound these signals when anchored in a special anchorage area.

A vessel aground shall give the bell signal and shall, in addition, give 3 separate and distinct strokes of the bell both before and after the rapid ringing of the bell.

MANEUVERING AND WARNING SIGNALS

Inland Rules:

> 1 short blast: I intend to leave you on my port side.
> 2 short blasts: I intend to leave you on my starboard side.
> 3 short blasts: I am backing
> 5 or more short and rapid blasts: DANGER

Response: If in agreement, upon hearing the 1 or 2 blast signal, a vessel shall sound the same signal and take the steps necessary to effect a safe passing. If in doubt sound the danger signal.

International Rules:

> 1 short blast: I am altering my course to starboard.
> 2 short blasts: I am altering my course to port.
> 2 prolonged, 1 short blast: I am overtaking you on your starboard side.
> 2 prolonged, 2 short blasts: I am overtaking you on your port side.

Response in overtaking: prolonged blast, short blast, prolonged blast, short blast if agreeable.

> 3 short blasts: I am backing
> 5 or more short and rapid blasts: DANGER

Why Tides and Currents Often Behave Differently
Frequently Asked Questions

We are often asked such questions as, **"Why are the times of high water and current change not the same?"** Shouldn't an ebb current begin right after a high tide? Although tides (vertical height of water) and currents (horizontal movement) are inextricably related, they often behave rather differently.

If the Earth had a uniform seabed and no land masses, it is likely that a high tide at one point would occur simultaneously with a change in the current direction. However, the existence of continents, a sea bottom which is anything but uniform, and the great ocean currents and different prevailing winds around the world, make the picture extremely complex.

As one example of how a time of high tide can differ greatly from the time of a current change, see the Relationship of High Water and Ebb Current, p. 161. Picture a fjord or long indentation into the coastline, with a narrow opening to the ocean. When a flood current is reaching its peak, or the tide is high outside the mouth of this fjord, the fjord is still filling, unable to keep pace with conditions on the outer coast.

Why do the heights of tides differ so much from one place to the next? Turn to Time of High Water at various ports, pp. 12-20, and compare the Rise in Feet of tides for Nova Scotia's outer coast — 2.6 to 4.8 feet — to those for the Bay of Fundy, just below, that range of up to 38.4 feet. Why the difference? The answer is geography, both above and below water. Tidal ranges of points out on the edge of an outer coast (Nantucket, for instance) tend to be moderate, while estuaries and deep bays with narrowing contours often experience a funneling effect which exaggerates the tidal range. Another explanation is proximity to the continental shelf: the closer a port is to the shelf, the more likely it is to experience a lower tidal range; the farther from the shelf, the more likely it is that a harbor is subject to surges, as when a wave crest hits the shallow water at a beach.

There are other anomalies between tides and currents. **Do stronger currents indicate higher tides?** Woods Hole, MA often has very strong currents through its narrow passage, sometimes as fast as 7 knots, but the tidal range is less than 2 feet. Conversely, Boston Harbor has a mean tidal range of about 9.6 feet, but the average currents at the opening, between Deer Island and Hull, do not exceed 2 knots. There is no necessary correlation between current strength and range of tide.

Why did the tidal or current prediction in ELDRIDGE differ from what I saw? Unless there was an error in the Government tables we take our data from, the answer is either (1) weather-related, as when a storm either retards or advances a tidal event, or (2) the discrepancy is small enough to be explained by the approximate nature of tide and current predictions, and figures are sometimes rounded off. We appreciate hearing from readers of any observed discrepancies or errors. Contact us by emailing pilot@eldridgetide.com, or calling 617-449-7393.

HOW TO USE THE TIDE AND CURRENT TABLES AND CURRENT CHARTS

High and Low Water Tide Tables

In addition to presenting tide tables for nine reference ports, from Portland to Miami, we show the approximate time of High Water and the mean (average) height of high at some 350 substations.

- On pp. 12-20, find your harbor, or the nearest one to it, and note the time difference between it and the reference port.
- Apply this time difference to the reference table for that date. On average the Low Water will follow by about 6 hours, 12 minutes.
- When the height of High Water in the reference table is higher or lower than the average, it will be correspondingly higher or lower at your harbor.

Current Tables

There are eight current tables covering from Massachusetts to the Chesapeake. At over 300 other points, on pp. 22-29, we show the approximate time of current change, the directions of ebb and flood, and the average maximum velocities.

- Find the place you are concerned with, or the listed position nearest to it, and note the time difference between it and the reference location.
- Apply this time difference to the reference table for that date. On average, the current will change approximately every 6 hours, 12 minutes.
- When the velocity of the current in the reference table exceeds the average maximum, the current in your area will also exceed the average maximum.

Naming Currents

While it is traditional to name currents as Ebb or Flood, these terms can easily confuse. We recommend using the direction as the name of the current. It is more helpful to refer to an Easterly current, which means it is Eastbound or runs toward the East, than it is to name it as an Ebb or Flood Current, which leaves the listener guessing its direction.

Current Charts and Diagrams

- Find the appropriate current chart and note the table to which it is refer-enced. For instance, the Long Island Sound charts (pp. 98-103) reference the Race tables.
- Turn to this table, which shows the time of start of Flood and start of Ebb, and find the time of the start of the advantageous current for that day.
- The difference between having a fair current or a head current means hours and dollars to the slower moving vessel such as a trawler or auxiliary sailboat. See Smarter Boating, p. 36.

Effect of the Moon

It is wise to pay particular attention to the phase or position of the Moon. "Astronomical" tides and currents occur around the times of full and new moons, especially when the Moon is at Perigee, or closest to the Earth. Tides will be both higher and lower than average, and currents will run stronger than average. See p. 236 & p. 238.

TIME OF HIGH WATER

Time figures shown are the *average* differences throughout the year. Rise in feet is mean range. (Low Water times are given *only* when they vary more than 20 min. from High Water times.)

> **NOTE: *Asterisk indicates that NOAA has recently dropped these substations from its listing because the data are judged to be of questionable accuracy. We have published NOAA's most recently available figures with this warning: Mariners are cautioned that the starred information is only approximate and not supported by NOAA or the Publishers of Eldridge.**

For **Canadian Ports**, *if your watch is set for Atlantic Time, use the time differences listed here; if your watch is set for Eastern Time, subtract one hour from these time differences.*

	Hr. Min.			Rise in feet
NOVA SCOTIA, Outer Coast				
Guysborough	3 00	before	PORTLAND	3.8
Whitehaven Harbour	3 15	"	"	3.7
Liscomb Harbour	3 20	"	"	4.2
Sheet Harbour	3 15	"	"	4.2
Ship Harbour	3 15	"	"	4.2
Jeddore Harbour	3 15	"	"	4.3
Halifax	3 10	"	"	4.4
Sable Island, north side	3 20	"	"	2.6
Sable Island, south side	3 15	"	"	3.9
Chester, Mahone Bay	3 10	"	"	4.4
Mahone Harbour, Mahone Bay	3 10	"	"	4.5
Lunenburg	3 05	"	"	4.2
Riverport, La Have River	3 00	"	"	4.5
Liverpool Bay	3 00	"	"	4.3
Lockeport	**high 2 45** before, low 3 10	"	"	4.6
Shelburne	2 40	"	"	4.8
NOVA SCOTIA & NEW BRUNSWICK, Bay of Fundy				
Lower E. Pubnico	1 10	before	PORTLAND	8.7
Yarmouth Harbour	0 25	"	"	11.5
Annapolis Royal, Annapolis R.	0 55	after	"	22.6
Parrsboro, Minas Basin, Partridge Is.	1 35	"	"	34.4
Burntcoat Head, Minas Basin	1 55	"	"	38.4
Amherst Point, Cumberland Basin	1 25	"	"	35.6
Grindstone Is, Petitcodiac River	1 10	"	"	31.1
Hopewell Cape, Petitcodiac River **high 1 00** after, low 1 25		"	"	33.2
Saint John	0 45	"	"	20.8
Indiantown, Saint John River **high 2 15** after, low 3 10		"	"	1.2
L'Etang Harbor	0 50	"	"	18.4

REVERSING FALLS, SAINT JOHN, N.B.

The most turbulence in the gorge occurs on days when the tides are largest. On largest tides the outward fall is between 15 and 16 1/2 feet and is accompanied by a greater turbulence than the inward fall which is between 11 and 12 1/2 feet. The outward fall is at its greatest between two hours before and one hour after low water at St. John; the inward fall is greater just before the time of high water. For complete tidal information of Canadian ports see Tide Tables of the Atlantic Coast of Canada. (Purchase tables from nautical dealers in Canadian ports or from the Queen's Printer, Department of Public Printing, Ottawa).

PORTLAND Tables, pp. 30-35

When a high tide exceeds avg. ht., the *following* low tide will be lower than avg.
*Times and Hts. are approximate. *Important*: See NOTE, top p. 12.

TIME OF HIGH WATER

Time figures shown are the *average* differences throughout the year. Rise in feet is mean range.
(Low Water times are given *only* when they vary more than 20 min. from High Water times.)

U.S. ATLANTIC COAST, from Maine southward

	Hr.	Min.			Rise in feet
MAINE					
Eastport	0	15	before	PORTLAND	18.4
Cutler, Little River	0	30	"	"	13.5
Shoppee Pt., Englishman Bay	0	25	"	"	12.1
Steele Harbor Island	0	25	"	"	11.6
*Jonesport	0	20	"	"	11.5
Green Island, Petit Manan Bar	0	40	"	"	10.6
Prospect Harbor	0	35	"	"	10.5
Winter Harbor, Frenchman Bay	0	10	"	"	10.1
Bar Harbor, Mt. Desert Island	0	20	"	"	10.6
Southwest Harbor, Mt. Desert Is. **high 0 20** *before, low* 0 45			"	"	10.2
Bass Harbor **high 0 15** *before, low* 0 45			"	"	9.9
Blue Hill Harbor, Blue Hill Bay	0	10	"	"	10.1
Burnt Coat Harbor, Swans Island	0	15	"	"	9.5
Penobscot Bay					
Center Harbor, Eggemoggin Reach	0	10	"	"	10.1
Little Deer Isle, Eggemoggin Reach	0	05	"	"	10.0
Isle Au Haut **high 0 20** *before, low* 0 45			"	"	9.3
Stonington, Deer Isle	0	10	"	"	9.7
Matinicus Harbor, Wheaton Is. ... **high 0 15** *before, low* 0 45			"	"	9.0
Vinalhaven	0	10	"	"	9.3
North Haven	0	10	"	"	9.7
Pulpit Harbor, North Haven Is.	0	10	"	"	9.9
Castine	0	05	"	"	10.1
Bucksport, Penobscott River	0	20	"	"	10.8
Bangor, Penobscot River **high 0 25** *before, low* same as				"	13.4
Belfast	0	15	before	"	10.2
*Camden	0	10	"	"	9.6
Rockland	0	10	"	"	9.8
MAINE, Outer Coast					
Tenants Harbor	0	10	before	PORTLAND	9.3
Monhegan Island	0	10	"	"	8.8
Port Clyde, St. George River	0	10	"	"	8.9
Thomaston, St. George River	0	05	"	"	9.4
New Harbor, Muscongus Bay	0	10	"	"	8.8
Friendship Harbor	0	15	"	"	9.0
Waldoboro, Medomak River	0	10	"	"	9.5
East Boothbay, Damariscotta River		same as		"	8.9
Boothbay Harbor	0	05	before	"	8.8
Wiscasset, Sheepscot River	0	10	after	"	9.4
Robinhood, Sasanoa River	0	15	"	"	8.8
Phippsburg, Kennebec River	0	25	"	"	8.0
Bath, Kennebec River	1	10	"	"	6.4
Casco Bay					
*Small Point Harbor	0	10	before	"	8.8
Cundy Harbor, New Meadows River		same as		"	8.9
South Harpswell, Potts Harbor		same as		"	8.9
South Freeport	0	10	after	"	9.0

PORTLAND Tables, pp. 30-35

When a high tide exceeds avg. ht., the *following* low tide will be lower than avg.
*Times and Hts. are approximate. *Important*: See NOTE, top p. 12.

TIDE STATIONS

TIME OF HIGH WATER

Time figures shown are the *average* differences throughout the year. Rise in feet is mean range. (Low Water times are given *only* when they vary more than 20 min. from High Water times.)

	Hr.	Min.			Rise in feet
MAINE, Cont.					
Falmouth Foreside	same as			*PORTLAND*	9.2
Great Chebeague Island	same as			"	9.1
Portland Head Light	same as			"	8.9
Cape Porpoise	0	15	after	"	8.7
Kennebunkport	0	05	"	"	8.8
York Harbor	0	10	"	"	8.6
NEW HAMPSHIRE					
Portsmouth	0	20	after	*PORTLAND*	7.8
Gosport Harbor, Isles of Shoals	same as			"	8.5
Hampton Harbor	0	20	after	"	8.3
MASSACHUSETTS, Outer Coast					
Newburyport, Merrimack River.. **high 0 30** *after, low*	1	10	after	*PORTLAND*	7.8
Plum Island Sound, S. End .... **high 0 10** *after, low*	0	35	"	"	8.6
Annisquam, Lobster Cove	0	10	"	"	8.8
Rockport	0	05	"	"	8.7
Gloucester Harbor	same as			*BOSTON*	8.8
*Manchester	same as			"	8.8
Salem	same as			"	8.9
*Marblehead	same as			"	9.1
Lynn, Lynn Harbor	same as			"	9.2
Neponset, Neponset R.	same as			"	9.5
Weymouth, Fore River Bridge	0	10	after	"	9.5
Hingham	0	10	"	"	9.5
Hull	0	05	"	"	9.3
Cohasset Harbor (White Head)	same as			"	8.8
Scituate, Scituate Harbor	same as			"	8.9
Cape Cod Bay					
Duxbury Harbor	**high 0 05** *after, low* 0 35		after	"	9.9
Plymouth	0	10	"	"	9.8
Cape Cod Canal, East Entrance	same as			"	8.7
Barnstable Harbor, Beach Point	0	20	after	"	9.5
Wellfleet	0	20	"	"	10.0
Provincetown	0	15	"	"	9.1
Cape Cod					
Stage Harbor, Chatham	**high 0 45** *after, low* 0 20		"	"	4.0
Chatham Hbr, Aunt Lydias Cove	1	05	"	"	5.8
Pleasant Bay, Chatham	**high 2 30** *after, low* 3 25		"	"	3.2
Nantucket Sound					
Wychmere Harbor	**high 0 50** *after, low* 0 25		"	"	3.7
Dennisport	**high 1 05** *after, low* 0 40		"	"	3.4
South Yarmouth, Bass River	1	45	"	"	2.8
Hyannis Port	**high 1 00** *after, low* 0 25		"	"	3.2
Cotuit Highlands	**high 1 15** *after, low* 0 45		"	"	2.5
Falmouth Heights	0	15	before	"	1.3
Nantucket Island					
Great Point	0	35	after	"	3.1
Nantucket	1	05	"	"	3.0
Muskeget Island, North side	0	20	"	"	2.0

PORTLAND Tables, pp. 30-35, BOSTON Tables, pp. 38-43

When a high tide exceeds avg. ht., the *following* low tide will be lower than avg.
*Times and Hts. are approximate. *Important*: See NOTE, top p. 12.

TIME OF HIGH WATER

Time figures shown are the *average* differences throughout the year. Rise in feet is mean range. (Low Water times are given *only* when they vary more than 20 min. from High Water times.)

	Hr.	Min.			Rise in feet
MASSACHUSETTS, Martha's Vineyard					
*Lake Tashmoo (inside).....................................2	2	30	before	BOSTON	2.0
Vineyard Haven..3	3	35	after	NEWPORT	1.6
Oak Bluffs..3	3	55	"	"	1.7
Edgartown...4	4	20	"	"	2.1
Wasque Point, Chappaquiddick.. **high 2 00** after, low 3	3	20	"	"	1.1
Squibnocket Point....................... **high 0 45** before, low..same as				"	2.9
Nomans Land............................ **high 0 20** before, low..0	0	20	after	"	3.0
Gay Head................................. **high 0 05** before, low..0	0	45	"	"	2.9
Cedar Tree Neck .... **high 0 10** after, low 1	1	30	"	"	2.2
*Menemsha Bight....................... **high** same as, low 0	0	35	"	"	2.7
Vineyard Sound					
Little Hbr., Woods Hole............... **high 0 30** after, low 2	2	20	"	"	1.4
Quick's Hole, N. side..0	0	10	before	"	3.5
Cuttyhunk..1	1	20	after	"	3.4
Buzzards Bay					
*Cuttyhunk Pond Entr....................................same as				"	3.4
W. Falmouth Harbor, Chappaquoit Pt. 0	0	05	after	"	3.8
*Pocasset Hbr., Barlows Landing 0	0	20	"	"	4.0
Monument Beach..0	0	20	"	"	4.0
*Wareham River..0	0	20	"	"	4.1
Great Hill...0	0	10	"	"	4.0
Marion, Sippican Harbor...0	0	10	"	"	4.0
Mattapoisett Harbor...0	0	15	"	"	3.9
Clarks Point..0	0	20	"	"	3.6
New Bedford..0	0	05	"	"	3.7
*South Dartmouth..0	0	30	"	"	3.7
Westport Harbor, Westport River. **high 0 10** after, low 0	0	35	"	"	3.0
RHODE ISLAND & MASS, Narragansett Bay					
Sakonnet, Sakonnet River........... **high 0 10** before, low..0	0	15	after	NEWPORT	3.2
Beavertail Point, Conanicut Island ....same as				"	3.3
Conanicut Point, Conanicut Island ....same as				"	3.8
Prudence Island (south end)......................................0	0	05	after	"	3.7
Bristol Harbor..0	0	10	"	"	4.1
Fall River, MA...0	0	10	"	"	4.4
Bay Spring, Bullock Cove...0	0	05	"	"	4.3
Providence, State Pier no. 1......................................0	0	05	"	"	4.4
Pawtucket, Seekonk River 0	0	15	"	"	4.6
East Greenwich...0	0	10	"	"	4.1
Wickford..same as				"	3.7
Narragansett Pier....................... **high 0 10** before, low..0	0	15	after	"	3.2
RHODE ISLAND, Outer Coast					
Pt. Judith, Harbor of Refuge....... **high** same as, low........0	0	35	after	NEWPORT	3.0
Block Island, Old Harbor........... **high 0 15** before, low..0	0	15	"	"	2.9
Watch Hill Pt. .... **high 0 40** after, low 1	1	15	"	"	2.6
CONNECTICUT, L.I. Sound					
*Stonington 2	2	15	before	BRIDGEPORT	2.7
*Noank...2	2	05	"	"	2.3
New London, Thames River (State Pier) 1	1	45	"	"	2.6
Norwich, Thames River...1	1	20	"	"	3.0

BOSTON Tables, pp. 38-43, NEWPORT Tables, pp. 84-89, BRIDGEPORT Tables, pp. 104-109

When a high tide exceeds avg. ht., the *following* low tide will be lower than avg.
*Times and Hts. are approximate. *Important*: See NOTE, top p. 12.

15

TIDE STATIONS

TIME OF HIGH WATER

Time figures shown are the *average* differences throughout the year. Rise in feet is mean range.
(Low Water times are given *only* when they vary more than 20 min. from High Water times.)

	Hr.	Min.			Rise in feet
CONNECTICUT, L.I. Sound, Cont.					
Saybrook Jetty, Connecticut Riv... **high 0 35** *before, low* .1	00	before	BRIDGEPORT	3.5
Essex, Connecticut River 0	05	"	"	3.0
Madison 0	25	"	"	4.9
Branford, Branford River 0	10	"	"	5.9
New Haven Harbor, New Haven Reach...........0	05	"	"	6.2
Milford Harbor.......................................*same as*			"	6.3
Sniffens Point, Housatonic River 0	10	after	"	6.4
South Norwalk 0	10	"	"	7.1
Stamford..0	05	"	"	7.2
Cos Cob Harbor 0	05	"	"	7.2
*Greenwich ....*same as*			"	7.4
NEW YORK, Long Island Sound, North Side					
Rye Beach 0	25	before	KINGS POINT	7.3
New Rochelle 0	15	"	"	7.3
Throgs Neck, Fort Schuyler....................*same as*			"	7.1
Whitestone, East River 0	10	after	"	7.1
College Point, Flushing Bay................................0	15	"	"	6.8
Hunts Point, East River 0	10	"	"	6.9
North Brother Island, East River 0	20	"	"	6.6
Port Morris, Stony Pt., East River 0	10	"	"	6.2
NEW YORK, Long Island, North Shore					
Willets Point..*same as*			KINGS POINT	7.2
Port Washington, Manhasset Bay........................0	10	before	"	7.3
Glen Cove, Hempstead Harbor............................0	25	"	"	7.3
Oyster Bay Harbor, Oyster Bay..........................0	10	after	BRIDGEPORT	7.3
Cold Spring Harbor, Oyster Bay........................0	05	before	"	7.3
Eatons Neck Point 0	05	after	"	7.1
Lloyd Harbor, Huntington Bay 0	05	"	"	7.0
Northport, Northport Bay ....*same as*			"	7.3
Port Jefferson Harbor Entrance............*same as*			"	6.6
Mattituck Inlet..0	10	after	"	5.0
Shelter Island Sound					
Orient..1	10	before	"	2.5
Greenport.................................. **high 0 30** *before, low* ..1	00	"	"	2.4
Southold 0	05	"	"	2.3
Sag Harbor 0	50	"	"	2.4
New Suffolk, Peconic Bay....................................0	35	after	"	2.6
South Jamesport, Peconic Bay............................0	55	"	"	2.8
Threemile Harbor, Entr., Gardiners Bay...........1	15	before	"	2.5
Montauk Harbor Entr. 2	05	"	"	1.9
Long Island, South Shore					
Shinnecock Inlet, Ocean .... **high 0 15** *before, low* ..1	10	before	SANDY HOOK	3.1
Moriches Inlet. Coast Guard Sta 0	45	after	"	2.2
Democrat Point, Fire Island Inlet......................0	35	before	"	2.6
Patchogue, Great South Bay 3	20	after	"	1.1
Bay Shore, Watchogue Creek Entrance...............2	20	"	"	1.0
Jones Inlet (Point Lookout) 0	20	before	"	3.6
Bellmore Creek, Hempstead Bay **high 1 30** *after, low* 2	00	after	"	2.0

BRIDGEPORT Tables, pp. 104-109, KINGS POINT Tables, pp. 110-115, SANDY HOOK Tables, pp. 140-145

When a high tide exceeds avg. ht., the *following* low tide will be lower than avg.
*Times and Hts. are approximate. *Important*: See NOTE, top p. 12.

TIME OF HIGH WATER

Time figures shown are the *average* differences throughout the year. Rise in feet is mean range.
(Low Water times are given *only* when they vary more than 20 min. from High Water times.)

	Hr. Min.			Rise in feet
NEW YORK, Long Island, South Shore, Cont.				
Freeport, Baldwin Bay 0 50		after	SANDY HOOK	3.0
E. Rockaway Inlet 0 10		before	"	4.1
Barren Is., Rockaway Inlet, Jamaica Bay .... same as			"	5.0
NEW YORK & NEW JERSEY				
New York Harbor				
Coney Island 0 10		before	SANDY HOOK	4.7
Fort Hamilton, The Narrows .... same as			"	4.7
Tarrytown, Hudson River 1 50		after	BATTERY	3.2
Poughkeepsie, Hudson River 4 40		"	"	3.1
Kingston, Hudson River 5 30		"	"	3.7
NY & NJ, the Kills and Newark Bay				
Constable Hook, Kill Van Kull 0 15		before	"	4.6
Port Elizabeth .... same as			"	5.1
Bellville, Passaic River .... **high 0 10** *after, low* 0 50		after	"	5.6
Kearny Pt., Hackensack River. 0 15		"	"	5.2
Hackensack, Hackensack River 1 05		"	"	6.0
Lower NY Bay, Raritan Bay				
Great Kills Harbor 0 05		after	SANDY HOOK	4.9
South Amboy, Raritan River .... same as			"	5.1
New Brunswick, Raritan River 0 40		after	"	5.7
Keyport .... same as			"	5.0
Atlantic Highlands, Sandy Hook Bay 0 10		before	"	4.7
Highlands, Shrewsbury R., Rte. 36 bridge, Sandy Hook .. 0 15		after	"	4.2
Red Bank, Navesink River, Sandy Hook Bay				
.... **high 1 20** *after, low* .. 2 00		"	"	3.5
Sea Bright, Shrewsbury River, Sandy Hook Bay 1 15		"	"	3.2
NEW JERSEY, Outer Coast				
Shark River Island, Fixed RR. Bridge, Shark River 0 10		before	"	4.3
Manasquan Inlet, USCG Station 0 20		"	"	4.0
Brielle, Rte. 35 bridge, Manasquan River 0 15		"	"	3.9
Barnegat Inlet,USCG Station, Barnegat Bay 0 05		"	"	2.2
Manahawkin Drawbridge .... **high 2 50** *after, low* 3 40		after	"	1.3
Beach Haven, USCG Station, Little Egg Harbor 1 20		"	"	2.2
Absecon Creek, Rte. 30 bridge 1 10		"	"	3.9
Atlantic City, Ocean 0 25		before	"	4.0
Beesleys Pt., Great Egg Hbr. Bay **high 0 30** *after, low* 1 05		after	"	3.6
Townsends Inlet, Ocean Dr. bridge .... same as			"	4.0
Stone Harbor, Great Channel, Hereford Inlet 0 40		after	"	4.0
Cape May Harbor, Cape May Inlet 0 05		"	"	4.5
NEW JERSEY & DELAWARE BAY				
Delaware Bay, Eastern Shore				
Brandywine Shoal Light .... **high 0 30** *after, low* 1 00		after	BATTERY	4.9
Cape May Point, Sunset Beach 0 25		"	"	4.8
Dennis Creek, 2.5 mi. above Entr.... **high 1 15** *after, low* 2 00		"	"	5.2
Mauricetown, Maurice R. .... **high 2 40** *after, low* 3 15		"	"	4.4
Millville, Maurice R. .... **high 3 55** *after, low* 4 20		"	"	5.0

SANDY HOOK Tables, pp. 140-145, BATTERY Tables, pp. 128-133

When a high tide exceeds avg. ht., the *following* low tide will be lower than avg.
*Times and Hts. are approximate. *Important*: See NOTE, top p. 12.

TIDE STATIONS

TIME OF HIGH WATER

Time figures shown are the *average* differences throughout the year. Rise in feet is mean range.
(Low Water times are given *only* when they vary more than 20 min. from High Water times.)

	Hr.	Min.			Rise in feet
NEW JERSEY & DELAWARE BAY, Cont.					
Delaware Bay, Western Shore					
*Cape Henlopen	0	10	after	BATTERY	4.1
Lewes (Breakwater Harbor) **high 0 20** *after, low*	0	45	"	"	4.1
*St. Jones River Ent. **high 1 10** *after, low*	1	55	"	"	4.8
Delaware River					
*Liston Point, Delaware	2	05	"	"	5.7
Salem, Salem River, NJ	3	55	"	"	4.2
Reedy Point, Delaware **high 3 05** *after, low*	3	25	"	"	5.3
C&D Summit Bridge, Delaware	2	35	"	"	3.5
Chesapeake City, MD	2	20	"	"	2.9
New Castle, Delaware **high 3 35** *after, low*	4	05	"	"	5.2
Wilmington Marine Terminal **high 3 55** *after, low*	4	30	"	"	5.3
Philadelphia, PA, USCG Station **high 5 30** *after, low*	5	50	"	"	6.0
Burlington, NJ **high 6 25** *after, low*	7	00	"	"	7.2
Trenton, NJ **high 6 45** *after, low*	7	45	"	"	8.2
DELAWARE, MARYLAND & VIRGINIA					
Indian River Inlet, USCG Station, Delaware					
high 0 55 *after, low*	0	25	after	SANDY HOOK	2.5
Ocean City Fishing Pier	0	20	before	"	3.4
Harbor of Refuge, Chincoteague Bay	0	10	after	"	2.4
Chincoteague Channel, south end	0	20	"	"	2.2
Chincoteague Island, USCG Station	0	40	"	"	1.6
Metompkin Inlet	0	30	"	"	3.6
Wachapreague, Wachapreague Channel	0	40	"	"	4.0
*Quinby Inlet Entrance	0	05	"	"	4.0
Great Machipongo Inlet, inside	0	40	"	"	3.9
Chesapeake Bay, Eastern Shore					
Cape Charles Harbor	0	40	after	BATTERY	2.3
Crisfield, Little Annemessex River	4	30	"	"	1.9
Salisbury, Wicomico River	7	10	"	"	3.0
Middle Hooper Island	4	40	before	BALTIMORE	1.5
Taylors Island, Little Choptank River, Slaughter Creek	3	10	"	"	1.3
*Sharps Is. Lt.	3	50	"	"	1.3
Cambridge, Choptank River	2	35	"	"	1.6
Dover Bridge, Choptank River	0	30	"	"	1.7
Oxford, Tred Avon River	2	50	"	"	1.4
Easton Pt., Tred Avon River	2	40	"	"	1.6
St. Michaels, Miles River	2	10	"	"	1.4
Kent Island Narrows	1	30	"	"	1.2
*Bloody Pt. Bar Lt.	2	40	"	"	1.1
Worton Creek Entrance	1	20	after	"	1.3
Town Point Wharf, Elk River	3	10	"	"	2.2
Chesapeake Bay, Western Shore					
Havre de Grace, Susquehanna River	3	20	after	"	1.9
*Pooles Is.	0	55	"	"	1.2
Annapolis, Severn River (US Naval Academy)	1	35	before	"	1.0
*Sandy Point	1	20	"	"	0.8
Thomas Pt. Shoal Lt.	2	00	"	"	0.9
*Drum Point, Pawtuxent River	4	50	"	"	1.2
Solomons Island, Pawtuxent River	4	40	"	"	1.2

BATTERY Tables, pp. 128-133, SANDY HOOK Tables, pp. 140-145, BALTIMORE Tables, pp. 162-165

When a high tide exceeds avg. ht., the *following* low tide will be lower than avg.
*Times and Hts. are approximate. *Important*: See NOTE, top p. 12.

TIME OF HIGH WATER

Time figures shown are the *average* differences throughout the year. Rise in feet is mean range.
(Low Water times are given *only* when they vary more than 20 min. from High Water times.)

	Hr.	Min.			Rise in feet
DELAWARE, MARYLAND & VIRGINIA, Cont.					
Point Lookout	5	30	before	BALTIMORE	1.2
Sunnybank, Little Wicomico River	6	30	after	BATTERY	0.8
Glebe Point, Great Wicomico River	4	10	"	"	1.2
Windmill Point, Rappahannock River	2	50	"	"	1.2
*Orchard Point, Rappahannock River	3	20	"	"	1.4
*New Point Comfort, Mobjack Bay	0	45	"	"	2.3
Tue Marshes Light, York River	0	50	"	"	2.2
*Perrin River, York River	1	05	"	"	2.3
Yorktown, Goodwin Neck, York River	1	05	"	"	2.2
Hampton Roads, Sewells Pt. .... **high 0 50** *after*, low	0	40	"	"	2.4
Norfolk, Elizabeth River	1	10	"	"	2.8
Newport News, James River	1	15	"	"	2.6
*Windmill Pt., James River	6	20	"	"	2.3
Chesapeake Bay Br. Tunnel	0	15	before	"	2.6
NORTH CAROLINA					
Roanoke Sound Channel	1	10	after	BATTERY	0.5
Oregon Inlet Marina	0	15	before	"	0.9
Oregon Inlet, USCG Station	0	50	"	"	1.9
Oregon Inlet Channel	0	35	"	"	1.2
Cape Hatteras Fishing Pier	1	05	"	"	3.0
Hatteras Inlet	0	55	"	"	2.0
Ocracoke Inlet	0	55	"	"	1.9
Beaufort Inlet Channel Range	0	55	"	"	3.2
Morehead City	0	40	"	"	3.1
Bogue Inlet	0	50	"	"	2.2
New River Inlet	0	50	"	"	3.0
*New Topsail Inlet ...... **high 0 40** *before*, low	0	10	"	"	3.0
Bald Head, Cape Fear River	0	55	"	"	4.5
Wilmington ...... **high 1 20** *after*, low	1	45	after	"	4.3
Lockwoods Folly Inlet	1	00	"	"	4.2
SOUTH CAROLINA					
Little River Neck, north end	1	30	after	BATTERY	4.7
Hog Inlet Pier	0	45	"	"	5.0
Myrtle Beach, Springmaid Pier	0	50	"	"	5.0
Pawleys Island Pier (ocean)	0	55	"	"	4.9
Winyah Bay Entrance, south jetty	0	50	before	"	4.6
South Island Plantation, C.G. Station	0	10	after	"	3.8
Georgetown, Sampit River ...... **high 1 00** *after*, low	1	40	"	"	3.7
North Santee River Inlet	0	30	before	"	4.5
Charleston (Custom House Wharf)	0	25	"	"	5.2
Folly River, north, Folly Island ... **high** same as, low	0	35	"	"	5.4
Rockville, Bohicket Creek, North Edisto River	0	15	"	"	5.8
Edisto Marina, Big Bay Creek entr., South Edisto River	0	25	"	"	6.0
Harbor River Bridge, St. Helena Sound	0	20	"	"	6.0
Hutchinson Island, Ashepoo River, St. Helena Sound ...... **high 0 15** *before*, low	0	25	after	"	6.0
Fripps Inlet, Hunting Island Bridge, St. Helena Sound	0	30	before	"	6.1
Port Royal Plantation, Hilton Head Is.	0	20	"	"	6.1

BATTERY Tables, pp. 128-133

When a high tide exceeds avg. ht., the *following* low tide will be lower than avg.
*Times and Hts. are approximate. *Important*: See NOTE, top p. 12.

TIME OF HIGH WATER

Time figures shown are the *average* differences throughout the year. Rise in feet is mean range.
(Low Water times are given *only* when they vary more than 20 min. from High Water times.)

	Hr. Min.			Rise in feet

SOUTH CAROLINA, Cont.

Battery Creek, Beaufort River Port Royal Sd, 4 mi. above entr.

	Hr. Min.			Rise in feet
.... **high 1 00** *after, low* 0 15		after	BATTERY	7.6
Beaufort, Beaufort River .... **high 0 55** *after, low* 0 30		"	"	7.4
Braddock Point, Hilton Head Island, Calibogue Sd. 0 10		before	"	6.7

GEORGIA

Savannah River Entrance, Fort Pulaski 0 15		before	BATTERY	6.9
Tybee Creek Entrance..0 20		"	"	6.8
Wilmington River, north entrance..................................0 25		after	"	7.6
Isle of Hope, Skidaway River ...... **high 0 35** *after, low* 0 10		"	"	7.8
Egg Islands, Ossabaw Sound 0 10		before	"	7.2
Walburg Creek Entr., St. Catherines Sd...........................same as			"	7.1
Blackbeard Island...same as			"	6.9
Blackbeard Creek, Blackbeard Island...............................0 15		after	"	6.5
Old Tower, Sapelo Island, Doboy Sound ....same as			"	6.8
Threemile Cut Entrance, Darien River............................0 30		after	"	7.1
St. Simons Sound Bar..0 15		before	"	6.5
Frederica River, St. Simons Sound.................................0 35		after	"	7.2
Brunswick, East River, Howe St. Pier, St. Simons Sound 0 20		"	"	7.1
Jekyll Is. Marina, Jekyll Creek, St. Andrew Sound 0 35		"	"	6.8
Cumberland Wharf, Cumberland River 0 30		after	"	6.8

FLORIDA, East Coast

St. Marys Entrance, north jetty, Cumberland Sd...............0 05		before	BATTERY	5.8
Fernandina Beach, Amelia R. ...... **high 0 30** *after, low* 0 05		after	"	6.0
Amelia City, South Amelia River....................................0 50		"	"	5.4
Nassau River Entrance .... **high 0 10** *after, low* 0 50		"	"	5.1
Mayport, (Bar Pilot Dock) .... **high 0 15** *after, low* 0 15		before	"	4.6
St. Augustine, City Dock...0 10		after	"	4.5
Ponce Inlet, Halifax River .... **high 0 05** *after, low* 0 30		after	MIAMI	2.8
Cape Canaveral .... **high 1 05** *before, low* ..0 45		before	"	3.5
Port Canaveral, Trident Pier..same as			"	3.5
Sebastian Inlet bridge................. **high 0 50** *before, low*..0 25		before	"	2.2
St. Lucie, Indian River .... **high 0 40** *after, low* 1 45		after	"	1.0
Vero Beach, ocean 0 45		before	"	3.4
Fort Pierce Inlet, south jetty...0 25		"	"	2.6
Stuart, St. Lucie River .... **high 2 15** *after, low* 3 30		after	"	0.9
Jupiter Inlet, south jetty...0 10		before	"	2.5
North Palm Beach, Lake Worth .. **high 0 15** *before, low*..0 15		after	"	2.8
Port of Palm Beach, Lake Worth . **high 0 20** *before, low*..0 05		"	"	2.7
Lake Worth Pier, ocean .... **high 0 45** *before, low*..0 20		before	"	2.7
Hillsboro Inlet, C.G. Light Station 0 10		"	"	2.5
Hillsboro Inlet Marina................ **high 0 05** *before, low*..0 25		after	"	2.5
Lauderdale-by-the-Sea, fish pier....................................0 25		before	"	2.6
Bahia Mar Yacht Club .... **high 0 05** *before, low*..0 35		after	"	2.4
Port Everglades, Turning Basin....................................0 20		before	"	2.5
North Miami Beach, fishing pier 0 10		"	"	2.5
Miami, Miamarina, Biscayne Bays **high 0 20** *after, low* 0 50		after	"	2.2
Dinner Key Marina, Biscayne Bay **high 0 55** *after, low* 1 50		"	"	1.9
Key Biscayne Yt. Club, Biscayne B **high 0 45** *after low* 1 30		"	"	2.0
Ocean Reef Hbr., Key Largo .... **high 0 10** *before, low*..0 15		"	"	2.3
Tavernier Harbor, Hawk Ch......... **high 0 05** *after, low* 0 25		"	"	2.0
Key West..0 50		before	BOSTON	1.3

BATTERY Tables, pp. 128-133, MIAMI Tables, pp. 166-169, BOSTON Tables, pp. 38-43
When a high tide exceeds avg. ht., the *following* low tide will be lower than avg.
*Times and Hts. are approximate. *Important*: See NOTE, top p. 12.

Piloting in a Cross Current

See also p. 58, Coping with Currents

When we are piloting in a body of water with an active current from ahead or astern, our course is not affected and the arithmetic for speed is easy. (See p. 36.) When the current comes at an angle to the bow or stern, unless our speed is far greater than the current, we need to alter course to compensate.

First, what not to do. When in a cross current it is a major mistake simply to steer toward our destination. The current will carry us more and more off course, with the heading or bearing to our destination changing all the time. We may finally get there, but we will have traveled considerably farther, on what is termed a hooked course, and possibly have entered dangerous water while doing so.

By GPS: With GPS it's all too easy to find the new heading. We enter our destination waypoint and press GoTo. There are several screens to choose from. First, carefully check the Map screen to see if there are any hazards or obstructions between us and our destination. The Highway screen, considered perhaps the most useful display, will show if we are on course by displaying the highway as straight ahead. The screen will also indicate how far to the left or right of our course we are. This is crosstrack error. We steer to that side which brings us back onto the center of the highway, and then continue to steer in such a way that we stay in the middle. We have changed our heading to achieve the desired COG, course over ground. Now the Course and Bearing numbers should be the same, and we have compensated for cross current.

By eye: Without the help of electronics but with good visibility, we know we need to alter course toward the current until a foreground object, let's say a point on the shore, remains steady in relation to an object farther away, perhaps a distant steeple. This alignment is called a range. Once we find the corrected heading, we can use our compass to maintain it, checking those objects periodically in case current or wind conditions change.

By a chart: With compromised visibility and again without electronics, the problem is solved the traditional way with a paper chart. First, consult the proper current table to determine the speed and direction of the current for the hour(s) in question. (Keep in mind that speeds and times are predictions only. They are approximate and can be altered by weather.) Plot the course, let's say 090°, as if there is no current. Then construct a one-hour vector diagram. From the departure point, construct a line in the direction of the current, let's say 180°, whose length is the distance the current would carry an object in one hour. If the predicted current is 2 knots, that's 2 n.m. Now we set our dividers for a distance which represents how far our boat speed will take us through the water in one hour, let's say 8 n.m. We will put one point of the dividers on the far end of the line representing current, and then swing the dividers until the second point intercepts the line of our intended course. The direction of that third line represents what our boat's heading needs to be (the course to steer) to maintain the original course we drew. The intercept point represents about where our boat will be along the intended course line (COG) at the end of one hour. If this leg is longer or shorter than one hour, it doesn't matter. The course to steer is the same as we determined in our one-hour vector plot, until conditions change.

TIME OF CURRENT CHANGE
(See Note at bottom of Boston Tables, pp. 38-43: Rule-of-Thumb for Current Velocities.)

CURRENTS IN THE GULF OF MAINE - In the Gulf of Maine, on the western side, the Flood Current splits at Cape Ann, Mass., and floods north and east along the shore towards the Bay of Fundy. At the same time, on the eastern side of the Gulf, at the southern tip of Nova Scotia, the Flood Current runs to the west and then north and eastwards along the shore into the Bay of Fundy. The Ebb Current is just the reverse. In addition to these large principal currents, along the Maine Coast, at least at the mouths of principal bays, there is a shoreward set during the Flood and an offshore set during the Ebb, although this set is of considerably less velocity.

West of Mount Desert, the average along-shore current is rarely more than a knot but the farther east one goes, the greater are the average velocities to be expected, up to 2 knots or more. When heading west, therefore, start off at the time shown for High Water in your area (see p. 13) and have a fair Ebb current for 6 hours. Headed east, start at the time for Low Water in your area (about 6 ½ hours after High Water) and carry the beneficial Flood current. East of Schoodic Point, the average currents are up to 2 knots and taking advantage of them will save considerable time and fuel.

Off shore, in the Gulf of Maine, unlike the along-shore currents that come to dead slack and _reverse_, there are so-called _rotary_ currents. These currents constantly change direction in a clockwise flow completing the circle in about 12 ½ hours. The maximum currents are when it is flooding in the northeasterly direction or ebbing in a southwesterly direction; minimum currents occur halfway between. There is no slack water.

Entering the Bay of Fundy through Grand Manan Channel, one finds that the average velocities are from 1-2 ½ knots, although in the narrower channels off the Bay, velocities are higher (Friar Roads at Eastport has average velocities of 3 knots of more). The Current in the Bay Floods to the Northeast and Ebbs to the Southwest.

In using this table, bear in mind that **actual times of Slack or Maximum occasionally differ from the predicted times** by as much as half an hour and in rare instances as much as an hour. Referring the Time of Current Change at the subordinate stations listed below, to the predicted Current Change at the reference station gives the _approximate_ time only. Therefore, to make make sure of getting the full advantage of a favorable current or slack water, the navigator should reach the entrance or strait at least half an hour before the predicted time. (This is essentially the same precautionary note found in the U.S. Tidal Currents Table Book.)

Figures shown below are **average maximum** velocities in knots. To find the Time of Current Change (Start of Flood and Start of Ebb) at a selected point, refer to the table heading that particular section (in bold type) and add or subtract the time listed.

TIME DIFFERENCES Flood Starts; Ebb Starts Hr. Min.	MAXIMUM FLOOD Dir.(true) in degrees	Avg. Max. in knots	MAXIMUM EBB Dir.(true) in degrees	Avg. Max. in knots
MAINE COAST – based on Portland, pp. 30-35				
(Flood starts at Low Water; Ebb starts at High Water)				
Isle Au Haut, 0.8 mi. E of Richs Pt. .... -0 10	336	1.4	139	1.5
Damariscotta R., off Cavis Pt. .... F+1 15, E+0 05	350	0.6	215	1.0
Sheepscot R., off Barter Is. .... F+1 15, E+0 15	005	0.8	200	1.1
Lowe Pt., NE of, Sasanoa R. .... F+1 15, E+0 45	327	1.7	152	1.8
Lower Hell Gate, Knubble Bay* F+1 40, E+0 45	290	3.0	155	3.5

*Velocities up to 9.0 kts. have been observed in the vicinity of the Boilers.

Important: **See NOTE, bottom p. 29.**

TIME OF CURRENT CHANGE
(See Note at bottom of Boston Tables, pp. 38-43: Rule-of-Thumb for Current Velocities.)

	TIME DIFFERENCES Flood Starts; Ebb Starts Hr. Min.	MAXIMUM FLOOD Dir.(true) in degrees	Avg. Max. in knots	MAXIMUM EBB Dir.(true) in degrees	Avg. Max. in knots
KENNEBEC RIVER – based on Portland, pp. 30-35					
(Fl. starts at Low Water; Ebb starts at High Water)					
Hunniwell Pt., NE of	F+2 10, E+1 35	332	2.4	151	2.9
Bald Head, 0.3 mi. SW of	F+2 30, E+1 25	321	1.6	153	2.3
Bluff Head, W of	F+2 40, E+1 55	014	2.3	184	3.4
Fiddler Ledge, N of	F+2 50, E+1 50	267	1.9	113	2.6
Doubling Pt., S of...........................	F+2 30, E+1 50	300	2.6	127	3.0
Bath Iron Works.............................	F+2 45, E+2 05	004	1.9	178	2.5
CASCO BAY – based on Portland, pp. 30-35					
(Flood starts at Low Water; Ebb starts at High Water)					
Broad Sound, W. of Eagle Is.	+0 15	010	0.9	168	1.3
Hussey Sound, Cow Islands.........	F-0 20, E+0 40	012	1.1	178	0.8
Portland Hbr. entr., 19ft depth.....	F+1 00, E+0 20	313	0.7	137	1.1
Portland, Fore River Bridge	F+0 50, E+0 05	229	0.5	065	0.4
PORTSMOUTH HARBOR – based on Boston, pp. 38-43					
(Flood starts at Low Water; Ebb starts at High Water)					
Portsmouth Hbr. entr.	F+2 05, E+1 30	342	1.2	194	1.5
Fort Point......................................	F+2 10, E+1 35	328	1.6	098	2.0
Clark Is., S of	+2 15	270	1.6	085	2.3
Henderson Pt., W of	F+2 35, E+2 00	285	2.4	138	2.8
MASSACHUSETTS COAST – based on Boston, pp. 38-43					
(Flood starts at Low Water; Ebb starts at High Water)					
Merrimack River entr.	+0 25	285	2.2	105	1.4
Newburyport, Merrimack R.	+0 50	288	1.5	098	1.4
Plum Is. Sound entr.	-0 05	316	1.6	184	1.5
Gloucester Hbr., Blynman Canal entr.	F-0 35, E-1 15	310	3.0	130	3.3
Marblehead Channel....................	F+0 20, E-0 30	280	0.3	171	0.3
Hypocrite Channel.........................	-0 15	262	0.9	070	1.0
BOSTON HARBOR – based on Boston, pp. 38-43					
(Flood starts at Low Water; Ebb starts at High Water)					
Pt. Allerton, 0.4 mi. NW.	-0 45	265	0.7	080	0.8
Deer Island Lt................................	F-0 20, E-0 55	264	1.3	112	1.2
Nantasket Rds					
Hull Gut	F-0 45, E-1 10	162	1.9	340	2.5
West Head (W. Gut) 0.2mi. SW	F-0 35, E+0 05	167	1.4	322	1.4
Weir R. entr., Worlds End, N of	-0 15	076	0.7	272	0.8
Bumkin Is., 0.4mi. W. of	-0 40	195	0.5	303	0.3
Weymouth Back R., betw. Grape I. and Lower Neck...	-0 45	094	0.7	281	0.9
CAPE COD BAY – based on Boston, pp. 38-43					
(Flood starts at Low Water; Ebb starts at High Water)					
Barnstable Harbor..........................	F-0 10, E-0 40	192	1.2	004	1.4
NANTUCKET SOUND – based on Pollock Rip Channel, pp. 66-71					
Pollock Rip Channel, E end	-0 20	053	2.0	212	1.8

Important: See NOTE, bottom p. 29.

(See Note at bottom of Boston Tables, pp. 38-43: Rule-of-Thumb for Current Velocities.)

	TIME DIFFERENCES Flood Starts; Ebb Starts Hr. Min.	MAXIMUM FLOOD Dir.(true) in degrees	Avg. Max. in knots	MAXIMUM EBB Dir.(true) in degrees	Avg. Max. in knots
*POLLOCK RIP CHANNEL at Butler Hole - See table, pp. 66-71					
Monomoy Point, 0.2 mi. W of	+0 10	170	1.7	346	2.0
Halfmoon Shoal, 3.5 mi. E of	+1 10	088	1.1	295	1.0
Great Point, 0.5 mi. W of	F+0 25, E+1 15	029	1.1	195	1.2
Tuckernuck Shoal, off E end	+1 15	113	0.9	287	0.9
Nantucket Hbr. entr. chan.	F+3 20, E+2 45	171	1.2	350	1.5
Muskeget Is. chan., 1 mi. NE of	F+1 30, E+1 00	108	1.1	295	1.5
Muskeget Rock, 1.3 mi. SW of	+1 05	024	1.3	192	1.0
Muskeget Channel	+1 35	021	3.8	200	3.3
Betw. Long Shoal-Norton Shoal	+1 30	100	1.4	260	1.1
Cape Poge Lt., 1.7 mi. SSE of	+0 55	025	1.6	215	1.3
Cross Rip Channel	+1 50	091	1.3	272	0.9
Cape Poge, 3.2 mi. NE of	+2 35	095	1.6	300	1.2
Betw. Broken Gr.-Horseshoe Sh.	F+1 45, E+1 15	107	1.1	276	0.9
Point Gammon, 1.2 mi. S of	+1 10	105	1.1	260	1.0
Lewis Bay entr. chan.	+2 45	004	0.9	184	1.3
Betw. Wreck Shoal-Eldridge Shoal	+1 45	062	1.7	245	1.4
Hedge Fence Lighted Gong Buoy 22	+2 45	108	1.4	268	1.2
Betw. E. Chop-Squash Meadow	F+2 10, E+1 45	131	1.4	329	1.8
East Chop, 1 mi. N of	+2 30	116	2.2	297	2.2
West Chop, 0.8 mi. N of	F+2 50, E+2 20	096	3.1	282	3.0
Betw. Hedge Fence-L'hommedieu Shoal	+2 15	106	2.1	276	2.2
Waquoit Bay entr.	+3 30	348	1.5	203	1.4
L'hommedieu Shoal, N of W end	+2 20	080	2.3	268	2.3
Nobska Point, 1.8 mi. E of	+2 05	063	2.3	240	1.7
VINEYARD SOUND – based on Pollock Rip Channel, pp. 66-71					
West Chop, 0.2 mi. W of	F+1 20, E+1 50	059	2.7	241	1.4
Nobska Point, 1 mi. SE of	+2 30	071	2.6	259	2.4
Norton Point, 0.5 mi. N of	+2 00	050	3.4	240	2.4
Tarpaulin Cove, 1.5 mi. E of	F+2 50, E+2 10	055	1.9	232	2.3
Robinsons Hole, 1.2 mi. SE of	+2 20	060	1.9	240	2.1
Gay Head, 3 mi. N of	+2 05	074	1.1	255	1.2
Gay Head, 1.5 mi. NW of	+1 35	012	2.0	249	2.0
VINEYARD SOUND-BUZZARDS BAY – based on Woods Hole, pp. 52-57					
Robinsons Hole, Naushon Pt.	+0 40	151	3.0	332	2.9
Quicks Hole, S end	F+1 20, E+0 30	140	1.9	300	2.0
Quicks Hole, Middle	F+1 30, E+1 00	157	2.3	327	1.8
Quicks Hole, N end	F+1 40, E+0 55	165	2.0	002	2.6
Canapitsit Channel	F+1 00, E+0 14	131	1.7	312	1.7
BUZZARDS BAY – based on Woods Hole, pp. 52-57					
Westport River entr.	-1 20	290	2.2	108	2.5

Gooseberry Nk., 2 mi. SSE of (41°27'N- 71°01'W) *Rotary current, no slack water. Avg. max. 0.6 kts, approx. dir. 52° true 3:20 hrs. after Flood starts at Pollock Rip. Avg. max. 0.5 kts, approx. dir. 232° true 2:45 hrs. after Ebb starts at Pollock Rip.*

Betw. Ribbon Reef-Sow &Pigs Rf.	F-1 45, E-3 45	062	0.8	237	1.2
Penikese Is., 0.8 mi. NW of	F-3 00, E-1 55	050	1.2	254	1.1
Betw. Gull Is.-Nashawena Is.	F-3 40, E-3 00	091	0.9	247	1.1
Dumpling Rocks, 0.2 mi. SE of	F-3 10, E-2 30	066	0.8	190	1.1
BUZZARDS BAY – based on Cape Cod Canal, pp. 46-51					
Abiels Ledge	F+0 10, E-0 20	069	1.3	236	1.8
CAPE COD CANAL - table, pp. 46-51		070	4.0	250	4.5

*See Tidal Current Chart Buzzards Bay, Vineyard and Nantucket Sounds, pp. 72-83

Important: **See NOTE, bottom p. 29.**

TIME OF CURRENT CHANGE
(See Note at bottom of Boston Tables, pp. 38-43: Rule-of-Thumb for Current Velocities.)

	TIME DIFFERENCES Flood Starts; Ebb Starts Hr. Min.	MAXIMUM FLOOD Dir.(true) in degrees	Avg. Max. in knots	MAXIMUM EBB Dir.(true) in degrees	Avg. Max. in knots
*NARRAGANSETT BAY – based on Pollock Rip Channel, pp. 66-71					
Tiverton, Stone Bridge, Sakonnet	F-3 00, E-2 25	010	2.7	190	2.7
Tiverton, RR Bridge, Sakonnet R.	F-3 25, E-2 50	000	2.3	180	2.4
Castle Hill, W of East Passage	F-0 05, E-1 05	013	0.7	237	1.2
Bull Point, E of	-1 10	001	1.2	206	1.5
Rose Is., NE of	F-1 55, E-1 15	310	0.8	124	1.0
Rose Is., W of	F-0 40, E-1 20	001	0.7	172	1.0
Dyer Is., W of	-1 00	023	0.8	216	1.0
Mount Hope Bridge	-1 15	047	1.1	230	1.4
Kickamuit R., Mt. Hope Bay	F-2 05, E-1 20	000	1.4	191	1.7
Warren R., Warren	-0 20	358	1.0	171	0.9
Beavertail Point, 0.8 mi NW of	F-0 10, E-1 30	003	0.5	188	1.0
Betw. Dutch Is.-Beaver Head	-1 55	030	1.0	233	1.0
Dutch Is., W of	-1 25	014	1.3	206	1.2
India Pt. RR Bridge, Seekonk R.	-1 40	020	1.0	180	1.4
BLOCK ISLAND SOUND – based on The Race, pp. 92-97					
Pt. Judith Pond entr.	-3 10	351	1.8	186	1.5
Sandy Pt., Block Is. 1.5 mi N of	F-0 25, E-1 05	315	1.9	063	2.1
Lewis Pt., 1.0 mi. SW of	F-1 30, E-0 25	298	1.9	136	1.8
Lewis Pt., 1.5 mi. W of	F-1 35, E-0 50	318	1.4	170	1.7
Southwest Ledge	-0 25	321	1.5	141	2.1
Watch Hill Pt., 2.2 mi. E of	F-0 30, E+0 45	260	1.2	086	0.7
Montauk Pt., 1.2 mi. E of	F-1 20, E-0 40	346	2.8	162	2.8
Montauk Pt., 1 mi. NE of	F-2 05, E-1 15	356	2.4	145	1.9
Betw. Shagwong Reef-Cerberus Shoal	-0 30	241	1.9	056	1.8
Betw. Cerberus Sh.-Fishers Is.	F-1 00, E+0 40	264	1.3	096	1.3
Gardiners Is., 3 mi. NE of	-0 35	305	0.9	138	1.0
GARDINERS BAY etc. – based on The Race, pp. 92-97					
Goff Point, 0.4 mi. NW of	-1 35	225	1.2	010	1.6
Acabonack Hbr. entr., 0.6 mi. ESE of	F-1 35, E-1 05	345	1.4	140	1.2
Gardiners Pt. Ruins, 1.1 mi. N of	-0 10	270	1.2	066	1.8
Betw. Gardiners Point-Plum Is.	-0 25	288	1.4	100	1.6
Jennings Pt., 0.2 mi. NNW of	+0 35	290	1.6	055	1.5
Cedar Pt., 0.2 mi. W of	F-0 10, E+0 30	195	1.8	005	1.6
North Haven Peninsula, N of	F+0 10, E+0 40	230	2.4	035	2.1
Paradise Pt., 0.4 mi. E of	+0 35	145	1.5	345	1.5
Little Peconic Bay entr.	+0 45	240	1.6	015	1.5
Robins Is., 0.5 mi. S of	F+0 30, E+0 55	245	1.7	065	0.6
FISHERS ISLAND SOUND – based on The Race, pp. 92-97					
Napatree Point, 0.7 mi. SW of	-0 50	284	1.7	113	2.2
Little Narragansett Bay entr.	-2 05	092	1.3	268	1.3
Ram Island Reef, S of	-0 50	255	1.3	088	1.6
LONG ISLAND SOUND – based on The Race, pp. 92-97					
**THE RACE (near Valiant Rock) – See pp. 92-97		291	3.3	106	4.2
Race Point, 0.4 mi. SW of	-0 25	288	2.6	135	3.5
Little Gull Is., 1.1 mi. ENE of	+0 05	301	4.0	130	4.7
Little Gull Is., 0.8 mi. NNW of	F+0 25, E-2 20	258	1.9	043	2.9
Great Gull Is., SW of	-0 40	320	2.3	147	3.3
New London St. Pier, Thames R.	-1 30	358	0.4	178	0.4
Goshen Pt., 1.9 mi. SSE of	-0 55	285	1.2	062	1.6
Bartlett Reef, 0.2 mi. S of	F-2 05, E-1 05	255	1.4	090	1.3
Twotree Is. Channel	F-1 00, E-0 35	267	1.2	099	1.6

*Floods somewhat unstable. Flood currents differing from predicted should be expected.
** See Tidal Current Chart Long Is. and Block Is. Sounds, pp. 98-103

Important: **See NOTE, bottom p. 29.**

CURRENT STATIONS

TIME OF CURRENT CHANGE
(See Note at bottom of Boston Tables, pp. 38-43: Rule-of-Thumb for Current Velocities.)

	TIME DIFFERENCES Flood Starts; Ebb Starts Hr. Min.	MAXIMUM FLOOD Dir.(true) in degrees	Avg. Max. in knots	MAXIMUM EBB Dir.(true) in degrees	Avg. Max. in knots
LONG ISLAND SOUND – based on The Race, pp. 92-97 (cont.)					
Black Point, 0.8 mi. S of	F-0 40, E-0 15	260	1.3	073	1.4
Betw. Black Pt.-Plum Is.	+0 35	236	2.1	076	2.4
Plum Is., 0.8 mi. NNW of	F+0 10,E-1 05	247	1.7	065	2.4
Plum Gut	-1 00	306	1.9	116	3.0
Hatchett Pt., 1.1 mi. WSW of	F-2 30, E-0 40	240	1.3	045	1.2
Saybrook Bkwtr., 1.5 mi. SE of	F-1 20, E-0 45	260	1.9	070	2.0
Conn. River I-95 Bridge	F+1 15, E+0 20	356	0.9	166	1.8
Mulford Pt., 3.1 mi. NW of	+0 05	269	1.9	066	2.3
Cornfield Point, 2.8 mi. SE of	F-1 30, E-0 30	249	1.9	085	1.4
Cornfield Point, 1.1 mi. S of	-0 50	293	1.4	108	1.6
Kelsey Point, 1 mi. S of	F-1 35, E-1 05	249	2.0	118	1.5
Six Mile Reef, 2 mi. E of	F-0 30, E+0 05	235	1.6	040	2.1
Sachem Head, 1 mi. SSE of	-0 30	255	1.1	065	1.0
New Haven Harbor entr.	-0 05	277	0.7	122	0.5
Housatonic R., Milford Pt., 0.2 mi. W of	+0 15	330	1.2	135	1.2
Point No Point, 2.1 mi. S of	-0 10	251	1.3	074	1.2
Port Jefferson Harbor entr.	-0 10	150	1.6	336	1.0
Crane Neck Point, 0.5 mi. NW of	F-0 45, E-1 40	256	1.3	016	1.5
Eatons Neck Pt., 1.3 mi. N of	+0 20	283	1.4	075	1.4
Lloyd Point, 1.3 mi. NNW of	+1 30	255	1.0	055	0.9
EAST RIVER – based on Hell Gate, pp. 116-121					
Cryders Pt., 0.4 mi. NNW of	-0 30	110	1.3	285	1.1
College Pt. Rf., .25 mi. NW of	-0 30	074	1.5	261	1.4
Rikers Is. Chann. off La Guardia Field	+0 05	088	1.1	261	1.3
Hunts Point, SW of	0 00	108	1.7	280	1.3
S. Brother Is. NW of	-0 10	054	1.5	252	1.2
Off Winthrop Ave., Astoria	0 00	040	3.4	220	2.5
Mill Rock, NE of	-0 25	103	2.3	288	0.6
Mill Rock, W of	F-0 25, E+0 00	000	1.2	180	1.0
HELL GATE (off Mill Rock) – table, pp. 116-121		050	3.4	230	4.6
Roosevelt Is., W of, off 75th St.	-0 05	037	3.8	215	4.7
Roosevelt Is., E of, off 36th Ave.	-0 10	030	3.5	210	3.4
Roosevelt Is., W of, off 67th St.	+0 10	011	3.6	230	4.0
Pier 67 (Off 19th St.)	-0 10	355	1.8	179	1.9
Williamsburg Br., 0.3 mi. N of	-0 05	020	2.7	220	2.9
Brooklyn Bridge, 0.1 mi. SW of	-0 10	046	2.9	222	3.5
LONG ISLAND, South Coast – based on The Narrows, pp. 122-127					
Shinnecock Inlet	F+0 05, E-0 40	350	2.5	170	2.3
Fire Is. Inlet, 0.5 mi. S. of Oak Bch.	+0 15	082	2.4	244	2.4
Jones Inlet	F-1 15, E-0 50	035	3.1	217	2.6
East Rockaway Inlet	F-1 35, E-1 10	042	2.2	227	2.3
JAMAICA BAY – based on The Narrows, pp. 122-127					
Rockaway Inlet entr.	-1 45	085	1.8	244	2.7
Barren Is., E of	F-1 50, E-2 10	004	1.2	192	1.7
Beach Channel (bridge)	F-1 40, E-1 05	062	1.9	225	2.0
Grass Hassock Channel	-1 10	052	1.0	228	1.0
NEW YORK HARBOR ENTRANCE – based on The Narrows, pp. 122-127					
Ambrose Channel	-0 40	303	1.6	123	1.7
Norton Pt., WSW of	+0 10	341	1.0	166	1.2
THE NARROWS (mid-ch.) – table, pp. 122-127		336	1.6	164	1.9

Important: See NOTE, bottom p. 29.

TIME OF CURRENT CHANGE
(See Note at bottom of Boston Tables, pp. 38-43: Rule-of-Thumb for Current Velocities.)

	TIME DIFFERENCES Flood Starts; Ebb Starts Hr. Min.	MAXIMUM FLOOD Dir.(true) in degrees	Avg. Max. in knots	MAXIMUM EBB Dir.(true) in degrees	Avg. Max. in knots
NEW YORK HARBOR, Upper Bay – based on The Narrows, pp. 122-127					
Bay Ridge, W of	F+0 00, E+0 35	354	1.4	185	1.5
Red Hook Channel	F-0 55, E-0 15	353	1.0	170	0.7
Robbins Reef Light, E of	F+0 25, E-0 05	016	1.3	204	1.6
Red Hook, 1 mi. W of	+0 45	024	1.3	206	2.3
Statue of Liberty, E of	+0 55	031	1.4	205	1.9
HUDSON RIVER, Midchannel – based on The Narrows, pp. 122-127					
George Washington Bridge	F+0 30, E+1 35	010	1.8	203	2.5
Spuyten Duyvil	F+0 25, E+1 45	020	1.6	–	2.1
Riverdale	F+1 25, E+1 50	015	1.4	200	2.0
Dobbs Ferry	F+1 45, E+2 10	010	1.3	–	1.7
Tarrytown	F+1 50, E+2 30	000	1.1	–	1.5
West Point, off Duck Is	F+2 45, E+3 40	010	1.0	–	1.1
NEW YORK HARBOR, Lower Bay – based on The Narrows, pp. 122-127					
Sandy Hook Channel	-1 20	286	1.6	094	1.9
Sandy Hook Channel, 0.4 mi. W of N. tip	-1 40	235	2.0	050	1.6
Coney Is. Lt., 1.5 mi. SSE of	-1 10	310	1.1	125	1.3
Rockaway Inlet Jetty, 1 mi. SW of	F-2 05, E-1 35	287	1.2	142	1.4
Coney Is. Channel, W end	F-1 15, E-0 30	293	1.1	102	1.2
SANDY HOOK BAY – based on The Narrows, pp. 122-127					
Highlands Bridge, Shrewsbury R.	+0 25	170	2.6	–	2.5
Sea Bright Br., Shrewsbury R.	F+1 05, E+0 45	185	1.4	–	1.7
RARITAN RIVER – based on The Narrows, pp. 122-127					
Washington Canal, N entr.	F-1 00, E-1 40	240	1.5	060	1.5
South River entr.	F-1 45, E-0 35	180	1.1	000	1.0
ARTHUR KILL & KILL VAN KULL – based on The Narrows, pp. 122-127					
Tottenville, Arthur Kill River	-0 50	023	1.0	211	1.1
Tufts Pt.-Smoking Pt.	-0 35	109	1.2	267	1.2
Elizabethport	+0 20	090	1.4	262	1.1
Bergen Pt., East Reach	-1 35	274	1.1	094	1.2
New Brighton	-1 35	262	1.3	072	1.9
NEW JERSEY COAST – based on Del. Bay Entr., pp. 146-151					
Manasquan Inlet	F-1 00, E-1 40	300	1.7	120	1.8
Manasquan R. Hwy. Br. Main Ch.	F-1 00, E-1 40	230	2.2	050	2.1
Pt. Pleasant Canal, north bridge*	F+1 30, E+0 20	170	1.8	350	2.0
Barnegat Inlet	F+0 40, E-0 10	270	2.2	090	2.5
Manahawkin Drawbridge	+2 05	030	1.1	210	0.9
McCrie Shoal	-1 05	280	1.3	100	1.4
Cape May Harbor entr.	-2 00	324	1.6	142	1.7
Cape May Canal, E end	-2 15	310	1.9	130	1.9
DELAWARE BAY & RIVER – based on Del. Bay Entr., pp. 146-151					
Cape May Channel	-1 35	306	1.5	150	2.3
DELAWARE BAY ENTR. – table, pp. 146-151		342	1.8	152	1.7
Cape Henlopen, 0.7 mi. ESE of	F-0 25, E-1 05	331	1.8	139	2.4
Cape Henlopen, 2 mi. NE of	F+0 00, E-0 30	315	2.0	145	2.3
Cape Henlopen, 5 mi. N of	+0 10	344	2.0	173	1.9

Waters are extremely turbulent. Currents of 6 to 7 knots have been reported near the bridges.

Important: See NOTE, bottom p. 29.

(Side tab: CURRENT STATIONS)

TIME OF CURRENT CHANGE

(See Note at bottom of Boston Tables, pp. 38-43: Rule-of-Thumb for Current Velocities.)

	TIME DIFFERENCES Flood Starts; Ebb Starts Hr. Min.	MAXIMUM FLOOD Dir.(true) in degrees	 Avg. Max. in knots	MAXIMUM EBB Dir.(true) in degrees	 Avg. Max. in knots
DELAWARE BAY & RIVER – based on Del. Bay Entr., pp. 146-151 (cont.)					
Mispillion River Mouth .... F+2 15, E+1 20		025	1.5	190	1.0
Bay Shore chan., City of Town Bank F-0 50, E-1 10		006	0.9	183	1.0
Fourteen Ft. Bk., Lt., 1.2 mi. E of .... -0 05		339	1.3	174	1.5
Maurice River entr. .... +0 30		012	1.1	192	1.0
Kelly Island, 1.5 mi. E of .... +0 20		348	0.9	164	1.2
Miah Maull rge. at Cross Ledge rge .... +1 00		335	1.5	160	1.8
False Egg Is. Pt., 2 mi. off .... -0 05		342	1.1	158	1.3
Ben Davis Pt. Shoal., SW of .... F+1 30, E+1 05		321	1.8	147	1.9
Cohansey R., 0.5 mi. above entr. .... +1 05		074	1.2	254	1.4
Arnold Point, 2.2 mi. WSW of .... +2 00		324	2.1	145	1.9
Smyrna River entr. .... +1 30		250	1.2	070	1.5
Stony Point chan., W of .... F+2 50, E+1 40		324	1.5	151	1.9
Appoquinimink R. entr. .... F+2 00, E+1 20		231	1.0	048	1.2
Reedy Is., off end of pier .... F+2 30, E+2 00		027	2.4	194	2.6
Alloway Creek entr., 0.2 mi. above .... F+1 50, E+1 20		129	2.1	325	2.1
Reedy Point, 0.85 mi. NE of .... F+3 00, E+2 05		341	1.6	163	2.2
Salem River entr. .... F+3 10, E+2 40		062	1.5	245	1.6
Bulkhead Sh. chan., off Del. City F+2 40, E+2 05		308	2.1	138	2.1
Pea Patch Is., chan., E of .... F+3 00, E+2 35		319	2.3	148	2.3
New Castle, chan., abreast of ..... F+3 00, E+2 10		051	1.9	230	2.4
CHESAPEAKE BAY – based on The Race, pp. 92-97					
(over 90% correlation within 15 min. throughout year)					
Cape Henry Light, 2.0 mi. N of .... +0 10		289	1.2	110	1.1
Chesapeake Bay entr., Buoy LB2CH .... -0 10		297	1.1	120	1.1
Cape Henry Light, 4.6 mi. N of .... -0 30		294	1.3	104	1.3
Cape Henry Light, 8.3 mi. NW of. F+0 10, E-0 15		329	1.0	133	1.1
Tail of the Horseshoe .... F+0 00, E-0 40		300	0.9	110	1.0
Chesapeake Channel (Bridge Tunnel) .... F+0 00, E-0 25		335	1.8	145	1.5
Fisherman Is., 1.7 mi. S of F-0 25, E-1 15		297	1.0	126	1.4
York Spit Channel N buoy "26". F+1 30, E+0 25		010	0.8	195	1.1
Old Plantation Flats Lt., 0.5 mi. W of .... F+1 30, E+0 55		005	1.2	175	1.3
Wolf Trap Lt., 0.5 mi. W of .... F+1 40, E+0 35		015	1.0	190	1.2
Stingray Point, 5.5 mi. E of .... +2 25		343	1.0	179	0.9
Stingray Point, 12.5 mi. E of .... F+2 15, E+1 10		030	1.0	175	0.8
Smith Point Lt., 6.0 mi. N of .... F+4 25, E+3 20		350	0.4	135	1.0
Cove Point - See Chesapeake Bay Current Diagram, p. 160					
Pooles Island - See Chesapeake Bay Current Diagram, p. 160					
Worton Point - See Chesapeake Bay Current Diagram, p. 160					
CHESAPEAKE & DELAWARE CANAL - **table, pp. 154-159**		097	2.0	278	1.9
HAMPTON ROADS – based on The Race, pp. 92-97					
(over 90% correlation within 15 min. throughout year)					
Thimble Shoal Channel (West End) F-0 20, E-1 00		293	0.9	116	1.2
Old Point Comfort, 0.2 mi. S of F-0 40, E-1 50		240	1.7	075	1.4
Willoughby Spit, 0.8 mi. NW of .... -1 40		260	0.7	040	1.0
Sewells Point, chan., W of F-0 45, E-2 20		195	0.9	000	1.2
Newport News, chan., middle F-0 45, E-1 10		244	1.1	076	1.1

Important: **See NOTE, bottom p. 29.**

TIME OF CURRENT CHANGE
(See Note at bottom of Boston Tables, pp. 38-43: Rule-of-Thumb for Current Velocities.)

	TIME DIFFERENCES Flood Starts; Ebb Starts Hr. Min.	MAXIMUM FLOOD Dir.(true) in degrees	Avg. Max. in knots	MAXIMUM EBB Dir.(true) in degrees	Avg. Max. in knots
C&D CANAL POINTS – based on C&D Canal, pp. 154-159					
Back Creek, 0.3 mi. W of Sandy Pt..............	-0 05	057	1.2	244	1.4
Reedy Point Radio Tower, S of......	F-1 05, E-0 10	078	1.9	263	1.3
VA, NC, SC, GA & FL, outer coast – based on Hell Gate, pp. 116-121					
(over 90% correlation within 15 min. throughout year)					
Hatteras Inlet	+0 50	307	2.1	148	2.0
Ocracoke Inlet chan. entr............	F+1 10, E+0 05	000	1.7	145	2.4
Beaufort Inlet Approach	F+0 25, E-1 00	358	0.3	161	1.4
Cape Fear R. Bald Head	-0 35	034	2.2	190	2.9
Winyah Bay entr.	F+0 05, E-0 35	320	1.9	140	2.0
North Santee R. entr.	F-0 40, E-1 35	010	1.5	165	1.8
South Santee R. entr.	-1 20	045	1.5	240	1.6
Charleston Hbr. entr., betw. jetties..............	-1 40	320	1.8	121	1.8
Charleston Hbr., off Ft. Sumter....................	-1 40	313	1.7	127	2.0
Charleston Hbr. S. ch. 0.8 mi.					
ENE of Ft. Johnson	F-0 55, E-1 50	275	0.8	115	2.6
Charleston Hbr., Drum Is., E of (bridge)...	-1 20	020	1.2	183	2.0
North Edisto River entr.	-0 35	332	2.9	142	3.7
South Edisto River entr.	F-1 20, E-1 50	350	1.8	146	2.2
Ashepoo R. off Jefford Cr. entr.....................	-0 40	016	1.5	197	1.6
Port Royal Sd., SE chan. entr........................	-2 00	310	1.3	150	1.6
Hilton Head...	-1 20	324	1.8	146	1.8
Beaufort River entr.	-1 20	010	1.3	195	1.4
Savannah River entr.......................................	-0 55	286	2.0	110	2.0
Vernon R. 1.2 mi. S of Possum Pt..	F-1 25, E-1 00	324	1.1	166	1.7
Raccoon Key & Egg Is. Shoal bet.	F-0 40, E -1 15	254	1.6	129	2.0
St. Catherines Sound entr.............	F-1 40, E-0 35	291	1.8	126	1.7
Sapelo Sound entr.........................	F-1 30, E-0 55	290	1.7	118	2.2
Doboy Sound entr...	-1 25	289	1.6	106	1.8
Altamaha Sd., 1 mi. SE of					
Onemile Cut................................	F-0 15, E-2 00	272	1.0	092	1.9
St. Simons Sound Bar Channel....	F-1 15, E-0 40	308	0.8	119	1.7
St. Andrews Sound entr.	F-1 20, E-0 50	268	2.1	103	2.2
Cumberland Sd., St. Mary's River,					
Ft. Clinch, 0.3 mi. N	F-1 15, E -0 50	275	1.4	087	1.6
Drum Point Is., rge. D chan............................	-0 35	350	1.1	170	1.5
Nassau Sd., midsound,					
1 mi. N of Sawpit Cr. entr.	-0 20	312	1.7	135	1.7
FLORIDA EAST COAST – based on The Narrows, pp. 122-127					
(over 90% correlation within 15 min. throughout year)					
St. Johns R. entr. betw. jetties......................	+0 20	262	2.0	081	2.0
Mayport...	+0 30	211	2.2	026	3.3
St. Johns Bluff..............................	F+0 55, E-0 05	244	1.6	059	2.4
FLORIDA EAST COAST – based on Hell Gate, pp. 116-121					
(over 90% correlation within 15 min. throughout year)					
Fort Pierce Inlet entr.	+0 40	258	2.7	080	2.8
Lake Worth Inlet, entr....................................	-0 55	267	1.6	086	1.3
Miami Hbr., Bakers Haulover Cut	-0 10	270	2.9	090	2.5
Miami Hbr. entr.	-0 15	293	2.3	114	2.4

NOTE: Velocities shown are from U.S. Gov't. figures. It is obvious, however, to local mariners and other observers, that coastal inlets may have far greater velocities than indicated here. Strong winds and opposing tides can cause even more dangerous conditions, and great caution should be used. Separate times for Flood and Ebb are given only when the times are more than 20 minutes apart.

CURRENT STATIONS

2019 HIGH & LOW WATER
PORTLAND, ME
43°39.4'N, 70°14.8'W

Standard Time   Standard Time

DAY OF MONTH	DAY OF WEEK	JANUARY HIGH a.m.	Ht.	HIGH p.m.	Ht.	LOW a.m.	LOW p.m.	DAY OF MONTH	DAY OF WEEK	FEBRUARY HIGH a.m.	Ht.	HIGH p.m.	Ht.	LOW a.m.	LOW p.m.
1	T	7:20	9.8	7:55	8.9	12:58	1:42	1	F	8:43	9.5	9:23	8.4	2:26	3:10
2	W	8:14	9.9	8:51	8.8	1:55	2:38	2	S	9:30	9.6	10:08	8.5	3:16	3:55
3	T	9:04	10.0	9:42	8.9	2:47	3:28	3	S	10:13	9.6	10:48	8.6	3:59	4:36
4	F	9:49	10.0	10:27	8.8	3:34	4:14	4	M	10:51	9.7	11:24	8.7	4:39	5:13
5	S	10:30	10.0	11:08	8.8	4:18	4:56	5	T	11:27	9.7	11:58	8.7	5:16	5:47
6	S	11:09	9.9	11:46	8.7	4:58	5:34	6	W	...	...	12:02	9.6	5:51	6:20
7	M	11:46	9.8	...	...	5:36	6:11	7	T	12:31	8.8	12:36	9.5	6:26	6:52
8	T	12:23	8.6	12:23	9.6	6:13	6:47	8	F	1:03	8.8	1:12	9.2	7:01	7:25
9	W	13:00	8.6	1:00	9.4	6:50	7:23	9	S	1:39	8.8	1:50	9.0	7:39	8:00
10	T	1:36	8.5	1:39	9.2	7:29	7:59	10	S	2:14	8.8	2:30	8.7	8:20	8:39
11	F	2:14	8.4	2:20	8.9	8:10	8:38	11	M	2:54	8.9	3:16	8.4	9:05	9:23
12	S	2:55	8.4	3:05	8.6	8:55	9:19	12	T	3:39	8.9	4:07	8.2	9:56	10:12
13	S	3:38	8.4	3:53	8.3	9:43	10:05	13	W	4:30	9.0	5:06	8.0	10:53	11:08
14	M	4:25	8.5	4:46	8.1	10:36	10:54	14	T	5:27	9.2	6:10	8.1	11:56	...
15	T	5:15	8.7	5:43	8.0	11:33	11:48	15	F	6:29	9.5	7:15	8.3	12:09	1:01
16	W	6:08	9.0	6:44	8.1	...	12:33	16	S	7:32	9.9	8:18	8.8	1:13	2:03
17	T	7:04	9.5	7:44	8.4	12:44	1:32	17	S	8:33	10.5	9:16	9.4	2:15	3:02
18	F	7:59	10.0	8:41	8.8	1:41	2:28	18	M	9:30	11.1	10:10	9.9	3:13	3:56
19	S	8:53	10.6	9:36	9.2	2:36	3:22	19	T	10:25	11.4	11:02	10.4	4:09	4:48
20	S	9:46	11.1	10:28	9.7	3:30	4:14	20	W	11:18	11.6	11:52	10.7	5:02	5:38
21	M	10:39	11.4	11:20	10.0	4:23	5:06	21	T	...	...	12:11	11.5	5:55	6:27
22	T	11:32	11.6	...	...	5:16	5:57	22	F	12:42	10.8	1:04	11.1	6:48	7:17
23	W	12:12	10.2	12:25	11.5	6:10	6:48	23	S	1:33	10.7	1:57	10.6	7:43	8:08
24	T	1:04	10.3	1:20	11.2	7:04	7:40	24	S	2:25	10.4	2:53	9.9	8:39	9:01
25	F	1:57	10.3	2:16	10.7	8:01	8:34	25	M	3:19	10.0	3:53	9.1	9:38	9:57
26	S	2:53	10.1	3:15	10.0	9:01	9:30	26	T	4:16	9.6	4:56	8.6	10:40	10:58
27	S	3:50	9.9	4:18	9.4	10:04	10:28	27	W	5:17	9.2	6:03	8.2	11:46	...
28	M	4:50	9.7	5:23	8.8	11:09	11:29	28	T	6:20	9.0	7:07	8.0	12:01	12:51
29	T	5:51	9.5	6:30	8.5	...	12:16								
30	W	6:52	9.4	7:34	8.3	12:31	1:20								
31	T	7:50	9.4	8:32	8.3	1:31	2:18								

Dates when Ht. of **Low** Water is below Mean Lower Low with Ht. of lowest given for each period and Date of lowest in ( ):

   2nd–6th: -0.4' (4th, 5th)   16th–25th: -2.0' (20th)
   18th–26th: -2.0' (22nd)

Average Rise and Fall 9.1 ft.

When a high tide exceeds avg. ht., the *following* low tide will be lower than avg.

2019 HIGH & LOW WATER
PORTLAND, ME
43°39.4'N, 70°14.8'W

*Daylight Time starts March 10 at 2 a.m.   Daylight Saving Time

DAY OF MONTH	DAY OF WEEK	MARCH HIGH a.m.	Ht.	HIGH p.m.	Ht.	LOW a.m.	LOW p.m.	DAY OF MONTH	DAY OF WEEK	APRIL HIGH a.m.	Ht.	HIGH p.m.	Ht.	LOW a.m.	LOW p.m.
1	F	7:22	8.9	8:06	8.1	1:04	1:51	1	M	9:34	8.9	10:07	8.6	3:22	3:54
2	S	8:18	9.0	8:58	8.2	2:02	2:44	2	T	10:19	9.1	10:46	8.9	4:08	4:35
3	S	9:07	9.2	9:42	8.5	2:53	3:30	3	W	10:59	9.3	11:21	9.2	4:48	5:10
4	M	9:50	9.4	10:21	8.7	3:37	4:10	4	T	11:36	9.4	11:54	9.4	5:25	5:43
5	T	10:29	9.5	10:56	8.9	4:17	4:46	5	F	...	...	12:11	9.4	6:00	6:15
6	W	11:04	9.6	11:28	9.0	4:53	5:18	6	S	12:25	9.6	12:46	9.4	6:34	6:47
7	T	11:38	9.6	11:59	9.1	5:27	5:49	7	S	12:57	9.8	1:22	9.3	7:10	7:21
8	F	...	...	12:12	9.5	6:01	6:20	8	M	1:31	9.9	2:00	9.2	7:48	7:58
9	S	12:31	9.2	12:46	9.3	6:35	6:52	9	T	2:10	9.9	2:43	9.0	8:29	8:40
10	S	1:03	9.3	*2:23	9.1	*8:12	*8:27	10	W	2:52	9.9	3:30	8.8	9:15	9:28
11	M	2:39	9.4	3:03	8.9	8:52	9:06	11	T	3:40	9.8	4:24	8.6	10:07	10:21
12	T	3:19	9.4	3:49	8.6	9:36	9:50	12	F	4:36	9.7	5:24	8.5	11:06	11:23
13	W	4:05	9.4	4:40	8.4	10:27	10:41	13	S	5:38	9.6	6:30	8.6	...	12:10
14	T	4:57	9.3	5:40	8.2	11:25	11:40	14	S	6:47	9.7	7:38	9.0	12:30	1:17
15	F	5:57	9.4	6:46	8.2	...	12:29	15	M	7:56	9.9	8:41	9.5	1:40	2:22
16	S	7:04	9.6	7:54	8.5	12:45	1:37	16	T	9:01	10.2	9:38	10.1	2:46	3:21
17	S	8:11	9.9	8:59	9.0	1:53	2:42	17	W	10:01	10.6	10:31	10.7	3:46	4:15
18	M	9:16	10.4	9:57	9.7	2:59	3:42	18	T	10:56	10.8	11:21	11.1	4:42	5:06
19	T	10:16	10.9	10:51	10.3	3:59	4:36	19	F	11:48	10.8	...	...	5:34	5:54
20	W	11:11	11.2	11:42	10.8	4:55	5:27	20	S	12:08	11.3	12:38	10.6	6:24	6:41
21	T	...	...	12:04	11.4	5:48	6:16	21	S	12:54	11.2	1:28	10.3	7:13	7:27
22	F	12:30	11.1	12:55	11.2	6:40	7:04	22	M	1:39	10.9	2:17	9.9	8:01	8:14
23	S	1:18	11.1	1:46	10.8	7:31	7:52	23	T	2:26	10.5	3:07	9.3	8:50	9:02
24	S	2:06	10.9	2:37	10.3	8:22	8:41	24	W	3:14	10.0	3:59	8.8	9:41	9:53
25	M	2:55	10.6	3:30	9.6	9:15	9:31	25	T	4:05	9.5	4:54	8.4	10:35	10:49
26	T	3:46	10.1	4:26	9.0	10:10	10:25	26	F	5:00	9.0	5:52	8.2	11:32	11:48
27	W	4:40	9.5	5:26	8.4	11:08	11:24	27	S	5:59	8.6	6:50	8.1	...	12:30
28	T	5:39	9.0	6:30	8.1	...	12:11	28	S	7:00	8.5	7:46	8.2	12:50	1:28
29	F	6:42	8.7	7:33	8.0	12:27	1:14	29	M	7:58	8.5	8:37	8.4	1:49	2:21
30	S	7:45	8.6	8:31	8.0	1:31	2:15	30	T	8:52	8.6	9:23	8.7	2:43	3:08
31	S	8:43	8.7	9:22	8.3	2:30	3:08								

Dates when Ht. of **Low** Water is below Mean Lower Low with Ht. of lowest given for each period and Date of lowest in ( ):

    17th–26th: -1.6' (20th, 21st, 22nd, 23rd)   15th–23rd: -1.5' (20th)

Average Rise and Fall 9.1 ft.

When a high tide exceeds avg. ht., the *following* low tide will be lower than avg.

2019 HIGH & LOW WATER
PORTLAND, ME
43°39.4'N, 70°14.8'W

| | | **Daylight Saving Time** | | | | | | | **Daylight Saving Time** | | | |

DAY OF MONTH	DAY OF WEEK	MAY					DAY OF MONTH	DAY OF WEEK	JUNE			
		HIGH		LOW					HIGH		LOW	
		a.m.	Ht.	p.m.	Ht.	a.m.	p.m.			a.m.	Ht.	p.m.	Ht.	a.m.	p.m.

DAY OF MONTH	DAY OF WEEK	a.m.	Ht.	p.m.	Ht.	a.m.	p.m.	DAY OF MONTH	DAY OF WEEK	a.m.	Ht.	p.m.	Ht.	a.m.	p.m.
1	W	9:40	8.8	10:03	9.1	3:30	3:49	1	S	10:26	8.8	10:35	10.0	4:16	4:21
2	T	10:23	9.0	10:40	9.4	4:13	4:27	2	S	11:09	9.0	11:15	10.4	4:58	5:02
3	F	11:03	9.1	11:15	9.8	4:53	5:03	3	M	11:53	9.2	11:57	10.7	5:40	5:44
4	S	11:41	9.2	11:50	10.0	5:30	5:38	4	T	...	...	12:37	9.3	6:23	6:28
5	S	...	...	12:19	9.3	6:07	6:14	5	W	12:41	10.8	1:24	9.4	7:08	7:15
6	M	12:25	10.3	12:59	9.3	6:46	6:53	6	T	1:28	10.9	2:13	9.4	7:56	8:06
7	T	1:04	10.4	1:41	9.3	7:27	7:35	7	F	2:19	10.8	3:06	9.5	8:48	9:00
8	W	1:46	10.4	2:27	9.2	8:11	8:21	8	S	3:14	10.6	4:02	9.5	9:42	9:59
9	T	2:34	10.4	3:18	9.1	9:00	9:12	9	S	4:14	10.4	5:01	9.6	10:39	11:02
10	F	3:25	10.2	4:13	9.0	9:54	10:09	10	M	5:16	10.1	6:02	9.7	11:39	...
11	S	4:23	10.1	5:14	9.0	10:53	11:12	11	T	6:21	9.8	7:03	9.9	12:09	12:40
12	S	5:26	9.9	6:18	9.2	11:55	...	12	W	7:28	9.6	8:03	10.2	1:16	1:40
13	M	6:34	9.8	7:22	9.5	12:20	12:59	13	T	8:32	9.5	8:59	10.5	2:20	2:38
14	T	7:42	9.8	8:22	9.9	1:28	2:01	14	F	9:32	9.5	9:52	10.7	3:20	3:33
15	W	8:47	9.9	9:19	10.4	2:33	2:59	15	S	10:28	9.5	10:41	10.8	4:15	4:24
16	T	9:47	10.1	10:11	10.8	3:33	3:53	16	S	11:20	9.4	11:27	10.7	5:06	5:12
17	F	10:42	10.1	11:00	11.1	4:29	4:44	17	M	...	...	12:07	9.4	5:53	5:58
18	S	11:34	10.1	11:46	11.1	5:20	5:32	18	T	12:11	10.6	12:52	9.2	6:38	6:42
19	S	...	...	12:23	10.0	6:08	6:18	19	W	12:54	10.4	1:36	9.0	7:21	7:25
20	M	12:31	11.0	1:10	9.7	6:55	7:03	20	T	1:36	10.1	2:19	8.9	8:03	8:08
21	T	1:15	10.7	1:57	9.4	7:41	7:48	21	F	2:18	9.8	3:01	8.7	8:45	8:52
22	W	1:59	10.3	2:43	9.1	8:27	8:34	22	S	3:01	9.5	3:44	8.6	9:27	9:37
23	T	2:45	9.9	3:31	8.7	9:13	9:22	23	S	3:46	9.2	4:29	8.5	10:10	10:25
24	F	3:32	9.5	4:20	8.5	10:01	10:13	24	M	4:33	8.9	5:14	8.5	10:54	11:16
25	S	4:22	9.1	5:11	8.3	10:51	11:07	25	T	5:23	8.6	6:01	8.6	11:40	...
26	S	5:15	8.7	6:03	8.3	11:42	...	26	W	6:15	8.4	6:49	8.8	12:09	12:27
27	M	6:11	8.5	6:55	8.4	12:03	12:34	27	T	7:09	8.2	7:37	9.0	1:03	1:15
28	T	7:07	8.4	7:44	8.6	1:00	1:24	28	F	8:03	8.2	8:24	9.4	1:56	2:04
29	W	8:01	8.4	8:31	8.9	1:55	2:12	29	S	8:57	8.4	9:11	9.8	2:48	2:53
30	T	8:53	8.5	9:15	9.2	2:45	2:57	30	S	9:48	8.6	9:58	10.2	3:38	3:41
31	F	9:41	8.6	9:55	9.6	3:32	3:39								

Dates when Ht. of **Low** Water is below Mean Lower Low with Ht. of lowest given for each period and Date of lowest in ( ):

    6th–10th: -0.5' (8th)   3rd–10th: -0.9' (6th)

    15th–22nd: -1.1' (19th)   14th–19th: -0.6' (16th, 17th)

Average Rise and Fall 9.1 ft.

When a high tide exceeds avg. ht., the *following* low tide will be lower than avg.

2019 HIGH & LOW WATER
PORTLAND, ME
43°39.4'N, 70°14.8'W

		Daylight Saving Time							**Daylight Saving Time**					

D A Y O F M O N T H	D A Y O F W E E K	JULY HIGH a.m.	Ht.	HIGH p.m.	Ht.	LOW a.m.	LOW p.m.	D A Y O F M O N T H	D A Y O F W E E K	AUGUST HIGH a.m.	Ht.	HIGH p.m.	Ht.	LOW a.m.	LOW p.m.
1	M	10:38	8.9	10:45	10.6	4:26	4:29	1	T	11:54	9.8	...	...	5:40	5:49
2	T	11:26	9.2	11:33	11.0	5:13	5:18	2	F	12:05	11.5	12:45	10.1	6:31	6:42
3	W	...	...	12:16	9.5	6:01	6:07	3	S	12:58	11.6	1:37	10.4	7:21	7:37
4	T	12:22	11.2	1:06	9.7	6:50	6:58	4	S	1:52	11.4	2:30	10.5	8:13	8:33
5	F	1:13	11.3	1:57	9.9	7:41	7:52	5	M	2:48	11.1	3:24	10.5	9:05	9:31
6	S	2:07	11.2	2:51	10.0	8:32	8:48	6	T	3:46	10.5	4:20	10.4	10:00	10:32
7	S	3:03	10.9	3:46	10.0	9:26	9:47	7	W	4:46	9.9	5:18	10.3	10:56	11:36
8	M	4:01	10.6	4:43	10.1	10:22	10:50	8	T	5:49	9.4	6:18	10.1	11:55	...
9	T	5:04	10.1	5:42	10.1	11:19	11:54	9	F	6:56	8.9	7:19	9.9	12:41	12:57
10	W	6:07	9.6	6:42	10.1	...	12:19	10	S	8:00	8.7	8:19	9.8	1:46	1:58
11	T	7:12	9.3	7:41	10.2	1:00	1:18	11	S	9:02	8.6	9:16	9.8	2:48	2:57
12	F	8:17	9.1	8:39	10.2	2:05	2:18	12	M	9:57	8.6	10:07	9.9	3:44	3:50
13	S	9:18	9.0	9:34	10.3	3:05	3:14	13	T	10:46	8.7	10:54	9.9	4:34	4:38
14	S	10:14	8.9	10:24	10.3	4:01	4:07	14	W	11:30	8.8	11:36	9.9	5:18	5:22
15	M	11:05	8.9	11:11	10.3	4:51	4:55	15	T	...	...	12:09	8.9	5:58	6:02
16	T	11:51	8.9	11:54	10.2	5:38	5:40	16	F	12:14	9.9	12:45	8.9	6:35	6:39
17	W	...	...	12:33	8.9	6:20	6:22	17	S	12:51	9.8	1:20	8.9	7:09	7:15
18	T	12:34	10.1	1:13	8.9	7:00	7:02	18	S	1:26	9.6	1:53	9.0	7:42	7:52
19	F	1:14	9.9	1:51	8.8	7:38	7:42	19	M	2:02	9.4	2:28	9.0	8:15	8:29
20	S	1:52	9.7	2:29	8.8	8:15	8:22	20	T	2:40	9.2	3:04	9.0	8:50	9:09
21	S	2:32	9.5	3:07	8.7	8:52	9:03	21	W	3:20	8.9	3:42	9.0	9:27	9:52
22	M	3:12	9.2	3:46	8.7	9:30	9:46	22	T	4:03	8.6	4:24	9.0	10:08	10:40
23	T	3:55	8.9	4:27	8.8	10:09	10:32	23	F	4:51	8.4	5:12	9.1	10:54	11:33
24	W	4:40	8.6	5:10	8.8	10:51	11:21	24	S	5:44	8.2	6:04	9.2	11:45	...
25	T	5:29	8.3	5:57	8.9	11:36	...	25	S	6:43	8.1	7:02	9.5	12:31	12:42
26	F	6:22	8.2	6:46	9.1	12:14	12:25	26	M	7:45	8.3	8:02	9.9	1:32	1:43
27	S	7:19	8.1	7:39	9.4	1:10	1:18	27	T	8:46	8.7	9:02	10.3	2:33	2:43
28	S	8:17	8.3	8:32	9.8	2:06	2:13	28	W	9:44	9.2	9:59	10.9	3:31	3:42
29	M	9:14	8.5	9:26	10.3	3:03	3:08	29	T	10:39	9.8	10:55	11.3	4:26	4:38
30	T	10:09	8.9	10:20	10.8	3:57	4:03	30	F	11:32	10.3	11:49	11.6	5:18	5:33
31	W	11:02	9.4	11:13	11.2	4:49	4:56	31	S	...	...	12:23	10.7	6:09	6:26

Dates when Ht. of **Low** Water is below Mean Lower Low with Ht. of lowest given for each period and Date of lowest in ( ):

2nd–9th: -1.3' (5th)　　　　　　1st–7th: -1.6' (3rd)
15th–17th: -0.2'　　　　　　　　28th–31st: -1.6' (31st)
30th–31st: -0.7' (31st)

Average Rise and Fall 9.1 ft.

When a high tide exceeds avg. ht., the *following* low tide will be lower than avg.

2019 HIGH & LOW WATER
PORTLAND, ME
43°39.4'N, 70°14.8'W

Daylight Saving Time   **Daylight Saving Time**

D A Y O F M O N T H	D A Y O F W E E K	SEPTEMBER						D A Y O F M O N T H	D A Y O F W E E K	OCTOBER					
		HIGH				LOW				HIGH				LOW	
		a.m.	Ht.	p.m.	Ht.	a.m.	p.m.			a.m.	Ht.	p.m.	Ht.	a.m.	p.m.
1	S	12:42	11.6	1:13	10.9	6:59	7:20	1	T	1:18	11.1	1:38	11.3	7:24	7:55
2	M	1:36	11.4	2:05	11.0	7:49	8:15	2	W	2:11	10.6	2:29	11.0	8:15	8:50
3	T	2:30	10.9	2:57	10.9	8:41	9:11	3	T	3:06	10.0	3:22	10.5	9:07	9:46
4	W	3:27	10.3	3:52	10.6	9:34	10:11	4	F	4:04	9.4	4:19	10.0	10:03	10:46
5	T	4:26	9.7	4:50	10.2	10:30	11:13	5	S	5:05	8.9	5:19	9.5	11:03	11:50
6	F	5:29	9.1	5:50	9.8	11:30	...	6	S	6:09	8.5	6:23	9.2	...	12:06
7	S	6:35	8.7	6:53	9.5	12:18	12:34	7	M	7:12	8.4	7:26	9.0	12:53	1:11
8	S	7:40	8.5	7:56	9.4	1:23	1:37	8	T	8:11	8.4	8:25	9.0	1:54	2:11
9	M	8:41	8.4	8:54	9.4	2:25	2:37	9	W	9:04	8.6	9:17	9.1	2:49	3:04
10	T	9:34	8.6	9:46	9.5	3:20	3:31	10	T	9:49	8.8	10:03	9.3	3:36	3:51
11	W	10:21	8.7	10:32	9.6	4:09	4:18	11	F	10:29	9.1	10:44	9.4	4:18	4:33
12	T	11:03	8.9	11:13	9.7	4:52	5:00	12	S	11:05	9.3	11:22	9.4	4:55	5:11
13	F	11:40	9.0	11:50	9.7	5:30	5:38	13	S	11:38	9.5	11:57	9.4	5:29	5:46
14	S	...	...	12:13	9.2	6:04	6:14	14	M	...	...	12:10	9.6	6:00	6:21
15	S	12:25	9.6	12:45	9.2	6:36	6:48	15	T	12:32	9.3	12:42	9.7	6:32	6:55
16	M	12:59	9.5	1:17	9.3	7:07	7:23	16	W	1:07	9.2	1:15	9.7	7:05	7:31
17	T	1:34	9.3	1:50	9.3	7:39	7:59	17	T	1:44	9.0	1:51	9.7	7:40	8:10
18	W	2:10	9.1	2:24	9.3	8:13	8:37	18	F	2:24	8.8	2:31	9.7	8:20	8:54
19	T	2:49	8.8	3:03	9.3	8:50	9:19	19	S	3:08	8.6	3:17	9.6	9:05	9:43
20	F	3:32	8.6	3:46	9.3	9:32	10:07	20	S	3:59	8.5	4:09	9.6	9:55	10:38
21	S	4:21	8.4	4:35	9.3	10:20	11:01	21	M	4:56	8.4	5:09	9.5	10:53	11:39
22	S	5:16	8.3	5:32	9.4	11:15	...	22	T	5:58	8.6	6:14	9.6	11:57	...
23	M	6:17	8.3	6:34	9.5	12:01	12:16	23	W	7:03	8.9	7:21	9.8	12:43	1:05
24	T	7:21	8.5	7:39	9.9	1:05	1:21	24	T	8:05	9.4	8:26	10.1	1:47	2:11
25	W	8:24	9.0	8:42	10.3	2:08	2:25	25	F	9:04	10.0	9:27	10.5	2:46	3:12
26	T	9:23	9.6	9:42	10.8	3:08	3:26	26	S	9:58	10.6	10:24	10.8	3:42	4:09
27	F	10:18	10.2	10:39	11.2	4:04	4:23	27	S	10:48	11.1	11:17	10.9	4:34	5:03
28	S	11:09	10.8	11:33	11.4	4:56	5:17	28	M	11:37	11.4	...	...	5:23	5:55
29	S	11:59	11.2	...	...	5:46	6:10	29	T	12:09	10.8	12:25	11.5	6:12	6:45
30	M	12:25	11.4	12:49	11.4	6:35	7:02	30	W	1:00	10.6	1:13	11.3	7:00	7:36
								31	T	1:52	10.1	2:02	10.9	7:49	8:27

Dates when Ht. of **Low** Water is below Mean Lower Low with Ht. of lowest given for each period and Date of lowest in ( ):

1st–4th: -1.6' (1st)   1st–3rd: -1.4' (1st)
26th–30th: -1.6' (30th)   25th–31st: -1.6' (28th, 29th)

Average Rise and Fall 9.1 ft.

When a high tide exceeds avg. ht., the *following* low tide will be lower than avg.

2019 HIGH & LOW WATER
PORTLAND, ME
43°39.4'N, 70°14.8'W

*Standard Time starts Nov. 3 at 2 a.m.   Standard Time

DAY OF MONTH	DAY OF WEEK	NOVEMBER						DAY OF MONTH	DAY OF WEEK	DECEMBER					
		HIGH				LOW				HIGH				LOW	
		a.m.	Ht.	p.m.	Ht.	a.m.	p.m.			a.m.	Ht.	p.m.	Ht.	a.m.	p.m.
1	F	2:44	9.6	2:53	10.4	8:40	9:21	1	S	2:11	8.9	2:15	9.6	8:04	8:44
2	S	3:39	9.1	3:47	9.8	9:34	10:16	2	M	3:02	8.6	3:07	9.1	8:56	9:35
3	S	*3:36	8.7	*3:44	9.3	*9:31	*10:15	3	T	3:54	8.4	4:01	8.7	9:51	10:28
4	M	4:35	8.4	4:45	8.9	10:32	11:15	4	W	4:48	8.2	4:58	8.4	10:49	11:21
5	T	5:35	8.3	5:47	8.7	11:35	...	5	T	5:41	8.3	5:56	8.3	11:48	...
6	W	6:31	8.3	6:45	8.6	12:13	12:35	6	F	6:32	8.4	6:52	8.2	12:13	12:44
7	T	7:23	8.5	7:39	8.7	1:06	1:29	7	S	7:20	8.7	7:44	8.3	1:02	1:36
8	F	8:09	8.8	8:27	8.8	1:54	2:18	8	S	8:04	9.0	8:32	8.4	1:48	2:23
9	S	8:51	9.1	9:10	9.0	2:37	3:01	9	M	8:46	9.4	9:16	8.6	2:30	3:06
10	S	9:27	9.4	9:50	9.1	3:15	3:40	10	T	9:24	9.7	9:57	8.8	3:10	3:46
11	M	10:01	9.7	10:28	9.1	3:50	4:17	11	W	10:02	10.0	10:38	8.9	3:49	4:25
12	T	10:35	9.9	11:05	9.1	4:24	4:53	12	T	10:41	10.3	11:18	9.0	4:28	5:05
13	W	11:09	10.0	11:42	9.1	4:58	5:29	13	F	11:21	10.4	...	...	5:09	5:47
14	T	11:45	10.1	...	...	5:34	6:07	14	S	12:01	9.1	12:04	10.5	5:52	6:31
15	F	12:21	9.0	12:24	10.1	6:13	6:49	15	S	12:46	9.1	12:51	10.5	6:39	7:18
16	S	1:04	8.9	1:08	10.1	6:56	7:34	16	M	1:35	9.2	1:42	10.4	7:29	8:09
17	S	1:50	8.8	1:57	10.0	7:44	8:25	17	T	2:27	9.2	2:38	10.1	8:24	9:03
18	M	2:43	8.8	2:51	9.8	8:38	9:20	18	W	3:23	9.3	3:38	9.8	9:25	10:01
19	T	3:40	8.8	3:52	9.7	9:38	10:20	19	T	4:23	9.4	4:43	9.6	10:30	11:02
20	W	4:42	8.9	4:58	9.6	10:43	11:23	20	F	5:25	9.6	5:51	9.4	11:37	...
21	T	5:45	9.2	6:05	9.6	11:51	...	21	S	6:27	9.9	6:58	9.3	12:04	12:45
22	F	6:46	9.7	7:11	9.8	12:25	12:58	22	S	7:26	10.2	8:01	9.3	1:05	1:48
23	S	7:45	10.2	8:13	10.0	1:25	2:00	23	M	8:22	10.5	9:00	9.4	2:03	2:46
24	S	8:39	10.8	9:11	10.1	2:21	2:57	24	T	9:15	10.8	9:54	9.5	2:57	3:40
25	M	9:30	11.1	10:04	10.2	3:14	3:50	25	W	10:04	10.9	10:44	9.5	3:48	4:29
26	T	10:18	11.3	10:55	10.1	4:04	4:41	26	T	10:50	10.8	11:30	9.4	4:36	5:16
27	W	11:06	11.3	11:45	9.9	4:52	5:30	27	F	11:35	10.6	...	...	5:22	6:00
28	T	11:52	11.0	...	...	5:39	6:18	28	S	12:15	9.2	12:18	10.3	6:06	6:44
29	F	12:33	9.6	12:38	10.6	6:26	7:05	29	S	12:58	9.0	1:01	9.9	6:50	7:26
30	S	1:22	9.3	1:26	10.1	7:14	7:54	30	M	1:41	8.8	1:45	9.5	7:34	8:09
								31	T	2:25	8.6	2:30	9.1	8:20	8:53

Dates when Ht. of **Low** Water is below Mean Lower Low with Ht. of lowest given for each period and Date of lowest in ( ):

1st: -0.3'
14th–16th: -0.2'
23rd–30th: -1.5' (26th)

11th–18th: -0.8' (14th)
22nd–29th: -1.1' (25th, 26th)

Average Rise and Fall 9.1 ft.

When a high tide exceeds avg. ht., the *following* low tide will be lower than avg.

Smarter Boating in Currents

If your vessel is a sailboat or a displacement powerboat your normal cruising speed is probably under 10 knots. In this range, current can become a significant factor. (See the Current Tables for the Cape Cod Canal and the Race, and the Current Diagrams for Vineyard Sound, showing some currents of 4 to 5 knots.) You can save a remarkable amount of time and, if under power, a great deal of fuel expense by using the current for maximum efficiency.

SAIL: Slow vs. Flow

The arithmetic is simple. If your 35' sailboat has a boat speed (BS) through the water of 5 knots under power or sail, then a 2-knot current directly against you means your speed made good (SMG) is 3 knots, and the same current going with you boosts that to 7 knots. Tacking into or with a current changes the simple arithmetic shown here. (See Coping With Currents, p. 58) The time difference can be great: a destination 10 miles away is 3 hours 20 minutes against the current, but only 1 hour 26 minutes with the current. Leaving earlier or later to go with the current leaves more time (almost 2 hours) to relax either at your departure point or destination. Of course if you're just out for a sail on a beautiful day, the arithmetic may not matter! If your sailboat is under power, keep reading.

POWER: Ego vs. Eco

As long as speed thrills, as we know it does, some boaters will demand it. But the trend is headed the other way. Today it is more about being economical, not egomaniacal. By far the most dramatic saving in fuel cost, or nautical miles per gallon (NMPG), comes from cutting back on the throttle; however, there are further savings from using the current to your advantage, especially with slower vessels.

Consider a trawler that burns 10 gallons of fuel per hour at a speed of 8 knots. If the cost of fuel is, say, $4 per gallon, that's $40 per hour. For a destination 24 nautical miles away, going directly against a current of 2 knots, her SMG is only 6 knots, requiring 4 hours for the trip, and costing her owner $160. If the skipper had gone with a current of 2 knots, then her SMG would be 10 knots, her transit time 2 hours 24 minutes, with a fuel expense of only $96. The time saved, 1 hour 36 minutes, allows more time for relaxation (TFR) either before departure or after arrival, and the $64 saved could buy a nice meal ashore. That's smarter boating!

Consult the table below for SMG and time/fuel consequences in currents.

SMG *WITH* CURRENT, and Time/Fuel GAINS

Current Speed Kts *With* +		+1 kt	+2 kts	+3 kts	+4 kts
Boat Speed: **4 kts**	SMG =	5 kts	6 kts	7 kts	8 kts
Time/Fuel **Gain**		20%	33%	43%	50%
Boat Speed: **6 kts**	SMG =	7 kts	8 kts	9 kts	10 kts
Time/Fuel **Gain**		14%	25%	33%	40%
Boat Speed: **8 kts**	SMG =	9 kts	10 kts	11 kts	12 kts
Time/Fuel **Gain**		11%	20%	28%	33%
Boat Speed: **10 kts**	SMG =	11 kts	12 kts	13 kts	14 kts
Time/Fuel **Gain**		9%	17%	24%	29%

SMG *AGAINST* CURRENT, and Time/Fuel LOSSES

Current Speed Kts *Against* -		-1 kt	-2 kts	-3 kts	-4 kts
Boat Speed: **4 kts**	SMG =	3 kts	2 kts	1 kts	0 kts
Time/Fuel **Loss**		33%	100%	300%	---
Boat Speed: **6 kts**	SMG =	5 kts	4 kts	3 kts	2 kts
Time/Fuel **Loss**		20%	50%	100%	200%
Boat Speed: **8 kts**	SMG =	7 kts	6 kts	5 kts	4 kts
Time/Fuel **Loss**		14%	33%	60%	100%
Boat Speed: **10 kts**	SMG =	9 kts	8 kts	7 kts	6 kts
Time/Fuel **Loss**		11%	25%	43%	67%

Boston Harbor Currents

This diagram shows the direction of the Flood Currents in Boston Harbor at the Maximum* Flood velocity, generally 3.5 hours after Low Water at Boston. The Ebb Currents flow in precisely the opposite direction (note one exception, shown by dotted arrow east of Winthrop), and reach these maximum velocities about 4 hours after High Water at Boston. The velocities of the Ebb Currents are about the same as those of the Flood Currents. Where the Ebb Current differs by .2 kts., the velocity of the Ebb is shown in parentheses.

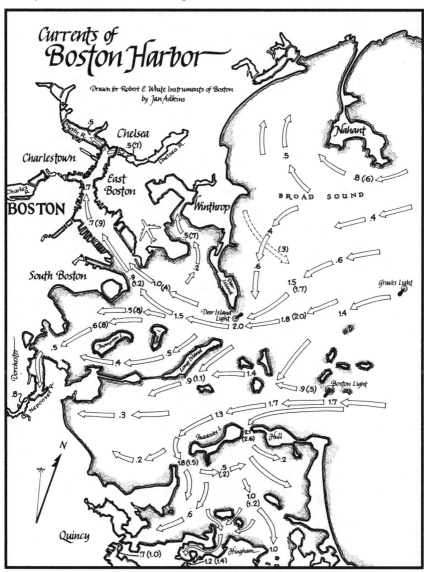

Currents of Boston Harbor

Drawn for Robert E. White Instruments of Boston by Jan Adkins

*The Velocities shown on this Current Diagram are the **maximums** normally encountered each month at Full Moon and at New Moon. At other times the velocities will be lower. As a rule of thumb, the velocities shown are those found on days when High Water at Boston is 11.0' to 11.5' (see Boston High Water Tables pp. 38-43). When the height of High Water is 10.5', subtract 10% from the velocities shown; at 10.0', subtract 20%; at 9.0', 30%; at 8.0', 40%; below 7.5', 50%.

2019 HIGH & LOW WATER
BOSTON, MA
42°21.3'N, 71°03'W

			Standard Time							Standard Time			

DAY OF MONTH	DAY OF WEEK	JANUARY				DAY OF MONTH	DAY OF WEEK	FEBRUARY					
		HIGH		LOW				HIGH			LOW		
		a.m.	Ht.	p.m.	Ht.	a.m.	p.m.			a.m.	Ht.	p.m.	Ht.	a.m.	p.m.

DAY OF MONTH	DAY OF WEEK	a.m.	Ht.	p.m.	Ht.	a.m.	p.m.	DAY OF MONTH	DAY OF WEEK	a.m.	Ht.	p.m.	Ht.	a.m.	p.m.
1	T	7:22	10.1	7:57	9.1	12:58	1:41	1	F	8:45	9.8	9:26	8.6	2:23	3:11
2	W	8:16	10.2	8:54	9.1	1:54	2:38	2	S	9:33	9.9	10:11	8.7	3:13	3:57
3	T	9:07	10.3	9:45	9.1	2:46	3:30	3	S	10:17	10.0	10:52	8.9	3:59	4:38
4	F	9:53	10.4	10:30	9.1	3:34	4:16	4	M	10:57	10.1	11:29	9.0	4:40	5:15
5	S	10:35	10.4	11:12	9.1	4:19	4:58	5	T	11:35	10.1	...	...	5:20	5:52
6	S	11:15	10.3	11:52	9.0	5:01	5:37	6	W	12:05	9.1	12:12	10.1	5:59	6:28
7	M	11:55	10.2	...	...	5:42	6:16	7	T	12:41	9.2	12:49	10.0	6:38	7:05
8	T	12:30	9.0	12:34	10.1	6:22	6:55	8	F	1:17	9.2	1:28	9.8	7:18	7:42
9	W	1:09	8.9	1:13	9.9	7:03	7:34	9	S	1:55	9.2	2:08	9.5	7:59	8:21
10	T	1:48	8.9	1:54	9.6	7:45	8:14	10	S	2:33	9.3	2:50	9.2	8:42	9:03
11	F	2:28	8.8	2:38	9.3	8:29	8:56	11	M	3:14	9.3	3:37	8.9	9:29	9:48
12	S	3:11	8.8	3:23	9.0	9:15	9:40	12	T	4:00	9.3	4:29	8.6	10:21	10:38
13	S	3:55	8.8	4:12	8.8	10:04	10:27	13	W	4:51	9.4	5:26	8.5	11:17	11:34
14	M	4:43	8.9	5:05	8.6	10:57	11:17	14	T	5:47	9.6	6:26	8.5	...	12:17
15	T	5:33	9.1	6:01	8.5	11:53	...	15	F	6:46	10.0	7:28	8.8	12:32	1:17
16	W	6:25	9.5	6:59	8.6	12:10	12:50	16	S	7:46	10.5	8:29	9.2	1:32	2:17
17	T	7:19	9.9	7:56	8.8	1:05	1:47	17	S	8:45	11.0	9:26	9.8	2:31	3:13
18	F	8:13	10.5	8:53	9.2	2:00	2:42	18	M	9:41	11.6	10:20	10.3	3:27	4:07
19	S	9:07	11.0	9:47	9.6	2:54	3:36	19	T	10:36	11.9	11:12	10.8	4:22	4:59
20	S	10:00	11.6	10:40	10.1	3:47	4:28	20	W	11:29	12.1	...	...	5:15	5:49
21	M	10:52	11.9	11:32	10.4	4:40	5:19	21	T	12:03	11.1	12:22	12.0	6:07	6:38
22	T	11:45	12.1	...	...	5:32	6:09	22	F	12:53	11.3	1:14	11.6	6:59	7:27
23	W	12:24	10.7	12:38	12.0	6:24	7:00	23	S	1:42	11.2	2:06	11.1	7:52	8:17
24	T	1:15	10.8	1:31	11.7	7:18	7:51	24	S	2:33	10.9	3:01	10.3	8:46	9:08
25	F	2:08	10.8	2:26	11.2	8:12	8:43	25	M	3:26	10.5	3:58	9.6	9:42	10:02
26	S	3:01	10.6	3:23	10.5	9:09	9:37	26	T	4:21	10.0	4:58	8.9	10:41	10:59
27	S	3:57	10.4	4:23	9.8	10:08	10:32	27	W	5:20	9.6	6:02	8.5	11:44	11:59
28	M	4:55	10.1	5:26	9.2	11:10	11:30	28	T	6:21	9.3	7:07	8.3	...	12:48
29	T	5:54	9.9	6:31	8.8	...	12:14								
30	W	6:54	9.7	7:35	8.6	12:30	1:18								
31	T	7:52	9.7	8:34	8.5	1:28	2:18								

Dates when Ht. of **Low** Water is below Mean Lower Low with Ht. of lowest given for each period and Date of lowest in ( ):

4th–6th: -0.3' (5th)   16th–25th: -2.1' (20th)
18th–26th: -2.2' (22nd)

Average Rise and Fall 9.5 ft.
When a high tide exceeds avg. ht., the *following* low tide will be lower than avg.
Since there is a high degree of correlation between the height of High Water and the velocities of the Flood and Ebb Currents for that same day, we offer a rough rule of thumb for estimating the current velocities, for ALL the Current Charts and Diagrams in this book. **Rule of Thumb:** Refer to Boston High Water. If the height of High Water is 11.0' or over, use the Current Chart velocities as shown. When the height is 10.5', subtract 10%; at 10.0', subtract 20%; at 9.0', 30%; at 8.0', 40%; below 7.5', 50%.

2019 HIGH & LOW WATER
BOSTON, MA
42°21.3'N, 71°03'W

Daylight Time starts March 10 at 2 a.m.   **Daylight Saving Time**

DAY OF MONTH	DAY OF WEEK	MARCH HIGH a.m.	Ht.	HIGH p.m.	Ht.	LOW a.m.	LOW p.m.	DAY OF MONTH	DAY OF WEEK	APRIL HIGH a.m.	Ht.	HIGH p.m.	Ht.	LOW a.m.	LOW p.m.
1	F	7:22	9.3	8:07	8.3	12:59	1:50	1	M	9:36	9.3	10:09	8.9	3:18	3:53
2	S	8:19	9.3	9:00	8.5	1:57	2:45	2	T	10:22	9.5	10:50	9.2	4:05	4:35
3	S	9:09	9.5	9:45	8.7	2:49	3:31	3	W	11:04	9.7	11:27	9.5	4:48	5:13
4	M	9:53	9.7	10:25	9.0	3:35	4:11	4	T	11:44	9.9	...	...	5:29	5:50
5	T	10:34	9.9	11:01	9.2	4:17	4:48	5	F	12:02	9.8	12:22	9.9	6:08	6:26
6	W	11:12	10.0	11:36	9.4	4:56	5:23	6	S	12:37	10.0	12:59	9.9	6:47	7:03
7	T	11:48	10.1	...	...	5:35	5:59	7	S	1:13	10.2	1:38	9.9	7:26	7:42
8	F	12:10	9.6	12:25	10.0	6:13	6:34	8	M	1:49	10.3	2:18	9.7	8:07	8:22
9	S	12:46	9.7	1:02	9.8	6:52	7:11	9	T	2:30	10.3	3:02	9.5	8:51	9:05
10	S	1:20	9.8	*2:41	9.6	*8:32	*8:50	10	W	3:12	10.3	3:49	9.2	9:38	9:53
11	M	2:58	9.8	3:23	9.3	9:14	9:31	11	T	4:01	10.2	4:42	9.0	10:30	10:46
12	T	3:40	9.8	4:09	9.0	10:00	10:17	12	F	4:56	10.1	5:41	8.9	11:27	11:46
13	W	4:26	9.8	5:01	8.8	10:52	11:08	13	S	5:57	10.1	6:44	9.1	...	12:28
14	T	5:19	9.8	5:59	8.6	11:48	...	14	S	7:01	10.2	7:47	9.4	12:49	1:31
15	F	6:17	9.8	7:02	8.7	12:06	12:50	15	M	8:07	10.4	8:48	9.9	1:53	2:32
16	S	7:20	10.1	8:06	9.0	1:07	1:52	16	T	9:09	10.7	9:45	10.5	2:55	3:29
17	S	8:24	10.4	9:08	9.5	2:10	2:54	17	W	10:08	11.0	10:38	11.1	3:54	4:23
18	M	9:26	10.9	10:06	10.1	3:12	3:51	18	T	11:04	11.2	11:28	11.5	4:49	5:14
19	T	10:25	11.4	11:00	10.7	4:10	4:46	19	F	11:56	11.3	...	...	5:41	6:02
20	W	11:20	11.7	11:51	11.2	5:05	5:37	20	S	12:16	11.7	12:46	11.1	6:31	6:49
21	T	...	...	12:13	11.8	5:58	6:26	21	S	1:02	11.6	1:35	10.8	7:20	7:36
22	F	12:40	11.5	1:04	11.7	6:50	7:14	22	M	1:48	11.4	2:24	10.3	8:08	8:23
23	S	1:28	11.6	1:55	11.3	7:40	8:02	23	T	2:35	11.0	3:13	9.8	8:57	9:11
24	S	2:15	11.4	2:45	10.8	8:30	8:50	24	W	3:23	10.4	4:04	9.3	9:46	10:01
25	M	3:04	11.1	3:37	10.1	9:21	9:39	25	T	4:13	9.9	4:57	8.8	10:38	10:53
26	T	3:54	10.5	4:31	9.4	10:14	10:31	26	F	5:07	9.4	5:53	8.5	11:32	11:49
27	W	4:47	9.9	5:28	8.8	11:10	11:26	27	S	6:04	9.1	6:50	8.4	...	12:29
28	T	5:44	9.4	6:29	8.4	...	12:09	28	S	7:03	8.9	7:46	8.5	12:48	1:25
29	F	6:44	9.1	7:31	8.2	12:25	1:11	29	M	8:01	8.9	8:38	8.7	1:45	2:19
30	S	7:45	9.0	8:30	8.3	1:26	2:12	30	T	8:54	9.1	9:25	9.1	2:39	3:07
31	S	8:44	9.1	9:23	8.5	2:24	3:06								

Dates when Ht. of **Low** Water is below Mean Lower Low with Ht. of lowest given for each period and Date of lowest in ( ):

17th–26th: -1.7' (21st–23rd)   8th: -0.2'
                                      15th–23rd: -1.6' (20th)

Average Rise and Fall 9.5 ft.
When a high tide exceeds avg. ht., the *following* low tide will be lower than avg.
Since there is a high degree of correlation between the height of High Water and the velocities of the Flood and Ebb Currents for that same day, we offer a rough rule of thumb for estimating the current velocities, for ALL the Current Charts and Diagrams in this book. **Rule of Thumb:** Refer to Boston High Water. If the height of High Water is 11.0' or over, use the Current Chart velocities as shown. When the height is 10.5', subtract 10%; at 10.0', subtract 20%; at 9.0', 30%; at 8.0', 40%; below 7.5', 50%.

2019 HIGH & LOW WATER
BOSTON, MA
42°21.3'N, 71°03'W

		Daylight Saving Time							Daylight Saving Time				

DAY OF MONTH	DAY OF WEEK	MAY							DAY OF MONTH	DAY OF WEEK	JUNE					
		HIGH				LOW					HIGH				LOW	
		a.m.	Ht.	p.m.	Ht.	a.m.	p.m.				a.m.	Ht.	p.m.	Ht.	a.m.	p.m.
1	W	9:43	9.3	10:07	9.5	3:29	3:51	1	S	10:35	9.3	10:47	10.4	4:23	4:35
2	T	10:28	9.5	10:47	9.8	4:14	4:33	2	S	11:20	9.5	11:29	10.8	5:08	5:19
3	F	11:11	9.6	11:25	10.2	4:57	5:13	3	M	...	...	12:05	9.7	5:53	6:03
4	S	11:52	9.8	...	...	5:39	5:52	4	T	12:13	11.1	12:51	9.8	6:38	6:49
5	S	12:03	10.5	12:33	9.8	6:20	6:32	5	W	12:58	11.3	1:38	9.9	7:25	7:36
6	M	12:41	10.7	1:14	9.8	7:02	7:14	6	T	1:45	11.3	2:28	9.9	8:13	8:27
7	T	1:21	10.8	1:58	9.8	7:45	7:58	7	F	2:36	11.3	3:20	9.9	9:04	9:20
8	W	2:05	10.9	2:44	9.6	8:31	8:44	8	S	3:30	11.1	4:15	9.9	9:57	10:16
9	T	2:53	10.8	3:34	9.5	9:20	9:35	9	S	4:29	10.8	5:12	10.0	10:53	11:16
10	F	3:44	10.7	4:29	9.4	10:13	10:31	10	M	5:28	10.5	6:11	10.1	11:50	...
11	S	4:41	10.5	5:27	9.4	11:10	11:31	11	T	6:31	10.2	7:10	10.3	12:18	12:48
12	S	5:42	10.3	6:28	9.6	...	12:09	12	W	7:35	10.0	8:07	10.6	1:21	1:46
13	M	6:46	10.3	7:29	9.9	12:34	1:10	13	T	8:37	9.9	9:03	10.8	2:23	2:43
14	T	7:51	10.3	8:28	10.3	1:37	2:09	14	F	9:36	9.9	9:55	11.0	3:22	3:37
15	W	8:53	10.4	9:24	10.8	2:39	3:06	15	S	10:32	9.8	10:45	11.1	4:17	4:28
16	T	9:52	10.5	10:16	11.2	3:38	3:59	16	S	11:23	9.8	11:32	11.1	5:08	5:17
17	F	10:47	10.5	11:06	11.4	4:33	4:50	17	M	...	...	12:11	9.7	5:56	6:03
18	S	11:39	10.5	11:53	11.5	5:24	5:39	18	T	12:17	10.9	12:57	9.6	6:41	6:48
19	S	...	...	12:28	10.4	6:13	6:25	19	W	1:01	10.8	1:41	9.4	7:25	7:32
20	M	12:38	11.4	1:16	10.1	7:00	7:11	20	T	1:44	10.5	2:24	9.3	8:08	8:17
21	T	1:23	11.1	2:02	9.8	7:46	7:57	21	F	2:28	10.2	3:07	9.1	8:51	9:02
22	W	2:08	10.7	2:49	9.5	8:32	8:43	22	S	3:12	9.9	3:52	9.0	9:34	9:48
23	T	2:54	10.3	3:36	9.1	9:18	9:31	23	S	3:59	9.6	4:37	8.9	10:19	10:37
24	F	3:42	9.9	4:25	8.9	10:06	10:21	24	M	4:47	9.2	5:24	8.9	11:05	11:28
25	S	4:32	9.5	5:16	8.7	10:56	11:13	25	T	5:38	9.0	6:12	9.0	11:53	...
26	S	5:25	9.1	6:07	8.6	11:46	...	26	W	6:30	8.8	7:00	9.2	12:20	12:41
27	M	6:20	8.9	6:59	8.8	12:08	12:38	27	T	7:23	8.7	7:48	9.4	1:14	1:31
28	T	7:15	8.8	7:49	9.0	1:03	1:29	28	F	8:16	8.8	8:36	9.8	2:07	2:21
29	W	8:08	8.9	8:36	9.3	1:57	2:18	29	S	9:08	8.9	9:24	10.2	2:58	3:10
30	T	9:00	9.0	9:21	9.7	2:48	3:05	30	S	9:59	9.1	10:11	10.6	3:49	3:59
31	F	9:48	9.1	10:05	10.1	3:37	3:50								

Dates when Ht. of **Low** Water is below Mean Lower Low with Ht. of lowest given for each period and Date of lowest in ( ):

5th–10th: -0.6' (7th, 8th)   3rd–10th: -1.0' (6th)
15th–22nd: -1.1' (18th, 19th)   14th–19th: -0.6' (16th, 17th)

Average Rise and Fall 9.5 ft.
When a high tide exceeds avg. ht., the *following* low tide will be lower than avg.
Since there is a high degree of correlation between the height of High Water and the velocities of the Flood and Ebb Currents for that same day, we offer a rough rule of thumb for estimating the current velocities, for ALL the Current Charts and Diagrams in this book. **Rule of Thumb:** Refer to Boston High Water. If the height of High Water is 11.0' or over, use the Current Chart velocities as shown. When the height is 10.5', subtract 10%; at 10.0', subtract 20%; at 9.0', 30%; at 8.0', 40%; below 7.5', 50%.

2019 HIGH & LOW WATER
BOSTON, MA
42°21.3'N, 71°03'W

		Daylight Saving Time						Daylight Saving Time				

DAY OF MONTH	DAY OF WEEK	JULY							DAY OF MONTH	DAY OF WEEK	AUGUST						
		HIGH				LOW					HIGH				LOW		
		a.m.	Ht.	p.m.	Ht.	a.m.	p.m.				a.m.	Ht.	p.m.	Ht.	a.m.	p.m.	
1	M	10:49	9.4	10:59	11.0	4:38	4:48		1	T	...	...	12:06	10.3	5:53	6:06	
2	T	11:39	9.7	11:48	11.4	5:27	5:37		2	F	12:19	11.9	12:57	10.6	6:43	6:59	
3	W	...	...	12:29	9.9	6:16	6:26		3	S	1:11	12.0	1:48	10.9	7:34	7:52	
4	T	12:37	11.6	1:19	10.2	7:05	7:17		4	S	2:05	11.9	2:40	11.0	8:24	8:46	
5	F	1:28	11.7	2:10	10.3	7:55	8:10		5	M	3:00	11.5	3:33	11.0	9:16	9:42	
6	S	2:21	11.6	3:02	10.4	8:46	9:04		6	T	3:56	10.9	4:28	10.9	10:09	10:40	
7	S	3:16	11.4	3:56	10.5	9:38	10:00		7	W	4:55	10.3	5:24	10.7	11:03	11:40	
8	M	4:13	11.0	4:52	10.5	10:32	11:00		8	T	5:56	9.8	6:22	10.5	...	12:01	
9	T	5:14	10.5	5:49	10.5	11:28	...		9	F	7:00	9.3	7:22	10.3	12:43	12:59	
10	W	6:15	10.0	6:47	10.5	12:01	12:25		10	S	8:03	9.0	8:21	10.2	1:46	1:58	
11	T	7:18	9.7	7:45	10.6	1:03	1:23		11	S	9:04	8.9	9:17	10.1	2:47	2:56	
12	F	8:21	9.4	8:42	10.6	2:06	2:20		12	M	10:00	8.9	10:09	10.2	3:44	3:49	
13	S	9:21	9.3	9:36	10.6	3:05	3:15		13	T	10:50	9.0	10:56	10.2	4:34	4:38	
14	S	10:17	9.2	10:27	10.6	4:01	4:08		14	W	11:33	9.1	11:39	10.2	5:18	5:23	
15	M	11:08	9.2	11:14	10.6	4:52	4:57		15	T	...	...	12:13	9.2	5:59	6:04	
16	T	11:54	9.2	11:58	10.5	5:38	5:43		16	F	12:19	10.2	12:50	9.3	6:36	6:45	
17	W	...	...	12:37	9.2	6:21	6:26		17	S	12:58	10.2	1:27	9.4	7:13	7:25	
18	T	12:40	10.4	1:17	9.2	7:02	7:09		18	S	1:36	10.0	2:03	9.4	7:50	8:05	
19	F	1:21	10.3	1:57	9.2	7:42	7:51		19	M	2:15	9.9	2:40	9.5	8:28	8:46	
20	S	2:02	10.1	2:36	9.2	8:21	8:33		20	T	2:56	9.6	3:19	9.5	9:07	9:29	
21	S	2:44	9.9	3:16	9.2	9:01	9:17		21	W	3:38	9.3	4:00	9.4	9:47	10:14	
22	M	3:26	9.6	3:58	9.2	9:42	10:02		22	T	4:23	9.0	4:44	9.5	10:31	11:03	
23	T	4:11	9.3	4:41	9.2	10:25	10:49		23	F	5:12	8.8	5:32	9.5	11:19	11:56	
24	W	4:58	9.0	5:26	9.2	11:10	11:40		24	S	6:05	8.6	6:24	9.7	...	12:11	
25	T	5:48	8.8	6:14	9.4	11:58	...		25	S	7:02	8.6	7:20	9.9	12:52	1:07	
26	F	6:41	8.6	7:03	9.6	12:32	12:48		26	M	8:01	8.8	8:17	10.3	1:50	2:05	
27	S	7:36	8.6	7:55	9.9	1:27	1:41		27	T	8:59	9.2	9:15	10.8	2:48	3:02	
28	S	8:32	8.8	8:47	10.3	2:22	2:34		28	W	9:56	9.7	10:12	11.4	3:44	3:59	
29	M	9:27	9.0	9:40	10.8	3:17	3:28		29	T	10:50	10.2	11:07	11.8	4:38	4:54	
30	T	10:21	9.4	10:33	11.2	4:10	4:21		30	F	11:43	10.8	...	...	5:30	5:47	
31	W	11:14	9.8	11:26	11.7	5:02	5:14		31	S	12:01	12.0	12:34	11.2	6:21	6:40	

Dates when Ht. of **Low** Water is below Mean Lower Low with Ht. of lowest given for each period and Date of lowest in ( ):

1st–9th: -1.4' (5th)
30th–31st: -0.9' (31st)

1st–7th: -1.7' (3rd)
28th–31st: -1.7' (31st)

Average Rise and Fall 9.5 ft.
When a high tide exceeds avg. ht., the *following* low tide will be lower than avg.
Since there is a high degree of correlation between the height of High Water and the velocities of the Flood and Ebb Currents for that same day, we offer a rough rule of thumb for estimating the current velocities, for ALL the Current Charts and Diagrams in this book. **Rule of Thumb:** Refer to Boston High Water. If the height of High Water is 11.0' or over, use the Current Chart velocities as shown. When the height is 10.5', subtract 10%; at 10.0', subtract 20%; at 9.0', 30%; at 8.0', 40%; below 7.5', 50%.

2019 HIGH & LOW WATER
BOSTON, MA
42°21.3'N, 71°03'W

Daylight Saving Time   Daylight Saving Time

DAY OF MONTH	DAY OF WEEK	SEPTEMBER HIGH a.m.	Ht.	SEPTEMBER HIGH p.m.	Ht.	SEPTEMBER LOW a.m.	SEPTEMBER LOW p.m.	DAY OF MONTH	DAY OF WEEK	OCTOBER HIGH a.m.	Ht.	OCTOBER HIGH p.m.	Ht.	OCTOBER LOW a.m.	OCTOBER LOW p.m.
1	S	12:54	12.1	1:24	11.5	7:10	7:33	1	T	1:28	11.5	1:48	11.8	7:35	8:05
2	M	1:47	11.8	2:15	11.5	8:00	8:26	2	W	2:20	11.0	2:38	11.5	8:24	8:58
3	T	2:41	11.4	3:06	11.4	8:51	9:21	3	T	3:14	10.4	3:30	11.0	9:15	9:52
4	W	3:36	10.8	4:00	11.1	9:43	10:17	4	F	4:10	9.8	4:25	10.5	10:09	10:49
5	T	4:33	10.1	4:56	10.6	10:37	11:16	5	S	5:09	9.2	5:23	9.9	11:05	11:49
6	F	5:34	9.5	5:54	10.2	11:34	...	6	S	6:11	8.8	6:25	9.5	...	12:05
7	S	6:37	9.0	6:56	9.9	12:18	12:34	7	M	7:13	8.6	7:27	9.4	12:51	1:07
8	S	7:42	8.8	7:57	9.7	1:22	1:35	8	T	8:13	8.7	8:25	9.3	1:52	2:07
9	M	8:44	8.7	8:55	9.7	2:24	2:34	9	W	9:07	8.9	9:18	9.4	2:48	3:01
10	T	9:37	8.8	9:48	9.8	3:21	3:28	10	T	9:52	9.1	10:05	9.6	3:35	3:50
11	W	10:25	9.0	10:34	9.9	4:10	4:17	11	F	10:32	9.4	10:48	9.7	4:17	4:33
12	T	11:06	9.2	11:16	10.0	4:52	5:00	12	S	11:10	9.7	11:27	9.8	4:56	5:13
13	F	11:44	9.4	11:55	10.1	5:30	5:40	13	S	11:45	9.9	...	...	5:32	5:52
14	S	...	...	12:19	9.6	6:06	6:19	14	M	12:05	9.8	12:20	10.1	6:09	6:31
15	S	12:33	10.1	12:54	9.7	6:42	6:58	15	T	12:43	9.8	12:55	10.2	6:45	7:10
16	M	1:10	9.9	1:29	9.8	7:18	7:37	16	W	1:21	9.6	1:31	10.2	7:23	7:50
17	T	1:48	9.8	2:05	9.8	7:55	8:17	17	T	2:01	9.5	2:09	10.2	8:02	8:32
18	W	2:27	9.5	2:42	9.8	8:33	8:58	18	F	2:43	9.3	2:51	10.1	8:44	9:17
19	T	3:08	9.3	3:22	9.8	9:13	9:43	19	S	3:28	9.1	3:38	10.1	9:30	10:06
20	F	3:53	9.0	4:07	9.7	9:57	10:31	20	S	4:19	8.9	4:30	10.0	10:21	11:01
21	S	4:42	8.8	4:57	9.7	10:46	11:25	21	M	5:15	8.8	5:28	10.0	11:18	11:59
22	S	5:37	8.7	5:52	9.8	11:41	...	22	T	6:15	9.0	6:30	10.1	...	12:19
23	M	6:36	8.7	6:52	10.0	12:23	12:40	23	W	7:16	9.3	7:34	10.3	1:00	1:22
24	T	7:37	9.0	7:54	10.4	1:23	1:41	24	T	8:16	9.8	8:36	10.6	2:00	2:24
25	W	8:36	9.4	8:54	10.8	2:23	2:42	25	F	9:12	10.5	9:35	10.9	2:57	3:23
26	T	9:34	10.1	9:53	11.3	3:20	3:40	26	S	10:06	11.1	10:32	11.2	3:51	4:19
27	F	10:28	10.7	10:49	11.6	4:15	4:35	27	S	10:57	11.6	11:26	11.3	4:43	5:12
28	S	11:19	11.3	11:43	11.8	5:06	5:29	28	M	11:46	11.9	...	...	5:33	6:04
29	S	...	...	12:09	11.7	5:57	6:22	29	T	12:18	11.2	12:35	12.0	6:22	6:54
30	M	12:35	11.8	12:59	11.9	6:46	7:13	30	W	1:09	10.9	1:23	11.8	7:10	7:44
								31	T	2:00	10.5	2:11	11.4	7:59	8:35

Dates when Ht. of **Low** Water is below Mean Lower Low with Ht. of lowest given for each period and Date of lowest in ( ):

1st–4th: -1.7' (1st)   1st–3rd: -1.5' (1st)
26th–30th: -1.7' (30th)   25th–31st: -1.7' (28th, 29th)

Average Rise and Fall 9.5 ft.
When a high tide exceeds avg. ht., the *following* low tide will be lower than avg. Since there is a high degree of correlation between the height of High Water and the velocities of the Flood and Ebb Currents for that same day, we offer a rough rule of thumb for estimating the current velocities, for ALL the Current Charts and Diagrams in this book. **Rule of Thumb:** Refer to Boston High Water. If the height of High Water is 11.0' or over, use the Current Chart velocities as shown. When the height is 10.5', subtract 10%; at 10.0', subtract 20%; at 9.0', 30%; at 8.0', 40%; below 7.5', 50%.

2019 HIGH & LOW WATER
BOSTON, MA
42°21.3'N, 71°03'W

*Standard Time starts Nov. 3 at 2 a.m.   **Standard Time**

DAY OF MONTH	DAY OF WEEK	NOVEMBER HIGH a.m.	Ht.	HIGH p.m.	Ht.	LOW a.m.	LOW p.m.	DAY OF MONTH	DAY OF WEEK	DECEMBER HIGH a.m.	Ht.	HIGH p.m.	Ht.	LOW a.m.	LOW p.m.
1	F	2:51	10.0	3:02	10.8	8:49	9:26	1	S	2:17	9.3	2:23	10.1	8:11	8:48
2	S	3:44	9.5	3:54	10.2	9:40	10:19	2	M	3:07	8.9	3:14	9.6	9:02	9:38
3	S	*3:40	9.0	*3:50	9.7	*9:35	*10:15	3	T	3:59	8.7	4:08	9.1	9:55	10:30
4	M	4:37	8.7	4:48	9.3	10:32	11:13	4	W	4:51	8.6	5:03	8.8	10:51	11:22
5	T	5:36	8.6	5:48	9.0	11:32	...	5	T	5:44	8.6	5:59	8.7	11:47	...
6	W	6:32	8.6	6:46	9.0	12:10	12:31	6	F	6:35	8.8	6:54	8.6	12:14	12:43
7	T	7:24	8.9	7:40	9.1	1:04	1:26	7	S	7:24	9.1	7:47	8.7	1:03	1:35
8	F	8:11	9.1	8:29	9.2	1:52	2:16	8	S	8:09	9.4	8:36	8.8	1:51	2:24
9	S	8:54	9.5	9:14	9.3	2:36	3:01	9	M	8:53	9.8	9:22	9.0	2:36	3:10
10	S	9:32	9.8	9:56	9.5	3:17	3:43	10	T	9:34	10.1	10:06	9.2	3:20	3:54
11	M	10:10	10.1	10:36	9.5	3:56	4:24	11	W	10:14	10.4	10:49	9.3	4:02	4:37
12	T	10:47	10.3	11:16	9.6	4:35	5:04	12	T	10:56	10.7	11:32	9.4	4:45	5:20
13	W	11:24	10.5	11:56	9.5	5:14	5:44	13	F	11:38	10.9	...	...	5:29	6:04
14	T	...	...	12:02	10.6	5:54	6:26	14	S	12:16	9.5	12:22	11.0	6:13	6:49
15	F	12:38	9.4	12:43	10.6	6:36	7:09	15	S	1:02	9.6	1:09	11.0	7:01	7:37
16	S	1:21	9.3	1:27	10.5	7:20	7:56	16	M	1:51	9.6	2:00	10.8	7:51	8:27
17	S	2:09	9.2	2:16	10.4	8:09	8:46	17	T	2:42	9.6	2:54	10.6	8:45	9:20
18	M	3:00	9.1	3:10	10.3	9:01	9:40	18	W	3:37	9.7	3:53	10.3	9:42	10:16
19	T	3:56	9.2	4:09	10.1	9:59	10:38	19	T	4:35	9.8	4:55	10.0	10:43	11:14
20	W	4:55	9.3	5:12	10.1	11:01	11:37	20	F	5:34	10.0	5:59	9.8	11:47	...
21	T	5:56	9.7	6:16	10.1	...	12:04	21	S	6:33	10.3	7:03	9.7	12:13	12:50
22	F	6:55	10.1	7:19	10.2	12:36	1:07	22	S	7:31	10.6	8:05	9.7	1:11	1:51
23	S	7:52	10.7	8:20	10.4	1:34	2:07	23	M	8:27	10.9	9:04	9.7	2:07	2:49
24	S	8:45	11.2	9:17	10.5	2:29	3:03	24	T	9:19	11.1	9:58	9.8	3:01	3:43
25	M	9:37	11.6	10:11	10.5	3:21	3:57	25	W	10:09	11.2	10:49	9.8	3:52	4:33
26	T	10:26	11.7	11:02	10.5	4:11	4:47	26	T	10:56	11.2	11:36	9.7	4:41	5:20
27	W	11:13	11.7	11:51	10.3	5:00	5:36	27	F	11:42	11.0	...	...	5:28	6:05
28	T	...	...	12:01	11.5	5:48	6:24	28	S	12:21	9.6	12:26	10.8	6:13	6:49
29	F	12:40	10.0	12:47	11.1	6:35	7:12	29	S	1:05	9.4	1:10	10.4	6:58	7:33
30	S	1:28	9.6	1:35	10.6	7:23	8:00	30	M	1:48	9.2	1:54	10.0	7:43	8:16
								31	T	2:32	9.0	2:40	9.6	8:30	9:01

Dates when Ht. of **Low** Water is below Mean Lower Low with Ht. of lowest given for each period and Date of lowest in ( ):

1st: -0.4'
13th–17th: -0.3' (14th–16th)
23rd–30th: -1.5' (26th, 27th)

11th–19th: -0.9' (14th, 15th)
22nd–29th: -1.1' (25th, 26th)

Average Rise and Fall 9.5 ft.
When a high tide exceeds avg. ht., the *following* low tide will be lower than avg.
Since there is a high degree of correlation between the height of High Water and the velocities of the Flood and Ebb Currents for that same day, we offer a rough rule of thumb for estimating the current velocities, for ALL the Current Charts and Diagrams in this book. **Rule of Thumb:** Refer to Boston High Water. If the height of High Water is 11.0' or over, use the Current Chart velocities as shown. When the height is 10.5', subtract 10%; at 10.0', subtract 20%; at 9.0', 30%; at 8.0', 40%; below 7.5', 50%.

Cape Cod Canal

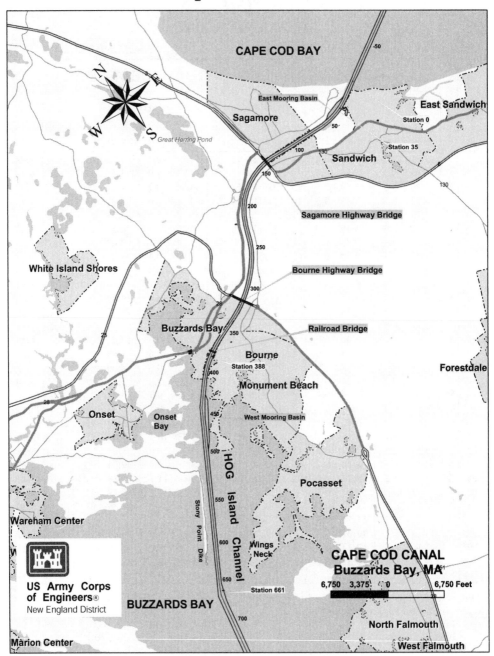

SMALL BOAT BASINS ON EITHER END OF THE CANAL: On E. end, 13-ft. mean low water, on S. side of Sandwich, available for mooring small boat traffic; On W. end, channel 13-ft. at mean low water, 100 ft. wide leads from NE side of Hog Is. Ch. abreast of Hog Is. to harbor in Onset Bay. Fuel, supplies and phone services at both locations.

See Cape Cod Canal Currents pp. 46-51.

Cape Cod Canal Regulations

For complete regulations see 33 CFR, Part 207 and 36 CFR, Part 327

Call on **Channel 13** to establish contact

No excessive wake – Speed Limit 10 m.p.h. (8.7 kts.)

Vessels going *with* the current have right of way over those going *against* it.

Clearance under all bridges: 135 feet at mean high water. Available clearance can be reduced by construction work on the bridges so mariners are advised to contact the Marine Traffic Controller for current clearance dimensions prior to transit. Buzzards Bay Railroad Bridge is maintained in up, or open position, except when lowered for trains or maintenance.

Obtaining Clearance

Vessels 65 feet and over shall not enter the Canal until clearance has been given by radio from the Marine Traffic Controller. These vessels shall request clearance at least 15 minutes prior to entering the Canal at any point.

Vessels of any kind unable to make a through transit of the Canal against a head current of 6 kts. within a time limit of 2-1/2 hrs. are required to obtain helper tug assistance or wait for a fair current prior to receiving clearance from the Controller.

Two-way traffic through the Canal for all vessels is allowed when Controller on duty considers conditions suitable.

Communications

Direct communications are available at all hours by VHF radio or by phoning 978-318-8500. Call on Channel 13 to establish contact. Transmissions may then be switched to Channel 14 as the working channel. Channel 16 is also available but should be limited to emergency situations. Vessels shall maintain a radio guard on Channel 13 during the entire passage.

Traffic Lights

Traffic Lights are at Eastern End at Sandwich (Cape Cod Bay entrance) and at Western End near Wings Neck (Buzzards Bay entrance). When traffic lights are extinguished: all vessels over 65 feet are cautioned not to enter Canal until clearance given, as above.

Entering From EASTERN END: (Lights on South side of entrance to Canal.)

RED LIGHT: Any type of vessel 65 feet in length and over must stop clear of the Cape Cod Bay entrance channel.

YELLOW LIGHT: Vessels 65 feet in length and over and drawing less than 25 feet may proceed as far as the East Mooring Basin where they must stop.

GREEN LIGHT: Vessels may proceed westward through the Canal.

Entering From WESTERN END: (Lights near Wings Neck at West Entrance to Hog Is. Channel)

RED LIGHT: Vessels 65 feet and over in length and drawing less than 25 feet must keep southerly of Hog Island Channel Entrance Buoys Nos. 1 and 2 and utilize the general anchorage areas adjacent to the improved channel. Vessel traffic drawing 25 feet and over are directed not to enter the Canal channel at the Cleveland Ledge Light entrance and shall lay to or anchor in Buzzards Bay until clearance is granted by the Marine Traffic Controller or a green traffic light at Wings Neck is displayed.

YELLOW LIGHT: Vessels may proceed through Hog Island Channel as far as the West Mooring Basin where they must stop.

GREEN LIGHT: Vessels may proceed eastward through the Canal.

Prohibited Activities

Jet skis, sea planes, paddle-driven craft and sailing vessels not under power are prohibited from transiting the Canal.

Fishing from a vessel within the channel limits of the Canal is prohibited.

Anchoring within the channel limits of the Canal, except in emergencies with notice given to the Traffic Controller, is prohibited.

2019 CURRENT TABLE
CAPE COD CANAL
41°44.56'N, 70°36.85'W at R.R. Bridge

Standard Time   Standard Time

JANUARY							FEBRUARY					
D A Y O F M O N T H	D A Y O F W E E K	CURRENT TURNS TO						CURRENT TURNS TO				
		EAST Flood Starts			WEST Ebb Starts		D A Y O F M O N T H	D A Y O F W E E K	EAST Flood Starts			WEST Ebb Starts	
		a.m.	p.m.	Kts.	a.m.	p.m.	Kts.			a.m.	p.m.	Kts.	a.m.	p.m.	Kts.

D.M.	D.W.	a.m.	p.m.	Kts.	a.m.	p.m.	Kts.	D.M.	D.W.	a.m.	p.m.	Kts.	a.m.	p.m.	Kts.
1	T	11:54	...	4.2	5:42	6:18	a4.7	1	F	12:42	1:18	p4.5	7:06	7:48	a4.7
2	W	12:12	12:48	p4.4	6:36	7:12	a4.8	2	S	1:36	2:06	p4.7	7:54	8:36	a4.8
3	T	1:06	1:42	p4.7	7:30	8:06	a5.0	3	S	2:30	2:54	p4.7	8:42	9:24	a4.9
4	F	2:00	2:30	p4.8	8:18	9:00	a5.2	4	M	3:12	3:42	p4.5	9:30	10:06	a4.8
5	S	2:48	3:18	p4.8	9:06	9:48	a5.2	5	T	4:00	4:24	p4.3	10:12	10:48	a4.8
6	S	3:36	4:06	p4.6	9:54	10:36	a5.1	6	W	4:42	5:00	a4.2	10:54	11:30	a4.8
7	M	4:24	4:48	p4.4	10:36	11:18	a5.0	7	T	5:24	5:42	4.2	11:36	...	4.8
8	T	5:12	5:36	p4.1	11:24	...	4.8	8	F	6:00	6:18	4.2	12:06	12:12	p4.8
9	W	5:55	6:18	a4.0	12:06	12:06	p4.7	9	S	6:43	6:54	p4.3	12:48	12:54	p4.9
10	T	6:36	7:00	3.9	12:48	12:48	p4.5	10	S	7:24	7:36	p4.3	1:24	1:36	p4.8
11	F	7:24	7:42	3.8	1:30	1:30	p4.4	11	M	8:06	8:18	p4.4	2:00	2:18	p4.8
12	S	8:06	8:18	p3.8	2:06	2:12	p4.4	12	T	8:54	9:06	p4.4	2:42	3:12	4.4
13	S	8:48	9:06	p3.9	2:48	3:00	p4.3	13	W	9:48	10:06	p4.4	3:30	4:06	a4.7
14	M	9:36	9:48	p4.1	3:30	3:48	p4.3	14	T	10:42	11:06	p4.5	4:24	5:06	a4.8
15	T	10:24	10:42	p4.3	4:12	4:36	p4.4	15	F	11:42	...	4.4	5:24	6:12	a5.0
16	W	11:18	11:30	p4.5	5:00	5:36	4.5	16	S	12:06	12:42	4.6	6:18	7:06	a5.2
17	T	...	12:12	4.3	5:54	6:30	a4.8	17	S	1:00	1:36	p4.8	7:18	8:06	a5.5
18	F	12:24	1:00	a4.7	6:42	7:30	a5.2	18	M	2:00	2:30	p5.0	8:18	9:00	a5.9
19	S	1:18	1:54	4.9	7:36	8:24	a5.6	19	T	2:54	3:24	p5.2	9:12	9:48	a6.1
20	S	2:12	2:48	p5.2	8:30	9:18	a6.0	20	W	3:42	4:12	5.2	10:06	10:42	a6.2
21	M	3:06	3:36	p5.3	9:24	10:06	a6.2	21	T	4:36	5:06	a5.2	10:54	11:30	a6.2
22	T	4:00	4:30	5.3	10:18	11:00	a6.3	22	F	5:24	5:54	a5.1	11:48	...	6.0
23	W	4:54	5:24	5.2	11:12	11:54	a6.3	23	S	6:18	6:42	a4.8	12:24	12:42	a5.7
24	T	5:42	6:12	a5.1	...	12:06	6.1	24	S	7:12	7:36	a4.4	1:12	1:36	a5.5
25	F	6:36	7:06	a4.8	12:48	1:00	p5.8	25	M	8:06	8:30	4.0	2:06	2:36	a5.1
26	S	7:36	8:00	4.4	1:36	2:00	a5.4	26	T	9:06	9:30	a3.8	2:54	3:30	a4.7
27	S	8:30	9:00	4.1	2:30	2:54	a5.1	27	W	10:06	10:30	a3.8	3:48	4:30	a4.4
28	M	9:30	9:54	3.9	3:24	3:54	a4.8	28	T	11:06	11:24	a4.0	4:48	5:30	a4.1
29	T	10:30	10:54	a3.9	4:18	4:54	a4.5								
30	W	11:30	11:48	a4.1	5:12	5:54	a4.4								
31	T	...	12:24	4.3	6:12	6:54	a4.5								

The Kts. (knots) columns show the **maximum** predicted velocities of the stronger one of the Flood Currents and the stronger one of the Ebb Currents for each day.

The letter "a" means the velocity shown should occur **after** the a.m. Current Change. The letter "p" means the velocity shown should occur **after** the p.m. Current Change (even if next morning). No "a" or "p" means a.m. and p.m. velocities are the same for that day.

Avg. Max. Velocity: Flood 4.0 Kts., Ebb 4.5 Kts.

Max. Flood 3 hrs. after Flood Starts, ±20 min.

Max. Ebb 3 hrs. after Ebb Starts, ±20 min.

Average rise and fall: canal east end, 8.7 ft. (time of high water same as Boston); west end, at Monument Beach, 4.0 ft. (time of high water 15 min. after Newport).

See pp. 22-29 for Current Change at other points.

2019 CURRENT TABLE
CAPE COD CANAL

41°44.56'N, 70°36.85'W at R.R. Bridge

Daylight Time starts Mar. 10 at 2 a.m.   **Daylight Saving Time**

		MARCH									APRIL					
DAY OF MONTH	**DAY OF WEEK**	CURRENT TURNS TO						**DAY OF MONTH**	**DAY OF WEEK**	CURRENT TURNS TO						
		EAST Flood Starts			WEST Ebb Starts					EAST Flood Starts			WEST Ebb Starts		
		a.m.	**p.m.**	Kts.	a.m.	**p.m.**	Kts.			a.m.	**p.m.**	Kts.	a.m.	**p.m.**	Kts.
1	F	...	**12:01**	4.2	5:42	**6:30**	a4.1	1	M	1:48	**2:12**	p4.1	8:00	**8:36**	p4.2
2	S	12:24	**12:54**	p4.3	6:36	**7:24**	4.3	2	T	2:36	**2:54**	p4.0	8:48	**9:24**	4.2
3	S	1:12	**1:42**	p4.4	7:30	**8:12**	4.5	3	W	3:18	**3:36**	p4.0	9:30	**10:00**	a4.4
4	M	2:06	**2:30**	p4.4	8:18	**8:54**	a4.6	4	T	4:00	**4:12**	p4.3	10:12	**10:36**	a4.6
5	T	2:48	**3:12**	p4.2	9:00	**9:36**	a4.6	5	F	4:36	**4:48**	p4.6	10:48	**11:12**	a4.9
6	W	3:30	**3:54**	p4.2	9:42	**10:12**	a4.7	6	S	5:12	**5:24**	p4.8	11:24	**11:42**	5.2
7	T	4:12	**4:30**	4.3	10:24	**10:54**	a4.8	7	S	5:48	**6:00**	p5.0	...	**12:06**	5.3
8	F	4:48	**5:06**	p4.5	11:00	**11:24**	a5.0	8	M	6:24	**6:42**	p5.1	12:24	**12:48**	p5.5
9	S	5:25	**5:36**	p4.7	11:36	**...**	5.1	9	T	7:07	**7:24**	p5.0	1:00	**1:36**	a5.6
10	S	*7:00	***7:12**	p4.7	12:01	***1:18**	p5.2	10	W	7:54	**8:18**	4.8	1:48	**2:30**	a5.7
11	M	7:42	**7:54**	p4.7	1:42	**2:00**	p5.2	11	T	8:48	**9:12**	4.6	2:36	**3:24**	a5.6
12	T	8:24	**8:42**	p4.6	2:18	**2:54**	a5.2	12	F	9:48	**10:18**	a4.5	3:36	**4:24**	a5.4
13	W	9:12	**9:36**	p4.5	3:06	**3:48**	a5.2	13	S	10:54	**11:24**	a4.4	4:36	**5:30**	a5.2
14	T	10:12	**10:36**	p4.4	4:00	**4:42**	a5.1	14	S	...	**12:01**	4.4	5:42	**6:30**	a5.0
15	F	11:18	**11:42**	p4.4	4:54	**5:48**	a5.1	15	M	12:30	**1:00**	4.4	6:48	**7:30**	a5.1
16	S	...	**12:18**	4.4	6:00	**6:48**	a5.0	16	T	1:30	**2:00**	p4.7	7:48	**8:24**	5.2
17	S	12:48	**1:18**	p4.5	7:00	**7:48**	a5.1	17	W	2:24	**2:54**	p4.9	8:42	**9:18**	p5.6
18	M	1:48	**2:18**	p4.7	8:00	**8:48**	a5.4	18	T	3:18	**3:42**	p5.0	9:36	**10:06**	p5.8
19	T	2:42	**3:12**	p5.0	9:00	**9:42**	a5.7	19	F	4:06	**4:30**	5.0	10:30	**10:54**	p5.9
20	W	3:36	**4:06**	p5.1	9:54	**10:30**	a5.9	20	S	5:00	**5:18**	a5.0	11:24	**11:42**	p5.9
21	T	4:24	**4:54**	5.2	10:48	**11:18**	a6.0	21	S	5:48	**6:06**	a4.8	...	**12:12**	5.4
22	F	5:18	**5:42**	5.1	11:42	**...**	6.0	22	M	6:36	**6:54**	a4.6	12:30	**1:06**	a5.7
23	S	6:06	**6:30**	a5.0	12:06	**12:30**	a5.9	23	T	7:24	**7:48**	a4.3	1:18	**2:00**	a5.4
24	S	6:54	**7:18**	a4.7	12:54	**1:24**	a5.8	24	W	8:18	**8:42**	a4.0	2:12	**2:54**	a5.0
25	M	7:48	**8:12**	a4.3	1:48	**2:18**	a5.5	25	T	9:12	**9:42**	a3.9	3:00	**3:48**	a4.6
26	T	8:42	**9:06**	a4.0	2:36	**3:12**	a5.1	26	F	10:12	**10:36**	a3.8	3:54	**4:42**	a4.1
27	W	9:42	**10:06**	a3.9	3:30	**4:12**	a4.7	27	S	11:06	**11:36**	a3.7	4:48	**5:36**	a3.8
28	T	10:36	**11:06**	a3.8	4:24	**5:06**	a4.2	28	S	...	**12:01**	3.7	5:42	**6:30**	3.6
29	F	11:36	**...**	3.9	5:18	**6:06**	a3.9	29	M	12:30	**12:54**	p3.7	6:36	**7:18**	p3.7
30	S	12:01	**12:36**	p4.0	6:18	**7:00**	p3.9	30	T	1:18	**1:36**	p3.6	7:24	**8:00**	p3.8
31	S	1:00	**1:24**	p4.1	7:12	**7:54**	p4.1								

The Kts. (knots) columns show the **maximum** predicted velocities of the stronger one of the Flood Currents and the stronger one of the Ebb Currents for each day.

The letter "a" means the velocity shown should occur **after** the **a.m.** Current Change. The letter "p" means the velocity shown should occur **after** the **p.m.** Current Change (even if next morning). No "a" or "p" means a.m. and p.m. velocities are the same for that day.

Avg. Max. Velocity: Flood 4.0 Kts., Ebb 4.5 Kts.

Max. Flood 3 hrs. after Flood Starts, ±20 min.

Max. Ebb 3 hrs. after Ebb Starts, ±20 min.

Average rise and fall: canal east end, 8.7 ft. (time of high water same as Boston); west end, at Monument Beach, 4.0 ft. (time of high water 15 min. after Newport).

See pp. 22-29 for Current Change at other points.

2019 CURRENT TABLE
CAPE COD CANAL
41°44.56'N, 70°36.85'W at R.R. Bridge
Daylight Saving Time   **Daylight Saving Time**

DAY OF MONTH	DAY OF WEEK	EAST Flood Starts a.m.	**p.m.**	Kts.	WEST Ebb Starts a.m.	**p.m.**	Kts.	DAY OF MONTH	DAY OF WEEK	EAST Flood Starts a.m.	**p.m.**	Kts.	WEST Ebb Starts a.m.	**p.m.**	Kts.
1	W	2:00	**2:18**	p3.7	8:12	**8:42**	3.9	1	S	2:48	**2:54**	p4.6	9:00	**9:12**	p5.0
2	T	2:42	**3:00**	p4.0	8:54	**9:18**	p4.3	2	S	3:24	**3:36**	p4.9	9:42	**9:54**	p5.5
3	F	3:24	**3:36**	p4.4	9:36	**9:54**	p4.7	3	M	4:06	**4:24**	p5.2	10:30	**10:36**	p5.9
4	S	4:00	**4:12**	p4.8	10:12	**10:30**	p5.2	4	T	4:48	**5:06**	p5.3	11:18	**11:24**	p6.1
5	S	4:36	**4:48**	p5.1	10:54	**11:06**	p5.6	5	W	5:36	**5:54**	5.3	...	**12:06**	5.7
6	M	5:18	**5:30**	p5.2	11:36	**11:48**	p5.9	6	T	6:24	**6:48**	a5.3	12:12	**1:00**	a6.2
7	T	5:54	**6:12**	5.2	...	**12:24**	5.6	7	F	7:18	**7:42**	a5.2	1:06	**1:54**	a6.2
8	W	6:42	**7:06**	a5.2	12:30	**1:18**	a6.0	8	S	8:12	**8:42**	a4.9	2:00	**2:48**	a6.0
9	T	7:31	**8:00**	a5.0	1:24	**2:12**	a6.0	9	S	9:13	**9:42**	a4.6	3:00	**3:48**	a5.7
10	F	8:30	**9:00**	a4.8	2:18	**3:06**	a5.9	10	M	10:12	**10:48**	a4.4	4:00	**4:48**	a5.4
11	S	9:30	**10:00**	a4.6	3:18	**4:06**	a5.6	11	T	11:18	**11:48**	a4.3	5:06	**5:42**	a5.0
12	S	10:36	**11:06**	a4.4	4:18	**5:06**	a5.3	12	W	...	**12:18**	4.3	6:06	**6:42**	p4.9
13	M	11:36	...	4.4	5:24	**6:06**	a5.1	13	T	12:48	**1:12**	p4.4	7:06	**7:36**	p5.0
14	T	12:12	**12:42**	p4.4	6:24	**7:06**	a5.0	14	F	1:42	**2:06**	p4.5	8:06	**8:30**	p5.2
15	W	1:06	**1:36**	p4.6	7:30	**8:00**	p5.2	15	S	2:36	**2:54**	a4.7	9:00	**9:18**	p5.4
16	T	2:06	**2:30**	p4.7	8:24	**8:54**	p5.5	16	S	3:30	**3:48**	a4.9	9:54	**10:06**	p5.5
17	F	3:00	**3:18**	4.8	9:18	**9:42**	p5.7	17	M	4:18	**4:36**	a4.9	10:48	**10:54**	p5.5
18	S	3:48	**4:06**	a4.9	10:12	**10:30**	p5.8	18	T	5:06	**5:24**	a4.9	11:36	**11:42**	p5.3
19	S	4:36	**5:00**	a4.9	11:06	**11:18**	p5.7	19	W	5:54	**6:12**	a4.7	...	**12:24**	4.8
20	M	5:24	**5:48**	a4.8	11:54	...	5.1	20	T	6:42	**7:06**	a4.4	12:30	**1:12**	a5.1
21	T	6:12	**6:36**	a4.6	12:06	**12:48**	a5.5	21	F	7:30	**7:54**	a4.1	1:18	**2:00**	a4.9
22	W	7:06	**7:24**	a4.4	12:54	**1:36**	a5.3	22	S	8:18	**8:42**	a3.8	2:06	**2:48**	a4.6
23	T	7:54	**8:18**	a4.1	1:42	**2:30**	a4.9	23	S	9:06	**9:30**	a3.6	2:54	**3:36**	a4.3
24	F	8:48	**9:12**	a3.9	2:36	**3:18**	a4.5	24	M	9:54	**10:24**	a3.5	3:42	**4:18**	a4.0
25	S	9:36	**10:06**	a3.7	3:24	**4:12**	a4.1	25	T	10:36	**11:12**	a3.4	4:30	**5:06**	a3.8
26	S	10:30	**11:00**	a3.5	4:18	**5:00**	a3.8	26	W	11:24	...	3.5	5:18	**5:48**	a3.7
27	M	11:24	**11:54**	a3.4	5:06	**5:48**	a3.6	27	T	12:01	**12:12**	p3.7	6:06	**6:30**	p3.8
28	T	...	**12:12**	3.3	6:00	**6:36**	a3.5	28	F	12:42	**12:54**	p4.0	6:54	**7:12**	p4.1
29	W	12:42	**12:54**	p3.5	6:48	**7:18**	3.6	29	S	1:30	**1:36**	p4.3	7:42	**7:54**	p4.6
30	T	1:24	**1:36**	p3.8	7:30	**8:00**	p3.9	30	S	2:12	**2:24**	p4.6	8:30	**8:42**	p5.2
31	F	2:06	**2:18**	p4.2	8:18	**8:36**	p4.4								

The Kts. (knots) columns show the **maximum** predicted velocities of the stronger one of the Flood Currents and the stronger one of the Ebb Currents for each day.

The letter "a" means the velocity shown should occur **after** the a.m. Current Change. The letter "p" means the velocity shown should occur **after** the p.m. Current Change (even if next morning). No "a" or "p" means a.m. and p.m. velocities are the same for that day.

Avg. Max. Velocity: Flood 4.0 Kts., Ebb 4.5 Kts.

Max. Flood 3 hrs. after Flood Starts, ±20 min.

Max. Ebb 3 hrs. after Ebb Starts, ±20 min.

Average rise and fall: canal east end, 8.7 ft. (time of high water same as Boston); west end, at Monument Beach, 4.0 ft. (time of high water 15 min. after Newport).

See pp. 22-29 for Current Change at other points.

2019 CURRENT TABLE
CAPE COD CANAL

41°44.56'N, 70°36.85'W at R.R. Bridge

Daylight Saving Time   Daylight Saving Time

DAY OF MONTH	DAY OF WEEK	CURRENT TURNS TO						DAY OF MONTH	DAY OF WEEK	CURRENT TURNS TO					
		EAST Flood Starts			WEST Ebb Starts					EAST Flood Starts			WEST Ebb Starts		
		a.m.	p.m.	Kts.	a.m.	p.m.	Kts.			a.m.	p.m.	Kts.	a.m.	p.m.	Kts.
1	M	2:54	3:12	p4.9	9:18	9:24	p5.6	1	T	4:12	4:30	p5.4	10:42	10:48	p6.3
2	T	3:42	4:00	p5.2	10:06	10:12	p6.0	2	F	5:00	5:24	5.4	11:30	11:42	p6.4
3	W	4:30	4:48	p5.4	11:00	11:06	p6.3	3	S	5:54	6:12	a5.4	...	12:24	6.0
4	T	5:18	5:36	5.4	11:48	11:54	p6.4	4	S	6:42	7:06	a5.3	12:36	1:18	a6.3
5	F	6:06	6:30	a5.4	...	12:42	5.8	5	M	7:36	8:00	a5.0	1:30	2:06	a6.1
6	S	7:00	7:24	a5.2	12:48	1:36	a6.3	6	T	8:30	9:00	a4.7	2:30	3:00	a5.7
7	S	7:54	8:24	a5.0	1:48	2:30	a6.1	7	W	9:24	10:00	a4.3	3:24	3:54	a5.2
8	M	8:54	9:24	a4.7	2:48	3:24	a5.8	8	T	10:24	11:00	a4.0	4:24	4:48	p4.7
9	T	9:49	10:24	a4.4	3:42	4:18	a5.3	9	F	11:25	...	3.8	5:24	5:48	p4.5
10	W	10:48	11:24	a4.2	4:42	5:18	a4.9	10	S	12:01	12:24	a4.0	6:24	6:42	p4.4
11	T	11:48	...	4.1	5:48	6:12	p4.7	11	S	1:00	1:18	a4.2	7:24	7:36	p4.6
12	F	12:24	12:48	a4.1	6:48	7:06	p4.8	12	M	1:54	2:12	a4.5	8:24	8:30	p4.8
13	S	1:24	1:42	a4.3	7:48	8:00	p4.9	13	T	2:48	3:06	a4.7	9:18	9:24	p5.0
14	S	2:18	2:36	a4.6	8:42	8:54	p5.1	14	W	3:36	3:54	a4.8	10:06	10:12	p5.0
15	M	3:06	3:24	a4.8	9:36	9:48	p5.2	15	T	4:24	4:42	a4.8	10:48	10:54	p5.0
16	T	4:00	4:18	a4.9	10:30	10:36	p5.2	16	F	5:06	5:24	a4.6	11:36	11:42	p4.9
17	W	4:48	5:06	a4.9	11:18	11:18	p5.2	17	S	5:48	6:06	a4.3	...	12:12	4.6
18	T	5:30	5:54	a4.7	...	12:01	4.8	18	S	6:30	6:48	4.2	12:24	12:54	a4.9
19	F	6:18	6:36	a4.4	12:06	12:48	a5.0	19	M	7:06	7:30	a4.2	1:00	1:36	a4.8
20	S	7:00	7:24	a4.1	12:54	1:30	a4.9	20	T	7:48	8:12	a4.2	1:42	2:12	a4.7
21	S	7:42	8:06	a4.0	1:36	2:12	a4.7	21	W	8:24	8:54	a4.2	2:24	2:48	a4.6
22	M	8:24	8:54	a3.8	2:18	2:54	a4.5	22	T	9:06	9:36	a4.1	3:06	3:30	a4.5
23	T	9:06	9:36	a3.8	3:00	3:36	a4.3	23	F	9:48	10:24	a4.1	3:54	4:12	4.4
24	W	9:54	10:24	a3.8	3:48	4:18	a4.1	24	S	10:42	11:18	a4.1	4:48	5:00	p4.5
25	T	10:36	11:12	a3.8	4:30	5:00	a4.0	25	S	11:42	...	4.2	5:42	5:54	p4.7
26	F	11:24	...	4.0	5:24	5:42	p4.1	26	M	12:18	12:36	p4.4	6:42	6:54	p4.9
27	S	12:01	12:12	p4.1	6:12	6:30	p4.4	27	T	1:12	1:36	p4.6	7:42	7:48	p5.3
28	S	12:48	1:06	p4.4	7:06	7:18	p4.8	28	W	2:06	2:30	p4.9	8:36	8:48	p5.7
29	M	1:42	1:54	p4.6	8:06	8:12	p5.2	29	T	3:00	3:24	p5.2	9:30	9:42	p6.1
30	T	2:30	2:48	p4.9	8:54	9:06	p5.7	30	F	3:54	4:18	p5.4	10:24	10:36	p6.3
31	W	3:18	3:42	p5.2	9:48	9:54	p6.1	31	S	4:48	5:06	5.4	11:12	11:30	p6.3

The Kts. (knots) columns show the **maximum** predicted velocities of the stronger one of the Flood Currents and the stronger one of the Ebb Currents for each day.

The letter "a" means the velocity shown should occur **after** the **a.m.** Current Change. The letter "p" means the velocity shown should occur **after** the **p.m.** Current Change (even if next morning). No "a" or "p" means a.m. and p.m. velocities are the same for that day.

Avg. Max. Velocity: Flood 4.0 Kts., Ebb 4.5 Kts.

Max. Flood 3 hrs. after Flood Starts, ±20 min.

Max. Ebb 3 hrs. after Ebb Starts, ±20 min.

Average rise and fall: canal east end, 8.7 ft. (time of high water same as Boston); west end, at Monument Beach, 4.0 ft. (time of high water 15 min. after Newport).

See pp. 22-29 for Current Change at other points.

2019 CURRENT TABLE
CAPE COD CANAL
41°44.56'N, 70°36.85'W at R.R. Bridge

Daylight Saving Time   Daylight Saving Time

SEPTEMBER						OCTOBER					

D A Y O F M O N T H	D A Y O F W E E K	CURRENT TURNS TO						D A Y O F M O N T H	D A Y O F W E E K	CURRENT TURNS TO					
		EAST Flood Starts			WEST Ebb Starts					EAST Flood Starts			WEST Ebb Starts		
		a.m.	**p.m.**	Kts.	a.m.	**p.m.**	Kts.			a.m.	**p.m.**	Kts.	a.m.	**p.m.**	Kts.
1	S	5:36	**6:00**	a5.4	...	**12:01**	6.1	1	T	6:06	**6:30**	a5.1	12:06	**12:30**	p6.0
2	M	6:24	**6:48**	a5.2	12:18	**12:54**	a6.2	2	W	6:54	**7:24**	a4.8	1:00	**1:18**	p5.8
3	T	7:12	**7:42**	a4.9	1:12	**1:42**	a5.9	3	T	7:42	**8:18**	a4.4	1:54	**2:06**	p5.4
4	W	8:06	**8:36**	a4.6	2:12	**2:36**	5.5	4	F	8:36	**9:12**	a4.0	2:48	**3:00**	p5.0
5	T	9:00	**9:36**	a4.2	3:06	**3:30**	p5.0	5	S	9:36	**10:12**	p3.9	3:42	**3:54**	p4.5
6	F	10:00	**10:36**	p3.9	4:06	**4:24**	p4.6	6	S	10:36	**11:12**	p4.0	4:42	**4:54**	p4.1
7	S	11:00	**11:36**	p4.0	5:06	**5:18**	p4.3	7	M	11:36	...	3.4	5:42	**5:54**	p3.9
8	S	...	**12:01**	3.5	6:06	**6:18**	p4.1	8	T	12:06	**12:36**	a4.1	6:36	**6:48**	4.0
9	M	12:37	**1:00**	a4.2	7:06	**7:12**	p4.3	9	W	1:07	**1:30**	a4.2	7:30	**7:42**	4.2
10	T	1:30	**1:54**	a4.4	8:00	**8:06**	p4.5	10	T	1:54	**2:18**	a4.3	8:18	**8:30**	4.4
11	W	2:24	**2:42**	a4.6	8:48	**9:00**	p4.7	11	F	2:42	**3:00**	a4.3	9:06	**9:18**	4.5
12	T	3:12	**3:30**	a4.6	9:36	**9:48**	4.8	12	S	3:24	**3:42**	a4.2	9:48	**10:00**	p4.6
13	F	3:54	**4:18**	a4.6	10:18	**10:30**	p4.8	13	S	4:00	**4:24**	4.2	10:24	**10:36**	p4.7
14	S	4:36	**4:54**	4.3	11:00	**11:12**	p4.8	14	M	4:36	**5:00**	4.4	11:00	**11:18**	p4.8
15	S	5:18	**5:36**	4.3	11:36	**11:48**	p4.9	15	T	5:12	**5:36**	a4.6	11:36	**11:54**	p5.0
16	M	5:54	**6:12**	4.4	...	**12:12**	4.6	16	W	5:48	**6:12**	a4.7	...	**12:06**	5.1
17	T	6:30	**6:54**	a4.5	12:30	**12:48**	a4.9	17	T	6:24	**6:54**	a4.8	12:36	**12:42**	p5.3
18	W	7:06	**7:30**	a4.5	1:06	**1:24**	a4.9	18	F	7:06	**7:36**	a4.8	1:18	**1:24**	p5.4
19	T	7:42	**8:06**	a4.5	1:48	**2:00**	4.9	19	S	7:54	**8:24**	a4.7	2:06	**2:12**	p5.4
20	F	8:24	**8:54**	a4.4	2:36	**2:42**	p5.0	20	S	8:48	**9:18**	a4.5	3:00	**3:06**	p5.3
21	S	9:12	**9:48**	a4.3	3:24	**3:30**	p4.9	21	M	9:48	**10:18**	4.4	3:54	**4:06**	p5.2
22	S	10:12	**10:48**	a4.3	4:18	**4:24**	p4.9	22	T	10:54	**11:24**	4.4	4:54	**5:06**	p5.1
23	M	11:12	**11:48**	4.3	5:18	**5:30**	p4.9	23	W	11:54	...	4.4	5:54	**6:12**	p5.1
24	T	...	**12:18**	4.4	6:18	**6:30**	p5.0	24	T	12:30	**12:54**	4.5	6:54	**7:12**	p5.2
25	W	12:48	**1:18**	p4.6	7:18	**7:30**	p5.3	25	F	1:24	**1:54**	p4.7	7:54	**8:12**	p5.5
26	T	1:48	**2:12**	p4.8	8:18	**8:30**	p5.6	26	S	2:24	**2:48**	p4.9	8:48	**9:12**	p5.7
27	F	2:42	**3:06**	p5.1	9:12	**9:24**	p5.9	27	S	3:12	**3:42**	p5.1	9:36	**10:06**	5.8
28	S	3:36	**4:00**	p5.3	10:00	**10:18**	p6.1	28	M	4:06	**4:30**	5.1	10:30	**10:54**	a6.0
29	S	4:24	**4:48**	5.3	10:48	**11:12**	6.1	29	T	4:54	**5:18**	5.0	11:18	**11:48**	a6.0
30	M	5:12	**5:36**	5.2	11:42	...	6.1	30	W	5:42	**6:12**	a4.8	...	**12:06**	5.9
								31	T	6:30	**7:00**	4.5	12:42	**12:54**	p5.6

The Kts. (knots) columns show the **maximum** predicted velocities of the stronger one of the Flood Currents and the stronger one of the Ebb Currents for each day.

The letter "a" means the velocity shown should occur **after** the **a.m.** Current Change. The letter "p" means the velocity shown should occur **after** the **p.m.** Current Change (even if next morning). No "a" or "p" means a.m. and p.m. velocities are the same for that day.

Avg. Max. Velocity: Flood 4.0 Kts., Ebb 4.5 Kts.

Max. Flood 3 hrs. after Flood Starts, ±20 min.

Max. Ebb 3 hrs. after Ebb Starts, ±20 min.

Average rise and fall: canal east end, 8.7 ft. (time of high water same as Boston); west end, at Monument Beach, 4.0 ft. (time of high water 15 min. after Newport).

See pp. 22-29 for Current Change at other points.

2019 CURRENT TABLE
CAPE COD CANAL
41°44.56'N, 70°36.85'W at R.R. Bridge

*Standard Time starts Nov. 3 at 2 a.m.   Standard Time

NOVEMBER

D A Y O F M O N T H	D A Y O F W E E K	CURRENT TURNS TO					
		EAST Flood Starts			WEST Ebb Starts		
		a.m.	p.m.	Kts.	a.m.	p.m.	Kts.
1	F	7:24	7:54	4.2	1:36	1:42	p5.3
2	S	8:18	8:48	p4.0	2:30	2:36	p4.9
3	S	*8:12	*8:42	p4.0	*2:24	*2:30	p4.4
4	M	9:12	9:42	p3.9	3:18	3:24	p4.0
5	T	10:12	10:36	p3.9	4:12	4:24	3.8
6	W	11:06	11:30	p3.9	5:06	5:18	a3.8
7	T	...	12:01	3.5	5:54	6:06	a4.0
8	F	12:18	12:48	a3.9	6:42	6:54	a4.1
9	S	1:07	1:30	a3.8	7:30	7:42	4.1
10	S	1:42	2:12	3.9	8:06	8:24	p4.3
11	M	2:24	2:48	4.2	8:42	9:06	p4.6
12	T	3:00	3:30	4.5	9:18	9:42	4.8
13	W	3:36	4:06	4.7	9:54	10:24	a5.2
14	T	4:18	4:42	4.9	10:30	11:06	a5.5
15	F	4:54	5:24	5.0	11:12	11:54	a5.7
16	S	5:42	6:06	5.0	11:54	...	5.8
17	S	6:30	7:00	a4.9	12:48	12:48	p5.8
18	M	7:30	7:54	4.7	1:42	1:48	p5.7
19	T	8:30	9:00	a4.6	2:36	2:48	p5.5
20	W	9:30	10:06	p4.5	3:36	3:48	p5.3
21	T	10:36	11:06	p4.5	4:36	4:54	p5.1
22	F	11:36	...	4.4	5:30	5:54	p5.1
23	S	12:06	12:36	a4.6	6:30	6:54	a5.2
24	S	1:00	1:30	4.7	7:24	7:54	a5.4
25	M	1:54	2:24	p4.8	8:12	8:48	a5.7
26	T	2:42	3:12	p4.9	9:06	9:42	a5.8
27	W	3:30	4:00	p4.9	9:54	10:30	a5.8
28	T	4:24	4:54	p4.8	10:42	11:24	a5.7
29	F	5:12	5:42	p4.6	11:30	...	5.5
30	S	6:06	6:30	p4.3	12:18	12:24	p5.2

DECEMBER

D A Y O F M O N T H	D A Y O F W E E K	CURRENT TURNS TO					
		EAST Flood Starts			WEST Ebb Starts		
		a.m.	p.m.	Kts.	a.m.	p.m.	Kts.
1	S	6:54	7:24	p4.1	1:06	1:12	p4.8
2	M	7:48	8:18	p4.0	2:00	2:06	p4.4
3	T	8:48	9:12	p3.8	2:48	3:00	p4.1
4	W	9:42	10:00	p3.6	3:42	3:48	p3.8
5	T	10:36	10:54	p3.5	4:30	4:42	3.6
6	F	11:24	11:42	p3.5	5:18	5:30	p3.6
7	S	...	12:12	3.3	6:00	6:18	p3.6
8	S	12:24	12:54	a3.6	6:42	7:06	p3.8
9	M	1:07	1:36	a3.9	7:24	7:48	4.1
10	T	1:42	2:12	4.2	8:00	8:30	4.5
11	W	2:24	2:54	4.5	8:42	9:12	a5.0
12	T	3:06	3:36	p4.9	9:18	10:00	a5.5
13	F	3:48	4:18	5.1	10:00	10:48	a5.8
14	S	4:36	5:00	5.2	10:48	11:36	a6.0
15	S	5:24	5:48	5.2	11:36	...	6.1
16	M	6:12	6:42	5.1	12:24	12:30	p6.1
17	T	7:06	7:36	4.9	1:18	1:30	p6.0
18	W	8:06	8:36	4.7	2:18	2:30	p5.7
19	T	9:12	9:42	4.5	3:12	3:30	p5.3
20	F	10:12	10:42	p4.4	4:12	4:30	5.0
21	S	11:12	11:42	p4.4	5:06	5:36	a5.0
22	S	...	12:12	4.3	6:06	6:36	a5.0
23	M	12:36	1:12	p4.5	7:00	7:36	a5.2
24	T	1:30	2:00	p4.8	7:54	8:30	a5.4
25	W	2:24	2:54	p4.9	8:42	9:24	a5.5
26	T	3:12	3:42	p4.9	9:30	10:12	a5.5
27	F	4:06	4:30	p4.9	10:18	11:06	a5.5
28	S	4:54	5:18	p4.7	11:12	11:54	a5.3
29	S	5:42	6:06	p4.4	...	12:01	5.1
30	M	6:30	6:54	p4.1	12:42	12:48	p4.8
31	T	7:24	7:48	3.8	1:30	1:36	p4.5

The Kts. (knots) columns show the **maximum** predicted velocities of the stronger one of the Flood Currents and the stronger one of the Ebb Currents for each day.

The letter "a" means the velocity shown should occur **after** the **a.m.** Current Change. The letter "p" means the velocity shown should occur **after** the **p.m.** Current Change (even if next morning). No "a" or "p" means a.m. and p.m. velocities are the same for that day.

Avg. Max. Velocity: Flood 4.0 Kts., Ebb 4.5 Kts.

Max. Flood 3 hrs. after Flood Starts, ±20 min.

Max. Ebb 3 hrs. after Ebb Starts, ±20 min.

Average rise and fall: canal east end, 8.7 ft. (time of high water same as Boston); west end, at Monument Beach, 4.0 ft. (time of high water 15 min. after Newport).

See pp. 22-29 for Current Change at other points.

2019 CURRENT TABLE
WOODS HOLE, MA, The Strait
41°31.16'N, 70°40.97'W

		Standard Time					Standard Time		
		JANUARY					**FEBRUARY**		
D A Y O F M O N T H	D A Y O F W E E K	CURRENT TURNS TO			D A Y O F M O N T H	D A Y O F W E E K	CURRENT TURNS TO		
		SOUTHEAST Flood Starts	NORTHWEST Ebb Starts				SOUTHEAST Flood Starts	NORTHWEST Ebb Starts	
		a.m. **p.m.** Kts.	a.m. **p.m.** Kts.				a.m. **p.m.** Kts.	a.m. **p.m.** Kts.	
1	T	12:12 **12:54** a3.6	6:36 **7:06** a3.1		1	F	1:30 **2:12** p3.6	8:00 **8:30** a3.2	
2	W	1:06 **1:48** p3.7	7:30 **8:06** a3.3		2	S	2:18 **3:00** p3.7	8:48 **9:18** a3.2	
3	T	2:00 **2:36** p3.8	8:24 **8:54** a3.4		3	S	3:06 **3:48** p3.7	9:30 **10:06** a3.2	
4	F	2:48 **3:30** p3.9	9:12 **9:48** a3.4		4	M	3:54 **4:30** p3.5	10:18 **10:48** a3.3	
5	S	3:36 **4:12** p3.9	10:00 **10:30** a3.4		5	T	4:36 **5:12** p3.3	11:00 **11:30** a3.3	
6	S	4:18 **5:00** p3.7	10:42 **11:18** a3.4		6	W	5:18 **5:48** a3.2	11:42 ... 3.4	
7	M	5:06 **5:42** p3.5	11:30 ... 3.4		7	T	6:00 **6:24** 3.2	12:12 **12:24** p3.5	
8	T	5:48 **6:24** p3.2	12:06 **12:12** p3.4		8	F	6:42 **7:00** a3.3	12:54 **1:00** p3.6	
9	W	6:31 **7:00** 3.0	12:48 **12:54** p3.4		9	S	7:25 **7:42** p3.3	1:36 **1:42** p3.6	
10	T	7:18 **7:42** 3.0	1:30 **1:36** p3.3		10	S	8:06 **8:18** p3.4	2:12 **2:24** p3.6	
11	F	8:00 **8:24** 3.0	2:12 **2:18** p3.3		11	M	9:00 **9:06** p3.5	2:54 **3:12** p3.5	
12	S	8:48 **9:06** p3.1	2:54 **3:00** p3.3		12	T	9:54 **9:54** p3.5	3:42 **4:06** 3.4	
13	S	9:36 **9:48** p3.2	3:36 **3:48** p3.2		13	W	10:48 **10:54** p3.5	4:30 **5:00** a3.4	
14	M	10:30 **10:36** p3.3	4:18 **4:36** p3.1		14	T	11:48 **11:48** p3.5	5:24 **6:00** a3.4	
15	T	11:24 **11:24** p3.4	5:06 **5:30** p3.1		15	F	... **12:42** 3.3	6:18 **7:00** a3.5	
16	W	... **12:12** 3.2	5:54 **6:24** 3.2		16	S	12:48 **1:36** a3.6	7:18 **8:00** a3.7	
17	T	12:18 **1:06** a3.5	6:48 **7:24** 3.4		17	S	1:42 **2:36** 3.7	8:12 **8:54** a4.0	
18	F	1:06 **2:00** a3.6	7:42 **8:18** a3.8		18	M	2:42 **3:30** p3.9	9:06 **9:48** a4.2	
19	S	2:00 **2:54** 3.7	8:36 **9:12** a4.1		19	T	3:36 **4:18** p4.1	10:00 **10:36** a4.3	
20	S	2:54 **3:42** 3.9	9:24 **10:06** a4.3		20	W	4:30 **5:12** p4.2	10:54 **11:30** a4.4	
21	M	3:48 **4:36** p4.1	10:18 **11:00** a4.5		21	T	5:24 **6:00** p4.2	11:48 ... 4.4	
22	T	4:42 **5:30** p4.1	11:12 **11:48** a4.5		22	F	6:18 **6:54** p4.0	12:24 **12:42** p4.2	
23	W	5:42 **6:18** p4.1	... **12:06** 4.5		23	S	7:12 **7:42** p3.9	1:12 **1:36** 4.0	
24	T	6:36 **7:12** p4.0	12:42 **1:00** p4.4		24	S	8:12 **8:36** 3.6	2:06 **2:30** a3.8	
25	F	7:30 **8:06** p3.9	1:36 **1:54** p4.1		25	M	9:06 **9:30** 3.4	2:54 **3:24** a3.5	
26	S	8:30 **9:00** p3.8	2:30 **2:48** 3.8		26	T	10:06 **10:24** a3.3	3:48 **4:18** a3.1	
27	S	9:30 **10:00** p3.6	3:24 **3:48** a3.5		27	W	11:06 **11:18** a3.2	4:42 **5:18** a2.8	
28	M	10:36 **10:54** p3.4	4:18 **4:42** a3.2		28	T	... **12:01** 3.2	5:42 **6:18** a2.7	
29	T	11:30 **11:48** 3.3	5:12 **5:42** a2.9						
30	W	... **12:30** 3.4	6:12 **6:42** a2.9						
31	T	12:42 **1:24** p3.5	7:06 **7:42** a3.1						

See the Woods Hole Current Diagram on pp. 60-65.

Mariners should exercise great caution when transiting Woods Hole Passage as velocities have been reported to exceed NOAA's predictions.

To hold longest fair current from Buzzards Bay headed East through Vineyard and Nantucket Sounds go through Woods Hole 2 1/2 hrs. after flood starts SE in Woods Hole. (Any earlier means adverse currents in the Sounds.)

2019 CURRENT TABLE
WOODS HOLE, MA, The Strait
41°31.16'N, 70°40.97'W

*Daylight Time starts Mar. 10 at 2 a.m. Daylight Saving Time

DAY OF MONTH	DAY OF WEEK	SOUTHEAST Flood Starts a.m.	**p.m.**	Kts.	NORTHWEST Ebb Starts a.m.	**p.m.**	Kts.	DAY OF MONTH	DAY OF WEEK	SOUTHEAST Flood Starts a.m.	**p.m.**	Kts.	NORTHWEST Ebb Starts a.m.	**p.m.**	Kts.
		MARCH								APRIL					
1	F	12:12	**12:54**	p3.3	6:36	**7:12**	a2.8	1	M	2:24	**2:54**	p3.1	8:48	**9:18**	2.7
2	S	1:06	**1:42**	p3.4	7:30	**8:06**	a2.9	2	T	3:12	**3:36**	p3.1	9:36	**10:06**	p2.9
3	S	1:54	**2:30**	p3.4	8:18	**8:54**	a3.0	3	W	3:54	**4:18**	p3.0	10:18	**10:42**	3.1
4	M	2:42	**3:12**	p3.4	9:06	**9:36**	a3.0	4	T	4:36	**4:54**	3.2	10:54	**11:24**	3.3
5	T	3:24	**3:54**	p3.3	9:48	**10:18**	a3.1	5	F	5:18	**5:30**	3.4	11:36	**...**	3.6
6	W	4:06	**4:36**	3.1	10:30	**11:00**	a3.3	6	S	5:54	**6:12**	3.6	12:01	**12:18**	p3.8
7	T	4:48	**5:12**	3.3	11:06	**11:36**	a3.5	7	S	6:36	**6:48**	p3.8	12:36	**1:00**	p3.9
8	F	5:30	**5:48**	3.4	11:48	**...**	3.7	8	M	7:18	**7:24**	p3.8	1:18	**1:42**	4.0
9	S	6:07	**6:24**	3.5	12:18	**12:30**	p3.8	9	T	8:07	**8:06**	3.7	2:00	**2:30**	a4.1
10	S	*7:48	***8:00**	p3.6	12:54	***2:12**	p3.9	10	W	8:54	**9:00**	p3.7	2:48	**3:24**	a4.1
11	M	8:30	**8:42**	p3.6	2:36	**2:54**	p3.9	11	T	9:48	**10:00**	3.6	3:36	**4:18**	a4.0
12	T	9:24	**9:24**	p3.6	3:18	**3:42**	3.8	12	F	10:54	**11:06**	3.5	4:30	**5:18**	a3.9
13	W	10:18	**10:24**	p3.6	4:06	**4:36**	a3.8	13	S	...	**12:01**	3.5	5:30	**6:18**	a3.7
14	T	11:18	**11:24**	p3.5	4:54	**5:36**	a3.7	14	S	12:12	**1:00**	3.5	6:36	**7:18**	a3.5
15	F	...	**12:18**	3.4	5:54	**6:36**	a3.5	15	M	1:18	**2:00**	p3.6	7:36	**8:18**	3.5
16	S	12:30	**1:18**	a3.5	6:54	**7:36**	a3.5	16	T	2:18	**2:54**	p3.8	8:36	**9:12**	3.7
17	S	1:30	**2:18**	3.5	7:54	**8:36**	a3.6	17	W	3:12	**3:48**	p4.1	9:36	**10:06**	p3.9
18	M	2:30	**3:12**	p3.7	8:54	**9:36**	a3.8	18	T	4:06	**4:36**	p4.2	10:30	**10:54**	p4.0
19	T	3:30	**4:06**	p4.0	9:54	**10:24**	a4.0	19	F	5:00	**5:30**	4.2	11:24	**11:48**	p4.1
20	W	4:24	**5:00**	p4.2	10:48	**11:18**	a4.2	20	S	5:54	**6:18**	a4.2	...	**12:12**	3.9
21	T	5:18	**5:48**	p4.3	11:36	**...**	4.2	21	S	6:48	**7:06**	a4.1	12:36	**1:06**	a4.0
22	F	6:12	**6:42**	p4.2	12:06	**12:30**	p4.2	22	M	7:36	**7:54**	a3.9	1:24	**1:54**	a3.9
23	S	7:06	**7:30**	4.0	1:00	**1:24**	a4.1	23	T	8:24	**8:42**	a3.7	2:12	**2:48**	a3.6
24	S	7:54	**8:18**	a3.8	1:48	**2:18**	a4.0	24	W	9:18	**9:30**	a3.5	3:06	**3:36**	a3.4
25	M	8:48	**9:06**	a3.7	2:42	**3:06**	a3.7	25	T	10:12	**10:30**	a3.3	3:54	**4:30**	a3.0
26	T	9:42	**10:00**	a3.5	3:30	**4:00**	a3.4	26	F	11:06	**11:24**	a3.1	4:48	**5:24**	a2.7
27	W	10:42	**10:54**	a3.3	4:24	**4:54**	a3.1	27	S	...	**12:01**	2.9	5:36	**6:18**	a2.5
28	T	11:36	**11:54**	a3.2	5:18	**5:54**	a2.7	28	S	12:12	**12:48**	p2.8	6:30	**7:06**	2.3
29	F	...	**12:30**	3.1	6:12	**6:48**	a2.4	29	M	1:06	**1:30**	p2.8	7:24	**8:00**	p2.5
30	S	12:42	**1:24**	p3.1	7:06	**7:42**	2.5	30	T	1:54	**2:18**	p2.7	8:12	**8:42**	p2.6
31	S	1:36	**2:12**	p3.1	8:00	**8:36**	a2.7								

See the Woods Hole Current Diagram on pp. 60-65.

Mariners should exercise great caution when transiting Woods Hole Passage as velocities have been reported to exceed NOAA's predictions.

CAUTION: Going *from* Buzzards Bay *into* Vineyard Sound, whether through Woods Hole, or Robinsons Hole or Quicks Hole, *Red* Buoys must be kept on the LEFT or PORT hand, *Green* Buoys kept on the RIGHT or STARBOARD hand. You are considered to be proceeding seaward and should thus follow the rules for LEAVING a harbor.

See pp. 22-29 for Current Change at other points.

2019 CURRENT TABLE
WOODS HOLE, MA, The Strait
41°31.16'N, 70°40.97'W

| Daylight Saving Time | Daylight Saving Time |

MAY						JUNE				
DAY OF MONTH	DAY OF WEEK	CURRENT TURNS TO			DAY OF MONTH	DAY OF WEEK	CURRENT TURNS TO			
		SOUTHEAST Flood Starts		NORTHWEST Ebb Starts				SOUTHEAST Flood Starts		NORTHWEST Ebb Starts	
		a.m. **p.m.** Kts.		a.m. **p.m.** Kts.				a.m. **p.m.** Kts.		a.m. **p.m.** Kts.	

D	W	2:36 **3:00** p2.8	9:00 **9:24** p2.9	D	S	3:30 **3:36** p3.5	9:54 **10:06** p3.7
1	W	2:36 **3:00** p2.8	9:00 **9:24** p2.9	1	S	3:30 **3:36** p3.5	9:54 **10:06** p3.7
2	T	3:24 **3:36** 3.0	9:42 **10:06** p3.2	2	S	4:18 **4:18** p3.7	10:36 **10:48** p4.0
3	F	4:06 **4:18** p3.3	10:24 **10:42** p3.5	3	M	5:00 **5:00** p3.9	11:24 **11:36** p4.3
4	S	4:48 **4:54** p3.6	11:06 **11:24** p3.8	4	T	5:48 **5:48** p4.0	... **12:12** 4.0
5	S	5:30 **5:30** p3.8	11:48 ... 3.8	5	W	6:36 **6:36** 4.0	12:18 **1:00** a4.5
6	M	6:12 **6:12** p3.9	12:06 **12:36** a4.1	6	T	7:24 **7:30** a4.0	1:12 **1:54** a4.6
7	T	6:54 **7:00** 3.9	12:48 **1:18** a4.3	7	F	8:18 **8:30** a3.9	2:00 **2:48** a4.5
8	W	7:42 **7:48** a3.9	1:30 **2:12** a4.4	8	S	9:12 **9:30** a3.8	2:54 **3:42** a4.4
9	T	8:31 **8:42** a3.8	2:18 **3:06** a4.4	9	S	10:13 **10:36** a3.8	3:54 **4:36** a4.1
10	F	9:30 **9:42** a3.7	3:12 **4:00** a4.2	10	M	11:12 **11:42** a3.7	4:54 **5:36** a3.8
11	S	10:36 **10:54** a3.6	4:12 **4:54** a4.0	11	T	... **12:12** 3.6	5:54 **6:30** a3.5
12	S	11:36 ... 3.6	5:12 **5:54** a3.8	12	W	12:42 **1:12** p3.7	6:54 **7:30** 3.3
13	M	12:01 **12:36** p3.6	6:12 **6:54** a3.5	13	T	1:42 **2:06** p3.8	8:00 **8:30** p3.5
14	T	1:00 **1:36** p3.7	7:18 **7:54** 3.4	14	F	2:42 **3:00** p3.8	8:54 **9:24** p3.6
15	W	2:00 **2:30** p3.9	8:18 **8:48** p3.6	15	S	3:36 **3:48** a4.0	9:54 **10:12** p3.7
16	T	3:00 **3:24** p4.0	9:18 **9:42** p3.8	16	S	4:30 **4:36** a4.1	10:42 **11:00** p3.7
17	F	3:54 **4:12** p4.1	10:12 **10:36** p3.9	17	M	5:18 **5:24** a4.2	11:36 **11:48** p3.7
18	S	4:48 **5:00** a4.2	11:06 **11:24** p3.9	18	T	6:06 **6:12** a4.0	... **12:24** 3.2
19	S	5:36 **5:54** a4.2	11:54 ... 3.5	19	W	6:54 **7:00** a3.9	12:36 **1:12** a3.6
20	M	6:24 **6:36** a4.1	12:12 **12:48** a3.9	20	T	7:36 **7:48** a3.6	1:24 **2:00** a3.5
21	T	7:12 **7:24** a3.9	1:00 **1:36** a3.7	21	F	8:18 **8:36** a3.4	2:06 **2:48** a3.3
22	W	8:00 **8:12** a3.7	1:48 **2:24** a3.5	22	S	9:06 **9:24** a3.1	2:54 **3:30** a3.2
23	T	8:48 **9:06** a3.5	2:36 **3:12** a3.3	23	S	9:48 **10:12** a2.8	3:42 **4:18** a3.0
24	F	9:42 **9:54** a3.2	3:24 **4:06** a3.1	24	M	10:36 **11:00** a2.8	4:24 **5:00** a2.9
25	S	10:30 **10:48** a3.0	4:12 **4:54** a2.8	25	T	11:24 **11:54** a2.8	5:12 **5:48** a2.8
26	S	11:18 **11:42** a2.8	5:00 **5:42** a2.6	26	W	... **12:06** 2.9	6:00 **6:36** a2.7
27	M	... **12:06** 2.6	5:54 **6:30** a2.5	27	T	12:42 **12:48** p3.0	6:48 **7:18** 2.7
28	T	12:30 **12:48** 2.6	6:42 **7:18** 2.4	28	F	1:30 **1:30** p3.2	7:42 **8:06** p3.0
29	W	1:18 **1:36** p2.8	7:30 **8:06** p2.6	29	S	2:18 **2:18** p3.4	8:30 **8:54** p3.4
30	T	2:06 **2:12** p3.0	8:18 **8:48** p2.9	30	S	3:06 **3:00** p3.6	9:24 **9:36** p3.8
31	F	2:48 **2:54** p3.2	9:06 **9:30** p3.3				

See the Woods Hole Current Diagram on pp. 60-65.

Mariners should exercise great caution when transiting Woods Hole Passage as velocities have been reported to exceed NOAA's predictions.

To hold longest fair current from Buzzards Bay headed East through Vineyard and Nantucket Sounds go through Woods Hole 2 1/2 hrs. after flood starts SE in Woods Hole. (Any earlier means adverse currents in the Sounds.)

		Daylight Saving Time						Daylight Saving Time		
		JULY						**AUGUST**		
		CURRENT TURNS TO						CURRENT TURNS TO		
D A Y O F M O N T H	D A Y O F W E E K	SOUTHEAST Flood Starts			NORTHWEST Ebb Starts						
		a.m.	**p.m.**	Kts.	a.m.	**p.m.**	Kts.	a.m.	**p.m.**	Kts.

D A Y O F M O N T H	D A Y O F W E E K	SOUTHEAST Flood Starts a.m.	**p.m.**	Kts.	NORTHWEST Ebb Starts a.m.	**p.m.**	Kts.	D A Y O F M O N T H	D A Y O F W E E K	SOUTHEAST Flood Starts a.m.	**p.m.**	Kts.	NORTHWEST Ebb Starts a.m.	**p.m.**	Kts.
1	M	3:48	**3:48**	p3.7	10:12	**10:24**	p4.1	1	T	5:06	**5:18**	p4.1	11:30	**11:42**	p4.5
2	T	4:36	**4:42**	p3.9	11:00	**11:12**	p4.4	2	F	6:00	**6:12**	4.1	...	**12:24**	4.2
3	W	5:24	**5:30**	p4.0	11:48	...	4.0	3	S	6:48	**7:06**	a4.2	12:36	**1:12**	a4.6
4	T	6:18	**6:24**	4.1	12:01	**12:42**	a4.5	4	S	7:42	**8:00**	a4.1	1:30	**2:06**	a4.6
5	F	7:06	**7:18**	a4.1	12:54	**1:36**	a4.6	5	M	8:36	**9:00**	a4.0	2:24	**3:00**	a4.4
6	S	8:00	**8:12**	a4.0	1:48	**2:24**	a4.6	6	T	9:30	**10:00**	a3.8	3:18	**3:54**	a4.1
7	S	8:54	**9:12**	a3.9	2:42	**3:18**	a4.4	7	W	10:24	**11:00**	a3.6	4:12	**4:48**	a3.7
8	M	9:54	**10:18**	a3.8	3:36	**4:12**	a4.2	8	T	11:24	...	3.5	5:12	**5:42**	a3.3
9	T	10:49	**11:24**	a3.7	4:36	**5:12**	a3.8	9	F	12:07	**12:18**	p3.4	6:12	**6:42**	2.9
10	W	11:48	...	3.6	5:36	**6:06**	a3.4	10	S	1:00	**1:12**	a3.4	7:12	**7:36**	p3.0
11	T	12:24	**12:42**	p3.6	6:36	**7:06**	3.1	11	S	2:00	**2:06**	a3.5	8:12	**8:36**	p3.2
12	F	1:24	**1:42**	p3.6	7:36	**8:06**	p3.2	12	M	2:54	**3:00**	a3.7	9:12	**9:24**	p3.2
13	S	2:24	**2:30**	3.6	8:36	**9:00**	p3.4	13	T	3:42	**3:48**	a3.8	10:00	**10:12**	p3.3
14	S	3:18	**3:24**	a3.8	9:30	**9:48**	p3.4	14	W	4:30	**4:36**	a3.9	10:48	**11:00**	p3.3
15	M	4:06	**4:12**	a4.0	10:24	**10:36**	p3.5	15	T	5:12	**5:24**	a3.8	11:36	**11:42**	p3.4
16	T	4:54	**5:00**	a4.1	11:12	**11:24**	p3.5	16	F	5:54	**6:06**	a3.6	...	**12:18**	3.1
17	W	5:42	**5:48**	a4.0	...	**12:01**	3.1	17	S	6:36	**6:48**	a3.3	12:24	**1:00**	a3.4
18	T	6:24	**6:36**	a3.8	12:12	**12:48**	a3.5	18	S	7:12	**7:30**	p3.2	1:06	**1:42**	a3.5
19	F	7:06	**7:18**	a3.5	12:54	**1:30**	a3.4	19	M	7:48	**8:12**	p3.2	1:48	**2:18**	a3.5
20	S	7:48	**8:00**	a3.2	1:42	**2:18**	a3.4	20	T	8:24	**8:54**	a3.2	2:30	**3:00**	a3.5
21	S	8:30	**8:48**	2.9	2:24	**3:00**	a3.3	21	W	9:06	**9:42**	a3.2	3:12	**3:42**	a3.5
22	M	9:12	**9:30**	2.9	3:06	**3:42**	a3.3	22	T	9:48	**10:30**	a3.3	3:54	**4:24**	a3.4
23	T	9:48	**10:24**	a3.0	3:48	**4:24**	a3.2	23	F	10:36	**11:24**	a3.3	4:42	**5:06**	a3.3
24	W	10:36	**11:12**	a3.1	4:30	**5:06**	a3.1	24	S	11:30	...	3.4	5:36	**6:00**	p3.2
25	T	11:18	...	3.2	5:18	**5:48**	a3.0	25	S	12:18	**12:24**	p3.4	6:36	**6:54**	p3.3
26	F	12:06	**12:06**	p3.2	6:12	**6:36**	2.9	26	M	1:18	**1:18**	p3.5	7:30	**7:48**	p3.5
27	S	12:54	**12:54**	p3.3	7:06	**7:24**	p3.1	27	T	2:12	**2:18**	p3.6	8:30	**8:48**	p3.8
28	S	1:42	**1:42**	p3.5	8:00	**8:18**	p3.5	28	W	3:06	**3:12**	p3.7	9:24	**9:42**	p4.1
29	M	2:36	**2:36**	p3.6	8:54	**9:12**	p3.8	29	T	4:00	**4:06**	p3.9	10:18	**10:36**	p4.3
30	T	3:24	**3:30**	p3.7	9:48	**10:00**	p4.1	30	F	4:48	**5:00**	p4.1	11:12	**11:24**	p4.5
31	W	4:18	**4:24**	p3.9	10:42	**10:48**	p4.4	31	S	5:42	**5:54**	a4.2	...	**12:01**	4.2

See the Woods Hole Current Diagram on pp. 60-65.

Mariners should exercise great caution when transiting Woods Hole Passage as velocities have been reported to exceed NOAA's predictions.

CAUTION: Going *from* Buzzards Bay *into* Vineyard Sound, whether through Woods Hole, or Robinsons Hole or Quicks Hole, *Red* Buoys must be kept on the LEFT or PORT hand, *Green* Buoys kept on the RIGHT or STARBOARD hand. You are considered to be proceeding seaward and should thus follow the rules for LEAVING a harbor.

See pp. 22-29 for Current Change at other points.

2019 CURRENT TABLE
WOODS HOLE, MA, The Strait
41°31.16'N, 70°40.97'W

Daylight Saving Time   Daylight Saving Time

		SEPTEMBER CURRENT TURNS TO						OCTOBER CURRENT TURNS TO					
		SOUTHEAST Flood Starts			NORTHWEST Ebb Starts			SOUTHEAST Flood Starts			NORTHWEST Ebb Starts		
DAY OF MONTH	DAY OF WEEK	a.m.	p.m.	Kts.	a.m.	p.m.	Kts.	a.m.	p.m.	Kts.	a.m.	p.m.	Kts.
1	S/T	6:30	6:48	a4.2	12:18	12:54	a4.5	7:00	7:30	a4.0	12:54	1:24	4.2
2	M/W	7:24	7:42	a4.1	1:12	1:42	a4.4	7:48	8:24	3.8	1:48	2:12	4.0
3	T/T	8:12	8:42	a3.9	2:06	2:36	a4.2	8:42	9:18	p3.6	2:42	3:06	3.7
4	W/F	9:06	9:36	a3.7	3:00	3:30	a3.9	9:36	10:18	p3.5	3:36	3:54	3.3
5	T/S	10:00	10:42	a3.5	3:54	4:24	a3.5	10:30	11:12	p3.3	4:30	4:48	2.9
6	F/S	11:00	11:42	3.3	4:54	5:18	a3.1	11:30	...	2.9	5:30	5:48	2.6
7	S/M	11:54	...	3.1	5:54	6:12	2.7	12:12	12:24	a3.3	6:24	6:42	p2.6
8	S/T	12:36	12:48	a3.3	6:48	7:12	p2.8	1:06	1:18	a3.3	7:24	7:36	p2.7
9	M/W	1:37	1:42	a3.4	7:48	8:06	p2.9	1:55	2:06	a3.3	8:12	8:30	p2.8
10	T/T	2:24	2:36	a3.5	8:42	9:00	p3.0	2:42	2:54	a3.3	9:06	9:18	p2.9
11	W/F	3:12	3:24	a3.6	9:36	9:48	p3.1	3:24	3:36	a3.3	9:48	10:00	p3.0
12	T/S	4:00	4:06	a3.6	10:18	10:30	p3.1	4:06	4:24	a3.2	10:30	10:42	p3.2
13	F/S	4:42	4:54	a3.5	11:00	11:12	p3.3	4:42	5:06	p3.2	11:06	11:24	p3.4
14	S/M	5:18	5:36	a3.3	11:42	11:54	p3.4	5:18	5:42	p3.4	11:48	...	3.4
15	S/T	6:00	6:18	p3.3	...	12:24	3.3	5:54	6:24	p3.5	12:06	12:24	p3.6
16	M/W	6:36	6:54	p3.4	12:36	1:06	a3.5	6:30	7:06	3.6	12:48	1:00	p3.8
17	T/T	7:12	7:36	3.4	1:18	1:42	a3.6	7:12	7:48	3.6	1:30	1:42	p3.9
18	W/F	7:48	8:18	3.4	2:00	2:18	a3.7	7:48	8:30	a3.6	2:12	2:24	p4.0
19	T/S	8:24	9:00	a3.5	2:42	3:00	a3.7	8:36	9:24	a3.6	3:00	3:12	p4.0
20	F/S	9:06	9:54	a3.4	3:24	3:42	3.6	9:30	10:24	3.5	3:54	4:00	p3.9
21	S/M	10:00	10:54	a3.4	4:18	4:30	p3.6	10:36	11:24	3.5	4:48	5:00	p3.7
22	S/T	11:00	11:54	a3.4	5:12	5:24	p3.5	11:42	...	3.5	5:48	6:00	p3.6
23	M/W	...	12:01	3.4	6:06	6:24	p3.4	12:24	12:42	3.5	6:48	7:06	p3.5
24	T/T	12:48	1:00	p3.5	7:06	7:24	p3.5	1:24	1:42	3.6	7:42	8:06	p3.7
25	W/F	1:48	2:00	p3.6	8:06	8:24	p3.7	2:18	2:42	3.7	8:42	9:06	p3.8
26	T/S	2:42	3:00	p3.7	9:06	9:24	p4.0	3:12	3:42	3.9	9:36	10:00	p4.0
27	F/S	3:36	3:54	p3.9	10:00	10:18	p4.2	4:06	4:36	4.1	10:30	10:54	a4.1
28	S/M	4:30	4:48	4.1	10:48	11:12	p4.3	5:00	5:30	4.2	11:18	11:48	a4.2
29	S/T	5:18	5:42	a4.2	11:42	...	4.3	5:48	6:18	4.1	...	12:06	4.2
30	M/W	6:12	6:36	a4.2	12:06	12:30	4.3	6:36	7:12	p4.0	12:36	1:00	p4.1
31	/T							7:24	8:00	p3.8	1:30	1:48	p3.9

See the Woods Hole Current Diagram on pp. 60-65.

Mariners should exercise great caution when transiting Woods Hole Passage as velocities have been reported to exceed NOAA's predictions.

To hold longest fair current from Buzzards Bay headed East through Vineyard and Nantucket Sounds go through Woods Hole 2 1/2 hrs. after flood starts SE in Woods Hole. (Any earlier means adverse currents in the Sounds.)

2019 CURRENT TABLE
WOODS HOLE, MA, The Strait
41°31.16'N, 70°40.97'W

*Standard Time starts Nov. 3 at 2 a.m.   Standard Time

		NOVEMBER									DECEMBER					
D A Y O F M O N T H	D A Y O F W E E K	CURRENT TURNS TO						D A Y O F M O N T H	D A Y O F W E E K	CURRENT TURNS TO					
		SOUTHEAST Flood Starts			NORTHWEST Ebb Starts					SOUTHEAST Flood Starts			NORTHWEST Ebb Starts		
		a.m.	p.m.	Kts.	a.m.	p.m.	Kts.			a.m.	p.m.	Kts.	a.m.	p.m.	Kts.
1	F	8:18	8:54	p3.7	2:24	2:42	p3.6	1	S	7:42	8:18	p3.5	1:54	2:06	p3.3
2	S	9:12	9:48	p3.5	3:18	3:30	p3.3	2	M	8:36	9:12	p3.3	2:42	2:54	p3.0
3	S	*9:06	*9:42	p3.3	*3:06	*3:24	p2.9	3	T	9:30	10:00	p3.0	3:36	3:42	p2.8
4	M	10:00	10:36	p3.2	4:00	4:18	2.6	4	W	10:24	10:48	p2.8	4:24	4:36	p2.6
5	T	10:54	11:30	p3.1	4:54	5:12	2.4	5	T	11:12	11:36	p2.7	5:12	5:24	p2.4
6	W	11:48	...	2.7	5:48	6:06	2.4	6	F	...	12:01	2.5	6:00	6:18	p2.4
7	T	12:18	12:36	a3.0	6:42	6:54	a2.6	7	S	12:18	12:48	a2.7	6:48	7:06	p2.6
8	F	1:00	1:24	a2.9	7:30	7:42	a2.7	8	S	1:00	1:36	2.8	7:30	7:54	p2.8
9	S	1:43	2:06	2.8	8:12	8:30	p2.9	9	M	1:43	2:18	3.0	8:12	8:36	3.0
10	S	2:24	2:48	p3.0	8:54	9:12	p3.1	10	T	2:24	3:00	3.2	8:54	9:24	a3.4
11	M	3:00	3:30	p3.2	9:30	9:54	3.3	11	W	3:00	3:48	3.4	9:36	10:06	a3.7
12	T	3:42	4:12	p3.4	10:12	10:36	a3.6	12	T	3:42	4:30	3.7	10:12	10:54	a4.0
13	W	4:18	4:54	3.6	10:48	11:18	a3.8	13	F	4:30	5:12	3.8	11:00	11:36	a4.2
14	T	5:00	5:36	3.7	11:30	...	4.0	14	S	5:18	6:00	3.9	11:48	...	4.4
15	F	5:36	6:18	3.8	12:01	12:12	p4.2	15	S	6:06	6:48	3.9	12:30	12:36	p4.5
16	S	6:24	7:06	a3.8	12:48	12:54	p4.3	16	M	7:00	7:42	p3.9	1:18	1:30	p4.5
17	S	7:12	8:00	3.7	1:42	1:48	p4.2	17	T	7:54	8:36	3.8	2:12	2:24	p4.3
18	M	8:12	9:00	p3.7	2:30	2:42	p4.1	18	W	9:00	9:36	p3.8	3:06	3:18	p4.1
19	T	9:18	10:00	p3.7	3:24	3:42	p3.9	19	T	10:06	10:36	p3.7	4:00	4:18	p3.8
20	W	10:24	11:00	p3.6	4:24	4:42	p3.7	20	F	11:12	11:36	p3.6	5:00	5:24	3.5
21	T	11:30	...	3.5	5:24	5:42	3.5	21	S	...	12:12	3.4	6:00	6:24	a3.4
22	F	12:01	12:30	a3.6	6:24	6:48	3.5	22	S	12:30	1:12	3.6	6:54	7:24	a3.5
23	S	12:54	1:30	a3.7	7:18	7:48	3.6	23	M	1:30	2:06	p3.8	7:54	8:24	a3.6
24	S	1:48	2:24	p3.9	8:12	8:42	a3.8	24	T	2:18	3:00	p4.1	8:48	9:18	a3.7
25	M	2:42	3:18	p4.1	9:06	9:36	a4.0	25	W	3:12	3:54	p4.2	9:36	10:12	a3.8
26	T	3:36	4:12	p4.2	9:54	10:30	a4.0	26	T	4:06	4:42	p4.2	10:24	11:00	a3.7
27	W	4:24	5:06	p4.2	10:48	11:24	a4.0	27	F	4:54	5:30	p4.1	11:12	11:54	a3.7
28	T	5:18	5:54	p4.1	11:36	...	3.9	28	S	5:42	6:18	p3.9	...	12:01	3.6
29	F	6:06	6:42	p3.9	12:12	12:24	p3.7	29	S	6:30	7:06	p3.6	12:42	12:48	p3.5
30	S	6:54	7:30	p3.7	1:06	1:18	p3.5	30	M	7:18	7:48	p3.4	1:30	1:36	p3.3
								31	T	8:06	8:36	p3.0	2:12	2:24	p3.1

See the Woods Hole Current Diagram on pp. 60-65.

Mariners should exercise great caution when transiting Woods Hole Passage as velocities have been reported to exceed NOAA's predictions.

CAUTION: Going *from* Buzzards Bay *into* Vineyard Sound, whether through Woods Hole, or Robinsons Hole or Quicks Hole, *Red* Buoys must be kept on the LEFT or PORT hand, *Green* Buoys kept on the RIGHT or STARBOARD hand. You are considered to be proceeding seaward and should thus follow the rules for LEAVING a harbor.

See pp. 22-29 for Current Change at other points.

57

Coping with Currents

See also p. 21, Piloting in a Cross Current

When going directly with or against a current, our piloting problems are simple. (See Smarter Boating, p. 36.) There is no change in course, and our speed over the bottom is easily figured. However, we tend to guess a bit when the current is at some other angle. Where these currents are strong, as between New York and Nantucket, it will be vital to figure the factors carefully, especially in haze or fog.

The Table below tells 1) how many degrees to change your course; 2) by what percent your speed is decreased, with the current off the Bow; 3) or by what percent it is increased, with the current off the Stern.

First: estimate your boat's speed through the water. Then refer to the appropriate TIDAL CURRENT CHART (see pp. 72-83 or pp. 98-103) and estimate the current's speed. Put these two in the form of a ratio, for example: boat speed is 8 kts, current 2 kts; ratio is 4 to 1.

Second: using the same CURRENT CHART, estimate the relative direction of the current to the nearest 15°. Example: your desired course is 60°, the current is from the East, or a relative angle of 30° on your starboard bow.

Third: Enter the Tables under Ratio of 4.0; drop down to the 30° block of numbers (indicated in the left margin). The top figure in the block shows you must change your course 7°, always toward the current, and in this example, to 67°. The middle figure, 22%, is the amount by which your speed over the bottom will be decreased if the current is off your bow, i.e. from 8 kts down to 6.25 kts. Had the figure been 30% off your stern, instead of your bow, you would apply the third figure, 21%, adding it to your 8 kts, making your true speed about 9.7 kts.

RATIOS OF BOAT SPEED TO CURRENT SPEED

Relative Angle of Current		2	2½	3	3½	4	5	6	7	8	10	12	15	20
0° from	°	0	0	0	0	0	0	0	0	0	0	0	0	0
Bow	−%	50	40	33	29	25	20	17	14	12	10	8.3	6.7	5.0
Stern	+%	50	40	33	29	25	20	17	14	12	10	8.3	6.7	5.0
15° from	°	7.0	6.0	5.0	4.0	3.5	3.0	2.5	2.0	1.5	1.5	1.0	1.0	0.5
Bow	−%	49	39	33	28	24	20	16	14	12	10	8.0	6.4	4.8
Stern	+%	48	38	32	27	24	19	16	14	12	10	8.0	6.4	4.8
30° from	°	14	11	9.5	8.0	7.0	5.5	4.5	4.0	3.0	2.5	2.0	2.0	1.0
Bow	−%	46	36	30	26	22	18	15	13	11	8.8	7.3	5.9	4.3
Stern	+%	40	33	28	24	21	17	14	12	11	8.6	7.1	5.7	4.3
45° from	°	20	16	13	11	10	8.0	7.0	5.5	5.0	4.0	3.0	2.5	1.5
Bow	−%	42	32	26	22	19	15	12	11	9.2	7.4	6.1	4.9	3.6
Stern	+%	29	24	21	18	16	13	11	10	8.4	6.8	5.7	4.5	3.4
60° from	°	25	20	16	14	12	9.5	8.0	7.0	6.0	4.5	3.5	3.0	2.0
Bow	−%	34	26	21	18	15	11	9.3	7.8	6.7	5.4	4.4	3.5	2.6
Stern	+%	16	14	13	11	10	8.6	7.3	6.4	5.7	4.6	3.8	3.1	2.4
75° from	°	29	23	18	16	14	10	9.0	7.5	6.5	5.0	4.0	3.5	2.5
Bow	−%	25	18	14	11	9.1	6.8	5.5	4.5	3.8	3.0	2.5	1.9	1.4
Stern	+%	0.8	2.5	3.7	3.8	3.6	3.6	3.1	2.9	2.6	2.2	1.9	1.5	1.2
90°	°	30	24	19	17	14	11	9.5	8.0	7.0	5.5	4.5	3.5	2.5
Abeam	−%	13	8.6	5.4	4.1	3.0	1.8	1.4	1.0	0.7	0.4	0.3	0.2	0.1

Note: In general, while rounding a headland where head current is strong, hug the shore as far as safety will permit or go well out. (Current is usually apt to be strongest between these two points.)

58

Woods Hole and Surrounds

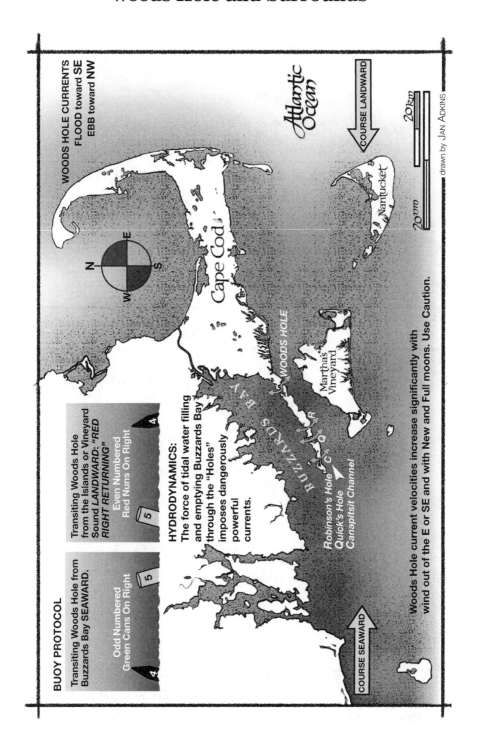

WOODS HOLE CURRENTS
FLOOD toward SE
EBB toward NW

COURSE LANDWARD

Atlantic Ocean

Nantucket

20km

20nm

drawn by JAN ADKINS

Cape Cod

WOODS HOLE

Martha's Vineyard

BUZZARDS BAY

Robinson's Hole
Quick's Hole
Canapitsit Channel

COURSE SEAWARD

BUOY PROTOCOL

Transiting Woods Hole from Buzzards Bay SEAWARD.

Odd Numbered Green Cans On Right

Transiting Woods Hole from the Islands or Vineyard Sound *LANDWARD: "RED RIGHT RETURNING"*

Even Numbered Red Nuns On Right

HYDRODYNAMICS:
The force of tidal water filling and emptying Buzzards Bay through the "Holes" imposes dangerously powerful currents.

Woods Hole current velocities increase significantly with wind out of the E or SE and with New and Full moons. Use Caution.

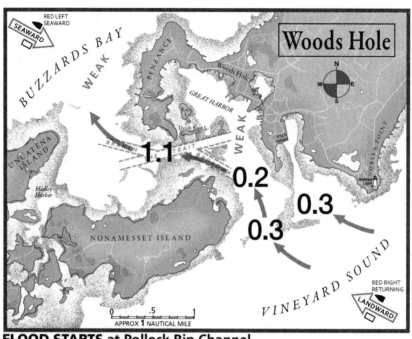

FLOOD STARTS at Pollock Rip Channel
4 hours AFTER HIGH WATER at Boston

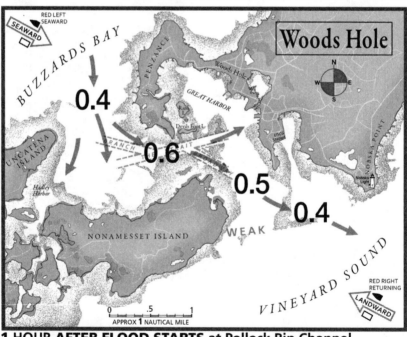

1 HOUR AFTER FLOOD STARTS at Pollock Rip Channel
5 hours AFTER HIGH WATER at Boston

Woods Hole velocities increase significantly with wind out of the E or SE and with New and Full Moons. Use Caution. Velocities shown are at Spring Tides. See note at bottom of Boston Tables: Rule-of-Thumb for Current Velocities.

Adapted from Buzzards Bay, Vineyard, and Nantucket Sounds chart on pp. 72–83.

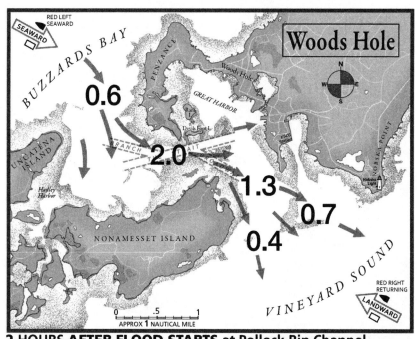

2 HOURS AFTER FLOOD STARTS at Pollock Rip Channel
LOW WATER at Boston

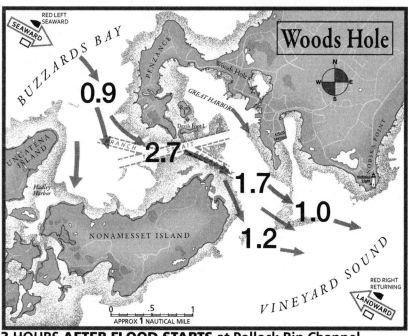

3 HOURS AFTER FLOOD STARTS at Pollock Rip Channel
1 HOUR AFTER LOW WATER at Boston

Woods Hole velocities increase significantly with wind out of the E or SE and with New and Full Moons. Use Caution. Velocities shown are at Spring Tides. See note at bottom of Boston Tables: Rule-of-Thumb for Current Velocities.

Adapted from Buzzards Bay, Vineyard, and Nantucket Sounds chart on pp. 72–83.

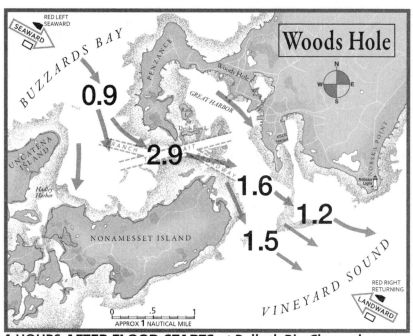

4 HOURS AFTER FLOOD STARTS at Pollock Rip Channel
2 HOURS AFTER LOW WATER at Boston

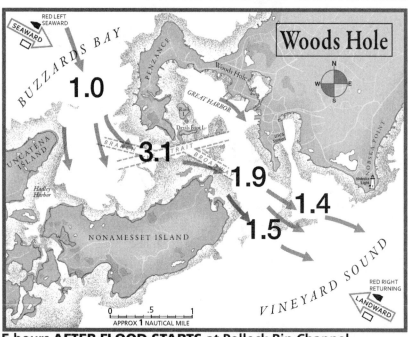

5 hours AFTER FLOOD STARTS at Pollock Rip Channel
3 hours AFTER LOW WATER at Boston

Woods Hole velocities increase significantly with wind out of the E or SE and with New and Full Moons. Use Caution. Velocities shown are at Spring Tides. See note at bottom of Boston Tables: Rule-of-Thumb for Current Velocities.

Adapted from Buzzards Bay, Vineyard, and Nantucket Sounds chart on pp. 72–83.

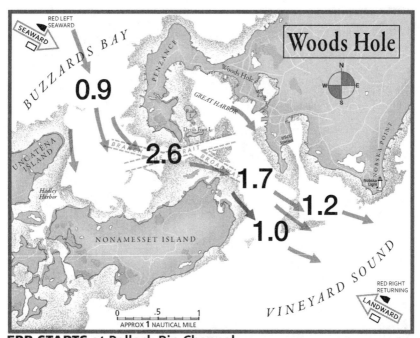

EBB STARTS at Pollock Rip Channel
4 hours **AFTER LOW WATER** at Boston

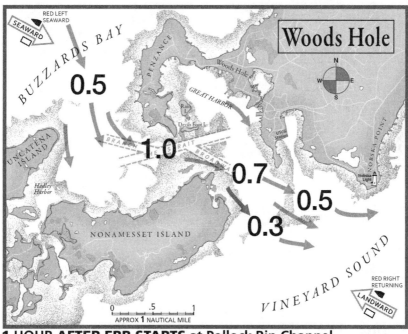

1 HOUR AFTER EBB STARTS at Pollock Rip Channel
5 hours **AFTER LOW WATER** at Boston

Woods Hole velocities increase significantly with wind out of the E or SE and with New and Full Moons. Use Caution. Velocities shown are at Spring Tides. See note at bottom of Boston Tables: Rule-of-Thumb for Current Velocities.

Adapted from Buzzards Bay, Vineyard, and Nantucket Sounds chart on pp. 72–83.

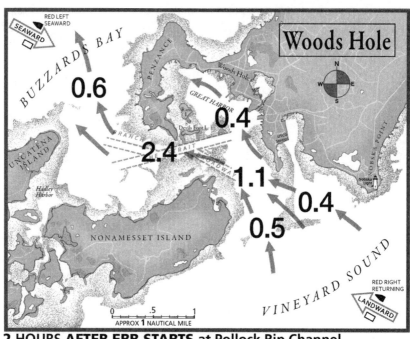

2 HOURS AFTER EBB STARTS at Pollock Rip Channel
HIGH WATER at Boston

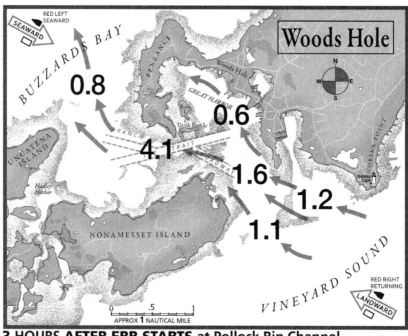

3 HOURS AFTER EBB STARTS at Pollock Rip Channel
1 HOUR AFTER HIGH WATER at Boston

Woods Hole velocities increase significantly with wind out of the E or SE and with New and Full Moons. Use Caution. Velocities shown are at Spring Tides. See note at bottom of Boston Tables: Rule-of-Thumb for Current Velocities.

Adapted from Buzzards Bay, Vineyard, and Nantucket Sounds chart on pp. 72–83.

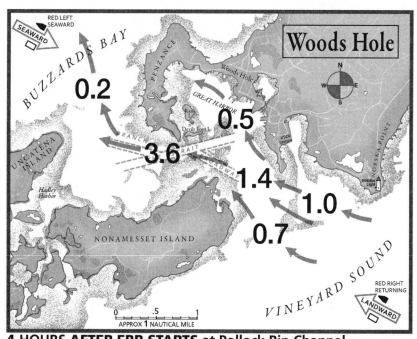

4 HOURS AFTER EBB STARTS at Pollock Rip Channel
2 HOURS AFTER HIGH WATER at Boston

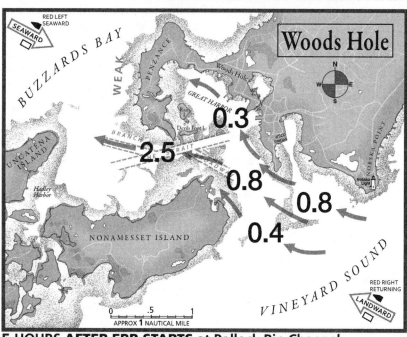

5 HOURS AFTER EBB STARTS at Pollock Rip Channel
3 HOURS AFTER HIGH WATER at Boston

Woods Hole velocities increase significantly with wind out of the E or SE and with New and Full Moons. Use Caution. Velocities shown are at Spring Tides. See note at bottom of Boston Tables: Rule-of-Thumb for Current Velocities.

Adapted from Buzzards Bay, Vineyard, and Nantucket Sounds chart on pp. 72–83.

2019 CURRENT TABLE
POLLOCK RIP CHANNEL, MA

41°33'N, 69°59'W SE of Monomoy Pt. at Butler Hole

Standard Time   Standard Time

JANUARY | FEBRUARY

DAY OF MONTH	DAY OF WEEK	NORTHEAST Flood Starts a.m.	p.m.	Kts.	SOUTHWEST Ebb Starts a.m.	p.m.	Kts.	DAY OF MONTH	DAY OF WEEK	NORTHEAST Flood Starts a.m.	p.m.	Kts.	SOUTHWEST Ebb Starts a.m.	p.m.	Kts.
1	T	11:36	...	2.1	5:36	6:12	a1.7	1	F	12:42	1:00	p2.2	7:00	7:42	a1.7
2	W	12:06	12:36	p2.2	6:30	7:06	a1.8	2	S	1:36	1:54	p2.2	7:48	8:30	a1.7
3	T	1:06	1:24	p2.2	7:24	8:00	a1.8	3	S	2:24	2:36	p2.2	8:36	9:12	a1.7
4	F	1:54	2:12	p2.3	8:12	8:48	a1.8	4	M	3:06	3:12	p2.2	9:18	9:48	a1.8
5	S	2:42	2:54	p2.3	8:54	9:36	a1.8	5	T	3:42	3:48	p2.2	9:54	10:30	a1.8
6	S	3:24	3:36	p2.2	9:36	10:12	a1.8	6	W	4:18	4:24	p2.2	10:30	11:06	1.8
7	M	4:06	4:12	p2.2	10:18	10:54	a1.8	7	T	4:48	5:00	p2.2	11:12	11:42	1.8
8	T	4:42	4:48	p2.1	10:54	11:30	a1.8	8	F	5:24	5:36	p2.1	11:48	...	1.9
9	W	5:19	5:24	p2.1	11:36	...	1.8	9	S	6:07	6:18	p2.0	12:18	12:30	1.8
10	T	6:00	6:06	p2.0	12:12	12:18	1.7	10	S	6:42	7:00	p2.0	1:00	1:18	1.8
11	F	6:42	6:48	p2.0	12:54	1:06	1.7	11	M	7:30	7:42	1.8	1:42	2:06	1.7
12	S	7:24	7:36	p1.9	1:36	1:54	a1.7	12	T	8:12	8:36	a1.8	2:30	3:00	a1.7
13	S	8:12	8:24	p1.8	2:24	2:42	a1.7	13	W	9:06	9:36	a1.7	3:18	3:54	a1.6
14	M	9:00	9:18	p1.8	3:12	3:36	a1.6	14	T	10:06	10:36	a1.7	4:18	4:54	a1.6
15	T	9:54	10:12	1.7	4:00	4:30	a1.6	15	F	11:06	11:36	a1.8	5:12	5:54	a1.6
16	W	10:48	11:06	1.7	4:54	5:30	a1.6	16	S	...	12:06	1.9	6:12	6:54	1.6
17	T	11:36	...	1.8	5:48	6:24	a1.6	17	S	12:42	1:00	p2.1	7:06	7:48	a1.8
18	F	12:06	12:30	p2.0	6:36	7:18	a1.7	18	M	1:36	1:54	p2.3	8:00	8:42	a1.9
19	S	1:00	1:24	p2.1	7:24	8:06	a1.8	19	T	2:30	2:48	p2.4	8:48	9:30	2.0
20	S	1:54	2:12	p2.2	8:18	9:00	a1.9	20	W	3:18	3:36	p2.5	9:42	10:18	a2.2
21	M	2:42	3:00	p2.4	9:06	9:48	a2.0	21	T	4:06	4:30	p2.5	10:30	11:06	a2.2
22	T	3:36	3:48	p2.4	9:54	10:36	a2.1	22	F	5:00	5:18	p2.4	11:24	11:54	a2.2
23	W	4:24	4:42	p2.5	10:42	11:24	a2.2	23	S	5:48	6:12	p2.3	...	12:12	2.1
24	T	5:18	5:36	p2.4	11:36	...	2.1	24	S	6:36	7:06	2.1	12:48	1:12	a2.0
25	F	6:12	6:30	p2.3	12:18	12:36	2.0	25	M	7:36	8:00	a2.0	1:42	2:12	a1.8
26	S	7:06	7:24	p2.2	1:12	1:30	1.9	26	T	8:30	9:06	a1.9	2:36	3:12	a1.7
27	S	8:06	8:30	2.0	2:06	2:36	a1.8	27	W	9:36	10:12	a1.9	3:36	4:18	a1.6
28	M	9:06	9:30	1.9	3:06	3:36	a1.7	28	T	10:36	11:18	a1.9	4:36	5:18	a1.5
29	T	10:06	10:36	1.9	4:06	4:42	a1.6								
30	W	11:12	11:42	a2.0	5:06	5:48	a1.6								
31	T	...	12:12	2.1	6:06	6:48	a1.6								

The Kts. (knots) columns show the **maximum** predicted velocities of the stronger one of the Flood Currents and the stronger one of the Ebb Currents for each day.

The letter "a" means the velocity shown should occur **after** the **a.m.** Current Change. The letter "p" means the velocity shown should occur **after** the **p.m.** Current Change (even if next morning). No "a" or "p" means a.m. and p.m. velocities are the same for that day.

Avg. Max. Velocity: Flood 2.0 Kts., Ebb 1.8 Kts.

Max. Flood 3 hrs. 20 min. after Flood Starts, ±15 min.

Max. Ebb 2 hrs. 45 min. after Ebb Starts, ±15 min.

Gay Head (1 1/2 mi. NW of): avg. max velocity, Flood 2.0 kts., Ebb 2.0 kts. Time of Flood and Ebb 1 hr. 35 min. after Pollock Rip. Cross Rip: avg. max. velocity, Flood 1.3 kts., Ebb 0.9 kts. Time of Flood and Ebb 1 hr. 50 min. after Pollock Rip. Use POLLOCK RIP tables with current charts on pp. 72-83. See pp. 22-29 for Current Change at other points.

2019 CURRENT TABLE
POLLOCK RIP CHANNEL, MA
41°33'N, 69°59'W SE of Monomoy Pt. at Butler Hole

*Daylight Time starts March 10 at 2 a.m.   Daylight Saving Time

		MARCH							APRIL				
		CURRENT TURNS TO							CURRENT TURNS TO				
		NORTHEAST Flood Starts			SOUTHWEST Ebb Starts				NORTHEAST Flood Starts			SOUTHWEST Ebb Starts	
D A Y O F M O N T H	D A Y O F W E E K	a.m.	**p.m.**	Kts.	a.m.	**p.m.**	Kts.	D A Y O F M O N T H	D A Y O F W E E K	a.m.	**p.m.**	Kts.	a.m.	**p.m.**	Kts.

D.M.	D.W.	a.m.	p.m.	Kts.	a.m.	p.m.	Kts.	D.M.	D.W.	a.m.	p.m.	Kts.	a.m.	p.m.	Kts.
1	F	11:42	...	2.0	5:36	**6:18**	1.5	1	M	1:36	**1:48**	p2.1	7:54	**8:24**	1.6
2	S	12:18	**12:36**	p2.1	6:30	**7:12**	a1.6	2	T	2:24	**2:36**	p2.2	8:42	**9:06**	1.7
3	S	1:12	**1:24**	p2.2	7:24	**8:00**	1.6	3	W	3:00	**3:12**	p2.2	9:24	**9:48**	1.8
4	M	1:54	**2:06**	p2.2	8:06	**8:42**	1.7	4	T	3:42	**3:54**	p2.2	10:00	**10:24**	p1.9
5	T	2:36	**2:48**	p2.2	8:48	**9:18**	a1.8	5	F	4:12	**4:24**	2.1	10:36	**11:00**	1.9
6	W	3:12	**3:24**	p2.2	9:30	**9:54**	1.8	6	S	4:48	**5:00**	2.1	11:12	**11:30**	1.9
7	T	3:48	**3:54**	p2.2	10:06	**10:30**	1.9	7	S	5:18	**5:36**	2.1	11:54	...	1.9
8	F	4:18	**4:30**	p2.2	10:42	**11:06**	1.9	8	M	5:54	**6:18**	a2.1	12:06	**12:30**	1.9
9	S	4:55	**5:06**	p2.1	11:18	**11:42**	1.9	9	T	6:31	**7:00**	a2.1	12:48	**1:18**	a1.9
10	S	*6:30	*6:42	2.0	...	*1:00	1.9	10	W	7:18	**7:48**	a2.0	1:30	**2:06**	a1.9
11	M	7:06	**7:24**	a2.0	1:24	**1:42**	a1.9	11	T	8:06	**8:42**	a2.0	2:18	**3:00**	a1.8
12	T	7:48	**8:12**	a1.9	2:06	**2:30**	a1.8	12	F	9:00	**9:48**	a1.9	3:18	**4:00**	a1.6
13	W	8:36	**9:06**	a1.9	2:48	**3:24**	a1.7	13	S	10:06	**10:54**	a1.8	4:18	**5:06**	a1.6
14	T	9:30	**10:06**	a1.8	3:42	**4:24**	a1.6	14	S	11:12	...	1.9	5:24	**6:12**	1.5
15	F	10:30	**11:12**	a1.8	4:42	**5:30**	a1.5	15	M	12:01	**12:24**	p2.0	6:30	**7:12**	1.6
16	S	11:36	...	1.8	5:48	**6:30**	1.5	16	T	1:06	**1:24**	p2.1	7:30	**8:06**	p1.8
17	S	12:18	**12:42**	p1.9	6:48	**7:30**	1.6	17	W	2:00	**2:24**	p2.3	8:24	**9:00**	1.9
18	M	1:24	**1:42**	p2.1	7:48	**8:30**	1.7	18	T	2:54	**3:18**	p2.3	9:18	**9:48**	2.0
19	T	2:18	**2:42**	p2.3	8:42	**9:18**	1.9	19	F	3:42	**4:06**	2.3	10:12	**10:36**	p2.1
20	W	3:12	**3:30**	p2.4	9:36	**10:12**	2.0	20	S	4:30	**4:54**	a2.4	11:00	**11:18**	2.0
21	T	4:00	**4:24**	p2.4	10:24	**10:54**	2.1	21	S	5:12	**5:42**	a2.3	11:48	...	2.0
22	F	4:48	**5:12**	p2.4	11:12	**11:42**	a2.2	22	M	6:00	**6:30**	a2.3	12:06	**12:36**	a2.0
23	S	5:36	**6:00**	2.3	...	12:06	2.1	23	T	6:48	**7:18**	a2.2	12:54	**1:30**	a1.9
24	S	6:24	**6:48**	a2.3	12:30	**12:54**	2.0	24	W	7:36	**8:12**	a2.0	1:42	**2:24**	a1.7
25	M	7:12	**7:42**	a2.2	1:18	**1:48**	a1.9	25	T	8:30	**9:12**	a1.9	2:36	**3:18**	a1.6
26	T	8:06	**8:36**	a2.1	2:12	**2:48**	a1.8	26	F	9:24	**10:06**	a1.9	3:30	**4:12**	a1.5
27	W	9:00	**9:36**	a1.9	3:06	**3:42**	a1.6	27	S	10:24	**11:06**	a1.9	4:30	**5:12**	1.4
28	T	10:00	**10:42**	a1.9	4:06	**4:48**	a1.5	28	S	11:24	...	1.9	5:30	**6:06**	p1.5
29	F	11:00	**11:42**	a1.9	5:06	**5:48**	1.4	29	M	12:06	**12:18**	p2.0	6:24	**7:00**	p1.6
30	S	...	12:06	1.9	6:06	**6:48**	1.4	30	T	12:54	**1:06**	p2.0	7:18	**7:42**	p1.7
31	S	12:42	**1:00**	p2.0	7:00	**7:36**	1.5								

The Kts. (knots) columns show the **maximum** predicted velocities of the stronger one of the Flood Currents and the stronger one of the Ebb Currents for each day.

The letter "a" means the velocity shown should occur **after** the a.m. Current Change. The letter "p" means the velocity shown should occur **after** the p.m. Current Change (even if next morning). No "a" or "p" means a.m. and p.m. velocities are the same for that day.

Avg. Max. Velocity: Flood 2.0 Kts., Ebb 1.8 Kts.

Max. Flood 3 hrs. 20 min. after Flood Starts, ±15 min.

Max. Ebb 2 hrs. 45 min. after Ebb Starts, ±15 min.

Gay Head (1 1/2 mi. NW of): avg. max velocity, Flood 2.0 kts., Ebb 2.0 kts. Time of Flood and Ebb 1 hr. 35 min. after Pollock Rip. Cross Rip: avg. max. velocity, Flood 1.3 kts., Ebb 0.9 kts. Time of Flood and Ebb 1 hr. 50 min. after Pollock Rip. Use POLLOCK RIP tables with current charts on pp. 72-83. See pp. 22-29 for Current Change at other points.

2019 CURRENT TABLE
POLLOCK RIP CHANNEL, MA
41°33'N, 69°59'W SE of Monomoy Pt. at Butler Hole

Daylight Saving Time   Daylight Saving Time

DAY OF MONTH	DAY OF WEEK	CURRENT TURNS TO						DAY OF MONTH	DAY OF WEEK	CURRENT TURNS TO					
		NORTHEAST Flood Starts			SOUTHWEST Ebb Starts					NORTHEAST Flood Starts			SOUTHWEST Ebb Starts		
		a.m.	**p.m.**	Kts.	a.m.	**p.m.**	Kts.			a.m.	**p.m.**	Kts.	a.m.	**p.m.**	Kts.
1	W	1:42	**1:54**	p2.1	8:06	**8:30**	p1.8	1	S	2:24	**2:42**	a2.0	8:54	**9:06**	p1.8
2	T	2:24	**2:36**	p2.1	8:48	**9:06**	p1.8	2	S	3:00	**3:24**	a2.1	9:42	**9:48**	p1.9
3	F	3:00	**3:18**	2.1	9:30	**9:48**	p1.9	3	M	3:42	**4:06**	a2.1	10:24	**10:30**	p1.9
4	S	3:36	**3:54**	a2.1	10:06	**10:24**	p1.9	4	T	4:18	**4:48**	a2.2	11:06	**11:12**	p2.0
5	S	4:12	**4:30**	a2.1	10:48	**11:00**	p2.0	5	W	5:00	**5:30**	a2.2	11:48	**11:54**	p2.0
6	M	4:48	**5:12**	a2.2	11:30	**11:36**	p2.0	6	T	5:48	**6:24**	a2.2	...	**12:36**	1.8
7	T	5:24	**5:54**	a2.2	...	**12:12**	1.9	7	F	6:36	**7:12**	a2.2	12:42	**1:30**	a1.9
8	W	6:06	**6:36**	a2.2	12:18	**12:54**	a1.9	8	S	7:30	**8:12**	a2.2	1:36	**2:24**	a1.9
9	T	6:55	**7:30**	a2.1	1:06	**1:48**	a1.9	9	S	8:31	**9:12**	a2.1	2:36	**3:24**	a1.8
10	F	7:42	**8:30**	a2.1	1:54	**2:42**	a1.8	10	M	9:30	**10:18**	a2.0	3:42	**4:24**	1.7
11	S	8:42	**9:30**	a2.0	2:54	**3:42**	a1.7	11	T	10:36	**11:24**	a2.0	4:48	**5:24**	1.7
12	S	9:48	**10:36**	a1.9	4:00	**4:48**	1.6	12	W	11:42	...	2.0	5:54	**6:24**	1.7
13	M	10:54	**11:42**	a2.0	5:06	**5:48**	1.6	13	T	12:24	**12:48**	p2.1	6:54	**7:24**	p1.8
14	T	...	**12:06**	2.0	6:12	**6:48**	p1.7	14	F	1:24	**1:48**	2.1	7:54	**8:12**	p1.8
15	W	12:48	**1:06**	p2.1	7:12	**7:42**	p1.8	15	S	2:18	**2:42**	a2.2	8:48	**9:06**	p1.9
16	T	1:42	**2:06**	p2.2	8:12	**8:36**	p1.9	16	S	3:06	**3:36**	a2.3	9:42	**9:54**	p1.9
17	F	2:36	**3:00**	2.2	9:06	**9:24**	p2.0	17	M	3:54	**4:24**	a2.3	10:30	**10:36**	p1.8
18	S	3:24	**3:48**	a2.3	9:54	**10:12**	p2.0	18	T	4:36	**5:06**	a2.3	11:18	**11:24**	p1.8
19	S	4:12	**4:36**	a2.3	10:48	**11:00**	1.9	19	W	5:18	**5:54**	a2.2	...	**12:01**	1.6
20	M	4:54	**5:24**	a2.3	11:36	**11:42**	p1.9	20	T	6:00	**6:36**	a2.1	12:06	**12:48**	a1.7
21	T	5:36	**6:12**	a2.2	...	**12:18**	1.7	21	F	6:42	**7:18**	a2.1	12:48	**1:30**	a1.7
22	W	6:24	**7:00**	a2.1	12:30	**1:06**	a1.8	22	S	7:24	**8:06**	a2.0	1:36	**2:12**	a1.7
23	T	7:06	**7:48**	a2.1	1:18	**2:00**	a1.7	23	S	8:12	**8:54**	a2.0	2:24	**3:00**	1.6
24	F	8:00	**8:36**	a2.0	2:06	**2:48**	a1.6	24	M	9:00	**9:42**	a1.9	3:18	**3:48**	1.6
25	S	8:48	**9:30**	a1.9	3:00	**3:42**	1.5	25	T	9:54	**10:30**	a1.9	4:06	**4:36**	p1.6
26	S	9:42	**10:24**	a1.9	3:54	**4:30**	1.5	26	W	10:42	**11:24**	a1.8	5:00	**5:30**	p1.6
27	M	10:36	**11:18**	a1.9	4:48	**5:24**	1.5	27	T	11:36	...	1.8	5:54	**6:18**	p1.6
28	T	11:30	...	1.9	5:42	**6:12**	p1.6	28	F	12:12	**12:30**	1.8	6:48	**7:06**	p1.7
29	W	12:12	**12:24**	p1.9	6:36	**7:00**	p1.7	29	S	1:00	**1:18**	a1.9	7:36	**7:48**	p1.7
30	T	1:00	**1:12**	1.9	7:24	**7:48**	p1.7	30	S	1:42	**2:06**	a2.0	8:24	**8:36**	p1.8
31	F	1:42	**2:00**	1.9	8:12	**8:30**	p1.8								

The Kts. (knots) columns show the **maximum** predicted velocities of the stronger one of the Flood Currents and the stronger one of the Ebb Currents for each day.

The letter "a" means the velocity shown should occur **after** the a.m. Current Change. The letter "p" means the velocity shown should occur **after** the p.m. Current Change (even if next morning). No "a" or "p" means a.m. and p.m. velocities are the same for that day.

Avg. Max. Velocity: Flood 2.0 Kts., Ebb 1.8 Kts.

Max. Flood 3 hrs. 20 min. after Flood Starts, ±15 min.

Max. Ebb 2 hrs. 45 min. after Ebb Starts, ±15 min.

Gay Head (1 1/2 mi. NW of): avg. max velocity, Flood 2.0 kts., Ebb 2.0 kts. Time of Flood and Ebb 1 hr. 35 min. after Pollock Rip. Cross Rip: avg. max. velocity, Flood 1.3 kts., Ebb 0.9 kts. Time of Flood and Ebb 1 hr. 50 min. after Pollock Rip. Use POLLOCK RIP tables with current charts on pp. 72-83. See pp. 22-29 for Current Change at other points.

2019 CURRENT TABLE
POLLOCK RIP CHANNEL, MA
41°33'N, 69°59'W SE of Monomoy Pt. at Butler Hole

Daylight Saving Time   Daylight Saving Time

		JULY								AUGUST					
		CURRENT TURNS TO								CURRENT TURNS TO					
		NORTHEAST Flood Starts			SOUTHWEST Ebb Starts					NORTHEAST Flood Starts			SOUTHWEST Ebb Starts		
DAY OF MONTH	DAY OF WEEK	a.m.	p.m.	Kts.	a.m.	p.m.	Kts.	DAY OF MONTH	DAY OF WEEK	a.m.	p.m.	Kts.	a.m.	p.m.	Kts.
1	M	2:30	2:54	a2.0	9:12	9:18	p1.9	1	T	3:36	4:06	a2.3	10:24	10:30	p2.1
2	T	3:12	3:42	a2.1	10:00	10:00	p1.9	2	F	4:24	5:00	a2.4	11:12	11:18	p2.1
3	W	3:54	4:30	a2.2	10:42	10:48	p2.0	3	S	5:12	5:48	a2.4	...	12:01	2.0
4	T	4:42	5:18	a2.3	11:30	11:36	p2.0	4	S	6:06	6:36	a2.4	12:12	12:48	a2.1
5	F	5:30	6:06	a2.3	...	12:18	1.9	5	M	7:00	7:30	a2.3	1:06	1:42	a2.1
6	S	6:18	7:00	a2.3	12:24	1:12	a2.0	6	T	7:54	8:30	a2.2	2:00	2:36	a2.0
7	S	7:12	7:54	a2.3	1:24	2:06	a2.0	7	W	8:54	9:30	a2.1	3:00	3:36	1.8
8	M	8:12	8:54	a2.2	2:18	3:00	a1.9	8	T	10:00	10:36	p2.0	4:06	4:36	1.7
9	T	9:13	9:54	a2.1	3:24	4:00	1.8	9	F	11:07	11:36	p2.0	5:12	5:36	1.6
10	W	10:18	11:00	a2.0	4:24	5:00	1.7	10	S	...	12:12	1.8	6:18	6:36	p1.6
11	T	11:24	...	2.0	5:30	6:00	p1.7	11	S	12:42	1:18	a2.1	7:18	7:36	p1.7
12	F	12:01	12:30	2.0	6:36	7:00	p1.7	12	M	1:36	2:12	a2.2	8:18	8:30	p1.7
13	S	1:00	1:30	a2.1	7:36	7:54	p1.8	13	T	2:30	3:06	a2.2	9:06	9:18	p1.8
14	S	2:00	2:30	a2.2	8:36	8:48	p1.8	14	W	3:18	3:48	a2.3	9:54	10:00	p1.8
15	M	2:48	3:24	a2.2	9:30	9:36	p1.8	15	T	4:00	4:24	a2.3	10:36	10:42	p1.8
16	T	3:36	4:06	a2.3	10:18	10:18	p1.8	16	F	4:36	5:00	a2.2	11:12	11:18	p1.8
17	W	4:18	4:48	a2.2	11:00	11:00	p1.8	17	S	5:12	5:36	a2.2	11:48	11:54	p1.8
18	T	5:00	5:30	a2.2	11:42	11:42	p1.8	18	S	5:48	6:12	a2.1	...	12:24	1.8
19	F	5:36	6:06	a2.2	...	12:18	1.7	19	M	6:24	6:48	a2.1	12:36	1:00	1.8
20	S	6:18	6:48	a2.1	12:24	1:00	1.7	20	T	7:00	7:30	a2.0	1:18	1:42	1.8
21	S	6:54	7:30	a2.1	1:06	1:42	1.7	21	W	7:42	8:12	a1.9	2:00	2:24	1.7
22	M	7:36	8:12	a2.0	1:48	2:24	1.7	22	T	8:30	8:54	1.8	2:48	3:12	1.7
23	T	8:24	8:54	a1.9	2:36	3:06	1.7	23	F	9:18	9:48	1.7	3:42	4:00	1.6
24	W	9:06	9:42	a1.9	3:24	3:54	1.6	24	S	10:12	10:42	p1.7	4:36	4:54	p1.6
25	T	10:00	10:36	a1.8	4:18	4:42	p1.6	25	S	11:12	11:42	p1.8	5:36	5:48	p1.5
26	F	10:54	11:24	1.7	5:12	5:36	p1.6	26	M	...	12:12	1.6	6:30	6:48	p1.6
27	S	11:48	...	1.7	6:06	6:24	p1.6	27	T	12:36	1:12	a1.9	7:30	7:42	p1.7
28	S	12:18	12:42	a1.8	7:00	7:18	p1.7	28	W	1:36	2:06	a2.0	8:24	8:30	p1.8
29	M	1:06	1:36	a1.9	7:54	8:06	p1.7	29	T	2:30	3:00	a2.2	9:12	9:24	p2.0
30	T	2:00	2:30	a2.0	8:48	8:54	p1.8	30	F	3:18	3:48	a2.3	10:00	10:12	p2.1
31	W	2:48	3:18	a2.1	9:36	9:42	p2.0	31	S	4:06	4:36	a2.4	10:48	11:00	p2.2

The Kts. (knots) columns show the **maximum** predicted velocities of the stronger one of the Flood Currents and the stronger one of the Ebb Currents for each day.

The letter "a" means the velocity shown should occur **after** the **a.m.** Current Change. The letter "p" means the velocity shown should occur **after** the **p.m.** Current Change (even if next morning). No "a" or "p" means a.m. and p.m. velocities are the same for that day.

Avg. Max. Velocity: Flood 2.0 Kts., Ebb 1.8 Kts.

Max. Flood 3 hrs. 20 min. after Flood Starts, ±15 min.

Max. Ebb 2 hrs. 45 min. after Ebb Starts, ±15 min.

Gay Head (1 1/2 mi. NW of): avg. max velocity, Flood 2.0 kts., Ebb 2.0 kts. Time of Flood and Ebb 1 hr. 35 min. after Pollock Rip. Cross Rip: avg. max. velocity, Flood 1.3 kts., Ebb 0.9 kts. Time of Flood and Ebb 1 hr. 50 min. after Pollock Rip. Use POLLOCK RIP tables with current charts on pp. 72-83. See pp. 22-29 for Current Change at other points.

2019 CURRENT TABLE
POLLOCK RIP CHANNEL, MA
41°33'N, 69°59'W SE of Monomoy Pt. at Butler Hole

Daylight Saving Time								Daylight Saving Time						

SEPTEMBER / OCTOBER

DAY OF MONTH	DAY OF WEEK	CURRENT TURNS TO						DAY OF MONTH	DAY OF WEEK	CURRENT TURNS TO					
		NORTHEAST Flood Starts			SOUTHWEST Ebb Starts					NORTHEAST Flood Starts			SOUTHWEST Ebb Starts		
		a.m.	p.m.	Kts.	a.m.	p.m.	Kts.			a.m.	p.m.	Kts.	a.m.	p.m.	Kts.
1	S	5:00	5:24	a2.5	11:36	11:54	p2.2	1	T	5:30	5:54	2.3	...	12:01	2.1
2	M	5:48	6:18	a2.4	...	12:24	2.1	2	W	6:24	6:42	2.2	12:30	12:48	a2.1
3	T	6:42	7:06	a2.3	12:48	1:18	a2.1	3	T	7:18	7:36	p2.1	1:24	1:42	a1.9
4	W	7:36	8:00	2.1	1:42	2:12	a2.0	4	F	8:12	8:36	p2.0	2:18	2:42	1.7
5	T	8:36	9:00	2.0	2:42	3:06	a1.8	5	S	9:12	9:36	p1.9	3:18	3:42	a1.6
6	F	9:36	10:06	p1.9	3:42	4:06	1.6	6	S	10:18	10:42	p1.9	4:24	4:42	p1.5
7	S	10:42	11:12	p2.0	4:48	5:12	1.5	7	M	11:24	11:42	p2.0	5:24	5:42	p1.5
8	S	11:54	...	1.8	5:54	6:12	1.5	8	T	...	12:24	1.8	6:24	6:42	1.5
9	M	12:13	12:54	a2.0	6:54	7:12	p1.6	9	W	12:43	1:18	a2.1	7:18	7:36	1.6
10	T	1:12	1:48	a2.1	7:54	8:06	p1.7	10	T	1:30	2:06	a2.2	8:06	8:24	1.7
11	W	2:06	2:36	a2.2	8:42	8:54	1.7	11	F	2:18	2:48	a2.2	8:48	9:06	1.8
12	T	2:54	3:18	a2.3	9:24	9:36	p1.8	12	S	3:00	3:24	a2.2	9:30	9:48	1.8
13	F	3:30	4:00	a2.3	10:06	10:12	1.8	13	S	3:36	4:00	a2.2	10:06	10:24	1.9
14	S	4:06	4:30	a2.2	10:42	10:54	p1.9	14	M	4:12	4:30	2.1	10:42	11:00	1.9
15	S	4:42	5:06	a2.2	11:18	11:30	p1.9	15	T	4:48	5:06	2.1	11:18	11:36	1.9
16	M	5:18	5:36	a2.1	11:48	...	1.9	16	W	5:24	5:36	p2.1	11:54	...	1.9
17	T	5:54	6:12	a2.1	12:06	12:24	1.9	17	T	6:00	6:12	p2.1	12:18	12:30	p1.9
18	W	6:30	6:48	2.0	12:42	1:06	1.8	18	F	6:42	6:54	p2.0	1:00	1:12	1.8
19	T	7:12	7:30	1.9	1:24	1:48	1.8	19	S	7:24	7:42	p1.9	1:48	2:00	1.7
20	F	7:54	8:12	1.8	2:12	2:30	1.7	20	S	8:18	8:36	p1.9	2:36	2:48	1.6
21	S	8:42	9:06	p1.8	3:06	3:24	1.6	21	M	9:18	9:36	p1.8	3:36	3:48	1.5
22	S	9:42	10:06	p1.7	4:00	4:18	1.5	22	T	10:24	10:42	p1.8	4:36	4:54	1.5
23	M	10:48	11:06	p1.8	5:06	5:18	p1.5	23	W	11:30	11:48	p1.9	5:42	6:00	p1.6
24	T	11:48	...	1.5	6:06	6:18	p1.6	24	T	...	12:30	1.8	6:42	7:00	p1.7
25	W	12:12	12:54	a1.9	7:06	7:18	p1.7	25	F	12:54	1:30	a2.1	7:36	7:54	1.8
26	T	1:12	1:48	a2.0	8:00	8:12	p1.9	26	S	1:48	2:24	a2.2	8:30	8:48	p2.0
27	F	2:06	2:42	a2.2	8:48	9:06	p2.0	27	S	2:42	3:12	2.3	9:18	9:42	p2.1
28	S	3:00	3:30	a2.3	9:42	9:54	p2.1	28	M	3:36	4:00	p2.4	10:06	10:30	2.1
29	S	3:54	4:18	a2.4	10:24	10:48	p2.2	29	T	4:24	4:48	p2.4	10:54	11:24	a2.1
30	M	4:42	5:06	2.4	11:12	11:36	p2.2	30	W	5:12	5:30	p2.3	11:36	...	2.0
								31	T	6:06	6:18	p2.2	12:12	12:24	1.9

The Kts. (knots) columns show the **maximum** predicted velocities of the stronger one of the Flood Currents and the stronger one of the Ebb Currents for each day.

The letter "a" means the velocity shown should occur **after** the **a.m.** Current Change. The letter "p" means the velocity shown should occur **after** the **p.m.** Current Change (even if next morning). No "a" or "p" means a.m. and p.m. velocities are the same for that day.

Avg. Max. Velocity: Flood 2.0 Kts., Ebb 1.8 Kts.

Max. Flood 3 hrs. 20 min. after Flood Starts, ±15 min.

Max. Ebb 2 hrs. 45 min. after Ebb Starts, ±15 min.

Gay Head (1 1/2 mi. NW of): avg. max velocity, Flood 2.0 kts., Ebb 2.0 kts. Time of Flood and Ebb 1 hr. 35 min. after Pollock Rip. Cross Rip: avg. max. velocity, Flood 1.3 kts., Ebb 0.9 kts. Time of Flood and Ebb 1 hr. 50 min. after Pollock Rip. Use POLLOCK RIP tables with current charts on pp. 72-83. See pp. 22-29 for Current Change at other points.

2019 CURRENT TABLE
POLLOCK RIP CHANNEL, MA
41°33'N, 69°59'W SE of Monomoy Pt. at Butler Hole

Standard Time starts Nov. 3 at 2 a.m.   **Standard Time**

NOVEMBER

DAY OF MONTH	DAY OF WEEK	NORTHEAST Flood Starts a.m.	**p.m.**	Kts.	SOUTHWEST Ebb Starts a.m.	**p.m.**	Kts.
1	F	6:54	**7:12**	p2.1	1:06	**1:18**	1.8
2	S	7:48	**8:06**	p2.0	2:00	**2:12**	1.6
3	S	*7:48	***8:06**	p1.9	*1:54	***2:12**	1.5
4	M	8:48	**9:06**	p1.9	2:54	**3:12**	1.4
5	T	9:48	**10:06**	p1.9	3:54	**4:12**	1.4
6	W	10:48	**11:00**	p2.0	4:48	**5:06**	1.5
7	T	11:42	**11:54**	p2.1	5:42	**6:00**	1.6
8	F	...	**12:30**	2.0	6:30	**6:48**	a1.7
9	S	12:43	**1:12**	2.1	7:12	**7:36**	a1.8
10	S	1:24	**1:48**	2.1	7:54	**8:18**	1.8
11	M	2:06	**2:24**	2.1	8:30	**8:54**	a1.9
12	T	2:42	**3:00**	p2.1	9:06	**9:36**	a1.9
13	W	3:18	**3:30**	p2.2	9:42	**10:12**	a1.9
14	T	3:54	**4:06**	p2.2	10:18	**10:54**	a1.9
15	F	4:36	**4:48**	p2.1	11:00	**11:36**	a1.9
16	S	5:18	**5:30**	p2.1	11:42	...	1.9
17	S	6:06	**6:18**	p2.0	12:24	**12:30**	p1.8
18	M	7:00	**7:12**	p2.0	1:18	**1:24**	1.7
19	T	8:00	**8:12**	p1.9	2:12	**2:24**	1.6
20	W	9:00	**9:18**	p1.9	3:12	**3:30**	1.6
21	T	10:06	**10:24**	p2.0	4:12	**4:36**	1.6
22	F	11:12	**11:30**	p2.0	5:12	**5:42**	1.7
23	S	...	**12:12**	2.0	6:12	**6:42**	1.8
24	S	12:30	**1:06**	p2.2	7:06	**7:36**	1.9
25	M	1:30	**1:54**	p2.3	7:54	**8:30**	a2.0
26	T	2:24	**2:42**	p2.4	8:42	**9:18**	a2.0
27	W	3:12	**3:30**	p2.4	9:30	**10:06**	a2.0
28	T	4:00	**4:18**	p2.3	10:18	**11:00**	a1.9
29	F	4:48	**5:00**	p2.2	11:06	**11:48**	a1.9
30	S	5:36	**5:48**	p2.1	11:54	...	1.8

DECEMBER

DAY OF MONTH	DAY OF WEEK	NORTHEAST Flood Starts a.m.	**p.m.**	Kts.	SOUTHWEST Ebb Starts a.m.	**p.m.**	Kts.
1	S	6:30	**6:36**	p2.0	12:36	**12:42**	p1.7
2	M	7:18	**7:30**	p2.0	1:30	**1:36**	p1.6
3	T	8:12	**8:24**	p1.9	2:18	**2:36**	1.5
4	W	9:06	**9:18**	p1.9	3:12	**3:30**	1.5
5	T	10:00	**10:12**	p1.9	4:06	**4:24**	1.5
6	F	10:54	**11:06**	p1.9	4:54	**5:18**	a1.6
7	S	11:42	...	1.9	5:42	**6:12**	a1.6
8	S	12:01	**12:30**	p2.0	6:30	**7:00**	a1.7
9	M	12:43	**1:12**	p2.0	7:12	**7:42**	a1.8
10	T	1:30	**1:48**	p2.1	7:54	**8:24**	a1.8
11	W	2:12	**2:30**	p2.1	8:36	**9:06**	a1.9
12	T	2:48	**3:06**	p2.2	9:12	**9:48**	a1.9
13	F	3:30	**3:42**	p2.2	9:54	**10:30**	a1.9
14	S	4:12	**4:24**	p2.2	10:36	**11:18**	a2.0
15	S	5:00	**5:12**	p2.2	11:18	...	2.0
16	M	5:48	**6:00**	p2.2	12:06	**12:12**	p1.9
17	T	6:42	**6:54**	p2.1	12:54	**1:06**	1.8
18	W	7:36	**7:54**	p2.0	1:48	**2:06**	p1.8
19	T	8:42	**9:00**	p2.0	2:48	**3:12**	1.7
20	F	9:42	**10:06**	p2.0	3:48	**4:18**	a1.7
21	S	10:48	**11:12**	p2.0	4:48	**5:18**	a1.7
22	S	11:48	...	2.0	5:48	**6:24**	1.7
23	M	12:18	**12:48**	p2.2	6:42	**7:24**	a1.8
24	T	1:18	**1:42**	p2.3	7:36	**8:18**	a1.9
25	W	2:12	**2:30**	p2.3	8:30	**9:06**	a1.9
26	T	3:00	**3:18**	p2.3	9:18	**9:54**	a1.9
27	F	3:48	**4:00**	p2.3	10:00	**10:42**	a1.9
28	S	4:36	**4:42**	p2.2	10:48	**11:30**	a1.8
29	S	5:18	**5:24**	p2.2	11:30	...	1.8
30	M	6:00	**6:12**	p2.1	12:12	**12:18**	1.7
31	T	6:48	**6:54**	p2.0	12:54	**1:06**	p1.7

The Kts. (knots) columns show the **maximum** predicted velocities of the stronger one of the Flood Currents and the stronger one of the Ebb Currents for each day.
The letter "a" means the velocity shown should occur **after** the **a.m.** Current Change. The letter "p" means the velocity shown should occur **after** the **p.m.** Current Change (even if next morning). No "a" or "p" means a.m. and p.m. velocities are the same for that day.
Avg. Max. Velocity: Flood 2.0 Kts., Ebb 1.8 Kts.
Max. Flood 3 hrs. 20 min. after Flood Starts, ±15 min.
Max. Ebb 2 hrs. 45 min. after Ebb Starts, ±15 min.
Gay Head (1 1/2 mi. NW of): avg. max velocity, Flood 2.0 kts., Ebb 2.0 kts. Time of Flood and Ebb 1 hr. 35 min. after Pollock Rip. Cross Rip: avg. max. velocity, Flood 1.3 kts., Ebb 0.9 kts. Time of Flood and Ebb 1 hr. 50 min. after Pollock Rip. Use POLLOCK RIP tables with current charts on pp. 72-83. See pp. 22-29 for Current Change at other points.

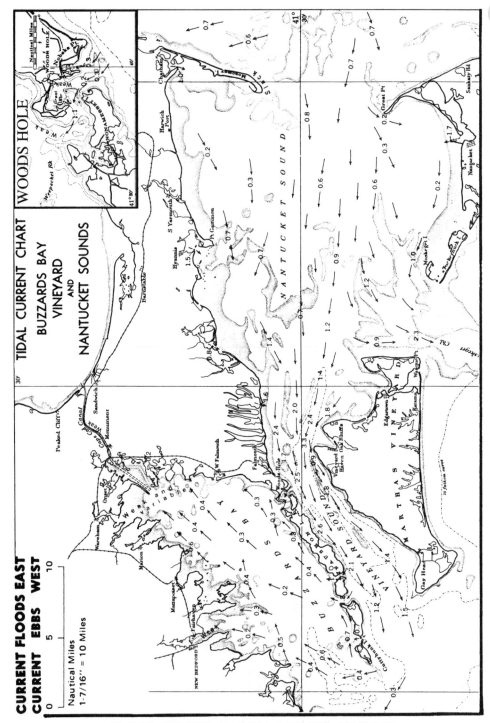

FLOOD STARTS AT POLLOCK RIP CHANNEL
OR: 4 HOURS **AFTER** HIGH WATER AT BOSTON

Velocities shown are at Spring Tides. See note at bottom of Boston Tables: Rule-of-
Thumb for Current Velocities. See pp. 60–65 for an enlarged version of Woods Hole inset.
Pollock Rip Ch. is SE of Monomoy Pt.

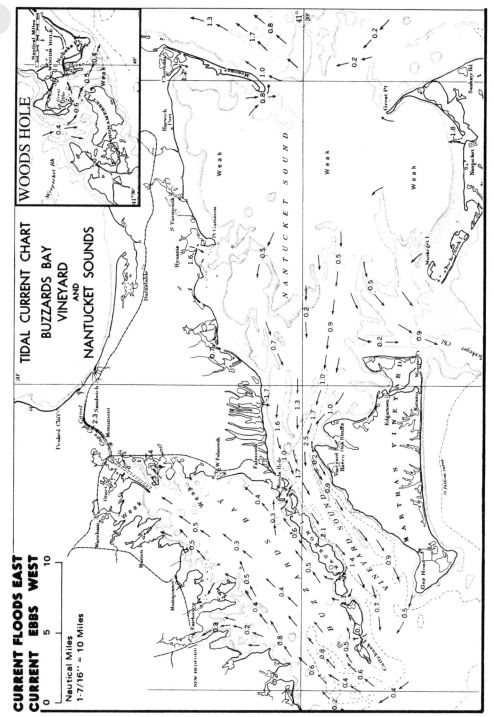

CURRENT FLOODS EAST
CURRENT EBBS WEST

WOODS HOLE

TIDAL CURRENT CHART
BUZZARDS BAY
VINEYARD
AND
NANTUCKET SOUNDS

Nautical Miles
1-7/16'' = 10 Miles

1 HOUR **AFTER** FLOOD STARTS AT POLLOCK RIP CHANNEL
OR: 5 HOURS **AFTER** HIGH WATER AT BOSTON

Velocities shown are at Spring Tides. See note at bottom of Boston Tables: Rule-of-Thumb for Current Velocities. See pp. 60–65 for an enlarged version of Woods Hole inset.
Pollock Rip Ch. is SE of Monomoy Pt.

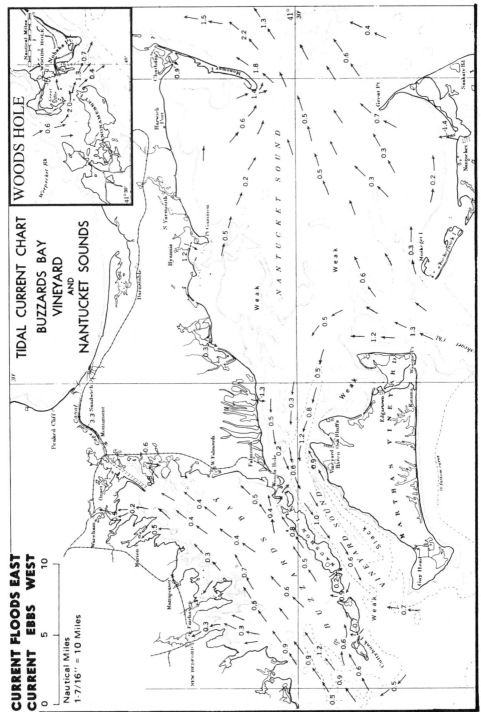

2 HOURS **AFTER** FLOOD STARTS AT POLLOCK RIP CHANNEL
OR: LOW WATER AT BOSTON

Velocities shown are at Spring Tides. See note at bottom of Boston Tables: Rule-of-Thumb for Current Velocities. See pp. 60–65 for an enlarged version of Woods Hole inset.
Pollock Rip Ch. is SE of Monomoy Pt.

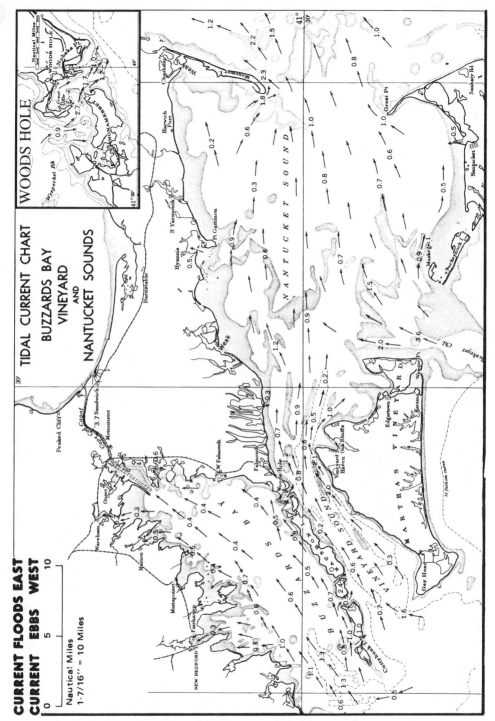

3 HOURS **AFTER** FLOOD STARTS AT POLLOCK RIP CHANNEL
OR: 1 HOUR **AFTER** LOW WATER AT BOSTON

Velocities shown are at Spring Tides. See note at bottom of Boston Tables: Rule-of-Thumb for Current Velocities. See pp. 60–65 for an enlarged version of Woods Hole inset.
Pollock Rip Ch. is SE of Monomoy Pt.

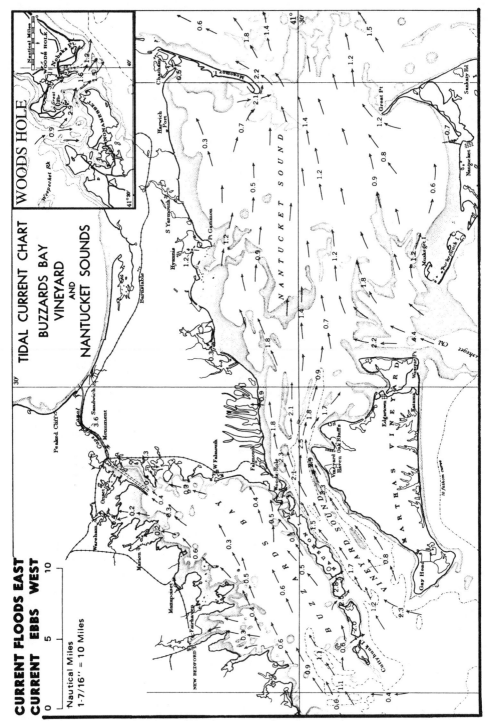

4 HOURS **AFTER** FLOOD STARTS AT POLLOCK RIP CHANNEL
OR: 2 HOURS **AFTER** LOW WATER AT BOSTON

Velocities shown are at Spring Tides. See note at bottom of Boston Tables: Rule-of-Thumb for Current Velocities. See pp. 60–65 for an enlarged version of Woods Hole inset.
Pollock Rip Ch. is SE of Monomoy Pt.

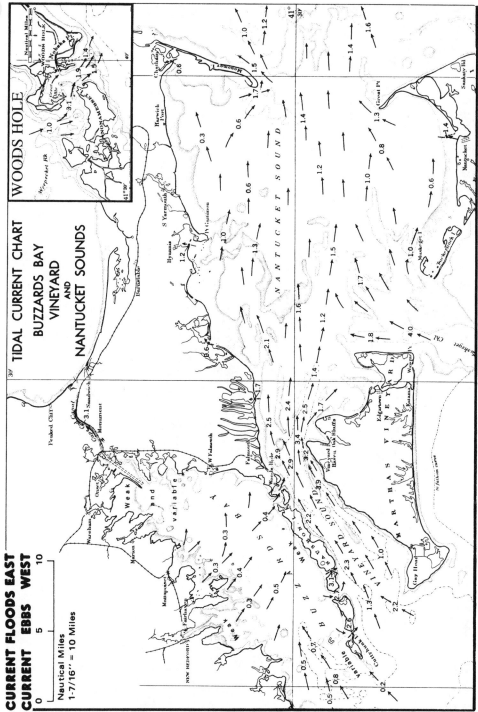

5 HOURS **AFTER** FLOOD STARTS AT POLLOCK RIP CHANNEL
OR: 3 HOURS **AFTER** LOW WATER AT BOSTON

Velocities shown are at Spring Tides. See note at bottom of Boston Tables: Rule-of-Thumb for Current Velocities. See pp. 60–65 for an enlarged version of Woods Hole inset.

Pollock Rip Ch. is SE of Monomoy Pt.

77

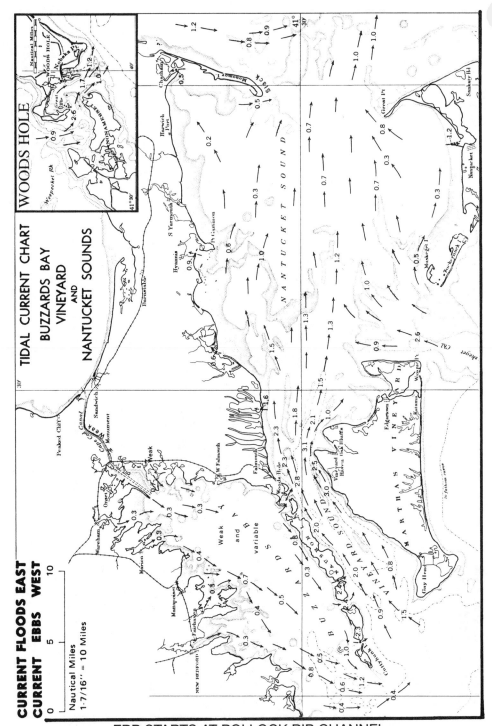

EBB STARTS AT POLLOCK RIP CHANNEL
OR: 4 HOURS **AFTER** LOW WATER AT BOSTON

Velocities shown are at Spring Tides. See note at bottom of Boston Tables: Rule-of-Thumb for Current Velocities. See pp. 60–65 for an enlarged version of Woods Hole inset.
Pollock Rip Ch. is SE of Monomoy Pt.

78

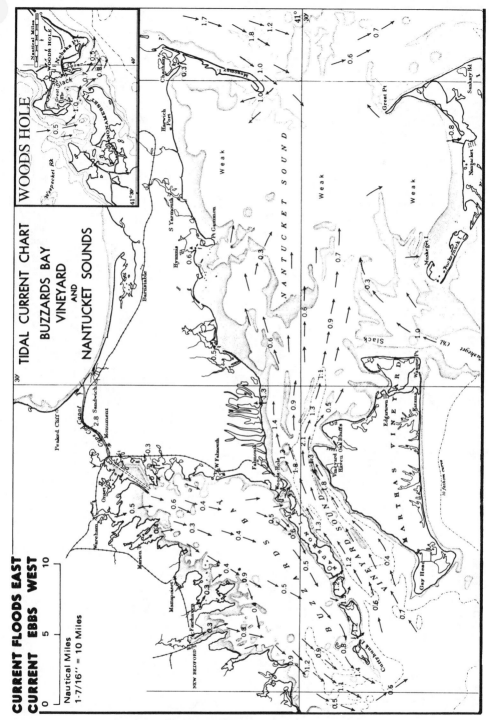

1 HOUR **AFTER** EBB STARTS AT POLLOCK RIP CHANNEL
OR: 5 HOURS **AFTER** LOW WATER AT BOSTON

Velocities shown are at Spring Tides. See note at bottom of Boston Tables: Rule-of-Thumb for Current Velocities. See pp. 60–65 for an enlarged version of Woods Hole inset.
Pollock Rip Ch. is SE of Monomoy Pt.

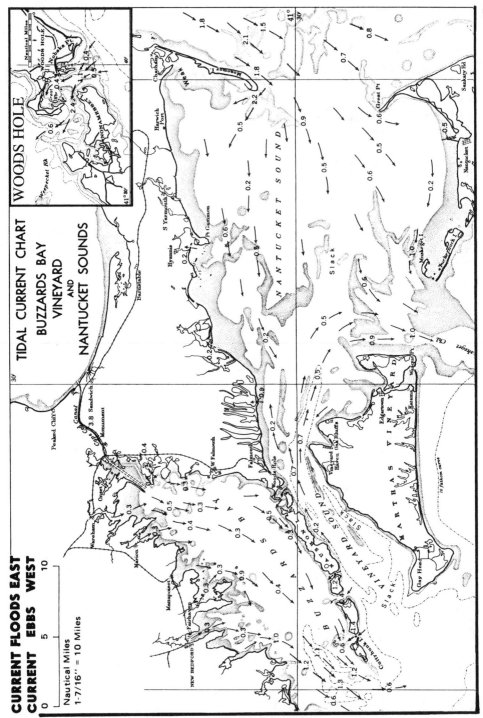

2 HOURS **AFTER** EBB STARTS AT POLLOCK RIP CHANNEL
OR: HIGH WATER AT BOSTON

Velocities shown are at Spring Tides. See note at bottom of Boston Tables: Rule-of-Thumb for Current Velocities. See pp. 60–65 for an enlarged version of Woods Hole inset.
Pollock Rip Ch. is SE of Monomoy Pt.

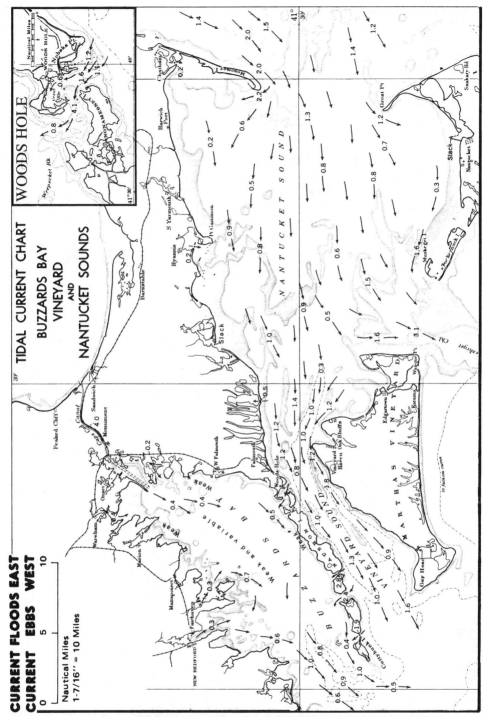

3 HOURS **AFTER** EBB STARTS AT POLLOCK RIP CHANNEL
OR: 1 HOUR **AFTER** HIGH WATER AT BOSTON

Velocities shown are at Spring Tides. See note at bottom of Boston Tables: Rule-of-Thumb for Current Velocities. See pp. 60–65 for an enlarged version of Woods Hole inset.
Pollock Rip Ch. is SE of Monomoy Pt.

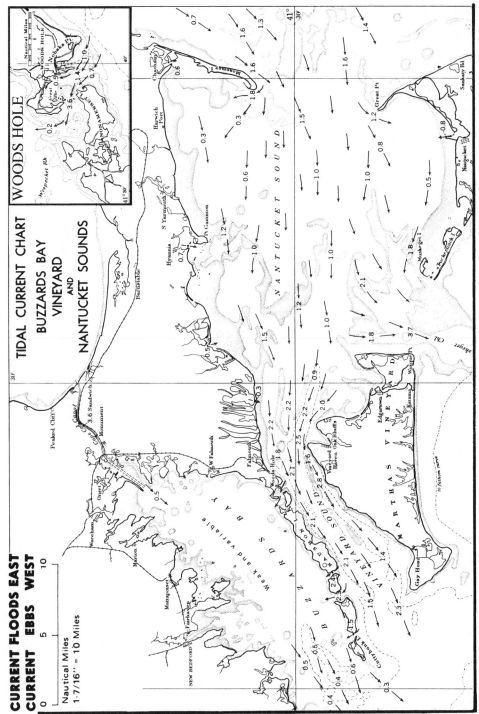

4 HOURS **AFTER** EBB STARTS AT POLLOCK RIP CHANNEL
OR: 2 HOURS **AFTER** HIGH WATER AT BOSTON

Velocities shown are at Spring Tides. See note at bottom of Boston Tables: Rule-of-Thumb for Current Velocities. See pp. 60–65 for an enlarged version of Woods Hole inset.
Pollock Rip Ch. is SE of Monomoy Pt.

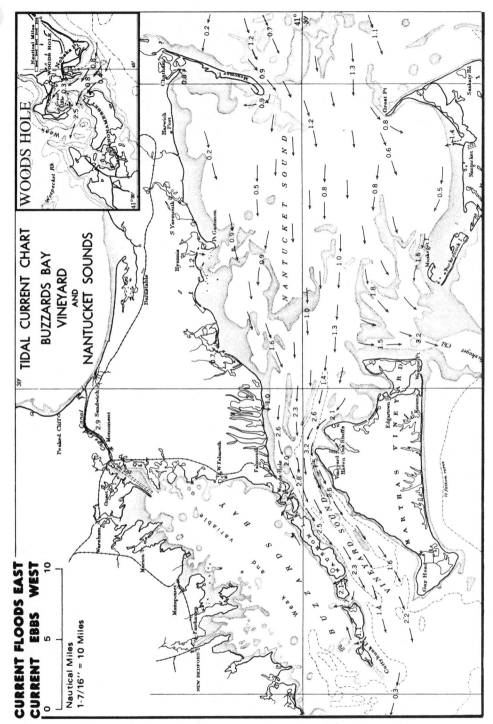

5 HOURS **AFTER** EBB STARTS AT POLLOCK RIP CHANNEL
OR: 3 HOURS **AFTER** HIGH WATER AT BOSTON

Velocities shown are at Spring Tides. See note at bottom of Boston Tables: Rule-of-Thumb for Current Velocities. See pp. 60–65 for an enlarged version of Woods Hole inset.

Pollock Rip Ch. is SE of Monomoy Pt.

83

2019 HIGH & LOW WATER
NEWPORT, RI
41°30.3'N, 71°19.6'W

		Standard Time							Standard Time				

<table>
<tr><th rowspan="3">D A Y O F M O N T H</th><th rowspan="3">D A Y O F W E E K</th><th colspan="6">JANUARY</th><th rowspan="3">D A Y O F M O N T H</th><th rowspan="3">D A Y O F W E E K</th><th colspan="6">FEBRUARY</th></tr>
<tr><th colspan="4">HIGH</th><th colspan="2">LOW</th><th colspan="4">HIGH</th><th colspan="2">LOW</th></tr>
<tr><th>a.m.</th><th>Ht.</th><th>p.m.</th><th>Ht.</th><th>a.m.</th><th>p.m.</th><th>a.m.</th><th>Ht.</th><th>p.m.</th><th>Ht.</th><th>a.m.</th><th>p.m.</th></tr>
<tr><td>1</td><td>T</td><td>3:58</td><td>3.7</td><td>4:22</td><td>3.0</td><td>10:42</td><td>10:07</td><td>1</td><td>F</td><td>5:29</td><td>3.4</td><td>5:47</td><td>2.9</td><td>11:42</td><td>11:03</td></tr>
<tr><td>2</td><td>W</td><td>4:56</td><td>3.8</td><td>5:17</td><td>3.1</td><td>11:24</td><td>10:41</td><td>2</td><td>S</td><td>6:15</td><td>3.5</td><td>6:31</td><td>3.0</td><td>-A-</td><td>12:12</td></tr>
<tr><td>3</td><td>T</td><td>5:47</td><td>3.8</td><td>6:06</td><td>3.2</td><td>11:59</td><td>11:17</td><td>3</td><td>S</td><td>6:56</td><td>3.5</td><td>7:11</td><td>3.2</td><td>...</td><td>12:44</td></tr>
<tr><td>4</td><td>F</td><td>6:33</td><td>3.9</td><td>6:51</td><td>3.2</td><td>...</td><td>12:31</td><td>4</td><td>M</td><td>7:34</td><td>3.5</td><td>7:49</td><td>3.2</td><td>12:25</td><td>1:18</td></tr>
<tr><td>5</td><td>S</td><td>7:15</td><td>3.8</td><td>7:33</td><td>3.2</td><td>12:01</td><td>1:04</td><td>5</td><td>T</td><td>8:09</td><td>3.5</td><td>8:25</td><td>3.2</td><td>1:08</td><td>1:52</td></tr>
<tr><td>6</td><td>S</td><td>7:55</td><td>3.8</td><td>8:13</td><td>3.2</td><td>12:38</td><td>1:39</td><td>6</td><td>W</td><td>8:42</td><td>3.4</td><td>9:00</td><td>3.2</td><td>1:50</td><td>2:25</td></tr>
<tr><td>7</td><td>M</td><td>8:33</td><td>3.6</td><td>8:52</td><td>3.1</td><td>1:21</td><td>2:15</td><td>7</td><td>T</td><td>9:16</td><td>3.3</td><td>9:35</td><td>3.1</td><td>2:29</td><td>2:56</td></tr>
<tr><td>8</td><td>T</td><td>9:10</td><td>3.5</td><td>9:30</td><td>3.0</td><td>2:04</td><td>2:50</td><td>8</td><td>F</td><td>9:50</td><td>3.1</td><td>10:11</td><td>3.0</td><td>3:06</td><td>3:26</td></tr>
<tr><td>9</td><td>W</td><td>9:47</td><td>3.3</td><td>10:09</td><td>2.9</td><td>2:46</td><td>3:24</td><td>9</td><td>S</td><td>10:29</td><td>3.0</td><td>10:50</td><td>3.0</td><td>3:42</td><td>3:56</td></tr>
<tr><td>10</td><td>T</td><td>10:23</td><td>3.1</td><td>10:49</td><td>2.8</td><td>3:26</td><td>3:58</td><td>10</td><td>S</td><td>11:11</td><td>2.8</td><td>11:34</td><td>3.0</td><td>4:19</td><td>4:30</td></tr>
<tr><td>11</td><td>F</td><td>11:03</td><td>2.9</td><td>11:31</td><td>2.8</td><td>4:06</td><td>4:34</td><td>11</td><td>M</td><td>11:58</td><td>2.7</td><td>...</td><td>...</td><td>5:01</td><td>5:11</td></tr>
<tr><td>12</td><td>S</td><td>11:45</td><td>2.8</td><td>...</td><td>...</td><td>4:49</td><td>5:13</td><td>12</td><td>T</td><td>12:21</td><td>3.0</td><td>12:49</td><td>2.6</td><td>5:56</td><td>6:03</td></tr>
<tr><td>13</td><td>S</td><td>12:14</td><td>2.8</td><td>12:30</td><td>2.7</td><td>5:41</td><td>5:59</td><td>13</td><td>W</td><td>1:13</td><td>3.1</td><td>1:45</td><td>2.6</td><td>7:10</td><td>7:07</td></tr>
<tr><td>14</td><td>M</td><td>12:59</td><td>2.8</td><td>1:20</td><td>2.6</td><td>6:48</td><td>6:54</td><td>14</td><td>T</td><td>2:13</td><td>3.2</td><td>2:49</td><td>2.7</td><td>8:42</td><td>8:17</td></tr>
<tr><td>15</td><td>T</td><td>1:49</td><td>3.0</td><td>2:15</td><td>2.6</td><td>8:07</td><td>7:54</td><td>15</td><td>F</td><td>3:20</td><td>3.3</td><td>3:57</td><td>2.9</td><td>9:57</td><td>9:26</td></tr>
<tr><td>16</td><td>W</td><td>2:46</td><td>3.1</td><td>3:18</td><td>2.7</td><td>9:21</td><td>8:54</td><td>16</td><td>S</td><td>4:29</td><td>3.6</td><td>5:01</td><td>3.3</td><td>10:54</td><td>10:29</td></tr>
<tr><td>17</td><td>T</td><td>3:50</td><td>3.4</td><td>4:23</td><td>2.9</td><td>10:19</td><td>9:52</td><td>17</td><td>S</td><td>5:31</td><td>4.0</td><td>5:58</td><td>3.7</td><td>11:45</td><td>11:27</td></tr>
<tr><td>18</td><td>F</td><td>4:52</td><td>3.7</td><td>5:22</td><td>3.2</td><td>11:10</td><td>10:46</td><td>18</td><td>M</td><td>6:25</td><td>4.3</td><td>6:51</td><td>4.1</td><td>...</td><td>12:34</td></tr>
<tr><td>19</td><td>S</td><td>5:48</td><td>4.1</td><td>6:16</td><td>3.5</td><td>11:59</td><td>11:39</td><td>19</td><td>T</td><td>7:17</td><td>4.5</td><td>7:42</td><td>4.3</td><td>12:24</td><td>1:22</td></tr>
<tr><td>20</td><td>S</td><td>6:41</td><td>4.4</td><td>7:08</td><td>3.8</td><td>...</td><td>12:52</td><td>20</td><td>W</td><td>8:07</td><td>4.6</td><td>8:32</td><td>4.5</td><td>1:19</td><td>2:06</td></tr>
<tr><td>21</td><td>M</td><td>7:33</td><td>4.6</td><td>7:59</td><td>4.1</td><td>12:33</td><td>1:42</td><td>21</td><td>T</td><td>8:57</td><td>4.5</td><td>9:23</td><td>4.5</td><td>2:13</td><td>2:47</td></tr>
<tr><td>22</td><td>T</td><td>8:24</td><td>4.6</td><td>8:51</td><td>4.2</td><td>1:27</td><td>2:30</td><td>22</td><td>F</td><td>9:47</td><td>4.2</td><td>10:15</td><td>4.3</td><td>3:04</td><td>3:26</td></tr>
<tr><td>23</td><td>W</td><td>9:15</td><td>4.5</td><td>9:44</td><td>4.2</td><td>2:22</td><td>3:14</td><td>23</td><td>S</td><td>10:39</td><td>3.9</td><td>11:09</td><td>4.1</td><td>3:52</td><td>4:04</td></tr>
<tr><td>24</td><td>T</td><td>10:08</td><td>4.3</td><td>10:38</td><td>4.1</td><td>3:14</td><td>3:56</td><td>24</td><td>S</td><td>11:32</td><td>3.5</td><td>...</td><td>...</td><td>4:42</td><td>4:44</td></tr>
<tr><td>25</td><td>F</td><td>11:02</td><td>3.9</td><td>11:35</td><td>4.0</td><td>4:06</td><td>4:39</td><td>25</td><td>M</td><td>12:04</td><td>3.8</td><td>12:27</td><td>3.2</td><td>5:41</td><td>5:32</td></tr>
<tr><td>26</td><td>S</td><td>11:57</td><td>3.6</td><td>...</td><td>...</td><td>5:04</td><td>5:27</td><td>26</td><td>T</td><td>1:00</td><td>3.5</td><td>1:23</td><td>2.9</td><td>7:24</td><td>6:31</td></tr>
<tr><td>27</td><td>S</td><td>12:31</td><td>3.8</td><td>12:53</td><td>3.3</td><td>6:22</td><td>6:24</td><td>27</td><td>W</td><td>1:59</td><td>3.2</td><td>2:23</td><td>2.7</td><td>9:00</td><td>7:48</td></tr>
<tr><td>28</td><td>M</td><td>1:29</td><td>3.6</td><td>1:50</td><td>3.0</td><td>8:16</td><td>7:34</td><td>28</td><td>T</td><td>3:03</td><td>3.1</td><td>3:28</td><td>2.6</td><td>9:59</td><td>9:12</td></tr>
<tr><td>29</td><td>T</td><td>2:29</td><td>3.5</td><td>2:52</td><td>2.8</td><td>9:31</td><td>8:45</td><td></td><td></td><td></td><td></td><td></td><td></td><td></td><td></td></tr>
<tr><td>30</td><td>W</td><td>3:33</td><td>3.4</td><td>3:57</td><td>2.7</td><td>10:26</td><td>9:39</td><td></td><td></td><td></td><td></td><td></td><td></td><td></td><td></td></tr>
<tr><td>31</td><td>T</td><td>4:35</td><td>3.3</td><td>4:56</td><td>2.8</td><td>11:09</td><td>10:23</td><td></td><td></td><td></td><td></td><td></td><td></td><td></td><td></td></tr>
</table>

A also at 11:43 p.m.

Dates when Ht. of **Low** Water is below Mean Lower Low with Ht. of lowest given for each period and Date of lowest in ( ):

17th–25th: -0.9' (21st–23rd)

5th–8th: -0.2'
15th–23rd: -0.9' (19th–21st)

Average Rise and Fall 3.5 ft.

When a high tide exceeds avg. ht., the *following* low tide will be lower than avg.

2019 HIGH & LOW WATER
NEWPORT, RI
41°30.3'N, 71°19.6'W

*Daylight Time starts March 10 at 2 a.m.   Daylight Saving Time

DAY OF MONTH	DAY OF WEEK	MARCH						DAY OF MONTH	DAY OF WEEK	APRIL					
		HIGH		LOW						HIGH		LOW			
		a.m.	Ht.	p.m.	Ht.	a.m.	p.m.			a.m.	Ht.	p.m.	Ht.	a.m.	p.m.
1	F	4:10	3.0	4:31	2.7	10:41	10:08	1	M	6:21	3.0	6:37	3.1	...	12:04
2	S	5:07	3.1	5:24	2.9	11:14	10:51	2	T	7:00	3.2	7:15	3.3	12:13	12:36
3	S	5:53	3.2	6:08	3.0	11:43	11:32	3	W	7:35	3.3	7:50	3.5	12:54	1:09
4	M	6:33	3.3	6:46	3.2	...	12:14	4	T	8:08	3.4	8:23	3.6	1:34	1:42
5	T	7:08	3.4	7:22	3.3	12:12	12:47	5	F	8:42	3.4	8:56	3.7	2:13	2:15
6	W	7:41	3.4	7:55	3.4	12:53	1:21	6	S	9:17	3.4	9:31	3.8	2:51	2:47
7	T	8:13	3.4	8:28	3.4	1:33	1:53	7	S	9:56	3.4	10:09	3.8	3:26	3:20
8	F	8:46	3.4	9:02	3.4	2:11	2:23	8	M	10:38	3.3	10:52	3.7	4:01	3:55
9	S	9:22	3.2	9:38	3.4	2:46	2:53	9	T	11:26	3.2	11:39	3.6	4:36	4:33
10	S	*11:00	3.1	*11:17	3.3	*4:20	*4:23	10	W	...	...	12:17	3.1	5:17	5:17
11	M	11:45	3.0	...	...	4:54	4:58	11	T	12:34	3.5	1:13	3.0	6:07	6:09
12	T	12:02	3.3	12:34	2.8	5:34	5:38	12	F	1:32	3.5	2:11	3.1	7:15	7:17
13	W	12:52	3.2	1:28	2.8	6:24	6:29	13	S	2:34	3.5	3:13	3.2	9:01	8:39
14	T	1:48	3.2	2:25	2.8	7:33	7:35	14	S	3:40	3.5	4:19	3.5	10:25	10:06
15	F	2:50	3.3	3:29	2.9	9:13	8:52	15	M	4:49	3.7	5:23	3.8	11:17	11:17
16	S	3:58	3.4	4:37	3.1	10:42	10:11	16	T	5:53	3.9	6:22	4.2	11:59	...
17	S	5:09	3.7	5:42	3.5	11:38	11:20	17	W	6:49	4.1	7:14	4.6	12:15	12:39
18	M	6:13	4.0	6:40	3.9	...	12:25	18	T	7:40	4.2	8:04	4.8	1:08	1:19
19	T	7:08	4.3	7:33	4.3	12:20	1:10	19	F	8:28	4.2	8:52	4.8	1:59	1:59
20	W	7:59	4.4	8:23	4.6	1:16	1:53	20	S	9:16	4.1	9:39	4.7	2:47	2:39
21	T	8:48	4.5	9:12	4.7	2:10	2:35	21	S	10:03	3.9	10:27	4.5	3:32	3:19
22	F	9:36	4.3	10:01	4.7	3:02	3:14	22	M	10:52	3.7	11:15	4.1	4:12	3:59
23	S	10:25	4.1	10:51	4.5	3:49	3:52	23	T	11:42	3.4	...	...	4:51	4:40
24	S	11:15	3.8	11:42	4.2	4:33	4:30	24	W	12:06	3.8	12:34	3.2	5:33	5:24
25	M	...	...	12:07	3.4	5:17	5:09	25	T	12:59	3.4	1:28	3.0	6:22	6:16
26	T	12:35	3.8	1:01	3.1	6:04	5:54	26	F	1:53	3.1	2:21	2.8	7:30	7:23
27	W	1:30	3.4	1:56	2.9	7:06	6:48	27	S	2:46	2.9	3:15	2.8	8:59	8:53
28	T	2:27	3.1	2:53	2.7	9:01	8:01	28	S	3:43	2.8	4:13	2.8	9:58	10:11
29	F	3:27	2.9	3:54	2.7	10:13	9:37	29	M	4:42	2.8	5:09	3.0	10:40	11:04
30	S	4:33	2.8	4:58	2.7	10:58	10:46	30	T	5:34	2.9	5:57	3.2	11:17	11:47
31	S	5:34	2.9	5:53	2.9	11:33	11:32								

Dates when Ht. of **Low** Water is below Mean Lower Low with Ht. of lowest given for each period and Date of lowest in ( ):

6th–10th: -0.3' (8th)   5th–8th: -0.2'
17th–24th: -0.8' (21st, 22nd)   17th–22nd: -0.5' (18th–20th)

Average Rise and Fall 3.5 ft.

When a high tide exceeds avg. ht., the *following* low tide will be lower than avg.

2019 HIGH & LOW WATER
NEWPORT, RI
41°30.3'N, 71°19.6'W

| | | Daylight Saving Time | | | | | | | | Daylight Saving Time | | | | | |

DAY OF MONTH	DAY OF WEEK	MAY						DAY OF MONTH	DAY OF WEEK	JUNE					
		HIGH				LOW				HIGH				LOW	
		a.m.	Ht.	p.m.	Ht.	a.m.	p.m.			a.m.	Ht.	p.m.	Ht.	a.m.	p.m.
1	W	6:17	3.0	6:37	3.4	11:51	...	1	S	6:56	3.3	7:15	4.0	12:40	12:20
2	T	6:55	3.2	7:13	3.7	12:28	12:25	2	S	7:40	3.4	7:57	4.2	1:22	1:00
3	F	7:32	3.3	7:49	3.9	1:08	1:00	3	M	8:26	3.6	8:42	4.3	2:06	1:44
4	S	8:10	3.4	8:25	4.0	1:49	1:36	4	T	9:13	3.7	9:29	4.4	2:51	2:29
5	S	8:50	3.5	9:05	4.1	2:29	2:13	5	W	10:02	3.7	10:18	4.4	3:35	3:17
6	M	9:33	3.5	9:47	4.1	3:08	2:52	6	T	10:54	3.7	11:12	4.3	4:19	4:05
7	T	10:19	3.5	10:33	4.0	3:46	3:33	7	F	11:49	3.8	...	...	5:04	4:56
8	W	11:09	3.4	11:24	4.0	4:25	4:16	8	S	12:08	4.1	12:46	3.8	5:56	5:54
9	T	...	...	12:03	3.4	5:08	5:04	9	S	1:07	4.0	1:44	3.9	7:00	7:06
10	F	12:21	3.8	1:00	3.4	6:00	5:59	10	M	2:04	3.8	2:41	4.0	8:18	8:46
11	S	1:20	3.8	1:59	3.5	7:10	7:08	11	T	3:03	3.7	3:41	4.1	9:24	10:15
12	S	2:20	3.7	2:58	3.6	8:48	8:38	12	W	4:05	3.6	4:43	4.2	10:15	11:17
13	M	3:22	3.7	4:01	3.8	9:59	10:10	13	T	5:08	3.5	5:43	4.3	10:57	...
14	T	4:28	3.7	5:04	4.1	10:48	11:17	14	F	6:07	3.6	6:37	4.5	12:07	-A-
15	W	5:31	3.8	6:02	4.4	11:29	...	15	S	7:00	3.7	7:26	4.5	12:52	12:15
16	T	6:28	3.9	6:55	4.6	12:11	12:06	16	S	7:49	3.7	8:13	4.5	1:34	12:56
17	F	7:20	3.9	7:44	4.8	1:00	12:44	17	M	8:36	3.7	8:58	4.4	2:15	1:39
18	S	8:08	4.0	8:32	4.8	1:46	1:24	18	T	9:21	3.6	9:42	4.2	2:53	2:24
19	S	8:55	3.9	9:18	4.6	2:31	2:06	19	W	10:06	3.5	10:25	3.9	3:29	3:09
20	M	9:42	3.8	10:04	4.4	3:13	2:49	20	T	10:50	3.4	11:08	3.7	4:05	3:54
21	T	10:29	3.6	10:50	4.0	3:51	3:32	21	F	11:36	3.3	11:52	3.4	4:41	4:38
22	W	11:17	3.4	11:38	3.7	4:28	4:15	22	S	...	...	12:21	3.2	5:20	5:23
23	T	...	...	12:07	3.2	5:07	4:59	23	S	12:35	3.2	1:06	3.1	6:02	6:15
24	F	12:27	3.4	12:57	3.1	5:50	5:49	24	M	1:17	3.0	1:49	3.1	6:48	7:18
25	S	1:15	3.2	1:46	3.0	6:42	6:49	25	T	1:59	2.9	2:31	3.1	7:40	8:32
26	S	2:02	3.0	2:33	2.9	7:44	8:06	26	W	2:42	2.8	3:15	3.2	8:33	9:41
27	M	2:48	2.8	3:21	3.0	8:47	9:25	27	T	3:32	2.8	4:06	3.3	9:24	10:38
28	T	3:37	2.8	4:12	3.1	9:38	10:26	28	F	4:29	2.9	5:01	3.5	10:12	11:26
29	W	4:30	2.8	5:04	3.2	10:22	11:15	29	S	5:28	3.0	5:54	3.8	10:59	...
30	T	5:23	2.9	5:50	3.5	11:02	11:58	30	S	6:23	3.2	6:45	4.1	12:12	-B-
31	F	6:11	3.1	6:33	3.8	11:41	...								

A also at 11:36 a.m.   **B** also at 11:45 a.m.

Dates when Ht. of **Low** Water is below Mean Lower Low with Ht. of lowest given for each period and Date of lowest in ( ):

5th–6th: -0.2'   3rd–5th: -0.2'
17th–19th: -0.2'

Average Rise and Fall 3.5 ft.

When a high tide exceeds avg. ht., the *following* low tide will be lower than avg.

2019 HIGH & LOW WATER
NEWPORT, RI
41°30.3'N, 71°19.6'W

<table>
<tr><td colspan="6" align="center">Daylight Saving Time</td><td colspan="6" align="center">Daylight Saving Time</td></tr>
<tr><th rowspan="4">D A Y O F M O N T H</th><th rowspan="4">D A Y O F W E E K</th><th colspan="6">JULY</th><th rowspan="4">D A Y O F M O N T H</th><th rowspan="4">D A Y O F W E E K</th><th colspan="6">AUGUST</th></tr>
<tr><th colspan="4">HIGH</th><th colspan="2">LOW</th><th colspan="4">HIGH</th><th colspan="2">LOW</th></tr>
<tr><th>a.m.</th><th>Ht.</th><th>p.m.</th><th>Ht.</th><th>a.m.</th><th>p.m.</th><th>a.m.</th><th>Ht.</th><th>p.m.</th><th>Ht.</th><th>a.m.</th><th>p.m.</th></tr>
<tr><td>1</td><td>M</td><td>7:13</td><td>3.5</td><td>7:34</td><td>4.3</td><td>12:57</td><td>12:32</td><td>1</td><td>T</td><td>8:34</td><td>4.2</td><td>8:56</td><td>4.8</td><td>2:14</td><td>1:59</td></tr>
<tr><td>2</td><td>T</td><td>8:03</td><td>3.7</td><td>8:23</td><td>4.5</td><td>1:44</td><td>1:21</td><td>2</td><td>F</td><td>9:25</td><td>4.4</td><td>9:47</td><td>4.8</td><td>3:02</td><td>2:55</td></tr>
<tr><td>3</td><td>W</td><td>8:53</td><td>3.9</td><td>9:13</td><td>4.6</td><td>2:34</td><td>2:12</td><td>3</td><td>S</td><td>10:17</td><td>4.5</td><td>10:39</td><td>4.7</td><td>3:48</td><td>3:50</td></tr>
<tr><td>4</td><td>T</td><td>9:44</td><td>4.0</td><td>10:04</td><td>4.6</td><td>3:22</td><td>3:05</td><td>4</td><td>S</td><td>11:11</td><td>4.6</td><td>11:33</td><td>4.4</td><td>4:30</td><td>4:43</td></tr>
<tr><td>5</td><td>F</td><td>10:37</td><td>4.1</td><td>10:57</td><td>4.5</td><td>4:08</td><td>3:58</td><td>5</td><td>M</td><td>...</td><td>...</td><td>12:06</td><td>4.5</td><td>5:13</td><td>5:40</td></tr>
<tr><td>6</td><td>S</td><td>11:31</td><td>4.2</td><td>11:52</td><td>4.3</td><td>4:53</td><td>4:51</td><td>6</td><td>T</td><td>12:28</td><td>4.1</td><td>1:03</td><td>4.4</td><td>5:58</td><td>6:50</td></tr>
<tr><td>7</td><td>S</td><td>...</td><td>...</td><td>12:28</td><td>4.2</td><td>5:40</td><td>5:49</td><td>7</td><td>W</td><td>1:24</td><td>3.8</td><td>2:00</td><td>4.3</td><td>6:50</td><td>8:37</td></tr>
<tr><td>8</td><td>M</td><td>12:49</td><td>4.1</td><td>1:25</td><td>4.2</td><td>6:33</td><td>7:03</td><td>8</td><td>T</td><td>2:21</td><td>3.5</td><td>2:58</td><td>4.1</td><td>7:53</td><td>10:00</td></tr>
<tr><td>9</td><td>T</td><td>1:46</td><td>3.9</td><td>2:22</td><td>4.2</td><td>7:35</td><td>8:48</td><td>9</td><td>F</td><td>3:21</td><td>3.3</td><td>3:59</td><td>4.0</td><td>9:04</td><td>11:02</td></tr>
<tr><td>10</td><td>W</td><td>2:42</td><td>3.6</td><td>3:20</td><td>4.2</td><td>8:41</td><td>10:11</td><td>10</td><td>S</td><td>4:24</td><td>3.2</td><td>5:03</td><td>3.9</td><td>10:09</td><td>11:50</td></tr>
<tr><td>11</td><td>T</td><td>3:42</td><td>3.5</td><td>4:21</td><td>4.1</td><td>9:39</td><td>11:12</td><td>11</td><td>S</td><td>5:27</td><td>3.2</td><td>6:02</td><td>3.9</td><td>10:59</td><td>...</td></tr>
<tr><td>12</td><td>F</td><td>4:46</td><td>3.3</td><td>5:23</td><td>4.2</td><td>10:29</td><td>11:59</td><td>12</td><td>M</td><td>6:23</td><td>3.3</td><td>6:52</td><td>3.9</td><td>12:29</td><td>-B-</td></tr>
<tr><td>13</td><td>S</td><td>5:47</td><td>3.4</td><td>6:19</td><td>4.2</td><td>11:12</td><td>...</td><td>13</td><td>T</td><td>7:11</td><td>3.5</td><td>7:37</td><td>4.0</td><td>1:00</td><td>12:23</td></tr>
<tr><td>14</td><td>S</td><td>6:42</td><td>3.4</td><td>7:10</td><td>4.2</td><td>12:44</td><td>-A-</td><td>14</td><td>W</td><td>7:55</td><td>3.6</td><td>8:17</td><td>4.0</td><td>1:29</td><td>1:05</td></tr>
<tr><td>15</td><td>M</td><td>7:31</td><td>3.5</td><td>7:56</td><td>4.2</td><td>1:21</td><td>12:36</td><td>15</td><td>T</td><td>8:35</td><td>3.6</td><td>8:55</td><td>3.9</td><td>2:00</td><td>1:49</td></tr>
<tr><td>16</td><td>T</td><td>8:16</td><td>3.6</td><td>8:39</td><td>4.2</td><td>1:55</td><td>1:19</td><td>16</td><td>F</td><td>9:13</td><td>3.7</td><td>9:30</td><td>3.8</td><td>2:34</td><td>2:32</td></tr>
<tr><td>17</td><td>W</td><td>8:59</td><td>3.6</td><td>9:20</td><td>4.0</td><td>2:30</td><td>2:05</td><td>17</td><td>S</td><td>9:50</td><td>3.6</td><td>10:05</td><td>3.7</td><td>3:08</td><td>3:14</td></tr>
<tr><td>18</td><td>T</td><td>9:41</td><td>3.5</td><td>9:59</td><td>3.9</td><td>3:05</td><td>2:50</td><td>18</td><td>S</td><td>10:25</td><td>3.5</td><td>10:39</td><td>3.5</td><td>3:40</td><td>3:54</td></tr>
<tr><td>19</td><td>F</td><td>10:21</td><td>3.5</td><td>10:37</td><td>3.7</td><td>3:39</td><td>3:34</td><td>19</td><td>M</td><td>11:01</td><td>3.5</td><td>11:16</td><td>3.3</td><td>4:12</td><td>4:32</td></tr>
<tr><td>20</td><td>S</td><td>11:02</td><td>3.4</td><td>11:15</td><td>3.5</td><td>4:13</td><td>4:16</td><td>20</td><td>T</td><td>11:39</td><td>3.4</td><td>11:56</td><td>3.2</td><td>4:44</td><td>5:10</td></tr>
<tr><td>21</td><td>S</td><td>11:42</td><td>3.3</td><td>11:54</td><td>3.3</td><td>4:47</td><td>4:58</td><td>21</td><td>W</td><td>...</td><td>...</td><td>12:19</td><td>3.3</td><td>5:17</td><td>5:51</td></tr>
<tr><td>22</td><td>M</td><td>...</td><td>...</td><td>12:23</td><td>3.2</td><td>5:22</td><td>5:42</td><td>22</td><td>T</td><td>12:41</td><td>3.0</td><td>1:03</td><td>3.3</td><td>5:55</td><td>6:42</td></tr>
<tr><td>23</td><td>T</td><td>12:34</td><td>3.1</td><td>1:03</td><td>3.2</td><td>6:00</td><td>6:32</td><td>23</td><td>F</td><td>1:29</td><td>3.0</td><td>1:51</td><td>3.4</td><td>6:42</td><td>7:50</td></tr>
<tr><td>24</td><td>W</td><td>1:16</td><td>3.0</td><td>1:44</td><td>3.2</td><td>6:42</td><td>7:33</td><td>24</td><td>S</td><td>2:21</td><td>2.9</td><td>2:45</td><td>3.5</td><td>7:40</td><td>9:15</td></tr>
<tr><td>25</td><td>T</td><td>2:01</td><td>2.9</td><td>2:29</td><td>3.3</td><td>7:32</td><td>8:47</td><td>25</td><td>S</td><td>3:20</td><td>3.0</td><td>3:47</td><td>3.6</td><td>8:47</td><td>10:30</td></tr>
<tr><td>26</td><td>F</td><td>2:51</td><td>2.9</td><td>3:19</td><td>3.4</td><td>8:27</td><td>9:57</td><td>26</td><td>M</td><td>4:25</td><td>3.2</td><td>4:54</td><td>3.8</td><td>9:55</td><td>11:25</td></tr>
<tr><td>27</td><td>S</td><td>3:48</td><td>2.9</td><td>4:18</td><td>3.6</td><td>9:26</td><td>10:55</td><td>27</td><td>T</td><td>5:30</td><td>3.5</td><td>5:58</td><td>4.2</td><td>10:59</td><td>...</td></tr>
<tr><td>28</td><td>S</td><td>4:52</td><td>3.0</td><td>5:21</td><td>3.8</td><td>10:23</td><td>11:46</td><td>28</td><td>W</td><td>6:29</td><td>3.8</td><td>6:55</td><td>4.5</td><td>12:14</td><td>12:00</td></tr>
<tr><td>29</td><td>M</td><td>5:54</td><td>3.3</td><td>6:20</td><td>4.1</td><td>11:18</td><td>...</td><td>29</td><td>T</td><td>7:22</td><td>4.2</td><td>7:47</td><td>4.8</td><td>1:01</td><td>12:52</td></tr>
<tr><td>30</td><td>T</td><td>6:50</td><td>3.6</td><td>7:13</td><td>4.4</td><td>12:34</td><td>12:11</td><td>30</td><td>F</td><td>8:14</td><td>4.6</td><td>8:38</td><td>4.9</td><td>1:47</td><td>1:48</td></tr>
<tr><td>31</td><td>W</td><td>7:42</td><td>4.0</td><td>8:05</td><td>4.7</td><td>1:23</td><td>1:04</td><td>31</td><td>S</td><td>9:05</td><td>4.8</td><td>9:28</td><td>4.8</td><td>2:34</td><td>2:44</td></tr>
</table>

A also at 11:54 a.m.   B also at 11:42 a.m.

Dates when Ht. of **Low** Water is below Mean Lower Low with Ht. of lowest given for each period and Date of lowest in ( ):

2nd–6th: -0.3' (3rd, 4th)   1st–5th: -0.4' (1st, 2nd)
30th–31st: -0.3' (31st)   28th–31st: -0.5' (30th, 31st)

Average Rise and Fall 3.5 ft.

When a high tide exceeds avg. ht., the *following* low tide will be lower than avg.

2019 HIGH & LOW WATER
NEWPORT, RI
41°30.3'N, 71°19.6'W

Daylight Saving Time

Daylight Saving Time

DAY OF MONTH	DAY OF WEEK	SEPTEMBER						DAY OF MONTH	DAY OF WEEK	OCTOBER					
		HIGH				LOW				HIGH				LOW	
		a.m.	Ht.	p.m.	Ht.	a.m.	p.m.			a.m.	Ht.	p.m.	Ht.	a.m.	p.m.
1	S	9:56	4.9	10:19	4.7	3:18	3:38	1	T	10:25	5.0	10:49	4.2	3:26	4:13
2	M	10:48	4.9	11:11	4.4	3:59	4:30	2	W	11:17	4.7	11:42	3.9	4:08	5:01
3	T	11:42	4.7	...	...	4:40	5:23	3	T	...	...	12:12	4.3	4:50	5:52
4	W	12:06	4.0	12:38	4.4	5:23	6:25	4	F	12:38	3.6	1:10	4.0	5:35	7:11
5	T	1:02	3.7	1:36	4.2	6:10	8:11	5	S	1:36	3.3	2:08	3.7	6:30	9:08
6	F	1:59	3.5	2:34	3.9	7:08	9:41	6	S	2:34	3.2	3:08	3.5	7:46	10:11
7	S	2:58	3.2	3:35	3.7	8:27	10:43	7	M	3:34	3.1	4:10	3.3	9:41	10:55
8	S	4:01	3.2	4:40	3.6	9:59	11:29	8	T	4:37	3.1	5:11	3.3	10:41	11:26
9	M	5:06	3.2	5:41	3.6	10:55	11:59	9	W	5:35	3.3	6:01	3.4	11:21	11:51
10	T	6:01	3.3	6:31	3.7	11:36	...	10	T	6:21	3.4	6:43	3.5	11:58	...
11	W	6:49	3.5	7:13	3.8	12:30	12:13	11	F	7:01	3.6	7:19	3.6	12:18	12:35
12	T	7:30	3.6	7:51	3.8	12:56	12:52	12	S	7:36	3.8	7:52	3.6	12:48	1:14
13	F	8:07	3.7	8:25	3.8	1:25	1:32	13	S	8:10	3.9	8:26	3.6	1:20	1:53
14	S	8:42	3.8	8:58	3.8	1:58	2:13	14	M	8:42	3.9	9:00	3.6	1:54	2:32
15	S	9:16	3.8	9:31	3.7	2:31	2:54	15	T	9:15	3.9	9:37	3.5	2:27	3:09
16	M	9:49	3.8	10:06	3.5	3:04	3:31	16	W	9:51	3.9	10:17	3.4	3:01	3:44
17	T	10:23	3.7	10:44	3.4	3:36	4:07	17	T	10:30	3.8	11:01	3.2	3:36	4:19
18	W	11:00	3.6	11:26	3.2	4:07	4:42	18	F	11:15	3.7	11:51	3.2	4:12	4:56
19	T	11:42	3.5	...	...	4:41	5:19	19	S	...	...	12:07	3.6	4:53	5:42
20	F	12:13	3.1	12:30	3.5	5:19	6:05	20	S	12:46	3.1	1:04	3.6	5:41	6:42
21	S	1:05	3.0	1:23	3.5	6:05	7:07	21	M	1:44	3.1	2:04	3.6	6:43	8:15
22	S	2:00	3.0	2:21	3.5	7:06	8:40	22	T	2:43	3.3	3:06	3.7	8:01	9:50
23	M	2:59	3.1	3:24	3.7	8:19	10:10	23	W	3:45	3.5	4:12	3.8	9:27	10:44
24	T	4:04	3.3	4:33	3.9	9:37	11:07	24	T	4:50	3.8	5:17	4.0	10:42	11:27
25	W	5:09	3.7	5:38	4.2	10:47	11:52	25	F	5:50	4.3	6:15	4.2	11:43	...
26	T	6:09	4.1	6:35	4.4	11:48	...	26	S	6:44	4.7	7:08	4.4	12:08	12:36
27	F	7:03	4.5	7:28	4.7	12:35	12:43	27	S	7:35	5.0	7:59	4.4	12:48	1:28
28	S	7:54	4.9	8:18	4.8	1:18	1:38	28	M	8:24	5.1	8:48	4.4	1:29	2:19
29	S	8:44	5.1	9:08	4.7	2:01	2:32	29	T	9:13	5.1	9:37	4.2	2:12	3:08
30	M	9:34	5.1	9:57	4.5	2:44	3:24	30	W	10:02	4.8	10:27	4.0	2:55	3:54
								31	T	10:53	4.5	11:18	3.7	3:38	4:37

Dates when Ht. of **Low** Water is below Mean Lower Low with Ht. of lowest given for each period and Date of lowest in ( ):

1st–3rd: -0.4' (1st)
27th–30th: -0.5' (28th, 29th)

1st: -0.3'
26th–30th: -0.4' (27th–29th)

Average Rise and Fall 3.5 ft.

When a high tide exceeds avg. ht., the *following* low tide will be lower than avg.

2019 HIGH & LOW WATER
NEWPORT, RI
41°30.3'N, 71°19.6'W

*Standard Time starts Nov. 3 at 2 a.m.   Standard Time

DAY OF MONTH	DAY OF WEEK	NOVEMBER						DAY OF MONTH	DAY OF WEEK	DECEMBER					
		HIGH				LOW				HIGH				LOW	
		a.m.	Ht.	p.m.	Ht.	a.m.	p.m.			a.m.	Ht.	p.m.	Ht.	a.m.	p.m.
1	F	11:46	4.1	...	...	4:21	5:21	1	S	11:10	3.5	11:38	3.1	3:42	4:34
2	S	12:13	3.4	12:41	3.8	5:06	6:13	2	M	...	...	12:01	3.2	4:29	5:23
3	S	1:09	3.2	*12:37	3.4	*4:58	*6:39	3	T	12:30	3.0	12:51	3.0	5:26	6:25
4	M	1:05	3.1	1:33	3.2	6:04	8:11	4	W	1:21	2.9	1:39	2.8	6:41	7:32
5	T	2:01	3.0	2:29	3.1	7:45	8:59	5	T	2:11	2.9	2:28	2.7	8:10	8:26
6	W	2:59	3.0	3:26	3.0	9:06	9:34	6	F	3:04	2.9	3:20	2.7	9:16	9:11
7	T	3:56	3.1	4:19	3.0	9:54	10:05	7	S	3:56	3.0	4:12	2.7	10:05	9:51
8	F	4:45	3.3	5:03	3.1	10:35	10:37	8	S	4:43	3.2	4:59	2.9	10:48	10:30
9	S	5:27	3.5	5:42	3.2	11:13	11:10	9	M	5:25	3.5	5:42	3.0	11:28	11:08
10	S	6:02	3.7	6:18	3.3	11:52	11:43	10	T	6:03	3.7	6:24	3.2	-A-	12:08
11	M	6:36	3.8	6:54	3.4	...	12:31	11	W	6:42	3.9	7:06	3.3	...	12:49
12	T	7:10	3.9	7:32	3.5	12:18	1:10	12	T	7:23	4.0	7:50	3.4	12:27	1:31
13	W	7:46	4.0	8:12	3.5	12:54	1:48	13	F	8:06	4.1	8:36	3.5	1:09	2:12
14	T	8:25	4.0	8:55	3.4	1:32	2:26	14	S	8:52	4.1	9:25	3.5	1:54	2:52
15	F	9:08	3.9	9:42	3.3	2:11	3:03	15	S	9:42	4.0	10:17	3.5	2:40	3:34
16	S	9:57	3.8	10:34	3.2	2:52	3:43	16	M	10:36	3.9	11:12	3.5	3:27	4:18
17	S	10:50	3.8	11:30	3.2	3:37	4:29	17	T	11:32	3.8	...	...	4:19	5:10
18	M	11:48	3.7	...	...	4:27	5:27	18	W	12:10	3.5	12:30	3.6	5:20	6:15
19	T	12:28	3.3	12:48	3.6	5:29	6:49	19	T	1:08	3.6	1:29	3.5	6:41	7:32
20	W	1:26	3.4	1:48	3.6	6:49	8:18	20	F	2:07	3.7	2:29	3.4	8:27	8:38
21	T	2:27	3.7	2:51	3.6	8:25	9:15	21	S	3:09	3.9	3:34	3.3	9:45	9:31
22	F	3:30	3.9	3:55	3.7	9:43	10:00	22	S	4:12	4.1	4:36	3.4	10:42	10:16
23	S	4:31	4.3	4:55	3.8	10:41	10:40	23	M	5:10	4.2	5:33	3.5	11:31	10:59
24	S	5:26	4.6	5:50	3.9	11:32	11:20	24	T	6:02	4.4	6:24	3.6	-B-	12:17
25	M	6:18	4.8	6:41	4.0	...	12:20	25	W	6:51	4.4	7:13	3.6	...	1:00
26	T	7:07	4.8	7:29	4.0	12:01	1:08	26	T	7:38	4.3	7:59	3.6	12:24	1:39
27	W	7:54	4.8	8:17	3.9	12:44	1:53	27	F	8:23	4.2	8:45	3.5	1:09	2:16
28	T	8:42	4.5	9:05	3.7	1:29	2:35	28	S	9:08	3.9	9:30	3.4	1:54	2:50
29	F	9:30	4.2	9:54	3.5	2:13	3:13	29	S	9:52	3.7	10:15	3.2	2:37	3:24
30	S	10:19	3.9	10:45	3.3	2:57	3:52	30	M	10:36	3.4	11:02	3.0	3:20	4:00
								31	T	11:20	3.1	11:50	2.9	4:04	4:40

A also at 11:46 p.m.   B also at 11:41 p.m.

Dates when Ht. of **Low** Water is below Mean Lower Low with Ht. of lowest given for each period and Date of lowest in ( ):

23rd–28th: -0.4' (26th)   10th: -0.2'
                                           12th–16th: -0.4' (14th)
                                           23rd–28th: -0.2'

Average Rise and Fall 3.5 ft.

When a high tide exceeds avg. ht., the *following* low tide will be lower than avg.

Narragansett Bay Currents

This current diagram shows current **directions** and **average maximum velocities** when the tides have a normal (3.5 ft.) range at Newport. (pp. 84-89).

Average maximum Ebb currents occur about 3 hours *after* High Water at Newport and are shown by light arrows.

Average maximum Flood currents occur about 2 1/2 hours *before* High Water at Newport and are shown by black arrows.

When height of High Water at Newport is 3.0 ft., subtract 30% from velocities shown. When height is 4.0 ft., add 20%; when 4.5 ft., add 40%; when 5.0 ft., add 60%.

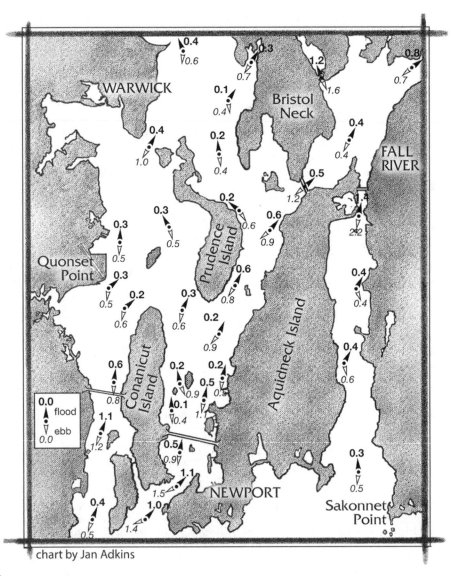

chart by Jan Adkins

Holding a Fair Current Between Eastern Long Island and Nantucket

There is a curious phenomenon which can be used to advantage by every vessel, and particularly the slower cruiser or auxiliary, in making the passage *either* way between eastern Long Island Sound, on the west, and Buzzards Bay, Vineyard and Nantucket Sounds on the east.

Note in the very simplified diagram below, that in Long Island Sound, the Ebb Current flows to the *east*, and in Buzzards Bay, Vineyard and Nantucket Sounds the Ebb Current flows to the *west*. (Off Newport, these opposed Ebb Currents merge and flow *south*.) The reverse is also true: the Flood Current flows *west* through Long Island Sound and *east* through Buzzards Bay, Vineyard and Nantucket Sounds. (Half arrow indicates Ebb Current, whole arrow indicates Flood Current.)

In making a *complete* passage through the area of the diagram, simply ride the favoring Ebb Current toward Newport from either direction and, pick up the favoring Flood Current in leaving the Newport area.

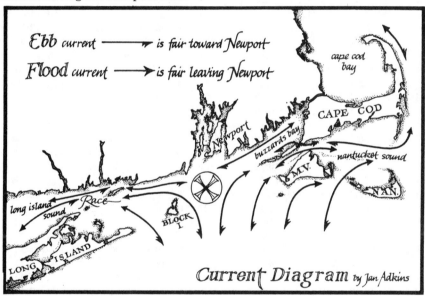

Current Diagram by Jan Adkins

Arrive at "X" at the times shown for "Current Turns to Northwest at The Race," tables pp. 92-97.

The E-W currents between Pt. Judith and Cuttyhunk are only 1/2 to 1 kt., while those to the West of Pt. Judith and to the East of Cuttyhunk are much greater. Bearing this in mind, those making *only a partial trip* through the area may find it better even to buck a slight head current in the Pt. Judith-Cuttyhunk area so as to pick up the maximum hours of strong favoring currents beyond those points.

For example, if headed for the Cape Cod Canal, refer to the Tidal Current Chart Buzzards Bay, Vineyard & Nantucket Sound, pp. 72-83 and arrive just N. of Cuttyhunk as Flood Starts at Pollock Rip, pp. 66-71 to ensure the most favorable currents. If headed for Nantucket, refer to the same Charts and arrive just S. of Cuttyhunk at 3 hours after Flood Starts at Pollock Rip, pp. 66-71. If headed into Long Island Sound, refer to the Tidal Current Chart Long Island Sound and Block Island Sound, pp. 98-103 and arrive at Pt. Judith when Flood Current turns West at The Race, p. 101.

Standard Time   Standard Time

JANUARY | FEBRUARY

JANUARY

DAY OF MONTH	DAY OF WEEK	NORTHWEST Flood Starts a.m.	**p.m.**	Kts.	SOUTHEAST Ebb Starts a.m.	**p.m.**	Kts.
1	T	1:54	**2:42**	a3.4	7:54	**8:36**	a4.5
2	W	2:48	**3:36**	a3.5	8:48	**9:30**	a4.6
3	T	3:42	**4:24**	a3.5	9:36	**10:18**	a4.7
4	F	4:30	**5:12**	a3.5	10:24	**11:00**	a4.6
5	S	5:12	**5:54**	3.4	11:06	**11:42**	a4.5
6	S	6:00	**6:30**	3.3	11:42	...	4.4
7	M	6:36	**7:06**	3.2	12:18	**12:24**	p4.2
8	T	7:18	**7:42**	p3.2	12:54	**1:00**	p4.1
9	W	8:01	**8:18**	p3.1	1:30	**1:36**	p3.9
10	T	8:36	**8:54**	p3.0	2:06	**2:12**	3.8
11	F	9:24	**9:36**	p3.0	2:48	**2:54**	a3.8
12	S	10:06	**10:18**	p2.9	3:24	**3:36**	a3.7
13	S	10:54	**11:00**	p2.9	4:12	**4:24**	a3.7
14	M	11:48	**11:54**	p3.0	5:00	**5:18**	a3.8
15	T	...	**12:42**	2.6	5:48	**6:18**	a3.9
16	W	12:48	**1:36**	a3.1	6:42	**7:18**	a4.1
17	T	1:42	**2:36**	a3.2	7:42	**8:18**	a4.4
18	F	2:36	**3:24**	a3.5	8:36	**9:18**	a4.8
19	S	3:30	**4:18**	a3.8	9:36	**10:12**	a5.1
20	S	4:30	**5:12**	a4.1	10:30	**11:06**	a5.4
21	M	5:24	**6:00**	a4.3	11:24	...	5.5
22	T	6:18	**6:54**	4.3	12:01	**12:12**	p5.5
23	W	7:12	**7:42**	p4.3	12:48	**1:06**	p5.4
24	T	8:06	**8:36**	p4.2	1:42	**2:00**	5.1
25	F	9:06	**9:30**	p3.9	2:36	**3:00**	a5.0
26	S	10:12	**10:30**	p3.7	3:36	**4:00**	a4.7
27	S	11:12	**11:30**	p3.4	4:30	**5:00**	a4.5
28	M	...	**12:18**	2.9	5:30	**6:06**	a4.3
29	T	12:30	**1:24**	a3.2	6:30	**7:12**	a4.2
30	W	1:30	**2:24**	a3.1	7:30	**8:12**	a4.2
31	T	2:30	**3:18**	a3.1	8:24	**9:06**	a4.2

FEBRUARY

DAY OF MONTH	DAY OF WEEK	NORTHWEST Flood Starts a.m.	**p.m.**	Kts.	SOUTHEAST Ebb Starts a.m.	**p.m.**	Kts.
1	F	3:18	**4:06**	3.1	9:18	**9:54**	a4.3
2	S	4:06	**4:48**	3.2	10:00	**10:36**	a4.3
3	S	4:54	**5:24**	p3.3	10:42	**11:12**	a4.2
4	M	5:36	**6:00**	p3.3	11:18	**11:48**	a4.2
5	T	6:12	**6:36**	p3.3	11:54	...	4.1
6	W	6:48	**7:12**	p3.3	12:24	**12:30**	p4.1
7	T	7:30	**7:42**	p3.3	1:00	**1:06**	a4.1
8	F	8:06	**8:18**	p3.3	1:30	**1:42**	a4.1
9	S	8:49	**8:54**	p3.2	2:12	**2:24**	a4.1
10	S	9:30	**9:36**	p3.1	2:48	**3:06**	a4.1
11	M	10:18	**10:24**	p3.1	3:30	**3:54**	a4.0
12	T	11:12	**11:18**	p3.0	4:24	**4:48**	a4.0
13	W	...	**12:12**	2.6	5:18	**5:48**	a4.0
14	T	12:18	**1:06**	a3.1	6:12	**6:54**	a4.1
15	F	1:18	**2:06**	a3.2	7:18	**7:54**	a4.3
16	S	2:18	**3:06**	a3.5	8:18	**8:54**	a4.7
17	S	3:12	**4:00**	a3.8	9:18	**9:54**	a5.0
18	M	4:12	**4:48**	4.1	10:12	**10:48**	a5.3
19	T	5:06	**5:42**	p4.4	11:06	**11:36**	a5.5
20	W	6:00	**6:30**	p4.5	...	**12:01**	5.5
21	T	6:54	**7:24**	p4.5	12:30	**12:54**	a5.4
22	F	7:48	**8:12**	p4.3	1:24	**1:42**	a5.3
23	S	8:48	**9:06**	p3.9	2:12	**2:42**	a5.1
24	S	9:48	**10:00**	p3.5	3:06	**3:36**	a4.8
25	M	10:48	**11:00**	p3.2	4:00	**4:36**	a4.4
26	T	11:54	...	2.8	5:00	**5:42**	a4.1
27	W	12:06	**12:54**	a2.9	6:00	**6:42**	a3.9
28	T	1:06	**1:54**	a2.8	7:00	**7:42**	a3.8

The Kts. (knots) columns show the **maximum** predicted velocities of the stronger one of the Flood Currents and the stronger one of the Ebb Currents for each day.
The letter "a" means the velocity shown should occur **after** the **a.m.** Current Change. The letter "p" means the velocity shown should occur **after** the **p.m.** Current Change (even if next morning). No "a" or "p" means a.m. and p.m. velocities are the same for that day.
Avg. Max. Velocity: Flood 3.3 Kts., Ebb 4.2 Kts.
Max. Flood 2 hrs. 45 min. after Flood Starts, ±15 min.
Max. Ebb 3 hrs. 25 min. after Ebb Starts, ±15 min.
Use THE RACE tables with current charts pp. 98-103

See pp. 22-29 for Current Change at other points.

2019 CURRENT TABLE
THE RACE, LONG ISLAND SOUND
41°13.69'N, 72°03.75'W 0.2 nm E.N.E. of Valiant Rock

Daylight Time starts March 10 at 2 a.m.   Daylight Saving Time

DAY OF MONTH	DAY OF WEEK	NORTHWEST Flood Starts a.m.	**p.m.**	Kts.	SOUTHEAST Ebb Starts a.m.	**p.m.**	Kts.	DAY OF MONTH	DAY OF WEEK	NORTHWEST Flood Starts a.m.	**p.m.**	Kts.	SOUTHEAST Ebb Starts a.m.	**p.m.**	Kts.
		MARCH								**APRIL**					
1	F	2:06	**2:48**	2.8	8:00	**8:36**	a3.8	1	M	4:12	**4:36**	p2.9	10:00	**10:24**	p3.8
2	S	2:54	**3:36**	p2.9	8:48	**9:24**	a3.9	2	T	4:54	**5:18**	p3.1	10:42	**11:00**	p4.0
3	S	3:42	**4:18**	p3.0	9:36	**10:06**	a3.9	3	W	5:36	**5:54**	p3.3	11:18	**11:36**	p4.3
4	M	4:30	**4:54**	p3.2	10:18	**10:42**	a4.0	4	T	6:12	**6:24**	p3.4	...	**12:01**	4.0
5	T	5:06	**5:30**	p3.3	10:54	**11:18**	p4.1	5	F	6:54	**7:00**	p3.5	12:12	**12:36**	a4.5
6	W	5:48	**6:06**	p3.4	11:30	**11:48**	p4.3	6	S	7:30	**7:36**	p3.6	12:48	**1:12**	a4.7
7	T	6:24	**6:36**	p3.4	...	**12:06**	4.1	7	S	8:06	**8:12**	p3.6	1:24	**1:54**	a4.7
8	F	7:00	**7:12**	p3.5	12:24	**12:42**	a4.4	8	M	8:48	**8:54**	p3.5	2:06	**2:36**	a4.7
9	S	7:37	**7:42**	p3.5	1:00	**1:18**	a4.4	9	T	9:37	**9:42**	p3.4	2:48	**3:24**	a4.6
10	S	*9:18	***9:24**	p3.4	1:36	***3:00**	a4.5	10	W	10:24	**10:36**	p3.2	3:36	**4:12**	a4.5
11	M	10:00	**10:06**	p3.3	3:18	**3:42**	a4.4	11	T	11:18	**11:36**	p3.1	4:30	**5:12**	a4.3
12	T	10:48	**10:54**	p3.2	4:00	**4:30**	a4.3	12	F	...	**12:24**	2.9	5:30	**6:12**	a4.1
13	W	11:42	**11:54**	p3.1	4:54	**5:24**	a4.1	13	S	12:42	**1:24**	3.0	6:36	**7:18**	a4.1
14	T	...	**12:42**	2.7	5:48	**6:24**	a4.1	14	S	1:48	**2:24**	p3.2	7:42	**8:18**	4.2
15	F	12:54	**1:42**	a3.1	6:54	**7:30**	a4.1	15	M	2:48	**3:24**	p3.5	8:48	**9:18**	p4.6
16	S	2:00	**2:48**	a3.2	7:54	**8:36**	a4.2	16	T	3:48	**4:18**	p3.9	9:48	**10:18**	p5.0
17	S	3:00	**3:42**	3.4	9:00	**9:36**	4.5	17	W	4:48	**5:06**	p4.2	10:42	**11:06**	p5.3
18	M	4:00	**4:36**	p3.8	10:00	**10:36**	4.9	18	T	5:42	**6:00**	p4.4	11:36	...	5.0
19	T	5:00	**5:30**	p4.2	11:00	**11:30**	p5.3	19	F	6:30	**6:48**	p4.4	12:01	**12:30**	a5.5
20	W	5:54	**6:18**	p4.5	11:48	...	5.3	20	S	7:24	**7:36**	p4.2	12:48	**1:18**	a5.5
21	T	6:48	**7:06**	p4.5	12:18	**12:42**	a5.5	21	S	8:12	**8:24**	p4.0	1:36	**2:06**	a5.4
22	F	7:42	**8:00**	p4.4	1:06	**1:36**	a5.6	22	M	9:06	**9:18**	3.6	2:18	**2:54**	a5.0
23	S	8:30	**8:48**	p4.2	2:00	**2:24**	a5.4	23	T	9:54	**10:06**	a3.3	3:06	**3:48**	a4.6
24	S	9:24	**9:42**	p3.8	2:48	**3:18**	a5.2	24	W	10:48	**11:06**	a2.9	4:00	**4:36**	a4.2
25	M	10:18	**10:36**	3.3	3:36	**4:12**	a4.8	25	T	11:42	...	2.6	4:48	**5:30**	a3.7
26	T	11:18	**11:36**	a3.0	4:30	**5:06**	a4.3	26	F	12:01	**12:36**	p2.5	5:42	**6:24**	a3.4
27	W	...	**12:18**	2.7	5:24	**6:06**	a3.9	27	S	1:00	**1:30**	p2.4	6:36	**7:18**	3.1
28	T	12:36	**1:18**	a2.6	6:24	**7:06**	a3.6	28	S	2:00	**2:24**	p2.4	7:36	**8:12**	p3.3
29	F	1:36	**2:18**	2.5	7:24	**8:06**	a3.4	29	M	2:48	**3:06**	p2.6	8:30	**8:54**	p3.5
30	S	2:36	**3:12**	p2.6	8:18	**8:54**	a3.4	30	T	3:36	**3:54**	p2.8	9:18	**9:42**	p3.8
31	S	3:24	**3:54**	p2.7	9:12	**9:42**	3.5								

The Kts. (knots) columns show the **maximum** predicted velocities of the stronger one of the Flood Currents and the stronger one of the Ebb Currents for each day.

The letter "a" means the velocity shown should occur **after** the a.m. Current Change. The letter "p" means the velocity shown should occur **after** the p.m. Current Change (even if next morning). No "a" or "p" means a.m. and p.m. velocities are the same for that day.

Avg. Max. Velocity: Flood 3.3 Kts., Ebb 4.2 Kts.

Max. Flood 2 hrs. 45 min. after Flood Starts, ±15 min.

Max. Ebb 3 hrs. 25 min. after Ebb Starts, ±15 min.

Use THE RACE tables with current charts pp. 98-103

See pp. 22-29 for Current Change at other points.

2019 CURRENT TABLE
THE RACE, LONG ISLAND SOUND
41°13.69'N, 72°03.75'W 0.2 nm E.N.E. of Valiant Rock

Daylight Saving Time   **Daylight Saving Time**

		MAY								JUNE				
		CURRENT TURNS TO								CURRENT TURNS TO				
		NORTHWEST Flood Starts			SOUTHEAST Ebb Starts					NORTHWEST Flood Starts			SOUTHEAST Ebb Starts		
DAY OF MONTH	DAY OF WEEK	a.m.	p.m.	Kts.	a.m.	p.m.	Kts.	DAY OF MONTH	DAY OF WEEK	a.m.	p.m.	Kts.	a.m.	p.m.	Kts.
1	W	4:18	4:30	p3.0	10:00	10:18	p4.1	1	S	5:06	5:12	p3.5	10:54	11:06	p4.8
2	T	5:00	5:12	p3.2	10:42	11:00	p4.4	2	S	5:48	5:54	p3.7	11:36	11:48	p5.0
3	F	5:42	5:48	p3.4	11:24	11:36	p4.7	3	M	6:36	6:42	p3.8	...	12:24	4.3
4	S	6:18	6:24	p3.6	...	12:06	4.1	4	T	7:18	7:24	p3.9	12:36	1:12	a5.1
5	S	7:00	7:06	p3.7	12:18	12:48	a4.9	5	W	8:06	8:18	3.8	1:24	2:00	a5.2
6	M	7:42	7:48	p3.7	1:00	1:30	a5.0	6	T	8:54	9:12	3.7	2:12	2:54	a5.1
7	T	8:24	8:36	p3.7	1:42	2:18	a5.0	7	F	9:48	10:06	a3.6	3:06	3:48	a4.9
8	W	9:12	9:24	3.5	2:30	3:06	a4.8	8	S	10:42	11:12	a3.5	4:00	4:42	a4.6
9	T	10:07	10:18	3.3	3:18	4:00	a4.7	9	S	11:43	...	3.4	5:00	5:42	a4.4
10	F	11:00	11:24	a3.2	4:12	4:54	a4.4	10	M	12:18	12:42	p3.4	6:06	6:42	p4.3
11	S	...	12:01	3.1	5:12	6:00	a4.2	11	T	1:24	1:42	p3.5	7:12	7:42	p4.5
12	S	12:30	1:06	p3.2	6:18	7:00	4.1	12	W	2:24	2:42	p3.6	8:18	8:42	p4.7
13	M	1:36	2:06	p3.4	7:24	8:00	p4.4	13	T	3:30	3:36	p3.7	9:18	9:36	p4.9
14	T	2:42	3:00	p3.6	8:30	9:00	p4.7	14	F	4:24	4:30	p3.8	10:18	10:30	p5.0
15	W	3:42	3:54	p3.9	9:30	10:00	p5.0	15	S	5:18	5:24	p3.9	11:12	11:18	p5.1
16	T	4:36	4:48	p4.1	10:30	10:48	p5.3	16	S	6:06	6:12	p3.8	...	12:01	4.3
17	F	5:30	5:36	p4.2	11:24	11:36	p5.4	17	M	6:54	7:00	3.7	12:06	12:42	a5.0
18	S	6:18	6:30	p4.1	...	12:12	4.6	18	T	7:36	7:42	a3.6	12:48	1:30	a4.8
19	S	7:06	7:18	p4.0	12:24	1:00	a5.3	19	W	8:18	8:30	a3.4	1:36	2:12	a4.6
20	M	7:54	8:06	a3.8	1:12	1:48	a5.1	20	T	9:00	9:12	a3.2	2:12	2:54	a4.3
21	T	8:42	8:54	a3.5	1:54	2:36	a4.8	21	F	9:42	10:00	a3.1	2:54	3:30	a4.0
22	W	9:30	9:42	a3.2	2:42	3:18	a4.4	22	S	10:24	10:48	a2.9	3:36	4:12	a3.7
23	T	10:12	10:30	a3.0	3:24	4:06	a4.0	23	S	11:06	11:36	a2.7	4:18	4:54	3.4
24	F	11:00	11:24	a2.7	4:12	4:54	a3.7	24	M	11:48	...	2.7	5:06	5:42	p3.4
25	S	11:54	...	2.5	5:00	5:42	a3.3	25	T	12:24	12:36	p2.6	5:54	6:24	p3.4
26	S	12:18	12:42	p2.5	5:48	6:30	p3.2	26	W	1:18	1:24	p2.7	6:42	7:12	p3.6
27	M	1:12	1:30	p2.5	6:42	7:18	p3.3	27	T	2:06	2:12	p2.8	7:36	8:00	p3.8
28	T	2:06	2:18	p2.6	7:36	8:06	p3.5	28	F	3:00	3:00	p3.0	8:36	8:54	p4.1
29	W	2:54	3:00	p2.7	8:30	8:48	p3.8	29	S	3:48	3:48	p3.2	9:30	9:42	p4.5
30	T	3:42	3:42	p3.0	9:18	9:36	p4.1	30	S	4:36	4:36	p3.5	10:24	10:36	p4.8
31	F	4:24	4:30	p3.2	10:06	10:18	p4.5								

The Kts. (knots) columns show the **maximum** predicted velocities of the stronger one of the Flood Currents and the stronger one of the Ebb Currents for each day.

The letter "a" means the velocity shown should occur **after** the **a.m.** Current Change. The letter "p" means the velocity shown should occur **after** the **p.m.** Current Change (even if next morning). No "a" or "p" means a.m. and p.m. velocities are the same for that day.

Avg. Max. Velocity: Flood 3.3 Kts., Ebb 4.2 Kts.

Max. Flood 2 hrs. 45 min. after Flood Starts, ±15 min.

Max. Ebb 3 hrs. 25 min. after Ebb Starts, ±15 min.

Use THE RACE tables with current charts pp. 98-103

See pp. 22-29 for Current Change at other points.

THE RACE, LONG ISLAND SOUND
41°13.69'N, 72°03.75'W 0.2 nm E.N.E. of Valiant Rock

		Daylight Saving Time						Daylight Saving Time				

		JULY							AUGUST				

DAY OF MONTH	DAY OF WEEK	CURRENT TURNS TO						DAY OF MONTH	DAY OF WEEK	CURRENT TURNS TO				
		NORTHWEST Flood Starts			SOUTHEAST Ebb Starts					NORTHWEST Flood Starts			SOUTHEAST Ebb Starts		
		a.m.	p.m.	Kts.	a.m.	p.m.	Kts.			a.m.	p.m.	Kts.	a.m.	p.m.	Kts.
1	M	5:24	5:24	p3.8	11:12	11:24	p5.1	1	T	6:36	6:48	p4.3	...	12:30	5.0
2	T	6:12	6:18	p4.0	...	12:01	4.4	2	F	7:24	7:42	4.3	12:48	1:24	a5.5
3	W	7:00	7:06	p4.1	12:12	12:54	a5.3	3	S	8:12	8:36	a4.3	1:42	2:12	a5.4
4	T	7:48	8:00	p4.1	1:06	1:42	a5.3	4	S	9:06	9:36	a4.3	2:30	3:06	a5.2
5	F	8:36	8:54	a4.0	1:54	2:36	a5.3	5	M	10:00	10:36	a4.1	3:30	4:00	4.9
6	S	9:30	9:54	a4.0	2:48	3:30	a5.1	6	T	10:54	11:42	a3.8	4:24	5:00	p4.7
7	S	10:24	10:54	a3.8	3:48	4:24	a4.8	7	W	11:54	...	3.5	5:30	6:00	p4.4
8	M	11:18	...	3.7	4:42	5:24	4.5	8	T	12:48	1:00	p3.3	6:30	7:00	p4.3
9	T	12:02	12:18	p3.6	5:48	6:24	p4.4	9	F	1:55	2:00	p3.2	7:42	8:00	p4.2
10	W	1:06	1:18	p3.5	6:54	7:24	p4.4	10	S	2:54	3:00	p3.2	8:42	9:00	p4.3
11	T	2:12	2:18	p3.4	8:00	8:24	p4.5	11	S	3:54	4:00	p3.2	9:42	9:54	p4.3
12	F	3:12	3:18	p3.5	9:00	9:18	p4.6	12	M	4:42	4:48	p3.3	10:30	10:42	p4.4
13	S	4:12	4:12	p3.5	10:00	10:12	p4.7	13	T	5:30	5:36	3.3	11:18	11:30	p4.4
14	S	5:00	5:06	p3.6	10:54	11:06	p4.7	14	W	6:12	6:18	a3.4	...	12:01	4.0
15	M	5:48	5:54	p3.6	11:42	11:48	p4.7	15	T	6:48	7:00	a3.4	12:12	12:36	a4.3
16	T	6:36	6:42	3.5	...	12:24	4.1	16	F	7:24	7:42	a3.4	12:48	1:12	a4.2
17	W	7:18	7:24	a3.5	12:30	1:06	a4.6	17	S	8:00	8:18	a3.4	1:24	1:48	4.1
18	T	7:54	8:06	a3.4	1:12	1:42	a4.4	18	S	8:30	8:54	a3.3	1:54	2:18	p4.1
19	F	8:30	8:48	a3.3	1:48	2:18	a4.2	19	M	9:06	9:30	a3.3	2:30	2:54	p4.1
20	S	9:06	9:24	a3.2	2:24	2:54	a4.0	20	T	9:42	10:12	a3.2	3:06	3:30	p4.0
21	S	9:42	10:06	a3.1	3:00	3:36	3.8	21	W	10:18	11:00	a3.1	3:48	4:12	p4.0
22	M	10:18	10:54	a3.0	3:42	4:12	p3.7	22	T	11:06	11:48	a3.0	4:36	5:00	p3.9
23	T	11:00	11:42	a2.9	4:24	4:54	p3.7	23	F	11:54	...	2.9	5:24	5:48	p3.8
24	W	11:42	...	2.8	5:06	5:36	p3.7	24	S	12:42	12:48	p2.9	6:24	6:48	p3.9
25	T	12:30	12:36	p2.8	6:00	6:24	p3.7	25	S	1:42	1:48	p3.0	7:24	7:48	p4.1
26	F	1:24	1:24	p2.9	6:54	7:18	p3.9	26	M	2:42	2:48	p3.2	8:24	8:48	p4.4
27	S	2:18	2:18	p3.0	7:54	8:18	p4.1	27	T	3:36	3:48	p3.5	9:24	9:48	p4.7
28	S	3:12	3:12	p3.2	8:54	9:12	p4.4	28	W	4:30	4:42	p3.9	10:24	10:42	p5.1
29	M	4:06	4:12	p3.5	9:54	10:06	p4.8	29	T	5:24	5:42	p4.2	11:18	11:36	p5.3
30	T	4:54	5:00	p3.8	10:48	11:00	p5.1	30	F	6:12	6:36	p4.4	...	12:12	5.3
31	W	5:48	5:54	p4.1	11:42	11:54	p5.3	31	S	7:00	7:24	a4.5	12:30	1:00	5.5

The Kts. (knots) columns show the **maximum** predicted velocities of the stronger one of the Flood Currents and the stronger one of the Ebb Currents for each day.
The letter "a" means the velocity shown should occur **after** the a.m. Current Change. The letter "p" means the velocity shown should occur **after** the p.m. Current Change (even if next morning). No "a" or "p" means a.m. and p.m. velocities are the same for that day.
Avg. Max. Velocity: Flood 3.3 Kts., Ebb 4.2 Kts.
Max. Flood 2 hrs. 45 min. after Flood Starts, ±15 min.
Max. Ebb 3 hrs. 25 min. after Ebb Starts, ±15 min.
Use THE RACE tables with current charts pp. 98-103

See pp. 22-29 for Current Change at other points.

THE RACE, LONG ISLAND SOUND
41°13.69'N, 72°03.75'W 0.2 nm E.N.E. of Valiant Rock

Daylight Saving Time							Daylight Saving Time				

SEPTEMBER / OCTOBER

DAY OF MONTH	DAY OF WEEK	CURRENT TURNS TO						DAY OF MONTH	DAY OF WEEK	CURRENT TURNS TO					
		NORTHWEST Flood Starts			SOUTHEAST Ebb Starts					NORTHWEST Flood Starts			SOUTHEAST Ebb Starts		
		a.m.	p.m.	Kts.	a.m.	p.m.	Kts.			a.m.	p.m.	Kts.	a.m.	p.m.	Kts.
1	S	7:54	8:18	a4.5	1:24	1:54	p5.5	1	T	8:18	9:00	a4.4	2:00	2:18	p5.4
2	M	8:42	9:18	a4.4	2:18	2:42	p5.4	2	W	9:12	9:54	a4.0	2:54	3:12	p5.1
3	T	9:36	10:12	a4.1	3:12	3:36	p5.1	3	T	10:06	10:54	a3.6	3:48	4:06	p4.6
4	W	10:30	11:18	a3.8	4:06	4:30	p4.7	4	F	11:06	11:54	a3.2	4:42	5:00	p4.2
5	T	11:30	...	3.4	5:06	5:30	p4.3	5	S	...	12:12	2.9	5:42	6:00	p3.8
6	F	12:24	12:36	p3.1	6:12	6:30	p4.0	6	S	12:54	1:12	a2.7	6:42	7:00	p3.6
7	S	1:24	1:42	p2.9	7:12	7:36	p3.9	7	M	1:54	2:12	a2.7	7:42	8:00	p3.5
8	S	2:30	2:42	p2.9	8:18	8:36	p3.9	8	T	2:48	3:12	a2.7	8:42	9:00	3.5
9	M	3:25	3:36	2.9	9:12	9:30	p4.0	9	W	3:43	4:00	a2.8	9:30	9:48	3.6
10	T	4:18	4:30	3.0	10:06	10:18	p4.0	10	T	4:24	4:42	2.9	10:12	10:30	a3.9
11	W	5:00	5:12	3.1	10:48	11:06	p4.0	11	F	5:00	5:24	a3.1	10:48	11:12	a4.1
12	T	5:42	5:54	3.2	11:30	11:42	a4.1	12	S	5:42	6:06	3.2	11:24	11:48	a4.4
13	F	6:18	6:36	3.3	...	12:06	4.2	13	S	6:12	6:42	3.3	...	12:01	4.4
14	S	6:48	7:12	a3.4	12:18	12:36	p4.3	14	M	6:48	7:18	a3.4	12:24	12:36	p4.5
15	S	7:24	7:48	a3.4	12:54	1:12	p4.4	15	T	7:24	7:54	a3.5	1:00	1:12	p4.6
16	M	7:54	8:24	a3.4	1:30	1:42	p4.4	16	W	8:00	8:30	a3.5	1:36	1:48	p4.6
17	T	8:30	9:00	a3.4	2:06	2:18	p4.4	17	T	8:36	9:12	a3.4	2:18	2:30	p4.5
18	W	9:06	9:42	a3.3	2:42	3:00	p4.3	18	F	9:18	10:00	a3.3	3:00	3:12	p4.4
19	T	9:48	10:24	a3.2	3:24	3:42	p4.2	19	S	10:12	10:48	a3.2	3:48	4:00	p4.2
20	F	10:30	11:18	a3.1	4:06	4:24	p4.1	20	S	11:06	11:48	a3.0	4:42	5:00	p4.1
21	S	11:24	...	3.0	5:00	5:18	p4.0	21	M	...	12:06	3.0	5:36	6:00	p4.0
22	S	12:12	12:24	p2.9	5:54	6:18	p3.9	22	T	12:48	1:12	p3.0	6:42	7:06	p4.0
23	M	1:12	1:30	p3.0	7:00	7:24	p4.0	23	W	1:48	2:18	p3.2	7:42	8:06	p4.2
24	T	2:12	2:30	p3.2	8:00	8:24	p4.3	24	T	2:48	3:18	3.4	8:42	9:12	4.5
25	W	3:12	3:30	p3.5	9:06	9:30	p4.6	25	F	3:42	4:18	3.7	9:42	10:12	a4.9
26	T	4:06	4:30	p3.8	10:00	10:24	p5.0	26	S	4:36	5:12	a4.1	10:36	11:06	a5.3
27	F	5:00	5:24	p4.1	10:54	11:24	5.2	27	S	5:30	6:06	a4.3	11:30	...	5.5
28	S	5:48	6:18	a4.4	11:48	...	5.5	28	M	6:18	6:54	a4.4	12:01	12:18	p5.6
29	S	6:36	7:12	a4.6	12:12	12:36	p5.7	29	T	7:06	7:48	a4.4	12:48	1:06	p5.6
30	M	7:30	8:06	a4.6	1:06	1:30	p5.6	30	W	8:00	8:36	a4.2	1:42	1:54	p5.3
								31	T	8:48	9:30	a3.8	2:36	2:48	p4.9

The Kts. (knots) columns show the **maximum** predicted velocities of the stronger one of the Flood Currents and the stronger one of the Ebb Currents for each day.

The letter "a" means the velocity shown should occur **after** the **a.m.** Current Change. The letter "p" means the velocity shown should occur **after** the **p.m.** Current Change (even if next morning). No "a" or "p" means a.m. and p.m. velocities are the same for that day.

Avg. Max. Velocity: Flood 3.3 Kts., Ebb 4.2 Kts.

Max. Flood 2 hrs. 45 min. after Flood Starts, ±15 min.

Max. Ebb 3 hrs. 25 min. after Ebb Starts, ±15 min.

Use THE RACE tables with current charts pp. 98-103

See pp. 22-29 for Current Change at other points.

*Standard Time starts Nov. 3 at 2 a.m.   Standard Time

DAY OF MONTH	DAY OF WEEK	NORTHWEST Flood Starts			SOUTHEAST Ebb Starts			DAY OF MONTH	DAY OF WEEK	NORTHWEST Flood Starts			SOUTHEAST Ebb Starts		
		a.m.	**p.m.**	Kts.	a.m.	**p.m.**	Kts.			a.m.	**p.m.**	Kts.	a.m.	**p.m.**	Kts.
1	F	9:42	**10:24**	a3.4	3:24	**3:36**	p4.5	1	S	9:12	**9:48**	p3.0	2:48	**3:00**	p3.9
2	S	10:42	**11:18**	a3.0	4:18	**4:30**	p4.0	2	M	10:06	**10:36**	p2.7	3:36	**3:48**	3.6
3	S	*10:42	***11:18**	2.7	*4:12	***4:24**	p3.6	3	T	11:06	**11:24**	p2.6	4:30	**4:36**	a3.4
4	M	11:42	...	2.4	5:06	**5:24**	3.3	4	W	...	**12:01**	2.2	5:18	**5:30**	a3.3
5	T	12:12	**12:42**	a2.6	6:06	**6:18**	a3.3	5	T	12:12	**12:54**	a2.5	6:06	**6:24**	a3.3
6	W	1:06	**1:36**	a2.6	6:54	**7:12**	a3.4	6	F	1:00	**1:42**	a2.6	6:48	**7:18**	a3.5
7	T	1:54	**2:24**	a2.6	7:42	**8:06**	a3.5	7	S	1:48	**2:30**	a2.6	7:36	**8:06**	a3.7
8	F	2:36	**3:12**	a2.8	8:24	**8:54**	a3.8	8	S	2:30	**3:12**	a2.8	8:18	**8:54**	a3.9
9	S	3:19	**3:54**	a2.9	9:06	**9:36**	a4.0	9	M	3:13	**3:54**	a3.0	9:06	**9:36**	a4.2
10	S	4:00	**4:30**	a3.1	9:48	**10:12**	a4.3	10	T	3:54	**4:36**	3.2	9:48	**10:24**	a4.5
11	M	4:36	**5:12**	a3.3	10:24	**10:54**	a4.5	11	W	4:36	**5:18**	3.4	10:30	**11:06**	a4.7
12	T	5:12	**5:48**	3.4	11:00	**11:36**	a4.7	12	T	5:24	**6:00**	3.6	11:12	**11:54**	a4.9
13	W	5:54	**6:24**	3.5	11:42	...	4.8	13	F	6:06	**6:48**	3.7	...	**12:01**	5.0
14	T	6:30	**7:06**	a3.6	12:12	**12:24**	p4.8	14	S	6:54	**7:30**	a3.8	12:36	**12:48**	p5.0
15	F	7:12	**7:54**	a3.5	1:00	**1:06**	p4.8	15	S	7:42	**8:18**	a3.7	1:24	**1:36**	p4.9
16	S	8:00	**8:36**	a3.5	1:42	**1:54**	p4.6	16	M	8:36	**9:12**	p3.6	2:18	**2:30**	p4.7
17	S	8:54	**9:30**	a3.3	2:30	**2:42**	p4.4	17	T	9:36	**10:06**	p3.5	3:12	**3:24**	p4.5
18	M	9:48	**10:24**	3.2	3:24	**3:42**	p4.3	18	W	10:36	**11:06**	p3.5	4:06	**4:24**	a4.3
19	T	10:54	**11:24**	p3.2	4:24	**4:42**	p4.1	19	T	11:42	...	3.1	5:06	**5:30**	a4.3
20	W	...	**12:01**	3.0	5:24	**5:48**	a4.1	20	F	12:06	**12:48**	a3.5	6:06	**6:36**	a4.4
21	T	12:24	**1:06**	a3.3	6:24	**6:54**	a4.3	21	S	1:06	**1:54**	a3.5	7:06	**7:42**	a4.6
22	F	1:24	**2:06**	a3.5	7:24	**7:54**	a4.6	22	S	2:00	**2:54**	a3.6	8:06	**8:42**	a4.8
23	S	2:18	**3:06**	a3.8	8:24	**8:54**	a4.9	23	M	3:00	**3:48**	a3.8	9:00	**9:42**	a5.0
24	S	3:18	**4:00**	a4.0	9:18	**9:54**	a5.2	24	T	3:54	**4:42**	a3.9	9:54	**10:30**	a5.1
25	M	4:06	**4:54**	a4.1	10:12	**10:48**	a5.4	25	W	4:42	**5:30**	a3.9	10:42	**11:24**	a5.1
26	T	5:00	**5:42**	a4.2	11:00	**11:36**	a5.4	26	T	5:36	**6:18**	a3.9	11:30	...	5.0
27	W	5:48	**6:30**	a4.1	11:48	...	5.3	27	F	6:24	**7:00**	3.7	12:06	**12:18**	p4.8
28	T	6:42	**7:18**	a3.9	12:24	**12:36**	p5.1	28	S	7:12	**7:42**	3.5	12:54	**1:00**	p4.6
29	F	7:30	**8:06**	a3.7	1:12	**1:24**	p4.8	29	S	8:00	**8:24**	p3.3	1:36	**1:42**	p4.3
30	S	8:24	**8:54**	a3.3	2:00	**2:12**	p4.4	30	M	8:42	**9:06**	p3.1	2:18	**2:24**	3.9
								31	T	9:30	**9:48**	p2.7	3:00	**3:06**	a3.7

The Kts. (knots) columns show the **maximum** predicted velocities of the stronger one of the Flood Currents and the stronger one of the Ebb Currents for each day.
The letter "a" means the velocity shown should occur **after** the a.m. Current Change. The letter "p" means the velocity shown should occur **after** the p.m. Current Change (even if next morning). No "a" or "p" means a.m. and p.m. velocities are the same for that day.
Avg. Max. Velocity: Flood 3.3 Kts., Ebb 4.2 Kts.
Max. Flood 2 hrs. 45 min. after Flood Starts, ±15 min.
Max. Ebb 3 hrs. 25 min. after Ebb Starts, ±15 min.
Use THE RACE tables with current charts pp. 98-103

See pp. 22-29 for Current Change at other points.

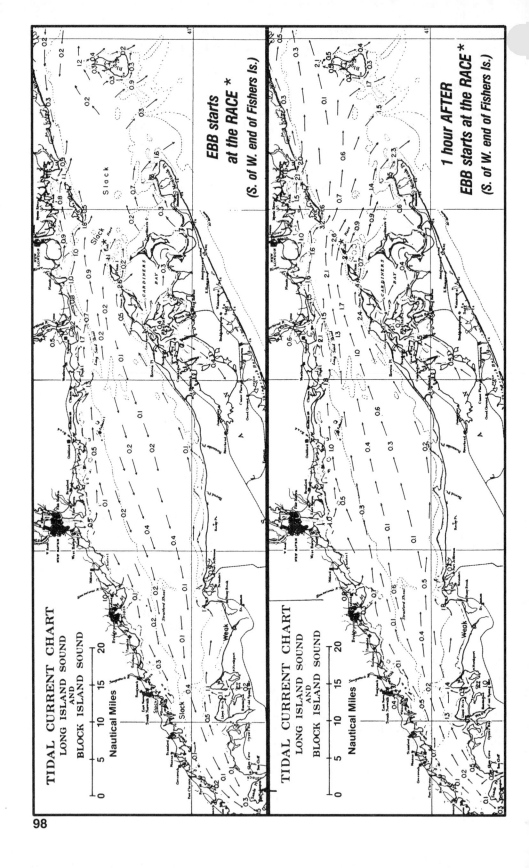

TIDAL CURRENT CHART
LONG ISLAND SOUND
AND
BLOCK ISLAND SOUND

Nautical Miles

EBB starts
at the RACE *
(S. of W. end of Fishers Is.)

TIDAL CURRENT CHART
LONG ISLAND SOUND
AND
BLOCK ISLAND SOUND

Nautical Miles

1 hour AFTER
EBB starts at the RACE *
(S. of W. end of Fishers Is.)

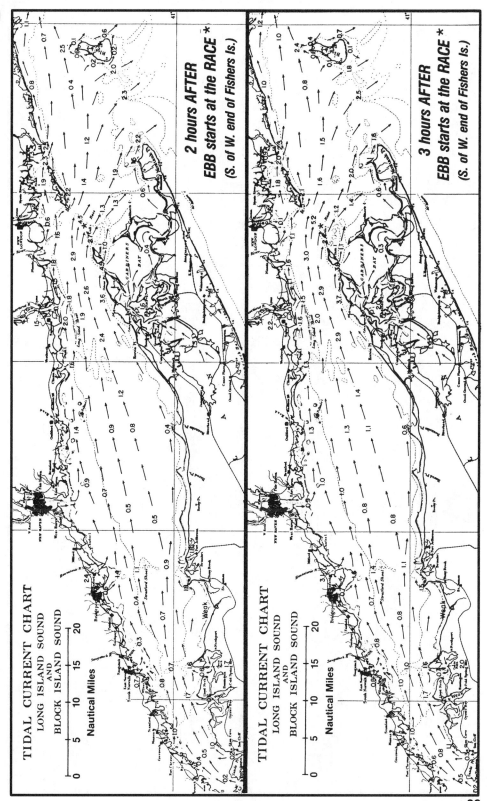

TIDAL CURRENT CHART
LONG ISLAND SOUND
AND
BLOCK ISLAND SOUND

Nautical Miles
0   5   10   15   20

2 hours AFTER
EBB starts at the RACE *
(S. of W. end of Fishers Is.)

TIDAL CURRENT CHART
LONG ISLAND SOUND
AND
BLOCK ISLAND SOUND

Nautical Miles
0   5   10   15   20

3 hours AFTER
EBB starts at the RACE *
(S. of W. end of Fishers Is.)

99

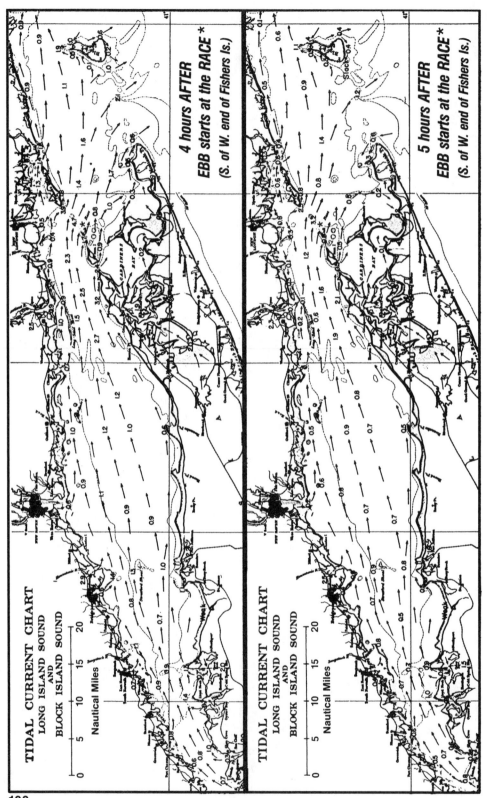

TIDAL CURRENT CHART
LONG ISLAND SOUND
AND
BLOCK ISLAND SOUND

Nautical Miles

4 hours AFTER
EBB starts at the RACE *
(S. of W. end of Fishers Is.)

TIDAL CURRENT CHART
LONG ISLAND SOUND
AND
BLOCK ISLAND SOUND

Nautical Miles

5 hours AFTER
EBB starts at the RACE *
(S. of W. end of Fishers Is.)

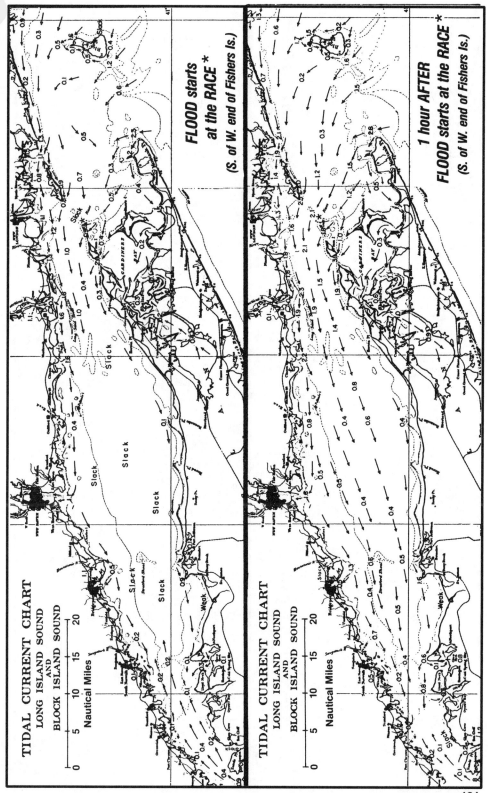

TIDAL CURRENT CHART
LONG ISLAND SOUND
AND
BLOCK ISLAND SOUND

Nautical Miles

FLOOD starts
at the RACE *
(S. of W. end of Fishers Is.)

1 hour AFTER
FLOOD starts at the RACE *
(S. of W. end of Fishers Is.)

101

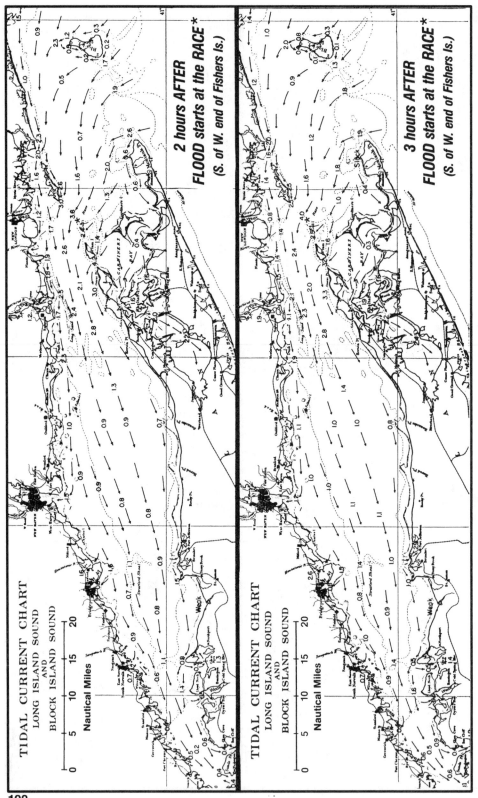

TIDAL CURRENT CHART
LONG ISLAND SOUND
AND
BLOCK ISLAND SOUND

Nautical Miles
0   5   10   15   20

2 hours AFTER
FLOOD starts at the RACE*
(S. of W. end of Fishers Is.)

TIDAL CURRENT CHART
LONG ISLAND SOUND
AND
BLOCK ISLAND SOUND

Nautical Miles
0   5   10   15   20

3 hours AFTER
FLOOD starts at the RACE*
(S. of W. end of Fishers Is.)

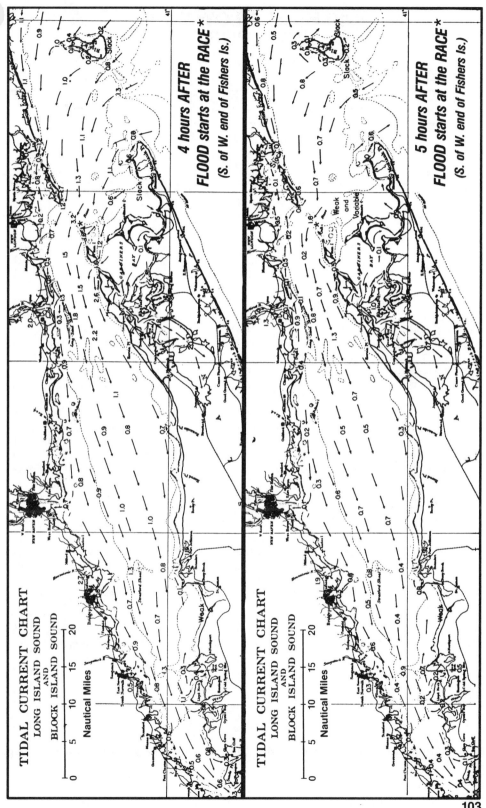

TIDAL CURRENT CHART
LONG ISLAND SOUND
AND
BLOCK ISLAND SOUND

Nautical Miles
0   5   10   15   20

4 hours AFTER
FLOOD starts at the RACE*
(S. of W. end of Fishers Is.)

TIDAL CURRENT CHART
LONG ISLAND SOUND
AND
BLOCK ISLAND SOUND

Nautical Miles
0   5   10   15   20

5 hours AFTER
FLOOD starts at the RACE*
(S. of W. end of Fishers Is.)

2019 HIGH & LOW WATER
BRIDGEPORT, CT
41°10.4'N, 73°10.9'W

		Standard Time								Standard Time					
DAY OF MONTH	**DAY OF WEEK**	**JANUARY**						**DAY OF MONTH**	**DAY OF WEEK**	**FEBRUARY**					
		HIGH				LOW				HIGH				LOW	
		a.m.	Ht.	p.m.	Ht.	a.m.	p.m.			a.m.	Ht.	p.m.	Ht.	a.m.	p.m.
1	T	7:26	7.2	7:58	6.3	1:13	1:56	1	F	8:47	6.8	9:18	6.2	2:36	3:15
2	W	8:18	7.2	8:51	6.4	2:07	2:49	2	S	9:33	6.8	10:03	6.3	3:24	3:59
3	T	9:07	7.3	9:39	6.4	2:57	3:37	3	S	10:16	6.9	10:43	6.4	4:08	4:39
4	F	9:52	7.2	10:23	6.4	3:43	4:20	4	M	10:56	6.9	11:21	6.5	4:48	5:16
5	S	10:35	7.2	11:05	6.5	4:26	5:01	5	T	11:34	6.9	11:58	6.6	5:27	5:52
6	S	11:15	7.1	11:44	6.4	5:07	5:40	6	W	...	...	12:11	6.8	6:04	6:27
7	M	11:55	7.0	...	...	5:47	6:17	7	T	12:34	6.6	12:48	6.7	6:42	7:02
8	T	12:23	6.4	12:34	6.8	6:26	6:55	8	F	1:10	6.6	1:26	6.6	7:20	7:38
9	W	1:03	6.4	1:13	6.6	7:06	7:32	9	S	1:48	6.6	2:05	6.4	8:01	8:16
10	T	1:42	6.3	1:54	6.4	7:48	8:12	10	S	2:26	6.6	2:49	6.2	8:45	8:59
11	F	2:23	6.3	2:38	6.2	8:32	8:54	11	M	3:08	6.5	3:38	6.0	9:34	9:46
12	S	3:06	6.2	3:24	6.0	9:20	9:39	12	T	3:57	6.5	4:33	5.8	10:29	10:40
13	S	3:52	6.2	4:16	5.8	10:13	10:28	13	W	4:52	6.6	5:34	5.8	11:30	11:40
14	M	4:42	6.3	5:12	5.8	11:09	11:21	14	T	5:53	6.7	6:37	5.9	...	12:33
15	T	5:35	6.4	6:10	5.8	...	12:07	15	F	6:56	6.9	7:39	6.1	12:43	1:35
16	W	6:30	6.7	7:09	5.9	12:17	1:05	16	S	7:58	7.2	8:37	6.5	1:45	2:34
17	T	7:26	6.9	8:06	6.1	1:13	2:02	17	S	8:56	7.6	9:32	6.9	2:45	3:29
18	F	8:21	7.3	9:00	6.4	2:09	2:57	18	M	9:52	7.9	10:24	7.3	3:41	4:21
19	S	9:15	7.6	9:53	6.8	3:04	3:49	19	T	10:45	8.1	11:15	7.7	4:35	5:11
20	S	10:08	7.9	10:44	7.1	3:57	4:41	20	W	11:37	8.1	...	...	5:28	5:59
21	M	11:00	8.1	11:34	7.3	4:50	5:31	21	T	12:04	7.9	12:27	8.0	6:20	6:47
22	T	11:52	8.1	...	...	5:43	6:21	22	F	12:54	8.0	1:18	7.7	7:12	7:36
23	W	12:25	7.5	12:45	8.0	6:36	7:11	23	S	1:44	7.8	2:10	7.3	8:06	8:26
24	T	1:17	7.5	1:38	7.7	7:31	8:02	24	S	2:35	7.6	3:05	6.8	9:01	9:19
25	F	2:10	7.5	2:33	7.3	8:28	8:55	25	M	3:30	7.2	4:02	6.4	9:59	10:15
26	S	3:05	7.3	3:30	6.8	9:27	9:50	26	T	4:27	6.9	5:03	6.0	10:59	11:15
27	S	4:02	7.2	4:31	6.4	10:28	10:48	27	W	5:27	6.6	6:06	5.9	...	12:01
28	M	5:01	7.0	5:33	6.2	11:31	11:47	28	T	6:29	6.4	7:07	5.9	12:17	1:02
29	T	6:00	6.9	6:35	6.0	...	12:33								
30	W	6:59	6.8	7:35	6.0	12:46	1:33								
31	T	7:55	6.8	8:30	6.1	1:43	2:27								

Dates when Ht. of **Low** Water is below Mean Lower Low with Ht. of lowest given for each period and Date of lowest in ( ):

1st–7th: -0.4' (4th)   3rd–5th: -0.2'
18th–26th: -1.3' (22nd)   16th–24th: -1.3' (20th)

Average Rise and Fall 6.8 ft.

When a high tide exceeds avg. ht., the *following* low tide will be lower than avg.

2019 HIGH & LOW WATER
BRIDGEPORT, CT
41°10.4'N, 73°10.9'W

*Daylight Time starts March 10 at 2 a.m.   **Daylight Saving Time**

DAY OF MONTH	DAY OF WEEK	MARCH HIGH a.m.	Ht.	p.m.	Ht.	LOW a.m.	p.m.	DAY OF MONTH	DAY OF WEEK	APRIL HIGH a.m.	Ht.	p.m.	Ht.	LOW a.m.	p.m.
1	F	7:28	6.4	8:03	6.0	1:17	1:58	1	M	9:40	6.5	10:04	6.6	3:32	3:55
2	S	8:22	6.5	8:52	6.2	2:12	2:48	2	T	10:25	6.6	10:45	6.9	4:17	4:36
3	S	9:11	6.6	9:37	6.4	3:02	3:31	3	W	11:05	6.8	11:23	7.1	4:59	5:14
4	M	9:54	6.7	10:17	6.6	3:46	4:11	4	T	11:44	6.9	11:58	7.3	5:38	5:50
5	T	10:34	6.8	10:55	6.8	4:26	4:48	5	F	...	...	12:21	6.9	6:15	6:26
6	W	11:11	6.9	11:30	6.9	5:04	5:23	6	S	12:33	7.4	12:58	6.9	6:53	7:02
7	T	11:47	6.9	...	...	5:41	5:57	7	S	1:08	7.4	1:36	6.9	7:31	7:39
8	F	12:04	7.0	12:23	6.8	6:18	6:31	8	M	1:44	7.4	2:17	6.8	8:11	8:19
9	S	12:40	7.0	1:00	6.7	6:55	7:07	9	T	2:25	7.4	3:01	6.6	8:55	9:03
10	S	1:13	7.0	*2:39	6.6	*8:34	*8:45	10	W	3:08	7.3	3:51	6.4	9:44	9:54
11	M	2:51	7.0	3:22	6.4	9:16	9:27	11	T	4:00	7.1	4:47	6.3	10:40	10:53
12	T	3:33	6.9	4:10	6.2	10:04	10:15	12	F	5:00	7.0	5:49	6.3	11:42	11:58
13	W	4:22	6.8	5:05	6.0	10:59	11:11	13	S	6:07	6.9	6:54	6.4	...	12:47
14	T	5:20	6.8	6:08	6.0	...	12:01	14	S	7:16	7.0	7:57	6.8	1:07	1:50
15	F	6:25	6.8	7:13	6.1	12:15	1:07	15	M	8:21	7.2	8:56	7.2	2:13	2:50
16	S	7:33	6.9	8:17	6.4	1:22	2:12	16	T	9:22	7.4	9:51	7.7	3:14	3:44
17	S	8:39	7.2	9:17	6.8	2:27	3:12	17	W	10:18	7.6	10:42	8.1	4:11	4:36
18	M	9:40	7.6	10:12	7.3	3:29	4:08	18	T	11:10	7.8	11:31	8.3	5:04	5:24
19	T	10:36	7.8	11:04	7.8	4:26	4:59	19	F	...	...	12:01	7.8	5:55	6:11
20	W	11:28	8.0	11:53	8.1	5:20	5:48	20	S	12:18	8.4	12:48	7.6	6:43	6:56
21	T	...	...	12:19	8.0	6:12	6:35	21	S	1:04	8.3	1:35	7.4	7:31	7:42
22	F	12:41	8.3	1:08	7.9	7:02	7:22	22	M	1:50	8.1	2:23	7.1	8:18	8:29
23	S	1:29	8.3	1:57	7.6	7:52	8:09	23	T	2:36	7.7	3:12	6.8	9:06	9:18
24	S	2:17	8.1	2:47	7.2	8:42	8:57	24	W	3:25	7.2	4:03	6.5	9:56	10:10
25	M	3:05	7.7	3:38	6.8	9:34	9:48	25	T	4:18	6.8	4:57	6.2	10:48	11:06
26	T	3:57	7.3	4:33	6.4	10:27	10:42	26	F	5:14	6.4	5:54	6.1	11:43	...
27	W	4:52	6.8	5:31	6.1	11:24	11:41	27	S	6:13	6.2	6:51	6.2	12:06	12:39
28	T	5:51	6.5	6:31	5.9	...	12:24	28	S	7:13	6.1	7:46	6.3	1:06	1:34
29	F	6:53	6.2	7:32	6.0	12:43	1:24	29	M	8:09	6.2	8:37	6.5	2:03	2:25
30	S	7:54	6.2	8:28	6.1	1:45	2:20	30	T	9:01	6.3	9:24	6.8	2:55	3:11
31	S	8:50	6.3	9:19	6.4	2:41	3:10								

Dates when Ht. of **Low** Water is below Mean Lower Low with Ht. of lowest given for each period and Date of lowest in ( ):

    17th–25th: -1.2' (21st, 22nd)   7th: -0.2'
                                          16th–23rd: -1.0' (19th, 20th)

Average Rise and Fall 6.8 ft.

When a high tide exceeds avg. ht., the *following* low tide will be lower than avg.

2019 HIGH & LOW WATER
BRIDGEPORT, CT
41°10.4'N, 73°10.9'W

<table>
<tr><td colspan="7" align="center">Daylight Saving Time</td><td colspan="7" align="center">Daylight Saving Time</td></tr>
</table>

DAY OF MONTH	DAY OF WEEK	MAY						DAY OF MONTH	DAY OF WEEK	JUNE					
		HIGH				LOW				HIGH				LOW	
		a.m.	Ht.	p.m.	Ht.	a.m.	p.m.			a.m.	Ht.	p.m.	Ht.	a.m.	p.m.
1	W	9:48	6.5	10:07	7.1	3:43	3:54	1	S	10:39	6.6	10:49	7.6	4:35	4:39
2	T	10:31	6.6	10:46	7.3	4:26	4:35	2	S	11:24	6.8	11:31	7.8	5:19	5:23
3	F	11:13	6.8	11:24	7.5	5:08	5:15	3	M	...	...	12:08	6.9	6:03	6:07
4	S	11:53	6.9	...	...	5:48	5:54	4	T	12:15	7.9	12:54	7.0	6:48	6:54
5	S	12:01	7.6	12:33	6.9	6:28	6:33	5	W	1:00	8.0	1:41	7.1	7:35	7:42
6	M	12:39	7.7	1:15	6.9	7:09	7:15	6	T	1:49	7.9	2:30	7.1	8:24	8:34
7	T	1:20	7.7	1:58	6.9	7:52	7:59	7	F	2:41	7.8	3:23	7.1	9:16	9:31
8	W	2:04	7.7	2:45	6.8	8:38	8:47	8	S	3:36	7.6	4:19	7.1	10:10	10:31
9	T	2:53	7.6	3:37	6.7	9:29	9:41	9	S	4:37	7.4	5:18	7.2	11:07	11:35
10	F	3:47	7.4	4:34	6.7	10:25	10:42	10	M	5:39	7.2	6:17	7.3	...	12:06
11	S	4:48	7.2	5:34	6.7	11:25	11:47	11	T	6:42	7.0	7:17	7.5	12:39	1:04
12	S	5:53	7.1	6:36	6.9	...	12:27	12	W	7:45	6.9	8:14	7.7	1:43	2:02
13	M	7:00	7.0	7:38	7.2	12:54	1:28	13	T	8:45	6.9	9:08	7.9	2:43	2:57
14	T	8:04	7.1	8:36	7.6	1:58	2:26	14	F	9:41	6.9	10:00	8.0	3:39	3:49
15	W	9:04	7.2	9:30	7.9	2:59	3:20	15	S	10:33	7.0	10:48	8.0	4:31	4:39
16	T	9:59	7.3	10:21	8.2	3:56	4:12	16	S	11:22	7.0	11:35	7.9	5:20	5:26
17	F	10:52	7.4	11:09	8.3	4:48	5:00	17	M	...	...	12:09	7.0	6:05	6:12
18	S	11:41	7.3	11:55	8.3	5:37	5:47	18	T	12:19	7.8	12:53	6.9	6:49	6:56
19	S	...	...	12:28	7.3	6:24	6:33	19	W	1:03	7.6	1:37	6.8	7:31	7:39
20	M	12:40	8.1	1:14	7.1	7:10	7:18	20	T	1:46	7.4	2:19	6.8	8:12	8:23
21	T	1:25	7.9	2:00	6.9	7:54	8:03	21	F	2:29	7.1	3:03	6.7	8:54	9:08
22	W	2:10	7.5	2:46	6.8	8:39	8:50	22	S	3:14	6.8	3:48	6.6	9:36	9:56
23	T	2:57	7.2	3:33	6.6	9:25	9:39	23	S	4:01	6.6	4:34	6.6	10:20	10:46
24	F	3:45	6.8	4:23	6.4	10:12	10:31	24	M	4:50	6.3	5:22	6.6	11:06	11:39
25	S	4:37	6.5	5:14	6.3	11:01	11:26	25	T	5:42	6.2	6:11	6.7	11:54	...
26	S	5:32	6.2	6:07	6.4	11:52	...	26	W	6:35	6.1	7:01	6.8	12:33	12:44
27	M	6:27	6.1	7:00	6.5	12:23	12:43	27	T	7:30	6.1	7:51	6.9	1:28	1:34
28	T	7:23	6.1	7:51	6.7	1:19	1:34	28	F	8:23	6.1	8:40	7.2	2:21	2:25
29	W	8:16	6.2	8:39	6.9	2:13	2:23	29	S	9:16	6.3	9:28	7.4	3:12	3:16
30	T	9:06	6.3	9:24	7.2	3:03	3:09	30	S	10:06	6.5	10:16	7.7	4:02	4:05
31	F	9:54	6.4	10:07	7.4	3:50	3:55								

Dates when Ht. of **Low** Water is below Mean Lower Low with Ht. of lowest given for each period and Date of lowest in ( ):

5th–8th: -0.3' (6th, 7th)   3rd–8th: -0.4' (4th–6th)
16th–21st: -0.7' (18th, 19th)   14th–18th: -0.4' (16th)

Average Rise and Fall 6.8 ft.

When a high tide exceeds avg. ht., the *following* low tide will be lower than avg.

2019 HIGH & LOW WATER
BRIDGEPORT, CT
41°10.4'N, 73°10.9'W

Daylight Saving Time

Daylight Saving Time

DAY OF MONTH	DAY OF WEEK	JULY						DAY OF MONTH	DAY OF WEEK	AUGUST					
		HIGH				LOW				HIGH				LOW	
		a.m.	Ht.	p.m.	Ht.	a.m.	p.m.			a.m.	Ht.	p.m.	Ht.	a.m.	p.m.
1	M	10:55	6.7	11:05	7.9	4:51	4:55	1	T	...	...	12:10	7.5	6:06	6:17
2	T	11:44	7.0	11:53	8.1	5:39	5:44	2	F	12:26	8.4	1:01	7.7	6:55	7:11
3	W	...	...	12:32	7.2	6:28	6:35	3	S	1:18	8.3	1:51	7.9	7:45	8:05
4	T	12:43	8.2	1:22	7.3	7:17	7:27	4	S	2:11	8.1	2:43	8.0	8:35	9:01
5	F	1:34	8.2	2:13	7.4	8:07	8:21	5	M	3:05	7.8	3:37	8.0	9:27	9:58
6	S	2:28	8.0	3:05	7.5	8:58	9:18	6	T	4:01	7.4	4:32	7.9	10:20	10:58
7	S	3:23	7.8	4:00	7.6	9:51	10:17	7	W	5:00	7.1	5:30	7.7	11:17	...
8	M	4:21	7.5	4:57	7.6	10:46	11:19	8	T	6:01	6.7	6:29	7.5	12:01	12:15
9	T	5:22	7.1	5:55	7.6	11:42	...	9	F	7:05	6.5	7:29	7.4	1:03	1:15
10	W	6:23	6.9	6:54	7.7	12:22	12:40	10	S	8:05	6.5	8:27	7.3	2:04	2:14
11	T	7:25	6.7	7:52	7.7	1:24	1:38	11	S	9:03	6.5	9:22	7.3	3:01	3:10
12	F	8:25	6.6	8:48	7.7	2:24	2:35	12	M	9:55	6.6	10:12	7.3	3:53	4:02
13	S	9:22	6.6	9:40	7.7	3:21	3:29	13	T	10:43	6.7	10:57	7.3	4:40	4:49
14	S	10:15	6.7	10:30	7.7	4:13	4:20	14	W	11:26	6.8	11:39	7.3	5:22	5:32
15	M	11:04	6.8	11:16	7.6	5:01	5:08	15	T	...	...	12:06	6.9	6:01	6:13
16	T	11:49	6.8	...	...	5:46	5:52	16	F	12:19	7.3	12:44	7.0	6:38	6:51
17	W	12:01	7.5	12:31	6.8	6:27	6:35	17	S	12:58	7.2	1:21	7.1	7:13	7:30
18	T	12:42	7.4	1:12	6.8	7:06	7:16	18	S	1:35	7.1	1:57	7.1	7:48	8:09
19	F	1:22	7.3	1:51	6.8	7:44	7:57	19	M	2:13	6.9	2:34	7.1	8:24	8:49
20	S	2:03	7.1	2:31	6.8	8:22	8:38	20	T	2:53	6.7	3:13	7.0	9:02	9:31
21	S	2:44	6.9	3:11	6.8	9:00	9:22	21	W	3:35	6.5	3:54	7.0	9:42	10:18
22	M	3:26	6.7	3:53	6.8	9:40	10:07	22	T	4:22	6.3	4:39	6.9	10:27	11:10
23	T	4:11	6.4	4:37	6.8	10:22	10:56	23	F	5:13	6.2	5:30	6.9	11:18	...
24	W	4:59	6.2	5:23	6.8	11:08	11:49	24	S	6:10	6.1	6:27	7.0	12:06	12:14
25	T	5:51	6.1	6:13	6.8	11:57	...	25	S	7:11	6.2	7:27	7.2	1:06	1:15
26	F	6:47	6.1	7:06	7.0	12:44	12:51	26	M	8:11	6.4	8:28	7.4	2:07	2:15
27	S	7:44	6.1	8:00	7.2	1:41	1:46	27	T	9:09	6.7	9:26	7.8	3:05	3:15
28	S	8:40	6.3	8:55	7.4	2:37	2:42	28	W	10:04	7.1	10:22	8.1	4:00	4:11
29	M	9:35	6.5	9:49	7.7	3:32	3:37	29	T	10:56	7.5	11:16	8.3	4:52	5:06
30	T	10:28	6.8	10:42	8.0	4:25	4:31	30	F	11:47	7.9	...	...	5:42	6:00
31	W	11:20	7.2	11:34	8.2	5:16	5:24	31	S	12:08	8.4	12:37	8.2	6:31	6:53

Dates when Ht. of **Low** Water is below Mean Lower Low with Ht. of lowest given for each period and Date of lowest in ( ):

2nd–8th: -0.6' (4th–6th)
31st: -0.4'

1st–6th: -0.8' (2nd, 3rd)
29th–31st: -0.8' (31st)

Average Rise and Fall 6.8 ft.

When a high tide exceeds avg. ht., the *following* low tide will be lower than avg.

2019 HIGH & LOW WATER
BRIDGEPORT, CT
41°10.4'N, 73°10.9'W

Daylight Saving Time | Daylight Saving Time

D A Y O F M O N T H	D A Y O F W E E K	SEPTEMBER						D A Y O F M O N T H	D A Y O F W E E K	OCTOBER					
		HIGH				LOW				HIGH				LOW	
		a.m.	Ht.	p.m.	Ht.	a.m.	p.m.			a.m.	Ht.	p.m.	Ht.	a.m.	p.m.
1	S	12:59	8.4	1:27	8.4	7:20	7:46	1	T	1:30	7.9	1:51	8.5	7:42	8:18
2	M	1:51	8.1	2:18	8.4	8:09	8:40	2	W	2:21	7.6	2:42	8.2	8:32	9:11
3	T	2:44	7.8	3:10	8.2	9:00	9:36	3	T	3:15	7.2	3:35	7.8	9:25	10:07
4	W	3:39	7.3	4:05	7.9	9:53	10:34	4	F	4:11	6.8	4:32	7.3	10:22	11:06
5	T	4:37	6.9	5:02	7.6	10:50	11:35	5	S	5:11	6.5	5:33	7.0	11:22	...
6	F	5:38	6.6	6:03	7.3	11:50	...	6	S	6:12	6.3	6:35	6.7	12:07	12:25
7	S	6:40	6.4	7:04	7.1	12:37	12:52	7	M	7:13	6.3	7:36	6.7	1:07	1:26
8	S	7:42	6.4	8:05	7.0	1:38	1:53	8	T	8:10	6.5	8:32	6.7	2:03	2:23
9	M	8:41	6.5	9:00	7.0	2:36	2:50	9	W	9:01	6.7	9:21	6.8	2:53	3:14
10	T	9:31	6.6	9:50	7.1	3:27	3:41	10	T	9:46	6.9	10:06	6.9	3:38	4:00
11	W	10:17	6.8	10:35	7.2	4:12	4:27	11	F	10:27	7.1	10:47	7.0	4:18	4:42
12	T	10:59	7.0	11:15	7.2	4:53	5:09	12	S	11:05	7.3	11:26	7.0	4:56	5:21
13	F	11:37	7.1	11:54	7.2	5:31	5:48	13	S	11:41	7.4	...	...	5:32	5:58
14	S	...	...	12:14	7.2	6:06	6:25	14	M	12:03	7.0	12:16	7.4	6:07	6:35
15	S	12:31	7.2	12:49	7.3	6:40	7:02	15	T	12:40	7.0	12:50	7.4	6:43	7:13
16	M	1:08	7.1	1:23	7.3	7:15	7:40	16	W	1:18	6.9	1:26	7.4	7:19	7:52
17	T	1:45	6.9	1:58	7.3	7:50	8:18	17	T	1:57	6.7	2:04	7.3	7:58	8:34
18	W	2:23	6.8	2:35	7.2	8:27	9:00	18	F	2:40	6.6	2:46	7.2	8:41	9:21
19	T	3:05	6.6	3:16	7.1	9:08	9:46	19	S	3:28	6.4	3:36	7.1	9:29	10:14
20	F	3:51	6.4	4:02	7.0	9:54	10:38	20	S	4:22	6.3	4:33	7.0	10:26	11:14
21	S	4:44	6.2	4:57	7.0	10:47	11:37	21	M	5:21	6.3	5:37	7.0	11:29	...
22	S	5:43	6.2	5:58	7.0	11:48	...	22	T	6:24	6.4	6:44	7.1	12:17	12:35
23	M	6:45	6.3	7:03	7.1	12:39	12:52	23	W	7:26	6.8	7:49	7.3	1:19	1:40
24	T	7:47	6.6	8:07	7.4	1:42	1:56	24	T	8:25	7.2	8:49	7.5	2:18	2:42
25	W	8:46	7.0	9:07	7.7	2:41	2:57	25	F	9:20	7.7	9:46	7.7	3:13	3:39
26	T	9:41	7.4	10:04	8.0	3:36	3:55	26	S	10:12	8.1	10:39	7.8	4:04	4:33
27	F	10:33	7.9	10:57	8.2	4:28	4:49	27	S	11:01	8.5	11:30	7.9	4:53	5:25
28	S	11:24	8.3	11:49	8.3	5:18	5:42	28	M	11:50	8.6	...	...	5:41	6:16
29	S	...	...	12:13	8.6	6:06	6:34	29	T	12:19	7.8	12:37	8.6	6:29	7:05
30	M	12:39	8.1	1:02	8.6	6:54	7:26	30	W	1:09	7.5	1:25	8.3	7:17	7:55
								31	T	1:59	7.2	2:15	7.9	8:06	8:45

Dates when Ht. of **Low** Water is below Mean Lower Low with Ht. of lowest given for each period and Date of lowest in ( ):

1st–3rd: -0.8' (1st)   1st–2nd: -0.6' (1st)
27th–30th: -0.9' (29th)   25th–31st: -1.0' (28th)

Average Rise and Fall 6.8 ft.

When a high tide exceeds avg. ht., the *following* low tide will be lower than avg.

2019 HIGH & LOW WATER
BRIDGEPORT, CT
41°10.4'N, 73°10.9'W

*Standard Time starts Nov. 3 at 2 a.m.   Standard Time

DAY OF MONTH	DAY OF WEEK	NOVEMBER						DAY OF MONTH	DAY OF WEEK	DECEMBER					
		HIGH				LOW				HIGH				LOW	
		a.m.	Ht.	p.m.	Ht.	a.m.	p.m.			a.m.	Ht.	p.m.	Ht.	a.m.	p.m.
1	F	2:50	6.9	3:06	7.5	8:57	9:38	1	S	2:14	6.5	2:29	6.8	8:21	8:57
2	S	3:43	6.6	4:01	7.0	9:52	10:33	2	M	3:05	6.3	3:22	6.4	9:15	9:47
3	S	*3:40	6.4	*3:59	6.6	*9:50	*10:30	3	T	3:58	6.2	4:17	6.2	10:11	10:39
4	M	4:38	6.2	4:59	6.4	10:51	11:26	4	W	4:52	6.2	5:14	6.0	11:09	11:31
5	T	5:36	6.2	5:59	6.3	11:52	...	5	T	5:46	6.3	6:10	5.9	...	12:05
6	W	6:32	6.4	6:54	6.3	12:21	12:48	6	F	6:37	6.4	7:03	6.0	12:21	12:59
7	T	7:22	6.6	7:45	6.4	1:11	1:40	7	S	7:25	6.6	7:53	6.1	1:10	1:49
8	F	8:08	6.8	8:32	6.5	1:56	2:27	8	S	8:10	6.8	8:39	6.2	1:56	2:35
9	S	8:52	7.1	9:15	6.6	2:39	3:10	9	M	8:54	7.1	9:24	6.3	2:40	3:19
10	S	9:30	7.3	9:55	6.7	3:19	3:51	10	T	9:34	7.2	10:07	6.5	3:23	4:02
11	M	10:07	7.4	10:35	6.8	3:57	4:30	11	W	10:15	7.4	10:49	6.6	4:05	4:44
12	T	10:44	7.5	11:14	6.8	4:35	5:09	12	T	10:55	7.5	11:32	6.7	4:48	5:26
13	W	11:21	7.5	11:54	6.7	5:13	5:48	13	F	11:38	7.5	...	...	5:31	6:10
14	T	11:59	7.5	...	...	5:53	6:29	14	S	12:16	6.7	12:23	7.5	6:17	6:57
15	F	12:35	6.7	12:40	7.4	6:35	7:14	15	S	1:02	6.7	1:12	7.4	7:06	7:46
16	S	1:20	6.6	1:26	7.3	7:21	8:03	16	M	1:52	6.7	2:05	7.3	7:59	8:38
17	S	2:09	6.5	2:18	7.2	8:12	8:56	17	T	2:46	6.7	3:02	7.1	8:57	9:34
18	M	3:04	6.4	3:17	7.0	9:10	9:55	18	W	3:43	6.8	4:04	6.8	9:59	10:32
19	T	4:03	6.5	4:21	6.9	10:14	10:56	19	T	4:43	6.9	5:08	6.7	11:04	11:32
20	W	5:04	6.7	5:26	6.9	11:20	11:56	20	F	5:43	7.1	6:12	6.6	...	12:09
21	T	6:05	7.0	6:31	7.0	...	12:25	21	S	6:42	7.3	7:13	6.6	12:30	1:11
22	F	7:04	7.3	7:31	7.1	12:54	1:27	22	S	7:39	7.6	8:12	6.7	1:27	2:10
23	S	7:59	7.8	8:28	7.2	1:49	2:24	23	M	8:33	7.7	9:06	6.8	2:22	3:04
24	S	8:51	8.1	9:22	7.3	2:41	3:18	24	T	9:24	7.8	9:57	6.8	3:14	3:55
25	M	9:41	8.3	10:12	7.3	3:32	4:10	25	W	10:12	7.8	10:45	6.8	4:03	4:43
26	T	10:29	8.3	11:01	7.3	4:20	4:58	26	T	10:59	7.7	11:31	6.8	4:50	5:28
27	W	11:16	8.2	11:49	7.1	5:07	5:46	27	F	11:44	7.5	...	...	5:36	6:12
28	T	...	...	12:03	7.9	5:55	6:33	28	S	12:15	6.7	12:28	7.3	6:21	6:54
29	F	12:37	6.9	12:50	7.6	6:42	7:20	29	S	12:59	6.6	1:13	7.0	7:05	7:36
30	S	1:25	6.7	1:39	7.2	7:31	8:07	30	M	1:43	6.4	1:58	6.7	7:51	8:19
								31	T	2:28	6.3	2:44	6.3	8:38	9:04

Dates when Ht. of **Low** Water is below Mean Lower Low with Ht. of lowest given for each period and Date of lowest in ( ):

23rd–29th: -1.0' (26th)   10th–17th: -0.5' (12th–14th)
                                  21st–28th: -0.8' (24th, 25th)

Average Rise and Fall 6.8 ft.

When a high tide exceeds avg. ht., the *following* low tide will be lower than avg.

2019 HIGH & LOW WATER
KINGS POINT, NY
40°48.7'N, 73°45.9'W

		Standard Time							Standard Time				
		JANUARY							**FEBRUARY**				
DAY OF MONTH	DAY OF WEEK	HIGH				LOW		DAY OF MONTH	DAY OF WEEK	HIGH				LOW	

DAY OF MONTH	DAY OF WEEK	a.m.	Ht.	p.m.	Ht.	a.m.	p.m.	DAY OF MONTH	DAY OF WEEK	a.m.	Ht.	p.m.	Ht.	a.m.	p.m.
1	T	8:01	8.0	**8:34**	7.1	2:01	**2:41**	1	F	9:23	7.6	**9:52**	7.0	3:25	**4:00**
2	W	8:53	8.1	**9:25**	7.1	2:55	**3:33**	2	S	10:08	7.7	**10:36**	7.1	4:13	**4:44**
3	T	9:40	8.1	**10:12**	7.2	3:45	**4:21**	3	S	10:49	7.6	**11:16**	7.1	4:56	**5:25**
4	F	10:24	8.0	**10:55**	7.2	4:32	**5:06**	4	M	11:26	7.6	**11:51**	7.1	5:35	**6:02**
5	S	11:04	7.9	**11:35**	7.1	5:15	**5:48**	5	T	11:56	7.5	...	...	6:07	**6:31**
6	S	11:40	7.7	...	...	5:54	**6:26**	6	W	12:20	7.1	**12:16**	7.3	6:25	**6:40**
7	M	12:13	7.0	**12:11**	7.5	6:25	**6:58**	7	T	12:36	7.0	**12:35**	7.3	6:36	**6:52**
8	T	12:45	6.9	**12:33**	7.3	6:37	**7:11**	8	F	12:54	7.1	**1:06**	7.2	7:06	**7:22**
9	W	1:10	6.8	**12:59**	7.2	6:54	**7:21**	9	S	1:26	7.2	**1:43**	7.1	7:43	**8:00**
10	T	1:31	6.7	**1:33**	7.0	7:29	**7:53**	10	S	2:03	7.2	**2:26**	7.0	8:26	**8:43**
11	F	2:02	6.8	**2:13**	6.9	8:11	**8:33**	11	M	2:46	7.3	**3:13**	6.8	9:14	**9:30**
12	S	2:41	6.8	**2:58**	6.7	8:57	**9:18**	12	T	3:33	7.3	**4:05**	6.6	10:06	**10:22**
13	S	3:24	6.8	**3:47**	6.5	9:48	**10:07**	13	W	4:26	7.3	**5:04**	6.4	11:06	**11:20**
14	M	4:12	6.9	**4:41**	6.4	10:44	**10:59**	14	T	5:25	7.3	**6:10**	6.4	...	**12:15**
15	T	5:05	7.0	**5:40**	6.3	11:45	**11:55**	15	F	6:30	7.4	**7:23**	6.7	12:23	**1:45**
16	W	6:02	7.2	**6:45**	6.4	...	**12:53**	16	S	7:41	7.7	**8:34**	7.1	1:33	**3:05**
17	T	7:02	7.5	**7:51**	6.7	12:54	**2:11**	17	S	8:49	8.1	**9:34**	7.6	2:49	**4:03**
18	F	8:03	7.9	**8:51**	7.0	1:55	**3:19**	18	M	9:50	8.5	**10:28**	8.0	3:59	**4:55**
19	S	9:00	8.3	**9:46**	7.4	2:57	**4:16**	19	T	10:45	8.8	**11:19**	8.4	4:58	**5:43**
20	S	9:55	8.6	**10:38**	7.7	3:58	**5:07**	20	W	11:38	8.8	...	...	5:52	**6:30**
21	M	10:49	8.8	**11:30**	7.9	4:57	**5:57**	21	T	12:10	8.6	**12:31**	8.7	6:46	**7:17**
22	T	11:43	8.8	...	...	5:53	**6:46**	22	F	1:01	8.6	**1:25**	8.3	7:40	**8:05**
23	W	12:24	8.1	**12:39**	8.6	6:49	**7:37**	23	S	1:53	8.5	**2:22**	7.9	8:38	**8:58**
24	T	1:19	8.1	**1:37**	8.3	7:49	**8:31**	24	S	2:48	8.2	**3:23**	7.4	9:41	**9:58**
25	F	2:17	8.1	**2:39**	7.9	8:56	**9:29**	25	M	3:48	7.8	**4:30**	6.9	10:47	**11:04**
26	S	3:19	7.9	**3:46**	7.4	10:07	**10:32**	26	T	4:55	7.4	**5:40**	6.6	11:51	**...**
27	S	4:24	7.8	**4:58**	7.0	11:15	**11:36**	27	W	6:04	7.2	**6:46**	6.5	12:09	**12:52**
28	M	5:31	7.6	**6:09**	6.7	...	**12:20**	28	T	7:10	7.1	**7:47**	6.6	1:11	**1:50**
29	T	6:37	7.5	**7:14**	6.7	12:38	**1:20**								
30	W	7:37	7.5	**8:13**	6.7	1:37	**2:17**								
31	T	8:33	7.6	**9:05**	6.9	2:33	**3:11**								

Dates when Ht. of **Low** Water is below Mean Lower Low with Ht. of lowest given for each period and Date of lowest in ( ):

1st–7th: -0.8' (2nd–4th)	1st–5th: -0.5' (1st–3rd)
18th–31st: -1.4' (21st, 22nd)	16th–25th: -1.5' (20th)

Average Rise and Fall 7.1 ft.

When a high tide exceeds avg. ht., the *following* low tide will be lower than avg.

2019 HIGH & LOW WATER
KINGS POINT, NY
40°48.7'N, 73°45.9'W

*Daylight Time starts March 10 at 2 a.m.   Daylight Saving Time

D A Y O F M O N T H	D A Y O F W E E K	MARCH						D A Y O F M O N T H	D A Y O F W E E K	APRIL					
		HIGH				LOW				HIGH				LOW	
		a.m.	Ht.	p.m.	Ht.	a.m.	p.m.			a.m.	Ht.	p.m.	Ht.	a.m.	p.m.
1	F	8:09	7.1	8:40	6.8	2:08	2:44	1	M	10:18	7.2	10:41	7.3	4:20	4:44
2	S	9:01	7.3	9:28	7.0	3:01	3:33	2	T	11:00	7.4	11:19	7.5	5:04	5:23
3	S	9:47	7.4	10:11	7.2	3:49	4:18	3	W	11:36	7.5	11:50	7.6	5:43	5:57
4	M	10:28	7.5	10:50	7.3	4:33	4:58	4	T	...	...	12:06	7.5	6:17	6:19
5	T	11:05	7.5	11:24	7.4	5:12	5:33	5	F	12:09	7.7	12:26	7.5	6:41	6:28
6	W	11:35	7.5	11:49	7.4	5:45	5:58	6	S	12:20	7.9	12:45	7.5	6:56	6:52
7	T	11:54	7.4	11:59	7.4	6:06	6:05	7	S	12:46	8.0	1:16	7.5	7:22	7:27
8	F	...	...	12:11	7.4	6:17	6:22	8	M	1:22	8.1	1:54	7.5	7:58	8:06
9	S	12:20	7.6	12:40	7.4	6:43	6:53	9	T	2:04	8.2	2:38	7.4	8:39	8:50
10	S	12:52	7.7	*2:17	7.3	*8:19	*8:31	10	W	2:49	8.1	3:26	7.3	9:26	9:39
11	M	2:30	7.8	2:59	7.2	9:00	9:14	11	T	3:40	7.9	4:20	7.1	10:20	10:35
12	T	3:14	7.7	3:47	7.1	9:46	10:01	12	F	4:36	7.7	5:21	6.9	11:23	11:40
13	W	4:03	7.7	4:39	6.8	10:38	10:54	13	S	5:40	7.5	6:34	7.0	...	12:49
14	T	4:57	7.5	5:38	6.7	11:39	11:55	14	S	6:57	7.4	8:03	7.3	1:01	2:27
15	F	5:58	7.4	6:46	6.7	...	12:52	15	M	8:29	7.6	9:15	7.8	2:45	3:31
16	S	7:08	7.4	8:07	6.9	1:04	2:37	16	T	9:41	8.0	10:11	8.4	3:55	4:26
17	S	8:29	7.7	9:24	7.4	2:28	3:50	17	W	10:38	8.3	11:01	8.8	4:52	5:17
18	M	9:45	8.1	10:24	7.9	3:56	4:46	18	T	11:29	8.5	11:47	9.1	5:45	6:04
19	T	10:46	8.5	11:16	8.5	5:00	5:37	19	F	...	...	12:18	8.5	6:34	6:49
20	W	11:39	8.7	...	...	5:55	6:24	20	S	12:31	9.1	1:05	8.3	7:22	7:32
21	T	12:04	8.8	12:29	8.7	6:46	7:09	21	S	1:15	9.0	1:53	8.0	8:09	8:15
22	F	12:51	9.0	1:19	8.6	7:35	7:54	22	M	1:59	8.6	2:42	7.7	8:56	8:58
23	S	1:38	8.9	2:10	8.2	8:25	8:39	23	T	2:44	8.2	3:34	7.3	9:46	9:45
24	S	2:26	8.7	3:02	7.8	9:18	9:26	24	W	3:33	7.7	4:29	7.0	10:41	10:47
25	M	3:16	8.3	3:59	7.3	10:14	10:22	25	T	4:29	7.2	5:30	6.7	11:40	11:58
26	T	4:10	7.8	5:00	6.9	11:15	11:29	26	F	5:40	6.8	6:34	6.6	...	12:39
27	W	5:14	7.3	6:07	6.6	...	12:18	27	S	6:53	6.6	7:35	6.7	1:03	1:36
28	T	6:27	6.9	7:13	6.5	12:37	1:19	28	S	7:57	6.6	8:31	6.8	2:01	2:29
29	F	7:36	6.8	8:15	6.6	1:40	2:17	29	M	8:53	6.8	9:20	7.1	2:55	3:17
30	S	8:38	6.8	9:09	6.8	2:39	3:11	30	T	9:41	6.9	10:03	7.4	3:45	4:01
31	S	9:31	7.0	9:58	7.1	3:32	4:00								

Dates when Ht. of **Low** Water is below Mean Lower Low with Ht. of lowest given for each period and Date of lowest in ( ):

4th–5th: -0.2'   6th–9th: -0.3' (7th, 8th)
17th–25th: -1.4' (21st, 22nd)   16th–23rd: -1.3' (19th, 20th)

Average Rise and Fall 7.1 ft.

When a high tide exceeds avg. ht., the *following* low tide will be lower than avg.

2019 HIGH & LOW WATER
KINGS POINT, NY
40°48.7'N, 73°45.9'W

<table>
<tr><td colspan="2" align="center">Daylight Saving Time</td><td></td><td></td><td></td><td></td><td></td><td></td><td colspan="4" align="center">Daylight Saving Time</td></tr>
</table>

DAY OF MONTH	DAY OF WEEK	MAY HIGH a.m.	Ht.	MAY HIGH p.m.	Ht.	MAY LOW a.m.	MAY LOW p.m.	DAY OF MONTH	DAY OF WEEK	JUNE HIGH a.m.	Ht.	JUNE HIGH p.m.	Ht.	JUNE LOW a.m.	JUNE LOW p.m.
1	W	10:24	7.1	10:39	7.6	4:29	4:40	1	S	10:48	7.2	10:35	8.1	5:07	4:35
2	T	11:01	7.3	11:06	7.8	5:10	5:10	2	S	11:18	7.4	11:11	8.4	5:41	5:16
3	F	11:31	7.4	11:20	8.0	5:45	5:28	3	M	11:53	7.6	11:53	8.6	6:14	5:59
4	S	11:53	7.4	11:43	8.2	6:12	5:50	4	T	...	...	12:34	7.7	6:51	6:44
5	S	...	...	12:19	7.6	6:34	6:24	5	W	12:38	8.7	1:20	7.7	7:33	7:32
6	M	12:17	8.4	12:54	7.6	7:04	7:03	6	T	1:27	8.7	2:10	7.8	8:20	8:23
7	T	12:57	8.5	1:35	7.6	7:42	7:46	7	F	2:20	8.5	3:05	7.7	9:13	9:20
8	W	1:42	8.5	2:21	7.6	8:25	8:33	8	S	3:16	8.2	4:05	7.7	10:14	10:28
9	T	2:32	8.3	3:13	7.5	9:15	9:26	9	S	4:19	7.9	5:13	7.7	11:28	...
10	F	3:25	8.1	4:09	7.3	10:12	10:26	10	M	5:31	7.6	6:30	7.9	12:01	12:43
11	S	4:24	7.8	5:14	7.3	11:23	11:40	11	T	6:59	7.4	7:42	8.1	1:22	1:48
12	S	5:31	7.6	6:34	7.4	...	12:56	12	W	8:15	7.4	8:44	8.4	2:29	2:48
13	M	6:58	7.4	7:56	7.7	1:26	2:09	13	T	9:18	7.5	9:39	8.6	3:29	3:44
14	T	8:26	7.6	9:01	8.2	2:42	3:10	14	F	10:14	7.7	10:29	8.8	4:24	4:37
15	W	9:32	7.8	9:55	8.6	3:44	4:05	15	S	11:04	7.8	11:15	8.8	5:16	5:27
16	T	10:27	8.0	10:44	8.9	4:40	4:56	16	S	11:52	7.8	11:59	8.6	6:04	6:14
17	F	11:17	8.1	11:30	9.1	5:31	5:44	17	M	...	...	12:37	7.7	6:50	6:58
18	S	...	...	12:05	8.1	6:20	6:30	18	T	12:41	8.4	1:21	7.6	7:34	7:39
19	S	12:13	9.0	12:51	8.0	7:07	7:14	19	W	1:20	8.1	2:03	7.4	8:15	8:16
20	M	12:55	8.8	1:37	7.8	7:52	7:56	20	T	1:57	7.8	2:43	7.3	8:52	8:40
21	T	1:37	8.4	2:23	7.5	8:36	8:35	21	F	2:32	7.6	3:21	7.1	9:20	9:00
22	W	2:18	8.0	3:09	7.3	9:19	9:10	22	S	3:07	7.3	3:56	7.0	9:29	9:38
23	T	3:00	7.6	3:57	7.0	10:04	9:43	23	S	3:46	7.0	4:30	6.9	10:01	10:25
24	F	3:46	7.2	4:48	6.8	10:50	10:34	24	M	4:30	6.8	5:08	6.9	10:43	11:18
25	S	4:37	6.9	5:44	6.7	11:41	...	25	T	5:19	6.6	5:53	7.0	11:31	...
26	S	5:43	6.6	6:42	6.7	12:07	12:35	26	W	6:15	6.5	6:42	7.1	12:18	12:21
27	M	6:57	6.5	7:38	6.8	1:11	1:26	27	T	7:19	6.5	7:33	7.3	1:28	1:14
28	T	7:59	6.5	8:28	7.0	2:08	2:13	28	F	8:23	6.6	8:23	7.6	2:40	2:07
29	W	8:53	6.6	9:11	7.3	3:00	2:53	29	S	9:16	6.8	9:11	7.9	3:36	3:01
30	T	9:38	6.8	9:43	7.5	3:47	3:25	30	S	10:02	7.1	9:58	8.2	4:26	3:55
31	F	10:17	7.0	10:06	7.8	4:29	3:58								

Dates when Ht. of **Low** Water is below Mean Lower Low with Ht. of lowest given for each period and Date of lowest in ( ):

5th–8th: -0.4' (6th, 7th)	3rd–7th: -0.5' (5th)
15th–21st: -1.1' (18th)	13th–19th: -0.8' (15th, 16th)

Average Rise and Fall 7.1 ft.

When a high tide exceeds avg. ht., the *following* low tide will be lower than avg.

112

2019 HIGH & LOW WATER
KINGS POINT, NY
40°48.7'N, 73°45.9'W

Daylight Saving Time   **Daylight Saving Time**

DAY OF MONTH	DAY OF WEEK	JULY HIGH a.m.	Ht.	JULY HIGH p.m.	Ht.	JULY LOW a.m.	JULY LOW p.m.	DAY OF MONTH	DAY OF WEEK	AUGUST HIGH a.m.	Ht.	AUGUST HIGH p.m.	Ht.	AUGUST LOW a.m.	AUGUST LOW p.m.
1	M	10:46	7.4	10:45	8.5	5:11	4:48	1	T	...	...	12:02	8.2	6:28	6:24
2	T	11:30	7.6	11:34	8.8	5:56	5:39	2	F	12:13	9.0	12:53	8.4	7:16	7:20
3	W	...	...	12:17	7.8	6:41	6:31	3	S	1:08	9.0	1:47	8.6	8:04	8:18
4	T	12:24	8.9	1:07	8.0	7:28	7:24	4	S	2:04	8.8	2:42	8.7	8:55	9:21
5	F	1:16	8.8	2:00	8.1	8:17	8:19	5	M	3:03	8.4	3:41	8.6	9:50	10:30
6	S	2:12	8.6	2:57	8.2	9:10	9:22	6	T	4:08	8.0	4:43	8.5	10:51	11:40
7	S	3:11	8.4	3:58	8.2	10:09	10:38	7	W	5:19	7.6	5:50	8.3	11:58	...
8	M	4:15	8.0	5:04	8.2	11:15	11:57	8	T	6:32	7.3	6:59	8.1	12:47	1:03
9	T	5:31	7.6	6:14	8.2	...	12:21	9	F	7:43	7.2	8:05	8.1	1:50	2:06
10	W	6:49	7.4	7:22	8.2	1:07	1:26	10	S	8:45	7.2	9:04	8.1	2:49	3:06
11	T	8:00	7.3	8:25	8.3	2:11	2:27	11	S	9:41	7.3	9:58	8.1	3:45	4:01
12	F	9:03	7.3	9:22	8.4	3:10	3:25	12	M	10:31	7.5	10:47	8.1	4:37	4:52
13	S	9:59	7.4	10:14	8.4	4:06	4:20	13	T	11:17	7.6	11:31	8.1	5:24	5:39
14	S	10:49	7.5	11:02	8.4	4:58	5:11	14	W	11:59	7.7	...	...	6:08	6:21
15	M	11:36	7.6	11:47	8.3	5:46	5:58	15	T	12:11	8.0	12:38	7.7	6:47	6:59
16	T	...	...	12:20	7.6	6:31	6:42	16	F	12:46	7.9	1:12	7.6	7:21	7:31
17	W	12:28	8.2	1:01	7.5	7:13	7:21	17	S	1:15	7.8	1:37	7.6	7:44	7:46
18	T	1:05	8.0	1:40	7.5	7:50	7:55	18	S	1:35	7.6	1:52	7.6	7:45	8:00
19	F	1:38	7.8	2:13	7.4	8:21	8:13	19	M	1:58	7.5	2:15	7.6	8:08	8:32
20	S	2:04	7.6	2:39	7.3	8:29	8:28	20	T	2:32	7.4	2:48	7.7	8:43	9:11
21	S	2:32	7.4	3:01	7.3	8:45	9:03	21	W	3:12	7.2	3:28	7.7	9:24	9:56
22	M	3:06	7.2	3:32	7.3	9:19	9:45	22	T	3:56	7.1	4:13	7.7	10:09	10:46
23	T	3:47	7.0	4:10	7.3	10:00	10:32	23	F	4:45	6.9	5:02	7.6	10:59	11:41
24	W	4:32	6.9	4:54	7.3	10:46	11:24	24	S	5:40	6.8	5:57	7.6	11:54	...
25	T	5:22	6.7	5:42	7.4	11:35	...	25	S	6:41	6.8	6:59	7.7	12:44	12:54
26	F	6:18	6.6	6:36	7.5	12:21	12:29	26	M	7:49	6.9	8:05	7.9	1:57	1:58
27	S	7:19	6.6	7:33	7.6	1:23	1:25	27	T	8:59	7.3	9:12	8.3	3:22	3:08
28	S	8:24	6.8	8:32	7.9	2:33	2:24	28	W	10:00	7.8	10:13	8.7	4:27	4:19
29	M	9:25	7.1	9:31	8.3	3:47	3:26	29	T	10:55	8.3	11:10	9.0	5:21	5:22
30	T	10:20	7.5	10:26	8.6	4:47	4:27	30	F	11:46	8.7	...	...	6:10	6:20
31	W	11:11	7.9	11:20	8.9	5:39	5:27	31	S	12:04	9.1	12:36	9.0	6:56	7:14

Dates when Ht. of **Low** Water is below Mean Lower Low with Ht. of lowest given for each period and Date of lowest in ( ):

2nd–8th: -0.7' (4th, 5th)	1st–5th: -0.9' (2nd, 3rd)
12th–17th: -0.5' (14th, 15th)	12th–14th: -0.2'
31st: -0.4'	29th–31st: -0.9' (31st)

Average Rise and Fall 7.1 ft.

When a high tide exceeds avg. ht., the *following* low tide will be lower than avg.

2019 HIGH & LOW WATER
KINGS POINT, NY
40°48.7'N, 73°45.9'W

Daylight Saving Time	Daylight Saving Time

DAY OF MONTH	DAY OF WEEK	SEPTEMBER						DAY OF MONTH	DAY OF WEEK	OCTOBER					
		HIGH				LOW				HIGH				LOW	
		a.m.	Ht.	p.m.	Ht.	a.m.	p.m.			a.m.	Ht.	p.m.	Ht.	a.m.	p.m.
1	S	12:57	9.0	1:27	9.1	7:43	8:10	1	T	1:37	8.6	1:55	9.2	8:06	8:51
2	M	1:52	8.8	2:20	9.1	8:31	9:08	2	W	2:33	8.2	2:47	8.8	8:57	9:50
3	T	2:50	8.4	3:16	8.9	9:24	10:12	3	T	3:33	7.7	3:45	8.4	9:56	10:53
4	W	3:53	7.9	4:16	8.5	10:24	11:18	4	F	4:38	7.3	4:52	7.9	11:06	11:56
5	T	5:01	7.5	5:23	8.1	11:33	...	5	S	5:46	7.1	6:05	7.5	...	12:15
6	F	6:12	7.2	6:34	7.8	12:24	12:41	6	S	6:53	7.0	7:14	7.3	12:58	1:19
7	S	7:20	7.1	7:42	7.7	1:26	1:45	7	M	7:55	7.0	8:16	7.3	1:56	2:18
8	S	8:22	7.1	8:44	7.7	2:25	2:44	8	T	8:50	7.2	9:10	7.4	2:50	3:12
9	M	9:19	7.3	9:38	7.8	3:20	3:39	9	W	9:40	7.5	9:58	7.6	3:40	4:02
10	T	10:08	7.5	10:26	7.9	4:11	4:29	10	T	10:23	7.8	10:41	7.7	4:25	4:47
11	W	10:52	7.7	11:09	7.9	4:57	5:15	11	F	11:02	7.9	11:20	7.7	5:05	5:28
12	T	11:33	7.8	11:48	7.9	5:39	5:57	12	S	11:36	8.0	11:53	7.7	5:41	6:05
13	F	...	...	12:09	7.9	6:17	6:34	13	S	...	...	12:01	8.0	6:07	6:35
14	S	12:22	7.8	12:39	7.9	6:47	7:04	14	M	12:18	7.6	12:11	8.0	6:15	6:51
15	S	12:48	7.7	12:55	7.8	7:00	7:18	15	T	12:34	7.5	12:31	8.1	6:33	7:08
16	M	1:04	7.6	1:08	7.9	7:07	7:32	16	W	12:59	7.5	1:02	8.2	7:05	7:39
17	T	1:27	7.5	1:36	7.9	7:35	8:03	17	T	1:34	7.4	1:41	8.2	7:44	8:18
18	W	2:01	7.4	2:12	8.0	8:11	8:42	18	F	2:16	7.3	2:25	8.1	8:26	9:02
19	T	2:41	7.3	2:53	7.9	8:53	9:26	19	S	3:02	7.2	3:14	8.0	9:14	9:53
20	F	3:26	7.2	3:40	7.9	9:39	10:16	20	S	3:54	7.1	4:08	7.8	10:07	10:52
21	S	4:16	7.0	4:31	7.8	10:30	11:12	21	M	4:51	7.0	5:08	7.6	11:08	...
22	S	5:12	6.9	5:29	7.7	11:27	...	22	T	5:57	7.0	6:16	7.6	12:02	12:18
23	M	6:15	6.9	6:34	7.7	12:18	12:31	23	W	7:15	7.3	7:36	7.7	1:33	1:47
24	T	7:28	7.1	7:46	7.9	1:38	1:43	24	T	8:33	7.8	8:55	8.0	2:49	3:13
25	W	8:43	7.5	9:01	8.2	3:06	3:06	25	F	9:33	8.4	9:58	8.3	3:48	4:16
26	T	9:46	8.1	10:05	8.6	4:08	4:20	26	S	10:25	8.9	10:52	8.5	4:40	5:12
27	F	10:39	8.7	11:01	8.9	5:00	5:19	27	S	11:12	9.3	11:42	8.6	5:28	6:03
28	S	11:28	9.1	11:53	8.9	5:48	6:13	28	M	11:58	9.4	...	...	6:14	6:53
29	S	...	...	12:16	9.4	6:34	7:05	29	T	12:32	8.4	12:44	9.3	7:00	7:42
30	M	12:44	8.8	1:05	9.4	7:20	7:57	30	W	1:23	8.2	1:31	9.0	7:45	8:33
								31	T	2:15	7.8	2:21	8.6	8:33	9:27

Dates when Ht. of **Low** Water is below Mean Lower Low with Ht. of lowest given for each period and Date of lowest in ( ):

1st–3rd: -0.9' (1st)	1st–2nd: -0.8' (1st)
27th–30th: -1.1' (29th)	25th–31st: -1.2' (27th, 28th)

Average Rise and Fall 7.1 ft.

When a high tide exceeds avg. ht., the *following* low tide will be lower than avg.

2019 HIGH & LOW WATER
KINGS POINT, NY
40°48.7'N, 73°45.9'W

*Standard Time starts Nov. 3 at 2 a.m.   Standard Time

DAY OF MONTH	DAY OF WEEK	NOVEMBER						DAY OF MONTH	DAY OF WEEK	DECEMBER					
		HIGH				LOW				HIGH				LOW	
		a.m.	Ht.	p.m.	Ht.	a.m.	p.m.			a.m.	Ht.	p.m.	Ht.	a.m.	p.m.
1	F	3:12	7.5	3:15	8.0	9:29	10:24	1	S	2:41	7.0	2:40	7.3	8:56	9:44
2	S	4:12	7.1	4:18	7.5	10:35	11:24	2	M	3:36	6.8	3:38	6.9	9:59	10:38
3	S	*4:15	6.9	*4:28	7.1	*10:43	*11:24	3	T	4:34	6.6	4:43	6.6	11:03	11:31
4	M	5:19	6.8	5:37	6.9	11:47	...	4	W	5:32	6.6	5:48	6.4	...	12:02
5	T	6:19	6.9	6:39	6.9	12:20	12:45	5	T	6:28	6.7	6:48	6.4	12:22	12:58
6	W	7:14	7.1	7:35	6.9	1:12	1:39	6	F	7:19	6.9	7:42	6.5	1:10	1:49
7	T	8:04	7.3	8:24	7.1	2:01	2:29	7	S	8:05	7.1	8:29	6.6	1:54	2:37
8	F	8:48	7.6	9:08	7.2	2:45	3:15	8	S	8:43	7.3	9:10	6.8	2:32	3:21
9	S	9:28	7.8	9:47	7.3	3:25	3:56	9	M	9:14	7.5	9:45	6.9	3:01	4:00
10	S	9:58	7.9	10:21	7.3	3:59	4:34	10	T	9:32	7.7	10:12	7.0	3:26	4:35
11	M	10:18	7.9	10:46	7.3	4:20	5:05	11	W	9:59	8.0	10:39	7.1	4:00	5:03
12	T	10:32	8.1	11:05	7.3	4:34	5:25	12	T	10:34	8.2	11:13	7.2	4:39	5:33
13	W	10:59	8.2	11:34	7.3	5:03	5:47	13	F	11:16	8.3	11:54	7.3	5:20	6:09
14	T	11:36	8.3	...	...	5:40	6:20	14	S	...	...	12:01	8.3	6:05	6:51
15	F	12:12	7.3	12:18	8.3	6:21	7:01	15	S	12:40	7.3	12:50	8.2	6:53	7:38
16	S	12:55	7.3	1:05	8.2	7:06	7:47	16	M	1:30	7.4	1:43	8.0	7:45	8:31
17	S	1:44	7.2	1:56	8.0	7:56	8:39	17	T	2:25	7.3	2:40	7.7	8:44	9:32
18	M	2:37	7.1	2:52	7.8	8:52	9:40	18	W	3:26	7.4	3:43	7.4	9:55	10:47
19	T	3:37	7.1	3:53	7.5	9:57	10:56	19	T	4:35	7.4	4:58	7.1	11:34	...
20	W	4:46	7.2	5:05	7.4	11:20	...	20	F	5:54	7.6	6:28	7.0	12:05	12:52
21	T	6:07	7.5	6:32	7.4	12:23	1:00	21	S	7:06	7.9	7:42	7.1	1:11	1:56
22	F	7:21	7.9	7:50	7.6	1:30	2:08	22	S	8:06	8.2	8:42	7.3	2:11	2:55
23	S	8:20	8.4	8:50	7.8	2:28	3:07	23	M	9:00	8.5	9:35	7.5	3:07	3:49
24	S	9:11	8.9	9:44	8.0	3:22	4:01	24	T	9:50	8.6	10:25	7.6	3:59	4:39
25	M	9:59	9.1	10:33	8.0	4:12	4:52	25	W	10:36	8.6	11:12	7.5	4:49	5:27
26	T	10:44	9.1	11:22	7.9	5:00	5:41	26	T	11:20	8.4	11:57	7.4	5:36	6:13
27	W	11:29	8.9	...	...	5:46	6:28	27	F	...	...	12:03	8.2	6:20	6:56
28	T	12:10	7.8	12:14	8.6	6:31	7:15	28	S	12:41	7.3	12:44	7.8	7:01	7:38
29	F	12:59	7.5	1:00	8.2	7:16	8:03	29	S	1:25	7.1	1:23	7.5	7:38	8:16
30	S	1:49	7.2	1:48	7.7	8:02	8:52	30	M	2:06	6.9	2:01	7.2	8:06	8:45
								31	T	2:47	6.8	2:40	6.8	8:33	9:02

Dates when Ht. of **Low** Water is below Mean Lower Low with Ht. of lowest given for each period and Date of lowest in ( ):

  13th–14th: -0.2'   10th–17th: -0.5' (12th–14th)
  23rd–29th: -1.3' (26th)   21st–28th: -1.2' (24th, 25th)

Average Rise and Fall 7.1 ft.

When a high tide exceeds avg. ht., the *following* low tide will be lower than avg.

2019 CURRENT TABLE
HELL GATE, NY (EAST RIVER)

40°46.7'N, 73°56.3'W Off Mill Rock

Standard Time   Standard Time

JANUARY   ## FEBRUARY

DAY OF MONTH	DAY OF WEEK	CURRENT TURNS TO						DAY OF MONTH	DAY OF WEEK	CURRENT TURNS TO					
		NORTHEAST Flood Starts			SOUTHWEST Ebb Starts					NORTHEAST Flood Starts			SOUTHWEST Ebb Starts		
		a.m.	**p.m.**	Kts.	a.m.	**p.m.**	Kts.			a.m.	**p.m.**	Kts.	a.m.	**p.m.**	Kts.
1	T	12:18	**12:54**	3.3	6:12	**6:42**	a4.6	1	F	1:36	**2:06**	3.2	7:30	**7:54**	a4.5
2	W	1:12	**1:42**	3.3	7:06	**7:30**	a4.7	2	S	2:18	**2:48**	3.3	8:18	**8:42**	4.5
3	T	2:00	**2:30**	3.4	7:54	**8:18**	a4.7	3	S	3:00	**3:30**	a3.4	9:00	**9:18**	4.6
4	F	2:42	**3:18**	a3.5	8:36	**9:00**	a4.8	4	M	3:42	**4:12**	a3.5	9:42	**10:00**	4.7
5	S	3:30	**3:54**	a3.5	9:18	**9:42**	a4.8	5	T	4:18	**4:48**	a3.5	10:18	**10:36**	a4.8
6	S	4:06	**4:36**	a3.5	10:00	**10:24**	a4.8	6	W	5:00	**5:24**	a3.5	11:00	**11:18**	a4.8
7	M	4:48	**5:18**	a3.5	10:42	**11:06**	a4.8	7	T	5:36	**6:00**	a3.5	11:36	**11:54**	a4.8
8	T	5:24	**5:54**	a3.4	11:24	**11:42**	a4.8	8	F	6:12	**6:36**	a3.4	...	**12:12**	4.7
9	W	6:07	**6:36**	a3.3	...	**12:01**	4.7	9	S	6:49	**7:12**	a3.4	12:30	**12:54**	a4.7
10	T	6:48	**7:12**	a3.2	12:24	**12:42**	4.6	10	S	7:30	**7:54**	a3.2	1:12	**1:36**	a4.6
11	F	7:30	**7:54**	a3.1	1:00	**1:24**	4.5	11	M	8:12	**8:36**	3.1	1:54	**2:24**	a4.6
12	S	8:12	**8:42**	a3.0	1:48	**2:12**	4.4	12	T	9:06	**9:30**	3.0	2:42	**3:12**	a4.5
13	S	9:00	**9:30**	a2.9	2:30	**3:00**	a4.4	13	W	10:06	**10:30**	3.0	3:36	**4:12**	a4.4
14	M	9:54	**10:18**	2.9	3:18	**3:48**	a4.4	14	T	11:12	**11:30**	p3.2	4:36	**5:12**	a4.5
15	T	10:54	**11:12**	p3.0	4:12	**4:48**	a4.4	15	F	...	**12:18**	3.2	5:42	**6:18**	4.5
16	W	11:48	**...**	3.0	5:12	**5:42**	a4.5	16	S	12:36	**1:18**	3.4	6:48	**7:18**	4.7
17	T	12:06	**12:48**	p3.2	6:06	**6:42**	a4.7	17	S	1:36	**2:18**	3.6	7:48	**8:18**	4.9
18	F	1:06	**1:42**	p3.4	7:06	**7:36**	a4.8	18	M	2:36	**3:12**	3.8	8:42	**9:12**	5.1
19	S	2:00	**2:36**	3.6	8:00	**8:30**	a5.0	19	T	3:30	**4:00**	4.0	9:36	**10:00**	5.2
20	S	2:54	**3:30**	a3.8	8:54	**9:24**	a5.2	20	W	4:24	**4:54**	a4.1	10:30	**10:54**	5.3
21	M	3:42	**4:18**	a3.9	9:48	**10:18**	a5.3	21	T	5:12	**5:42**	a4.1	11:24	**11:42**	5.2
22	T	4:36	**5:12**	a4.0	10:42	**11:06**	a5.3	22	F	6:06	**6:36**	a4.0	...	**12:12**	5.1
23	W	5:30	**6:06**	a4.0	11:36	**...**	5.2	23	S	7:00	**7:24**	a3.8	12:36	**1:06**	a5.1
24	T	6:24	**7:00**	a3.9	12:01	**12:30**	5.1	24	S	7:54	**8:18**	a3.6	1:30	**2:00**	a4.9
25	F	7:24	**7:54**	a3.7	12:54	**1:24**	a5.0	25	M	8:54	**9:18**	a3.3	2:24	**2:54**	a4.6
26	S	8:18	**8:48**	a3.5	1:48	**2:18**	a4.8	26	T	9:54	**10:18**	a3.1	3:18	**3:54**	a4.3
27	S	9:24	**9:48**	a3.3	2:48	**3:18**	a4.6	27	W	10:54	**11:18**	3.0	4:18	**4:54**	a4.1
28	M	10:24	**10:48**	3.1	3:48	**4:18**	a4.5	28	T	11:54	**...**	2.9	5:18	**5:48**	a4.1
29	T	11:30	**11:48**	3.1	4:48	**5:18**	a4.4								
30	W	...	**12:24**	3.1	5:42	**6:18**	a4.3								
31	T	12:48	**1:18**	3.1	6:42	**7:06**	a4.4								

The Kts. (knots) columns show the **maximum** predicted velocities of the stronger one of the Flood Currents and the stronger one of the Ebb Currents for each day.

The letter "a" means the velocity shown should occur **after** the a.m. Current Change. The letter "p" means the velocity shown should occur **after** the p.m. Current Change (even if next morning). No "a" or "p" means a.m. and p.m. velocities are the same for that day.

Avg. Max. Velocity: Flood 3.4 Kts., Ebb 4.6 Kts.

Max. Flood 3 hrs. after Flood Starts, ±10 min.

Max. Ebb 3 hrs. after Ebb Starts, ±10 min.

At **City Island** the Current turns 2 hours before Hell Gate. At **Throg's Neck** the Current turns 1 hour before Hell Gate. At **Whitestone Pt.** the Current turns 35 min. before Hell Gate. At **College Pt.** the Current turns 30 min. before Hell Gate.

HELL GATE, NY (EAST RIVER)

40°46.7'N, 73°56.3'W Off Mill Rock

*Daylight Time starts March 10 at 2 a.m.   Daylight Saving Time

		MARCH						APRIL			
		CURRENT TURNS TO						CURRENT TURNS TO			
DAY OF MONTH	DAY OF WEEK	NORTHEAST Flood Starts			SOUTHWEST Ebb Starts		DAY OF MONTH	DAY OF WEEK	NORTHEAST Flood Starts			SOUTHWEST Ebb Starts	
		a.m.	p.m.	Kts.	a.m.	p.m.	Kts.			a.m.	p.m.	Kts.	a.m.	p.m.	Kts.

DAY OF MONTH	DAY OF WEEK	a.m.	p.m.	Kts.	a.m.	p.m.	Kts.	DAY OF MONTH	DAY OF WEEK	a.m.	p.m.	Kts.	a.m.	p.m.	Kts.
1	F	12:12	12:48	3.0	6:12	6:42	a4.1	1	M	2:18	2:42	p3.2	8:24	8:42	4.2
2	S	1:06	1:36	3.1	7:06	7:30	4.2	2	T	3:00	3:24	3.3	9:06	9:24	p4.5
3	S	1:54	2:18	3.2	7:54	8:12	4.3	3	W	3:42	4:06	3.5	9:48	10:06	p4.6
4	M	2:36	3:00	a3.4	8:36	8:54	4.5	4	T	4:18	4:42	3.6	10:24	10:42	p4.8
5	T	3:12	3:36	3.5	9:18	9:36	4.6	5	F	4:54	5:12	a3.7	11:06	11:18	p4.9
6	W	3:48	4:12	a3.6	9:54	10:12	4.7	6	S	5:30	5:48	3.7	11:42	11:54	p4.9
7	T	4:24	4:48	a3.7	10:36	10:48	4.8	7	S	6:12	6:24	a3.7	...	12:18	4.8
8	F	5:00	5:24	a3.7	11:12	11:24	4.8	8	M	6:48	7:00	3.6	12:30	1:00	a4.9
9	S	5:37	5:54	a3.6	11:48	...	4.8	9	T	7:31	7:42	3.5	1:12	1:42	a4.9
10	S	*7:12	*7:30	a3.6	12:01	*1:24	a4.8	10	W	8:18	8:30	3.4	2:00	2:30	a4.8
11	M	7:54	8:12	a3.4	1:42	2:06	a4.8	11	T	9:12	9:30	3.2	2:48	3:24	a4.6
12	T	8:36	8:54	a3.3	2:24	2:54	a4.7	12	F	10:12	10:36	p3.2	3:48	4:30	a4.5
13	W	9:30	9:48	3.2	3:12	3:48	a4.6	13	S	11:24	11:48	p3.2	5:00	5:36	a4.4
14	T	10:36	10:54	3.1	4:12	4:48	a4.5	14	S	...	12:36	3.2	6:06	6:42	4.4
15	F	11:42	...	3.1	5:12	5:54	a4.4	15	M	1:00	1:36	p3.5	7:12	7:42	4.6
16	S	12:06	12:54	3.2	6:24	7:00	a4.5	16	T	2:06	2:36	p3.7	8:18	8:42	p4.9
17	S	1:12	1:54	3.4	7:30	8:00	4.6	17	W	3:00	3:30	3.9	9:12	9:36	p5.1
18	M	2:18	2:54	p3.7	8:30	9:00	p4.9	18	T	3:54	4:18	4.0	10:06	10:24	p5.2
19	T	3:18	3:48	3.9	9:30	9:54	p5.1	19	F	4:48	5:06	4.1	10:54	11:12	p5.2
20	W	4:12	4:42	a4.1	10:24	10:48	p5.2	20	S	5:36	5:54	a4.1	11:42	...	5.0
21	T	5:06	5:30	a4.2	11:12	11:36	p5.3	21	S	6:24	6:42	3.9	12:06	12:30	a5.2
22	F	5:54	6:18	a4.2	...	12:06	5.2	22	M	7:12	7:30	a3.7	12:48	1:18	a5.0
23	S	6:48	7:06	a4.0	12:24	12:54	a5.2	23	T	8:00	8:18	a3.5	1:36	2:06	a4.8
24	S	7:36	7:54	a3.8	1:12	1:42	a5.1	24	W	8:54	9:12	a3.2	2:24	2:54	a4.5
25	M	8:30	8:48	a3.6	2:06	2:36	a4.8	25	T	9:48	10:06	a3.0	3:18	3:48	a4.2
26	T	9:18	9:42	a3.3	2:54	3:30	a4.5	26	F	10:42	11:06	2.8	4:12	4:42	a4.0
27	W	10:18	10:42	3.0	3:48	4:24	a4.2	27	S	11:36	...	2.8	5:06	5:36	a3.9
28	T	11:18	11:42	2.9	4:48	5:18	a4.0	28	S	12:01	12:30	2.8	6:00	6:30	3.9
29	F	...	12:18	2.8	5:48	6:18	a3.9	29	M	12:54	1:24	2.9	6:54	7:18	4.0
30	S	12:36	1:12	2.9	6:42	7:12	3.9	30	T	1:42	2:06	p3.1	7:42	8:06	p4.3
31	S	1:30	2:00	3.0	7:36	8:00	4.0								

The Kts. (knots) columns show the **maximum** predicted velocities of the stronger one of the Flood Currents and the stronger one of the Ebb Currents for each day.

The letter "a" means the velocity shown should occur **after** the a.m. Current Change. The letter "p" means the velocity shown should occur **after** the p.m. Current Change (even if next morning). No "a" or "p" means a.m. and p.m. velocities are the same for that day.

Avg. Max. Velocity: Flood 3.4 Kts., Ebb 4.6 Kts.

Max. Flood 3 hrs. after Flood Starts, ±10 min.

Max. Ebb 3 hrs. after Ebb Starts, ±10 min.

See pp. 22-29 for Current Change at other points.

2019 CURRENT TABLE
HELL GATE, NY (EAST RIVER)

40°46.7'N, 73°56.3'W Off Mill Rock

Daylight Saving Time   Daylight Saving Time

		MAY							JUNE			
D A Y O F M O N T H	D A Y O F W E E K	CURRENT TURNS TO				D A Y O F M O N T H	D A Y O F W E E K	CURRENT TURNS TO					
		NORTHEAST Flood Starts		SOUTHWEST Ebb Starts				NORTHEAST Flood Starts			SOUTHWEST Ebb Starts		
		a.m.	**p.m.**	Kts.	a.m.	**p.m.**	Kts.	a.m.	**p.m.**	Kts.	a.m.	**p.m.**	Kts.

D.O.M.	D.O.W.	a.m.	p.m.	Kts.	a.m.	p.m.	Kts.	D.O.M.	D.O.W.	a.m.	p.m.	Kts.	a.m.	p.m.	Kts.
1	W	2:24	**2:48**	p3.3	8:30	**8:48**	p4.5	1	S	3:18	**3:30**	p3.5	9:18	**9:30**	p4.9
2	T	3:06	**3:30**	3.4	9:12	**9:30**	p4.7	2	S	4:00	**4:12**	p3.6	10:00	**10:18**	p5.0
3	F	3:48	**4:06**	3.5	9:54	**10:06**	p4.8	3	M	4:42	**4:54**	p3.7	10:42	**11:00**	p5.1
4	S	4:30	**4:42**	3.6	10:30	**10:48**	p5.0	4	T	5:30	**5:36**	p3.7	11:30	**11:48**	p5.1
5	S	5:06	**5:18**	3.7	11:12	**11:24**	p5.0	5	W	6:12	**6:24**	p3.7	...	**12:12**	4.9
6	M	5:48	**6:00**	3.7	11:54	...	4.8	6	T	7:06	**7:18**	3.6	12:36	**1:06**	a5.1
7	T	6:30	**6:42**	3.6	12:06	**12:36**	a5.0	7	F	7:54	**8:12**	3.5	1:24	**2:00**	a5.0
8	W	7:12	**7:24**	3.5	12:54	**1:24**	a5.0	8	S	8:54	**9:18**	3.4	2:24	**2:54**	a4.8
9	T	8:07	**8:18**	3.4	1:42	**2:12**	a4.9	9	S	9:55	**10:24**	3.3	3:24	**3:54**	a4.7
10	F	9:00	**9:18**	3.3	2:36	**3:12**	a4.7	10	M	11:00	**11:30**	3.3	4:24	**5:00**	a4.6
11	S	10:06	**10:30**	3.2	3:36	**4:12**	a4.6	11	T	...	**12:01**	3.3	5:30	**6:00**	p4.6
12	S	11:12	**11:42**	p3.3	4:42	**5:18**	a4.5	12	W	12:36	**1:00**	3.4	6:36	**7:00**	p4.7
13	M	...	**12:18**	3.3	5:48	**6:24**	4.5	13	T	1:36	**2:00**	3.5	7:36	**8:00**	p4.8
14	T	12:48	**1:18**	p3.5	6:54	**7:24**	p4.7	14	F	2:30	**2:48**	p3.6	8:30	**8:48**	p4.9
15	W	1:48	**2:18**	3.6	7:54	**8:18**	p4.9	15	S	3:24	**3:42**	p3.7	9:18	**9:42**	p4.9
16	T	2:48	**3:12**	p3.8	8:48	**9:12**	p5.0	16	S	4:12	**4:24**	p3.7	10:06	**10:24**	p5.0
17	F	3:42	**4:00**	p3.9	9:42	**10:00**	p5.1	17	M	5:00	**5:12**	p3.7	10:54	**11:12**	p4.9
18	S	4:30	**4:48**	3.9	10:30	**10:48**	p5.1	18	T	5:42	**5:54**	3.6	11:36	**11:54**	p4.8
19	S	5:18	**5:36**	3.8	11:18	**11:36**	p5.1	19	W	6:30	**6:42**	3.5	...	**12:24**	4.6
20	M	6:06	**6:18**	3.7	...	**12:06**	4.8	20	T	7:12	**7:24**	3.3	12:42	**1:06**	a4.7
21	T	6:48	**7:06**	a3.6	12:24	**12:48**	a4.9	21	F	7:54	**8:06**	3.2	1:24	**1:48**	a4.6
22	W	7:36	**7:54**	a3.4	1:06	**1:36**	a4.7	22	S	8:36	**8:54**	a3.1	2:06	**2:30**	a4.5
23	T	8:24	**8:42**	a3.2	1:54	**2:24**	a4.5	23	S	9:24	**9:42**	2.9	2:54	**3:18**	a4.3
24	F	9:12	**9:30**	a3.0	2:42	**3:12**	a4.3	24	M	10:12	**10:30**	p2.9	3:42	**4:06**	4.2
25	S	10:06	**10:24**	2.8	3:30	**4:00**	a4.2	25	T	11:00	**11:24**	p2.9	4:30	**4:54**	4.2
26	S	10:54	**11:18**	2.8	4:24	**4:54**	a4.1	26	W	11:48	...	2.9	5:24	**5:42**	4.2
27	M	11:48	...	2.8	5:18	**5:42**	4.0	27	T	12:12	**12:36**	p3.0	6:12	**6:36**	p4.3
28	T	12:12	**12:36**	2.8	6:06	**6:30**	4.1	28	F	1:06	**1:24**	p3.1	7:06	**7:24**	p4.5
29	W	1:00	**1:24**	p3.0	7:00	**7:18**	p4.3	29	S	1:54	**2:12**	p3.3	7:54	**8:12**	p4.7
30	T	1:48	**2:06**	p3.2	7:48	**8:06**	p4.5	30	S	2:42	**3:00**	p3.5	8:42	**9:00**	p4.9
31	F	2:36	**2:48**	3.3	8:30	**8:48**	p4.7								

The Kts. (knots) columns show the **maximum** predicted velocities of the stronger one of the Flood Currents and the stronger one of the Ebb Currents for each day.

The letter "a" means the velocity shown should occur **after** the **a.m.** Current Change. The letter "p" means the velocity shown should occur **after** the **p.m.** Current Change (even if next morning). No "a" or "p" means a.m. and p.m. velocities are the same for that day.

Avg. Max. Velocity: Flood 3.4 Kts., Ebb 4.6 Kts.

Max. Flood 3 hrs. after Flood Starts, ±10 min.

Max. Ebb 3 hrs. after Ebb Starts, ±10 min.

At **City Island** the Current turns 2 hours before Hell Gate. At **Throg's Neck** the Current turns 1 hour before Hell Gate. At **Whitestone Pt.** the Current turns 35 min. before Hell Gate. At **College Pt.** the Current turns 30 min. before Hell Gate.

2019 CURRENT TABLE
HELL GATE, NY (EAST RIVER)
40°46.7'N, 73°56.3'W Off Mill Rock

Daylight Saving Time   Daylight Saving Time

DAY OF MONTH	DAY OF WEEK	NORTHEAST Flood Starts a.m.	**p.m.**	Kts.	SOUTHWEST Ebb Starts a.m.	**p.m.**	Kts.	DAY OF MONTH	DAY OF WEEK	NORTHEAST Flood Starts a.m.	**p.m.**	Kts.	SOUTHWEST Ebb Starts a.m.	**p.m.**	Kts.
JULY								**AUGUST**							
1	M	3:30	**3:42**	p3.6	9:30	**9:48**	p5.0	1	T	4:48	**5:06**	p4.0	10:54	**11:18**	p5.2
2	T	4:18	**4:30**	p3.7	10:18	**10:42**	p5.1	2	F	5:36	**5:54**	p4.0	11:42	...	5.1
3	W	5:06	**5:24**	p3.8	11:06	**11:30**	p5.1	3	S	6:30	**6:48**	p4.0	12:12	**12:36**	5.1
4	T	6:00	**6:12**	p3.8	...	**12:01**	5.0	4	S	7:24	**7:48**	3.9	1:06	**1:30**	a5.1
5	F	6:48	**7:06**	p3.8	12:24	**12:48**	a5.1	5	M	8:18	**8:42**	3.7	2:00	**2:24**	4.9
6	S	7:42	**8:00**	p3.7	1:18	**1:42**	a5.0	6	T	9:12	**9:42**	a3.6	2:54	**3:24**	4.7
7	S	8:36	**9:00**	3.5	2:12	**2:42**	a4.9	7	W	10:12	**10:48**	3.4	3:54	**4:18**	4.5
8	M	9:36	**10:06**	3.4	3:12	**3:42**	a4.8	8	T	11:12	**11:48**	3.3	4:54	**5:24**	p4.4
9	T	10:37	**11:12**	a3.4	4:12	**4:42**	4.6	9	F	...	**12:12**	3.3	5:54	**6:24**	p4.3
10	W	11:36	...	3.3	5:12	**5:42**	4.5	10	S	12:48	**1:12**	p3.3	6:54	**7:18**	p4.3
11	T	12:12	**12:36**	p3.4	6:12	**6:42**	p4.5	11	S	1:48	**2:06**	p3.4	7:48	**8:12**	p4.4
12	F	1:18	**1:36**	p3.4	7:12	**7:36**	p4.6	12	M	2:42	**2:54**	p3.5	8:42	**9:06**	p4.4
13	S	2:12	**2:30**	p3.5	8:06	**8:30**	p4.7	13	T	3:24	**3:42**	p3.5	9:30	**9:48**	p4.5
14	S	3:06	**3:18**	p3.5	9:00	**9:18**	p4.7	14	W	4:06	**4:24**	p3.6	10:12	**10:30**	p4.6
15	M	3:54	**4:06**	p3.6	9:48	**10:06**	p4.7	15	T	4:48	**5:00**	p3.6	10:48	**11:12**	p4.6
16	T	4:36	**4:48**	p3.6	10:30	**10:54**	p4.7	16	F	5:24	**5:36**	p3.6	11:30	**11:48**	p4.7
17	W	5:18	**5:30**	p3.6	11:12	**11:36**	p4.7	17	S	6:06	**6:18**	p3.6	...	**12:06**	4.6
18	T	6:00	**6:12**	3.5	11:54	...	4.6	18	S	6:42	**6:54**	p3.6	12:30	**12:48**	4.6
19	F	6:36	**6:48**	p3.5	12:12	**12:36**	a4.7	19	M	7:18	**7:30**	p3.5	1:06	**1:24**	4.6
20	S	7:18	**7:30**	p3.4	12:54	**1:18**	a4.6	20	T	7:54	**8:06**	p3.4	1:48	**2:00**	4.5
21	S	8:00	**8:12**	p3.3	1:36	**1:54**	a4.5	21	W	8:30	**8:48**	3.2	2:30	**2:42**	4.4
22	M	8:36	**8:54**	3.1	2:18	**2:42**	a4.5	22	T	9:12	**9:36**	3.1	3:12	**3:30**	4.3
23	T	9:18	**9:42**	3.0	3:00	**3:24**	4.3	23	F	10:00	**10:36**	3.1	4:00	**4:24**	p4.3
24	W	10:06	**10:30**	3.0	3:48	**4:12**	4.3	24	S	10:54	**11:36**	3.1	5:00	**5:18**	p4.3
25	T	10:54	**11:24**	p3.0	4:36	**5:00**	p4.3	25	S	11:54	...	3.2	5:54	**6:24**	p4.3
26	F	11:42	...	3.0	5:30	**5:54**	p4.3	26	M	12:42	**1:00**	p3.3	6:54	**7:24**	p4.5
27	S	12:18	**12:36**	p3.1	6:24	**6:48**	p4.4	27	T	1:42	**2:00**	p3.6	7:54	**8:24**	p4.7
28	S	1:18	**1:30**	p3.3	7:24	**7:48**	p4.6	28	W	2:42	**3:00**	p3.8	8:54	**9:18**	p4.9
29	M	2:12	**2:24**	p3.5	8:18	**8:42**	p4.8	29	T	3:36	**3:54**	p4.0	9:48	**10:12**	p5.0
30	T	3:06	**3:18**	p3.7	9:12	**9:36**	p4.9	30	F	4:24	**4:48**	p4.1	10:36	**11:06**	5.1
31	W	3:54	**4:12**	p3.9	10:00	**10:24**	p5.1	31	S	5:18	**5:42**	p4.2	11:30	...	5.2

The Kts. (knots) columns show the **maximum** predicted velocities of the stronger one of the Flood Currents and the stronger one of the Ebb Currents for each day.

The letter "a" means the velocity shown should occur **after** the **a.m.** Current Change. The letter "p" means the velocity shown should occur **after** the **p.m.** Current Change (even if next morning). No "a" or "p" means a.m. and p.m. velocities are the same for that day.

Avg. Max. Velocity: Flood 3.4 Kts., Ebb 4.6 Kts.

Max. Flood 3 hrs. after Flood Starts, ±10 min.

Max. Ebb 3 hrs. after Ebb Starts, ±10 min.

See pp. 22-29 for Current Change at other points.

2019 CURRENT TABLE
HELL GATE, NY (EAST RIVER)
40°46.7'N, 73°56.3'W Off Mill Rock

Daylight Saving Time **Daylight Saving Time**

SEPTEMBER

Day of Month	Day of Week	NORTHEAST Flood Starts a.m.	**p.m.**	Kts.	SOUTHWEST Ebb Starts a.m.	**p.m.**	Kts.
1	S	6:06	6:30	4.1	12:01	12:18	p5.2
2	M	7:00	7:24	4.0	12:48	1:12	5.1
3	T	7:48	8:18	a3.9	1:42	2:06	4.9
4	W	8:42	9:18	a3.7	2:36	3:00	4.6
5	T	9:42	10:18	a3.5	3:36	4:00	4.4
6	F	10:42	11:24	a3.3	4:36	5:00	p4.2
7	S	11:42	...	3.2	5:36	6:00	p4.0
8	S	12:24	12:42	p3.2	6:36	7:00	p4.0
9	M	1:19	1:42	p3.3	7:30	7:54	p4.1
10	T	2:12	2:30	p3.4	8:18	8:42	p4.2
11	W	3:00	3:12	p3.5	9:06	9:24	p4.4
12	T	3:36	3:54	p3.6	9:48	10:06	p4.5
13	F	4:18	4:30	p3.7	10:24	10:48	p4.6
14	S	4:54	5:06	p3.7	11:00	11:24	4.6
15	S	5:30	5:42	3.7	11:36	...	4.7
16	M	6:00	6:18	p3.7	12:01	12:12	4.7
17	T	6:36	6:54	3.6	12:36	12:48	p4.7
18	W	7:12	7:30	3.5	1:18	1:30	4.6
19	T	7:48	8:12	3.4	1:54	2:12	p4.5
20	F	8:30	9:00	a3.3	2:42	2:54	p4.4
21	S	9:18	10:00	a3.2	3:30	3:48	p4.3
22	S	10:18	11:06	3.1	4:24	4:54	p4.2
23	M	11:24	...	3.2	5:30	6:00	p4.3
24	T	12:12	12:36	p3.4	6:36	7:06	p4.4
25	W	1:18	1:42	p3.6	7:36	8:06	p4.6
26	T	2:18	2:42	p3.9	8:30	9:00	p4.9
27	F	3:12	3:36	p4.1	9:24	9:54	5.0
28	S	4:06	4:30	p4.2	10:18	10:48	a5.2
29	S	4:54	5:24	4.2	11:06	11:36	a5.2
30	M	5:48	6:12	4.2	...	12:01	5.2

OCTOBER

Day of Month	Day of Week	NORTHEAST Flood Starts a.m.	**p.m.**	Kts.	SOUTHWEST Ebb Starts a.m.	**p.m.**	Kts.
1	T	6:36	7:06	a4.1	12:30	12:48	p5.1
2	W	7:24	8:00	a3.9	1:18	1:42	p4.9
3	T	8:18	8:54	a3.6	2:12	2:36	4.6
4	F	9:12	9:54	a3.4	3:06	3:30	4.3
5	S	10:12	10:54	a3.2	4:06	4:30	4.0
6	S	11:18	11:54	3.0	5:06	5:30	p3.9
7	M	...	12:18	3.0	6:06	6:30	p3.9
8	T	12:48	1:12	p3.1	7:00	7:24	p4.0
9	W	1:43	2:00	p3.3	7:48	8:12	p4.1
10	T	2:24	2:42	p3.4	8:30	8:54	p4.3
11	F	3:06	3:24	p3.5	9:12	9:36	p4.5
12	S	3:42	4:00	p3.6	9:54	10:12	4.6
13	S	4:18	4:36	p3.7	10:30	10:54	4.7
14	M	4:54	5:12	3.7	11:06	11:30	a4.8
15	T	5:30	5:48	3.7	11:42	...	4.8
16	W	6:06	6:24	3.6	12:06	12:18	p4.8
17	T	6:36	7:06	a3.6	12:42	12:54	p4.8
18	F	7:18	7:48	a3.5	1:24	1:36	p4.7
19	S	8:00	8:42	a3.3	2:12	2:24	p4.5
20	S	8:54	9:36	a3.2	3:00	3:24	p4.4
21	M	10:00	10:48	a3.2	4:00	4:30	p4.3
22	T	11:12	11:54	3.2	5:06	5:36	p4.3
23	W	...	12:24	3.4	6:12	6:42	p4.5
24	T	1:00	1:30	p3.6	7:12	7:42	p4.7
25	F	2:00	2:30	p3.8	8:12	8:42	p4.9
26	S	2:54	3:24	p4.0	9:06	9:36	5.0
27	S	3:48	4:18	4.1	9:54	10:24	a5.2
28	M	4:36	5:06	4.1	10:48	11:18	a5.3
29	T	5:24	6:00	a4.1	11:36	...	5.2
30	W	6:12	6:48	a4.0	12:06	12:24	p5.1
31	T	7:06	7:36	a3.8	12:54	1:12	p4.9

The Kts. (knots) columns show the **maximum** predicted velocities of the stronger one of the Flood Currents and the stronger one of the Ebb Currents for each day.

The letter "a" means the velocity shown should occur **after** the **a.m.** Current Change. The letter "p" means the velocity shown should occur **after** the **p.m.** Current Change (even if next morning). No "a" or "p" means a.m. and p.m. velocities are the same for that day.

Avg. Max. Velocity: Flood 3.4 Kts., Ebb 4.6 Kts.

Max. Flood 3 hrs. after Flood Starts, ±10 min.

Max. Ebb 3 hrs. after Ebb Starts, ±10 min.

At **City Island** the Current turns 2 hours before Hell Gate. At **Throg's Neck** the Current turns 1 hour before Hell Gate. At **Whitestone Pt.** the Current turns 35 min. before Hell Gate. At **College Pt.** the Current turns 30 min. before Hell Gate.

2019 CURRENT TABLE
HELL GATE, NY (EAST RIVER)
40°46.7'N, 73°56.3'W Off Mill Rock

*Standard Time starts Nov. 3 at 2 a.m.   **Standard Time**

NOVEMBER							DECEMBER					

D A Y O F M O N T H	D A Y O F W E E K	CURRENT TURNS TO					D A Y O F M O N T H	D A Y O F W E E K	CURRENT TURNS TO			
		NORTHEAST Flood Starts			SOUTHWEST Ebb Starts				NORTHEAST Flood Starts			SOUTHWEST Ebb Starts
		a.m.	**p.m.**	Kts.	a.m.	**p.m.**	Kts.			a.m.	**p.m.**	Kts.	a.m.	**p.m.**	Kts.

D.O.M	D.O.W	a.m.	p.m.	Kts.	a.m.	p.m.	Kts.	D.O.M	D.O.W	a.m.	p.m.	Kts.	a.m.	p.m.	Kts.
1	F	7:54	8:30	a3.5	1:42	2:06	4.6	1	S	7:24	8:00	a3.2	1:00	1:24	p4.5
2	S	8:48	9:24	a3.3	2:36	3:00	4.3	2	M	8:18	8:48	a3.0	1:54	2:12	p4.3
3	S	*8:48	*9:24	a3.0	*2:30	*2:54	4.1	3	T	9:12	9:42	2.8	2:42	3:06	4.1
4	M	9:48	10:24	a2.9	3:30	3:54	3.9	4	W	10:06	10:36	2.7	3:36	4:00	4.0
5	T	10:48	11:18	2.9	4:24	4:48	p3.9	5	T	11:00	11:30	2.8	4:24	4:54	4.0
6	W	11:42	...	2.9	5:18	5:42	p4.0	6	F	11:48	...	2.8	5:18	5:42	4.1
7	T	12:06	12:30	p3.1	6:06	6:30	p4.1	7	S	12:12	12:36	p3.0	6:06	6:30	4.3
8	F	12:54	1:12	p3.2	6:54	7:18	p4.3	8	S	1:00	1:24	3.1	6:48	7:18	4.4
9	S	1:37	1:54	p3.4	7:36	8:00	p4.5	9	M	1:43	2:06	p3.3	7:36	8:00	4.6
10	S	2:12	2:36	p3.5	8:12	8:36	4.6	10	T	2:18	2:48	3.4	8:18	8:42	a4.8
11	M	2:48	3:12	p3.6	8:54	9:18	a4.8	11	W	3:00	3:30	3.5	8:54	9:24	a5.0
12	T	3:24	3:48	3.6	9:30	9:54	a4.9	12	T	3:36	4:12	a3.6	9:36	10:06	a5.1
13	W	4:00	4:30	3.6	10:06	10:36	a5.0	13	F	4:18	4:54	3.6	10:24	10:48	a5.1
14	T	4:36	5:06	3.6	10:48	11:12	a5.0	14	S	5:06	5:42	a3.6	11:06	11:36	a5.1
15	F	5:18	5:48	a3.6	11:30	11:54	a4.9	15	S	5:48	6:30	a3.6	11:54	...	5.0
16	S	6:00	6:36	a3.5	...	12:12	4.9	16	M	6:42	7:24	a3.5	12:24	12:48	p4.9
17	S	6:48	7:30	a3.4	12:42	1:06	p4.7	17	T	7:42	8:18	a3.4	1:18	1:42	p4.8
18	M	7:48	8:30	a3.3	1:36	2:00	p4.6	18	W	8:42	9:18	a3.3	2:18	2:48	p4.7
19	T	8:54	9:36	a3.2	2:36	3:06	p4.5	19	T	9:54	10:24	3.2	3:18	3:48	4.6
20	W	10:00	10:42	3.2	3:42	4:12	p4.5	20	F	11:00	11:30	p3.3	4:24	4:54	4.6
21	T	11:12	11:48	p3.4	4:48	5:18	4.5	21	S	...	12:06	3.3	5:24	6:00	a4.7
22	F	...	12:18	3.5	5:48	6:18	4.7	22	S	12:30	1:06	p3.5	6:24	6:54	a4.8
23	S	12:42	1:18	p3.7	6:48	7:18	a4.9	23	M	1:24	2:00	3.6	7:18	7:54	a4.9
24	S	1:42	2:12	3.8	7:42	8:12	5.0	24	T	2:18	2:54	a3.7	8:12	8:42	a5.0
25	M	2:30	3:06	3.9	8:36	9:06	a5.2	25	W	3:06	3:42	3.7	9:06	9:30	a5.1
26	T	3:24	3:54	3.9	9:24	9:54	a5.2	26	T	3:54	4:24	a3.7	9:48	10:18	a5.1
27	W	4:12	4:42	a3.9	10:12	10:42	a5.2	27	F	4:42	5:12	a3.7	10:36	11:00	a5.0
28	T	5:00	5:30	a3.8	11:00	11:30	a5.1	28	S	5:24	5:54	a3.6	11:24	11:48	a4.9
29	F	5:48	6:18	a3.7	11:48	...	4.9	29	S	6:12	6:42	a3.4	...	12:06	4.8
30	S	6:36	7:06	a3.4	12:12	12:36	p4.7	30	M	6:54	7:24	a3.3	12:30	12:48	4.6
								31	T	7:42	8:12	a3.1	1:12	1:36	p4.5

The Kts. (knots) columns show the **maximum** predicted velocities of the stronger one of the Flood Currents and the stronger one of the Ebb Currents for each day.

The letter "a" means the velocity shown should occur **after** the **a.m.** Current Change. The letter "p" means the velocity shown should occur **after** the **p.m.** Current Change (even if next morning). No "a" or "p" means a.m. and p.m. velocities are the same for that day.

Avg. Max. Velocity: Flood 3.4 Kts., Ebb 4.6 Kts.

Max. Flood 3 hrs. after Flood Starts, ±10 min.

Max. Ebb 3 hrs. after Ebb Starts, ±10 min.

See pp. 22-29 for Current Change at other points.

2019 CURRENT TABLE
THE NARROWS, NY HARBOR
40°36.56'N, 74°02.77'W Mid-Channel

| Standard Time | | | | | | | Standard Time | | | | | |

JANUARY								FEBRUARY					

DAY OF MONTH	DAY OF WEEK	CURRENT TURNS TO											
		NORTH Flood Starts			SOUTH Ebb Starts		DAY OF MONTH	DAY OF WEEK	NORTH Flood Starts			SOUTH Ebb Starts	

D A Y O F M O N T H	D A Y O F W E E K	NORTH Flood Starts a.m.	**p.m.**	Kts.	SOUTH Ebb Starts a.m.	**p.m.**	Kts.	D A Y O F M O N T H	D A Y O F W E E K	NORTH Flood Starts a.m.	**p.m.**	Kts.	SOUTH Ebb Starts a.m.	**p.m.**	Kts.
1	T	12:24	**1:12**	a1.4	6:24	**6:42**	1.7	1	F	1:48	**2:54**	a1.5	7:54	**8:18**	a1.8
2	W	1:12	**2:06**	a1.5	7:18	**7:36**	a1.8	2	S	2:36	**3:36**	a1.5	8:36	**9:00**	a1.8
3	T	2:00	**3:00**	a1.6	8:06	**8:24**	a1.8	3	S	3:18	**4:12**	a1.4	9:12	**9:36**	a1.7
4	F	2:48	**3:42**	a1.6	8:48	**9:06**	a1.8	4	M	3:48	**4:36**	a1.4	9:42	**10:06**	a1.7
5	S	3:24	**4:24**	a1.6	9:24	**9:48**	a1.8	5	T	4:24	**5:06**	a1.4	10:12	**10:36**	a1.7
6	S	4:00	**5:00**	a1.5	10:00	**10:24**	a1.8	6	W	4:54	**5:30**	a1.4	10:48	**11:12**	a1.7
7	M	4:36	**5:36**	a1.4	10:36	**11:06**	a1.8	7	T	5:30	**6:00**	a1.4	11:24	**11:48**	a1.8
8	T	5:18	**6:12**	a1.4	11:18	**11:48**	a1.8	8	F	6:12	**6:36**	a1.5	...	**12:06**	1.9
9	W	6:01	**6:48**	a1.4	...	**12:01**	1.8	9	S	6:55	**7:18**	1.5	12:30	**12:48**	p1.9
10	T	6:48	**7:30**	a1.4	12:30	**12:42**	p1.8	10	S	7:48	**8:06**	p1.6	1:18	**1:36**	p2.0
11	F	7:36	**8:12**	a1.4	1:12	**1:30**	p1.8	11	M	8:48	**8:54**	p1.8	2:00	**2:24**	p1.9
12	S	8:36	**9:00**	1.5	2:00	**2:18**	p1.8	12	T	9:48	**9:48**	p1.9	2:54	**3:12**	p1.9
13	S	9:30	**9:48**	p1.6	2:48	**3:06**	p1.9	13	W	10:48	**10:42**	p1.9	3:48	**4:12**	p1.9
14	M	10:24	**10:36**	p1.8	3:42	**4:00**	p1.9	14	T	11:48	**11:36**	p2.0	4:48	**5:18**	1.9
15	T	11:24	**11:24**	p1.9	4:36	**4:54**	p2.0	15	F	...	**12:42**	1.6	5:48	**6:18**	a2.1
16	W	...	**12:18**	1.6	5:30	**5:54**	p2.1	16	S	12:36	**1:42**	a2.0	6:48	**7:18**	a2.3
17	T	12:12	**1:12**	a2.0	6:24	**6:48**	2.2	17	S	1:30	**2:30**	a2.1	7:42	**8:12**	a2.4
18	F	1:06	**2:06**	a2.1	7:18	**7:42**	a2.4	18	M	2:30	**3:24**	a2.3	8:36	**9:00**	a2.5
19	S	1:54	**3:00**	a2.3	8:06	**8:30**	a2.5	19	T	3:24	**4:06**	a2.3	9:24	**9:54**	a2.5
20	S	2:48	**3:48**	a2.3	8:54	**9:24**	a2.5	20	W	4:18	**4:54**	a2.3	10:18	**10:42**	a2.5
21	M	3:36	**4:36**	a2.3	9:42	**10:12**	a2.5	21	T	5:06	**5:48**	a2.1	11:06	**11:36**	a2.4
22	T	4:30	**5:24**	a2.2	10:36	**11:06**	a2.4	22	F	6:06	**6:42**	1.9	...	**12:01**	2.3
23	W	5:24	**6:12**	a2.0	11:30	...	2.3	23	S	7:06	**7:36**	1.8	12:36	**1:00**	2.1
24	T	6:24	**7:12**	a1.8	12:01	**12:24**	2.1	24	S	8:12	**8:42**	p1.7	1:30	**1:54**	1.9
25	F	7:30	**8:12**	1.6	12:54	**1:18**	1.9	25	M	9:24	**9:42**	p1.6	2:30	**2:54**	a1.8
26	S	8:36	**9:12**	p1.6	1:54	**2:18**	1.8	26	T	10:30	**10:42**	p1.5	3:30	**3:54**	a1.7
27	S	9:42	**10:12**	p1.5	2:54	**3:12**	p1.7	27	W	11:42	**11:42**	p1.4	4:36	**5:06**	a1.7
28	M	10:54	**11:12**	p1.5	4:00	**4:18**	1.6	28	T	...	**12:42**	1.2	5:48	**6:18**	a1.7
29	T	...	**12:01**	1.2	5:06	**5:24**	1.6								
30	W	12:06	**1:00**	a1.4	6:12	**6:30**	a1.7								
31	T	1:00	**2:00**	a1.4	7:06	**7:30**	a1.7								

The Kts. (knots) columns show the **maximum** predicted velocities of the stronger one of the Flood Currents and the stronger one of the Ebb Currents for each day.

The letter "a" means the velocity shown should occur **after** the **a.m.** Current Change. The letter "p" means the velocity shown should occur **after** the **p.m.** Current Change (even if next morning). No "a" or "p" means a.m. and p.m. velocities are the same for that day.

Avg. Max. Velocity: Flood 1.7 Kts., Ebb 2.0 Kts.

Max. Flood 2 hrs. 25 min. after Flood Starts, ±30 min.

Max. Ebb 3 hrs. 15 min. after Ebb Starts, ±10 min.

At **The Battery, Desbrosses St., & Chelsea Dock** Current turns 1 1/2 hrs. after the Narrows. At **42nd St.** and the **George Washington Bridge**, the Current turns 1 3/4 hrs. after the Narrows. See pp. 22-29 for Current Change at other points.

*Daylight Time starts March 10 at 2 a.m.   Daylight Saving Time

		MARCH						APRIL			
		CURRENT TURNS TO						CURRENT TURNS TO			
		NORTH Flood Starts			SOUTH Ebb Starts			NORTH Flood Starts			SOUTH Ebb Starts		
DAY OF MONTH	DAY OF WEEK	a.m.	**p.m.**	Kts.	a.m.	**p.m.**	Kts.	DAY OF MONTH	DAY OF WEEK	a.m.	**p.m.**	Kts.	a.m.	**p.m.**	Kts.

*Daylight Time starts March 10 at 2 a.m.   Daylight Saving Time

MARCH / APRIL

CURRENT TURNS TO

Day of Month	Day of Week	NORTH Flood Starts a.m.	**p.m.**	Kts.	SOUTH Ebb Starts a.m.	**p.m.**	Kts.	Day of Month	Day of Week	NORTH Flood Starts a.m.	**p.m.**	Kts.	SOUTH Ebb Starts a.m.	**p.m.**	Kts.
1	F	12:42	**1:42**	a1.4	6:48	**7:18**	a1.7	1	M	2:54	**3:36**	a1.4	8:48	**9:18**	a1.8
2	S	1:36	**2:36**	a1.4	7:36	**8:06**	a1.8	2	T	3:36	**4:06**	a1.4	9:24	**9:48**	a1.8
3	S	2:24	**3:12**	a1.4	8:18	**8:48**	a1.8	3	W	4:12	**4:30**	a1.5	9:54	**10:12**	1.8
4	M	3:00	**3:42**	a1.4	8:54	**9:18**	a1.7	4	T	4:42	**4:48**	a1.5	10:24	**10:42**	1.8
5	T	3:36	**4:06**	a1.4	9:18	**9:42**	a1.7	5	F	5:12	**5:12**	p1.6	10:54	**11:06**	1.9
6	W	4:06	**4:30**	a1.4	9:48	**10:06**	a1.7	6	S	5:42	**5:42**	p1.7	11:24	**11:42**	1.9
7	T	4:36	**4:48**	a1.4	10:18	**10:36**	a1.8	7	S	6:18	**6:12**	p1.8	...	**12:01**	2.0
8	F	5:06	**5:18**	a1.5	10:54	**11:12**	a1.9	8	M	7:00	**6:54**	p1.8	12:18	**12:42**	p2.0
9	S	5:43	**5:48**	p1.6	11:30	**11:48**	a1.9	9	T	7:49	**7:42**	p1.8	1:06	**1:30**	a2.0
10	S	*7:24	***7:30**	p1.7	...	***1:12**	2.0	10	W	8:48	**8:36**	p1.7	1:54	**2:24**	a1.9
11	M	8:12	**8:18**	p1.7	1:36	**2:00**	p2.0	11	T	9:48	**9:36**	p1.7	2:42	**3:18**	a1.8
12	T	9:12	**9:06**	p1.8	2:24	**2:48**	1.9	12	F	10:54	**10:42**	p1.6	3:36	**4:18**	a1.7
13	W	10:12	**10:06**	p1.8	3:12	**3:42**	1.8	13	S	11:54	**11:54**	p1.6	4:36	**5:24**	a1.7
14	T	11:18	**11:06**	p1.8	4:06	**4:42**	a1.8	14	S	...	**12:54**	1.4	5:48	**6:30**	1.7
15	F	...	**12:18**	1.4	5:06	**5:48**	a1.8	15	M	1:00	**1:48**	a1.6	6:54	**7:30**	1.9
16	S	12:12	**1:18**	a1.8	6:12	**6:54**	a1.9	16	T	2:00	**2:36**	p1.8	7:54	**8:30**	p2.2
17	S	1:12	**2:12**	a1.8	7:18	**7:54**	a2.1	17	W	3:00	**3:30**	p2.0	8:54	**9:18**	p2.4
18	M	2:12	**3:06**	a2.0	8:18	**8:48**	2.3	18	T	3:54	**4:12**	p2.1	9:42	**10:12**	p2.5
19	T	3:12	**3:54**	a2.1	9:12	**9:42**	2.4	19	F	4:42	**5:00**	p2.2	10:30	**11:00**	p2.5
20	W	4:06	**4:42**	a2.2	10:06	**10:30**	2.5	20	S	5:36	**5:48**	p2.1	11:18	**11:48**	2.4
21	T	5:00	**5:30**	2.2	10:54	**11:18**	2.5	21	S	6:24	**6:36**	p2.0	...	**12:12**	2.2
22	F	5:54	**6:18**	2.1	11:42	...	2.4	22	M	7:24	**7:30**	p1.8	12:42	**1:06**	a2.3
23	S	6:48	**7:06**	2.0	12:12	**12:36**	a2.4	23	T	8:24	**8:30**	p1.6	1:36	**2:06**	a2.1
24	S	7:42	**8:06**	1.8	1:06	**1:30**	a2.3	24	W	9:30	**9:36**	p1.5	2:30	**3:06**	a1.9
25	M	8:48	**9:06**	p1.7	2:06	**2:30**	a2.1	25	T	10:36	**10:42**	p1.4	3:24	**4:06**	a1.7
26	T	10:00	**10:12**	p1.6	3:00	**3:30**	a1.8	26	F	11:42	**11:42**	p1.4	4:24	**5:12**	a1.7
27	W	11:06	**11:12**	p1.5	4:00	**4:36**	a1.7	27	S	...	**12:36**	1.3	5:24	**6:18**	a1.7
28	T	...	**12:12**	1.3	5:06	**5:42**	a1.7	28	S	12:42	**1:24**	1.3	6:24	**7:12**	a1.7
29	F	12:18	**1:12**	a1.4	6:12	**6:54**	a1.7	29	M	1:30	**2:06**	1.3	7:18	**8:00**	a1.8
30	S	1:12	**2:12**	a1.4	7:12	**7:54**	a1.7	30	T	2:18	**2:42**	1.4	8:06	**8:36**	1.8
31	S	2:06	**3:00**	a1.4	8:06	**8:42**	a1.8								

The Kts. (knots) columns show the **maximum** predicted velocities of the stronger one of the Flood Currents and the stronger one of the Ebb Currents for each day.

The letter "a" means the velocity shown should occur **after** the a.m. Current Change. The letter "p" means the velocity shown should occur **after** the p.m. Current Change (even if next morning). No "a" or "p" means a.m. and p.m. velocities are the same for that day.

Avg. Max. Velocity: Flood 1.7 Kts., Ebb 2.0 Kts.

Max. Flood 2 hrs. 25 min. after Flood Starts, ±30 min.

Max. Ebb 3 hrs. 15 min. after Ebb Starts, ±10 min.

See pp. 22-29 for Current Change at other points.

2019 CURRENT TABLE
THE NARROWS, NY HARBOR
40°36.56'N, 74°02.77'W Mid-Channel

Daylight Saving Time   Daylight Saving Time

DAY OF MONTH	DAY OF WEEK	NORTH Flood Starts a.m.	**p.m.**	Kts.	SOUTH Ebb Starts a.m.	**p.m.**	Kts.	DAY OF MONTH	DAY OF WEEK	NORTH Flood Starts a.m.	**p.m.**	Kts.	SOUTH Ebb Starts a.m.	**p.m.**	Kts.
		MAY								**JUNE**					
1	W	3:00	3:18	1.5	8:42	9:12	1.9	1	S	3:48	3:36	p1.9	9:18	9:42	p2.2
2	T	3:42	3:42	p1.6	9:18	9:42	p2.0	2	S	4:30	4:12	p2.1	10:00	10:18	p2.2
3	F	4:18	4:12	p1.7	9:48	10:12	2.0	3	M	5:06	4:48	p2.1	10:36	11:00	p2.2
4	S	4:48	4:42	p1.8	10:24	10:42	2.0	4	T	5:48	5:30	p2.0	11:18	11:42	p2.2
5	S	5:24	5:12	p1.9	11:00	11:18	p2.1	5	W	6:36	6:12	p1.9	...	12:06	1.9
6	M	6:06	5:48	p1.9	11:36	11:54	2.0	6	T	7:24	7:06	p1.7	12:24	1:00	a2.1
7	T	6:48	6:30	p1.8	...	12:24	1.9	7	F	8:18	8:06	p1.5	1:18	1:54	a1.9
8	W	7:36	7:18	p1.7	12:42	1:12	a2.0	8	S	9:18	9:12	p1.4	2:12	2:48	a1.8
9	T	8:31	8:12	p1.6	1:30	2:06	a1.9	9	S	10:19	10:24	1.3	3:06	3:48	a1.6
10	F	9:30	9:18	p1.5	2:24	3:00	a1.8	10	M	11:18	11:36	1.3	4:06	4:48	a1.5
11	S	10:36	10:30	p1.4	3:18	4:00	a1.6	11	T	...	12:12	1.4	5:06	5:54	1.5
12	S	11:36	11:42	p1.4	4:18	5:06	a1.6	12	W	12:42	1:06	p1.4	6:12	7:00	p1.7
13	M	...	12:30	1.4	5:24	6:12	1.6	13	T	1:42	1:54	p1.6	7:18	7:54	p1.8
14	T	12:48	1:24	p1.5	6:30	7:12	p1.8	14	F	2:36	2:42	p1.7	8:12	8:48	p2.0
15	W	1:48	2:12	p1.7	7:36	8:12	p2.0	15	S	3:30	3:30	p1.8	9:00	9:36	p2.1
16	T	2:48	3:06	p1.9	8:30	9:00	p2.2	16	S	4:24	4:18	p1.9	9:54	10:18	p2.1
17	F	3:42	3:48	p2.0	9:18	9:48	p2.3	17	M	5:06	5:00	p1.8	10:42	11:00	p2.1
18	S	4:30	4:36	p2.1	10:06	10:36	p2.3	18	T	5:54	5:42	p1.7	11:24	11:48	p2.0
19	S	5:18	5:18	p2.0	10:54	11:24	p2.3	19	W	6:42	6:30	p1.6	...	12:18	1.7
20	M	6:06	6:06	p1.9	11:48	...	2.0	20	T	7:30	7:18	p1.5	12:36	1:06	a1.9
21	T	7:00	7:00	p1.7	12:12	12:42	a2.2	21	F	8:24	8:18	p1.4	1:24	2:00	a1.9
22	W	8:00	7:54	p1.6	1:06	1:36	a2.0	22	S	9:12	9:12	p1.4	2:12	2:48	a1.8
23	T	9:00	8:54	p1.4	1:54	2:36	a1.9	23	S	10:00	10:12	p1.4	3:00	3:42	a1.7
24	F	10:00	10:00	p1.4	2:48	3:30	a1.8	24	M	10:48	11:06	p1.4	3:48	4:30	a1.7
25	S	10:54	11:00	p1.4	3:42	4:30	a1.7	25	T	11:30	...	1.4	4:36	5:18	a1.7
26	S	11:48	11:54	1.3	4:36	5:24	a1.7	26	W	12:01	12:12	p1.5	5:30	6:12	a1.8
27	M	...	12:30	1.3	5:30	6:18	a1.7	27	T	12:48	12:54	p1.6	6:24	7:00	1.9
28	T	12:48	1:12	1.3	6:24	7:06	a1.8	28	F	1:42	1:36	p1.8	7:12	7:48	p2.1
29	W	1:36	1:48	1.4	7:12	7:48	p1.9	29	S	2:30	2:18	p1.9	8:00	8:30	p2.2
30	T	2:24	2:24	p1.6	8:00	8:30	p2.0	30	S	3:18	3:00	p2.1	8:48	9:12	p2.3
31	F	3:06	3:00	p1.8	8:42	9:06	p2.1								

The Kts. (knots) columns show the **maximum** predicted velocities of the stronger one of the Flood Currents and the stronger one of the Ebb Currents for each day.

The letter "a" means the velocity shown should occur **after** the **a.m.** Current Change. The letter "p" means the velocity shown should occur **after** the **p.m.** Current Change (even if next morning). No "a" or "p" means a.m. and p.m. velocities are the same for that day.

Avg. Max. Velocity: Flood 1.7 Kts., Ebb 2.0 Kts.

Max. Flood 2 hrs. 25 min. after Flood Starts, ±30 min.

Max. Ebb 3 hrs. 15 min. after Ebb Starts, ±10 min.

At **The Battery, Desbrosses St., & Chelsea Dock** Current turns 1 1/2 hrs. after the Narrows. At **42nd St.** and the **George Washington Bridge**, the Current turns 1 3/4 hrs. after the Narrows. See pp. 22-29 for Current Change at other points.

2019 CURRENT TABLE
THE NARROWS, NY HARBOR

40°36.56'N, 74°02.77'W Mid-Channel

Daylight Saving Time							Daylight Saving Time					

		JULY							AUGUST			
D A Y O F M O N T H	D A Y O F W E E K	CURRENT TURNS TO				D A Y O F M O N T H	D A Y O F W E E K	CURRENT TURNS TO			
		NORTH Flood Starts		SOUTH Ebb Starts					NORTH Flood Starts		SOUTH Ebb Starts	
		a.m. **p.m.** Kts.		a.m. **p.m.** Kts.					a.m. **p.m.** Kts.		a.m. **p.m.** Kts.
1	M	4:00 **3:48** p2.2		9:36 **9:54** p2.4		1	T		5:12 **5:06** p2.2		10:48 **11:12** p2.4	
2	T	4:48 **4:30** p2.2		10:18 **10:42** p2.3		2	F		5:54 **5:54** p2.1		11:36 ... 2.2	
3	W	5:30 **5:18** p2.1		11:06 **11:24** p2.3		3	S		6:42 **6:54** p1.9		12:01 **12:30** a2.3	
4	T	6:18 **6:06** p2.0		11:54 ... 2.0		4	S		7:36 **7:54** 1.7		12:54 **1:24** a2.2	
5	F	7:06 **7:00** p1.8		12:12 **12:48** a2.2		5	M		8:30 **9:00** a1.6		1:48 **2:18** a2.0	
6	S	8:00 **8:00** p1.6		1:06 **1:42** a2.0		6	T		9:30 **10:06** a1.6		2:42 **3:18** a1.8	
7	S	9:00 **9:12** 1.4		2:00 **2:36** a1.8		7	W		10:30 **11:18** a1.5		3:36 **4:18** a1.7	
8	M	9:54 **10:18** a1.4		3:00 **3:36** a1.7		8	T		11:30 ... 1.5		4:36 **5:24** a1.6	
9	T	10:55 **11:30** a1.4		3:54 **4:36** a1.6		9	F		12:25 **12:30** p1.4		5:42 **6:30** p1.6	
10	W	11:54 ... 1.4		4:54 **5:42** 1.5		10	S		1:30 **1:30** p1.4		6:54 **7:36** p1.7	
11	T	12:30 **12:48** p1.4		5:54 **6:48** 1.6		11	S		2:30 **2:24** p1.4		8:00 **8:30** p1.7	
12	F	1:36 **1:42** p1.5		7:00 **7:42** p1.7		12	M		3:24 **3:12** p1.5		8:54 **9:18** p1.8	
13	S	2:36 **2:30** p1.5		8:00 **8:36** p1.8		13	T		4:12 **4:00** p1.5		9:42 **9:54** p1.8	
14	S	3:30 **3:18** p1.6		8:54 **9:24** p1.9		14	W		4:54 **4:42** p1.5		10:24 **10:30** p1.8	
15	M	4:18 **4:06** p1.6		9:42 **10:06** p1.9		15	T		5:24 **5:12** p1.4		10:54 **11:06** p1.8	
16	T	5:00 **4:48** p1.6		10:30 **10:48** p1.9		16	F		5:54 **5:48** p1.4		11:30 **11:36** p1.8	
17	W	5:42 **5:30** p1.5		11:12 **11:24** p1.9		17	S		6:24 **6:24** p1.4		... **12:01** 1.6	
18	T	6:18 **6:06** p1.5		11:54 ... 1.6		18	S		6:48 **7:00** p1.4		12:12 **12:36** a1.8	
19	F	7:00 **6:48** p1.4		12:06 **12:36** a1.8		19	M		7:24 **7:42** p1.4		12:54 **1:18** a1.8	
20	S	7:36 **7:36** p1.4		12:48 **1:18** a1.8		20	T		8:00 **8:36** 1.4		1:36 **2:00** a1.9	
21	S	8:18 **8:30** p1.4		1:30 **2:06** a1.8		21	W		8:42 **9:30** a1.5		2:18 **2:42** a1.9	
22	M	9:00 **9:24** p1.4		2:18 **2:48** a1.8		22	T		9:30 **10:24** a1.7		3:06 **3:30** a1.9	
23	T	9:42 **10:18** 1.4		3:00 **3:36** a1.8		23	F		10:24 **11:24** a1.8		3:54 **4:24** 1.8	
24	W	10:30 **11:12** 1.5		3:48 **4:24** a1.8		24	S		11:18 ... 1.8		4:48 **5:24** p1.9	
25	T	11:18 ... 1.7		4:36 **5:12** a1.8		25	S		12:24 **12:18** p1.9		5:54 **6:24** p2.0	
26	F	12:06 **12:06** p1.8		5:30 **6:12** 1.9		26	M		1:18 **1:12** p1.9		6:54 **7:24** p2.2	
27	S	1:00 **12:54** p1.9		6:30 **7:06** p2.1		27	T		2:18 **2:12** p2.1		7:54 **8:18** p2.3	
28	S	1:54 **1:42** p2.0		7:24 **7:54** p2.2		28	W		3:06 **3:06** p2.2		8:48 **9:12** p2.5	
29	M	2:48 **2:36** p2.1		8:18 **8:48** p2.4		29	T		4:00 **4:00** p2.3		9:42 **10:00** p2.5	
30	T	3:36 **3:24** p2.2		9:12 **9:36** p2.4		30	F		4:42 **4:54** p2.3		10:30 **10:54** p2.5	
31	W	4:24 **4:12** p2.3		10:00 **10:24** p2.5		31	S		5:30 **5:42** p2.2		11:18 **11:42** 2.4	

The Kts. (knots) columns show the **maximum** predicted velocities of the stronger one of the Flood Currents and the stronger one of the Ebb Currents for each day.

The letter "a" means the velocity shown should occur **after** the a.m. Current Change. The letter "p" means the velocity shown should occur **after** the p.m. Current Change (even if next morning). No "a" or "p" means a.m. and p.m. velocities are the same for that day.

Avg. Max. Velocity: Flood 1.7 Kts., Ebb 2.0 Kts.

Max. Flood 2 hrs. 25 min. after Flood Starts, ±30 min.

Max. Ebb 3 hrs. 15 min. after Ebb Starts, ±10 min.

See pp. 22-29 for Current Change at other points.

2019 CURRENT TABLE
THE NARROWS, NY HARBOR

40°36.56'N, 74°02.77'W Mid-Channel

Daylight Saving Time | Daylight Saving Time

		SEPTEMBER							OCTOBER					
		CURRENT TURNS TO							CURRENT TURNS TO					
		NORTH			SOUTH					NORTH			SOUTH		
		Flood Starts			Ebb Starts					Flood Starts			Ebb Starts		
DAY OF MONTH	DAY OF WEEK	a.m.	p.m.	Kts.	a.m.	p.m.	Kts.	DAY OF MONTH	DAY OF WEEK	a.m.	p.m.	Kts.	a.m.	p.m.	Kts.
1	S	6:18	6:36	2.0	...	12:06	2.4	1	T	6:36	7:18	a2.1	12:06	12:36	2.4
2	M	7:06	7:36	a1.9	12:36	1:00	a2.3	2	W	7:30	8:18	a1.9	1:00	1:36	2.2
3	T	8:00	8:42	a1.8	1:24	2:00	a2.1	3	T	8:30	9:24	a1.8	2:00	2:30	a2.0
4	W	9:00	9:48	a1.7	2:24	2:54	a1.9	4	F	9:36	10:36	a1.6	3:00	3:30	p1.8
5	T	10:06	11:00	a1.6	3:18	3:54	1.7	5	S	10:42	11:48	a1.5	4:06	4:36	p1.7
6	F	11:12	...	1.5	4:18	5:00	1.6	6	S	11:54	...	1.4	5:12	5:42	p1.7
7	S	12:06	12:12	p1.4	5:30	6:12	p1.6	7	M	12:48	12:54	p1.4	6:30	6:48	p1.8
8	S	1:12	1:12	p1.4	6:48	7:18	p1.7	8	T	1:48	1:54	p1.4	7:36	7:48	p1.8
9	M	2:19	2:12	p1.4	7:54	8:12	p1.8	9	W	2:43	2:42	1.4	8:30	8:36	p1.8
10	T	3:12	3:06	p1.4	8:48	9:00	p1.8	10	T	3:24	3:30	p1.5	9:12	9:12	p1.8
11	W	3:54	3:48	p1.5	9:30	9:42	p1.8	11	F	3:54	4:06	p1.5	9:42	9:42	p1.8
12	T	4:30	4:24	p1.4	10:06	10:12	p1.7	12	S	4:24	4:36	p1.4	10:06	10:12	p1.8
13	F	5:00	5:00	p1.4	10:36	10:42	p1.7	13	S	4:42	5:06	1.4	10:30	10:42	1.8
14	S	5:24	5:30	p1.4	11:00	11:12	p1.7	14	M	5:06	5:36	a1.5	11:00	11:12	1.8
15	S	5:42	6:00	p1.4	11:30	11:42	p1.8	15	T	5:24	6:06	a1.6	11:24	11:42	p1.9
16	M	6:06	6:30	1.4	...	12:01	1.7	16	W	5:54	6:42	a1.7	...	12:01	1.9
17	T	6:36	7:06	a1.5	12:12	12:36	a1.9	17	T	6:30	7:30	a1.8	12:24	12:42	1.9
18	W	7:12	7:54	a1.6	12:54	1:18	a1.9	18	F	7:18	8:18	a1.8	1:06	1:24	1.9
19	T	7:54	8:48	a1.7	1:36	2:00	1.9	19	S	8:06	9:18	a1.7	2:00	2:18	p1.9
20	F	8:42	9:48	a1.7	2:24	2:48	a1.9	20	S	9:06	10:24	a1.7	2:54	3:12	p1.8
21	S	9:42	10:48	a1.8	3:18	3:42	1.8	21	M	10:12	11:24	a1.7	3:48	4:06	p1.7
22	S	10:42	11:54	a1.8	4:18	4:42	p1.8	22	T	11:24	...	1.6	4:54	5:12	p1.8
23	M	11:42	...	1.8	5:18	5:42	p1.9	23	W	12:24	12:30	p1.7	6:00	6:24	p1.9
24	T	12:48	12:48	p1.8	6:24	6:48	p2.0	24	T	1:18	1:30	p1.7	7:00	7:24	p2.1
25	W	1:48	1:48	p1.9	7:30	7:54	p2.2	25	F	2:06	2:30	p1.9	8:00	8:24	2.2
26	T	2:36	2:48	p2.1	8:24	8:48	p2.4	26	S	3:00	3:24	2.0	8:54	9:18	2.4
27	F	3:30	3:42	p2.2	9:18	9:42	p2.5	27	S	3:48	4:18	a2.2	9:42	10:06	a2.5
28	S	4:12	4:36	p2.3	10:06	10:30	2.5	28	M	4:30	5:06	a2.3	10:30	10:54	a2.5
29	S	5:00	5:24	2.2	10:54	11:18	a2.6	29	T	5:18	6:00	a2.3	11:18	11:42	a2.5
30	M	5:48	6:18	a2.2	11:42	...	2.5	30	W	6:06	6:54	a2.2	...	12:12	2.4
								31	T	7:00	7:54	a2.0	12:36	1:06	p2.2

The Kts. (knots) columns show the **maximum** predicted velocities of the stronger one of the Flood Currents and the stronger one of the Ebb Currents for each day.

The letter "a" means the velocity shown should occur **after** the **a.m.** Current Change. The letter "p" means the velocity shown should occur **after** the **p.m.** Current Change (even if next morning). No "a" or "p" means a.m. and p.m. velocities are the same for that day.

Avg. Max. Velocity: Flood 1.7 Kts., Ebb 2.0 Kts.

Max. Flood 2 hrs. 25 min. after Flood Starts, ±30 min.

Max. Ebb 3 hrs. 15 min. after Ebb Starts, ±10 min.

At **The Battery, Desbrosses St., & Chelsea Dock** Current turns 1 1/2 hrs. after the Narrows. At **42nd St.** and the **George Washington Bridge**, the Current turns 1 3/4 hrs. after the Narrows. See pp. 22-29 for Current Change at other points.

2019 CURRENT TABLE
THE NARROWS, NY HARBOR
40°36.56'N, 74°02.77'W Mid-Channel

*Standard Time starts Nov. 3 at 2 a.m.   Standard Time

		NOVEMBER							DECEMBER					
		CURRENT TURNS TO							CURRENT TURNS TO					
		NORTH Flood Starts			SOUTH Ebb Starts				NORTH Flood Starts			SOUTH Ebb Starts		
DAY OF MONTH	DAY OF WEEK	a.m.	**p.m.**	Kts.	a.m.	**p.m.**	Kts.	DAY OF MONTH	DAY OF WEEK	a.m.	**p.m.**	Kts.	a.m.	**p.m.**	Kts.
1	F	8:00	**9:06**	a1.8	1:36	**2:06**	p2.0	1	S	7:36	**8:36**	a1.6	1:12	**1:30**	p1.9
2	S	9:06	**10:12**	a1.6	2:36	**3:00**	p1.8	2	M	8:42	**9:36**	a1.5	2:12	**2:24**	p1.8
3	S	*9:18	***10:18**	a1.5	*2:42	***3:00**	p1.7	3	T	9:42	**10:30**	1.4	3:12	**3:24**	p1.7
4	M	10:24	**11:18**	1.4	3:48	**4:06**	p1.7	4	W	10:42	**11:18**	a1.4	4:12	**4:18**	p1.7
5	T	11:24	...	1.4	5:00	**5:06**	p1.8	5	T	11:36	...	1.4	5:06	**5:12**	p1.7
6	W	12:06	**12:18**	1.4	6:00	**6:06**	p1.8	6	F	12:01	**12:24**	1.3	6:00	**6:00**	p1.8
7	T	12:54	**1:06**	1.4	6:48	**6:54**	p1.8	7	S	12:42	**1:12**	1.4	6:42	**6:48**	1.8
8	F	1:36	**1:54**	1.4	7:30	**7:36**	1.8	8	S	1:18	**1:54**	a1.5	7:18	**7:30**	1.9
9	S	2:07	**2:36**	1.4	8:06	**8:06**	1.8	9	M	1:49	**2:36**	a1.6	7:54	**8:06**	a2.0
10	S	2:36	**3:06**	a1.5	8:36	**8:42**	a1.9	10	T	2:24	**3:18**	a1.8	8:30	**8:42**	a2.1
11	M	3:00	**3:42**	a1.6	9:00	**9:12**	1.9	11	W	2:54	**3:54**	a1.9	9:06	**9:18**	a2.1
12	T	3:30	**4:12**	a1.7	9:30	**9:42**	1.9	12	T	3:30	**4:30**	a2.0	9:42	**10:00**	a2.1
13	W	3:54	**4:48**	a1.8	10:00	**10:18**	a2.0	13	F	4:06	**5:12**	a2.0	10:18	**10:42**	a2.1
14	T	4:30	**5:24**	a1.9	10:36	**11:00**	a2.0	14	S	4:48	**5:54**	a1.9	11:00	**11:30**	a2.1
15	F	5:06	**6:12**	a1.8	11:18	**11:48**	a2.0	15	S	5:36	**6:48**	a1.8	11:48	...	2.0
16	S	5:48	**7:00**	a1.8	...	**12:01**	2.0	16	M	6:36	**7:42**	a1.6	12:24	**12:42**	p1.9
17	S	6:42	**8:00**	a1.7	12:36	**12:54**	p1.9	17	T	7:36	**8:36**	a1.5	1:18	**1:36**	p1.7
18	M	7:48	**9:00**	a1.6	1:36	**1:48**	p1.8	18	W	8:48	**9:36**	1.4	2:18	**2:30**	p1.6
19	T	8:54	**10:00**	a1.5	2:30	**2:48**	p1.7	19	T	9:54	**10:30**	1.4	3:12	**3:30**	p1.6
20	W	10:06	**10:54**	a1.5	3:30	**3:48**	p1.7	20	F	11:00	**11:24**	p1.5	4:12	**4:30**	p1.6
21	T	11:12	**11:48**	1.5	4:36	**4:54**	p1.7	21	S	...	**12:06**	1.3	5:18	**5:36**	p1.7
22	F	...	**12:18**	1.5	5:36	**6:00**	p1.9	22	S	12:18	**1:06**	a1.6	6:18	**6:36**	1.8
23	S	12:42	**1:12**	a1.7	6:36	**7:00**	p2.1	23	M	1:12	**2:00**	a1.7	7:12	**7:30**	a2.0
24	S	1:30	**2:12**	a1.9	7:30	**7:48**	2.2	24	T	2:00	**2:54**	a1.8	8:06	**8:24**	a2.1
25	M	2:18	**3:00**	a2.1	8:24	**8:42**	a2.3	25	W	2:48	**3:42**	a1.9	8:54	**9:12**	a2.1
26	T	3:06	**3:54**	a2.2	9:12	**9:30**	a2.4	26	T	3:36	**4:30**	a1.9	9:42	**10:06**	a2.2
27	W	3:54	**4:42**	a2.2	10:00	**10:24**	a2.4	27	F	4:24	**5:18**	a1.9	10:24	**10:54**	a2.1
28	T	4:42	**5:36**	a2.1	10:48	**11:18**	a2.3	28	S	5:12	**6:12**	a1.7	11:12	**11:48**	a2.1
29	F	5:36	**6:36**	a1.9	11:42	...	2.2	29	S	6:06	**7:00**	a1.6	...	**12:06**	2.0
30	S	6:30	**7:36**	a1.7	12:12	**12:36**	p2.0	30	M	7:00	**7:54**	a1.5	12:42	**1:00**	p1.9
								31	T	8:00	**8:48**	a1.4	1:36	**1:48**	p1.8

The Kts. (knots) columns show the **maximum** predicted velocities of the stronger one of the Flood Currents and the stronger one of the Ebb Currents for each day.
The letter "a" means the velocity shown should occur **after** the **a.m.** Current Change. The letter "p" means the velocity shown should occur **after** the **p.m.** Current Change (even if next morning). No "a" or "p" means a.m. and p.m. velocities are the same for that day.
Avg. Max. Velocity: Flood 1.7 Kts., Ebb 2.0 Kts.
Max. Flood 2 hrs. 25 min. after Flood Starts, ±30 min.
Max. Ebb 3 hrs. 15 min. after Ebb Starts, ±10 min.

See pp. 22-29 for Current Change at other points.

2019 HIGH & LOW WATER
THE BATTERY, NY HARBOR
40°42'N, 74°00.8'W

<table>
<tr><td colspan="2"></td><td colspan="5" align="center">Standard Time</td><td colspan="2"></td><td colspan="5" align="center">Standard Time</td></tr>
<tr>
<th>DAY OF MONTH</th><th>DAY OF WEEK</th>
<th colspan="5">JANUARY</th>
<th>DAY OF MONTH</th><th>DAY OF WEEK</th>
<th colspan="5">FEBRUARY</th>
</tr>
<tr>
<th></th><th></th>
<th colspan="3">HIGH</th><th colspan="2">LOW</th>
<th></th><th></th>
<th colspan="3">HIGH</th><th colspan="2">LOW</th>
</tr>
<tr>
<th></th><th></th>
<th>a.m.</th><th>Ht.</th><th>p.m.</th><th>Ht.</th><th>a.m.</th><th>p.m.</th>
<th></th><th></th>
<th>a.m.</th><th>Ht.</th><th>p.m.</th><th>Ht.</th><th>a.m.</th><th>p.m.</th>
</tr>
<tr><td>1</td><td>T</td><td>4:32</td><td>4.8</td><td>4:52</td><td>4.0</td><td>10:56</td><td>11:08</td><td>1</td><td>F</td><td>5:52</td><td>4.6</td><td>6:18</td><td>3.9</td><td>...</td><td>12:13</td></tr>
<tr><td>2</td><td>W</td><td>5:25</td><td>4.9</td><td>5:47</td><td>4.1</td><td>11:47</td><td>11:56</td><td>2</td><td>S</td><td>6:38</td><td>4.8</td><td>7:03</td><td>4.0</td><td>12:20</td><td>12:59</td></tr>
<tr><td>3</td><td>T</td><td>6:13</td><td>5.0</td><td>6:36</td><td>4.1</td><td>...</td><td>12:36</td><td>3</td><td>S</td><td>7:19</td><td>4.8</td><td>7:44</td><td>4.1</td><td>1:05</td><td>1:42</td></tr>
<tr><td>4</td><td>F</td><td>6:57</td><td>5.1</td><td>7:21</td><td>4.1</td><td>12:42</td><td>1:22</td><td>4</td><td>M</td><td>7:58</td><td>4.8</td><td>8:23</td><td>4.2</td><td>1:48</td><td>2:23</td></tr>
<tr><td>5</td><td>S</td><td>7:38</td><td>5.1</td><td>8:03</td><td>4.1</td><td>1:27</td><td>2:06</td><td>5</td><td>T</td><td>8:35</td><td>4.8</td><td>9:01</td><td>4.2</td><td>2:29</td><td>3:01</td></tr>
<tr><td>6</td><td>S</td><td>8:17</td><td>5.0</td><td>8:45</td><td>4.1</td><td>2:10</td><td>2:48</td><td>6</td><td>W</td><td>9:11</td><td>4.7</td><td>9:38</td><td>4.1</td><td>3:08</td><td>3:37</td></tr>
<tr><td>7</td><td>M</td><td>8:56</td><td>4.9</td><td>9:27</td><td>4.0</td><td>2:50</td><td>3:28</td><td>7</td><td>T</td><td>9:46</td><td>4.6</td><td>10:13</td><td>4.1</td><td>3:44</td><td>4:10</td></tr>
<tr><td>8</td><td>T</td><td>9:35</td><td>4.7</td><td>10:10</td><td>3.9</td><td>3:29</td><td>4:06</td><td>8</td><td>F</td><td>10:20</td><td>4.4</td><td>10:45</td><td>4.0</td><td>4:18</td><td>4:41</td></tr>
<tr><td>9</td><td>W</td><td>10:16</td><td>4.5</td><td>10:53</td><td>3.8</td><td>4:06</td><td>4:42</td><td>9</td><td>S</td><td>10:55</td><td>4.2</td><td>11:16</td><td>4.0</td><td>4:51</td><td>5:09</td></tr>
<tr><td>10</td><td>T</td><td>10:55</td><td>4.3</td><td>11:34</td><td>3.7</td><td>4:41</td><td>5:18</td><td>10</td><td>S</td><td>11:31</td><td>4.0</td><td>11:51</td><td>4.1</td><td>5:25</td><td>5:38</td></tr>
<tr><td>11</td><td>F</td><td>11:34</td><td>4.1</td><td>...</td><td>...</td><td>5:16</td><td>5:53</td><td>11</td><td>M</td><td>...</td><td>...</td><td>12:14</td><td>3.9</td><td>6:09</td><td>6:16</td></tr>
<tr><td>12</td><td>S</td><td>12:12</td><td>3.7</td><td>12:13</td><td>4.0</td><td>5:56</td><td>6:33</td><td>12</td><td>T</td><td>12:34</td><td>4.2</td><td>1:04</td><td>3.8</td><td>7:26</td><td>7:16</td></tr>
<tr><td>13</td><td>S</td><td>12:49</td><td>3.8</td><td>12:55</td><td>3.8</td><td>6:59</td><td>7:24</td><td>13</td><td>W</td><td>1:24</td><td>4.3</td><td>2:03</td><td>3.7</td><td>8:47</td><td>8:39</td></tr>
<tr><td>14</td><td>M</td><td>1:29</td><td>3.9</td><td>1:43</td><td>3.7</td><td>8:17</td><td>8:25</td><td>14</td><td>T</td><td>2:24</td><td>4.4</td><td>3:12</td><td>3.7</td><td>9:52</td><td>9:48</td></tr>
<tr><td>15</td><td>T</td><td>2:15</td><td>4.0</td><td>2:39</td><td>3.7</td><td>9:23</td><td>9:23</td><td>15</td><td>F</td><td>3:34</td><td>4.6</td><td>4:27</td><td>3.9</td><td>10:51</td><td>10:50</td></tr>
<tr><td>16</td><td>W</td><td>3:10</td><td>4.3</td><td>3:45</td><td>3.7</td><td>10:21</td><td>10:18</td><td>16</td><td>S</td><td>4:48</td><td>4.9</td><td>5:33</td><td>4.2</td><td>11:46</td><td>11:48</td></tr>
<tr><td>17</td><td>T</td><td>4:12</td><td>4.6</td><td>4:52</td><td>3.9</td><td>11:15</td><td>11:11</td><td>17</td><td>S</td><td>5:52</td><td>5.2</td><td>6:31</td><td>4.6</td><td>...</td><td>12:39</td></tr>
<tr><td>18</td><td>F</td><td>5:13</td><td>4.9</td><td>5:52</td><td>4.1</td><td>...</td><td>12:08</td><td>18</td><td>M</td><td>6:48</td><td>5.6</td><td>7:23</td><td>4.9</td><td>12:44</td><td>1:31</td></tr>
<tr><td>19</td><td>S</td><td>6:09</td><td>5.3</td><td>6:46</td><td>4.4</td><td>12:05</td><td>1:00</td><td>19</td><td>T</td><td>7:40</td><td>5.7</td><td>8:14</td><td>5.2</td><td>1:39</td><td>2:21</td></tr>
<tr><td>20</td><td>S</td><td>7:01</td><td>5.6</td><td>7:38</td><td>4.6</td><td>12:59</td><td>1:52</td><td>20</td><td>W</td><td>8:31</td><td>5.8</td><td>9:05</td><td>5.3</td><td>2:31</td><td>3:09</td></tr>
<tr><td>21</td><td>M</td><td>7:52</td><td>5.7</td><td>8:29</td><td>4.8</td><td>1:53</td><td>2:42</td><td>21</td><td>T</td><td>9:23</td><td>5.6</td><td>9:58</td><td>5.3</td><td>3:22</td><td>3:56</td></tr>
<tr><td>22</td><td>T</td><td>8:44</td><td>5.7</td><td>9:24</td><td>4.9</td><td>2:45</td><td>3:31</td><td>22</td><td>F</td><td>10:17</td><td>5.4</td><td>10:52</td><td>5.3</td><td>4:13</td><td>4:42</td></tr>
<tr><td>23</td><td>W</td><td>9:39</td><td>5.6</td><td>10:21</td><td>4.9</td><td>3:37</td><td>4:19</td><td>23</td><td>S</td><td>11:12</td><td>5.0</td><td>11:46</td><td>5.1</td><td>5:04</td><td>5:30</td></tr>
<tr><td>24</td><td>T</td><td>10:36</td><td>5.4</td><td>11:18</td><td>4.9</td><td>4:29</td><td>5:08</td><td>24</td><td>S</td><td>...</td><td>...</td><td>12:07</td><td>4.6</td><td>5:59</td><td>6:22</td></tr>
<tr><td>25</td><td>F</td><td>11:33</td><td>5.1</td><td>...</td><td>...</td><td>5:23</td><td>6:00</td><td>25</td><td>M</td><td>12:39</td><td>4.9</td><td>1:02</td><td>4.3</td><td>7:00</td><td>7:20</td></tr>
<tr><td>26</td><td>S</td><td>12:15</td><td>4.8</td><td>12:30</td><td>4.7</td><td>6:23</td><td>6:57</td><td>26</td><td>T</td><td>1:33</td><td>4.7</td><td>1:58</td><td>4.0</td><td>8:05</td><td>8:22</td></tr>
<tr><td>27</td><td>S</td><td>1:10</td><td>4.8</td><td>1:26</td><td>4.4</td><td>7:28</td><td>7:56</td><td>27</td><td>W</td><td>2:28</td><td>4.5</td><td>2:58</td><td>3.8</td><td>9:08</td><td>9:23</td></tr>
<tr><td>28</td><td>M</td><td>2:05</td><td>4.6</td><td>2:24</td><td>4.0</td><td>8:34</td><td>8:56</td><td>28</td><td>T</td><td>3:28</td><td>4.3</td><td>4:02</td><td>3.7</td><td>10:06</td><td>10:18</td></tr>
<tr><td>29</td><td>T</td><td>3:03</td><td>4.6</td><td>3:25</td><td>3.8</td><td>9:37</td><td>9:51</td><td></td><td></td><td></td><td></td><td></td><td></td><td></td><td></td></tr>
<tr><td>30</td><td>W</td><td>4:02</td><td>4.5</td><td>4:29</td><td>3.7</td><td>10:33</td><td>10:44</td><td></td><td></td><td></td><td></td><td></td><td></td><td></td><td></td></tr>
<tr><td>31</td><td>T</td><td>5:00</td><td>4.6</td><td>5:27</td><td>3.8</td><td>11:25</td><td>11:33</td><td></td><td></td><td></td><td></td><td></td><td></td><td></td><td></td></tr>
</table>

Dates when Ht. of **Low** Water is below Mean Lower Low with Ht. of lowest given for each period and Date of lowest in ( ):

1st–8th: -0.4' (5th)
18th–27th: -1.2' (22nd, 23rd)

3rd–7th: -0.3' (4th–6th)
16th–24th: -1.3' (20th)

Average Rise and Fall 4.6 ft.

When a high tide exceeds avg. ht., the *following* low tide will be lower than avg.

2019 HIGH & LOW WATER
THE BATTERY, NY HARBOR
40°42'N, 74°00.8'W

*Daylight Time starts March 10 at 2 a.m.   Daylight Saving Time

DAY OF MONTH	DAY OF WEEK	MARCH HIGH a.m.	Ht.	p.m.	Ht.	LOW a.m.	p.m.	DAY OF MONTH	DAY OF WEEK	APRIL HIGH a.m.	Ht.	p.m.	Ht.	LOW a.m.	p.m.
1	F	4:29	4.3	5:03	3.8	10:58	11:09	1	M	6:42	4.5	7:11	4.4	12:29	12:56
2	S	5:26	4.4	5:55	4.0	11:46	11:56	2	T	7:27	4.6	7:51	4.6	1:14	1:38
3	S	6:14	4.6	6:40	4.2	...	12:31	3	W	8:06	4.8	8:26	4.8	1:58	2:18
4	M	6:56	4.7	7:20	4.3	12:41	1:13	4	T	8:42	4.8	8:58	4.9	2:40	2:55
5	T	7:35	4.8	7:57	4.5	1:25	1:53	5	F	9:16	4.8	9:26	5.0	3:20	3:31
6	W	8:11	4.8	8:32	4.5	2:06	2:30	6	S	9:48	4.7	9:52	5.0	4:00	4:05
7	T	8:45	4.8	9:03	4.5	2:45	3:06	7	S	10:22	4.6	10:21	5.1	4:37	4:37
8	F	9:17	4.7	9:31	4.5	3:22	3:38	8	M	11:00	4.4	10:56	5.1	5:15	5:09
9	S	9:50	4.5	9:57	4.5	3:57	4:07	9	T	11:46	4.3	11:41	5.0	5:55	5:44
10	S	*11:23	4.3	*11:28	4.6	*5:31	*5:35	10	W	...	...	12:37	4.2	6:41	6:27
11	M	...	...	12:02	4.2	6:06	6:04	11	T	12:35	4.9	1:36	4.1	7:44	7:29
12	T	12:08	4.6	12:48	4.0	6:49	6:42	12	F	1:37	4.9	2:38	4.2	8:58	8:58
13	W	12:56	4.6	1:42	3.9	7:55	7:39	13	S	2:43	4.8	3:46	4.3	10:06	10:15
14	T	1:52	4.6	2:44	3.9	9:18	9:10	14	S	3:57	4.8	4:55	4.5	11:06	11:19
15	F	2:56	4.6	3:55	3.9	10:28	10:29	15	M	5:12	5.0	6:00	4.9	...	12:01
16	S	4:11	4.7	5:09	4.2	11:28	11:34	16	T	6:19	5.2	6:57	5.3	12:18	12:53
17	S	5:29	4.9	6:17	4.5	...	12:24	17	W	7:16	5.4	7:47	5.7	1:13	1:43
18	M	6:37	5.2	7:14	5.0	12:33	1:17	18	T	8:07	5.5	8:34	5.9	2:07	2:31
19	T	7:34	5.5	8:06	5.3	1:29	2:08	19	F	8:56	5.4	9:20	6.0	2:59	3:18
20	W	8:25	5.7	8:55	5.6	2:23	2:57	20	S	9:44	5.3	10:06	5.9	3:48	4:03
21	T	9:14	5.7	9:43	5.8	3:16	3:44	21	S	10:34	5.0	10:54	5.7	4:36	4:48
22	F	10:04	5.5	10:32	5.7	4:06	4:30	22	M	11:27	4.8	11:44	5.4	5:23	5:32
23	S	10:56	5.3	11:23	5.6	4:55	5:15	23	T	...	...	12:21	4.5	6:10	6:17
24	S	11:49	4.9	...	...	5:44	6:00	24	W	12:35	5.1	1:15	4.3	7:01	7:08
25	M	12:15	5.3	12:43	4.6	6:35	6:49	25	T	1:26	4.8	2:08	4.1	7:57	8:08
26	T	1:07	5.0	1:38	4.3	7:30	7:44	26	F	2:18	4.5	3:01	4.0	8:57	9:13
27	W	1:59	4.7	2:33	4.0	8:32	8:47	27	S	3:12	4.3	3:57	4.0	9:55	10:14
28	T	2:53	4.5	3:31	3.9	9:35	9:51	28	S	4:09	4.2	4:53	4.1	10:47	11:08
29	F	3:51	4.3	4:31	3.8	10:34	10:49	29	M	5:07	4.2	5:46	4.3	11:33	11:57
30	S	4:52	4.2	5:31	3.9	11:26	11:41	30	T	6:01	4.3	6:33	4.5	...	12:17
31	S	5:51	4.3	6:25	4.1	...	12:13								

Dates when Ht. of **Low** Water is below Mean Lower Low with Ht. of lowest given for each period and Date of lowest in ( ):

6th–7th: -0.2'   16th–22nd: -0.8' (19th, 20th)
18th–25th: -1.0' (20th–22nd)

Average Rise and Fall 4.6 ft.

When a high tide exceeds avg. ht., the *following* low tide will be lower than avg.

2019 HIGH & LOW WATER
THE BATTERY, NY HARBOR
40°42'N, 74°00.8'W

		Daylight Saving Time								Daylight Saving Time				
DAY OF MONTH	DAY OF WEEK	MAY						DAY OF MONTH	DAY OF WEEK	JUNE				
		HIGH				LOW				HIGH				LOW
		a.m.	Ht.	p.m.	Ht.	a.m.	p.m.			a.m.	Ht.	p.m.	Ht.	a.m.	p.m.
1	W	6:49	4.5	7:14	4.8	12:43	12:58	1	S	7:33	4.4	7:42	5.4	1:42	1:38
2	T	7:31	4.6	7:49	5.0	1:28	1:38	2	S	8:14	4.5	8:17	5.6	2:28	2:22
3	F	8:09	4.7	8:21	5.2	2:12	2:17	3	M	8:55	4.6	8:55	5.7	3:14	3:07
4	S	8:45	4.7	8:50	5.3	2:55	2:56	4	T	9:40	4.6	9:38	5.7	3:59	3:52
5	S	9:21	4.7	9:20	5.4	3:37	3:34	5	W	10:30	4.6	10:27	5.7	4:45	4:38
6	M	9:59	4.6	9:55	5.5	4:18	4:12	6	T	11:27	4.6	11:24	5.5	5:32	5:27
7	T	10:44	4.5	10:37	5.4	5:00	4:51	7	F	...	...	12:27	4.6	6:22	6:21
8	W	11:36	4.4	11:28	5.3	5:44	5:34	8	S	12:26	5.4	1:26	4.7	7:18	7:25
9	T	...	...	12:34	4.4	6:34	6:24	9	S	1:29	5.2	2:23	4.8	8:18	8:36
10	F	12:28	5.2	1:34	4.4	7:33	7:30	10	M	2:28	5.0	3:21	5.0	9:20	9:45
11	S	1:32	5.1	2:34	4.5	8:40	8:49	11	T	3:30	4.9	4:20	5.1	10:18	10:48
12	S	2:37	5.0	3:36	4.6	9:44	10:01	12	W	4:34	4.7	5:19	5.3	11:11	11:46
13	M	3:44	4.9	4:39	4.9	10:43	11:04	13	T	5:38	4.7	6:15	5.6	...	12:02
14	T	4:53	4.9	5:41	5.2	11:36	...	14	F	6:37	4.7	7:06	5.7	12:40	12:52
15	W	5:58	5.0	6:37	5.5	12:02	12:27	15	S	7:30	4.7	7:53	5.8	1:32	1:41
16	T	6:56	5.0	7:27	5.8	12:57	1:17	16	S	8:19	4.7	8:37	5.8	2:23	2:28
17	F	7:48	5.1	8:13	6.0	1:50	2:05	17	M	9:06	4.7	9:20	5.7	3:10	3:15
18	S	8:37	5.1	8:58	6.0	2:41	2:52	18	T	9:53	4.6	10:03	5.5	3:56	3:59
19	S	9:25	4.9	9:42	5.8	3:30	3:38	19	W	10:42	4.5	10:48	5.2	4:39	4:42
20	M	10:13	4.8	10:27	5.6	4:17	4:22	20	T	11:31	4.4	11:34	5.0	5:21	5:23
21	T	11:05	4.6	11:15	5.3	5:02	5:06	21	F	...	...	12:20	4.3	6:02	6:05
22	W	11:57	4.4	...	...	5:46	5:49	22	S	12:21	4.8	1:08	4.2	6:44	6:50
23	T	12:04	5.0	12:49	4.2	6:32	6:35	23	S	1:07	4.6	1:52	4.2	7:29	7:43
24	F	12:54	4.8	1:40	4.2	7:21	7:28	24	M	1:51	4.4	2:35	4.2	8:17	8:46
25	S	1:43	4.6	2:29	4.1	8:14	8:30	25	T	2:34	4.2	3:17	4.3	9:08	9:47
26	S	2:32	4.4	3:18	4.1	9:10	9:33	26	W	3:20	4.1	4:01	4.4	9:58	10:43
27	M	3:22	4.2	4:08	4.2	10:02	10:30	27	T	4:12	4.0	4:47	4.6	10:45	11:34
28	T	4:15	4.2	4:58	4.3	10:49	11:21	28	F	5:09	4.0	5:35	4.8	11:30	...
29	W	5:10	4.2	5:46	4.6	11:32	...	29	S	6:06	4.1	6:22	5.2	12:23	12:16
30	T	6:02	4.2	6:29	4.8	12:09	12:14	30	S	6:58	4.3	7:07	5.4	1:12	1:04
31	F	6:50	4.3	7:07	5.1	12:56	12:56								

Dates when Ht. of **Low** Water is below Mean Lower Low with Ht. of lowest given for each period and Date of lowest in ( ):

15th–21st: -0.5' (18th, 19th)   4th–7th: -0.3' (5th, 6th)
                                                       16th–18th: -0.2'

Average Rise and Fall 4.6 ft.

When a high tide exceeds avg. ht., the *following* low tide will be lower than avg.

2019 HIGH & LOW WATER
THE BATTERY, NY HARBOR
40°42'N, 74°00.8'W

| | | Daylight Saving Time | | | | | | Daylight Saving Time | | | |

DAY OF MONTH	DAY OF WEEK	JULY				DAY OF MONTH	DAY OF WEEK	AUGUST			
		HIGH		LOW				HIGH		LOW	
		a.m.	Ht.	p.m.	Ht.	a.m.	p.m.			a.m.	Ht.	p.m.	Ht.	a.m.	p.m.

DAY OF MONTH	DAY OF WEEK	a.m.	Ht.	p.m.	Ht.	a.m.	p.m.	DAY OF MONTH	DAY OF WEEK	a.m.	Ht.	p.m.	Ht.	a.m.	p.m.
1	M	7:46	4.5	7:52	5.7	2:01	1:53	1	T	9:04	5.1	9:14	6.1	3:17	3:19
2	T	8:33	4.6	8:37	5.9	2:51	2:44	2	F	9:57	5.3	10:07	6.0	4:05	4:11
3	W	9:22	4.8	9:26	5.9	3:39	3:35	3	S	10:52	5.4	11:03	5.8	4:53	5:03
4	T	10:15	4.9	10:19	5.9	4:27	4:26	4	S	11:50	5.4	...	...	5:41	5:57
5	F	11:13	4.9	11:17	5.7	5:15	5:17	5	M	12:02	5.6	12:47	5.4	6:31	6:55
6	S	...	...	12:12	5.6	6:04	6:12	6	T	1:00	5.3	1:42	5.4	7:25	7:58
7	S	12:18	5.5	1:10	5.1	6:56	7:12	7	W	1:57	4.9	2:37	5.4	8:23	9:05
8	M	1:17	5.3	2:06	5.2	7:53	8:19	8	T	2:55	4.6	3:33	5.3	9:24	10:09
9	T	2:15	5.0	3:01	5.2	8:53	9:26	9	F	3:56	4.4	4:31	5.2	10:22	11:08
10	W	3:13	4.8	3:58	5.3	9:51	10:30	10	S	4:59	4.2	5:30	5.2	11:17	...
11	T	4:14	4.5	4:56	5.3	10:47	11:28	11	S	6:01	4.3	6:26	5.2	12:02	12:09
12	F	5:18	4.4	5:53	5.4	11:39	...	12	M	6:56	4.4	7:15	5.3	12:52	12:58
13	S	6:19	4.4	6:46	5.5	12:22	12:29	13	T	7:44	4.5	7:59	5.3	1:39	1:45
14	S	7:14	4.4	7:34	5.5	1:13	1:18	14	W	8:27	4.6	8:39	5.4	2:24	2:30
15	M	8:03	4.5	8:18	5.5	2:02	2:06	15	T	9:08	4.7	9:18	5.3	3:06	3:13
16	T	8:48	4.5	9:00	5.5	2:49	2:53	16	F	9:48	4.7	9:55	5.2	3:45	3:54
17	W	9:32	4.5	9:41	5.4	3:33	3:37	17	S	10:26	4.7	10:33	5.0	4:22	4:32
18	T	10:16	4.5	10:22	5.2	4:14	4:18	18	S	11:04	4.6	11:09	4.8	4:57	5:09
19	F	11:01	4.4	11:04	5.0	4:53	4:58	19	M	11:40	4.6	11:46	4.6	5:29	5:45
20	S	11:46	4.4	11:46	4.8	5:30	5:36	20	T	...	...	12:14	4.5	5:58	6:22
21	S	...	...	12:29	4.3	6:07	6:15	21	W	12:24	4.4	12:46	4.6	6:24	7:05
22	M	12:28	4.6	1:09	4.3	6:42	6:58	22	T	1:04	4.2	1:23	4.6	6:56	8:10
23	T	1:08	4.4	1:45	4.3	7:19	7:53	23	F	1:50	4.1	2:07	4.7	7:44	9:25
24	W	1:48	4.2	2:21	4.4	8:01	9:00	24	S	2:43	4.0	2:59	4.8	9:00	10:29
25	T	2:30	4.1	3:00	4.5	8:55	10:03	25	S	3:46	4.0	4:02	5.0	10:16	11:26
26	F	3:20	4.0	3:46	4.7	9:53	11:00	26	M	4:56	4.2	5:11	5.2	11:19	...
27	S	4:19	4.0	4:41	4.9	10:49	11:53	27	T	6:03	4.4	6:17	5.5	12:20	12:17
28	S	5:25	4.1	5:41	5.2	11:43	...	28	W	7:02	4.8	7:15	5.8	1:12	1:14
29	M	6:27	4.3	6:39	5.5	12:45	12:37	29	T	7:55	5.2	8:08	6.1	2:03	2:09
30	T	7:22	4.6	7:32	5.8	1:36	1:31	30	F	8:45	5.5	8:58	6.1	2:53	3:03
31	W	8:13	4.8	8:23	6.0	2:27	2:26	31	S	9:35	5.7	9:50	6.1	3:41	3:55

Dates when Ht. of **Low** Water is below Mean Lower Low with Ht. of lowest given for each period and Date of lowest in ( ):

2nd–8th: -0.6' (5th)   1st–6th: -0.8' (3rd)
31st: -0.2'   29th–31st: -0.8' (31st)

Average Rise and Fall 4.6 ft.

When a high tide exceeds avg. ht., the *following* low tide will be lower than avg.

2019 HIGH & LOW WATER
THE BATTERY, NY HARBOR
40°42'N, 74°00.8'W

| Daylight Saving Time | | | | | | | | Daylight Saving Time | | | | | |

DAY OF MONTH	DAY OF WEEK	SEPTEMBER						DAY OF MONTH	DAY OF WEEK	OCTOBER					
		HIGH				LOW				HIGH				LOW	
		a.m.	Ht.	p.m.	Ht.	a.m.	p.m.			a.m.	Ht.	p.m.	Ht.	a.m.	p.m.
1	S	10:28	5.8	10:44	5.8	4:28	4:47	1	T	10:55	6.0	11:19	5.2	4:48	5:20
2	M	11:23	5.8	11:41	5.5	5:15	5:39	2	W	11:49	5.8	...	...	5:35	6:13
3	T	...	...	12:19	5.7	6:03	6:34	3	T	12:18	4.9	12:45	5.5	6:25	7:09
4	W	12:39	5.1	1:15	5.6	6:55	7:35	4	F	1:17	4.6	1:41	5.2	7:20	8:11
5	T	1:37	4.8	2:10	5.4	7:52	8:40	5	S	2:15	4.3	2:37	5.0	8:24	9:16
6	F	2:36	4.5	3:06	5.2	8:55	9:45	6	S	3:14	4.2	3:34	4.8	9:29	10:16
7	S	3:36	4.3	4:05	5.0	9:57	10:45	7	M	4:14	4.1	4:33	4.7	10:30	11:09
8	S	4:39	4.2	5:05	4.9	10:55	11:38	8	T	5:13	4.2	5:31	4.7	11:23	11:56
9	M	5:41	4.2	6:02	5.0	11:48	...	9	W	6:08	4.4	6:22	4.8	...	12:11
10	T	6:35	4.4	6:52	5.1	12:27	12:36	10	T	6:53	4.6	7:06	4.9	12:39	12:56
11	W	7:21	4.6	7:36	5.2	1:12	1:22	11	F	7:34	4.8	7:46	5.0	1:20	1:40
12	T	8:03	4.8	8:15	5.2	1:54	2:06	12	S	8:10	5.0	8:23	5.0	1:59	2:22
13	F	8:41	4.9	8:52	5.2	2:34	2:48	13	S	8:43	5.1	8:57	4.9	2:37	3:03
14	S	9:16	4.9	9:27	5.1	3:12	3:29	14	M	9:13	5.2	9:30	4.8	3:13	3:43
15	S	9:50	4.9	10:00	5.0	3:48	4:07	15	T	9:39	5.2	10:02	4.6	3:47	4:21
16	M	10:20	4.9	10:33	4.8	4:22	4:44	16	W	10:04	5.1	10:36	4.4	4:18	4:59
17	T	10:47	4.9	11:07	4.6	4:52	5:20	17	T	10:34	5.1	11:17	4.3	4:48	5:37
18	W	11:15	4.8	11:45	4.3	5:19	5:55	18	F	11:14	5.0	...	...	5:20	6:19
19	T	11:50	4.8	...	...	5:45	6:35	19	S	12:08	4.1	12:06	5.0	5:58	7:15
20	F	12:30	4.2	12:35	4.8	6:19	7:33	20	S	1:08	4.0	1:06	4.9	6:49	8:28
21	S	1:22	4.1	1:28	4.9	7:06	8:52	21	M	2:10	4.1	2:12	4.9	8:12	9:38
22	S	2:21	4.0	2:29	4.9	8:24	10:02	22	T	3:15	4.2	3:21	4.9	9:40	10:39
23	M	3:27	4.1	3:37	5.0	9:55	11:02	23	W	4:22	4.4	4:33	5.1	10:48	11:33
24	T	4:37	4.3	4:50	5.2	11:03	11:56	24	T	5:27	4.8	5:41	5.2	11:47	...
25	W	5:45	4.7	5:59	5.5	...	12:02	25	F	6:25	5.3	6:41	5.4	12:24	12:43
26	T	6:44	5.1	6:59	5.8	12:48	12:58	26	S	7:17	5.7	7:34	5.6	1:13	1:37
27	F	7:36	5.5	7:51	5.9	1:38	1:53	27	S	8:05	6.0	8:23	5.6	2:02	2:30
28	S	8:25	5.9	8:41	6.0	2:27	2:47	28	M	8:52	6.2	9:13	5.4	2:50	3:22
29	S	9:13	6.1	9:31	5.8	3:15	3:39	29	T	9:39	6.1	10:03	5.2	3:37	4:12
30	M	10:03	6.1	10:23	5.6	4:02	4:30	30	W	10:28	5.9	10:57	4.9	4:23	5:01
								31	T	11:20	5.6	11:55	4.6	5:09	5:50

Dates when Ht. of **Low** Water is below Mean Lower Low with Ht. of lowest given for each period and Date of lowest in ( ):

1st–3rd: -0.8' (1st)
27th–30th: -0.8' (29th, 30th)

1st–2nd: -0.6' (1st)
25th–31st: -0.8' (28th)

Average Rise and Fall 4.6 ft.

When a high tide exceeds avg. ht., the *following* low tide will be lower than avg.

2019 HIGH & LOW WATER
THE BATTERY, NY HARBOR
40°42'N, 74°00.8'W

Standard Time starts Nov. 3 at 2 a.m.　　　　　　**Standard Time**

DAY OF MONTH	DAY OF WEEK	NOVEMBER HIGH a.m.	Ht.	HIGH p.m.	Ht.	LOW a.m.	LOW p.m.	DAY OF MONTH	DAY OF WEEK	DECEMBER HIGH a.m.	Ht.	HIGH p.m.	Ht.	LOW a.m.	LOW p.m.
1	F	...	...	12:15	5.3	5:57	6:42	1	S	11:38	4.7	...	...	5:18	6:04
2	S	12:53	4.3	1:10	5.0	6:48	7:39	2	M	12:20	4.0	12:30	4.5	6:10	6:58
3	S	1:50	4.1	*1:05	4.7	*6:48	*7:40	3	T	1:12	3.9	1:20	4.2	7:11	7:54
4	M	1:46	4.0	1:59	4.5	7:54	8:40	4	W	2:03	3.8	2:11	4.1	8:15	8:48
5	T	2:42	4.0	2:55	4.4	8:57	9:33	5	T	2:54	3.9	3:03	4.0	9:14	9:36
6	W	3:38	4.1	3:51	4.3	9:52	10:20	6	F	3:46	4.0	3:57	3.9	10:07	10:20
7	T	4:31	4.2	4:44	4.4	10:41	11:02	7	S	4:35	4.2	4:49	4.0	10:55	11:02
8	F	5:19	4.5	5:31	4.5	11:27	11:42	8	S	5:20	4.4	5:37	4.0	11:41	11:42
9	S	6:01	4.7	6:14	4.6	...	12:11	9	M	6:00	4.7	6:20	4.1	...	12:26
10	S	6:37	4.9	6:52	4.6	12:21	12:54	10	T	6:34	4.9	7:00	4.2	12:23	1:10
11	M	7:09	5.1	7:28	4.6	1:00	1:37	11	W	7:07	5.1	7:38	4.2	1:05	1:55
12	T	7:38	5.2	8:03	4.5	1:37	2:19	12	T	7:41	5.2	8:17	4.2	1:47	2:39
13	W	8:05	5.3	8:37	4.4	2:15	2:59	13	F	8:17	5.3	9:01	4.2	2:30	3:22
14	T	8:35	5.3	9:16	4.3	2:51	3:40	14	S	9:00	5.3	9:51	4.2	3:13	4:07
15	F	9:11	5.2	10:02	4.2	3:28	4:22	15	S	9:50	5.2	10:48	4.2	3:58	4:53
16	S	9:56	5.1	10:58	4.1	4:06	5:08	16	M	10:48	5.0	11:48	4.2	4:47	5:45
17	S	10:53	5.0	11:59	4.1	4:50	6:02	17	T	11:50	4.9	...	...	5:44	6:43
18	M	11:57	4.9	...	...	5:47	7:06	18	W	12:47	4.3	12:51	4.7	6:54	7:45
19	T	1:01	4.1	1:02	4.8	7:05	8:13	19	T	1:46	4.4	1:53	4.6	8:07	8:46
20	W	2:03	4.3	2:08	4.8	8:25	9:14	20	F	2:45	4.6	2:57	4.4	9:15	9:43
21	T	3:06	4.5	3:15	4.8	9:32	10:08	21	S	3:46	4.8	4:03	4.4	10:16	10:36
22	F	4:08	4.9	4:22	4.8	10:32	10:59	22	S	4:46	5.1	5:06	4.4	11:13	11:27
23	S	5:06	5.3	5:23	4.9	11:28	11:49	23	M	5:41	5.3	6:03	4.4	...	12:06
24	S	5:59	5.6	6:17	5.0	...	12:22	24	T	6:31	5.5	6:55	4.5	12:17	12:58
25	M	6:47	5.8	7:08	5.0	12:38	1:14	25	W	7:17	5.5	7:43	4.5	1:06	1:48
26	T	7:33	5.9	7:56	4.9	1:26	2:05	26	T	8:02	5.5	8:30	4.4	1:54	2:35
27	W	8:18	5.8	8:46	4.7	2:14	2:54	27	F	8:46	5.3	9:17	4.3	2:40	3:20
28	T	9:05	5.7	9:37	4.5	3:00	3:41	28	S	9:31	5.1	10:06	4.1	3:24	4:03
29	F	9:54	5.3	10:31	4.3	3:45	4:27	29	S	10:18	4.8	10:56	4.0	4:07	4:45
30	S	10:45	5.0	11:27	4.1	4:31	5:14	30	M	11:05	4.6	11:45	3.9	4:49	5:27
								31	T	11:52	4.3	...	...	5:33	6:11

Dates when Ht. of **Low** Water is below Mean Lower Low with Ht. of lowest given for each period and Date of lowest in ( ):

21st–29th: -0.8' (26th)　　　　　　11th–17th: -0.4' (13th, 14th)
　　　　　　　　　　　　　　　　19th–29th: -0.7' (25th, 26th)

Average Rise and Fall 4.6 ft.

When a high tide exceeds avg. ht., the *following* low tide will be lower than avg.

133

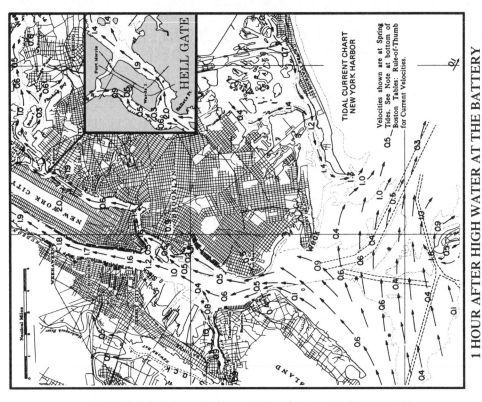

NEW YORK BAY CURRENTS

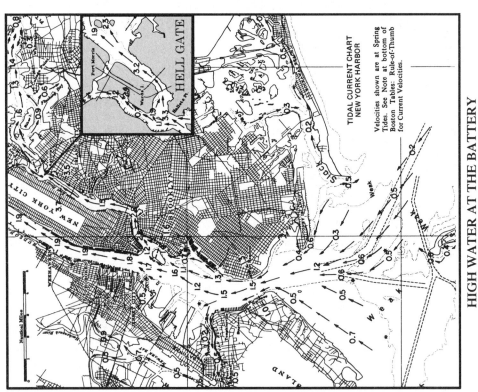

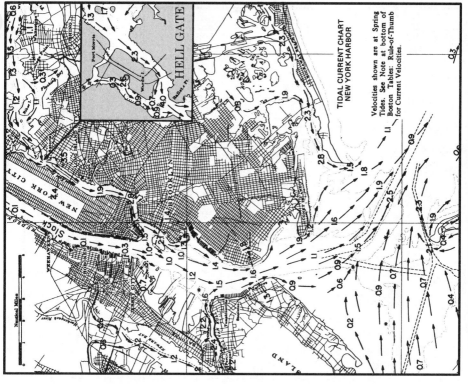

HELL GATE

TIDAL CURRENT CHART
NEW YORK HARBOR

Velocities shown are at Spring
Tides. See Note at bottom of
Boston Tables: Rule-of-Thumb
for Current Velocities.

NEW YORK BAY CURRENTS

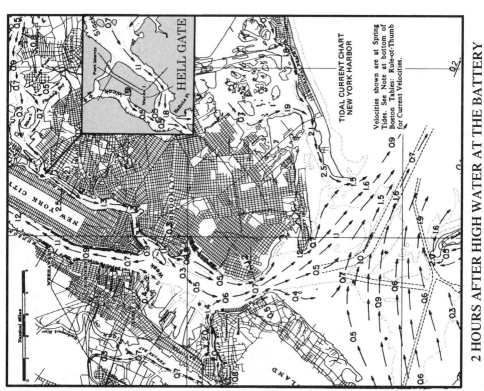

HELL GATE

TIDAL CURRENT CHART
NEW YORK HARBOR

Velocities shown are at Spring
Tides. See Note at bottom of
Boston Tables: Rule-of-Thumb
for Current Velocities.

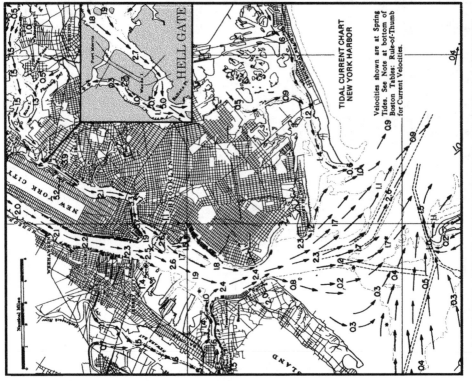

NEW YORK BAY CURRENTS

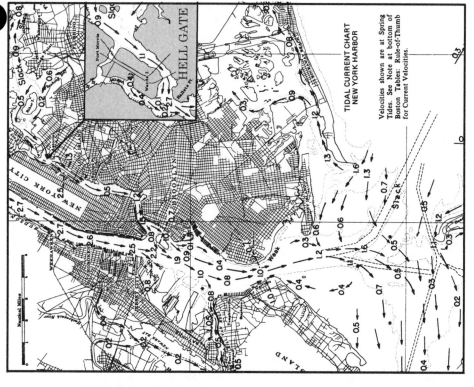

NEW YORK BAY CURRENTS

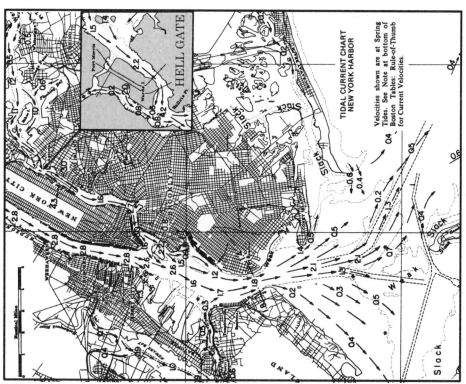

137

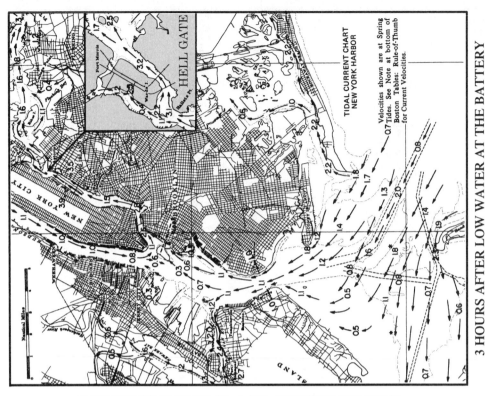

NEW YORK BAY CURRENTS

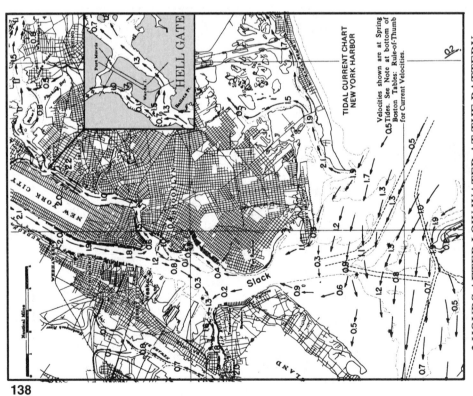

138

NEW YORK BAY CURRENTS

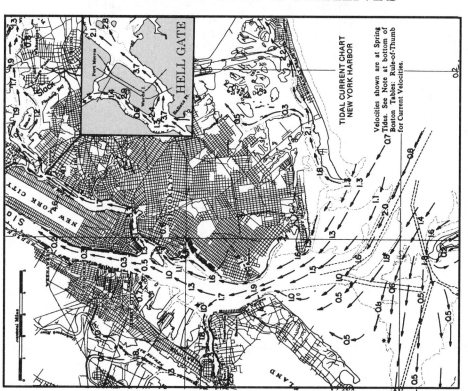

5 HOURS AFTER LOW WATER AT THE BATTERY

TIDAL CURRENT CHART
NEW YORK HARBOR

Velocities shown are at Spring
Tides. See Note at bottom of
Boston Tables: Rule-of-Thumb
for Current Velocities.

HELL GATE

4 HOURS AFTER LOW WATER AT THE BATTERY

TIDAL CURRENT CHART
NEW YORK HARBOR

Velocities shown are at Spring
Tides. See Note at bottom of
Boston Tables: Rule-of-Thumb
for Current Velocities.

HELL GATE

2019 HIGH & LOW WATER
SANDY HOOK, NJ
40°28.1'N, 74°00.6'W

Standard Time

Standard Time

D A Y O F M O N T H	D A Y O F W E E K	JANUARY HIGH a.m.	Ht.	p.m.	Ht.	LOW a.m.	p.m.	D A Y O F M O N T H	D A Y O F W E E K	FEBRUARY HIGH a.m.	Ht.	p.m.	Ht.	LOW a.m.	p.m.
1	T	3:56	4.9	4:14	4.2	10:27	10:38	1	F	5:16	4.8	5:41	4.0	11:44	11:48
2	W	4:50	5.0	5:10	4.2	11:18	11:24	2	S	6:03	4.9	6:28	4.1	...	12:29
3	T	5:40	5.1	6:01	4.2	...	12:06	3	S	6:46	5.0	7:10	4.2	12:33	1:12
4	F	6:25	5.2	6:47	4.2	12:09	12:52	4	M	7:26	5.0	7:49	4.3	1:16	1:52
5	S	7:07	5.2	7:30	4.2	12:53	1:36	5	T	8:04	5.0	8:27	4.3	1:57	2:30
6	S	7:47	5.2	8:11	4.2	1:36	2:17	6	W	8:40	4.9	9:04	4.3	2:36	3:05
7	M	8:26	5.1	8:52	4.1	2:17	2:56	7	T	9:16	4.8	9:40	4.2	3:13	3:39
8	T	9:05	4.9	9:34	4.0	2:56	3:33	8	F	9:52	4.6	10:15	4.2	3:48	4:10
9	W	9:45	4.7	10:15	3.9	3:34	4:09	9	S	10:29	4.4	10:51	4.2	4:23	4:41
10	T	10:24	4.5	10:57	3.8	4:10	4:44	10	S	11:08	4.2	11:31	4.2	4:59	5:13
11	F	11:05	4.3	11:39	3.8	4:47	5:19	11	M	11:54	4.0	...	...	5:42	5:52
12	S	11:47	4.1	...	...	5:28	5:58	12	T	12:17	4.3	12:46	3.9	6:45	6:48
13	S	12:21	3.9	12:33	4.0	6:22	6:46	13	W	1:09	4.4	1:44	3.8	8:05	8:02
14	M	1:05	4.0	1:22	3.9	7:33	7:45	14	T	2:09	4.6	2:50	3.9	9:17	9:14
15	T	1:54	4.2	2:18	3.8	8:45	8:46	15	F	3:16	4.8	4:00	4.1	10:19	10:17
16	W	2:49	4.4	3:20	3.9	9:47	9:44	16	S	4:24	5.1	5:05	4.4	11:16	11:16
17	T	3:49	4.8	4:25	4.0	10:43	10:39	17	S	5:27	5.5	6:03	4.8	...	12:10
18	F	4:49	5.1	5:25	4.3	11:37	11:34	18	M	6:23	5.8	6:57	5.2	12:13	1:02
19	S	5:46	5.5	6:21	4.6	...	12:31	19	T	7:15	6.0	7:48	5.4	1:09	1:53
20	S	6:39	5.8	7:13	4.8	12:29	1:23	20	W	8:06	6.1	8:38	5.6	2:02	2:41
21	M	7:30	6.0	8:05	5.0	1:23	2:14	21	T	8:56	5.9	9:30	5.6	2:54	3:27
22	T	8:21	6.0	8:57	5.1	2:16	3:03	22	F	9:48	5.6	10:23	5.5	3:44	4:12
23	W	9:14	5.9	9:52	5.1	3:08	3:51	23	S	10:41	5.2	11:16	5.3	4:34	4:58
24	T	10:09	5.6	10:49	5.1	4:00	4:39	24	S	11:35	4.8	...	...	5:26	5:47
25	F	11:04	5.3	11:44	5.0	4:53	5:29	25	M	12:09	5.1	12:29	4.4	6:24	6:42
26	S	11:59	4.9	...	...	5:50	6:22	26	T	1:01	4.9	1:23	4.1	7:29	7:44
27	S	12:39	4.9	12:54	4.6	6:53	7:21	27	W	1:55	4.6	2:20	3.9	8:35	8:47
28	M	1:33	4.8	1:50	4.2	8:01	8:21	28	T	2:52	4.5	3:21	3.8	9:36	9:45
29	T	2:29	4.7	2:48	4.0	9:06	9:19								
30	W	3:26	4.7	3:48	3.8	10:04	10:12								
31	T	4:23	4.7	4:48	3.9	10:56	11:01								

Dates when Ht. of **Low** Water is below Mean Lower Low with Ht. of lowest given for each period and Date of lowest in ( ):

1st–8th: -0.3' (4th–7th)   3rd–7th: -0.3' (5th)
17th–27th: -1.2' (22nd, 23rd)   16th–24th: -1.2' (20th, 21st)

Average Rise and Fall 4.6 ft.

When a high tide exceeds avg. ht., the *following* low tide will be lower than avg.

2019 HIGH & LOW WATER
SANDY HOOK, NJ
40°28.1'N, 74°00.6'W

*Daylight Time starts March 10 at 2 a.m.   **Daylight Saving Time**

DAY OF MONTH	DAY OF WEEK	MARCH HIGH a.m.	Ht.	MARCH HIGH p.m.	Ht.	MARCH LOW a.m.	MARCH LOW p.m.	DAY OF MONTH	DAY OF WEEK	APRIL HIGH a.m.	Ht.	APRIL HIGH p.m.	Ht.	APRIL LOW a.m.	APRIL LOW p.m.
1	F	3:50	4.5	4:22	3.8	10:29	10:37	1	M	6:04	4.6	6:34	4.4	...	12:25
2	S	4:47	4.6	5:17	4.0	11:16	11:25	2	T	6:51	4.8	7:16	4.7	12:43	1:06
3	S	5:38	4.7	6:04	4.2	...	12:01	3	W	7:32	4.9	7:53	4.9	1:26	1:46
4	M	6:22	4.9	6:46	4.4	12:10	12:42	4	T	8:10	5.0	8:27	5.1	2:09	2:24
5	T	7:02	5.0	7:24	4.6	12:53	1:22	5	F	8:46	5.0	9:00	5.2	2:50	3:00
6	W	7:39	5.0	7:59	4.7	1:34	1:59	6	S	9:21	4.9	9:31	5.2	3:29	3:35
7	T	8:14	5.0	8:32	4.7	2:14	2:34	7	S	9:57	4.8	10:04	5.2	4:07	4:09
8	F	8:48	4.9	9:04	4.7	2:51	3:07	8	M	10:36	4.6	10:41	5.2	4:45	4:42
9	S	9:23	4.7	9:36	4.7	3:27	3:38	9	T	11:23	4.4	11:27	5.2	5:24	5:19
10	S	*10:59	4.5	*11:10	4.7	*5:02	*5:08	10	W	...	...	12:15	4.3	6:09	6:02
11	M	11:40	4.3	11:52	4.7	5:38	5:40	11	T	12:21	5.1	1:13	4.2	7:05	6:59
12	T	...	...	12:28	4.2	6:20	6:19	12	F	1:22	5.0	2:15	4.2	8:18	8:19
13	W	12:41	4.7	1:24	4.0	7:17	7:13	13	S	2:27	5.0	3:19	4.4	9:32	9:39
14	T	1:39	4.8	2:25	4.0	8:35	8:32	14	S	3:35	5.1	4:25	4.7	10:36	10:47
15	F	2:42	4.8	3:31	4.1	9:52	9:53	15	M	4:44	5.2	5:29	5.0	11:32	11:48
16	S	3:52	4.9	4:41	4.3	10:57	11:01	16	T	5:48	5.4	6:26	5.5	...	12:24
17	S	5:03	5.2	5:47	4.7	11:54	...	17	W	6:46	5.6	7:19	5.9	12:44	1:13
18	M	6:08	5.5	6:46	5.1	12:02	12:48	18	T	7:38	5.7	8:07	6.1	1:38	2:01
19	T	7:06	5.8	7:38	5.6	12:59	1:39	19	F	8:26	5.7	8:53	6.2	2:29	2:48
20	W	7:58	6.0	8:28	5.9	1:54	2:28	20	S	9:14	5.5	9:39	6.1	3:19	3:33
21	T	8:47	6.0	9:16	6.0	2:46	3:15	21	S	10:02	5.2	10:26	5.9	4:06	4:16
22	F	9:36	5.8	10:05	6.0	3:37	4:00	22	M	10:53	4.9	11:14	5.6	4:52	4:58
23	S	10:25	5.5	10:54	5.8	4:25	4:44	23	T	11:45	4.6	...	...	5:37	5:41
24	S	11:17	5.1	11:45	5.5	5:13	5:28	24	W	12:04	5.2	12:38	4.3	6:25	6:28
25	M	...	...	12:10	4.7	6:02	6:13	25	T	12:54	4.9	1:31	4.1	7:17	7:23
26	T	12:36	5.2	1:03	4.4	6:54	7:03	26	F	1:45	4.7	2:23	4.0	8:16	8:29
27	W	1:28	4.9	1:57	4.1	7:53	8:03	27	S	2:38	4.5	3:17	4.0	9:18	9:36
28	T	2:20	4.6	2:53	3.9	8:59	9:11	28	S	3:32	4.4	4:12	4.1	10:13	10:34
29	F	3:15	4.4	3:51	3.9	10:01	10:14	29	M	4:27	4.4	5:05	4.3	11:01	11:25
30	S	4:13	4.4	4:50	4.0	10:55	11:09	30	T	5:22	4.4	5:55	4.6	11:44	...
31	S	5:11	4.4	5:45	4.2	11:42	11:57								

Dates when Ht. of **Low** Water is below Mean Lower Low with Ht. of lowest given for each period and Date of lowest in ( ):

    6th–7th: -0.2'   16th–22nd: -0.8' (19th, 20th)
    18th–25th: -1.0' (20th–22nd)

Average Rise and Fall 4.6 ft.

When a high tide exceeds avg. ht., the *following* low tide will be lower than avg.

2019 HIGH & LOW WATER
SANDY HOOK, NJ
40°28.1'N, 74°00.6'W

		Daylight Saving Time						Daylight Saving Time				
DAY OF MONTH	**DAY OF WEEK**	**MAY**				**DAY OF MONTH**	**DAY OF WEEK**	**JUNE**				
		HIGH		LOW				HIGH		LOW		
		a.m.	Ht.	p.m.	Ht.	a.m.	p.m.			a.m.	Ht.	p.m.	Ht.	a.m.	p.m.
1	W	6:11	4.6	6:38	4.9	12:11	12:25	1	S	7:02	4.6	7:18	5.5	1:11	1:07
2	T	6:56	4.7	7:17	5.2	12:56	1:05	2	S	7:46	4.7	7:58	5.8	1:57	1:51
3	F	7:37	4.8	7:53	5.4	1:41	1:45	3	M	8:30	4.8	8:38	5.9	2:44	2:37
4	S	8:16	4.8	8:27	5.5	2:24	2:25	4	T	9:16	4.8	9:22	5.9	3:30	3:23
5	S	8:54	4.8	9:02	5.6	3:07	3:04	5	W	10:05	4.8	10:11	5.9	4:15	4:10
6	M	9:35	4.8	9:40	5.7	3:48	3:43	6	T	10:59	4.8	11:06	5.7	5:02	4:58
7	T	10:20	4.7	10:23	5.6	4:30	4:24	7	F	11:58	4.8	...	...	5:51	5:51
8	W	11:11	4.6	11:14	5.5	5:14	5:07	8	S	12:05	5.6	12:56	4.8	6:44	6:51
9	T	...	...	12:07	4.5	6:01	5:56	9	S	1:05	5.4	1:54	4.9	7:44	8:00
10	F	12:12	5.4	1:07	4.5	6:57	6:56	10	M	2:03	5.2	2:51	5.1	8:47	9:11
11	S	1:14	5.2	2:06	4.6	8:03	8:11	11	T	3:02	5.1	3:48	5.3	9:47	10:17
12	S	2:16	5.2	3:07	4.7	9:11	9:27	12	W	4:02	4.9	4:47	5.5	10:41	11:16
13	M	3:19	5.1	4:08	5.0	10:12	10:33	13	T	5:03	4.8	5:43	5.7	11:32	...
14	T	4:23	5.1	5:09	5.3	11:07	11:33	14	F	6:02	4.8	6:35	5.9	12:11	12:21
15	W	5:26	5.2	6:05	5.7	11:58	...	15	S	6:57	4.8	7:23	6.0	1:03	1:09
16	T	6:24	5.2	6:57	6.0	12:28	12:47	16	S	7:46	4.8	8:08	6.0	1:53	1:56
17	F	7:17	5.3	7:45	6.2	1:21	1:34	17	M	8:34	4.8	8:51	5.8	2:41	2:42
18	S	8:06	5.2	8:30	6.2	2:12	2:21	18	T	9:19	4.7	9:34	5.7	3:26	3:26
19	S	8:53	5.1	9:14	6.1	3:00	3:06	19	W	10:06	4.6	10:18	5.4	4:08	4:08
20	M	9:40	4.9	9:59	5.8	3:46	3:50	20	T	10:53	4.4	11:02	5.2	4:48	4:49
21	T	10:29	4.7	10:44	5.5	4:30	4:32	21	F	11:41	4.3	11:48	4.9	5:28	5:29
22	W	11:20	4.5	11:32	5.2	5:13	5:14	22	S	...	...	12:28	4.2	6:07	6:11
23	T	...	...	12:11	4.3	5:56	5:57	23	S	12:34	4.7	1:14	4.2	6:49	7:00
24	F	12:21	4.9	1:02	4.2	6:42	6:45	24	M	1:19	4.5	1:58	4.3	7:34	8:00
25	S	1:10	4.7	1:51	4.1	7:32	7:44	25	T	2:04	4.4	2:42	4.3	8:25	9:05
26	S	1:59	4.5	2:39	4.1	8:28	8:51	26	W	2:51	4.2	3:27	4.5	9:18	10:06
27	M	2:48	4.4	3:28	4.2	9:23	9:53	27	T	3:41	4.2	4:15	4.7	10:09	11:00
28	T	3:39	4.3	4:18	4.4	10:13	10:47	28	F	4:37	4.2	5:06	5.0	10:57	11:51
29	W	4:32	4.3	5:08	4.7	10:58	11:37	29	S	5:34	4.3	5:56	5.3	11:44	...
30	T	5:25	4.4	5:54	4.9	11:41	...	30	S	6:29	4.4	6:45	5.6	12:41	12:33
31	F	6:16	4.5	6:37	5.3	12:24	12:24								

Dates when Ht. of **Low** Water is below Mean Lower Low with Ht. of lowest given for each period and Date of lowest in ( ):

15th–21st: -0.5' (18th, 19th)

4th–7th: -0.3' (5th, 6th)
16th–18th: -0.2'

Average Rise and Fall 4.6 ft.

When a high tide exceeds avg. ht., the *following* low tide will be lower than avg.

2019 HIGH & LOW WATER
SANDY HOOK, NJ
40°28.1'N, 74°00.6'W

		Daylight Saving Time							Daylight Saving Time				
DAY OF MONTH	DAY OF WEEK	JULY				DAY OF MONTH	DAY OF WEEK	AUGUST					
		HIGH		LOW				HIGH				LOW	
		a.m.	Ht.	p.m.	Ht.	a.m.	p.m.			a.m.	Ht.	p.m.	Ht.	a.m.	p.m.

Day	Wk	a.m.	Ht.	p.m.	Ht.	a.m.	p.m.	Day	Wk	a.m.	Ht.	p.m.	Ht.	a.m.	p.m.
1	M	7:19	4.6	7:32	5.9	1:31	1:23	1	T	8:39	5.3	8:53	6.3	2:48	2:50
2	T	8:09	4.8	8:20	6.1	2:21	2:14	2	F	9:31	5.5	9:45	6.3	3:37	3:43
3	W	8:58	5.0	9:08	6.2	3:10	3:06	3	S	10:25	5.6	10:39	6.1	4:25	4:35
4	T	9:49	5.1	10:00	6.1	3:58	3:57	4	S	11:20	5.6	11:34	5.8	5:12	5:27
5	F	10:44	5.1	10:55	6.0	4:46	4:48	5	M	...	...	12:16	5.6	6:00	6:22
6	S	11:42	5.2	11:52	5.8	5:34	5:41	6	T	12:30	5.5	1:11	5.6	6:51	7:23
7	S	...	...	12:39	5.2	6:25	6:39	7	W	1:26	5.1	2:06	5.5	7:48	8:31
8	M	12:50	5.5	1:35	5.3	7:20	7:44	8	T	2:22	4.8	3:01	5.4	8:49	9:38
9	T	1:47	5.2	2:30	5.4	8:19	8:53	9	F	3:21	4.5	3:57	5.3	9:49	10:39
10	W	2:42	4.9	3:26	5.4	9:18	9:59	10	S	4:20	4.4	4:55	5.3	10:46	11:34
11	T	3:41	4.7	4:23	5.5	10:15	10:59	11	S	5:22	4.3	5:50	5.3	11:38	...
12	F	4:41	4.6	5:19	5.5	11:08	11:53	12	M	6:19	4.4	6:41	5.4	12:23	12:27
13	S	5:42	4.5	6:13	5.6	11:58	...	13	T	7:09	4.6	7:27	5.5	1:10	1:13
14	S	6:38	4.5	7:03	5.7	12:44	12:47	14	W	7:53	4.7	8:08	5.5	1:54	1:58
15	M	7:28	4.6	7:48	5.7	1:33	1:34	15	T	8:34	4.8	8:47	5.5	2:35	2:41
16	T	8:14	4.6	8:30	5.7	2:19	2:20	16	F	9:13	4.8	9:25	5.4	3:14	3:22
17	W	8:58	4.7	9:11	5.6	3:02	3:04	17	S	9:51	4.8	10:02	5.2	3:50	4:00
18	T	9:41	4.6	9:52	5.4	3:43	3:45	18	S	10:29	4.7	10:39	5.0	4:24	4:37
19	F	10:24	4.5	10:33	5.2	4:21	4:25	19	M	11:05	4.7	11:17	4.8	4:57	5:13
20	S	11:07	4.5	11:14	5.0	4:57	5:03	20	T	11:42	4.7	11:56	4.5	5:27	5:50
21	S	11:49	4.4	11:55	4.8	5:32	5:41	21	W	...	...	12:20	4.7	5:58	6:31
22	M	...	...	12:31	4.4	6:07	6:22	22	T	12:40	4.3	1:01	4.7	6:33	7:26
23	T	12:37	4.5	1:11	4.4	6:43	7:11	23	F	1:28	4.2	1:49	4.8	7:20	8:39
24	W	1:20	4.4	1:52	4.5	7:25	8:14	24	S	2:22	4.1	2:43	4.9	8:27	9:51
25	T	2:06	4.2	2:35	4.7	8:16	9:22	25	S	3:23	4.2	3:44	5.1	9:41	10:53
26	F	2:56	4.1	3:24	4.8	9:16	10:24	26	M	4:30	4.3	4:50	5.4	10:47	11:49
27	S	3:54	4.1	4:20	5.1	10:15	11:20	27	T	5:35	4.6	5:54	5.7	11:46	...
28	S	4:57	4.2	5:19	5.3	11:11	...	28	W	6:35	5.0	6:52	6.1	12:42	12:43
29	M	5:59	4.4	6:17	5.7	12:13	12:06	29	T	7:29	5.4	7:45	6.3	1:34	1:39
30	T	6:56	4.7	7:11	6.0	1:06	1:01	30	F	8:20	5.7	8:36	6.4	2:24	2:34
31	W	7:48	5.1	8:03	6.2	1:58	1:56	31	S	9:10	6.0	9:26	6.3	3:13	3:27

Dates when Ht. of **Low** Water is below Mean Lower Low with Ht. of lowest given for each period and Date of lowest in ( ):

2nd–8th: -0.5' (4th–6th)
31st: -0.2'

1st–6th: -0.8' (3rd)
29th–31st: -0.8' (31st)

Average Rise and Fall 4.6 ft.

When a high tide exceeds avg. ht., the *following* low tide will be lower than avg.

2019 HIGH & LOW WATER
SANDY HOOK, NJ
40°28.1'N, 74°00.6'W

Daylight Saving Time   **Daylight Saving Time**

DAY OF MONTH	DAY OF WEEK	SEPTEMBER HIGH				LOW		DAY OF MONTH	DAY OF WEEK	OCTOBER HIGH				LOW	
		a.m.	Ht.	p.m.	Ht.	a.m.	p.m.			a.m.	Ht.	p.m.	Ht.	a.m.	p.m.
1	S	10:01	6.1	10:18	6.1	4:00	4:18	1	T	10:27	6.2	10:49	5.5	4:18	4:50
2	M	10:55	6.0	11:12	5.7	4:46	5:10	2	W	11:20	6.0	11:45	5.1	5:04	5:41
3	T	11:49	5.9	...	...	5:32	6:03	3	T	...	...	12:14	5.7	5:51	6:35
4	W	12:08	5.3	12:44	5.7	6:21	7:00	4	F	12:42	4.7	1:09	5.4	6:42	7:35
5	T	1:05	4.9	1:39	5.5	7:15	8:05	5	S	1:39	4.4	2:04	5.1	7:43	8:41
6	F	2:01	4.6	2:33	5.3	8:17	9:12	6	S	2:36	4.2	2:59	4.9	8:52	9:45
7	S	2:59	4.4	3:29	5.1	9:22	10:15	7	M	3:34	4.2	3:56	4.8	9:56	10:40
8	S	3:59	4.3	4:27	5.0	10:23	11:10	8	T	4:32	4.2	4:52	4.8	10:52	11:27
9	M	5:01	4.3	5:24	5.1	11:17	11:58	9	W	5:28	4.4	5:44	4.9	11:41	...
10	T	5:56	4.4	6:16	5.2	...	12:06	10	T	6:16	4.7	6:31	5.0	12:09	12:26
11	W	6:46	4.6	7:02	5.3	12:42	12:51	11	F	6:59	4.9	7:13	5.1	12:49	1:09
12	T	7:29	4.8	7:43	5.4	1:24	1:35	12	S	7:37	5.1	7:51	5.1	1:27	1:51
13	F	8:07	5.0	8:21	5.4	2:03	2:17	13	S	8:12	5.2	8:28	5.1	2:04	2:32
14	S	8:44	5.1	8:57	5.3	2:41	2:57	14	M	8:44	5.3	9:03	5.0	2:41	3:12
15	S	9:18	5.1	9:32	5.2	3:16	3:36	15	T	9:15	5.3	9:37	4.8	3:15	3:50
16	M	9:50	5.1	10:06	4.9	3:50	4:13	16	W	9:45	5.3	10:14	4.6	3:49	4:28
17	T	10:22	5.0	10:42	4.7	4:21	4:49	17	T	10:19	5.2	10:56	4.4	4:22	5:06
18	W	10:54	5.0	11:21	4.5	4:52	5:25	18	F	11:00	5.2	11:47	4.2	4:56	5:47
19	T	11:32	5.0	...	...	5:22	6:04	19	S	11:51	5.1	...	...	5:35	6:38
20	F	12:07	4.3	12:18	5.0	5:57	6:54	20	S	12:45	4.1	12:52	5.0	6:25	7:45
21	S	1:01	4.2	1:13	5.0	6:43	8:06	21	M	1:47	4.2	1:56	5.0	7:37	9:00
22	S	2:00	4.2	2:14	5.0	7:53	9:23	22	T	2:49	4.3	3:02	5.1	9:02	10:06
23	M	3:03	4.2	3:19	5.2	9:18	10:29	23	W	3:53	4.6	4:08	5.2	10:15	11:02
24	T	4:10	4.4	4:28	5.4	10:29	11:26	24	T	4:56	5.0	5:13	5.4	11:17	11:54
25	W	5:15	4.8	5:34	5.7	11:31	...	25	F	5:55	5.4	6:12	5.6	...	12:13
26	T	6:15	5.3	6:33	6.0	12:18	12:28	26	S	6:49	5.9	7:06	5.8	12:43	1:08
27	F	7:09	5.7	7:26	6.2	1:09	1:23	27	S	7:39	6.2	7:57	5.8	1:32	2:01
28	S	7:59	6.1	8:17	6.2	1:58	2:17	28	M	8:26	6.4	8:46	5.7	2:19	2:52
29	S	8:48	6.3	9:06	6.1	2:46	3:10	29	T	9:13	6.4	9:35	5.4	3:06	3:42
30	M	9:37	6.4	9:56	5.8	3:33	4:00	30	W	10:01	6.2	10:26	5.1	3:52	4:31
								31	T	10:51	5.8	11:21	4.7	4:37	5:19

Dates when Ht. of **Low** Water is below Mean Lower Low with Ht. of lowest given for each period and Date of lowest in ( ):

1st–3rd: -0.8' (1st)   1st–2nd: -0.6' (1st)
27th–30th: -0.8' (29th, 30th)   24th–31st: -0.8' (27th, 28th)

Average Rise and Fall 4.6 ft.

When a high tide exceeds avg. ht., the *following* low tide will be lower than avg.

2019 HIGH & LOW WATER
SANDY HOOK, NJ
40°28.1'N, 74°00.6'W

Standard Time starts Nov. 3 at 2 a.m.   **Standard Time**

DAY OF MONTH	DAY OF WEEK	NOVEMBER HIGH a.m.	Ht.	HIGH p.m.	Ht.	LOW a.m.	LOW p.m.	DAY OF MONTH	DAY OF WEEK	DECEMBER HIGH a.m.	Ht.	HIGH p.m.	Ht.	LOW a.m.	LOW p.m.
1	F	11:44	5.5	...	...	5:23	6:08	1	S	11:05	4.9	11:43	4.0	4:42	5:27
2	S	12:17	4.4	12:38	5.1	6:11	7:02	2	M	11:56	4.6	...	...	5:30	6:17
3	S	1:14	4.2	*12:31	4.8	*6:07	*7:02	3	T	12:35	3.9	12:46	4.4	6:27	7:13
4	M	1:09	4.1	1:25	4.6	7:13	8:04	4	W	1:25	3.9	1:35	4.2	7:33	8:08
5	T	2:03	4.1	2:18	4.5	8:20	9:00	5	T	2:15	4.0	2:26	4.1	8:37	8:59
6	W	2:57	4.1	3:12	4.4	9:19	9:47	6	F	3:05	4.1	3:18	4.1	9:32	9:45
7	T	3:50	4.3	4:05	4.5	10:10	10:30	7	S	3:54	4.3	4:10	4.1	10:22	10:28
8	F	4:39	4.5	4:54	4.6	10:56	11:10	8	S	4:41	4.6	5:01	4.2	11:09	11:09
9	S	5:25	4.8	5:39	4.7	11:40	11:48	9	M	5:26	4.8	5:47	4.2	11:54	11:51
10	S	6:03	5.1	6:20	4.7	...	12:23	10	T	6:05	5.1	6:30	4.3	...	12:39
11	M	6:39	5.2	6:59	4.7	12:27	1:06	11	W	6:43	5.3	7:12	4.4	12:33	1:24
12	T	7:12	5.4	7:36	4.7	1:05	1:48	12	T	7:21	5.4	7:54	4.4	1:17	2:09
13	W	7:45	5.4	8:14	4.6	1:44	2:29	13	F	8:01	5.5	8:38	4.4	2:01	2:53
14	T	8:19	5.4	8:54	4.4	2:22	3:10	14	S	8:45	5.5	9:28	4.3	2:45	3:37
15	F	8:57	5.4	9:40	4.3	3:01	3:51	15	S	9:34	5.4	10:22	4.3	3:31	4:23
16	S	9:43	5.3	10:35	4.2	3:41	4:36	16	M	10:30	5.2	11:21	4.3	4:19	5:12
17	S	10:38	5.2	11:34	4.2	4:26	5:26	17	T	11:29	5.1	...	...	5:14	6:07
18	M	11:40	5.1	...	...	5:19	6:28	18	W	12:19	4.4	12:28	4.9	6:18	7:09
19	T	12:35	4.2	12:43	5.0	6:29	7:36	19	T	1:17	4.6	1:28	4.8	7:31	8:12
20	W	1:35	4.4	1:45	5.0	7:48	8:41	20	F	2:15	4.8	2:28	4.6	8:43	9:11
21	T	2:35	4.7	2:48	5.0	9:00	9:37	21	S	3:14	5.0	3:30	4.6	9:46	10:05
22	F	3:36	5.0	3:51	5.0	10:02	10:29	22	S	4:13	5.3	4:32	4.5	10:43	10:56
23	S	4:35	5.4	4:52	5.1	10:58	11:19	23	M	5:09	5.5	5:30	4.6	11:37	11:45
24	S	5:29	5.8	5:47	5.2	11:52	...	24	T	6:00	5.7	6:22	4.6	...	12:29
25	M	6:19	6.1	6:38	5.2	12:07	12:45	25	W	6:48	5.7	7:11	4.6	12:34	1:19
26	T	7:06	6.2	7:27	5.1	12:55	1:35	26	T	7:33	5.7	7:58	4.5	1:22	2:06
27	W	7:52	6.1	8:16	4.9	1:42	2:24	27	F	8:17	5.5	8:44	4.4	2:08	2:50
28	T	8:38	5.9	9:05	4.7	2:28	3:11	28	S	9:01	5.3	9:31	4.3	2:52	3:32
29	F	9:25	5.6	9:57	4.4	3:13	3:56	29	S	9:46	5.0	10:19	4.1	3:34	4:12
30	S	10:14	5.2	10:50	4.2	3:57	4:41	30	M	10:32	4.7	11:08	4.0	4:15	4:52
								31	T	11:19	4.5	11:57	3.8	4:56	5:32

Dates when Ht. of **Low** Water is below Mean Lower Low with Ht. of lowest given for each period and Date of lowest in ( ):

21st–29th: -0.8' (26th)

11th–17th: -0.4' (13th, 14th)
19th–29th: -0.7' (25th, 26th)

Average Rise and Fall 4.6 ft.

When a high tide exceeds avg. ht., the *following* low tide will be lower than avg.

2019 CURRENT TABLE
DELAWARE BAY ENTRANCE
38°46.85'N, 75°02.58'W

			Standard Time								Standard Time			

JANUARY / FEBRUARY

DAY OF MONTH	DAY OF WEEK	CURRENT TURNS TO NORTHWEST Flood Starts			CURRENT TURNS TO SOUTHEAST Ebb Starts			DAY OF MONTH	DAY OF WEEK	CURRENT TURNS TO NORTHWEST Flood Starts			CURRENT TURNS TO SOUTHEAST Ebb Starts		
		a.m.	**p.m.**	Kts.	a.m.	**p.m.**	Kts.			a.m.	**p.m.**	Kts.	a.m.	**p.m.**	Kts.
1	T	...	**12:42**	1.2	6:12	**6:24**	a1.3	1	F	1:00	**2:24**	a1.3	7:30	**7:48**	a1.2
2	W	12:42	**1:42**	a1.5	7:06	**7:18**	a1.3	2	S	1:48	**3:06**	a1.3	8:18	**8:36**	a1.2
3	T	1:30	**2:36**	a1.5	7:54	**8:12**	a1.3	3	S	2:36	**3:48**	a1.3	9:06	**9:24**	a1.3
4	F	2:12	**3:24**	a1.5	8:36	**9:00**	a1.3	4	M	3:18	**4:30**	a1.4	9:48	**10:06**	a1.3
5	S	2:54	**4:12**	a1.4	9:24	**9:42**	a1.3	5	T	4:00	**5:06**	a1.4	10:24	**10:48**	a1.3
6	S	3:36	**4:54**	a1.4	10:06	**10:24**	a1.3	6	W	4:36	**5:36**	a1.4	11:06	**11:30**	a1.3
7	M	4:18	**5:30**	a1.4	10:42	**11:06**	a1.3	7	T	5:18	**6:06**	a1.3	11:42	...	1.3
8	T	4:54	**6:06**	a1.3	11:24	**11:48**	a1.3	8	F	6:00	**6:36**	a1.3	12:06	**12:18**	p1.3
9	W	5:31	**6:42**	a1.3	...	**12:01**	1.2	9	S	6:43	**7:12**	a1.2	12:42	**12:54**	p1.2
10	T	6:12	**7:12**	a1.2	12:30	**12:42**	p1.2	10	S	7:30	**7:48**	p1.2	1:24	**1:36**	p1.1
11	F	7:00	**7:48**	a1.1	1:12	**1:24**	p1.1	11	M	8:24	**8:30**	p1.3	2:06	**2:18**	1.1
12	S	7:48	**8:30**	1.0	1:54	**2:06**	p1.1	12	T	9:18	**9:18**	p1.4	2:54	**3:12**	1.1
13	S	8:48	**9:12**	p1.1	2:42	**2:54**	p1.0	13	W	10:24	**10:12**	p1.5	3:48	**4:12**	a1.2
14	M	9:48	**10:00**	p1.2	3:36	**3:48**	1.0	14	T	11:30	**11:12**	p1.6	4:42	**5:12**	a1.3
15	T	10:54	**10:48**	p1.4	4:30	**4:48**	1.1	15	F	...	**12:30**	1.3	5:42	**6:12**	a1.5
16	W	11:54	**11:42**	p1.5	5:24	**5:42**	a1.3	16	S	12:12	**1:30**	a1.8	6:42	**7:12**	a1.7
17	T	...	**12:54**	1.2	6:18	**6:42**	a1.5	17	S	1:12	**2:24**	a1.9	7:42	**8:12**	a1.8
18	F	12:36	**1:54**	a1.7	7:12	**7:36**	a1.7	18	M	2:12	**3:18**	a2.1	8:42	**9:06**	a2.0
19	S	1:30	**2:48**	a1.9	8:06	**8:30**	a1.8	19	T	3:12	**4:06**	a2.2	9:30	**10:00**	a2.1
20	S	2:30	**3:36**	a2.1	9:00	**9:24**	a2.0	20	W	4:06	**4:54**	a2.2	10:24	**10:48**	a2.1
21	M	3:24	**4:30**	a2.2	9:54	**10:18**	a2.1	21	T	5:00	**5:42**	a2.1	11:12	**11:42**	a2.0
22	T	4:18	**5:18**	a2.2	10:42	**11:12**	a2.1	22	F	5:54	**6:30**	a2.0	...	**12:01**	1.8
23	W	5:12	**6:06**	a2.2	11:36	...	2.0	23	S	6:48	**7:12**	a1.8	12:30	**12:54**	a1.7
24	T	6:06	**7:00**	a2.0	12:01	**12:24**	p1.9	24	S	7:42	**8:00**	1.5	1:18	**1:42**	a1.5
25	F	7:06	**7:48**	a1.8	12:54	**1:18**	p1.7	25	M	8:42	**8:48**	p1.4	2:12	**2:30**	a1.3
26	S	8:06	**8:36**	1.6	1:48	**2:06**	1.5	26	T	9:48	**9:42**	p1.2	3:12	**3:24**	a1.1
27	S	9:06	**9:30**	p1.5	2:48	**3:00**	a1.4	27	W	11:00	**10:36**	p1.1	4:06	**4:24**	a1.0
28	M	10:12	**10:24**	p1.4	3:48	**4:00**	1.2	28	T	-A-	**12:06**	0.8	5:12	**5:24**	a1.0
29	T	11:24	**11:18**	p1.3	4:48	**5:00**	a1.2								
30	W	...	**12:30**	0.9	5:42	**5:54**	a1.1								
31	T	12:06	**1:30**	a1.3	6:36	**6:54**	a1.2								

A also at 11:36 p.m. 1.1

The Kts. (knots) columns show the **maximum** predicted velocities of the stronger one of the Flood Currents and the stronger one of the Ebb Currents for each day.

The letter "a" means the velocity shown should occur **after** the **a.m.** Current Change. The letter "p" means the velocity shown should occur **after** the **p.m.** Current Change (even if next morning). No "a" or "p" means a.m. and p.m. velocities are the same for that day.

Avg. Max. Velocity: Flood 1.8 Kts., Ebb 1.9 Kts.
Max. Flood 3 hrs. 5 min. after Flood Starts, ±15 min.
Max. Ebb 3 hrs. 5 min. after Ebb Starts, ±15 min.

See pp. 22-29 for Current Change at other points.

2019 CURRENT TABLE
DELAWARE BAY ENTRANCE
38°46.85'N, 75°02.58'W

*Daylight Time starts March 10 at 2 a.m.   Daylight Saving Time

MARCH

DAY OF MONTH	DAY OF WEEK	NORTHWEST Flood Starts a.m.	p.m.	Kts.	SOUTHEAST Ebb Starts a.m.	p.m.	Kts.
1	F	...	1:06	0.8	6:12	6:24	a1.0
2	S	12:30	2:00	a1.1	7:06	7:24	a1.1
3	S	1:24	2:42	a1.2	8:00	8:18	a1.1
4	M	2:18	3:24	a1.3	8:42	9:00	a1.2
5	T	3:00	4:00	a1.3	9:24	9:42	a1.3
6	W	3:42	4:30	a1.4	10:06	10:24	a1.4
7	T	4:24	5:00	a1.4	10:42	11:00	a1.4
8	F	5:00	5:30	a1.4	11:18	11:36	a1.4
9	S	5:43	6:00	1.3	11:54	...	1.3
10	S	*7:24	*7:30	p1.4	12:12	*1:30	1.2
11	M	8:12	8:12	p1.4	1:48	2:06	1.2
12	T	9:00	8:54	p1.4	2:30	2:54	a1.2
13	W	10:00	9:48	p1.5	3:18	3:48	a1.2
14	T	11:00	10:48	p1.5	4:12	4:48	a1.3
15	F	11:59	11:48	p1.6	5:18	5:48	a1.4
16	S	...	1:06	1.4	6:18	6:54	a1.5
17	S	12:54	2:00	a1.8	7:24	7:54	a1.7
18	M	2:00	3:00	a1.9	8:24	8:48	a1.8
19	T	3:00	3:48	a2.0	9:18	9:42	a1.9
20	W	3:54	4:42	a2.1	10:12	10:36	a2.0
21	T	4:54	5:24	a2.1	11:00	11:24	a2.0
22	F	5:42	6:12	2.0	11:54	...	1.9
23	S	6:36	6:54	1.9	12:12	12:36	a1.8
24	S	7:30	7:36	p1.7	1:00	1:24	a1.7
25	M	8:24	8:24	p1.5	1:48	2:12	a1.4
26	T	9:18	9:06	p1.3	2:36	3:00	a1.2
27	W	10:24	9:54	p1.1	3:30	3:54	a1.1
28	T	11:30	10:54	p1.0	4:30	4:54	a0.9
29	F	...	12:36	0.7	5:30	5:54	a0.9
30	S	12:01	1:36	a1.0	6:36	7:00	a0.9
31	S	1:00	2:24	a1.0	7:36	7:54	a1.0

APRIL

DAY OF MONTH	DAY OF WEEK	NORTHWEST Flood Starts a.m.	p.m.	Kts.	SOUTHEAST Ebb Starts a.m.	p.m.	Kts.
1	M	2:00	3:06	a1.1	8:24	8:48	a1.1
2	T	2:54	3:42	a1.2	9:12	9:36	a1.2
3	W	3:42	4:18	a1.3	9:54	10:18	a1.3
4	T	4:24	4:48	1.3	10:36	10:54	1.3
5	F	5:06	5:18	1.4	11:12	11:30	1.4
6	S	5:48	5:48	p1.5	11:48	...	1.4
7	S	6:30	6:24	p1.5	12:06	12:30	a1.4
8	M	7:12	7:00	p1.6	12:42	1:06	a1.4
9	T	7:55	7:42	p1.6	1:24	1:48	a1.4
10	W	8:42	8:30	p1.5	2:06	2:36	a1.4
11	T	9:42	9:30	p1.5	2:54	3:30	a1.4
12	F	10:42	10:30	p1.6	3:54	4:30	a1.4
13	S	11:42	11:36	p1.6	4:54	5:30	a1.4
14	S	...	12:42	1.5	6:00	6:36	a1.5
15	M	12:42	1:36	a1.7	7:00	7:36	a1.7
16	T	1:48	2:30	1.8	8:00	8:30	a1.8
17	W	2:48	3:24	1.9	9:00	9:24	1.8
18	T	3:42	4:12	p2.0	9:48	10:18	p1.9
19	F	4:36	5:00	p2.0	10:42	11:00	p1.9
20	S	5:30	5:42	p1.9	11:30	11:48	p1.8
21	S	6:18	6:24	p1.8	...	12:12	1.5
22	M	7:12	7:00	p1.6	12:36	1:00	a1.6
23	T	8:00	7:42	p1.4	1:18	1:42	a1.4
24	W	8:54	8:24	p1.2	2:06	2:30	a1.2
25	T	9:48	9:12	p1.0	2:54	3:18	a1.0
26	F	10:48	10:06	p0.9	3:48	4:18	a0.9
27	S	11:54	11:18	p0.9	4:48	5:24	a0.8
28	S	...	12:48	0.7	5:54	6:24	a0.8
29	M	12:24	1:36	a0.9	6:48	7:24	a0.9
30	T	1:30	2:12	1.0	7:42	8:12	1.0

The Kts. (knots) columns show the **maximum** predicted velocities of the stronger one of the Flood Currents and the stronger one of the Ebb Currents for each day.

The letter "a" means the velocity shown should occur **after** the a.m. Current Change. The letter "p" means the velocity shown should occur **after** the p.m. Current Change (even if next morning). No "a" or "p" means a.m. and p.m. velocities are the same for that day.

Avg. Max. Velocity: Flood 1.8 Kts., Ebb 1.9 Kts.
Max. Flood 3 hrs. 5 min. after Flood Starts, ±15 min.
Max. Ebb 3 hrs. 5 min. after Ebb Starts, ±15 min.

See pp. 22-29 for Current Change at other points.

2019 CURRENT TABLE
DELAWARE BAY ENTRANCE
38°46.85'N, 75°02.58'W

Daylight Saving Time   **Daylight Saving Time**

MAY

Day of Month	Day of Week	NORTHWEST Flood Starts a.m.	**p.m.**	Kts.	SOUTHEAST Ebb Starts a.m.	**p.m.**	Kts.
1	W	2:24	**2:54**	1.1	8:36	**9:00**	p1.2
2	T	3:12	**3:24**	p1.3	9:18	**9:42**	p1.3
3	F	4:00	**4:00**	p1.4	10:00	**10:24**	p1.5
4	S	4:42	**4:36**	p1.5	10:42	**11:00**	p1.6
5	S	5:24	**5:12**	p1.6	11:24	**11:36**	p1.6
6	M	6:12	**5:54**	p1.7	...	**12:06**	1.3
7	T	6:54	**6:36**	p1.7	12:18	**12:48**	a1.6
8	W	7:42	**7:24**	p1.7	1:00	**1:30**	a1.6
9	T	8:31	**8:18**	p1.7	1:48	**2:18**	a1.6
10	F	9:24	**9:12**	p1.6	2:36	**3:18**	a1.5
11	S	10:18	**10:18**	p1.6	3:36	**4:18**	a1.5
12	S	11:18	**11:24**	p1.6	4:36	**5:18**	a1.5
13	M	...	**12:18**	1.6	5:42	**6:18**	a1.6
14	T	12:30	**1:12**	p1.7	6:42	**7:18**	1.6
15	W	1:36	**2:06**	p1.8	7:42	**8:12**	1.7
16	T	2:36	**2:54**	p1.9	8:36	**9:06**	1.7
17	F	3:30	**3:42**	p1.9	9:30	**9:54**	p1.8
18	S	4:24	**4:30**	p1.9	10:18	**10:42**	p1.7
19	S	5:18	**5:12**	p1.8	11:06	**11:24**	p1.6
20	M	6:06	**5:48**	p1.7	11:48	**...**	1.3
21	T	6:54	**6:30**	p1.5	12:06	**12:30**	a1.5
22	W	7:42	**7:06**	p1.3	12:48	**1:18**	a1.3
23	T	8:24	**7:48**	p1.2	1:36	**2:00**	a1.2
24	F	9:12	**8:36**	p1.0	2:18	**2:48**	a1.0
25	S	10:00	**9:30**	p0.9	3:12	**3:42**	a0.9
26	S	10:54	**10:36**	p0.9	4:06	**4:42**	a0.9
27	M	11:48	**11:42**	p0.9	5:06	**5:42**	a0.9
28	T	...	**12:30**	0.9	6:00	**6:42**	0.9
29	W	12:48	**1:12**	p1.0	6:54	**7:30**	1.0
30	T	1:48	**1:54**	p1.2	7:48	**8:18**	p1.2
31	F	2:42	**2:36**	p1.4	8:36	**9:06**	p1.4

JUNE

Day of Month	Day of Week	NORTHWEST Flood Starts a.m.	**p.m.**	Kts.	SOUTHEAST Ebb Starts a.m.	**p.m.**	Kts.
1	S	3:30	**3:18**	p1.5	9:24	**9:48**	p1.6
2	S	4:18	**4:00**	p1.7	10:12	**10:30**	p1.7
3	M	5:06	**4:42**	p1.8	10:54	**11:12**	p1.8
4	T	5:48	**5:30**	p1.9	11:42	**11:54**	p1.8
5	W	6:36	**6:18**	p1.9	...	**12:24**	1.4
6	T	7:24	**7:06**	p1.9	12:42	**1:12**	a1.8
7	F	8:12	**8:06**	p1.8	1:30	**2:06**	a1.7
8	S	9:06	**9:00**	p1.7	2:24	**3:00**	a1.7
9	S	10:01	**10:06**	1.6	3:18	**4:00**	a1.6
10	M	10:54	**11:12**	a1.6	4:18	**5:00**	a1.6
11	T	11:54	**...**	1.6	5:18	**6:00**	a1.5
12	W	12:18	**12:48**	p1.7	6:18	**7:00**	1.5
13	T	1:24	**1:36**	p1.7	7:18	**7:54**	p1.6
14	F	2:24	**2:30**	p1.7	8:12	**8:48**	p1.6
15	S	3:24	**3:18**	p1.7	9:06	**9:36**	p1.6
16	S	4:12	**4:00**	p1.7	9:54	**10:18**	p1.6
17	M	5:06	**4:42**	p1.6	10:42	**11:06**	p1.5
18	T	5:54	**5:24**	p1.5	11:24	**11:48**	p1.4
19	W	6:36	**6:00**	p1.4	...	**12:12**	1.0
20	T	7:18	**6:42**	p1.3	12:30	**12:54**	a1.3
21	F	8:00	**7:18**	p1.2	1:12	**1:36**	a1.2
22	S	8:36	**8:06**	p1.1	1:54	**2:24**	a1.1
23	S	9:18	**8:54**	p1.0	2:36	**3:12**	a1.0
24	M	9:54	**9:54**	p0.9	3:24	**4:06**	a1.0
25	T	10:42	**11:00**	0.9	4:18	**5:00**	a0.9
26	W	11:24	**...**	1.0	5:12	**5:54**	0.9
27	T	12:06	**12:12**	p1.1	6:06	**6:48**	p1.1
28	F	1:12	**1:00**	p1.3	7:00	**7:36**	p1.3
29	S	2:12	**1:48**	p1.5	7:54	**8:24**	p1.5
30	S	3:00	**2:36**	p1.6	8:48	**9:12**	p1.6

The Kts. (knots) columns show the **maximum** predicted velocities of the stronger one of the Flood Currents and the stronger one of the Ebb Currents for each day.

The letter "a" means the velocity shown should occur **after** the **a.m.** Current Change. The letter "p" means the velocity shown should occur **after** the **p.m.** Current Change (even if next morning). No "a" or "p" means a.m. and p.m. velocities are the same for that day.

Avg. Max. Velocity: Flood 1.8 Kts., Ebb 1.9 Kts.

Max. Flood 3 hrs. 5 min. after Flood Starts, ±15 min.

Max. Ebb 3 hrs. 5 min. after Ebb Starts, ±15 min.

See pp. 22-29 for Current Change at other points.

2019 CURRENT TABLE
DELAWARE BAY ENTRANCE
38°46.85'N, 75°02.58'W

Daylight Saving Time   Daylight Saving Time

JULY | AUGUST

DAY OF MONTH	DAY OF WEEK	NORTHWEST Flood Starts a.m.	p.m.	Kts.	SOUTHEAST Ebb Starts a.m.	p.m.	Kts.	DAY OF MONTH	DAY OF WEEK	NORTHWEST Flood Starts a.m.	p.m.	Kts.	SOUTHEAST Ebb Starts a.m.	p.m.	Kts.
1	M	3:54	3:30	p1.8	9:36	10:00	p1.8	1	T	5:06	4:54	p2.1	10:54	11:18	p2.0
2	T	4:42	4:18	p1.9	10:30	10:48	p1.9	2	F	5:54	5:48	p2.2	11:42	...	1.8
3	W	5:30	5:12	p2.0	11:18	11:36	p1.9	3	S	6:42	6:42	p2.1	12:06	12:36	a2.0
4	T	6:18	6:00	p2.0	...	12:06	1.6	4	S	7:30	7:36	1.9	1:00	1:30	a2.0
5	F	7:06	6:54	p2.0	12:24	12:54	a1.9	5	M	8:18	8:36	a1.8	1:48	2:18	a1.8
6	S	7:54	7:54	p1.9	1:18	1:48	a1.9	6	T	9:06	9:36	a1.7	2:42	3:18	a1.6
7	S	8:42	8:48	1.7	2:06	2:42	a1.8	7	W	10:00	10:42	a1.6	3:30	4:12	a1.5
8	M	9:36	9:54	a1.7	3:00	3:42	a1.7	8	T	10:54	11:48	a1.5	4:30	5:12	1.3
9	T	10:31	11:00	a1.6	4:00	4:42	a1.6	9	F	11:49	...	1.4	5:30	6:12	p1.2
10	W	11:24	...	1.6	4:54	5:42	1.4	10	S	12:54	12:42	p1.4	6:30	7:12	p1.2
11	T	12:06	12:18	p1.6	5:54	6:36	p1.4	11	S	2:00	1:36	p1.3	7:30	8:06	p1.2
12	F	1:12	1:12	p1.6	6:54	7:36	p1.4	12	M	3:00	2:30	p1.4	8:24	9:00	p1.3
13	S	2:12	2:00	p1.6	7:48	8:30	p1.4	13	T	3:48	3:18	p1.4	9:18	9:48	p1.3
14	S	3:12	2:54	p1.5	8:48	9:18	p1.4	14	W	4:30	4:06	p1.4	10:06	10:30	p1.3
15	M	4:06	3:36	p1.5	9:36	10:06	p1.4	15	T	5:12	4:48	p1.4	10:48	11:12	p1.3
16	T	4:54	4:24	p1.5	10:24	10:48	p1.4	16	F	5:48	5:24	p1.4	11:30	11:48	p1.3
17	W	5:36	5:00	p1.4	11:06	11:30	p1.4	17	S	6:24	6:06	p1.3	...	12:12	1.1
18	T	6:18	5:42	p1.4	11:48	...	1.0	18	S	6:48	6:42	p1.3	12:24	12:48	a1.3
19	F	6:54	6:18	p1.3	12:06	12:30	a1.3	19	M	7:18	7:24	p1.2	1:00	1:24	a1.2
20	S	7:24	7:00	p1.2	12:48	1:12	a1.2	20	T	7:48	8:12	1.1	1:36	2:06	a1.2
21	S	8:00	7:42	p1.1	1:24	1:54	a1.2	21	W	8:24	9:00	a1.1	2:18	2:42	a1.1
22	M	8:30	8:30	1.0	2:06	2:36	a1.1	22	T	9:06	9:54	a1.2	3:00	3:30	1.0
23	T	9:06	9:24	a1.0	2:48	3:24	a1.0	23	F	9:48	11:00	a1.2	3:48	4:18	p1.1
24	W	9:48	10:24	a1.0	3:36	4:12	a1.0	24	S	10:42	11:59	a1.3	4:42	5:18	p1.2
25	T	10:30	11:30	a1.1	4:24	5:06	1.0	25	S	11:42	...	1.4	5:48	6:18	p1.3
26	F	11:24	...	1.2	5:24	6:00	p1.1	26	M	1:00	12:42	p1.6	6:48	7:18	p1.5
27	S	12:36	12:12	p1.4	6:18	6:54	p1.3	27	T	2:00	1:42	p1.8	7:48	8:18	p1.7
28	S	1:36	1:12	p1.5	7:18	7:48	p1.5	28	W	2:54	2:48	p2.0	8:42	9:12	p1.9
29	M	2:30	2:06	p1.7	8:12	8:42	p1.7	29	T	3:48	3:42	p2.1	9:36	10:06	p2.0
30	T	3:24	3:06	p1.9	9:12	9:36	p1.8	30	F	4:36	4:42	p2.2	10:30	11:00	p2.1
31	W	4:18	4:00	p2.0	10:00	10:30	p2.0	31	S	5:24	5:36	p2.2	11:24	11:48	p2.1

The Kts. (knots) columns show the **maximum** predicted velocities of the stronger one of the Flood Currents and the stronger one of the Ebb Currents for each day.
The letter "a" means the velocity shown should occur **after** the a.m. Current Change. The letter "p" means the velocity shown should occur **after** the p.m. Current Change (even if next morning). No "a" or "p" means a.m. and p.m. velocities are the same for that day.
Avg. Max. Velocity: Flood 1.8 Kts., Ebb 1.9 Kts.
Max. Flood 3 hrs. 5 min. after Flood Starts, ±15 min.
Max. Ebb 3 hrs. 5 min. after Ebb Starts, ±15 min.

See pp. 22-29 for Current Change at other points.

2019 CURRENT TABLE
DELAWARE BAY ENTRANCE
38°46.85'N, 75°02.58'W

Daylight Saving Time							Daylight Saving Time						
SEPTEMBER							**OCTOBER**						

DAY OF MONTH	DAY OF WEEK	CURRENT TURNS TO						DAY OF MONTH	DAY OF WEEK	CURRENT TURNS TO					
		NORTHWEST Flood Starts			SOUTHEAST Ebb Starts					NORTHWEST Flood Starts			SOUTHEAST Ebb Starts		
		a.m.	**p.m.**	Kts.	a.m.	**p.m.**	Kts.			a.m.	**p.m.**	Kts.	a.m.	**p.m.**	Kts.
1	S	6:12	**6:30**	2.1	...	**12:12**	1.9	1	T	6:30	**7:06**	a2.0	12:12	**12:36**	p1.9
2	M	7:00	**7:24**	a2.0	12:36	**1:06**	a1.9	2	W	7:12	**8:00**	a1.9	1:00	**1:24**	p1.7
3	T	7:48	**8:18**	a1.9	1:24	**1:54**	a1.8	3	T	8:00	**8:54**	a1.7	1:48	**2:18**	1.4
4	W	8:36	**9:18**	a1.7	2:18	**2:48**	1.5	4	F	8:48	**10:00**	a1.4	2:42	**3:06**	p1.2
5	T	9:24	**10:18**	a1.6	3:06	**3:42**	1.3	5	S	9:36	**11:06**	a1.2	3:30	**4:06**	p1.0
6	F	10:18	**11:30**	a1.4	4:00	**4:42**	p1.2	6	S	10:36	...	1.1	4:30	**5:06**	p0.9
7	S	11:12	...	1.2	5:00	**5:42**	p1.1	7	M	12:12	**-A-**	0.8	5:36	**6:12**	p0.9
8	S	12:36	**12:12**	p1.2	6:06	**6:48**	p1.0	8	T	1:12	**12:48**	p1.0	6:36	**7:12**	p1.0
9	M	1:43	**1:12**	p1.2	7:06	**7:48**	p1.1	9	W	2:07	**1:48**	p1.1	7:36	**8:06**	p1.0
10	T	2:36	**2:12**	p1.2	8:06	**8:42**	p1.1	10	T	2:48	**2:42**	p1.2	8:30	**8:54**	p1.1
11	W	3:24	**3:00**	p1.3	8:54	**9:24**	p1.2	11	F	3:24	**3:30**	p1.2	9:18	**9:36**	p1.2
12	T	4:06	**3:48**	p1.3	9:42	**10:06**	p1.3	12	S	4:00	**4:12**	p1.3	10:00	**10:18**	p1.3
13	F	4:42	**4:30**	p1.3	10:24	**10:48**	p1.3	13	S	4:30	**4:54**	1.3	10:36	**10:54**	1.3
14	S	5:12	**5:12**	p1.4	11:06	**11:24**	p1.3	14	M	5:00	**5:30**	1.3	11:18	**11:36**	a1.4
15	S	5:42	**5:48**	p1.3	11:42	...	1.2	15	T	5:30	**6:12**	a1.4	11:54	...	1.4
16	M	6:12	**6:30**	1.3	12:01	**12:18**	a1.3	16	W	6:06	**6:54**	a1.4	12:12	**12:24**	p1.4
17	T	6:42	**7:06**	a1.3	12:36	**12:54**	a1.3	17	T	6:42	**7:36**	a1.5	12:48	**1:00**	p1.4
18	W	7:12	**7:54**	a1.3	1:12	**1:30**	1.2	18	F	7:18	**8:24**	a1.5	1:30	**1:42**	p1.3
19	T	7:48	**8:42**	a1.3	1:48	**2:12**	p1.2	19	S	8:06	**9:12**	a1.5	2:12	**2:30**	p1.3
20	F	8:30	**9:30**	a1.3	2:30	**2:54**	p1.2	20	S	9:00	**10:06**	a1.4	3:00	**3:24**	p1.3
21	S	9:18	**10:30**	a1.3	3:24	**3:48**	p1.2	21	M	10:00	**11:06**	a1.5	4:00	**4:24**	p1.4
22	S	10:18	**11:30**	a1.4	4:18	**4:48**	p1.3	22	T	11:00	...	1.5	5:00	**5:24**	p1.4
23	M	11:18	...	1.5	5:18	**5:48**	p1.4	23	W	12:06	**12:12**	p1.6	6:06	**6:30**	p1.6
24	T	12:36	**12:24**	p1.6	6:24	**6:54**	p1.5	24	T	1:06	**1:12**	p1.8	7:06	**7:30**	p1.7
25	W	1:30	**1:30**	p1.8	7:24	**7:54**	p1.7	25	F	2:00	**2:18**	p1.9	8:00	**8:24**	p1.8
26	T	2:30	**2:30**	p2.0	8:24	**8:48**	p1.9	26	S	2:54	**3:18**	1.9	8:54	**9:24**	p1.9
27	F	3:18	**3:30**	p2.1	9:18	**9:42**	p2.0	27	S	3:42	**4:12**	2.0	9:48	**10:12**	a1.9
28	S	4:12	**4:24**	p2.1	10:12	**10:36**	p2.0	28	M	4:30	**5:06**	a2.1	10:36	**11:00**	a2.0
29	S	5:00	**5:18**	2.1	11:00	**11:24**	2.0	29	T	5:12	**6:00**	a2.1	11:24	**11:48**	a1.9
30	M	5:42	**6:12**	a2.1	11:48	...	2.0	30	W	6:00	**6:48**	a2.0	...	**12:12**	1.8
								31	T	6:42	**7:42**	a1.8	12:36	**1:00**	p1.6

A also at 11:42 a.m. 1.0

The Kts. (knots) columns show the **maximum** predicted velocities of the stronger one of the Flood Currents and the stronger one of the Ebb Currents for each day.

The letter "a" means the velocity shown should occur **after** the **a.m.** Current Change. The letter "p" means the velocity shown should occur **after** the **p.m.** Current Change (even if next morning). No "a" or "p" means a.m. and p.m. velocities are the same for that day.

Avg. Max. Velocity: Flood 1.8 Kts., Ebb 1.9 Kts.

Max. Flood 3 hrs. 5 min. after Flood Starts, ±15 min.

Max. Ebb 3 hrs. 5 min. after Ebb Starts, ±15 min.

See pp. 22-29 for Current Change at other points.

2019 CURRENT TABLE
DELAWARE BAY ENTRANCE
38°46.85'N, 75°02.58'W

*Standard Time starts Nov. 3 at 2 a.m.   Standard Time

Day of Month	Day of Week	NOVEMBER — NORTHWEST Flood Starts a.m.	p.m.	Kts.	SOUTHEAST Ebb Starts a.m.	p.m.	Kts.	Day of Month	Day of Week	DECEMBER — NORTHWEST Flood Starts a.m.	p.m.	Kts.	SOUTHEAST Ebb Starts a.m.	p.m.	Kts.
1	F	7:24	8:36	a1.6	1:24	1:48	p1.4	1	S	6:36	8:00	a1.3	12:48	1:06	p1.1
2	S	8:12	9:30	a1.3	2:12	2:36	p1.1	2	M	7:24	8:48	a1.1	1:30	1:54	p1.0
3	S	*8:00	*9:30	a1.1	*2:00	*2:30	p1.0	3	T	8:18	9:36	a1.0	2:24	2:48	p0.9
4	M	8:54	10:30	a1.0	3:00	3:30	p0.9	4	W	9:18	10:24	a0.9	3:24	3:42	p0.9
5	T	10:00	11:30	a0.9	4:00	4:30	p0.9	5	T	10:24	11:12	0.9	4:24	4:42	p0.9
6	W	11:12	...	0.9	5:06	5:30	p0.9	6	F	11:30	11:54	p1.0	5:18	5:36	p0.9
7	T	12:18	12:12	p1.0	6:00	6:24	p1.0	7	S	...	12:36	0.9	6:12	6:30	1.0
8	F	12:54	1:12	1.0	6:54	7:12	p1.1	8	S	12:36	1:30	a1.1	7:00	7:18	1.1
9	S	1:37	2:00	1.1	7:42	8:00	1.1	9	M	1:19	2:18	a1.3	7:48	8:06	a1.3
10	S	2:12	2:48	1.2	8:24	8:42	a1.3	10	T	2:00	3:06	a1.4	8:30	8:54	a1.4
11	M	2:42	3:30	a1.3	9:06	9:24	a1.4	11	W	2:42	3:48	a1.5	9:12	9:42	a1.6
12	T	3:18	4:12	a1.4	9:42	10:06	a1.5	12	T	3:24	4:36	a1.6	9:54	10:24	a1.7
13	W	3:54	4:54	a1.5	10:24	10:48	a1.5	13	F	4:06	5:18	a1.7	10:36	11:06	a1.7
14	T	4:30	5:36	a1.6	11:00	11:30	a1.6	14	S	4:54	6:00	a1.8	11:18	11:54	a1.7
15	F	5:12	6:18	a1.6	11:42	...	1.5	15	S	5:42	6:48	a1.8	...	12:06	1.7
16	S	6:00	7:06	a1.6	12:12	12:24	p1.5	16	M	6:36	7:36	a1.8	12:42	12:54	p1.6
17	S	6:48	7:54	a1.6	12:54	1:12	p1.5	17	T	7:30	8:24	a1.7	1:30	1:48	p1.6
18	M	7:42	8:48	a1.6	1:48	2:06	p1.5	18	W	8:30	9:18	1.6	2:30	2:48	p1.6
19	T	8:42	9:48	a1.6	2:42	3:06	p1.5	19	T	9:36	10:18	p1.7	3:30	3:42	p1.5
20	W	9:48	10:42	a1.6	3:48	4:06	p1.5	20	F	10:42	11:12	p1.7	4:30	4:42	1.5
21	T	11:00	11:36	p1.7	4:48	5:06	p1.6	21	S	11:48	...	1.5	5:24	5:42	1.5
22	F	...	12:01	1.7	5:48	6:06	p1.6	22	S	12:06	12:54	a1.8	6:24	6:42	a1.6
23	S	12:30	1:06	a1.8	6:42	7:06	1.7	23	M	12:54	1:54	a1.8	7:18	7:36	a1.7
24	S	1:24	2:06	a1.9	7:36	8:00	a1.8	24	T	1:48	2:48	a1.8	8:06	8:30	a1.7
25	M	2:12	3:00	a2.0	8:30	8:48	a1.9	25	W	2:36	3:42	a1.8	9:00	9:18	a1.7
26	T	3:00	3:54	a2.0	9:18	9:42	a1.8	26	T	3:24	4:30	a1.7	9:42	10:06	a1.6
27	W	3:48	4:42	a1.9	10:00	10:30	a1.8	27	F	4:06	5:18	a1.7	10:30	10:54	a1.5
28	T	4:30	5:36	a1.8	10:48	11:12	a1.7	28	S	4:48	6:00	a1.6	11:12	11:36	a1.4
29	F	5:12	6:24	a1.7	11:36	...	1.5	29	S	5:30	6:42	a1.4	11:54	...	1.3
30	S	5:54	7:12	a1.5	12:01	12:18	p1.3	30	M	6:12	7:24	a1.3	12:18	12:36	p1.2
								31	T	6:54	8:00	a1.1	1:06	1:18	p1.1

The Kts. (knots) columns show the **maximum** predicted velocities of the stronger one of the Flood Currents and the stronger one of the Ebb Currents for each day.

The letter "a" means the velocity shown should occur **after** the **a.m.** Current Change. The letter "p" means the velocity shown should occur **after** the **p.m.** Current Change (even if next morning). No "a" or "p" means a.m. and p.m. velocities are the same for that day.

Avg. Max. Velocity: Flood 1.8 Kts., Ebb 1.9 Kts.

Max. Flood 3 hrs. 5 min. after Flood Starts, ±15 min.

Max. Ebb 3 hrs. 5 min. after Ebb Starts, ±15 min.

See pp. 22-29 for Current Change at other points.

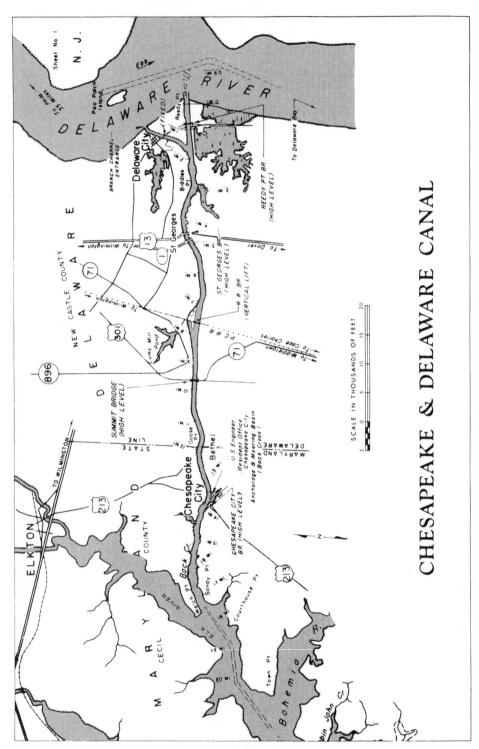

CHESAPEAKE & DELAWARE CANAL

See Chesapeake & Delaware Canal Current Tables, pp. 154-159

Chesapeake & Delaware Canal Regulations

(Traffic Dispatcher is located at Chesapeake City and monitors Channel 13.)

Philadelphia District Engineer issues notices periodically showing available channel depths and navigation conditions.

Projected Channel dimensions are 35 ft. deep and 450 ft. wide. (The branch to Delaware City is 8 ft. deep and 50 ft. wide.) The distance from the Delaware River Ship Channel to the Elk River is 19.1 miles.

1. Traffic controls, located at Reedy Point and Old Town Point Wharf, flash green when Canal is open, flash red when it is closed.
2. Vessel identification and monitoring are performed by TV cameras at Reedy Point and Old Town Point Wharf.
3. The following vessels, tugs and tows are required to have radiotelephones:
   a. Power vessels of 300 gross tons and upward.
   b. All commercial vessels of 100 gross tons and upward carrying 1 or more passengers for hire.
   c. Every towing vessel of 26 feet or over.
4. Vessels listed in 3. will not enter the Canal until radio communication is made with the dispatcher and clearance is received. Ships' captains will tell the dispatcher the estimated time of passing Reedy Point or Town Point. Communication is to be established on Channel 13 (156.65 MHz) two hours prior to entering the canal. Dispatcher also monitors Channel 16 (156.8 MHz) to respond to emergencies.
5. A westbound vessel must be able to pass Reedy Is. or Pea Patch Is. within1 hour of receiving clearance; an eastbound vessel must be able to pass Arnold Point within 1 hour. If passage is not made within 1 hour, a new clearance must be solicited. Vessels must also report to the dispatcher the time of passing the outer end of the jetties at Reedy Point and Old Town Point Wharf.
6. Maximum combined extreme breadth of vessels meeting and overtaking each other is 190 feet.
7. Vessels of all types are required to travel at a safe speed to avoid damage by suction or wash to wharves, landings, other boats, etc. Operators of yachts, motorboats, etc. are cautioned that there are many large, deep-draft ocean-going and commercial vessels using the Canal. There is "no anchoring" in the canal at any time. Moor or anchor outside of Reedy Point, near Arnold Point, or in Chesapeake City Basin.
8. Vessels proceeding *with* the current shall have the right-of-way but all small pleasure craft shall relinquish the right-of-way to deeper draft vessels which have a limited maneuvering ability.
9. Vessels under sail will not be permitted in the Canal.
10. Vessels difficult to handle must use the Canal during daylight hours and must have tug assistance. They should clear Reedy Point Bridge (going east) or Chesapeake City Bridge (going west) before dark.
11. Any tows over 760' contact dispatcher 72 hours prior to passage.

Anchorage and wharfage facilities for small vessels only are at Chesapeake City and permission to use them for more than 24 hours must be obtained from Chesapeake City.

The **railroad bridge** has a clearance when closed of 45 ft. at MHW. The bridge monitors Channel 13 and gives 30 minutes notice prior to lowering.

The **five highway bridges** are high level and fixed.

Normal tide range is 5.4 ft. at Delaware R. end of the Canal and 2.6 ft. at Chesapeake City. Local mean low water at Courthouse Pt. is 2.5 ft. and decreases gradually eastward to 0.6 ft. at Delaware R. (See pp. 18 and 19 for times of High Water in this area.)
Note: A violent northeast storm may raise tide 4 to 5 ft. above normal in the Canal; a westerly storm may cause low tide to fall slightly below normal at Chesapeake City and as much as 4.0 ft. below normal at Reedy Point.

2019 CURRENT TABLE
CHESAPEAKE & DELAWARE CANAL

39°31.83'N, 75°49.66'W at Chesapeake City

Standard Time							Standard Time					
JANUARY							**FEBRUARY**					
DAY OF MONTH	DAY OF WEEK	CURRENT TURNS TO					DAY OF MONTH	DAY OF WEEK	CURRENT TURNS TO			
		EAST Flood Starts			WEST Ebb Starts				EAST Flood Starts			WEST Ebb Starts
		a.m.	**p.m.**	Kts.	a.m.	**p.m.**	Kts.	a.m.	**p.m.**	Kts.	a.m.	**p.m.**	Kts.

D.M	D.W	a.m.	p.m.	Kts.	a.m.	p.m.	Kts.	D.M	D.W	a.m.	p.m.	Kts.	a.m.	p.m.	Kts.
1	T	12:01	**1:00**	p2.1	5:54	**7:30**	a2.5	1	F	1:06	**2:24**	p2.0	7:00	**9:00**	a2.4
2	W	12:48	**2:00**	p2.1	6:42	**8:30**	a2.5	2	S	2:00	**3:12**	p2.1	7:48	**9:48**	a2.4
3	T	1:36	**2:54**	p2.1	7:30	**9:24**	a2.6	3	S	2:54	**3:54**	p2.1	8:36	**10:30**	a2.4
4	F	2:24	**3:42**	p2.1	8:12	**10:12**	a2.5	4	M	3:42	**4:30**	p2.1	9:12	**11:12**	a2.4
5	S	3:12	**4:24**	p2.1	8:54	**11:00**	a2.5	5	T	4:30	**5:06**	p2.1	9:54	**11:42**	a2.3
6	S	3:54	**5:00**	p2.1	9:30	**11:42**	a2.5	6	W	5:12	**5:42**	p2.1	10:36	...	2.3
7	M	4:42	**5:30**	p2.1	10:06	...	2.4	7	T	5:48	**6:12**	p2.1	12:12	**-D-**	1.3
8	T	5:24	**6:06**	p2.1	12:18	**-A-**	1.0	8	F	6:24	**6:42**	p2.1	12:36	**12:06**	p2.0
9	W	6:07	**6:36**	p2.2	12:54	**-B-**	1.1	9	S	7:07	**7:12**	p2.1	12:54	**12:54**	p1.8
10	T	6:48	**7:06**	p2.2	1:24	**12:06**	p2.2	10	S	7:48	**7:42**	p2.1	1:18	**1:48**	a1.8
11	F	7:36	**7:42**	p2.2	1:54	**12:54**	p2.0	11	M	8:42	**8:18**	p2.1	1:48	**2:42**	a2.0
12	S	8:24	**8:24**	p2.1	2:18	**1:54**	p1.8	12	T	9:36	**9:00**	p2.1	2:24	**3:48**	a2.2
13	S	9:18	**9:00**	p2.1	2:48	**3:00**	a1.8	13	W	10:36	**9:54**	p2.1	3:12	**4:54**	a2.3
14	M	10:18	**9:48**	p2.1	3:18	**4:12**	a2.0	14	T	11:36	**10:54**	p2.1	4:06	**6:00**	a2.4
15	T	11:12	**10:30**	p2.1	4:00	**5:24**	a2.2	15	F	...	**12:42**	1.9	5:06	**7:06**	a2.5
16	W	**-C-**	**12:12**	1.8	4:42	**6:36**	a2.3	16	S	12:01	**1:42**	a2.1	6:06	**8:06**	a2.5
17	T	...	**1:12**	1.9	5:36	**7:42**	a2.5	17	S	1:18	**2:42**	p2.2	7:12	**9:00**	a2.6
18	F	12:24	**2:12**	a2.1	6:30	**8:36**	a2.6	18	M	2:24	**3:36**	p2.4	8:18	**9:54**	a2.7
19	S	1:30	**3:06**	p2.2	7:30	**9:30**	a2.7	19	T	3:30	**4:30**	p2.6	9:24	**10:42**	a2.7
20	S	2:36	**3:54**	p2.4	8:24	**10:24**	a2.8	20	W	4:30	**5:18**	p2.6	10:24	**11:24**	a2.6
21	M	3:42	**4:48**	p2.6	9:24	**11:12**	a2.8	21	T	5:24	**6:06**	2.5	11:24	...	2.5
22	T	4:42	**5:36**	p2.7	10:24	**11:59**	a2.8	22	F	6:18	**6:54**	a2.5	12:06	**12:24**	p2.3
23	W	5:42	**6:24**	p2.7	11:24	...	2.7	23	S	7:12	**7:36**	a2.5	12:48	**1:24**	a2.3
24	T	6:36	**7:18**	p2.6	12:48	**12:24**	p2.5	24	S	8:12	**8:24**	a2.3	1:30	**2:24**	a2.4
25	F	7:36	**8:06**	p2.4	1:30	**1:30**	p2.3	25	M	9:06	**9:12**	a2.1	2:12	**3:30**	a2.4
26	S	8:36	**8:54**	2.2	2:12	**2:36**	a2.2	26	T	10:06	**10:00**	a2.0	3:00	**4:30**	a2.3
27	S	9:36	**9:48**	a2.2	3:00	**3:48**	a2.3	27	W	11:06	**10:48**	a1.8	3:54	**5:36**	a2.3
28	M	10:36	**10:36**	a2.1	3:42	**4:54**	a2.3	28	T	**-E-**	**12:06**	1.8	4:42	**6:36**	a2.2
29	T	11:36	**11:24**	a2.0	4:30	**6:00**	a2.4								
30	W	...	**12:36**	1.9	5:24	**7:06**	a2.4								
31	T	12:12	**1:36**	p2.0	6:12	**8:06**	a2.4								

A also at 10:42 a.m. 2.4   B also at 11:18 a.m. 2.3   C also at 11:24 p.m. 2.1
D also at 11:18 a.m. 2.2   E also at 11:48 p.m. 1.6

The Kts. (knots) columns show the **maximum** predicted velocities of the stronger one of the Flood Currents and the stronger one of the Ebb Currents for each day.

The letter "a" means the velocity shown should occur **after** the **a.m.** Current Change. The letter "p" means the velocity shown should occur **after** the **p.m.** Current Change (even if next morning). No "a" or "p" means a.m. and p.m. velocities are the same for that day.

Avg. Max. Velocity: Flood 2.0 Kts., Ebb 1.9 Kts.

Max. Flood 3 hrs. 10 min. after Flood Starts ±45 min.

Max. Ebb 2 hrs. 45 min. after Ebb Starts ±45 min.

See pp. 22-29 for Current Change at other points.

Note *from NOS: These predictions should be considered questionable. Caution is advised.*

2019 CURRENT TABLE
CHESAPEAKE & DELAWARE CANAL

39°31.83'N, 75°49.66'W at Chesapeake City

*Daylight Time starts March 10 at 2 a.m.   Daylight Saving Time

	MARCH								APRIL					
DAY OF MONTH	DAY OF WEEK	CURRENT TURNS TO						DAY OF MONTH	DAY OF WEEK	CURRENT TURNS TO				
		EAST Flood Starts			WEST Ebb Starts					EAST Flood Starts			WEST Ebb Starts		
		a.m.	p.m.	Kts.	a.m.	p.m.	Kts.			a.m.	p.m.	Kts.	a.m.	p.m.	Kts.
1	F	...	1:00	1.8	5:42	7:36	a2.2	1	M	2:24	2:54	p2.0	8:06	9:24	a2.0
2	S	12:48	1:48	p1.9	6:36	8:24	a2.2	2	T	3:18	3:42	p2.0	9:00	10:06	a2.0
3	S	1:42	2:36	p2.0	7:30	9:12	a2.2	3	W	4:00	4:24	p2.0	9:54	10:36	a2.0
4	M	2:36	3:18	p2.1	8:18	9:54	a2.2	4	T	4:48	5:06	1.9	10:48	11:00	1.9
5	T	3:24	4:00	p2.1	9:06	10:30	a2.2	5	F	5:24	5:42	a2.1	11:36	11:24	p2.0
6	W	4:12	4:42	p2.0	9:54	11:00	a2.2	6	S	6:06	6:12	a2.1	-C-	12:24	1.6
7	T	4:48	5:12	p2.0	10:36	11:18	a2.1	7	S	6:42	6:36	a2.2	...	1:06	1.4
8	F	5:24	5:48	p2.0	11:24	11:36	a1.9	8	M	7:18	7:06	a2.1	12:06	1:48	a2.3
9	S	6:01	6:12	2.0	-A-	12:06	1.7	9	T	8:01	7:36	a2.1	12:42	2:36	a2.4
10	S	*7:36	*7:36	2.0	...	*1:54	1.6	10	W	8:48	8:24	a2.0	1:24	3:24	a2.4
11	M	8:18	8:06	p2.0	1:24	2:42	a2.1	11	T	9:42	9:24	a2.0	2:12	4:18	a2.4
12	T	9:06	8:42	p2.0	2:00	3:30	a2.3	12	F	10:42	10:36	a2.0	3:12	5:18	a2.3
13	W	10:06	9:30	p2.0	2:42	4:30	a2.3	13	S	11:42	11:48	a2.0	4:18	6:12	a2.2
14	T	11:06	10:36	p2.0	3:36	5:30	a2.4	14	S	...	12:48	2.1	5:36	7:12	a2.2
15	F	-B-	12:06	1.9	4:36	6:36	a2.3	15	M	1:00	1:48	p2.2	6:54	8:06	a2.2
16	S	...	1:12	2.0	5:42	7:36	a2.3	16	T	2:12	2:48	2.2	8:12	8:54	2.1
17	S	1:00	2:18	p2.1	6:54	8:36	a2.4	17	W	3:12	3:48	a2.4	9:18	9:36	p2.4
18	M	2:12	3:12	p2.2	8:12	9:30	a2.4	18	T	4:06	4:36	a2.6	10:24	10:18	p2.5
19	T	3:18	4:12	2.3	9:18	10:18	a2.4	19	F	5:00	5:24	a2.7	11:24	11:00	p2.6
20	W	4:18	5:06	a2.5	10:24	11:00	a2.4	20	S	5:54	6:06	a2.7	-D-	12:18	1.7
21	T	5:12	5:54	a2.6	11:24	11:42	p2.4	21	S	6:42	6:48	a2.6	...	1:12	1.5
22	F	6:06	6:42	a2.7	...	12:24	2.2	22	M	7:30	7:24	a2.4	12:18	2:00	a2.6
23	S	7:00	7:24	a2.7	12:24	1:18	a2.5	23	T	8:12	8:06	a2.2	1:00	2:54	a2.5
24	S	7:48	8:06	a2.5	1:00	2:12	a2.5	24	W	9:00	8:54	a2.0	1:42	3:42	a2.4
25	M	8:42	8:48	a2.3	1:42	3:12	a2.5	25	T	9:48	9:54	a1.9	2:24	4:36	a2.2
26	T	9:36	9:30	a2.1	2:30	4:06	a2.4	26	F	10:36	10:54	a1.9	3:18	5:24	a2.1
27	W	10:30	10:24	a1.9	3:18	5:06	a2.3	27	S	11:24	...	1.9	4:18	6:18	a2.0
28	T	11:24	11:18	a1.8	4:06	6:00	a2.1	28	S	12:01	12:18	p2.0	5:18	7:06	a1.9
29	F	...	12:18	1.8	5:00	7:00	a2.0	29	M	1:00	1:12	p2.0	6:30	7:54	a1.9
30	S	12:24	1:12	p1.8	6:00	7:54	a2.0	30	T	1:54	2:00	p2.0	7:36	8:36	a1.8
31	S	1:24	2:00	p1.9	7:00	8:42	a2.0								

A also at 11:54 p.m. 2.0   B also at 11:42 p.m. 2.0   C also at 11:42 p.m. 2.2
D also at 11:42 p.m. 2.7

The Kts. (knots) columns show the **maximum** predicted velocities of the stronger one of the Flood Currents and the stronger one of the Ebb Currents for each day.
The letter "a" means the velocity shown should occur **after** the **a.m.** Current Change. The letter "p" means the velocity shown should occur **after** the **p.m.** Current Change (even if next morning). No "a" or "p" means a.m. and p.m. velocities are the same for that day.
Avg. Max. Velocity: Flood 2.0 Kts., Ebb 1.9 Kts.
Max. Flood 3 hrs. 10 min. after Flood Starts ±45 min.
Max. Ebb 2 hrs. 45 min. after Ebb Starts ±45 min.
See pp. 22-29 for Current Change at other points.

Note *from NOS: These predictions should be considered questionable. Caution is advised.*

2019 CURRENT TABLE
CHESAPEAKE & DELAWARE CANAL

39°31.83'N, 75°49.66'W at Chesapeake City

Daylight Saving Time   **Daylight Saving Time**

| | | MAY | | | | | | JUNE | | | |

DAY OF MONTH	DAY OF WEEK	CURRENT TURNS TO				DAY OF MONTH	DAY OF WEEK	CURRENT TURNS TO			
		EAST Flood Starts		WEST Ebb Starts				EAST Flood Starts		WEST Ebb Starts	
		a.m. **p.m.** Kts.		a.m. **p.m.** Kts.				a.m. **p.m.** Kts.		a.m. **p.m.** Kts.	
1	W	2:48 **2:54** p1.9		8:42 **9:06** p1.9		1	S	3:48 **3:30** a2.0		10:18 **9:12** p2.5	
2	T	3:30 **3:42** 1.9		9:42 **9:36** p2.0		2	S	4:36 **4:12** a2.2		11:12 **9:48** p2.6	
3	F	4:18 **4:24** a2.0		10:36 **10:00** p2.2		3	M	5:24 **4:54** a2.3		11:59 **10:24** p2.7	
4	S	5:00 **5:00** a2.2		11:30 **10:30** p2.4		4	T	6:06 **5:42** a2.3		-E- **12:48** 1.1	
5	S	5:42 **5:36** a2.2		-A- **12:18** 1.3		5	W	6:48 **6:30** a2.4		... **1:30** 1.2	
6	M	6:24 **6:06** a2.3		-B- **1:00** 1.2		6	T	7:30 **7:24** a2.4		12:01 **2:12** a2.7	
7	T	7:06 **6:42** a2.2		... **1:42** 1.2		7	F	8:18 **8:24** a2.4		12:54 **3:00** a2.6	
8	W	7:48 **7:24** a2.2		12:12 **2:30** a2.6		8	S	9:12 **9:36** a2.4		1:54 **3:48** a2.5	
9	T	8:31 **8:24** a2.2		1:00 **3:18** a2.5		9	S	10:07 **10:42** a2.4		3:06 **4:36** a2.3	
10	F	9:24 **9:30** a2.2		2:00 **4:06** a2.4		10	M	11:06 **11:42** a2.3		4:24 **5:24** a2.1	
11	S	10:24 **10:42** a2.2		3:00 **5:00** a2.3		11	T	... **12:01** 2.2		5:42 **6:12** p2.2	
12	S	11:24 **11:54** a2.2		4:18 **5:54** a2.2		12	W	12:48 **1:00** 2.1		6:54 **7:00** p2.4	
13	M	... **12:24** 2.2		5:36 **6:42** 2.0		13	T	1:48 **1:54** a2.3		8:06 **7:48** p2.6	
14	T	1:00 **1:24** p2.2		7:00 **7:30** p2.2		14	F	2:48 **2:48** a2.3		9:12 **8:30** p2.7	
15	W	2:00 **2:24** a2.2		8:12 **8:18** p2.4		15	S	3:42 **3:36** a2.4		10:12 **9:18** p2.7	
16	T	3:00 **3:18** a2.4		9:18 **9:00** p2.6		16	S	4:36 **4:18** a2.4		11:12 **10:00** p2.7	
17	F	3:54 **4:06** a2.5		10:18 **9:42** p2.7		17	M	5:24 **5:00** a2.3		11:59 **10:36** 2.6	
18	S	4:48 **4:54** a2.6		11:18 **10:24** p2.7		18	T	6:06 **5:48** a2.2		-F- **12:42** 1.0	
19	S	5:36 **5:36** a2.5		-C- **12:12** 1.3		19	W	6:48 **6:30** a2.1		-G- **1:24** 1.0	
20	M	6:24 **6:12** a2.4		-D- **1:00** 1.2		20	T	7:18 **7:12** a2.1		... **2:06** 1.1	
21	T	7:06 **6:54** a2.2		... **1:48** 1.1		21	F	7:48 **8:00** a2.1		12:30 **2:42** a2.3	
22	W	7:48 **7:36** a2.1		12:24 **2:30** a2.5		22	S	8:24 **8:54** a2.2		1:12 **3:24** a2.2	
23	T	8:24 **8:24** a2.1		1:00 **3:18** a2.4		23	S	9:00 **9:48** a2.2		2:00 **4:00** a2.1	
24	F	9:00 **9:24** a2.1		1:42 **4:00** a2.2		24	M	9:42 **10:42** a2.2		3:00 **4:36** a2.0	
25	S	9:42 **10:24** a2.1		2:30 **4:48** a2.1		25	T	10:30 **11:42** a2.1		4:06 **5:12** a1.8	
26	S	10:30 **11:24** a2.1		3:30 **5:30** a2.0		26	W	11:18 **...** 2.1		5:24 **5:42** p1.9	
27	M	11:24 **...** 2.1		4:42 **6:12** a1.9		27	T	12:36 **12:06** p2.0		6:36 **6:18** p2.1	
28	T	12:24 **12:12** p2.0		5:54 **6:54** p1.8		28	F	1:30 **1:00** p1.9		7:48 **7:00** p2.3	
29	W	1:18 **1:06** p2.0		7:06 **7:30** p2.0		29	S	2:30 **1:48** p1.9		8:54 **7:42** p2.5	
30	T	2:12 **2:00** p1.9		8:18 **8:06** p2.1		30	S	3:18 **2:36** 1.9		9:54 **8:30** p2.6	
31	F	3:00 **2:48** a1.9		9:24 **8:36** p2.3							

A also at 10:54 p.m. 2.5   **B** also at 11:30 p.m. 2.5   **C** also at 11:06 p.m. 2.7
D also at 11:42 p.m. 2.6   **E** also at 11:12 p.m. 2.7   **F** also at 11:18 p.m. 2.5
G also at 11:54 p.m. 2.4

The Kts. (knots) columns show the **maximum** predicted velocities of the stronger one of the Flood Currents and the stronger one of the Ebb Currents for each day.

The letter "a" means the velocity shown should occur **after** the a.m. Current Change. The letter "p" means the velocity shown should occur **after** the p.m. Current Change (even if next morning). No "a" or "p" means a.m. and p.m. velocities are the same for that day.

Avg. Max. Velocity: Flood 2.0 Kts., Ebb 1.9 Kts.

Max. Flood 3 hrs. 10 min. after Flood Starts ±45 min.

Max. Ebb 2 hrs. 45 min. after Ebb Starts ±45 min.

See pp. 22-29 for Current Change at other points.

Note *from NOS: These predictions should be considered questionable. Caution is advised.*

2019 CURRENT TABLE
CHESAPEAKE & DELAWARE CANAL

39°31.83'N, 75°49.66'W at Chesapeake City

Daylight Saving Time   Daylight Saving Time

		JULY							AUGUST				
		CURRENT TURNS TO							CURRENT TURNS TO				
		EAST Flood Starts			WEST Ebb Starts				EAST Flood Starts			WEST Ebb Starts	
DAY OF MONTH	DAY OF WEEK	a.m.	**p.m.**	Kts.	a.m.	**p.m.**	Kts.	DAY OF MONTH	DAY OF WEEK	a.m.	**p.m.**	Kts.	a.m.	**p.m.**	Kts.
1	M	4:12	**3:30**	a2.1	10:48	**9:18**	p2.7	1	T	5:24	**5:12**	a2.4	11:48	**10:54**	p2.7
2	T	5:00	**4:24**	a2.2	11:36	**10:06**	p2.7	2	F	6:12	**6:12**	a2.6	-E-	**12:30**	1.7
3	W	5:48	**5:24**	a2.4	-A-	**12:18**	1.2	3	S	7:00	**7:06**	a2.6	...	**1:18**	1.9
4	T	6:30	**6:24**	a2.5	-B-	**1:06**	1.4	4	S	7:48	**8:06**	a2.6	1:00	**2:00**	a2.6
5	F	7:18	**7:24**	a2.6	...	**1:48**	1.5	5	M	8:36	**9:00**	a2.5	2:00	**2:42**	a2.4
6	S	8:06	**8:18**	a2.6	12:54	**2:36**	a2.6	6	T	9:30	**10:00**	2.3	3:06	**3:24**	p2.3
7	S	8:54	**9:24**	a2.5	2:00	**3:18**	a2.5	7	W	10:18	**11:06**	p2.2	4:18	**4:12**	p2.4
8	M	9:48	**10:24**	a2.4	3:06	**4:06**	a2.2	8	T	11:12	...	2.0	5:24	**5:00**	p2.4
9	T	10:43	**11:24**	a2.3	4:24	**4:48**	p2.2	9	F	12:07	**12:01**	a2.1	6:36	**5:54**	p2.4
10	W	11:36	...	2.1	5:36	**5:36**	p2.4	10	S	1:12	**12:54**	a2.0	7:42	**6:48**	p2.4
11	T	12:30	**12:30**	a2.2	6:48	**6:24**	p2.5	11	S	2:12	**1:48**	a2.0	8:42	**7:42**	p2.4
12	F	1:30	**1:24**	a2.2	8:00	**7:18**	p2.6	12	M	3:06	**2:42**	a2.0	9:36	**8:36**	p2.4
13	S	2:30	**2:12**	a2.2	9:00	**8:06**	p2.6	13	T	3:54	**3:36**	a2.1	10:24	**9:24**	p2.3
14	S	3:30	**3:06**	a2.2	10:00	**8:54**	p2.6	14	W	4:36	**4:30**	a2.1	11:12	**10:06**	p2.3
15	M	4:18	**3:54**	a2.2	10:54	**9:36**	p2.5	15	T	5:18	**5:18**	a2.1	11:48	**10:48**	p2.2
16	T	5:06	**4:42**	a2.2	11:42	**10:18**	p2.5	16	F	5:54	**6:00**	a2.1	-F-	**12:24**	1.3
17	W	5:48	**5:30**	a2.1	-C-	**12:24**	1.0	17	S	6:24	**6:36**	a2.1	...	**12:54**	1.4
18	T	6:18	**6:12**	a2.1	-D-	**1:00**	1.1	18	S	6:54	**7:12**	a2.1	12:12	**1:18**	a2.1
19	F	6:48	**7:00**	a2.1	...	**1:30**	1.2	19	M	7:24	**7:48**	a2.1	12:54	**1:36**	a2.0
20	S	7:18	**7:36**	a2.2	12:12	**2:06**	a2.3	20	T	7:54	**8:30**	a2.1	1:42	**2:00**	p1.9
21	S	7:54	**8:24**	a2.2	12:54	**2:36**	a2.2	21	W	8:24	**9:18**	a2.1	2:30	**2:24**	p2.0
22	M	8:24	**9:06**	a2.2	1:42	**3:00**	a2.0	22	T	9:00	**10:12**	a2.0	3:30	**3:00**	p2.2
23	T	9:06	**10:00**	a2.2	2:42	**3:30**	a1.9	23	F	9:36	**11:12**	a2.0	4:30	**3:48**	p2.3
24	W	9:42	**10:54**	a2.1	3:42	**4:00**	p2.0	24	S	10:24	...	2.0	5:30	**4:36**	p2.3
25	T	10:24	**11:54**	a2.0	4:54	**4:36**	p2.1	25	S	12:12	**-G-**	1.7	6:36	**5:36**	p2.3
26	F	11:12	...	2.0	6:00	**5:18**	p2.3	26	M	1:12	**12:30**	p2.0	7:42	**6:36**	p2.4
27	S	12:54	**12:01**	p2.0	7:12	**6:12**	p2.4	27	T	2:18	**1:42**	p2.0	8:42	**7:42**	p2.5
28	S	1:54	**12:54**	p2.0	8:18	**7:06**	p2.5	28	W	3:12	**2:54**	2.1	9:36	**8:54**	p2.5
29	M	2:48	**2:00**	p2.0	9:18	**8:00**	p2.6	29	T	4:06	**4:00**	2.3	10:24	**9:54**	p2.6
30	T	3:42	**3:06**	2.0	10:12	**9:00**	p2.7	30	F	5:00	**5:00**	p2.5	11:06	**10:54**	p2.6
31	W	4:36	**4:12**	a2.2	11:00	**10:00**	p2.7	31	S	5:48	**5:54**	p2.6	11:54	...	2.1

A also at 11:00 p.m. 2.8   **B** also at 11:54 p.m. 2.7   **C** also at 11:00 p.m. 2.4
D also at 11:36 p.m. 2.3   **E** also at 11:54 p.m. 2.7   **F** also at 11:30 p.m. 2.2
G also at 11:24 a.m. 2.0

The Kts. (knots) columns show the **maximum** predicted velocities of the stronger one of the Flood Currents and the stronger one of the Ebb Currents for each day.
The letter "a" means the velocity shown should occur **after** the **a.m.** Current Change. The letter "p" means the velocity shown should occur **after** the **p.m.** Current Change (even if next morning). No "a" or "p" means a.m. and p.m. velocities are the same for that day.
Avg. Max. Velocity: Flood 2.0 Kts., Ebb 1.9 Kts.
Max. Flood 3 hrs. 10 min. after Flood Starts ±45 min.
Max. Ebb 2 hrs. 45 min. after Ebb Starts ±45 min.
See pp. 22-29 for Current Change at other points.
Note *from NOS: These predictions should be considered questionable. Caution is advised.* **157**

2019 CURRENT TABLE
CHESAPEAKE & DELAWARE CANAL

39°31.83'N, 75°49.66'W at Chesapeake City

Daylight Saving Time · Daylight Saving Time

SEPTEMBER						OCTOBER				

DAY OF MONTH	DAY OF WEEK	CURRENT TURNS TO										DAY OF MONTH	DAY OF WEEK	CURRENT TURNS TO					

D A Y O F M O N T H	D A Y O F W E E K	EAST Flood Starts a.m.	**p.m.**	Kts.	WEST Ebb Starts a.m.	**p.m.**	Kts.	D A Y O F M O N T H	D A Y O F W E E K	EAST Flood Starts a.m.	**p.m.**	Kts.	WEST Ebb Starts a.m.	**p.m.**	Kts.
1	S	6:36	**6:48**	p2.7	12:01	**12:36**	a2.5	1	T	7:00	**7:24**	p2.7	12:54	**12:36**	p2.6
2	M	7:24	**7:42**	p2.6	1:00	**1:18**	2.4	2	W	7:42	**8:18**	p2.5	1:54	**1:18**	p2.6
3	T	8:12	**8:36**	p2.5	2:00	**2:00**	p2.5	3	T	8:30	**9:12**	p2.3	2:48	**2:00**	p2.5
4	W	9:00	**9:36**	p2.4	3:00	**2:42**	p2.5	4	F	9:18	**10:06**	p2.1	3:48	**2:54**	p2.4
5	T	9:48	**10:36**	p2.2	4:06	**3:36**	p2.4	5	S	10:12	**11:06**	p1.9	4:48	**3:48**	p2.2
6	F	10:42	**11:42**	p2.0	5:06	**4:24**	p2.3	6	S	11:06	...	1.5	5:42	**4:48**	p2.1
7	S	11:30	...	1.7	6:12	**5:24**	p2.2	7	M	12:01	**12:12**	a1.9	6:36	**5:48**	p2.0
8	S	12:42	**12:30**	a1.9	7:12	**6:18**	p2.2	8	T	12:54	**1:12**	a1.9	7:30	**6:48**	p1.9
9	M	1:37	**1:30**	a1.9	8:12	**7:18**	p2.2	9	W	1:43	**2:12**	a1.9	8:18	**7:48**	p1.9
10	T	2:30	**2:30**	a1.9	9:00	**8:12**	p2.1	10	T	2:30	**3:00**	a2.0	9:00	**8:48**	p1.9
11	W	3:18	**3:24**	a2.0	9:48	**9:06**	p2.1	11	F	3:18	**3:48**	a2.0	9:42	**9:42**	p1.9
12	T	4:00	**4:12**	a2.0	10:30	**9:54**	p2.1	12	S	4:00	**4:30**	a2.0	10:18	**10:36**	1.8
13	F	4:42	**5:00**	a2.0	11:06	**10:42**	p2.1	13	S	4:42	**5:12**	p2.0	10:42	**11:24**	a1.9
14	S	5:18	**5:36**	a2.0	11:36	**11:30**	p2.0	14	M	5:24	**5:48**	p2.1	11:06	...	2.1
15	S	5:54	**6:12**	a2.0	...	**12:01**	1.7	15	T	5:54	**6:30**	p2.1	12:12	**-A-**	1.6
16	M	6:30	**6:48**	2.0	12:12	**12:18**	1.9	16	W	6:24	**7:06**	p2.1	1:00	**-B-**	1.4
17	T	6:54	**7:24**	p2.0	12:54	**12:36**	p2.0	17	T	6:48	**7:42**	p2.0	1:42	**12:18**	p2.4
18	W	7:18	**8:00**	p2.0	1:42	**1:00**	p2.1	18	F	7:18	**8:24**	p2.0	2:24	**1:00**	p2.4
19	T	7:48	**8:48**	1.9	2:24	**1:36**	p2.3	19	S	7:54	**9:12**	p1.9	3:06	**1:42**	p2.4
20	F	8:18	**9:36**	a1.9	3:18	**2:18**	p2.3	20	S	8:48	**10:06**	p1.9	3:54	**2:42**	p2.3
21	S	9:06	**10:36**	a1.9	4:06	**3:06**	p2.3	21	M	10:00	**11:06**	p2.0	4:48	**3:42**	p2.2
22	S	10:00	**11:36**	a1.9	5:06	**4:06**	p2.3	22	T	11:12	...	1.8	5:42	**4:54**	p2.1
23	M	11:06	...	1.9	6:06	**5:06**	p2.2	23	W	12:06	**12:24**	a2.0	6:36	**6:18**	p2.1
24	T	12:36	**12:24**	1.9	7:06	**6:18**	p2.2	24	T	1:06	**1:36**	2.1	7:30	**7:36**	p2.1
25	W	1:42	**1:42**	2.0	8:00	**7:36**	p2.3	25	F	2:12	**2:36**	p2.3	8:18	**8:48**	a2.2
26	T	2:42	**2:48**	p2.2	8:54	**8:48**	p2.3	26	S	3:06	**3:36**	p2.5	9:06	**9:54**	a2.4
27	F	3:36	**3:48**	p2.4	9:42	**9:54**	p2.3	27	S	4:06	**4:30**	p2.7	9:48	**10:54**	a2.6
28	S	4:30	**4:48**	p2.7	10:30	**10:54**	2.3	28	M	4:54	**5:24**	p2.8	10:30	**11:54**	a2.7
29	S	5:24	**5:42**	p2.8	11:12	**11:54**	a2.5	29	T	5:42	**6:18**	p2.8	11:12	...	2.8
30	M	6:12	**6:30**	p2.8	11:54	...	2.6	30	W	6:30	**7:06**	p2.6	12:48	**-C-**	1.6
								31	T	7:12	**7:54**	p2.4	1:42	**12:42**	p2.6

A also at 11:24 a.m. 2.2   **B** also at 11:48 a.m. 2.3   **C** also at 11:54 a.m. 2.8

The Kts. (knots) columns show the **maximum** predicted velocities of the stronger one of the Flood Currents and the stronger one of the Ebb Currents for each day.

The letter "a" means the velocity shown should occur **after** the **a.m.** Current Change. The letter "p" means the velocity shown should occur **after** the **p.m.** Current Change (even if next morning). No "a" or "p" means a.m. and p.m. velocities are the same for that day.

Avg. Max. Velocity: Flood 2.0 Kts., Ebb 1.9 Kts.

Max. Flood 3 hrs. 10 min. after Flood Starts ±45 min.

Max. Ebb 2 hrs. 45 min. after Ebb Starts ±45 min.

See pp. 22-29 for Current Change at other points.

Note *from NOS: These predictions should be considered questionable. Caution is advised.*

*Standard Time starts Nov. 3 at 2 a.m. Standard Time

NOVEMBER

DAY OF MONTH	DAY OF WEEK	EAST Flood Starts a.m.	p.m.	Kts.	WEST Ebb Starts a.m.	p.m.	Kts.
1	F	7:54	8:42	p2.2	2:36	1:24	p2.5
2	S	8:42	9:30	p2.1	3:24	2:12	p2.3
3	S	*8:42	*9:18	p2.0	*3:18	*2:06	p2.1
4	M	9:42	10:06	p2.0	4:06	3:06	p2.0
5	T	10:48	10:54	p2.0	4:54	4:06	p1.9
6	W	11:48	11:48	p2.0	5:42	5:12	p1.8
7	T	...	12:42	1.4	6:30	6:24	p1.8
8	F	12:36	1:30	a2.0	7:12	7:24	a1.8
9	S	1:31	2:18	a2.0	7:48	8:24	a2.0
10	S	2:18	3:06	p2.0	8:18	9:24	a2.1
11	M	3:00	3:48	p2.1	8:48	10:12	a2.2
12	T	3:42	4:30	p2.2	9:12	11:06	a2.4
13	W	4:18	5:12	p2.2	9:36	11:54	a2.5
14	T	4:48	5:48	p2.2	10:12	...	2.5
15	F	5:18	6:30	p2.1	12:36	-A-	1.0
16	S	6:00	7:12	p2.1	1:12	-B-	1.0
17	S	6:48	7:54	p2.1	1:54	12:24	p2.4
18	M	7:54	8:48	p2.2	2:42	1:30	p2.3
19	T	9:06	9:42	p2.2	3:24	2:36	p2.2
20	W	10:18	10:42	p2.2	4:12	3:54	p2.0
21	T	11:24	11:42	p2.2	5:06	5:18	1.9
22	F	...	12:24	2.2	5:54	6:36	a2.2
23	S	12:42	1:24	p2.4	6:42	7:48	a2.5
24	S	1:42	2:24	p2.5	7:30	8:48	a2.6
25	M	2:36	3:18	p2.6	8:18	9:54	a2.8
26	T	3:24	4:12	p2.6	9:00	10:48	a2.8
27	W	4:12	5:06	p2.5	9:42	11:42	a2.8
28	T	4:54	5:48	p2.4	10:24	...	2.7
29	F	5:42	6:36	p2.2	12:30	-C-	1.2
30	S	6:24	7:12	p2.1	1:12	-D-	1.1

DECEMBER

DAY OF MONTH	DAY OF WEEK	EAST Flood Starts a.m.	p.m.	Kts.	WEST Ebb Starts a.m.	p.m.	Kts.
1	S	7:18	7:48	p2.1	2:00	12:36	p2.3
2	M	8:12	8:30	p2.1	2:42	1:24	p2.1
3	T	9:12	9:12	p2.1	3:24	2:24	p2.0
4	W	10:12	10:00	p2.1	4:12	3:30	p1.8
5	T	11:06	10:48	p2.1	4:54	4:36	p1.7
6	F	11:59	11:42	p2.0	5:30	5:48	a1.8
7	S	...	12:54	1.7	6:12	7:00	a2.0
8	S	12:36	1:42	a1.9	6:48	8:06	a2.2
9	M	1:25	2:36	p2.0	7:18	9:06	a2.3
10	T	2:12	3:24	p2.1	7:54	10:00	a2.4
11	W	2:54	4:06	p2.2	8:30	10:48	a2.5
12	T	3:30	4:54	p2.2	9:06	11:36	a2.6
13	F	4:18	5:36	p2.2	9:48	...	2.6
14	S	5:00	6:12	p2.3	12:18	-E-	1.0
15	S	5:54	6:54	p2.3	12:54	-F-	1.1
16	M	6:54	7:42	p2.3	1:36	12:24	p2.4
17	T	7:54	8:30	p2.3	2:18	1:30	p2.3
18	W	9:00	9:24	p2.3	3:00	2:42	p2.1
19	T	10:06	10:24	p2.2	3:48	4:00	a2.0
20	F	11:12	11:18	p2.2	4:36	5:18	a2.2
21	S	...	12:12	2.2	5:24	6:30	a2.4
22	S	12:18	1:12	p2.3	6:12	7:42	a2.6
23	M	1:12	2:12	p2.4	7:00	8:48	a2.7
24	T	2:06	3:12	p2.4	7:48	9:42	a2.8
25	W	2:54	4:00	p2.4	8:36	10:36	a2.8
26	T	3:42	4:48	p2.3	9:18	11:24	a2.7
27	F	4:30	5:30	p2.2	10:06	...	2.6
28	S	5:18	6:06	p2.2	12:06	-G-	1.1
29	S	6:06	6:42	p2.1	12:48	-H-	1.1
30	M	6:54	7:12	p2.2	1:24	12:06	p2.2
31	T	7:42	7:48	p2.2	2:00	12:54	p2.1

A also at 10:48 a.m. 2.5   B also at 11:36 a.m. 2.5   C also at 11:06 a.m. 2.6
D also at 11:48 a.m. 2.4   E also at 10:36 a.m. 2.6   F also at 11:24 a.m. 2.5
G also at 10:48 a.m. 2.4   H also at 11:24 a.m. 2.3

The Kts. (knots) columns show the **maximum** predicted velocities of the stronger one of the Flood Currents and the stronger one of the Ebb Currents for each day.
The letter "a" means the velocity shown should occur **after** the **a.m.** Current Change. The letter "p" means the velocity shown should occur **after** the **p.m.** Current Change (even if next morning). No "a" or "p" means a.m. and p.m. velocities are the same for that day.
Avg. Max. Velocity: Flood 2.0 Kts., Ebb 1.9 Kts.
Max. Flood 3 hrs. 10 min. after Flood Starts ±45 min.
Max. Ebb 2 hrs. 45 min. after Ebb Starts ±45 min.
See pp. 22-29 for Current Change at other points.

Note *from NOS: These predictions should be considered questionable. Caution is advised.*

Upper Chesapeake Bay Currents

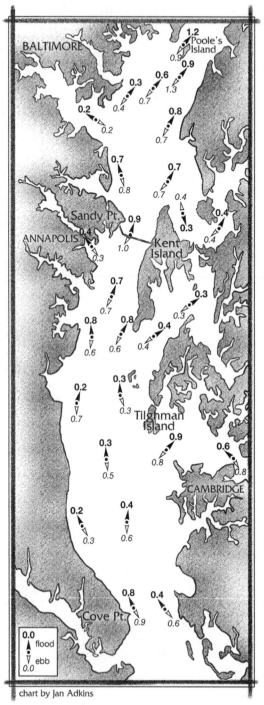

The arrows in this diagram denote **direction** and **average maximum velocities** for Flood (dark arrow) and Ebb (light arrow) currents.

Times of current change for the four areas listed below are in hours, before or after **High Water at Baltimore**, pp. 162-165.

West of Pooles Island:
Flood begins 3 1/2 before
Flood max. 1 1/2 before (1.2 kts.)
Ebb begins 2 1/2 after
Ebb max. 4 1/2 after (0.9 kts.)

Sandy Point:
Flood begins 3 1/2 before
Flood max. 1 1/2 before (0.9 kts.)
Ebb begins 1 1/2 after
Ebb max. 4 1/2 after (1.0 kts.)

off Tilghman Island:
Flood begins 5 1/2 before
Flood max. 3 1/2 before (0.3 kts.)
Ebb begins 1/2 after
Ebb max. 3 1/2 after (0.7 kts.)

off Cove Point:
Flood begins 6 1/2 before
Flood max. 4 1/2 before (0.9 kts.)
Ebb begins 1/2 before
Ebb max. 1 1/2 after (0.8 kts.)

Note:
From the beginning of the Flood Current at Cove Point until the Ebb Current begins off Baltimore, a north-bound vessel will have over 8 hours of fair current. A vessel bound southward from Sandy Point can expect only 4 hours of fair current.

chart by Jan Adkins

Relationship of High Water and Ebb Current

Many people wonder why the times of High Water and the start of Ebb Current at the mouths of bays and inlets are not simultaneous. (See p. 10, Why Tides and Currents Often Behave Differently.) The twelve diagrams below show the hourly stages of the Tide in the Ocean and a Bay connected by a narrow Inlet.

Picture the rising Tide, borne by the Flood Current, as a long wave. The wave enters the inlet and the crest reaches its maximum height in or at the inlet. But, the body of water inside the inlet - in the bay - has yet to be filled and the Flood Current continues to pour water through the inlet for a good period after the crest has already passed the inlet. The Ebb Current will not start until the level of the water in the ocean is lower than the water in the bay.

This does not necessarily apply to the mouths of small bays with wide entrances. The narrowness of the inlet and the size of the bay are the controlling factors.

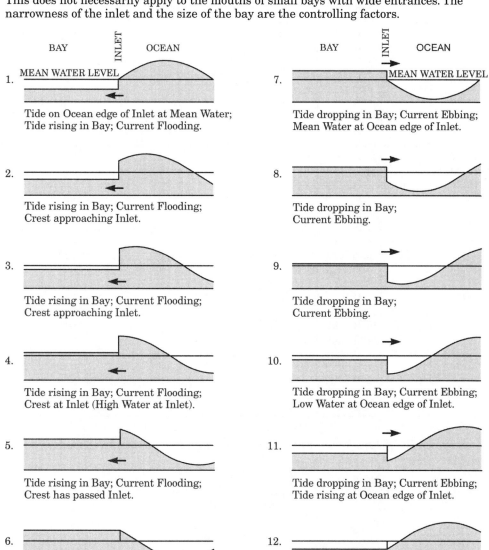

1. Tide on Ocean edge of Inlet at Mean Water; Tide rising in Bay; Current Flooding.

2. Tide rising in Bay; Current Flooding; Crest approaching Inlet.

3. Tide rising in Bay; Current Flooding; Crest approaching Inlet.

4. Tide rising in Bay; Current Flooding; Crest at Inlet (High Water at Inlet).

5. Tide rising in Bay; Current Flooding; Crest has passed Inlet.

6. High Water in Bay; Ebb Current about to start.

7. Tide dropping in Bay; Current Ebbing; Mean Water at Ocean edge of Inlet.

8. Tide dropping in Bay; Current Ebbing.

9. Tide dropping in Bay; Current Ebbing.

10. Tide dropping in Bay; Current Ebbing; Low Water at Ocean edge of Inlet.

11. Tide dropping in Bay; Current Ebbing; Tide rising at Ocean edge of Inlet.

12. Low Water in Bay; Flood Current about to start.

2019 HIGH WATER
BALTIMORE, MD
At Ft. McHenry 39°16'N, 76°34.7'W

		Standard Time					Standard Time					*Daylight Time starts Mar. 10 at 2 a.m.			

DAY OF MONTH	DAY OF WEEK	JANUARY a.m.	Ht.	p.m.	Ht.	DAY OF WEEK	FEBRUARY a.m.	Ht.	p.m.	Ht.	DAY OF WEEK	MARCH a.m.	Ht.	p.m.	Ht.	DAY OF MONTH
1	T	2:19	0.8	3:33	1.1	F	3:41	0.6	5:00	1.1	F	2:24	0.7	3:41	1.1	1
2	W	3:11	0.7	4:28	1.2	S	4:32	0.6	5:45	1.1	S	3:20	0.8	4:34	1.1	2
3	T	4:03	0.6	5:17	1.2	S	5:20	0.6	6:25	1.1	S	4:12	0.8	5:20	1.1	3
4	F	4:52	0.6	6:02	1.3	M	6:04	0.6	7:01	1.1	M	4:59	0.9	5:59	1.1	4
5	S	5:39	0.6	6:42	1.2	T	6:45	0.7	7:35	1.1	T	5:42	0.9	6:33	1.1	5
6	S	6:24	0.6	7:21	1.2	W	7:26	0.7	8:07	1.1	W	6:23	1.0	7:05	1.1	6
7	M	7:07	0.6	7:57	1.2	T	8:05	0.7	8:39	1.0	T	7:01	1.0	7:36	1.1	7
8	T	7:49	0.6	8:33	1.1	F	8:46	0.8	9:12	1.0	F	7:39	1.0	8:07	1.1	8
9	W	8:32	0.6	9:09	1.1	S	9:29	0.8	9:47	1.0	S	8:18	1.1	8:41	1.1	9
10	T	9:15	0.6	9:45	1.0	S	10:12	0.9	10:26	0.9	S	*9:56	1.2	*10:18	1.0	10
11	F	10:01	0.7	10:22	1.0	M	11:01	0.9	11:09	0.8	M	10:38	1.2	10:59	0.9	11
12	S	10:50	0.7	11:01	0.9	T	11:53	1.0	11:59	0.7	T	11:25	1.3	11:46	0.9	12
13	S	11:42	0.7	11:44	0.9	W	...	...	12:50	1.1	W	...	...	12:17	1.3	13
14	M	...	...	12:37	0.8	T	12:54	0.7	1:50	1.1	T	12:39	0.8	1:15	1.3	14
15	T	12:31	0.8	1:33	0.9	F	1:54	0.6	2:52	1.2	F	1:38	0.8	2:19	1.4	15
16	W	1:23	0.7	2:29	1.0	S	2:56	0.6	3:54	1.3	S	2:40	0.9	3:26	1.4	16
17	T	2:19	0.6	3:24	1.2	S	3:56	0.7	4:53	1.3	S	3:43	0.9	4:32	1.4	17
18	F	3:16	0.6	4:19	1.3	M	4:54	0.8	5:49	1.4	M	4:43	1.0	5:33	1.4	18
19	S	4:14	0.6	5:13	1.3	T	5:50	0.9	6:42	1.4	T	5:40	1.2	6:29	1.4	19
20	S	5:11	0.6	6:06	1.4	W	6:44	1.0	7:32	1.3	W	6:35	1.3	7:20	1.4	20
21	M	6:07	0.7	6:59	1.4	T	7:38	1.1	8:20	1.3	T	7:28	1.4	8:08	1.3	21
22	T	7:01	0.7	7:50	1.4	F	8:33	1.1	9:07	1.2	F	8:20	1.5	8:54	1.3	22
23	W	7:56	0.8	8:41	1.3	S	9:29	1.2	9:54	1.1	S	9:12	1.5	9:40	1.2	23
24	T	8:53	0.9	9:31	1.2	S	10:26	1.2	10:42	0.9	S	10:04	1.5	10:26	1.1	24
25	F	9:51	0.9	10:21	1.1	M	11:26	1.2	11:33	0.9	M	10:57	1.5	11:15	1.0	25
26	S	10:52	0.9	11:11	1.0	T	...	...	12:29	1.2	T	11:51	1.4	...	...	26
27	S	11:56	1.0	...	...	W	12:28	0.8	1:34	1.1	W	12:07	1.0	12:49	1.4	27
28	M	12:02	0.9	1:02	1.0	T	1:25	0.7	2:39	1.1	T	1:03	0.9	1:51	1.3	28
29	T	12:55	0.7	2:08	1.0						F	2:02	0.9	2:56	1.3	29
30	W	1:50	0.6	3:12	1.1						S	3:01	1.0	3:58	1.2	30
31	T	2:46	0.6	4:09	1.1						S	3:57	1.0	4:53	1.2	31

Dates when Ht. of **Low** Water is below Mean Low with Ht. of lowest given for each period and Date of lowest in ( ):

1st–10th: -0.4' (1st–6th)	1st–8th: -0.3' (1st–6th)	4th–5th: -0.2'
13th–31st: -0.6' (21st, 22nd)	10th–27th: -0.5' (19th, 20th)	18th–22nd: -0.2'

Average Rise and Fall 1.1 ft.

When a high tide exceeds avg. ht., the *following* low tide will be lower than avg.

2019 HIGH WATER
BALTIMORE, MD
At Ft. McHenry 39°16'N, 76°34.7'W

		Daylight Saving Time APRIL					Daylight Saving Time MAY					Daylight Saving Time JUNE				
DAY OF MONTH	DAY OF WEEK	a.m.	Ht.	p.m.	Ht.	DAY OF WEEK	a.m.	Ht.	p.m.	Ht.	DAY OF WEEK	a.m.	Ht.	p.m.	Ht.	DAY OF MONTH
1	M	4:48	1.1	5:39	1.2	W	5:07	1.5	5:25	1.3	S	5:57	1.8	6:00	1.2	1
2	T	5:35	1.2	6:18	1.2	T	5:50	1.5	6:04	1.2	S	6:36	1.9	6:48	1.1	2
3	W	6:18	1.2	6:53	1.2	F	6:30	1.6	6:43	1.2	M	7:17	2.0	7:37	1.1	3
4	T	6:58	1.3	7:26	1.2	S	7:07	1.7	7:23	1.2	T	7:59	2.0	8:27	1.1	4
5	F	7:35	1.4	8:00	1.2	S	7:44	1.8	8:04	1.2	W	8:44	2.1	9:19	1.2	5
6	S	8:12	1.5	8:35	1.2	M	8:22	1.9	8:48	1.1	T	9:32	2.0	10:12	1.2	6
7	S	8:48	1.5	9:13	1.1	T	9:03	1.9	9:36	1.1	F	10:24	2.0	11:08	1.3	7
8	M	9:27	1.6	9:54	1.1	W	9:48	1.9	10:26	1.1	S	11:19	1.9	...	...	8
9	T	10:11	1.6	10:40	1.0	T	10:39	1.9	11:21	1.2	S	12:08	1.4	12:17	1.7	9
10	W	10:57	1.6	11:31	1.0	F	11:33	1.8	...	...	M	1:09	1.5	1:16	1.6	10
11	T	11:51	1.6	...	...	S	12:19	1.2	12:33	1.7	T	2:11	1.6	2:15	1.5	11
12	F	12:28	1.0	12:51	1.6	S	1:20	1.3	1:37	1.6	W	3:12	1.8	3:13	1.4	12
13	S	1:29	1.1	1:56	1.5	M	2:22	1.4	2:41	1.5	T	4:11	1.9	4:09	1.3	13
14	S	2:31	1.2	3:04	1.5	T	3:23	1.6	3:42	1.5	F	5:06	2.0	5:04	1.2	14
15	M	3:32	1.3	4:09	1.5	W	4:22	1.7	4:40	1.4	S	5:57	2.0	5:57	1.2	15
16	T	4:32	1.4	5:09	1.5	T	5:17	1.8	5:33	1.4	S	6:44	2.1	6:48	1.2	16
17	W	5:28	1.5	6:03	1.4	F	6:09	1.9	6:23	1.3	M	7:28	2.1	7:38	1.2	17
18	T	6:21	1.7	6:53	1.4	S	6:58	2.0	7:12	1.2	T	8:11	2.0	8:26	1.2	18
19	F	7:13	1.8	7:40	1.3	S	7:45	2.0	8:00	1.2	W	8:52	2.0	9:14	1.2	19
20	S	8:03	1.8	8:26	1.3	M	8:30	2.0	8:48	1.2	T	9:32	1.9	10:00	1.2	20
21	S	8:51	1.8	9:13	1.2	T	9:14	2.0	9:37	1.2	F	10:13	1.8	10:48	1.3	21
22	M	9:38	1.8	10:01	1.1	W	9:58	1.9	10:26	1.2	S	10:54	1.7	11:37	1.3	22
23	T	10:26	1.8	10:50	1.1	T	10:43	1.8	11:17	1.2	S	11:36	1.6	...	...	23
24	W	11:16	1.7	11:43	1.1	F	11:30	1.6	...	...	M	12:28	1.4	12:19	1.5	24
25	T	...	...	12:08	1.5	S	12:10	1.2	12:19	1.5	T	1:21	1.5	1:03	1.4	25
26	F	12:38	1.1	1:04	1.5	S	1:04	1.3	1:09	1.5	W	2:13	1.5	1:50	1.4	26
27	S	1:36	1.2	2:03	1.4	M	2:00	1.4	2:00	1.4	T	3:04	1.6	2:40	1.3	27
28	S	2:33	1.2	3:02	1.3	T	2:54	1.4	2:50	1.3	F	3:53	1.7	3:33	1.2	28
29	M	3:28	1.3	3:55	1.3	W	3:46	1.5	3:39	1.3	S	4:38	1.9	4:28	1.1	29
30	T	4:20	1.4	4:42	1.3	T	4:33	1.6	4:26	1.2	S	5:22	2.0	5:23	1.1	30
31						F	5:17	1.7	5:13	1.2						31

Dates when Ht. of **Low** Water is below Mean Low with Ht. of lowest given for each period and Date of lowest in ( ):

Average Rise and Fall 1.1 ft.

When a high tide exceeds avg. ht., the *following* low tide will be lower than avg.

2019 HIGH WATER
BALTIMORE, MD
At Ft. McHenry 39°16'N, 76°34.7'W

		Daylight Saving Time JULY					Daylight Saving Time AUGUST					Daylight Saving Time SEPTEMBER				
DAY OF MONTH	DAY OF WEEK	a.m.	Ht.	p.m.	Ht.	DAY OF WEEK	a.m.	Ht.	p.m.	Ht.	DAY OF WEEK	a.m.	Ht.	p.m.	Ht.	DAY OF MONTH
1	M	6:07	2.0	6:19	1.1	T	7:23	2.1	7:45	1.4	S	8:42	1.9	9:15	1.8	1
2	T	6:53	2.1	7:13	1.1	F	8:13	2.1	8:40	1.5	M	9:29	1.8	10:10	1.9	2
3	W	7:40	2.1	8:06	1.2	S	9:03	2.0	9:35	1.6	T	10:16	1.7	11:08	1.9	3
4	T	8:29	2.1	9:00	1.3	S	9:53	1.9	10:32	1.7	W	11:06	1.5	...	...	4
5	F	9:19	2.0	9:55	1.4	M	10:42	1.8	11:31	1.8	T	12:06	2.0	12:00	1.4	5
6	S	10:11	2.0	10:52	1.5	T	11:32	1.6	...	...	F	1:07	2.0	12:56	1.3	6
7	S	11:03	1.8	11:51	1.6	W	12:32	1.8	12:25	1.5	S	2:10	1.9	1:58	1.2	7
8	M	11:57	1.7	...	...	T	1:35	1.9	1:20	1.4	S	3:12	1.9	3:03	1.2	8
9	T	12:54	1.7	12:51	1.6	F	2:39	1.9	2:19	1.3	M	4:12	1.9	4:05	1.2	9
10	W	1:56	1.8	1:47	1.4	S	3:39	2.0	3:21	1.2	T	5:04	1.9	5:02	1.3	10
11	T	2:58	1.9	2:44	1.3	S	4:36	2.0	4:22	1.2	W	5:50	1.8	5:52	1.4	11
12	F	3:58	2.0	3:42	1.2	M	5:27	2.0	5:20	1.2	T	6:29	1.8	6:38	1.4	12
13	S	4:53	2.0	4:40	1.2	T	6:14	2.0	6:12	1.2	F	7:04	1.8	7:20	1.5	13
14	S	5:44	2.0	5:36	1.1	W	6:55	1.9	6:59	1.3	S	7:37	1.7	8:00	1.5	14
15	M	6:30	2.0	6:29	1.2	T	7:33	1.9	7:43	1.4	S	8:07	1.7	8:38	1.6	15
16	T	7:13	2.0	7:19	1.2	F	8:08	1.8	8:25	1.4	M	8:38	1.6	9:16	1.7	16
17	W	7:53	2.0	8:05	1.2	S	8:40	1.8	9:06	1.5	T	9:11	1.6	9:53	1.7	17
18	T	8:31	1.9	8:49	1.3	S	9:12	1.7	9:46	1.5	W	9:46	1.5	10:32	1.8	18
19	F	9:08	1.8	9:33	1.3	M	9:45	1.7	10:27	1.6	T	10:25	1.4	11:15	1.8	19
20	S	9:44	1.8	10:17	1.4	T	10:19	1.6	11:10	1.6	F	11:11	1.3	...	...	20
21	S	10:20	1.7	11:02	1.4	W	10:56	1.5	11:54	1.7	S	12:02	1.9	12:03	1.2	21
22	M	10:56	1.6	11:49	1.5	T	11:37	1.4	...	...	S	12:54	1.9	1:04	1.2	22
23	T	11:34	1.5	...	...	F	12:41	1.8	12:26	1.3	M	1:53	1.9	2:09	1.2	23
24	W	12:38	1.5	12:15	1.4	S	1:32	1.8	1:22	1.2	T	2:54	1.9	3:14	1.3	24
25	T	1:27	1.6	1:01	1.4	S	2:26	1.9	2:25	1.2	W	3:56	1.9	4:18	1.4	25
26	F	2:18	1.7	1:54	1.2	M	3:23	2.0	3:31	1.2	T	4:55	1.9	5:17	1.5	26
27	S	3:08	1.8	2:52	1.2	T	4:21	2.0	4:34	1.2	F	5:50	1.9	6:14	1.6	27
28	S	3:58	1.9	3:54	1.1	W	5:18	2.1	5:34	1.4	S	6:40	1.9	7:08	1.8	28
29	M	4:49	2.0	4:55	1.1	T	6:12	2.1	6:30	1.5	S	7:29	1.8	8:02	1.9	29
30	T	5:41	2.1	5:54	1.2	F	7:04	2.0	7:25	1.6	M	8:15	1.7	8:55	2.0	30
31	W	6:32	2.1	6:50	1.3	S	7:54	2.0	8:20	1.7						31

Dates when Ht. of **Low** Water is below Mean Low with Ht. of lowest given for each period and Date of lowest in ( ):

Average Rise and Fall 1.1 ft.

When a high tide exceeds avg. ht., the *following* low tide will be lower than avg.

2019 HIGH WATER
BALTIMORE, MD
At Ft. McHenry 39°16'N, 76°34.7'W

Daylight Saving Time — *Standard Time starts Nov. 3 at 2 a.m.* — **Standard Time**

DAY OF MONTH	DAY OF WEEK	OCTOBER a.m.	Ht.	p.m.	Ht.	DAY OF WEEK	NOVEMBER a.m.	Ht.	p.m.	Ht.	DAY OF WEEK	DECEMBER a.m.	Ht.	p.m.	Ht.	DAY OF MONTH
1	T	9:02	1.6	**9:48**	2.0	F	10:16	1.1	**11:07**	1.8	S	9:44	0.8	**10:27**	1.4	1
2	W	9:50	1.5	**10:42**	2.0	S	11:10	1.0	**11:59**	1.7	M	10:38	0.8	**11:15**	1.3	2
3	T	10:40	1.4	**11:37**	2.0	S	*11:08	1.0	*11:56	1.6	T	11:35	0.8	...	...	3
4	F	11:34	1.2	...	...	M	...	...	**12:10**	1.0	W	12:04	1.2	**12:35**	0.9	4
5	S	12:35	1.9	**12:33**	1.2	T	12:52	1.5	**1:12**	1.1	T	12:51	1.1	**1:36**	0.9	5
6	S	1:35	1.8	**1:37**	1.2	W	1:47	1.4	**2:13**	1.1	F	1:37	1.0	**2:34**	1.0	6
7	M	2:36	1.8	**2:41**	1.2	T	2:36	1.4	**3:10**	1.2	S	2:22	1.0	**3:27**	1.1	7
8	T	3:35	1.7	**3:43**	1.2	F	3:21	1.3	**4:02**	1.3	S	3:06	0.9	**4:14**	1.2	8
9	W	4:28	1.7	**4:39**	1.3	S	4:02	1.3	**4:48**	1.4	M	3:51	0.9	**4:56**	1.3	9
10	T	5:12	1.6	**5:29**	1.4	S	4:38	1.2	**5:29**	1.4	T	4:34	0.8	**5:35**	1.3	10
11	F	5:51	1.6	**6:15**	1.5	M	5:15	1.2	**6:07**	1.5	W	5:19	0.8	**6:13**	1.4	11
12	S	6:25	1.6	**6:56**	1.5	T	5:53	1.1	**6:42**	1.6	T	6:05	0.7	**6:52**	1.5	12
13	S	6:58	1.5	**7:35**	1.6	W	6:32	1.0	**7:17**	1.6	F	6:52	0.7	**7:34**	1.5	13
14	M	7:30	1.5	**8:11**	1.7	T	7:14	1.0	**7:55**	1.7	S	7:41	0.7	**8:19**	1.5	14
15	T	8:04	1.4	**8:46**	1.7	F	7:59	0.9	**8:36**	1.7	S	8:31	0.7	**9:08**	1.5	15
16	W	8:40	1.3	**9:22**	1.8	S	8:47	0.9	**9:22**	1.7	M	9:25	0.7	**9:59**	1.4	16
17	T	9:19	1.2	**10:00**	1.8	S	9:39	0.9	**10:13**	1.6	T	10:23	0.8	**10:52**	1.3	17
18	F	10:03	1.2	**10:44**	1.8	M	10:37	0.9	**11:09**	1.6	W	11:24	0.9	**11:47**	1.2	18
19	S	10:53	1.1	**11:32**	1.8	T	11:39	1.0	...	...	T	...	...	**12:29**	0.9	19
20	S	11:49	1.1	...	...	W	12:08	1.5	**12:43**	1.0	F	12:43	1.1	**1:35**	1.0	20
21	M	12:27	1.8	**12:51**	1.1	T	1:08	1.4	**1:49**	1.1	S	1:39	1.0	**2:39**	1.2	21
22	T	1:28	1.8	**1:56**	1.1	F	2:06	1.4	**2:52**	1.3	S	2:34	0.9	**3:40**	1.3	22
23	W	2:31	1.7	**3:01**	1.2	S	3:02	1.3	**3:52**	1.4	M	3:29	0.8	**4:37**	1.4	23
24	T	3:32	1.7	**4:04**	1.4	S	3:55	1.2	**4:48**	1.6	T	4:22	0.7	**5:29**	1.4	24
25	F	4:30	1.7	**5:03**	1.5	M	4:46	1.1	**5:41**	1.7	W	5:14	0.7	**6:17**	1.5	25
26	S	5:23	1.6	**6:00**	1.7	T	5:35	1.0	**6:30**	1.7	T	6:05	0.7	**7:03**	1.4	26
27	S	6:13	1.5	**6:54**	1.8	W	6:24	0.9	**7:18**	1.7	F	6:53	0.6	**7:48**	1.4	27
28	M	7:01	1.5	**7:45**	1.9	T	7:13	0.9	**8:05**	1.7	S	7:41	0.6	**8:31**	1.3	28
29	T	7:48	1.4	**8:36**	1.9	F	8:02	0.9	**8:52**	1.6	S	8:28	0.6	**9:13**	1.2	29
30	W	8:36	1.2	**9:26**	1.9	S	8:52	0.8	**9:39**	1.5	M	9:15	0.7	**9:54**	1.1	30
31	T	9:25	1.2	**10:16**	1.9						T	10:04	0.7	**10:37**	1.0	31

Dates when Ht. of **Low** Water is below Mean Low with Ht. of lowest given for each period and Date of lowest in ( ):

25th–29th: -0.2'

9th–16th: -0.2'
20th–30th: -0.4' (23rd–27th)

Average Rise and Fall 1.1 ft.

When a high tide exceeds avg. ht., the *following* low tide will be lower than avg.

2019 HIGH WATER
MIAMI HARBOR ENTRANCE, FL
25°45.8'N, 80°07.8'W

		Standard Time — JANUARY					Standard Time — FEBRUARY					*Daylight Time starts Mar. 10 at 2 a.m. — MARCH				
Day of Month	Day of Week	a.m.	Ht.	p.m.	Ht.	Day of Week	a.m.	Ht.	p.m.	Ht.	Day of Week	a.m.	Ht.	p.m.	Ht.	Day of Month
1	T	5:01	2.3	5:09	2.2	F	6:24	2.1	6:27	2.0	F	5:02	1.9	5:09	1.9	1
2	W	5:56	2.4	6:01	2.2	S	7:08	2.1	7:12	2.0	S	5:55	2.0	6:02	1.9	2
3	T	6:45	2.4	6:48	2.2	S	7:49	2.2	7:53	2.1	S	6:41	2.1	6:48	2.0	3
4	F	7:29	2.4	7:32	2.2	M	8:26	2.2	8:32	2.1	M	7:21	2.2	7:30	2.1	4
5	S	8:10	2.4	8:13	2.2	T	9:02	2.2	9:10	2.1	T	7:58	2.2	8:09	2.2	5
6	S	8:49	2.4	8:52	2.2	W	9:37	2.2	9:48	2.1	W	8:33	2.3	8:47	2.2	6
7	M	9:26	2.4	9:31	2.2	T	10:11	2.2	10:26	2.1	T	9:08	2.3	9:25	2.3	7
8	T	10:03	2.3	10:10	2.1	F	10:46	2.1	11:05	2.0	F	9:42	2.3	10:02	2.3	8
9	W	10:40	2.2	10:49	2.0	S	11:22	2.1	11:46	2.0	S	10:17	2.2	10:40	2.3	9
10	T	11:16	2.2	11:31	2.0	S	11:58	2.0	...	...	S	*11:51	2.2	...	...	10
11	F	11:55	2.1	...	...	M	12:30	2.0	12:39	1.9	M	12:21	2.2	12:28	2.1	11
12	S	12:16	1.9	12:35	2.0	T	1:22	1.9	1:26	1.9	T	1:05	2.2	1:09	2.0	12
13	S	1:04	1.9	1:19	1.9	W	2:21	1.9	2:25	1.8	W	1:55	2.1	1:58	2.0	13
14	M	1:59	1.9	2:09	1.9	T	3:28	2.0	3:32	1.9	T	2:55	2.1	3:00	2.0	14
15	T	2:59	1.9	3:05	1.9	F	4:36	2.1	4:42	2.0	F	4:03	2.1	4:11	2.0	15
16	W	4:02	2.0	4:06	1.9	S	5:40	2.2	5:48	2.2	S	5:13	2.2	5:25	2.1	16
17	T	5:04	2.2	5:08	2.0	S	6:37	2.4	6:48	2.4	S	6:17	2.3	6:33	2.3	17
18	F	6:02	2.3	6:07	2.2	M	7:30	2.6	7:44	2.5	M	7:15	2.5	7:34	2.5	18
19	S	6:57	2.5	7:03	2.3	T	8:20	2.7	8:37	2.7	T	8:08	2.7	8:29	2.7	19
20	S	7:49	2.6	7:58	2.5	W	9:08	2.8	9:28	2.8	W	8:57	2.8	9:21	2.9	20
21	M	8:39	2.7	8:51	2.6	T	9:54	2.8	10:19	2.7	T	9:44	2.8	10:11	2.9	21
22	T	9:29	2.8	9:44	2.6	F	10:41	2.7	11:10	2.6	F	10:30	2.8	10:59	2.9	22
23	W	10:17	2.8	10:37	2.6	S	11:28	2.5	...	...	S	11:15	2.7	11:47	2.8	23
24	T	11:06	2.7	11:31	2.5	S	12:02	2.5	12:17	2.3	S	...	...	12:01	2.6	24
25	F	11:56	2.5	...	...	M	12:56	2.3	1:09	2.2	M	12:36	2.6	12:47	2.4	25
26	S	12:27	2.4	12:48	2.4	T	1:54	2.1	2:04	2.0	T	1:26	2.4	1:36	2.2	26
27	S	1:25	2.3	1:42	2.2	W	2:56	2.0	3:05	1.9	W	2:19	2.2	2:28	2.0	27
28	M	2:27	2.2	2:40	2.1	T	4:01	1.9	4:09	1.8	T	3:17	2.0	3:28	1.9	28
29	T	3:31	2.1	3:41	2.0						F	4:19	2.0	4:31	1.9	29
30	W	4:34	2.0	4:41	1.9						S	5:21	2.0	5:34	1.9	30
31	T	5:33	2.0	5:37	1.9						S	6:16	2.0	6:30	2.0	31

Dates when Ht. of **Low** Water is below Mean Low with Ht. of lowest given for each period and Date of lowest in ( ):

1st–2nd: -0.3'
4th–8th: -0.3' (4th–6th)
16th–17th: -0.4'
19th–31st: -0.8' (21st–23rd)

2nd–7th: -0.3' (3rd–6th)
14th–25th: -0.8' (19th–21st)

5th–10th: -0.2'
16th: -0.2'
18th–25th: -0.7' (21st, 22nd)

Average Rise and Fall 2.5 ft.

When a high tide exceeds avg. ht., the *following* low tide will be lower than avg.

2019 HIGH WATER
MIAMI HARBOR ENTRANCE, FL
25°45.8'N, 80°07.8'W

		Daylight Saving Time				Daylight Saving Time				Daylight Saving Time				
DAY OF MONTH	DAY OF WEEK	APRIL				DAY OF WEEK	MAY				DAY OF WEEK	JUNE				DAY OF MONTH
		a.m.	Ht.	p.m.	Ht.		a.m.	Ht.	p.m.	Ht.		a.m.	Ht.	p.m.	Ht.	
1	M	7:03	2.1	7:18	2.1	W	7:00	2.2	7:28	2.3	S	7:45	2.2	8:24	2.5	1
2	T	7:44	2.2	8:02	2.2	T	7:42	2.3	8:12	2.4	S	8:30	2.3	9:10	2.6	2
3	W	8:23	2.3	8:43	2.3	F	8:23	2.3	8:54	2.5	M	9:15	2.4	9:56	2.7	3
4	T	9:00	2.4	9:22	2.4	S	9:03	2.4	9:35	2.6	T	10:01	2.4	10:43	2.7	4
5	F	9:36	2.4	10:00	2.5	S	9:43	2.4	10:17	2.7	W	10:49	2.4	11:31	2.7	5
6	S	10:12	2.4	10:39	2.5	M	10:23	2.4	11:00	2.7	T	11:39	2.4	...	...	6
7	S	10:49	2.4	11:19	2.5	T	11:06	2.4	11:46	2.6	F	12:21	2.6	12:33	2.4	7
8	M	11:26	2.3	...	...	W	11:51	2.3	...	...	S	1:13	2.6	1:31	2.3	8
9	T	12:02	2.5	12:06	2.2	T	12:35	2.5	12:42	2.3	S	2:08	2.5	2:33	2.3	9
10	W	12:47	2.4	12:51	2.2	F	1:27	2.5	1:39	2.3	M	3:04	2.4	3:38	2.3	10
11	T	1:39	2.3	1:45	2.1	S	2:24	2.4	2:43	2.2	T	4:03	2.4	4:44	2.4	11
12	F	2:38	2.3	2:49	2.1	S	3:25	2.4	3:51	2.3	W	5:02	2.4	5:47	2.5	12
13	S	3:44	2.3	4:01	2.2	M	4:28	2.4	5:00	2.4	T	6:00	2.4	6:45	2.5	13
14	S	4:51	2.3	5:13	2.3	T	5:29	2.4	6:04	2.5	F	6:54	2.4	7:39	2.6	14
15	M	5:54	2.4	6:19	2.5	W	6:26	2.5	7:03	2.7	S	7:46	2.4	8:28	2.6	15
16	T	6:51	2.6	7:19	2.7	T	7:19	2.6	7:56	2.8	S	8:33	2.4	9:14	2.6	16
17	W	7:44	2.7	8:13	2.8	F	8:08	2.6	8:46	2.8	M	9:19	2.4	9:57	2.6	17
18	T	8:33	2.8	9:04	2.9	S	8:56	2.6	9:33	2.8	T	10:02	2.3	10:39	2.5	18
19	F	9:20	2.8	9:52	3.0	S	9:41	2.6	10:18	2.8	W	10:44	2.3	11:19	2.4	19
20	S	10:05	2.8	10:38	2.9	M	10:25	2.5	11:01	2.7	T	11:25	2.2	11:59	2.3	20
21	S	10:49	2.7	11:24	2.8	T	11:08	2.4	11:44	2.5	F	...	...	12:07	2.1	21
22	M	11:33	2.5	...	...	W	11:51	2.3	...	...	S	12:38	2.2	12:51	2.0	22
23	T	12:09	2.6	12:18	2.4	T	12:27	2.4	12:35	2.2	S	1:19	2.2	1:37	2.0	23
24	W	12:56	2.4	1:04	2.2	F	1:11	2.2	1:22	2.0	M	2:02	2.1	2:27	1.9	24
25	T	1:44	2.3	1:54	2.1	S	1:57	2.1	2:12	2.0	T	2:47	2.0	3:21	1.9	25
26	F	2:36	2.1	2:49	2.0	S	2:45	2.1	3:07	1.9	W	3:35	2.0	4:17	2.0	26
27	S	3:32	2.0	3:50	1.9	M	3:36	2.0	4:06	1.9	T	4:27	2.0	5:15	2.0	27
28	S	4:29	2.0	4:52	1.9	T	4:29	2.0	5:04	2.0	F	5:21	2.0	6:11	2.2	28
29	M	5:24	2.0	5:50	2.0	W	5:21	2.0	5:59	2.1	S	6:15	2.1	7:05	2.3	29
30	T	6:14	2.1	6:42	2.2	T	6:11	2.1	6:50	2.2	S	7:08	2.2	7:56	2.5	30
31						F	6:58	2.2	7:38	2.4						31

Dates when Ht. of **Low** Water is below Mean Low with Ht. of lowest given for each period and Date of lowest in ( ):

6th–9th: -0.2'
16th–22nd: -0.6' (19th, 20th)

4th–8th: -0.3' (6th, 7th)
15th–21st: -0.5' (17th–19th)

1st–8th: -0.4' (3rd–6th)
12th–19th: -0.4' (14th–17th)
30th: -0.3'

Average Rise and Fall 2.5 ft.

When a high tide exceeds avg. ht., the *following* low tide will be lower than avg.

167

2019 HIGH WATER
MIAMI HARBOR ENTRANCE, FL
25°45.8'N, 80°07.8'W

DAY OF MONTH	DAY OF WEEK	JULY a.m.	Ht.	JULY p.m.	Ht.	DAY OF WEEK	AUGUST a.m.	Ht.	AUGUST p.m.	Ht.	DAY OF WEEK	SEPTEMBER a.m.	Ht.	SEPTEMBER p.m.	Ht.	DAY OF MONTH
1	M	8:00	2.3	8:46	2.6	T	9:25	2.7	10:03	2.9	S	10:53	3.2	11:15	3.2	1
2	T	8:51	2.4	9:36	2.7	F	10:18	2.8	10:52	3.0	M	11:45	3.2	...	...	2
3	W	9:42	2.5	10:24	2.8	S	11:11	2.9	11:40	2.9	T	12:03	3.1	12:38	3.1	3
4	T	10:34	2.5	11:13	2.8	S	...	...	12:05	2.8	W	12:53	2.9	1:33	2.9	4
5	F	11:27	2.6	...	...	M	12:30	2.9	1:00	2.8	T	1:46	2.8	2:31	2.8	5
6	S	12:03	2.7	12:21	2.5	T	1:21	2.7	1:57	2.7	F	2:43	2.6	3:33	2.7	6
7	S	12:53	2.7	1:18	2.5	W	2:14	2.6	2:57	2.6	S	3:45	2.5	4:37	2.6	7
8	M	1:46	2.6	2:18	2.5	T	3:11	2.5	4:00	2.5	S	4:48	2.5	5:39	2.6	8
9	T	2:41	2.5	3:20	2.4	F	4:12	2.4	5:04	2.4	M	5:50	2.5	6:34	2.6	9
10	W	3:37	2.4	4:24	2.4	S	5:13	2.3	6:05	2.4	T	6:44	2.5	7:21	2.7	10
11	T	4:37	2.3	5:27	2.4	S	6:12	2.3	7:00	2.5	W	7:31	2.6	8:02	2.7	11
12	F	5:36	2.3	6:26	2.4	M	7:05	2.3	7:48	2.5	T	8:13	2.7	8:39	2.8	12
13	S	6:32	2.3	7:20	2.5	T	7:53	2.4	8:31	2.5	F	8:53	2.8	9:15	2.8	13
14	S	7:25	2.3	8:09	2.5	W	8:37	2.4	9:10	2.6	S	9:30	2.8	9:49	2.8	14
15	M	8:13	2.3	8:54	2.5	T	9:17	2.5	9:47	2.6	S	10:08	2.8	10:24	2.8	15
16	T	8:58	2.3	9:35	2.5	F	9:56	2.5	10:22	2.6	M	10:45	2.8	10:58	2.8	16
17	W	9:40	2.3	10:14	2.5	S	10:34	2.5	10:57	2.6	T	11:23	2.8	11:33	2.7	17
18	T	10:20	2.3	10:52	2.4	S	11:12	2.5	11:31	2.5	W	...	...	12:03	2.8	18
19	F	11:00	2.2	11:29	2.4	M	11:51	2.5	...	...	T	12:10	2.6	12:46	2.7	19
20	S	11:40	2.2	...	...	T	12:07	2.5	12:31	2.4	F	12:50	2.5	1:34	2.6	20
21	S	12:05	2.3	12:21	2.2	W	12:43	2.4	1:15	2.4	S	1:37	2.5	2:30	2.6	21
22	M	12:42	2.2	1:03	2.1	T	1:23	2.3	2:03	2.3	S	2:35	2.5	3:34	2.6	22
23	T	1:21	2.2	1:49	2.1	F	2:08	2.3	2:58	2.3	M	3:42	2.5	4:41	2.7	23
24	W	2:02	2.1	2:39	2.1	S	3:01	2.2	4:00	2.3	T	4:53	2.6	5:45	2.8	24
25	T	2:48	2.1	3:34	2.1	S	4:03	2.3	5:05	2.4	W	6:01	2.8	6:43	3.0	25
26	F	3:40	2.0	4:34	2.1	M	5:11	2.4	6:08	2.6	T	7:02	3.0	7:36	3.2	26
27	S	4:37	2.1	5:35	2.2	T	6:16	2.5	7:07	2.8	F	7:58	3.3	8:26	3.3	27
28	S	5:38	2.2	6:35	2.4	W	7:17	2.7	8:00	3.0	S	8:51	3.4	9:14	3.4	28
29	M	6:38	2.3	7:31	2.5	T	8:14	2.9	8:51	3.1	S	9:42	3.5	10:01	3.4	29
30	T	7:36	2.4	8:24	2.7	F	9:08	3.1	9:39	3.2	M	10:33	3.5	10:48	3.3	30
31	W	8:31	2.6	9:14	2.8	S	10:01	3.2	10:27	3.2						31

Dates when Ht. of **Low** Water is below Mean Low with Ht. of lowest given for each period and Date of lowest in ( ):

1st–17th: -0.6' (3rd)   1st–6th: -0.5' (1st, 2nd)   1st–2nd: -0.2'
29th–31st: -0.4' (31st)   29th–31st: -0.3' (30th)   30th: -0.2'

Average Rise and Fall 2.5 ft.

When a high tide exceeds avg. ht., the *following* low tide will be lower than avg.

2019 HIGH WATER
MIAMI HARBOR ENTRANCE, FL
25°45.8'N, 80°07.8'W

		Daylight Saving Time						*Standard Time starts Nov. 3 at 2 a.m.						Standard Time			

D A Y O F M O N T H	D A Y O F W E E K	OCTOBER				D A Y O F W E E K	NOVEMBER				D A Y O F W E E K	DECEMBER				D A Y O F M O N T H
		a.m.	Ht.	p.m.	Ht.		a.m.	Ht.	p.m.	Ht.		a.m.	Ht.	p.m.	Ht.	
1	T	11:23	3.4	11:36	3.2	F	...	...	12:38	3.0	S	11:56	2.6	...	...	1
2	W	...	...	12:13	3.3	S	12:48	2.8	1:30	2.8	M	12:08	2.3	12:43	2.4	2
3	T	12:26	3.0	1:06	3.1	S	1:42	2.6	*1:24	2.7	T	1:00	2.2	1:32	2.3	3
4	F	1:18	2.8	2:02	2.9	M	1:39	2.5	2:21	2.6	W	1:56	2.2	2:23	2.3	4
5	S	2:14	2.7	3:01	2.7	T	2:41	2.4	3:17	2.5	T	2:54	2.2	3:15	2.2	5
6	S	3:15	2.6	4:03	2.6	W	3:42	2.4	4:11	2.5	F	3:52	2.2	4:06	2.2	6
7	M	4:19	2.5	5:04	2.6	T	4:38	2.5	4:59	2.6	S	4:46	2.3	4:55	2.3	7
8	T	5:20	2.5	5:58	2.7	F	5:28	2.6	5:43	2.6	S	5:36	2.4	5:42	2.3	8
9	W	6:16	2.6	6:45	2.7	S	6:14	2.7	6:24	2.7	M	6:23	2.5	6:27	2.4	9
10	T	7:03	2.7	7:26	2.8	S	6:55	2.8	7:03	2.7	T	7:07	2.6	7:11	2.4	10
11	F	7:45	2.8	8:03	2.8	M	7:35	2.9	7:42	2.8	W	7:51	2.7	7:55	2.5	11
12	S	8:25	2.9	8:40	2.9	T	8:15	3.0	8:21	2.8	T	8:35	2.8	8:39	2.5	12
13	S	9:03	3.0	9:16	2.9	W	8:56	3.0	9:01	2.7	F	9:19	2.8	9:24	2.5	13
14	M	9:41	3.0	9:51	2.9	T	9:38	3.0	9:41	2.7	S	10:05	2.8	10:12	2.5	14
15	T	10:19	3.0	10:27	2.8	F	10:21	2.9	10:25	2.7	S	10:52	2.7	11:03	2.5	15
16	W	10:58	3.0	11:04	2.8	S	11:08	2.8	11:13	2.6	M	11:42	2.7	11:58	2.4	16
17	T	11:40	2.9	11:43	2.7	S	11:58	2.8	...	...	T	...	...	12:34	2.6	17
18	F	...	...	12:24	2.9	M	12:08	2.5	12:54	2.7	W	12:59	2.4	1:30	2.5	18
19	S	12:27	2.7	1:14	2.8	T	1:10	2.5	1:53	2.7	T	2:03	2.4	2:28	2.5	19
20	S	1:19	2.6	2:11	2.8	W	2:18	2.6	2:54	2.7	F	3:09	2.4	3:28	2.4	20
21	M	2:20	2.6	3:13	2.7	T	3:27	2.7	3:55	2.8	S	4:14	2.5	4:28	2.5	21
22	T	3:30	2.6	4:18	2.8	F	4:32	2.8	4:53	2.8	S	5:16	2.6	5:25	2.5	22
23	W	4:40	2.8	5:20	2.9	S	5:32	3.0	5:47	2.9	M	6:12	2.7	6:19	2.5	23
24	T	5:47	2.9	6:18	3.0	S	6:27	3.1	6:39	3.0	T	7:04	2.7	7:10	2.5	24
25	F	6:47	3.2	7:11	3.2	M	7:18	3.2	7:28	3.0	W	7:52	2.8	7:58	2.5	25
26	S	7:43	3.3	8:01	3.3	T	8:07	3.2	8:15	3.0	T	8:37	2.7	8:43	2.5	26
27	S	8:35	3.5	8:49	3.3	W	8:54	3.2	9:02	2.9	F	9:20	2.7	9:26	2.4	27
28	M	9:24	3.5	9:37	3.3	T	9:40	3.1	9:47	2.8	S	10:02	2.6	10:09	2.3	28
29	T	10:13	3.5	10:23	3.2	F	10:25	2.9	10:33	2.6	S	10:42	2.4	10:52	2.2	29
30	W	11:01	3.4	11:10	3.1	S	11:10	2.8	11:19	2.5	M	11:22	2.3	11:35	2.1	30
31	T	11:49	3.2	11:58	2.9						T	...	...	12:02	2.2	31

Dates when Ht. of **Low** Water is below Mean Low with Ht. of lowest given for each period and Date of lowest in ( ):

28th–29th: -0.2'   25th–28th: -0.3' (26th, 27th)   12th–15th: -0.2'
                                                                                                          21st–22nd: -0.3'
                                                                                                          24th–29th: -0.5' (25th)

Average Rise and Fall 2.5 ft.

When a high tide exceeds avg. ht., the *following* low tide will be lower than avg.

My dear Captain and Mr. Mate,

As I cannot talk with you, I will do the next best thing. I will write you a letter.

Do you know, Captain and Mr. Mate of a place on the Atlantic Coast that is called "The Graveyard"? I propose to tell you something about it, and do what I can to keep vessels out of it. "The Graveyard" so called, is that part of the coast which lies between Sow and Pigs Rocks and Naushon Island. This place has been called "The Graveyard" for many years, — because many a good craft has laid her bones there, and many a captain has lost his reputation there also. If a vessel gets into this graveyard, there must be a cause for it. Did it ever occur to you that seldom does a vessel go ashore on Gay Head, or on the south side of the Sound? but that hundreds of them have been piled up in "The Graveyard, or on the north side of the Sound? I will explain why this is so. if you are bound into Vineyard Sound in thick weather, you will probably refer to the "Gay Head and Cross Rip" table in this book, to see when the tide turns in or out. You will notice at the — head of each table that it says, "This table shows the time that the current turns Easterly and — Westerly, off Gay Head in ship channel." That — means off Gay Head when it bears about South. Now, as a rule, captains figure on the current's after they leave the Lightship, as running East-erly into the Sound, when as a matter of fact the first of the flood between the Lightship and Gay Head runs nearly North; and the current does not begin to run to the eastward until you are well into the Sound, as shewn by the chart on the opposite page. Vessels bound into — Vineyard Sound from the Westward will have the current of ebb on the starboard bow. (see arrows on the hulls in the chart on the opposite page)

I have explained this matter, and I leave the rest to your judgment and careful consideration; and thus you will undoubtedly keep your vessel out of "The Graveyard".

Yours for a fair tide,

Geo. W. Eldridge.

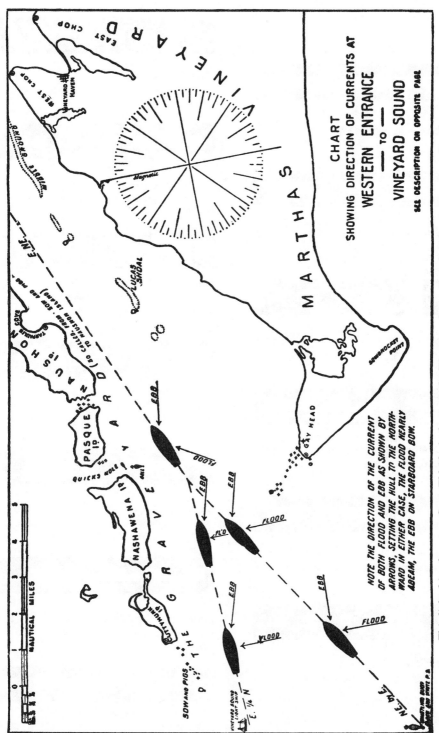

This lightship, shown on Capt. Eldridge's chart, on the Western edge, was replaced many years ago by a buoy.

CHARACTERISTICS OF LIGHT SIGNALS
(see footnote on next page for abbreviations used.)

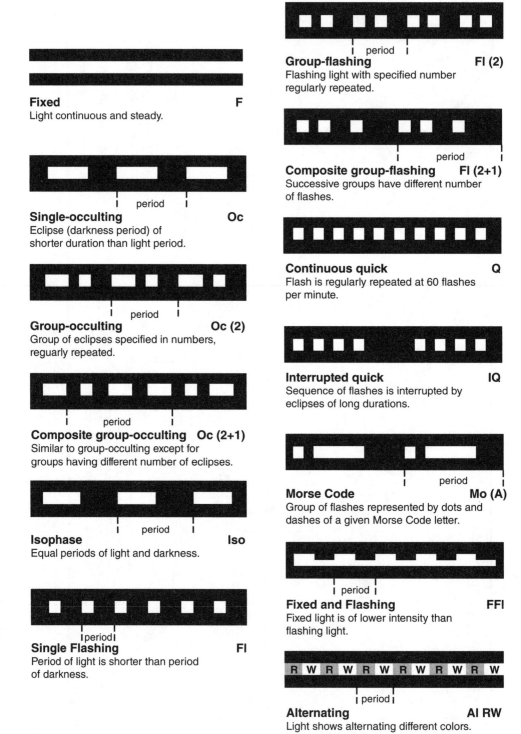

Fixed   **F**
Light continuous and steady.

Single-occulting   **Oc**
Eclipse (darkness period) of
shorter duration than light period.

Group-occulting   **Oc (2)**
Group of eclipses specified in numbers,
reguarly repeated.

Composite group-occulting   **Oc (2+1)**
Similar to group-occulting except for
groups having different number of eclipses.

Isophase   **Iso**
Equal periods of light and darkness.

Single Flashing   **Fl**
Period of light is shorter than period
of darkness.

Group-flashing   **Fl (2)**
Flashing light with specified number
regularly repeated.

Composite group-flashing   **Fl (2+1)**
Successive groups have different number
of flashes.

Continuous quick   **Q**
Flash is regularly repeated at 60 flashes
per minute.

Interrupted quick   **IQ**
Sequence of flashes is interrupted by
eclipses of long durations.

Morse Code   **Mo (A)**
Group of flashes represented by dots and
dashes of a given Morse Code letter.

Fixed and Flashing   **FFl**
Fixed light is of lower intensity than
flashing light.

Alternating   **Al RW**
Light shows alternating different colors.

LIGHTS, FOG SIGNALS and OFFSHORE BUOYS

NOVA SCOTIA, EAST COAST

Cranberry Is. Lt., off Cape Canso, S. part of Is. – Fl. W. ev. 15 s., 2 Horns 2 bl. ev. 60 s., Horns point 066° and 141°, Ht. 16.9 m. (56′), Rge. 21 mi., Racon (B), (45-19-29.6N/60-55-38.2W)

White Head Is. Lt., SW side of Is. – Fl. W. ev. 5 s., Horn 1 bl. ev. 30 s., Horn points 190°, Ht. 18.2 m. (60′), Rge. 12 mi., (45-11-49.1N/61-08-10.8W)

Country Is. Lt., S. side of Is. – Fl. W. ev. 20 s., Ht. 16.5 m. (54′), Rge. 10 mi., (45-05-59.8N/61-32-31.9W)

Liscomb Is. Lt., near Cranberry Pt. – Fl. W. ev. 10 s., Horn 1 bl. ev. 30 s., Ht. 21.9 m. (72′), Rge. 14 mi., (44-59-15.8N/61-57-58.4W)

Beaver Is. Lt., E. end of Is. – Fl. W. ev. 7 s., Horn 1 bl. ev. 60 s., Horn points 144°, Ht. 19.9 m. (66′), Rge. 14 mi., (44-49-29.2N/62-20-16W)

Ship Harbour Lt., on Wolfes Pt. – LFl. G. ev. 6 s., Ht. 18.2 m. (60′), Rge. 4 mi., (44-44-55.4N/62-45-23.6W)

Owls Head Lt., at end of head – Fl. W. ev. 4 s., Ht. 25.8 m. (84′), Rge. 6 mi., (44-43-14.6N/62-47-59.5W)

Egg Is. Lt., center of Is. – LFl. W. ev. 6 s., Ht. 7.6 m. (25′), Rge. 12 mi., (44-39-52.7N/62-51-48.4W)

Jeddore Rock Lt., summit of rock – LFl. W. ev. 12 s., Ht. 29.5 m. (97′), Rge. 8 mi., (44-39-47.1N/63-00-37.3)

Bear Cove Lt. & Bell By. "H6," NE of cove, Q. R., Racon (N), Red, (44-32-36.3N/63-31-19.6W)

Sambro Harbor Lt. & Wh. By. "HS," S. of SW breaker, Halifax Hbr. app. – Mo(A)W ev. 6 s., RWS, (44-24-30N/63-33-36.5W)

Chebucto Head Lt., on summit, Halifax Hbr. app. – Fl. W. ev. 20 s., Horn 2 bl. ev. 60 s., Horn points 113°, Ht. 47.8 m. (157′), Rge. 10 mi., Racon (Z), (44-30-26.6N/63-31-21.8W)

Halifax Alpha Lt. & Wh. By. "HA," Halifax app. – Mo(A)W ev. 6 s., RWS, (44-21-45N/63-24-15W)

Sambro Is. Lt., center of Is. – Fl. W. ev. 6 s., Ht. 42.7 m. (145′), Rge. 23 mi., (44-26-12N/63-33-48W)

Ketch Harbour Lt. By. "HE 19," Ketch Harbour entr. – Fl. G. ev 4 s., Green (44-28-19.6N/63-32-16W)

Betty Is. Lt., on Brig Pt. – LFl. W. ev. 15 s., Ht. 19.2 m. (63′), Rge. 13 mi., (44-26-19.7N/63-46-00.4W)

Pearl Is. Lt., off St. Margaret's & Mahone Bays – Fl. W. ev. 10 s., Ht. 19.0 m. (63′), Rge. 8 mi., (44-22-57.2N/64-02-54W)

East Ironbound Is. Lt., center of Is. – Iso. W. ev. 6 s., Ht. 44.5 m. (147′), Rge. 13 mi., (44-26-22.4N/64-04-59.7W)

East Point Island Lt., Mahone Bay – LFl G ev. 6 s., Ht. 9.6 m. (31′), Rge. 6 mi., (44-20-59.2N/64-12-15W)

Abbreviations: **Alt.,** Alternating; **App.,** Approach; **By.,** Buoy; **Ch.,** Channel; **Entr.,** Entrance; **ev.,** every; **F.,** Fixed; **fl.,** flash; **Fl.,** Flashing; **Fl(2),** Group Flashing; **LFl,** 2 s. flash.; **G.,** Green; **Hbr.,** Harbor or Harbour, **Ht.,** height; **Is.,** Island; **Iso.,** Isophase (Equal interval); **Iso. W.,** Isophase White (Red sector(s) of Lights warn of dangerous angle of approach. Bearings and ranges are <u>from</u> the observer <u>to</u> the aid.); **Jct.,** Junction; **Keyed,** Fog signal is radio activated. During times of reduced visibility, within ½ mile of the fog signal, turn VHF marine radio to channel 83A and 81A as alternate. Key microphone 5–10 times consecutively to activate fog signal for 45 minutes (Boston Lt. 60 minutes). **Lt.,** Light; **Ltd.,** Lighted.; **mi.,** miles; **Mo(A),** Morse Code "A," **Mo(U),** Morse Code "U"; **Oc.,** Occulting; **Pt.,** Point; **Q.,** Quick (Flashing); **RaRef.,** Radar Reflector; **R.,** Red; **rge.,** range; **RWS,** R.&W. Stripes; **RWSRST,** RWS with R. Spherical Topmarks; **s.,** seconds; **Wh.,** Whistle; **W.,** White; **Y.,** Yellow

Notices To Mariners: Keep informed of important changes. Visit **www.navcen.uscg.gov** to receive Local Notices to Mariners via email. When reporting discrepancies in navigational aids, contact nearest C.G. unit and give official name of the aid.

Table for Converting Seconds to Decimals of a Minute, p. 266, for standard GPS input of Lat/Lon.

See pp. 222-223 for Atlantic Coast Racon Information.   **173**

Rising Seas Along the Eastern Seaboard

Why, How Much, and How Fast?

by Jennifer Francis

The east coast of North America is experiencing some of the world's fastest rises in sea levels, exacerbating damage from recent storms such as Hurricanes Sandy and Matthew, as well as numerous destructive nor'easters. Coastal flooding events have increased about six-fold along the east coast just since the 1970s.[1] In some areas a storm is not even needed anymore to cause coastal inundation – "sunny day" flooding is becoming a regular occurrence in many low-lying areas during natural cycles of very high tides. Why are sea levels rising so fast, especially in "Eldridge country?"

Let's start with some historical context. The last ice age peaked about 20,000 years ago, when much of northern North America was buried in the massive Laurentide Ice Sheet. Sea levels back then were about 400 feet lower than today: George's Bank was dry land, and the northeast coastline was about 100 miles farther east.[2,3] As the Earth gradually warmed (owing to natural variations in the Earth's orbit), the ice sheet retreated northward, returning its meltwater back to the ocean. Seas rose steadily for the next 12,000 years before leveling off about 8,000 years ago at heights similar to today's. If only natural causes were still in control of the climate system, the Earth would now be in a cycle of gradual cooling, and sea levels would slowly begin to lower. But since the early 1900s, natural climate cycles have been increasingly overwhelmed by the influences of humans. Not only are global sea-levels now increasing – about seven inches since the early 1900s -- but the pace is accelerating.[4]

The big ice sheet is long gone, so why is this happening? There are three main contributors to the recent rise in global oceans, all directly related to the warming of the globe in response to increasing greenhouse gases that are produced mainly from burning coal, oil, and natural gas.

The largest source of rising seas (nearly half) is from melting glaciers – those rivers of ice that flow from ice fields in mountainous areas. In nearly every part of the world, glaciers have been getting shorter and thinner, as have their parent ice fields, and that lost meltwater adds directly to the mass of the ocean. The second biggest contribution is from the warming oceans. Extra heat trapped by those greenhouse gases goes mainly into the oceans, and warmer water expands. This so-called "thermal expansion" account for another third of the global sea-level rise. The third input is from melting ice sheets on Greenland and Antarctica. Both of these land masses are covered in a layer of ice that is over two miles thick in some areas, which recent studies indicate are also melting at an accelerating rate. Greenland's ice sheet is losing ice from its surface and from

---

1   Union of Concerned Scientists 2014, http://www.ucsusa.org/encroachingtides

2   https://www.usgs.gov/faqs/how-does-present-glacier-extent-and-sea-level-compare-extent-glaciers-and-global-sea-level?qt-news_science_products=0#qt-news_science_products

3   http://www.antarcticglaciers.org/glaciers-and-climate/sea-level-rise-2/sea-level-rise/

4   Hay, C.C., et al., Probabilistic reanalysis of twentieth-century sea-level rise. Nature, 2015. 517(7535): p. 481-484.

Continued on p. 176

Cross Is. Lt., E. Pt. of Is. – Fl. W. ev. 10 s., Ht. 24.9 m. (82′), Rge. 10 mi., (44-18-43.7N/64-10-06.4W)

West Ironbound Is. Lt., Entr. to La Have R. – Fl. W. ev. 12 s., Ht. 24.3 m. (80′), Rge. 8 mi., (44-13-43.7N/64-16-28W)

Mosher Is. Lt., W. side Entr. to La Have R. – F.W., Horn 1 bl. ev. 20 s., Ht. 23.3 m. (77′), Rge. 13 mi., (44-14-14.6N/64-18-59.1W)

Cherry Cove Lt., betw. Little Hbr. & Back Cove – Iso. G. ev. 4 s., Ht. 6.7 m. (22′), Rge. 8 mi., (44-09-29.8N/64-28-53.2W)

Medway Head Lt., W. side entr. to Pt. Medway – Fl. W. ev. 12 s., Ht. 24.2 m. (80′), Rge. 11 mi., (44-06-10.6N/64-32-23.3W)

Western Head Lt., W. side entr. to Liverpool Bay – Fl. W. ev. 15 s., Horn 1 bl. ev. 60 s., Horn points 104°, Ht. 16.8 m. (55′), Rge. 15 mi., (43-59-20.8N/64-39-44.5W)

Lockeport Lt., on Gull Rock, entr. to hbr. – LFl. W. ev. 15 s., Horn 1 bl. ev. 30 s., Ht. 16.7 m. (56′), Rge. 12 mi., (43-39-18.3N/65-05-55.9W)

Cape Roseway Lt., near SE Pt. of McNutt Is. – Fl. W. ev. 10 s., Ht. 33.1 m. (109′), Rge. 10 mi., (43-37-21.4N/65-15-50W)

Cape Negro Is. Lt., on SE end of Is. – Fl(2) W. ev. 15 s., Horn 1 bl. ev. 60 s., Ht. 28.3 m. (92′), Rge. 10 mi., (43-30-26.2N/65-20-44.2W)

The Salvages Lt., SE end of Is. – LFl. W. ev. 12 s., Horn 3 bl. ev. 60 s., Ht. 15.6 m. (51′), Rge. 10 mi., (43-28-08.1N/65-22-44W)

Baccaro Point Lt., E. side entr. to Barrington Bay – Mo(D)W ev. 10 s., Horn 1 bl. ev. 20 s., Horn points 200°, Ht. 15.0 m. (49′), Rge. 15 mi., (43-26-59N/65-28-15W)

Cape Sable Lt., on cape – Fl. W. ev. 5 s., Horn 1 bl. ev. 60 s., Horn points 150°, Ht. 29.7 m. (97′), Rge. 18 mi., Racon (C), (43-23-24N/65-37-16.9W)

West Head Lt., Cape Sable Is. – F.R., Horn 2 bl. ev. 60 s., Horn points 254°, Ht. 15.6 m. (51′), Rge. 7 mi., (43-27-23.8N/65-39-16.9W)

Outer Island Lt., on S. Pt. of Outer Is. – Fl. W. ev. 10 s., Ht. 13.7 m. (46′), Rge. 10 mi., (43-27-23.2N/65-44-36.2W)

Seal Is. Lt., S. Pt. of Is. – Fl. W. ev. 10 s., Horn 3 bl. ev. 60 s., Horn points 183°, Ht. 33.4 m. (110′), Rge. 19 mi., (43-23-40N/66-00-51W)

NOVA SCOTIA, WEST COAST

Peases Is. Lt., S. Pt. of one of the Tusket Is. – Fl. W. ev. 6 s., Horn 2 bl. ev. 60 s., Ht. 16 m. (53′), Rge. 9 mi., (43-37-42.6N/66-01-34.9W)

Cape Forchu Lt., E. Cape S. Pt. Yarmouth Sd. – LFl. W. ev. 12 s., Ht. 34.5 m. (113′), Rge. 12 mi., Racon (B), (43-47-38.8N/66-09-19.3W)

Lurcher Shoal Bifurcation Light By. "NM," W. of SW shoal – Fl.(2+1) R. ev. 6 s., Racon (K), R.G.R. marked "NM," (43-48-57.2N/66-29-58W)

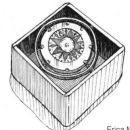

Erica M. Szuplat

Cape St. Marys Lt., E. side of Bay – Fl. W. ev. 5 s., Horn 1 bl. ev. 60 s., Horn points 251° 30′, Ht. 31.8 m (105′), Rge. 13 mi., (44-05-09.2N/66-12-39.6W)

Brier Is. Lt., on W. side of Is. R. & W. Tower – Fl(3) W. ev. 18 s., 2 Horns 2 bl. ev. 60 s., Horns point 270° and 315°, Ht. 22.2 m. (72′), Rge. 14 mi., (44-14-55N/66-23-32W)

Boars Head Lt., W. side of N. entr. to Petit Passage – Fl. W. ev. 5 s., Horn 3 bl. ev. 60 s., Horn points 315°, Ht. 28.0 m. (91′), Rge. 16 mi., (44-24-14.5N/66-12-55W)

Prim Pt. Lt., Digby Gut, W. Pt. of entr. to Annapolis Basin – Iso. W. ev. 6 s., Ht. 24.8 m. (82′), Rge. 12 mi., (44-41-28N/65-47-10.8W)

Ile Haute Lt., on highest Pt. – Fl. W. ev. 4 s., Ht. 112 m. (367′), Rge. 7 mi., (45-15-03.3N/65-00-19.8W)

For abbreviations see footnote p. 173

Continued from p. 174

the undersides of glaciers flowing into the warming ocean. If the entire ice sheet were to melt, sea levels would rise about 20 feet. Air temperatures over Antarctica are much colder than over Greenland, so surface melt is not yet an important factor, but the warming Southern Ocean is melting the undersides of massive ice shelves that extend seaward from the coasts, especially in West Antarctica. The ice sheet on Antarctica would raise sea levels about 60 feet if the whole thing were to melt. While these two ice sheets have come and gone through past ice ages and intervening warm epochs, their demise is not expected to occur within a few centuries. That said, their accelerated melting is the fastest growing contribution to rising seas.[5]

The factors discussed so far explain the rise in global sea levels, but why is the eastern seaboard experiencing even larger increases? Once again, there are three

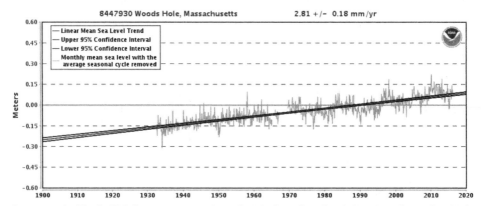

One example: Woods Hole has seen approximately 9 inches of sea level rise since the early 1900's.

main contributors: one is natural and two are related to human-caused warming. The natural cause goes back to the retreat of the Laurentide Ice Sheet. So much ice sat on top of northern North America that its weight depressed the land beneath it – like when someone lies on a waterbed – and land away from the ice sheet rose in compensation, again like the other side of the waterbed. As the ice receded, the land beneath it slowly rebounded toward its original elevation, like the waterbed returning to level when the weight is removed. In areas where land is rebounding, the increasing sea-levels are being offset, reducing the net pace of rising seas. Land south of the ice sheet, however, is sinking, which augments the effects of sea-level rise. The dividing line between rising and sinking land runs diagonally (SW to NE) right through New England.[6]

5   Church, J.A., P.U. Clark, A. Cazenave, J.M. Gregory, S. Jevrejeva, A. Levermann, M.A. Merrifield, G.A. Milne, R.S. Nerem, P.D. Nunn, A.J. Payne, W.T. Pfeffer, D. Stammer and A.S. Unnikrishnan, 2013: Sea Level Change. In: Climate Change 2013: The Physical Science Basis. Contribution of Working Group I to the Fifth Assessment Report of the Intergovernmental Panel on Climate Change [Stocker, T.F., D. Qin, G.-K. Plattner, M. Tignor, S.K. Allen, J. Boschung, A. Nauels, Y. Xia, V. Bex and P.M. Midgley (eds.)]. Cambridge University Press, Cambridge, United Kingdom and New York, NY, USA.

6   Sella, G.F. S. Stein, T.H. Dixon, M. Craymer, T.S. James, S. Mazzotti, and R.K. Dokka, 2007: Observation of glacial isostatic adjustment in "stable" North America with GPS. Geophys. Res. Lett., 34, doi:10.1029/2006GL027081.

 Continued on p. 178

NEW BRUNSWICK COAST

Cape Enrage Lt., at pitch of cape – Fl. G. ev. 6 s., Horn 3 bl. ev. 60 s., Horn points 220°, Ht. 40.7 m. (134'), Rge. 10 mi., (45-35-38.1N/64-46-47.7W)

Quaco Lt., tower on head – Fl. W. ev. 10 s., Horn 1 bl. ev. 30 s., Horn points 130°, Ht. 26.0 m. (86'), Rge. 21 mi., (45-19-25.3N/65-32-08.8W)

Cape Spencer Lt., pitch of cape – Fl. W. ev. 11 s., Horn 3 bl. ev. 60 s., Horn points 165°, Ht. 61.6 m. (203'), Rge. 14 mi., (45-11-42.5N/65-54-35.5W)

Partridge Is. Lt., highest pt. of Is., Saint John Harbour – Fl. W. ev. 7.5 s., Ht. 35.3 m. (116'), Rge. 19 mi., (45-14-21N/66-03-13.8W)

Musquash Head Lt., E. side entr. to Musquash Hbr. – Fl. W. ev. 3 s., Horn 1 bl. ev. 60 s., Horn points 180°, Ht. 35.1 m. (116'), Rge. 20 mi., (45-08-37.1N/66-14-14.2W)

Pt. Lepreau Lt., on point – Fl. W. ev. 5 s., Horn 3 bl. ev. 60 s., Horn points 190°, Ht. 25.5 m. (84'), Rge. 14 mi., (45-03-31.7N/66-27-31.3W)

Pea Pt. Lt., E. side entr. to Letang Hbr. – F.W. visible 251° thru N & E to 161°, Horn 2 bl. ev. 60 s., Horn points 180°, Ht. 17.2 m. (56'), Rge. 12 mi., (45-02-20.4N/66-48-28.2W)

Head Harbour Lt., outer rock of E. Quoddy Head – F.R., Horn 1 bl. ev. 60 s., Horn points 116°, Ht. 17.6 m. (58'), Rge. 13 mi., (44-57-28.6N/66-54-00.2W)

Swallowtail Lt., NE Pt. of Grand Manan – Oc. W. ev. 6 s., Horn 1 bl. ev. 20 s., Horn points 100°, Ht. 37.1 m. (122'), Rge. 12 mi., (44-45-51.1N/66-43-57.5W)

Great Duck Is. Lt., S. end of Is. – Fl. W. ev. 10 s., Horn 1 bl. ev. 60 s., Horn points 120°, Ht. 16.5 m. (54'), Rge. 18 mi., (44-41-03.5N/66-41-36.4W)

Southwest Head Lt., S. end of Grand Manan – Fl. W. ev. 10 s., Ht. 47.5 m. (156'), Rge. 16 mi., (44-36-02.9N/66-54-19.8W)

Gannet Rock North Lt. – Oc. W. ev. 3 s. visible 58° through E, S & W to 348°, Ht. 12.9 m. (42'), Rge. 11 mi., (44-30-38N/66-46-53.6W)

Gannet Rock South Lt. – Oc. W. ev. 3 s. visible 193° through W, N & E to 164°, Ht. 13.6 m. (44'), Rge. 11 mi., (44-30-37.2N/66-46-53.7W)

Machias Seal Is. Lt., On Is. summit – Fl. W. ev. 3 s., Ht. 25 m. (83'), Rge. 17 mi., (44-30-06.6N/67-06-04.1W)

MAINE

West Quoddy Head Lt., Entr. Quoddy Roads – Fl(2) W. ev. 15 s., Keyed (VHF 83A) Horn 2 bl. ev. 30 s., Ht. 83', Rge. 18 mi., ltd. 24 hrs., (44-48-54N/66-57-02W)

Libby Island Lt., Entr. Machias Bay – Fl(2) W. ev. 20 s., Horn 1 bl. ev. 15 s., Ht. 91', Rge. 18 mi., (44-34-06N/67-22-03W)

Moose Peak Lt., E. end Mistake Is. – Fl. W. ev. 30 s., Keyed (VHF 83A) Horn 2 bl. ev. 30 s., Ht. 72', Rge. 20 mi., (44-28-28N/67-31-55W)

Petit Manan Lt., E. Pt. of Is. – Fl. W. ev. 10 s., Horn 1 bl. ev. 30 s., Ht. 123', Rge. 19 mi., (44-22-03N/67-51-52W)

Prospect Harbor Point Lt. – Fl. R. ev. 6 s., (2 W. sect.), Ht. 42', Rge. R. 7 mi., W. 9 mi., ltd. 24 hrs., (44-24-12N/68-00-47W)

Mount Desert Lt., 20 mi. S. of island – Fl. W. ev. 15 s., Horn 2 bl. ev. 30 s., Ht. 75', Rge. 20 mi., (43-58-07N/68-07-42W)

Great Duck Island Lt., S. end of island – Fl. R. ev. 5 s., Horn 1 bl. ev. 15 s., Ht. 67', Rge. 19 mi., (44-08-31N/68-14-45W)

Frenchman Bay Ltd. By. "FB," Fl. (2+1) R. ev. 6 s., Rge. 4 mi., R&G Bands, Racon (B), (44-19-21N/68-07-24W)

Egg Rock Lt., Frenchman Bay – Fl. R. ev. 5 s., Keyed (VHF 83A) Horn 2 bl. ev. 30 s., Ht. 64', Rge. 18 mi., (44-21-14N/68-08-18W)

Baker Island Lt., SW Entr. Somes Sound – Fl. W. ev. 10 s., Ht. 105', Rge. 10 mi., (44-14-28N/68-11-56W)

Bass Harbor Head Lt., SW Pt. Mt. Desert Is. – Oc. R. ev. 4 s., Ht. 56', Rge. 13 mi., ltd. 24 hrs., (44-13-19N/68-20-14W)

For abbreviations see footnote p. 173

Continued from p. 176

The second reason that sea levels are rising faster along the east coast is that the ocean temperatures in the Gulf Stream – a strong current that begins in the Gulf of Mexico, flows along the eastern seaboard, then crosses the North Atlantic toward Europe – is warming faster than the Atlantic overall. Recent studies also suggest that the Gulf Stream's velocity is slowing down (owing at least partially to extra freshwater from Greenland's ice sheet), effectively piling up its warm waters along the east coast. All that extra warm water increases the thermal expansion effect, adding to sea-level rise.[7]

The third main cause of faster sea-level rise along the eastern seaboard is somewhat counterintuitive, and ties back to those melting ice sheets on Greenland and Antarctica. These heaps of ice are so massive that they actually exert gravity on surrounding waters, causing the ocean to bulge higher near their coasts. As the ice caps lose mass through melting, that gravitational pull is reduced, which lowers sea levels near the ice but raises it elsewhere.[5]

What does the future hold? Without a doubt, oceans will continue to rise. The open questions are: How much? and How fast? Those are difficult to answer because there is still much unknown about factors causing the great ice sheets to melt.

Another major unknown is how quickly we humans can kick our fossil fuel addiction, as this is the main source of increasing heat-trapping gases that are driving most of sea-level rise. If we do nothing to change our ways, oceans will rise at least six more inches by 2050 and three more feet by the end of this century. "Sunny day" flooding alone will threaten hundreds of billions of dollars in property and infrastructure, and that does not account for coasting flooding by storms.[1]

We must take a two-pronged approach to addressing this challenge. First, we need to get ready by bolstering our infrastructure, planning for evacuations, and stopping the practice of rebuilding in flood-prone areas of our coasts. Tax dollars are literally being washed into the sea whenever disaster funds are used to rebuild in areas that experience repeated flooding. Second, sea-level rise is just one symptom of the climate-change disease, and we need to treat that disease to slow its progression.

Every one of us must find ways to conserve energy in our personal lives, take actions to shift our communities to non-fossil energy sources, and elect leaders who accept the challenge of rising sea-levels. Coastal communities for generations to come will benefit from our actions today.

Jennifer Francis is a lifelong sailor and a Research Professor in the Department of Marine and Coastal Sciences at Rutgers University. Her recent research has explored connections between rapid Arctic warming and weather patterns in mid-latitudes.

7   Böning, C.W., E. Behrens, A. Biastoch, K. Getzla, and J.L. Bamber, 2016: Emerging impact of Greenland meltwater on deepwater formation in the North Atlantic Ocean. Nature Geosci., 9, doi: 10.1038/NGEO2740.

Blue Hill Bay Lt. #3, on Green Is. – Fl. G. ev. 4 s., Ht. 21', Rge. 5 mi., SG on tower, (44-14-55N/68-29-52W)

Burnt Coat Harbor Lt. – Oc. W. ev. 4 s., Ht. 75', Rge. 9 mi., (44-08-03N/68-26-50W)

Halibut Rocks Lt., Jericho Bay – Fl. W. ev. 6 s., Horn 1 bl. ev. 10 s., Ht. 25', Rge. 6 mi., NR on tower, (44-08-03N/68-31-32W)

Eggemoggin Ltd. Bell By. "EG" – Mo(A)W, Rge. 4 mi., RWSRST, (44-19-13N/68-44-34W)

Eggemoggin Reach Bell By. "ER" – RWSRST, (44-18-00N/68-46-29W)

Crotch Island Lt. #21, Deer Is. Thorofare – Fl. G. ev. 4 s., Ht. 20', Rge. 5 mi., SG on tower, (44-08-46N/68-40-39W)

Saddleback Ledge Lt., Isle au Haut Bay – Fl. W. ev. 6 s., Horn 1 bl. ev. 10 s., Ht. 52', Rge. 9 mi., (44-00-52N/68-43-35W)

Isle Au Haut Lt., Isle au Haut Bay – Fl. R. ev. 4 s., W. Sect. 034°-060°, Ht. 48', Rge. R. 6 mi., W. 8 mi., (44-03-53N/68-39-05W)

Deer Island Thorofare Lt., W. end of thorofare – Fl. W. ev. 6 s., Horn 1 bl. ev. 15 s., Ht. 52', Rge. 8 mi., Obscured from 240°-335°, (44-08-04N/68-42-12W)

Goose Rocks Lt., E. Entr. Fox Is. Thorofare – Fl. R. ev. 6 s., W. Sect. 301°-304°, Keyed (VHF 83A) Horn 1 bl. ev. 10 s., Ht. 51', Rge. R. 7 mi., W. 12 mi., (44-08-08N/68-49-50W)

Eagle Island Lt., E. Penobscot Bay – Fl. W. ev. 4 s., Ht. 106', Rge. 9 mi., (44-13-04N/68-46-04W)

Green Ledge Lt. #4, E. Penobscot Bay – Fl. R. ev. 6 s., Ht. 31', Rge. 5 mi., TR on tower, (44-17-25N/68-49-42W)

Heron Neck Lt., E. Entr. Hurricane Sound – F.R., W. Sect. 030°-063°, Keyed (VHF 83A) Horn 1 bl. ev. 30 s., Ht. 92', Rge. R. 7 mi., W. 9 mi., (44-01-30N/68-51-44W)

Matinicus Rock Lt., Penobscot Bay App. – Fl. W. ev. 10 s., Horn 1 bl. ev. 15 s., Ht. 90', Rge. 20 mi., (43-47-01N/68-51-18W)

Grindel Pt. Lt., West Penobscot Bay – Fl. W. ev. 4 s., Ht. 39', Rge. 7 mi., (44-16-53N/68-56-35W)

Two-Bush Island Lt., Two-Bush Ch. – Fl. W. ev. 5 s., R. Sect. 061°-247°, Keyed (VHF 83A) Horn 1 bl. ev. 15 s., Ht. 65', Rge. W. 21 mi., R. 15 mi., (43-57-51N/69-04-26W)

Two Bush Island Ltd. Wh. By. "TBI" – Mo(A)W, Rge. 6 mi., RWS, (43-58-17N/69-00-16W)

Whitehead Lt., W. side of S. entr. Muscle Ridge Ch. – Oc.G. ev. 4 s., Keyed (VHF 83A) Horn 2 bl. ev. 30 s., Ht. 75', Rge. 6 mi., (43-58-43N/69-07-27W)

Owls Head Lt., S. side Rockland Entr. – F.W., Keyed (VHF 83A) Horn 2 bl. ev. 20 s., Ht. 100', Rge. 16 mi., Obscured from 324°-354° by Monroe Island, ltd. 24 hrs., (44-05-32N/69-02-38W)

Rockland Harbor Breakwater Lt., S. end of breakwater – Fl. W. ev. 5 s., Keyed (VHF 83A) Horn 1 bl. ev. 15 s., Ht. 39', Rge. 17 mi., (44-06-15N/69-04-39W)

Lowell Rock Lt. #2, Rockport Entr. – Fl. R. ev. 6 s., Ht. 25', Rge. 5 mi., TR on spindle, (44-09-46N/69-03-37W)

Browns Head Lt., W. Entr. Fox Is. Thorofare – F.W., 2 R. Sect. 001°-050° and 061°-091°, Keyed (VHF 83A) Horn 1 bl. ev. 10 s., Ht. 39', Rge. R. 11 mi., F.W. 14 mi., ltd. 24 hrs., (44-06-42N/68-54-34W)

Curtis Island Lt., S. side Camden Entr. – Oc.G. ev. 4 s., Ht. 52', Rge. 6 mi., (44-12-05N/69-02-56W)

Northeast Point Lt. #2, Camden Entr. – Fl. R. ev. 4 s., Ht. 20', Rge. 5 mi., TR on white tower, (44-12-31N/69-02-47W)

Dice Head Lt., N. side Entr. to Castine – Fl. W. ev. 6 s., Ht. 134', Rge. 11 mi., White tower, (44-22-58N/68-49-08W)

Fort Point Lt., W. side Entr. to Penobscot R. – F.W., Keyed (VHF 83A) Horn 1 bl. ev. 10 s., Ht. 88', Rge. 15 mi., ltd. 24 hrs., (44-28-02N/68-48-42W)

For abbreviations see footnote p. 173

Marshall Point Lt., E. side of Pt. Clyde Hbr. S. Entr. – F.W., Keyed (VHF 83A) Horn 1 bl. ev. 10 s., Ht. 30', Rge. 13 mi., ltd. 24 hrs., (43-55-03N/69-15-41W)

Marshall Point Ltd. By. "MP" – Mo(A)W, Rge. 4 mi., RWSRST, (43-55-18N/69-10-52W)

Monhegan Island Lt., Penobscot Bay – Fl. W. ev. 15 s., Ht. 178', Rge. 20 mi., Obscured between west and southwest within 3 mi of island (43-45-53N/69-18-57W)

Franklin Is. Lt., Muscongus Bay – Fl. W. ev. 6 s., Ht. 57', Rge. 8 mi., Obscured from 253°-352° by trees (43-53-31N/69-22-29W)

Pemaquid Pt. Lt., W. side Muscongus Bay Entr. – Fl. W. ev. 6 s., Ht. 79', Rge. 14 mi., (43-50-12N/69-30-21W)

Ram Is. Lt., Fisherman Is. Passage S. side – Iso. R. ev. 6 s., 2 W. Sect. 258°-261° and 030°-046°, Covers fairways, Keyed (VHF 83A) Horn 1 bl. ev. 30 s., Ht. 36', Rge. W. 11 mi., R. 9 mi., W. 9 mi. (43-48-14N/69-35-57W)

Burnt Is. Lt., Boothbay Hbr. W. side Entr. – Fl. R. ev. 6 s., 2 W. Sect. 307°-316° and 355°-008°, Covers fairways. Keyed (VHF 83A) Horn 1 bl. ev. 10 s., Ht. 61', Rge. W. 8 mi., R. 6 mi., (43-49-31N/69-38-25W)

The Cuckolds Lt., Boothbay – Fl(2) W. ev. 6 s., Keyed (VHF 83A) Horn 1 bl. ev. 15 s., Ht. 59', Rge. 12 mi., (43-46-46N/69-39-00W)

Seguin Lt., 2 mi. S. of Kennebec R. mouth – F.W., Keyed (VHF 83A) Horn 2 bl. ev. 20 s., Ht. 180', Rge. 18 mi., (43-42-27N/69-45-29W)

Hendricks Head Lt., Sheepscot R. mouth E. side – F.W., R. Sect. 180°-000°, Ht. 43', Rge. R. 7 mi., F.W. 9 mi., (43-49-21N/69-41-23W)

Pond Is. Lt., Kennebec R. mouth W. side – Iso. W. ev. 6 s., Keyed (VHF 83A) Horn 2 bl. ev. 30 s., Ht. 52', Rge. 9 mi., Higher intensity beam up and down river (43-44-24N/69-46-13W)

Perkins Is. Lt., Kennebec R. – Fl. R. ev. 2.5 s., 2 W. Sect. 018° – 038°, 172° – 188°, Covers fairways, Ht. 41', Rge. R. 5 mi., W. 6 mi., (43-47-12N/69-47-07W)

Squirrel Pt. Lt., Kennebec R. – Iso. R. ev. 6 s., W. Sect. 321° - 324°, Covers fairway, Ht. 25', Rge. R. 7 mi., W. 9 mi., (43-48-59N/69-48-09W)

Fuller Rock Lt., off Cape Small – Fl. W. ev. 4 s., Ht. 39', Rge. 6 mi., NR on tower, (43-41-45N/69-50-01W)

White Bull Ltd. Gong By. "WB" – Mo(A)W, Rge. 6 mi., RWS, (43-42-49N/69-55-13W)

Whaleboat Island Lt., Broad Sd., Casco Bay – Fl. W. ev. 6 s., Ht. 47', Rge. 4 mi., NR on tower, (43-44-31N/70-03-40W)

Cow Island Ledge Lt., Portland to Merepoint – Fl. W. ev. 6 s., Ht. 23', Rge. 8 mi., RaRef., NR on spindle, (43-42-11N/70-11-19W)

Halfway Rock Lt., midway betw. Cape Small Pt. and Cape Eliz. – Fl. R. ev. 5 s., Keyed (VHF 83A) Horn 2 bl. ev. 30 s., Ht. 76', Rge. 19 mi., (43-39-21N/70-02-12W)

Portland Ltd. Wh. By. "P", Portland Hbr. App. – Mo(A)W, Rge. 6 mi., Racon (M), RWSRST, (43-31-36N/70-05-28W)

Ram Island Ledge Lt., N. side of Portland Hbr. Entr. – Fl. (2) W. ev. 6 s., Keyed (VHF 83A) Horn 1 bl. ev. 10 s., Ht. 77', Rge. 9 mi., (43-37-53N/70-11-15W)

Cape Elizabeth Lt., S. of Portland Hbr. Entr. – Fl(4) W. ev. 15 s., Keyed (VHF 83A) Horn 2 bl. ev. 60 s., Ht. 129', Rge. 15 mi., ltd. 24 hrs., (43-33-58N/70-12-00W)

Portland Head Lt., SW side Portland Hbr. Entr. – Fl. W. ev. 4 s., Keyed (VHF 83A) Horn 1 bl. ev. 15 s., Ht. 101', Rge. 24 mi., ltd. 24 hrs., (43-37-23N/70-12-28W)

Spring Pt. Ledge Lt., Portland main ch. W. side – Fl. W. ev. 6 s., 2 R. Sect., 2 W. Sectors 331°-337° Covers fairway entrance, and 074°-288°, Keyed (VHF 83A) Horn 1 bl. ev. 10 s., Ht. 54', Rge. R. 10 mi., W. 12 mi., ltd. 24 hrs., (43-39-08N/70-13-26W)

Wood Island Lt., S. Entr. Wood Is. Hbr. N. side – Alt. W. and G. ev. 10 s. (Night), Keyed (VHF 83A) Horn 2 bl. ev. 30 s., Ht. 71', Rge. W. 13 mi., G. 13 mi., (43-27-25N/70-19-45W)

Goat Is. Lt., Cape Porpoise Hbr. Entr. – Fl. W. ev. 6 s., Keyed (VHF 83A) Horn 1 bl. ev. 15 s., Ht. 38', Rge. 12 mi., (43-21-28N/70-25-30W)

Cape Neddick Lt., On N. side of Nubble – Iso. R. ev. 6 s., Keyed (VHF 83A) Horn 1 bl. ev. 10 s., Ht. 88', Rge. 13 mi., ltd. 24 hrs., (43-09-55N/70-35-28W)

Jaffrey Point Lt. #4 – Fl. R. ev. 4 s., Ht. 22', rge. 4 mi., TR on tower, (43-03-18N/70-42-49W)

Boon Is. Lt., 6.5 mi. off coast – Fl. W. ev. 5 s., Horn 1 bl. ev. 10 s., Ht. 137', Rge. 14 mi., (43-07-17N/70-28-35W)

York Harbor Ltd. Bell By. "YH" – Mo(A)W, Rge. 5 mi., RWSRST, (43-07-45N/70-37-01W)

NEW HAMPSHIRE

Whaleback Lt., Portsmouth Entr. NE side –Fl(2) W. ev. 10 s., Keyed (VHF 83A) Horn 2 bl. ev. 30 s., Ht. 59', Rge. 11 mi., (43-03-32N/70-41-47W)

Portsmouth Harbor Lt. (New Castle), on Fort Point – F. G., Keyed (VHF 83A) Horn 1 bl. ev. 10 s., Ht. 52', Rge. 12 mi., (43-04-16N/70-42-31W)

Rye Harbor Entr. Ltd. Wh. By. "RH" – Mo(A)W, Rge. 6 mi., RWSRST, (42-59-38N/70-43-45W)

Isles Of Shoals Lt., 5.5 mi. off coast – Fl. W. ev. 15 s., Horn 1 bl. ev. 30 s., Ht. 82', Rge. 14 mi., (42-58-02N/70-37-24W)

MASSACHUSETTS

Newburyport Harbor Lt., N. end of Plum Is. – Oc.(2) G. ev. 15 s., Obscured from 165°-192° and 313°-344°, Ht. 50', Rge. 10 mi., (42-48-55N/70-49-08W)

Merrimack River Entr. Ltd. Wh. By. "MR"– Mo(A)W, Rge. 4 mi., RWSRST, (42-48-34N/70-47-03W)

Ipswich Lt., Ipswich Entr. S. side – Oc.W. ev. 4 s., Ht. 30', Rge. 5 mi., NR on tower, (42-41-07N/70-45-58W)

Rockport Breakwater Lt. #6, W. side Entr. Rockport inner hbr. – Fl. R. ev. 4 s., Ht. 32', Rge. 4 mi., TR on spindle, (42-39-39N/70-36-43W)

Annisquam Harbor Lt., E. side Entr. – Fl. W. ev. 7.5 s., R. Sector 180°-217°, Horn 2 bl. ev. 60 s., Ht. 45', Rge. R. 11 mi., W. 14 mi., (42-39-43N/70-40-53W)

Straitsmouth Lt., Rockport Entr. S. side – Fl. G. ev. 6 s., Keyed (VHF 83A) Horn 1 bl. ev. 15 s., Ht. 46', Rge. 6 mi., (42-39-44N/70-35-17W)

Cape Ann Lt., E. side Thacher Is. – Fl. R. ev. 5 s., Horn 2 bl. ev. 60 s., Ht. 166', Rge. 17 mi., (42-38-12N/70-34-30W)

Eastern Point Ltd. Wh. By. #2 – Fl. R. ev. 4 s., Rge. 3 mi., (42-34-14N/70-39-50W)

Eastern Point Lt., Gloucester Entr. E. side – Fl. W. ev. 5 s., Ht. 57', Rge. 20 mi., (42-34-49N/70-39-52W)

Gloucester Breakwater Lt., W. end – Oc.R. ev. 4 s., Keyed (VHF 83A) Horn 1 bl. ev. 10 s., Ht. 45', Rge. 6 mi., (42-34-57N/70-40-20W)

Bakers Island Lt., Salem Ch. – Alt. Fl. W. and R. ev. 20 s., Horn 1 bl. ev. 30 s., Ht. 111', Rge. W. 16 mi., R. 14 mi., (42-32-11N/70-47-09W)

Hospital Point Range Front Lt., Beverly Cove W. side – F.W., Ht. 69', Higher intensity on range line (42-32-47N/70-51-21W)

The Graves Ltd. Wh. By. #5 – Fl. G. ev. 4 s., Rge. 4 mi., Green, (42-22-33N/70-51-28W)

Marblehead Lt., N. point Marblehead Neck – F.G., Ht. 130', Rge. 7 mi., (42-30-19N/70-50-01W)

The Graves Lt., Boston Hbr. S. Ch. Entr. – Fl(2) W. ev. 12 s., Keyed (VHF 83A) Horn 2 bl. ev. 20 s., Ht. 98', Rge. 15 mi., (42-21-54N/70-52-09W)

Boston App. Ltd. By. "BG"– Mo(A)W, Rge. 4 mi., RWSRST, (42-23-27N/70-51-29W)

Deer Island Lt., President Roads, Boston Hbr. – Alt. W. and R. ev. 10 s., Keyed (VHF 83A) Horn 1 bl. ev. 10 s., Ht. 53', Rge. 9 mi., (42-20-22N/70-57-16W)

Long Island Head Lt., President Roads, Boston Hbr. – Fl. W. ev. 2.5 s., Ht. 120', Rge. 6 mi., (42-19-49N/70-57-28W)

Boston Ltd. Wh. By. "B", Boston Hbr. Entr. – Mo(A)W, Rge. 6 mi., Racon (B), RWSRST, (42-22-42N/70-46-58W)

Boston App. Ltd. By. "BF" (NOAA-44013) –Fl(4) Y. ev. 20 sec, Rge. 7 mi., Yellow, (42-20-44N/70-39-04W)

Boston North Ch.Entr. Ltd. Wh. By. "NC" – Mo(A)W, Rge. 6 mi., RWSRST, Racon (N), (42-22-32N/70-54-18W)

Minots Ledge Lt., Boston Hbr. Entr. S. side – Fl(1+4+3) W. ev. 45 s., Keyed (VHF 83A) Horn 1 bl. ev. 10 s., Ht. 85', Rge. 10 mi., (42-16-11N/70-45-33W)

Boston Lt., SE side Little Brewster Is. – Fl. W. ev. 10 s., Keyed (VHF 83A) Horn 1 bl. ev. 30 s., Ht. 102', Rge. 27 mi., (42-19-41N/70-53-24W)

Scituate App. Ltd. Gong By. "SA"– Mo(A)W, Rge. 4 mi., RWSRST, (42-12-08N/70-41-49W)

Plymouth Lt. (Gurnet), N. side Entr. to hbr. – Fl(3) W. ev. 30 s., R. Sect. 323°-352°, Horn 2 bl. ev. 15 s., Ht. 102', Rge. R. 15 mi., W. 17 mi., (42-00-13N/70-36-02W)

Race Point Lt., NW Point of Cape Cod – Fl. W. ev. 10 s., Ht. 41', Rge. 14 mi., Obscured 220°-292°, (42-03-44N/70-14-35W)

Wood End Lt., Entr. to Provincetown – Fl. R. ev. 10 s., Keyed (VHF 83A) Horn 1 bl. ev. 30 s., Ht. 45', Rge. 13 mi., (42-01-17N/70-11-37W)

Long Point Lt., Provincetown Entr. SW side – Oc.G. ev. 4 s., Keyed (VHF 83A) Horn 1 bl. ev. 15 s., Ht. 36', Rge. 8 mi., (42-01-59N/70-10-07W)

Mary Ann Rocks Ltd. Wh. By. #12 – Fl. R. ev. 2.5 s., Rge. 4 mi., Red, (41-55-07N/70-30-22W)

Cape Cod Canal App. Ltd. Bell By. "CC" – Mo(A)W, Rge. 4 mi., RWSRST, (41-48-53N/70-27-39W)

Cape Cod Canal Breakwater Lt. #6, E. Entr. – Fl. R. ev. 5 s., Keyed (VHF 83A) Horn 1 bl. ev. 15 s., Ht. 43', Rge. 9 mi., (41-46-47N/70-29-23W)

Highland Lt., NE side of Cape Cod – Fl. W. ev. 5 s., Ht. 170', Rge. 14 mi., ltd. 24 hrs., (42-02-22N/70-03-39W)

Nauset Beach Lt., E. side of Cape Cod – Alt. W. R. ev. 10 s., Ht. 120', (41-51-36N/69-57-12W)

Chatham Beach Ltd. Wh. By. "C" – Mo(A)W, Rge. 4 mi., RWSRST, (41-39-12N/69-55-30W)

Chatham Lt., W. side of hbr. – Fl(2)W. ev. 10 s., Ht. 80', Rge. 24 mi., ltd. 24 hrs., (41-40-17N/69-57-01W)

Chatham Inlet Bar Guide Lt., Fl. Y. ev. 2.5 s., Ht. 62', Rge. 11 mi., (41-40-18N/69-57-00W)

Hyannis Harbor App. Ltd. Bell By. "HH" – Mo(A)W, Rge. 4 mi., RWSRST, (41-35-57N/70-17-22W)

Pollock Rip Ch. Ltd. By. #8 – Fl. R. ev. 6 s., Rge. 3 mi., Red, (41-32-43N/69-58-56W)

Cape Wind Meteorological Lt. Tower "MT"– Fl.Y. ev. 6 s., (41-28-20N/70-18-53W)

Nantucket Lt., (Great Point), Nantucket, N. end of Is., – Fl. W. ev. 5 s., R. sect. 084°-106° (Covers Cross Rip & Tuckernuck Shoals), Ht. 71', Rge. W. 14 mi., R. 12 mi., (41-23-25N/70-02-54W)

Sankaty Head Lt., E. end of Is. – Fl. W. ev. 7.5 s., Ht. 158', Rge. 24 mi., ltd. 24 hrs., (41-17-04N/69-57-58W)

Nantucket East Breakwater Lt. #3, Outer Entr. to hbr. – Fl. G. ev. 4 s., Ht. 30', Rge. 3 mi., (41-18-37N/70-06-00W)

Brant Point Lt., Hbr. Entr. W. side – Oc.R. ev. 4 s., Horn 1 bl. ev. 10 s., Ht. 26', Rge. 9 mi., (41-17-24N/70-05-25W)

Cape Poge Lt., NE point of Chappaquiddick Is. – Fl. W. ev. 6 s., Ht. 65', Rge. 9 mi., (41-25-10N/70-27-08W)

For abbreviations see footnote p. 173

Muskeget Ch. Ltd. Wh. By. "MC" – Mo(A)W, Rge. 4 mi., RWSRST, (41-15-00N/70-26-10W)

Edgartown Harbor Lt., Inner end of hbr. W. side – Fl. R. ev. 6 s., Ht. 45', Rge. 5 mi., (41-23-27N/70-30-11W)

East Chop Lt., E. side Vineyard Haven Hbr. Entr. – Iso. G. ev. 6 s., Ht. 79', Rge. 9 mi., (41-28-13N/70-34-03W)

West Chop Lt., W. side Vineyard Haven Hbr. Entr. – Oc.W. ev. 4 s., R. Sect. 281°-331° (covers Squash Meadow and Norton Shoals), Horn 1 bl. ev. 30 s., Ht. 84', Rge. R. 10 mi., W. 14 mi., (41-28-51N/70-35-59W)

Nobska Point Lt., Woods Hole E. Entr. – Fl. W. ev. 6 s., Obscured 125°-195°, R. Sect. 263°-289° (covers Hedge Fence and L'Hommedieu Shoal), Horn 2 bl. ev. 30 s., Ht. 87', Rge. R. 11 mi., W. 13 mi., ltd 24 hrs., (41-30-57N/70-39-18W)

Tarpaulin Cove Lt., SE side Naushon Is. – Fl. W. ev. 6 s., Ht. 78', Rge. 9 mi., (41-28-08N/70-45-27W)

Menemsha Creek Entr. Jetty Lt. #3 – Fl. G. ev. 4 s., Ht. 25', Rge. 5 mi., (41-21-16N/70-46-07W)

Gay Head Lt., W. point of Martha's Vineyard – Alt. W. and R. ev. 15 s., Ht. 175', Rge. W. 24 mi., R. 20 mi., Obscured 342°-359° by Nomans Land, ltd. 24 hrs., (41-20-54N/70-50-04W)

Cuttyhunk East Entr. Ltd. Bell By. "CH" – Mo(A)W, Rge. 4 mi., RWSRST, (41-26-34N/70-53-22W)

BUZZARDS BAY

Buzzards Bay Entr. Lt., W. Entr. – Fl. W. ev. 2.5 s., Keyed (VHF 83A) Horn 2 bl. ev. 30 s., Ht. 67', Rge. 14 mi., Racon (B), (41-23-49N/71-02-05W)

Dumpling Rocks Lt. #7, off Round Hill Pt. – Fl. G. ev. 6 s., Ht. 52', Rge. 8 mi., (41-32-18N/70-55-17W)

Buzzards Bay Midch. Ltd. Bell By. "BB" (east of Wilkes Ledge) – Mo(A)W, Rge. 4 mi., RWSRST, (41-30-33N/70-49-54W)

New Bedford West Barrier Lt. – Q.G., Horn 1 bl. ev. 10 s., Ht. 48', Rge. 8 mi., (41-37-27N/70-54-22W)

New Bedford East Barrier Lt. – Q. R., Ht. 33', Rge. 5 mi., (41-37-29N/70-54-19W)

Padanaram Breakwater Lt. #8 – Fl. R. ev. 4 s., Ht. 25', Rge. 5 mi., (41-34-27N/70-56-21W)

Cleveland East Ledge Lt., Cape Cod Canal App. E. side of S. Entr. – Fl. W. ev. 10 s., Horn 1 bl. ev. 15 s., Ht. 74', Rge. 14 mi., Racon (C), (41-37-51N/70-41-39W)

Ned Point Lt. – Iso. W. ev. 6 s., Ht. 41', Rge. 12 mi., (41-39-03N/70-47-44W)

Westport Harbor Entr. Lt. #7, W. side – Fl. G. ev. 6 s., Ht. 35', Rge. 9 mi., (41-30-27N/71-05-17W)

Westport Harbor App. Ltd. Bell By. 1, Fl. G. ev. 2.5s, Rge. 4 mi., (41-29-15N/71-04-04W)

RHODE ISLAND

Sakonnet Lt. – Fl. W. ev. 6 s., R. sect. 195°-350°, Ht. 70', Rge. W. 7 mi., R. 5 mi., (41-27-11N/71-12-09W)

Sakonnet Breakwater Lt. #2, Entr. to hbr. – Fl. R. ev. 4 s., Ht. 29', Rge. 6 mi., (41-28-00N/71-11-42W)

Narragansett Bay Entr. Ltd. Wh. By. "NB" – Mo(A)W, Rge. 6 mi., Racon (B), RWSRST, (41-23-00N/71-23-21W)

Beavertail Lt. – Narrag. Bay E. passage – Fl. W. ev. 10 s., Obscured 175°-215°, Horn 1 bl. ev. 30 s., Ht. 64', Rge. 15 mi., ltd. 24 hrs., (41-26-58N/71-23-58W)

Castle Hill Lt. – Iso R. 6 s., Keyed (VHF 83A) Horn 1 bl. ev. 10 s., Ht. 40', Rge. 9 mi., (41-27-44N/71-21-47W)

Fort Adams Lt. #2, Narrag. Bay E. passage – Fl. R. ev. 6 s., Horn 1 bl. ev. 15 s., Ht. 32', Rge. 7 mi., (41-28-54N/71-20-12W)

Newport Harbor Lt., N. end of breakwater – F.G., Ht. 33', Rge. 11 mi., (41-29-36N/71-19-38W)

Rose Is. Lt., Fl W. ev. 6 s., Ht. 48', (41-29-44N/71-20-34W)

Prudence Is. Lt. (Sandy Pt.), Narrag. Bay E. passage – Fl. G. ev. 6 s., Ht. 28', Rge. 6 mi., (41-36-21N/71-18-13W)

Hog Island Shoal Lt., N. side Entr. to Mt. Hope Bay – Iso. W. ev. 6 s., Keyed (VHF 83A) Horn 2 bl. ev 30s., Ht. 54', Rge. 12 mi., (41-37-56N/71-16-24W)

Musselbed Shoals Lt.#6A, Mt. Hope Bay Ch. – Fl. R. ev. 6 s., Ht. 26', Rge. 6 mi., (41-38-11N/71-15-36W)

Castle Is. Lt. #2, N. of Hog Is. – Fl. R. ev. 6 s., Ht. 26', Rge. 3 mi., (41-39-14N/71-17-10W)

Bristol Harbor Lt. #4 – F.R., Ht. 25', Rge. 11 mi., (41-39-58N/71-16-42W)

Conimicut Lt., Providence R. App. – Fl. W. ev. 2.5 s., R. Sect. 322°-349° covers Ohio Ledge, Keyed (VHF 83A) Horn 2 bl. ev. 30 s., Ht. 58', Rge. W. 8 mi., R. 5 mi., (41-43-01N/71-20-42W)

Bullock Point Lt. "BP", Prov. R. – Oc.W. ev. 4 s., Ht. 29', Rge. 6 mi., (41-44-16N/71-21-51W)

Pomham Rocks Lt., Prov. R. – F.R., Ht. 54', Rge. 6 mi., (41-46-39N/71-22-10W)

Providence River Ch. Lt. #42, off rock – Iso. R. ev. 6 s., Ht. 31', Rge. 4 mi., (41-47-39N/71-22-47W)

Mt. Hope Bay Jct. Ltd. Gong By. "MH" – Fl(2+1) R. 6 s., Rge., 3 mi., R. & G. Bands, (41-39-32N/71-14-03W)

Borden Flats Lt., Mt. Hope Bay – Fl. W. ev. 2.5 s., Ht. 47', Rge. 9 mi., (41-42-16N/71-10-28W)

Wickford Harbor Lt. #1, Narrag. Bay W. passage – Fl. G. ev. 6 s., Ht. 40', Rge. 6 mi., (41-34-21N/71-26-13W)

Warwick Lt., Greenwich Bay App. – Oc.G. ev. 4 s., Horn 1 bl. ev. 15 s., Ht. 66', Rge. 10 mi., ltd. 24 hrs., (41-40-02N/71-22-42W)

Point Judith Lt., Block Is. Sd. Entr. – Oc(3)W. ev. 15 s., Horn 1 bl. ev. 15 s., Ht. 65', Rge. 16 mi., (41-21-40N/71-28-53W)

Block Island North Lt., N. end of Is. – Fl. W. ev. 5 s., Ht. 58', (41-13-39N/71-34-33W)

Block Island Southeast Lt., SE end of Is. – Fl. G. ev. 5 s., Horn 1 bl. ev. 30 s., Ht. 261', Rge. 20 mi., ltd. 24 hrs., (41-09-10N/71-33-04W)

Pt. Judith Harbor of Refuge W. Entr. Lt. #3 – Fl. G. ev. 6 s., Keyed (VHF 83A) Horn 1 bl. ev. 30 s., Ht. 35', Rge. 5 mi., (41-21-56N/71-30-53W)

Block Is. Breakwater Lt. #3 – Q. G., Keyed (VHF 83A) Horn 2 bl. ev. 30 s., Ht. 27', Rge. 6mi., (41-10-38N/71-33-15W)

Watch Hill Lt., Fishers Is. Sd. E. Entr. – Alt. W. and R. ev. 5 s., Horn 1 bl. ev. 30 s., Ht. 61', Rge. 14 mi., ltd. 24 hrs., (41-18-14N/71-51-30W)

FISHERS ISLAND SOUND

Latimer Reef Lt., Fishers Is. Sd. main ch. – Fl. W. ev. 6 s., Bell 2 strokes ev. 15 s., Ht. 55', Rge. 9 mi., (41-18-16N/71-56-00W)

N. Dumpling Lt., Fishers Is. Sd. main ch. – F.W., Horn 1 bl. ev. 30 s., R. Sect. 257°-023°, Ht. 94', Rge. R. 7 mi., F.W. 9 mi., (41-17-17N/72-01-10W)

Stonington Outer Breakwater Lt. #4 – Fl. R. ev. 4 s., Horn 1 bl. ev. 10 s., Ht. 46', Rge. 5 mi., (41-19-00N/71-54-28W)

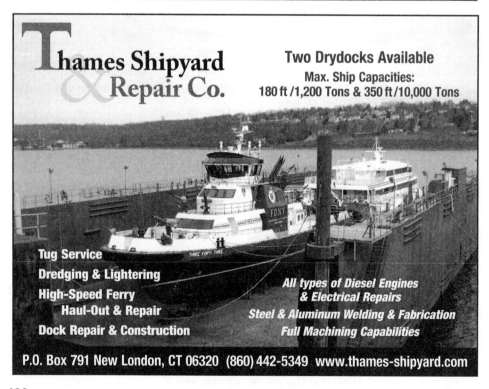

LONG ISLAND SOUND, NORTH SIDE

Race Rock Lt., SW end of Fishers Is. – Fl. R. ev. 10 s., Horn 2 bl. ev. 30 s., Ht. 67', Rge. 16 mi., (41-14-37N/72-02-50W)

Bartlett Reef Lt., S. end of reef – Fl. W. ev. 6 s., Keyed (VHF 83A) Horn 2 bl. ev. 60 s., Ht. 35', Rge. 8 mi., (41-16-28N/72-08-14W)

New London Ledge Lt., W. side of Southwest ledge –Fl(3+1) W. R. ev. 30 s., Horn 2 bl. ev. 20 s., Ht. 58', Rge. W. 17 mi., R. 14 mi., (41-18-21N/72-04-39W)

New London Harbor Lt., W. side Entr. – Iso. W. ev. 6 s., R. Sect. 000°-041° covers Sarah Ledge and shoals westward, Ht. 89', Rge. W. 17 mi., R. 14 mi., (41-19-00N/72-05-23W)

Saybrook Breakwater Lt., W. jetty – Fl. G. ev. 6 s., Horn 1 bl. ev. 30 s., Ht. 58', Rge. 14 mi., (41-15-48N/72-20-34W)

Lynde Pt. Lt., Conn. R. mouth W. side – F.W., Ht. 71', Rge. 14 mi., (41-16-17N/72-20-35W)

Twenty-Eight Foot Shoal Ltd. Wh. By. "TE" – Fl(2+1) R. ev. 6 s., , Rge. 4 mi., R&G Bands, (41-09-16N/72-30-25W)

Falkner Is. Lt., off Guilford Hbr. – Fl. W. ev. 10 s., Ht. 94', Rge. 13 mi., (41-12-43N/72-39-13W)

Branford Reef Lt., SE Entr. New Haven – Fl. W. ev. 6 s., Ht. 22', Rge. 7 mi., (41-13-17N/72-48-19W)

New Haven Hbr. Ltd. Wh. By. "NH" – Mo(A)W, Rge. 4 mi., RWSRST, (41-12-07N/72-53-47W)

Southwest Ledge Lt., E. side Entr. New Haven – Fl. R. ev. 5 s., Horn 1 bl. ev. 15 s., Ht. 57', Rge. 14 mi., (41-14-04N/72-54-44W)

New Haven Lt. – Fl. W. ev. 4 s., Ht. 27', Rge. 7 mi., (41-13-16N/72-56-32W)

Stratford Pt. Lt., W. side Entr. Housatonic R. –Fl(2)W. ev. 20 s., Ht. 52', Rge. 16 mi., (41-09-07N/73-06-12W)

Stratford Shoal Lt., Middle Ground – Fl. W. ev. 5 s., Horn 1 bl. ev. 15 s., Ht. 60', Rge. 13 mi., (41-03-35N/73-06-05W)

Tongue Pt. Lt., at Bridgeport Breakwater – Fl. G. ev. 4 s., Ht. 31', Rge. 5 mi., (41-10-00N/73-10-39W)

Penfield Reef Lt., S. side Entr. to Black Rock – Fl. R. ev. 6 s., Horn 1 bl. ev. 15 s., Ht. 51', Rge. 15 mi., (41-07-02N/73-13-20W)

Peck Ledge Lt., E. App. to Norwalk – Fl. G. ev. 2.5 s., Ht. 61', Rge. 5 mi., (41-04-39N/73-22-11W)

Greens Ledge Lt., W. end of ledge – Alt. Fl. W. and R. ev. 24 s., Horn 2 bl. ev. 20 s., Ht. 62', Rge. W. 18 mi., R. 15 mi., (41-02-30N/73-26-38W)

Stamford Harbor Ledge Obstruction Lt., on SW end of Harbor Ledge – Fl. W. ev. 4 s., (41-00-49N/73-32-34W)

Great Captain Is. Lt., SE Pt. of Is. – Alt. W. R. ev. 12 s., Horn 1 bl. ev. 15 s., Ht. 62', Rge. W. 14 mi., R. 14 mi., (40-58-57N/73-37-23W)

Larchmont Harbor Lt. #2, East Entr. – Fl. R. ev. 4 s., Ht. 26', Rge. 4 mi., (40-55-05N/73-43-52W)

LONG ISLAND SOUND, SOUTH SIDE

Little Gull Is. Lt., E. Entr. L.I. Sd. – Fl(2) W. ev. 15 s., Horn 1 bl. ev. 15 sec., Ht. 91', Rge. 18 mi., (41-12-23N/72-06-25W)

Plum Gut Lt. – Fl. W. ev. 2.5 s., Ht. 21' Rge. 5 mi., (41-10-26N/72-12-42W)

Plum Island Ltd. Wh. By. "PI" – Mo(A)W, Rge. 4 mi., RWSRST, (41-13-17N/72-10-48W)

Plum Is. Hbr. West Dolphin Lt., W. end of Is. – F.G., Horn 1 bl. ev. 10 s., (Maintained by U.S. Agr. Dept.), (41-10-17N/72-12-24W)

For abbreviations see footnote p. 173

AIS – An Overview

First developed in the 1990s, the Automatic Identification System is a comprehensive tracking system, in use internationally, to supplement the relatively modest amount of data offered by radar and GPS. AIS requires a vessel-mounted VHF transmitter-receiver, with input from onboard GPS and other electronic sensors, to allow tracking by AIS coastal base stations or satellites fitted with special receivers. It is required aboard all passenger ships and others of 300 gross tons or more. In addition to these, many yachts are now equipped with AIS.

A vessel's identification (name, MMSI, length, beam, draft, call sign), course, position, destination, and speed are tracked and exchanged via VHF with other vessels and base stations. The result is much greater safety for vessels in high-traffic areas, where they can "see" one another and anticipate navigation challenges. What was only a blip on a radar screen now has full identification, plus position, course, speed and more displayed on an AIS-enabled chartplotter.

Among the numerous applications for this service are collision avoidance, monitoring of fishing fleets, vessel traffic control, maritime security, aids to navigation, search and rescue, and accident investigation.

With regard to aids to navigation, AIS-equipped buoys, as one example, enable the USCG to monitor their positions, including the weather and sea state at each. Also, "virtual aids to navigation" can be made to appear on AIS screens even in the absence of an actual buoy. This ability will allow the USCG to remove buoys but cause their positions to appear on electronic charts, like a waypoint, as if they were there. AIS continues to grow in use and importance.

For a sample of AIS, see www.marinetraffic.com and www.navcen.uscg.gov/ais

Orient Pt. Lt., outer end of Oyster Pond Reef – Fl. W. ev. 5 s., Horn 2 bl. ev. 30 s., Ht. 64', Rge. 17 mi., (41-09-48N/72-13-25W)

Horton Pt. Lt., NW point of Horton Neck – Fl. G. ev. 10 s., Ht. 103', Rge. 14 mi., (41-05-06N/72-26-44W)

Mattituck Breakwater Lt. "MI" – Fl. W. ev. 4 s., Ht. 25', Rge. 6 mi., (41-00-55N/72-33-40W)

Old Field Pt. Lt. – Alt. Fl. R. and Fl. G. ev. 24 s., Ht. 74', Rge. 14 mi., (40-58-37N/73-07-07W)

Eatons Neck Lt., E. side Entr. Huntington Bay – F. W., Ht. 144', Rge. 14 mi., (40-57-14N/73-23-43W)

Cold Springs Hbr. Lt., on Pt. of shoal – F.W., R. Sect. 039°-125°, Ht. 37', Rge. W. Sect. 8 mi., R. Sect. 6 mi., (40-54-51N/73-29-35W)

Glen Cove Breakwater Lt. #5, E. side Entr. to hbr. – Fl. G. ev. 4 s., Ht. 24', Rge. 5 mi., (40-51-43N/73-39-37W)

Port Jefferson App. Ltd. Wh. By. "PJ" – Mo(A)W, Rge. 4 mi., RWSRST, (40-59-16N/73-06-27W)

Huntington Harbor Lt. – Iso. W. ev. 6 s., Horn 1 bl. ev. 15 s., Ht. 42', Rge. 9 mi., (40-54-39N/73-25-52W)

LONG ISLAND, OUTSIDE

Montauk Pt. Lt., E. end of L.I. – Fl. W. ev. 5 s., Horn 1 bl. ev. 15 s., Ht. 168', Rge. 18 mi., (41-04-15N/71-51-26W)

Montauk Hbr. Entr. Ltd. Bell By. "M" – Mo(A)W, Rge. 4 mi., RWSRST, (41-05-07N/71-56-23W)

Shinnecock Inlet App. Ltd. Wh. By. "SH" – Mo(A)W, Rge. 4 mi., RWSRST, (40-49-00N/72-28-35W)

Moriches Inlet App. Ltd. Wh. By. "M" – Mo(A)W, Rge. 6 mi., RWS, (40-44-08N/72-45-12W)

Shinnecock Lt., W. side of Inlet – Fl(2) W. ev. 15 s., Ht. 75', Rge. 11 mi., (40-50-31N/72-28-42W)

Jones Inlet Lt., end of breakwater – Fl. W. ev. 2.5 s., Ht. 33', Rge. 4 mi., (40-34-24N/73-34-32W)

Jones Inlet Ltd. Wh. By. "JI" – Mo(A)W, Rge. 4 mi., RWSRST, (40-33-37N/73-35-13W)

E. Rockaway Inlet Ltd. Bell By. "ER" – Mo(A)W, Rge. 5 mi., RWSRST, (40-34-17N/73-45-49W)

Fire Is. Lt., 5.5 mi. E. of inlet – Fl. W. ev. 7.5 s., Ht. 167', ltd. 24 hrs., (40-37-57N/73-13-07W)

Rockaway Point Breakwater Lt. #4, end of breakwater – Fl. R. ev. 4 s., Ht. 34', Rge. 5 mi., (40-32-25N/73-56-27W)

NEW YORK HARBOR & APPROACHES

Execution Rocks Lt. – Fl. W. ev. 10 s., Ht. 62', Rge. 14 mi., Racon (X), (40-52-41N/73-44-16W)

Hart Is. Lt. #46, off S. end of Is. – Fl. R. ev. 4 s., Ht. 23', Rge. 6 mi., (40-50-42N/73-46-00W)

Stepping Stones Lt., outer end of reef – Oc.G. ev. 4 s., Ht. 46', Rge. 8 mi., (40-49-28N/73-46-29W)

Throgs Neck Lt., Fort Schuyler – F. R., Ht. 60', Rge. 11 mi., (40-48-16N/73-47-26W)

Whitestone Pt. Lt. #1, East R. main ch. – Q.G., Ht. 56', Rge. 3 mi., (40-48-06N/73-49-10W)

Kings Pt. Lt. – (Private Aid), Iso. W. ev. 2 s., (40-48-42N/73-45-48W)

Hell Gate Lt. #15, East R. Hallets Pt. – Fl. G. ev. 2.5 s., Ht. 33', Rge. 4 mi., (40-46-41N/73-56-05W)

Mill Rock South Lt. #16, East R., main ch. – Fl. R. ev. 4 s., Ht. 37', Rge. 4 mi., (40-46-46N/73-56-22W)

For abbreviations see footnote p. 173

Governors Is. Lt. #2 – NW pt of Is. – 2 F.R. arranged vertically, Lower Lt. Obscured from 240°-243°, 254°-256°, 264°-360°, Ht. 75′, Rge. 7 mi., (40-41-35N/74-01-11W)

Verrazano-Narrows Bridge Sound Signal – (Private Aid), 2 Horns on bridge 1 bl. ev. 15 s., (40-36-31N/74-02-19W)

Coney Is. Lt., N.Y. Hbr. main ch. – Fl. R. ev. 5 s., Ht. 75′, Rge. 16 mi., ltd. 24 hrs., (40-34-36N/74-00-42W)

Romer Shoal Lt., N.Y. Hbr. S. App. – Fl(2) W. ev. 15 s., Horn 2 bl. ev. 30 s., Ht. 54′, Rge. 15 mi., (40-30-47N/74-00-49W)

West Bank (Range Front) Lt., Ambrose Ch. outer sect. – Iso. W. ev. 6 s., R. Sect. 004°-181° and W from 181° - 004°, Horn 2 bl. ev. 20 s., Ht. 69′, ltd. 24 hrs., (40-32-17N/74-02-34W)

Staten Island (Range Rear) Lt., Ambrose Ch. outer sect. – F. W. , Visible on range line only, Ht. 234′, ltd. 24 hrs., (40-34-34N/74-08-28W)

Old Orchard Shoal Lt., N.Y. Hbr. – Fl. W. ev. 6 s., R. Sect. 087°-203°, Ht. 20′, Rge. 4 mi.., (40-30-44N/74-05-55W)

Sandy Hook Lt. – F. W., Ht. 88′, Rge. 19 mi., ltd. 24 hrs., (40-27-42N/74-00-07W)

Sandy Hook Ch. (Range Front) Lt. – Q. W., G., and R. sectors, Red from 063°-073° and Green from 300.5°-315.5°, Ht. 45′, Rge. W. 6 mi., G. 4 mi., R. 4 mi. Racon (C), (40-29-15N/73-59-35W)

Southwest Spit Jct. Ltd. Gong By. "SP" – Fl(2+1) R. ev. 6 s., Rge. 3 mi., R. & G. Bands, (40-28-46N/74-03-18W)

Sandy Hook Pt. Lt. – Iso W. ev. 6 s., Ht. 38′, Rge. 7 mi., "NB" on Skeleton Tower, (40-28-15N/74-01-07W)

Scotland Ltd. Wh. By. "S", Sandy Hook Ch. App. – Mo(A)W, Rge. 7 mi., Racon (M), RWSRST, (40-26-33N/73-55-01W)

Ambrose Ch. Ltd. Wh. By. "A" – Mo(A)W, Rge. 7 mi., Racon (N), RWSRST, (40-27-28N/73-50-12W)

NEW JERSEY

Highlands Lt. – Iso W. ev. 10 s., Obscured 334°-140°, (40-23-48N/73-59-09W)

Atlantic Highlands Breakwater Lt. – Fl. W. ev. 4 s., Ht. 33′, Rge. 7 mi., (40-25-07N/74-01-10W)

Kill Van Kull Ch. Jct. Ltd. Wh. By. "KV" – Fl (2+1) R. ev. 6 s., Rge. 3 mi., R. & G. Bands, Racon (K), (40-39-02N/74-03-51W)

Kill Van Kull Ch. Jct. Ltd. By. "A" – Fl (2+1) G. ev. 6 s., Rge. 3 mi., G. & R. Bands (40-38-45N/74-10-07W)

Kill Van Kull Ch. East Jct. Ltd. By. "E" – Fl (2+1) G. ev. 6 s., Rge. 3 mi. G. & R. Bands (40-38-31N/74-09-15W)

Manasquan Inlet Lt. #3 - Fl. G. ev. 6 s., Keyed (VHF 83A) Horn 1 bl. ev. 30 s., Ht. 35′ Rge. 8 mi., (40-06-01N/74-01-54W)

Shark River Inlet Ltd. Wh. By. "SI" – Mo(A)W, Rge. 6 mi., RWSRST, (40-11-09N/74-00-03W)

Barnegat Inlet S. Breakwater Lt. #7 – Q. G., Ht. 35′, Rge. 5 mi., (39-45-26N/74-05-36W)

Barnegat Ltd. By. "B" – Fl. Y. ev. 6 s., Rge. 6 mi., Racon (B), Yellow, (39-45-48N/73-46-04W)

Barnegat Inlet Outer Ltd. Wh. By. "BI" – Mo(A)W, Rge. 6 mi., RWSRST, (39-44-28N/74-03-51W)

Little Egg Ltd. By. 3 – Q. G., Rge. 4 mi., Green, (39-28-26N/74-17-14W)

Brigantine Inlet Wreck Ltd. By. "WR2" (100 yards, 090° from wreck) – Q. R., Rge. 5 mi., Red, (39-24-48N/74-13-47W)

Great Egg Harbor Inlet Outer Ltd. Wh. By. "GE" – Mo(A)W, Rge. 5 mi., RWSRST, (39-16-14N/74-31-56W)

Hereford Inlet Lt., S. side – Fl. W. ev. 10 s., Ht. 57′, Rge. 24 mi., (39-00-24N/74-47-28W)

For abbreviations see footnote p. 173

Five Fathom Bank Ltd. By. "F" – Fl. Y. ev. 2.5 s., Rge. 6 mi., Racon (M), Yellow, (38-46-49N/74-34-32W)

Cape May Lt. – Fl. W. ev. 15 s., Ht. 165', Rge. 22 mi., (38-55-59N/74-57-37W)

NEW JERSEY, DELAWARE AND MARYLAND

Delaware Ltd. By. "D" – Fl. Y. ev. 6 s., Rge. 6 mi., Racon (K), Yellow, (38-27-18N/74-41-47W)

Delaware Traffic Lane Ltd. By. "DA" – Fl. Y. ev. 2.5 s., Rge. 6 mi., Yellow, (38-32-45N/74-46-56W)

Delaware Traffic Lane Ltd. By. "DB" – Fl. Y. ev. 4 s., Rge. 7 mi., Yellow, (38-38-12N/74-52-11W)

Delaware Traffic Lane Ltd. By. "DC" – Fl. Y. ev. 2.5 s., Rge. 7 mi., Yellow, (38-43-47N/74-57-33W)

Harbor of Refuge Lt., Del. Bay – Fl. W. ev. 10 s., 2 R. Sect. 325°-351° and 127°-175°, Horn 2 bl. ev. 30 s., (Mar. 15 - Dec. 15), Ht. 72', Rge. W. 19 mi., R. 16 mi., (38-48-52N/75-05-33W)

Brown Shoal Lt., Del. Bay main ch. – Fl. W. ev. 2.5 s., Ht. 23', Rge. 7 mi., Racon (B), (38-55-21N/75-06-01W)

Brandywine Shoal Lt., Del. Bay main ch. on shoal – Fl. W. ev. 10 s., R. Sect. 151°-338°, Horn 1 bl. ev. 15 s. (Mar. 15 - Dec. 15), Ht. 60', Rge. W. 19 mi., R. 13 mi., (38-59-10N/75-06-47W)

Fourteen Foot Bank Lt., Del. Bay main ch. – Fl. W. ev. 9 s., R. Sect. 332.5°-151°, Horn 1 bl. ev. 30 s., (Mar. 15-Dec. 1), Ht. 59', Rge. W. 13 mi., R. 10 mi., (39-02-54N/75-10-56W)

Miah Maull Shoal Lt., Del. Bay main ch. – Oc. W. ev. 4 s., R. Sect. 137.5°-333°, Horn 1 bl. ev. 10 s., (Mar. 15-Dec. 15), Ht. 59', Rge. W. 10 mi., R. 10 mi., Racon (M), (39-07-36N/75-12-31W)

Elbow of Cross Ledge Lt., Del. Bay main ch. – Iso. W. ev. 6 s., Horn 2 bl. ev. 20 s., (Mar. 15-Dec. 15), Ht. 61', Rge. 16 mi., (39-10-56N/75-16-06W)

Ship John Shoal Lt., Del. Bay main ch. – Fl. W. ev. 5 s., R. Sect. 138°-321.5°, Horn 1 bl. ev. 15 s. (Mar. 15 - Dec. 15), Ht. 50', Rge. W. 16 mi., R. 12 mi., Racon (O), (39-18-19N/75-22-36W)

Egg Island Point Lt., Del. Bay East side – Fl. W. ev. 4 s., Ht. 27', Rge. 7 mi., (39-10-21N/75-07-55W)

Old Reedy Is. Lt. – Iso. W. ev. 6 s., R. Sect. 353°-014°, Ht. 20', Rge. W. 8 mi., R. 6 mi., (39-30-03N/75-34-08W)

Fenwick Is. Lt. – Iso. W. ev. 8 s., Ht. 83', (38-27-06N/75-03-18W)

Ocean City Inlet Jetty Lt., on end of jetty – Iso. W. ev. 6 s., Keyed (VHF 81A) Horn 1 bl. ev. 10 s., Ht. 38', Rge. 6 mi., (38-19-27N/75-05-06)

VIRGINIA

Assateague Lt., S. side of Is. – Fl(2) W. ev. 5 s., Ht. 154', Rge. 22 mi., (37-54-40N/75-21-22W)

Wachapreague Inlet Ltd. Wh. By. "W" – Mo(A)W, Rge. 6 mi., RWSRST, (37-34-54N/75-33-37W)

Great Machipongo Inlet Lt. #5, S. side – Fl. G. ev. 4 s., Ht. 15', Rge. 4 mi., (37-21-40N/75-44-06W)

Cape Charles Lt., N. side of Entr. to Ches. Bay – Fl. W. ev. 5 s., Ht. 180', Rge. 18 mi., (37-07-23N/75-54-23W)

Chesapeake Lts. (2), off Entr. to Ches. Bay – Fl W. ev. 4 s., Ht. 84', (36-54-17N/75-42-46W)

Chesapeake Bay Entr. Ltd. Wh. By. "CH" – Mo(A)W, Rge. 6 mi., Racon (C), RWSRST, (36-56-08N/75-57-27W)

For abbreviations see footnote p. 173

Distance Table in Nautical Miles

*Approximate

Bar Harbor to

Halifax, N.S.	259
Yarmouth, N.S.	101
Saint John, N.B.	122
Machiasport	52
Rockland	62
Boothbay Harbor	86
Portland	115
Marblehead	169

Rockland to

Boothbay Harbor	42
Belfast	22
Bucksport	33

Boothbay Harbor to

Kennebec River	11
Monhegan	15
Portland	36

Portland Ltd. Buoy "P" to

Biddeford	17
Portsmouth	54
Cape Cod Light	99
Cape Cod Canal (E. Entr.)	118
Pollock Rip Slue	141

Portsmouth (Whaleback) to

York River	7
Biddeford Pool	30
Newburyport Entr.	15
Gloucester – via Annisquam	28

Gloucester to

Boston	26
Scituate	26
Plymouth	43
Cape Cod Canal (E. Entr.)	52
Provincetown	45

Marblehead to

Portsmouth	43
Biddeford Pool	68
Portland	87
Boothbay Harbor	104
Rockland	133
Plymouth	38
Cape Cod Canal (E. Entr.)	47

Boston (Commonwealth Pier)

Marblehead	17
Isles of Shoals	52
Portsmouth	58
Portland	95
Kennebec River	107
Boothbay Harbor	116
Rockland	149
North Haven	148
Bangor	194
St. John, N.B.	286
Halifax, N.S.	380
Cohasset	14
Cape Cod Canal, E. Entr.	50
Provincetown	50
Vineyard Haven	77
New Bedford	81
Fall River	107
Newport	122
New London	140
New York	234

**Western Entr., Cape Cod Canal to

East Entrance	8
Woods Hole	15
Quicks Hole	20
New Bedford	24
Newport	50
New London	83

Woods Hole to

Hyannis	19
Chatham	32
Cuttyhunk	14
Marion	11

Vineyard Haven to

Edgartown	9
Marblehead – around Cape	114
Canal – via Woods Hole	20
Newport	45
New London	77
New Haven	114
South Norwalk	140
City Island	153

*Each distance is by the shortest route that safe navigation permits between the two ports concerned.

Western entr., The beginning of the "land cut" at Bourne Neck, 7.3 nautical miles up the channel from Cleveland Ledge Lt.

Continued p. 200

Cape Henry Lt., S. side of Entr. to Ches. Bay – Mo (U) W ev. 20 s., R. Sect. 154°-233°, Ht. 164′, Rge. W. 17 mi., R. 15 mi., (36-55-35N/76-00-26W)

CHESAPEAKE BAY

Thimble Shoal Lt., Thimble Shoal Ch. – Fl. W. ev. 10 s., Ht. 55′, Rge. 18 mi., (37-00-52N/76-14-23W)

Worton Pt. Lt., Fl. W. ev. 6 s., Ht. 93′ Rge. 6 mi., (39-19-06N/76-11-11W)

Old Point Comfort Lt., N. side Entr. to Hampton Roads – Fl(2) R. ev. 12 s., W. Sect. 265°-038°, Ht. 54′, Rge. W. 16 mi., R. 14 mi., (37-00-06N/76-18-23W)

York Spit Lt., N. side Entr. to York R. – On pile, Fl. W. ev. 6 s., Ht. 30′, Rge. 8 mi., (37-12-35N/76-15-15W)

Stingray Pt. Lt., Ches. Ch. – Fl. W. ev. 4 s., Ht. 34′, Rge. 9 mi., (37-33-41N/76-16-12W)

Windmill Pt. Lt., Ches. Ch. – On pile. Fl. W. ev. 6 s., 2 R. Sectors 293°-082° and 091.5°-113°, Ht. 34′, Rge. W. 9 mi., R. 7 mi., (37-35-49N/76-14-10W)

Tangier Sound Lt., Ches. Ch. – Fl. W. ev. 6 s., R. Sect. 110°-192°, Ht. 45′, Rge. W. 12 mi., R. 9 mi., (37-47-17N/75-58-24W)

Smith Pt. Lt., Ches. Ch. – Fl. W. ev. 10 s., Ht. 52′, Rge. 15 mi., (37-52-48N/76-11-01W)

Point Lookout Lt., Ches. Ch. – Fl(2) W. ev. 5 s., Ht. 39′, Rge. 8 mi., (38-01-30N/76-19-25W)

Holland Is. Bar Lt., Ches. Ch. – Fl. W. ev. 2.5 s., Ht. 37′, Rge. 6 mi., (38-04-07N/76-05-45W)

Point No Point Lt., Ches. Ch. – Fl. W. ev. 6 s., Ht. 52′, Rge. 9 mi., (38-07-41N/76-17-25W)

Hooper Is. Lt., Ches. Ch. – Fl. W. ev. 6 s., Ht. 63′, Rge. 9 mi., (38-15-23N/76-14-59W)

Drum Pt. Lt.#4, Ches. Ch. – Fl. R. ev. 2.5 s., Ht. 17′, Rge. 5 mi., (38-19-08N/76-25-15W)

Cove Pt. Lt., Ches. Ch. – Fl. W. ev. 10 s., Ht. 45′, Rge. 12 mi., ltd. 24 hrs, (38-23-11N/76-22-54W)

Bloody Point Bar Warning Lt. – Fl. W. ev. 6 s., Ht. 22′, Rge. 7 mi., (38-50-00N/76-23-35W)

Thomas Pt. Shoal Lt., Ches. Ch. – Fl. W. ev. 5 s., 2 R. Sectors 011°-051.5° and 096.5°-202°, Horn 1 bl. ev. 15 s., Ht. 43′, Rge. W. 16 mi., R. 11 mi., (38-53-56N/76-26-09W)

Wm. P. Lane, Jr. Bridge West Ch. Fog Signal, on main ch. span – Horn 1 bl. ev. 15 s., 5 s. bl., Horn Points 017° & 197°, (38-59-36N/76-22-53W)

Wm. P. Lane, Jr. Bridge East Ch. Fog Signal, on main ch. span – Horn 1 bl. ev. 20 s., 2 s. bl., (38-59-18N/76-21-30W)

Sandy Pt. Shoal Lt., Ches. Ch. – Fl. W. ev. 6 s., Ht. 51′, Rge. 9 mi., (39-00-57N/76-23-04W)

Baltimore Lt. – Fl. W. ev. 2.5 s., R. Sector 082°- 160°, Ht. 52′, Rge. W. 7 mi., R. 5 mi., (39-03-33N/76-23-56W)

NORTH CAROLINA

Currituck Beach Lt. – Fl. W. ev. 20 s., Ht. 158′, Rge. 18 mi., (36-22-37N/75-49-47W)

Bodie Is. Lt. – Fl(2) W. ev. 30 s., Ht. 156′, Rge. 18 mi., (35-49-07N/75-33-48W)

Oregon Inlet Jetty Lt. – Fl. W. ev. 2.5 s., Ht. 28′, Rge. 7 mi., (35-46-26N/75-31-30W)

Cape Hatteras Lt., – Fl. W. ev. 7.5 s., Ht. 192′, Rge. 24 mi., (35-15-02N/75-31-44W)

Hatteras Inlet Lt. – Iso. W. ev. 6 s., Ht. 48′, Rge. 10 mi., (35-11-52N/75-43-56W)

Ocracoke Lt., on W. part of island – F.W., Ht. 75′, Rge. 15 mi., (35-06-32N/75-59-10W)

Cape Lookout Lt., on N. pt. of cape – Fl. W. ev. 15 s., Ht. 156′, Rge. 14 mi., (34-37-22N/76-31-28W)

Beaufort Inlet Ch. Ltd. Wh. By. "BM" – Mo(A)W, Rge. 6 mi., Racon (M), RWSRST, (34-34-49N/76-41-33W)

New River Inlet Ltd. Wh. By. "NR" – Mo(A)W, Rge. 6 mi., RWSRST, (34-31-02N/77-19-33W)

Distance Table in Nautical Miles

Continued from p. 198   *Approximate

Nantucket Entr. Bell NB to
Boston – around Cape	105
Boston – via Canal	94
Chatham	23
Edgartown	23
Hyannis	21
Woods Hole	30
Cape Cod Canal (W. Entr.)	45
Newport	71

New Bedford (State Pier) to
Woods Hole	14
Newport	38
New London	74
New York (Gov. Is.)	166

Newport to
Providence	21
Stonington	34
New London	48
New Haven	84
City Island	122

Block Island (FR Horn) to
Nantucket	79
Vineyard Haven	52
Cleveland Ledge Lt.	50
New Bedford	44
Newport	22
Race Point Lt.	21
New London	29

New London to
Greenport	25
New Haven	49
Bridgeport	60
City Island	86

Port Jefferson to
Larchmont	30
So. Norwalk	15
Milford	14
Old Saybrook	43
New London	53

City Island to
Governors Island	17
Execution Rocks	3

Execution Rocks to
Port Chester	8
Stamford	12
Oyster Bay Harbor	14
So. Norwalk	19
Bridgeport	29

Port Jefferson	30
Milford	37
New Haven	49
Conn. River	69
Mystic	84
Montauk Point	87

New York (Battery) to
Jones Inlet	34
Fire Island Inlet	47
Moriches Inlet	74
Shinnecock Inlet	88
Montauk Point	117
Keyport	22
Asbury Park	35
Manasquan	40
Little Egg Inlet	81
Atlantic City	97
Philadelphia	235
Chesapeake Lt. Stn	247
Cape Henry Lt.	262
Norfolk	288
Baltimore	418

Brielle-Manasquan to
E. Rockaway Inlet	32
Jones Inlet	35
Fire Island Inlet	45
Montauk Point	117
Barnegat Inlet	21
Atlantic City	51

Delaware Breakwater to
Reedy Pt. Entr. (C&D Canal)	51
Annapolis – via Canal	97
Norfolk	167
New York	150
New London	242
Providence	275
New Bedford	278
Boston (outside)	399
Portland (outside)	443

Old Point Comfort to
Baltimore	163
Philadelphia	240
New York	276
New London	363
Providence	392
New Bedford	397
Boston (outside)	512
Portland	553

Oak Is. Lt., on SE pt. of island – Fl(4) W. ev. 10 s., Ht. 169', Rge. 24 mi., (33-53-34N/78-02-06W)

Cape Fear River Entr. Ltd. Wh. By. "CF" – Mo(A)W, Rge. 6 mi., Racon (C), RWSRST, (33-46-17N/78-03-02W)

SOUTH CAROLINA

Little River Inlet Ltd. Wh. By. "LR" – Mo(A)W, Rge. 5 mi., RWSRST, (33-49-49N/78-32-27W)

Little River Inlet North Jetty Lt. #2 – Fl. R. ev. 4 s., Ht. 24', Rge. 5 mi., (33-50-31N/78-32-39W)

Winyah Bay Ltd. Wh. By. "WB" – Mo(A)W, Rge. 6 mi., RWSRST, (33-11-37N/79-05-11W)

Georgetown Lt., E. side Entr. to Winyah Bay – Fl(2) W. ev. 15 s., Ht. 85', Rge. 15 mi., (33-13-21N/79-11-06W)

Charleston Entr. Ltd. By. "C" – Mo(A)W, Rge. 6 mi., Racon (K), RWSRST, (32-37-05N/79-35-30W)

Charleston Lt., S. side of Sullivans Is. – Fl(2) W. ev. 30 s., Ht. 163', Rge. 26 mi., (32-45-29N/79-50-36W)

GEORGIA

Tybee Lt., NE end of Is. – F. W., Ht. 144', Rge. 19 mi., ltd. 24 hrs., (32-01-20N/80-50-44W)

Tybee Lighted Buoy "T" – Mo(A)W, Rge. 6 mi., Racon (G), RWSRST, (31-57-52N/80-43-10W)

St. Simons Ltd. By. "STS" – Mo(A)W, Rge. 7 mi., RWSRST, (31-02-49N/81-14-25W)

St. Simons Lt., N. side Entr. to St. Simons Sd. – F. Fl. W. ev. 60 s., Ht. 104', Rge. F. W. 18 mi., Fl. W. 23 mi., (31-08-03N/81-23-37W)

FLORIDA

Amelia Is. Lt., 2 mi. from N. end of Is. – Fl. W. ev. 10 s., R. Sect. 344°-360°, Ht. 107', Rge. W. 23 mi., R. 19 mi., (30-40-23N/81-26-33W)

St. Johns Lt., on shore – Fl(4) W. ev. 20 s., Obscured 179°-354°, Ht. 83', Rge. 19 mi., (30-23-10N/81-23-53W)

St. Johns Ltd. By. "STJ" – Mo(A)W, Rge. 6 mi., RWSRST, (30-23-35N/81-19-08W)

St. Augustine Lt., N. end of Anastasia Is. – F. Fl. W. ev. 30 s., Ht. 161', Rge. F. W. 19 mi., Fl. W. 24 mi., (29-53-08N/81-17-19W)

Ponce De Leon Inlet Lt., S. side on inlet – Fl(6) W. ev. 30 s., Ht. 159', (29-04-50N/80-55-41W)

Cape Canaveral Lt., on Cape – Fl(2) W. ev. 20 s., Ht. 137', Rge. 24 mi., (28-27-37N/80-32-36W)

Sebastian Inlet N. Jetty Lt. – Fl. R. ev. 4 s., Ht. 27', (27-51-41N/80-26-51W)

Jupiter Inlet Lt., N. side of inlet – Fl(2) W. ev. 30 s., Obscured 231°-234°, Ht. 146', Rge. 25 mi., (26-56-55N/80-04-55W)

Hillsboro Inlet Entr. Lt., N. side of inlet – Fl. (2) W. ev. 20 s., Obscured 114°-119°, Ht. 136', Rge. 28 mi., (26-15-33N/80-04-51W)

Port Everglades Ltd. By. "PE" - Mo(A)W, Rge. 7 mi., Racon (T), RWSRST, (26-05-30N/80-04-46W)

Miami Ltd. By. "M" – E. end of Miami Beach, Mo(A)W, Rge. 7 mi., Racon (M), RWSRST, (25-46-06N/80-05-00W)

Fowey Rocks Lt., Hawk Ch. – Fl. W. ev. 10 s., Ht. 110', Rge. 7 mi., (25-35-26N/80-05-48W)

Carysfort Reef Lt., outer line of reefs – Fl(3) W. ev. 60 s., Ht. 40', Rge. 13 mi., (25-13-37N/80-12-33W)

Alligator Reef Lt., – Fl(4) W. ev. 60 s., Ht. 16', Rge. 7 mi., (24-51-05N/80-37-04W)

Sombrero Key Lt., outer line of reefs – Fl(5) W. ev. 60 s., Ht. 19', Rge.7 mi. (24-37-40N/81-06-31W)

For abbreviations see footnote p. 173

American Shoal Lt. – Fl(4) W. ev. 60 s., Ht. 19', Rge. 7 mi., (24-31-32N/81-31-03W)
Key West Ltd. Wh. By. "KW" – Mo (A) W, Rge. 7, RWSRST, (24-27-26N/81-48-00W)
Sand Key Lt., Fl(2) W. ev. 15 s., Ht. 40', Rge. 13, (24-27-21N/81-52-38W)

BERMUDA – APPROACH LIGHTS FROM SEAWARD

North Rock Beacon – Fl(4)W. ev. 20 s. yellow, Ht. 70', Rge. 12 mi., RaRef, (32-28.5N/64-46.1W)

North East Breaker Beacon – Fl. W. ev. 2.5 s., Ht. 45', Rge. 12 mi., Racon (N), RaRef, (Red tower on red tripod base reading "Northeast," (32-28.7N/64-41.0W)

Kitchen Shoal Beacon – Fl(3)W. ev. 15 s., Ht. 45', Rge. 12 mi., RaRef, RWS, Red "Kitchen" on White background, (32-26.1N/64-37.6W)

Eastern Blue Cut Beacon – Fl. W. Mo(U) ev. 10 s., Ht. 60', Rge. 12 mi., RaRef, B&W Tower "Eastern Blue Cut" on white band, (32-23.9N/64-52.6W)

Chub Heads – Q. Fl(9) W. ev. 15 s., Ht. 60', Rge. 12 mi., RaRef, Yellow and Black Horizontal Stripe Tower with "Chub Heads" in White on Black Central band, Racon (C), (32-17.2N/64-58.9W)

Mills Breaker By. – Q. Fl(3)W. ev. 5 s., Black "Mills" on yellow background, (32-23.9N/64-36.9W)

Spit By. – Q. Fl(3) W. ev. 10 s., Black "Spit" on yellow, (32-22.7N/64-38.5W)

Sea By. –Mo(A)W ev. 6 s., RWS, Red "SB" in white on side, (32-22.9N/64-37.1W)

St. David's Is. Lighthouse – F. R. and G. Sectors below Fl(2) W. ev. 20 s., Ht. 212', Rge. W. 15 mi., R. and G. 20 mi., (32-21.8N/64-39.1W) Your bearing from seaward of G. Sector is 221°-276° True; remaining Sector is R. and partially obscured by land 044°-135° True.

Kindley Field Aero Beacon – Alt. W and G.; 1 White, 1 Green (rotating Aero Beacon), Ht. 140', Rge. 15 mi., (32-21.95N/64-40.55W)

Gibbs Hill Lighthouse – Fl. W. ev. 10 s., Ht. 354', Rge. 26 mi., (32-15.2N/64-50.1W)

Erica M. Szuplat

Foregoing information checked to date, September 2018. See page 4 for free supplement in June 2019.

Heaving the Lead

In tidal water where depths were doubtfully marked on the chart, or in thick weather off shore, soundings were made to determine the ship's position. The leadsman stood in the fore channels and swung the lead. [Aft] in the main and mizzen channels were other men who held the line as it led aft to the stern, where the mate stood by the line tub. The leadsman called, "All ready there?" to the next man, the mate shouted "Heave!" and the lead went spinning forward. Each man let go as the line tautened, and the mate grasped the line as it ran from the tub, and made the sounding. If the lead struck bottom before it reached him, one of the others took the sounding and called the marks. Markers on the line indicated the depth in fathoms, and an "arming" of tallow in the end of the lead showed the nature of the bottom.

Reprinted from Sail Ho! Windjammer Sketches Alow and Aloft, by Gordon Grant, 1931, William Farquhar Payson, Inc., NY

Traditional Markings for Leadlines

2 fathoms – a 2-ended scrap of leather

3 fathoms – a 3-ended scrap of leather

5 fathoms – a scrap of white calico

7 fathoms – a strip of red wool bunting

10 fathoms – leather with a round hole

13 fathoms – a piece of thick blue serge

15 fathoms – a piece of white calico

17 fathoms – a piece of red wool bunting

20 fathoms – a cord with 2 knots

30 fathoms – a cord with 3 knots

Tidal Heights and Depths

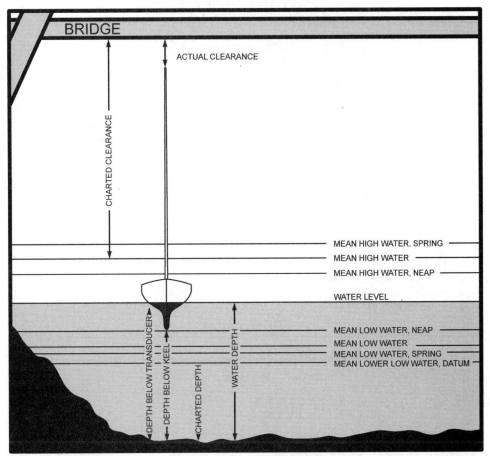

Mean High Water, Spring - the mean of high water heights of spring tides
Mean High Water - the mean of all high water heights; the charted clearance
of bridges is measured from this height
Mean High Water, Neap - the mean of high water heights of neap tides
Mean Low Water, Neap - the mean of low water heights of neap tides
Mean Low Water - the mean of all low water heights
Mean Low Water, Spring - the mean of low water heights of spring tides
Mean Lower Low Water Datum - the mean of lower low water heights;
charted depths originate from this reference height or datum

Spring Tides - tides of increased range, occurring twice a month, around the
times of the new and full moons
Neap Tides - tides of decreased range, occurring twice a month, around the
times of the half moons
Diurnal Inequality - the difference in height of the two daily low waters or
the two daily high waters, a result of the moon's (and to a lesser extent the
sun's) changing declination above and below the Equator

The Tide Cycle Simplified: The Rule of Twelfths

Since the average interval between high and low is just over six hours, we can divide the cycle into six segments of one hour each. On average the tide rises or falls approximately according to the fractions at right:

1st hour - 1/12
2nd hour - 2/12
3rd hour - 3/12
4th hour - 3/12
5th hour - 2/12
6th hour - 1/12

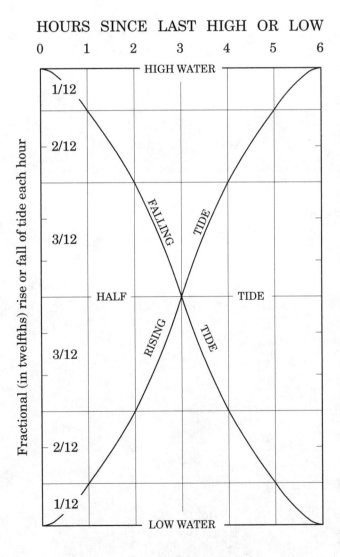

HOURS SINCE LAST HIGH OR LOW

0   1   2   3   4   5   6

Fractional (in twelfths) rise or fall of tide each hour

1/12
2/12
3/12
HALF   TIDE
3/12
2/12
1/12

HIGH WATER
FALLING TIDE
RISING TIDE
LOW WATER

Mean tidal heights by the hour at five ports				
9.6	3.5	4.6	5.2	6.9
8.8	3.2	4.2	4.8	6.3
7.2	2.6	3.4	3.9	5.2
Boston	Newport	New York	Charleston	Savannah
4.8	1.8	2.3	2.6	3.5
2.4	0.9	1.2	1.3	1.7
0.8	0.3	0.4	0.4	0.6
0.0	0.0	0.0	0.0	0.0

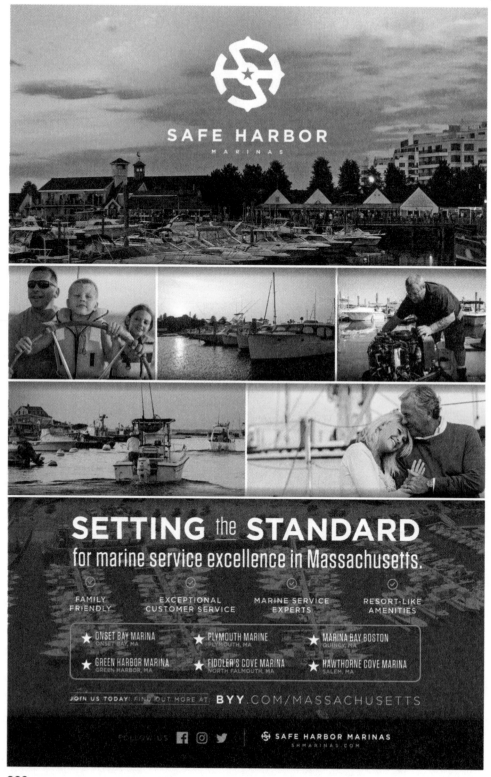

Using GPS to Adjust Your Compass

Nothing can equal the expert services of a professional Compass Adjuster, but if these services are not available, the information below can help you adjust a compass yourself.

As you used the GPS to create a Deviation Table (see p. 213), you can also use it to correct your steering compass to eliminate deviation.

Built-in Correctors - Most modern compasses are fitted with a magnetic corrector system attached inside the bottom of the compass or the binnacle cylinder. Such "B.I.C.'s" (Built-in Correctors) are easy to use and are capable of removing virtually all the deviations of a well-located compass. B.I.C.'s consist of two horizontal shafts, slotted at each end, one running Athwartship (port and starboard) and one running Fore and Aft. On each shaft are magnets. When these magnets are horizontal, they are in a neutral position. When a shaft is rotated to any angle, the magnets create correction. The usual B.I.C. can remove up to about 15° of deviation. The shaft which runs Athwartship corrects on North and South headings, and has zero effect on East and West. The Fore and Aft shaft corrects on East and West headings, and has zero effect on North and South.

Getting Started - Pick a quiet day and a swinging area with calm conditions. Have someone with a steady hand at the helm and the engine ticking over enough so there is good steering control. It is important to hold a steady heading for at least 30-45 seconds. You are looking at your GPS, and you are equipped with a non-magnetic screwdriver.

Adjusting your compass:

1. As steadily as possible steer within +/- 5° of a cardinal heading, let's say North. Slowly and with a non-magnetic screwdriver rotate the Athwartship B.I.C. until the compass reads the same as the GPS, creating zero error on North.
2. Turn 90° right to the next cardinal heading, let's say East. Turn the Fore/Aft B.I.C. to remove all of the existing error so the compass matches your GPS on East.
3. Turn 90° right to South. Compare your compass to the GPS. If the error is zero, move to step #4. If you have error, you will split the difference: if you have two (2) degrees of error, turn the Athwartship B.I.C. so you only have one (1) degree of error.
4. Turn 90° right to West. Compare your compass to the GPS. If the error is zero, move to step #5. If you have error, you will split the difference: if you have two (2) degrees of error, turn the Fore/Aft B.I.C. so you only have one (1) degree of error.
5. Return to North and confirm that you either have zero error, or if you had error on South and you split the difference to create an error of 1°, you have the same 1° of error on North.
6. Return to East and confirm that you either have zero error, or if you had error on West and you split the difference to create an error of 1°, you have the same 1° of error on East.

Check for deviation all around - Compare the steering compass to your GPS at least every 45° on all the cardinal (N, E, S, W) and intercardinal (NE, SE, SW, NW) points. If the steering compass reads too little (lower number of degrees), the deviation is Easterly on that heading, and the number of degrees must be subtracted when steering that magnetic course. If the steering compass reads too much (higher number of degrees), the deviation is Westerly on that heading, and the number of degrees must be added when steering that magnetic course.

Checking for Misalignment - After checking 8 headings, add up the total of Easterly deviations, subtract the total of Westerly, and divide by 8. The result tells you the amount by which your compass is misaligned. Let's say it is 1° Easterly. This means your lubbers line is off to port 1°. If you rotate the compass 1° clockwise, all your Easterly deviations will be reduced by 1°, your Westerly deviations will be increased by 1°, and your 0 deviations will become 1° Westerly. You will now find the total of your Easterly deviations is the very same as your Westerly total. You have eliminated misalignment error. Now you can trust your compass!

209

The Ship's Bell Code

Telling time by ship's bell has a romantic background that goes back hundreds of years. It is based in the workday routine of the ship's crew. A ship at sea requires a constant watch throughout the whole twenty-four hours of the day. To divide the duty, the day is broken up into six watches of four hours each and the crew into three divisions, or watches.

Each division of the crew stands two four-hour watches a day. In order to rotate the duty, so that a division does not have to stand the same watch day in and day out, the 4 to 8 watch in the afternoon is divided into two watches known as the dog watches.

The Mid-Watch - Midnight to 4 A.M.
The Morning Watch - 4 A.M. to 8 A.M.
The Forenoon Watch - 8 A.M. to 12 Noon
The Afternoon Watch - 12 Noon to 4 P.M.

The 1st Dog Watch - 4 P.M. to 6 P.M.
The 2nd Dog Watch - 6 P.M. to 8 P.M.
The First Watch - 8 P.M. to Midnight

To apprise the crew of the time, the ship's bell was struck by the watch officer at half hour intervals, the first half hour being one bell, the first hour two bells, hour and a half three bells, and so on up to eight bells, denoting time to relieve the watch. By this method of timekeeping eight bells marks 4, 8, or 12 o'clock.

8 Bells	4:00	8:00	12:00
1 Bell	4:30	8:30	12:30
2 Bells	5:00	9:00	1:00
3 Bells	5:30	9:30	1:30
4 Bells	6:00	10:00	2:00
5 Bells	6:30	10:30	2:30
6 Bells	7:00	11:00	3:00
7 Bells	7:30	11:30	3:30

Courtesy of Chelsea Clock Co., Chelsea, MA

Shoot To Shore

by Peter H. Spectre

"I thought you might appreciate this postcard," David Frantz wrote in a note accompanying this view of the old Deer Isle ferry. "It's a good reminder of the past. When I was a boy we first summered on Deer Isle from Philadelphia—train to New York, night boat to Boston, train to Rockland, steamer to Stonington. This was the program until the bridge was built, when we started driving. I remember seeing this ferry operation many times. The boat on the left in the photo cast off the scow, which slid up on the ramp. Great fun. Never saw them miss."

Sounds like a fine adventure to me—both the train-boat-train-steamer toodle-oo and the shoot-to-shore ferry across Eggemoggin Reach from Sargentville to Deer Isle—but believe me, it was far from boring after the Deer Isle Bridge put the ferry out of business. Here is a succinct description of the new reality from a newspaper account at the time of the new bridge's dedication:

Sway Not Dangerous

Many expressions of concern have been heard about the undulations, or waves in the floor of the new bridge, which have been quite noticeable when the wind was in a quartering direction and more or less gusty. As explained by Dr. Robinson, head of the engineering firm which designed the bridge, this movement is present in any light bridge of this type with comparatively lightweight floors and shallow stiffening girders. It does not indicate any lack of strength or safety in construction. Cross sway-cables, which are now in place and are being gradually tightened, will take care of this difficulty, it has been explained by Engineer Letourneau.

—from *The Messenger*, serving Deer Isle and Stonington, June 15, 1939

For a time in the late 1970s I was driving back and forth across the bridge once or twice a week, and I can assure you that while things are perhaps different now, in the new millennium, Engineer Letourneau's cables weren't doing the trick then. A good, stiff breeze from the right direction would set the bridge deck in motion—jumping, heaving, swaying—enough to make you seasick if you hung around long enough.

I didn't hang around. Rather, I gave new meaning to the phrase "shoot to shore." Each time I crossed the bridge I set a new speed record for getting from one end to the other. (One time, during a hard and gusty northwester, I didn't. I got stuck behind a school bus that had stalled out while struggling up the steep grade of the bridge deck. The structure rocked and rolled; my car did the same; my body felt like a tuning fork hit by a hammer; I developed a new, heretofore undiscovered religiosity.)

There's a persistent story on the coast of Maine—maybe apocryphal, maybe not—that the Deer Isle bridge was built to the same design as the Tacoma Narrows bridge in Washington state, the one that turned into a piece of limp spaghetti during a high wind back in 1940 and then disintegrated. No doubt you've seen the movie. If you haven't already, go to http://eldridgetide.com/tacoma where you can watch it, and weep. You'll have a newfound appreciation for David Frantz's good old days.

Peter H. Spectre of Spruce Head, Maine, is a freelance writer and editor. This article originally appeared in Maine Boats, Homes & Harbors magazine and appears here with the author's permission.

The Revolutionary Spherical Compass
Wilfrid O. White's Greatest Invention

Before the spherical compass, up until about 1930, all compasses were "flattops," having a flat glass on top. Although universally accepted, this design had severe limitations: the compass card was hard to read because there was no magnification, and the liquid inside swirled when the compass moved, making the card less steady.

A former publisher of ELDRIDGE, Wilfrid O. White (1878-1955), pioneered and patented in 1930 the most significant improvement in compass design since liquid was employed to steady the card. He experimented with a glass dome instead of flat glass, and found two huge advantages: with compass oil filling the compass, the dome acted as a magnifying lens for the compass card, making it far easier to read. Second, the oil inside was no longer turbulent when the compass turned or was jostled because the sphere of liquid inside (assuming the lower bowl was a hemisphere, too) remained undisturbed when the outer compass body moved. Now the compass card was far steadier, however active the motion of the boat.

Introduced at the New York Boat Show in 1931, and first advertised in ELDRIDGE in 1932, Wilfrid White's spherical compass was something of a sensation. His company, Kelvin & Wilfrid O. White Company, began production and sales increased rapidly, especially among recreational boaters. The U.S. Navy and Merchant Marine, both deeply committed to tradition, were slower to adopt the new design, but gradually accepted the spherical compass. It was not long before all compass manufacturers followed suit. Today, the flattop compass is most often found in antique shops or museums, and the spherical compass is found on virtually all pleasure craft around the world.

Using GPS to Create a Deviation Table

Most compasses are subject to onboard magnetic influences, called deviation. You can make your compass more trustworthy by using your GPS to create a deviation table.

Choose a day when the wind is light and sea as calm as possible. Find a large open area with little or no current and a minimum of boat traffic. Bring aboard an assistant. In a notebook create two columns: in pencil, label the left column GPS and the right column COMPASS. Down the right column, number each successive line using intervals of 15° [24 lines] up to 360°. You can concentrate on noting the four Cardinal and four Inter Cardinal headings (N, NE, E, SE, S, SW, W, NW) and safely interpolate and fill in the missing numbers for every 15°. Note that the Default setting on a GPS display is TRUE. For this exercise, make sure that your GPS is displaying MAGNETIC- Course Over Ground (COG) heading. This may require going into the GPS setup to insure that the COG is displaying a MAGNETIC heading.

Choose a speed which provides responsive steering and which will make any current or leeway a negligible factor. Proceed on any of the numbered courses for at least 30 seconds, giving the GPS time to report a consistent direction. Once you have held a steady course long enough to get a repeated reading, record it in the left column. Proceed to the next heading. Completing the circle results in a deviation table for your steering compass. Now, erase the penciled column headings and relabel the GPS column TO GO, and the COMPASS column STEER. Example: TO GO 094°, STEER 090°.

A deviation table admittedly falls far short of the ideal of a compensated compass; however, such a table will allow you to use your compass with a measure of confidence before an adjuster comes aboard. And that is much better than trying to steer by your GPS.

IALA BUOYAGE SYSTEM

Lateral Aids marking the sides of channels seen when entering from Seaward

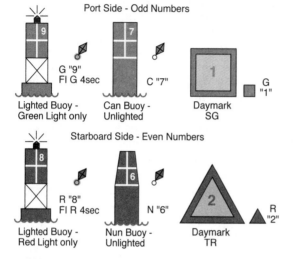

Port Side - Odd Numbers

G "9"
FI G 4sec

Lighted Buoy -
Green Light only

C "7"

Can Buoy -
Unlighted

Daymark
SG

G
"1"

Port- hand aids are Green, some with
Flashing Green Lights.
Daymarks:
1st letter "S" = Square
2nd letter "G" = color Green

Starboard Side - Even Numbers

R "8"
FI R 4sec

Lighted Buoy -
Red Light only

N "6"

Nun Buoy -
Unlighted

Daymark
TR

R
"2"

Starboard-hand aids are Red,
some with Flashing Red Lights.
Daymarks:
1st letter "T" = Triangle
2nd letter "R"= color Red

**Safe Water Aids Marking Mid-Channels & Fairways -
No Numbers - May Be Lettered:**

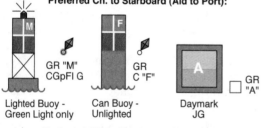

RW "E"
Mo (A)

Lighted
White Light

RW
SP "G"

Spherical Buoy -
Unlighted

Daymark
MR

RW
"A"

Red and White replaces vertical
stripes. Buoys are spherical; or
have a Red spherical topmark.
Flashing White Light only: Mo (A).
Daymarks:
1st letter "M" = Octagon
2nd letter "R" = color Red

**Preferred Channel Aids - Mark Bifurcations - No Numbers -
Preferred Ch. to Starboard (Aid to Port):**

GR "M"
CGpFI G

Lighted Buoy -
Green Light only

GR
C "F"

Can Buoy -
Unlighted

Daymark
JG

GR
"A"

Flashing Light (Red or Green) is
Composite Gp. Fl. (2 + 1).
Daymarks: 1st letter "J" = Square or
Triangle 2nd letter "R" or "G" is color
of top band

Preferred CH. to Port (Aid to Starboard):

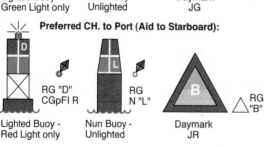

RG "D"
CGpFI R

Lighted Buoy -
Red Light only

RG
N "L"

Nun Buoy -
Unlighted

Daymark
JR

RG
"B"

Note: **ISOLATED DANGER BUOYS,
Black and Red with two Black spherical
topmarks - no numbers,**
may be lettered (if lighted, white light
only, FI (2) 5s). Stay Clear. **SPECIAL
AIDS BUOYS** will be all **YELLOW** (if
lighted, with yellow light only, Fixed
Flashing): Anchorage Areas, Fish Net
Areas, Spoil Grounds, Military Exercise
Zones, Dredging Buoys (where conven-
tional markers would be confusing),
Ocean Data Systems, some Traffic
Separations Zone Mid-Channel Buoys.

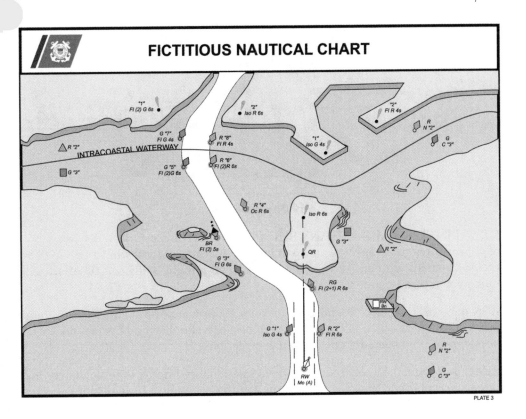

FICTITIOUS NAUTICAL CHART

"1"
Fl (2) G 6s

"2"
Iso R 6s

"2"
Fl R 4s

R
N "2"

G "7"
Fl G 4s

R "8"
Fl R 4s

"1"
Iso G 4s

G
C "3"

R "2"

INTRACOASTAL WATERWAY

R "6"
Fl (2)R 6s

G "3"

G "5"
Fl (2)G 6s

R "4"
Oc R 6s

Iso R 6s

R "2"

G "3"

BR
Fl (2) 5s

QR

G "3"
Fl G 6s

RG
Fl (2+1) R 6s

RW
Bn

G "1"
Iso G 4s

R "2"
Fl R 6s

R
N "2"

G
C "3"

RW
Mo (A)

PLATE 3

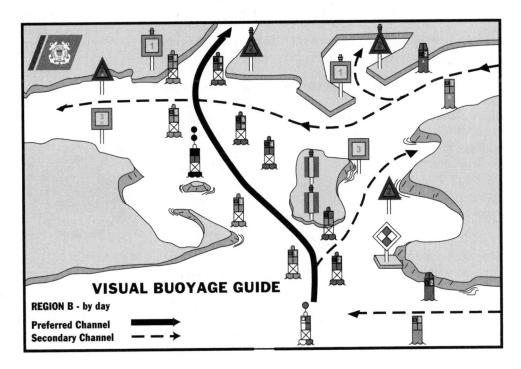

VISUAL BUOYAGE GUIDE

REGION B - by day

Preferred Channel ➡

Secondary Channel ⇢

Welcome Aboard
EARNING THE WELCOME

by Jan Adkins

BEING INVITED ABOARD ANY SKIPPER'S BOAT is a privilege. Expectations of your behavior as a boat guest are a bit more stringent than what's expected at cocktail parties, dinners, or quilting bees. Dread naught. Only a little effort will make you a come-again shipmate.

ASK to board the boat: "Permission to come aboard, captain?" This is traditional and polite and it's also OSHA-approved, because clambering between dock and deck can be unexpectedly tricky. Follow directions.

TIME is a critical factor. You can arrive fashionably late at a dinner party but tides, currents, and weather determine sailing schedules; if your skipper fixes 0945h (9:45 AM) as the time to leave the dock, BE THERE. On the other end of your voyage, time is less distinct. A boat's progress is affected by any number of causes beyond the skipper's control. Don't schedule a pedicure an hour after you expect to return to the dock, and avoid hectoring skipper and crew about your limited time. On the water you're in Neptune's lackadaisical hands; try to enjoy the open-ended nature of a day on the water.

DRESS sensibly. Non-marking soft-soled shoes are important because boat decks are often delicate, more often slippery. Even in summer, it's colder on the water than ashore; bring a fleece and windbreaker. Sun-glare comes from above and from the water's surface, so polarized sunglasses are smart wear, as well as a cap with a stiff bill or brim. Pin your cap to your collar with a safety pin and twine so it doesn't blow overboard. If rain is imminent, bring raingear. Ponchos and umbrellas are not useful in wind.

SUNSCREEN, SPF50, is important because the reflected water-glare can double your exposure. Soothing sunscreen can also prevent windburn. Drink plenty of water and find shade.

WEARING PFDs, "personal flotation devices," lifejackets, may or may not be compulsory. It's up to your skipper. The boat's skipper bears the legal and moral responsibility for everything that happens aboard his vessel; this responsibility obliges him to make the rules. It's not simple megalomania. If the captain orders a flogging, argue. Otherwise, listen well. Alcohol is occasionally a pleasant occasion but many prudent skippers keep the boat "dry" underway. The boat's rules apply to you.

FIND YOUR PERCH. Ask the skipper: "Where do you want me?" His place for you will keep you out of harm's way and out of the crew's way. Doubtless you'll wander around the boat but don't venture onto the foredeck without asking permission. The boat's motion is exaggerated up there and the footing is tricky. When you do move from your assigned perch, stay out of the crew's working traffic pattern. The hot spots are where the winches and sheets (lines that control sails) are handled. If you're on a sailboat, tacking (zigzagging toward the wind, alternately to starboard and port) is a frantic dance – letting go the jib sheet on one side, rushing across the cockpit as the boat turns 90°, and taking up the new lee-side (away from the wind) sheets rapidly, at first by hand, then wrapped around the winch drum and "cranked in." It's fast and not without danger: enormous forces are at work, there. Stand clear.

SEASICKNESS: avoid it. If you're predisposed to motion sickness, take Dramamine, Bonine, or whatever your doctor recommends long before you board the boat. Will it make you drowsy? Perhaps, but you need a rest. You'll find bags of advice on being sick; too little advice about feeling well! Seasickness is best defined as a disconnect between your eyes' perception and what your inner ear balance organs are reporting. It's wise to stay out in the breeze and focus on the horizon, to reassure your inner ear that your eyes are honest. Don't lay your head on the boat and close your eyes. Drink plenty of water and get a good night's sleep the night before your adventure. A few things help some folks: candied ginger, soda, hard candies, dry saltines. If you're really drowsy, go below to the main saloon and sleep (on the lee side of the boat). If the worst comes, expel yourself aft (toward the back of the vessel) and to leeward (on the side of the boat away from the wind). All sailors have performed this maneuver.

USEFUL TASKS aren't beyond even a first-sail shipmate. A sailboat always needs extra pairs of eyes to watch the water "under the jib": the skipper and helmsperson are watching the sail shape, the compass course, and the windvane, while a boat on a collision course might be maneuvering unseen behind the jib. No one will ever fault you for announcing an approaching vessel ahead or coming up from behind. Keeping the crew hydrated and fed is always welcome. You may be asked to fetch binoculars, bearing compass, charts, or hand-held VHF radio from the cabin. One way to show gratitude (and learn a few things) is to help clean up and wash down the boat after you return to dock.

Jan Adkins, nautical gadfly and touchy traditionalist, is a frequent contributor to ELDRIDGE. See pp. 262-263 for his comments on and drawings of essential knots. Charts drawn by him can be found throughout the book.

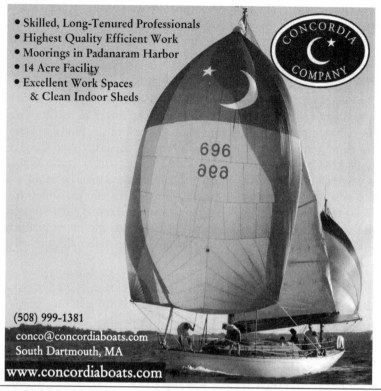
Yacht Flags and How To Fly Them

U.S. Ensign: 8 a.m. to sundown only. Not flown while racing.
At the stern staff of all vessels at anchor, or under way by power or sail.
At the leech of the aftermost sail, approximately 2/3 of the leech above the clew.
When the aftermost sail is gaff-rigged, the Ensign is flown immediately below the
peak of the gaff.

U.S. Power Squadron Ensign: 8 a.m. to sundown when flown at the stern staff in
place of the U.S. Ensign; otherwise, day and night from the starboard spreader. In
either case it is flown only when a Squadron member is in command.

Club Burgee: Day and night. Not flown while racing.
At the bow staff of power vessels with one mast.
At the main peak of yawls, ketches, sloops, cutters, and catboats.
At the fore peak of schooners and power vessels with two masts.

Private Signal: Day and night.
At the bow staff of power vessels without a mast.
At the masthead of power and sailing vessels with one mast.
At the mizzen peak of yawls and ketches.
At the main peak of schooners and power vessels with two masts.

Flag Officers' Flags: Day and night. Flown in place of the private signal on all rigs
except single-masted sailboats, when it is flown in place of the club burgee at the
masthead.

Union Jack: 8 a.m. to sundown, only at anchor, and only on Sundays, holidays, or oc-
casions for dressing ship, at the bow staff. Sailboats without a bow staff may fly it
from the forestay a few feet above the stem head.

International Signal Flags and Morse Code

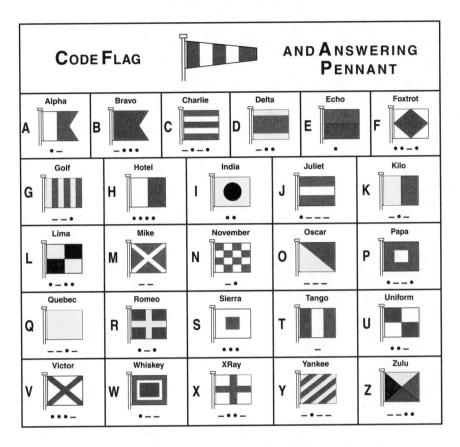

Numeral Pennants

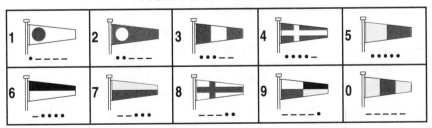

Repeaters

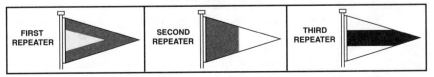

The International Code of Signals

The Code comprises 40 flags: 1 Code Flag; 26 letters; 10 numerals; 3 repeaters. With this Code it is possible to converse freely at sea with ships of different countries.

Single Flag Signals

A :: I have a diver down; keep well clear at slow speed.

B :: I am taking in, or discharging, or carrying dangerous goods.

C :: Yes

D :: Keep clear of me; I am maneuvering with difficulty.

E :: I am altering my course to starboard.

F :: I am disabled; communicate with me.

G :: I require a pilot. (When made by fishing vessels when operating in close proximity on the fishing grounds it means; "I am hauling nets.")

H :: I have a pilot on board.

I :: I am altering my course to port.

J :: I am on fire and have dangerous cargo on board; keep well clear of me.

K :: I wish to communicate with you.

L :: You should stop your vessel instantly.

M:: My vessel is stopped and making no way through water.

N :: No

O :: Man overboard.

P :: *In harbor*; All persons should report on board as the vessel is about to proceed to sea.

   At sea; It may be used by fishing vessels to mean "My nets have come fast upon an obstruction."

Q :: My vessel is healthy and I request free pratique.

R :: *nothing currently assigned*

S :: My engines are going astern.

T :: Keep clear of me; I am engaged in pair trawling.

U :: You are running into danger.

V :: I require assistance.

W:: I require medical assistance.

X :: Stop carrying out your intentions and watch for my signals.

Y :: I am dragging my anchor.

Z :: I require a tug. (When made by fishing vessels operating in close proximity on the fishing grounds it means : "I am shooting nets.")

Flags Showing "Diver Down"

There are two flags that may be flown to indicate diving operations, and each has a distinct meaning.

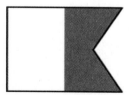

The **Alpha or "A" flag**, according to the U.S. Coast Guard, is to be flown on small vessels engaged in diving operations (1) whenever these vessels are restricted in their ability to maneuver (2) if divers are attached to the vessel. Generally, only vessels to which the divers are physically connected by communication lines, air hoses, or the like are affected by this requirement. The Alpha flag is a signal intended to *protect the vessel from collision*.

In sports diving, where divers are usually free-swimming, the Alpha flag does not have to be shown. The Coast Guard encourages the use of the traditional sports diver flag. The **sports diver flag** is an unofficial signal that, through custom, has come to be used to *protect the diver in the water*. To be most effective, the sports diver flag should be exhibited on a float in the water to mark the approximate location of the diver. Restrictions for nearby vessels vary from state to state, but typically they include a zone of 100' radius around the flag where no other boats are allowed, and a second larger zone in which speed is limited.

U.S. Storm Signals

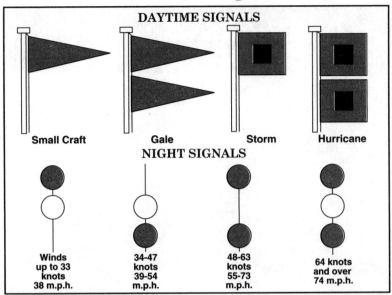

DAYTIME SIGNALS

Small Craft   Gale   Storm   Hurricane

NIGHT SIGNALS

| Winds up to 33 knots 38 m.p.h. | 34-47 knots 39-54 m.p.h. | 48-63 knots 55-73 m.p.h. | 64 knots and over 74 m.p.h. |

The above signals are displayed regularly on Light Vessels, at Coast Guard shore stations, and at many principal lighthouses. Each Coast and Geodetic Survey Chart lists those locations which appear within the area covered by that chart

Distance of Visibility

Given the curvature of the earth, can you see a 200' high headland from 20 miles away? (Answer below.) How far you can see depends on visibility, which we will assume is ideal, and the heights above water of your eye and the object.

To find the theoretical maximum distance of visibility, use the Table below. First, using your height of eye above water (say, 8'), the Table shows that at that height, your horizon is 3.2 n.m. away. Then, from our Lights, Fog Signals and Offshore Buoys (pp. 173-203), your chart, or the Light List, find the height of the object (say, 200'). The Table shows that object can be seen 16.2 n.m. from sea level. Add the two distances: 3.2 + 16.2 = 19.4 n.m. *Answer: not quite!*

(Heights below in feet, distance in nautical miles)

Ht.	Dist.	Ht.	Dist.	Ht.	Dist.	Ht.	Dist.	Ht.	Dist.
4	2.3	30	6.3	80	10.3	340	21.1	860	33.6
6	2.8	32	6.5	90	10.9	380	22.3	900	34.4
8	3.2	34	6.7	100	11.5	420	23.5	1000	36.2
10	3.6	36	6.9	120	12.6	460	24.6	1400	42.9
12	4.0	38	7.1	140	13.6	500	25.7	1800	48.6
14	4.3	40	7.3	160	14.5	540	26.7	2200	53.8
16	4.6	42	7.4	180	15.4	580	27.6	2600	58.5
18	4.9	44	7.6	200	16.2	620	28.6	3000	62.8
20	5.1	46	7.8	220	17.0	660	29.4	3400	66.9
22	5.4	48	8.0	240	17.8	700	30.4	3800	70.7
24	5.6	50	8.1	260	18.5	740	31.1	4200	74.3
26	5.9	60	8.9	280	19.2	780	32.0	4600	77.7
28	6.1	70	9.6	300	19.9	820	32.8	5000	81.0

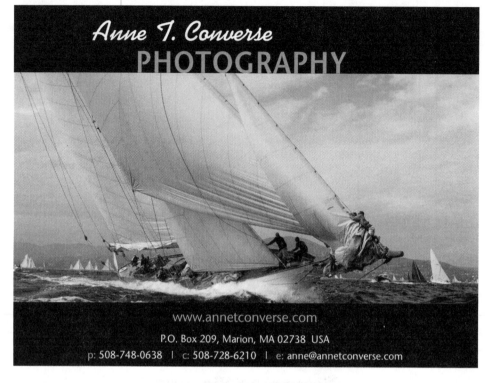
RACONS

RACONS are Radar Beacons operating in the marine radar frequency bands, 2900-3100 MHz (s-band) and 9300-9500 MHz (x-band). When triggered by a vessel's radar signal they provide a bearing by sending a coded reply (e.g. "T": –). This signal received takes the form of a single line or narrow sector extending radially towards the circumference of the radarscope from a point slightly beyond the spot formed by the echo from the lighthouse, buoy, etc. at the Racon site. Thus distance may be measured to the point at which the Racon coded flash begins. (The figure obtained will be a few hundred feet greater than the actual distance of the ship from the Racon due to the slight response delay in the Racon apparatus.)

Hours of transmission are continuous and coverage is all around the horizon unless otherwise stated. Their ranges depend on the effective range of the ship's radar and on the power and elevation of the Racon apparatus. Under conditions of abnormal radio activity, reliance should only be put on a Racon flash that is consistent and when the ship is believed to be within the area of the Racon's quoted range. Mariners are advised to turn off the interference controls of their radar when wishing to receive a Racon signal or else the signal may not come through to the ship.

See p. 223 **for list of Racons.**

Atlantic Coast RACONS

Location	RACON SITE	SIGNAL	LAT. N	LONG. W
NS	Cranberry Islands	– • • (B)	45-19-29.6	60-55-38.2
	Bear Cove Lt. & Bell By "H6"	– • (N)	44-32-36.3	63-31-19.6
	Chebucto Head	– – • • (Z)	44-30-26.6	63-31-21.8
	Cape Sable	– • – • (C)	43-23-24	65-37-16.9
	Cape Forchu	– • • (B)	43-47-38.8	66-09-19.3
	Lurcher Shoal Bifurcation Lt. By. "NM"	– • – (K)	43-48-57.2	66-29-58
NB	St. John Harbour. Lt. & Wh. By. "J"	– • (N)	45-12-55.3	66-02-36.9
	Gannet Rock	– – • (G)	44-30-37.1	66-46-52.9
ME	Frenchman Bay Ltd. By. "FB"	– • • (B)	44-19-21	68-07-24
	Portland Ltd. Wh. By. "P"	– – (M)	43-31-36	70-05-28
MA	Boston Ltd. Wh. By. "B"	– • • (B)	42-22-42	70-46-58
	Boston North Ch.Entr. Ltd. Wh. By. "NC"	– • (N)	42-22-32	70-54-18
	Cleveland East Ledge Lt.	– • – • (C)	41-37-51	70-41-39
	Buzzards Bay Entr. Lt., Horn	– • • (B)	41-23-49	71-02-05
RI	Narrag. Bay Entr. Ltd. Wh. By. "NB"	– • • (B)	41-23-00	71-23-21
	Newport - Pell Bridge	– • (N)	41-30-18	71-20-55
	Mount Hope Bay Bridge Racon "MH"	– – • • • • (MH)	41-38-24	71-15-28
NY	Valiant Rock Ltd. Wh. By. 11	– • • (B)	41-13-46	72-04-00
	Ambrose Ch. Ltd. Wh. By. "A"	– • (N)	40-27-28	73-50-12
	Tappan Zee Bridge	– • • (B)	41-04-17	73-52-52
	Kill van Kull Ch. Jct. Ltd. By. "KV"	– • – (K)	40-39-02	74-03-51
	Execution Rocks Lt.	– • • – (X)	40-52-41	73-44-16
NJ	Scotland Ltd. Wh. By. "S"	– – (M)	40-26-33	73-55-01
	Sandy Hook Ch. Rge. Front Lt.	– • – • (C)	40-29-15	73-59-35
	Barnegat Ltd. By. "B"	– • • (B)	39-45-48	73-46-04
DE	Del. Bay Appr. Ltd. Wh. By. "CH"	– • – (K)	38-46-14	75-01-20
	Del. Ltd. By. "D"	– • – (K)	38-27-18	74-41-47
	Del. River, Pea Patch Is.	– • • – (X)	39-36-42	75-34-54
	Five Fathom Bank Ltd. By. "F"	– – (M)	38-46-49	74-34-32
	Brown Shoal Lt.	– • • • (B)	38-55-21	75-06-01
	Miah Maull Shoal Lt.	– – (M)	39-07-36	75-12-31
	Ship John Shoal Lt.	– – – (O)	39-18-19	75-22-36
VA	Chesapeake Bay Ent. Ltd. Wh. By. "CB"	– • – (K)	36-49-00	75-45-36
	Ches. Ch. Ltd. By. #62	– • – – (Y)	37-46-28	76-10-16
	Chesapeake Bay Ent. Ltd. Wh. By. "CH"	– • – • (C)	36-56-08	75-57-27
	Ches. Ch. Ltd. By. #78	– – • – (Q)	38-33-19	76-25-39
	Ches. Ch. Ltd. By. #68	– • • – (X)	37-59-53	76-11-49
	Ches. Ch. Ltd. By. #42	– – – (O)	37-25-37	76-05-07
NC	Beaufort Inlet Ch. Ltd. Wh. By. "BM"	– – (M)	34-34-49	76-41-33
	Cape Fear River Ent. Ltd. Wh. By. "CF"	– • – • (C)	33-46-17	78-03-02
SC	Charleston Entr. Ltd. By. "C"	– • – (K)	32-37-05	79-35-30
GA	Tybee Ltd. By. "T"	– – • (G)	31-57-52	80-43-10
FL	Port Everglades Ltd. By. "PE"	– (T)	26-05-30	80-04-46
	Miami Ltd. By. "M"	– – (M)	25-46-06	80-05-00
Bermuda	North East Breaker Beacon	– • (N)	32-28.7	64-41.0
	Chub Heads Beacon	– • – • (C)	32-17.2	64-58.9

Range: Canada under 10 mi., US under 16 mi. **See p. 222** *for more on RACONS.*

Daily Moon Phases 2019

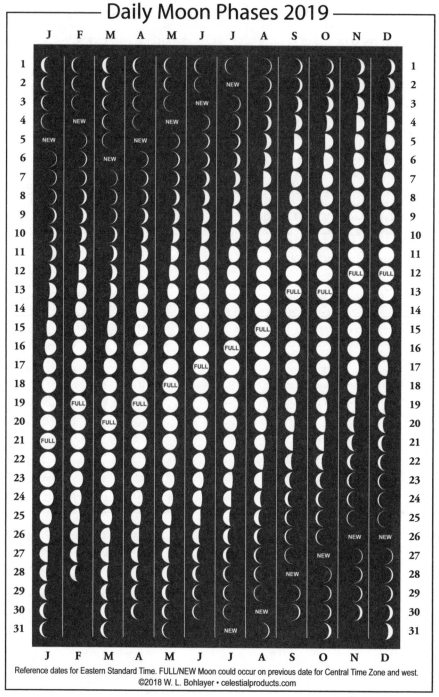

Reference dates for Eastern Standard Time. FULL/NEW Moon could occur on previous date for Central Time Zone and west.
©2018 W. L. Bohlayer • celestialproducts.com

Catalog of other moon calendars, cards, imprints and astronomy items available from Celestial Products.

800-235-3783

mooncalendar.com

If you have Easterly deviation, you must steer to the left of the desired Magnetic Course. If you have Westerly deviation, you must steer to the right of the desired Magnetic Course.

Table for Turning Compass Points into Degrees, and the Contrary
MERCHANT MARINE PRACTICE

NORTH----------	**0**	**EAST**-------------	**90**	**SOUTH** ----------	**180**	**WEST**------------	**270**
N. 1/4E. -----------	2 3/4	E. 1/4S. ------------	92 3/4	S. 1/4W. -----------	182 3/4	W. 1/4N. ----------	272 3/4
N. 1/2E. -----------	5 3/4	E. 1/2S. ------------	95 3/4	S. 1/2W. -----------	185 3/4	W. 1/2N. ----------	275 3/4
N. 3/4E. -----------	8 1/2	E. 3/4S. ------------	98 1/2	S. 3/4W. -----------	188 1/2	W. 3/4N. ----------	278 1/2
N. by E.-----------	11 1/4	E. by S. -----------	101 1/4	S. by W. -----------	191 1/4	W. by N.----------	281 1/4
N. by E. 1/4E. ----	14	E. by S. 1/4S.------	104	S. by W. 1/4W. ---	194	W. by N. 1/4N. ---	284
N. by E. 1/2E. ----	17	E. by S. 1/2S.-----	107	S. by W. 1/2W. ---	197	W. by N. 1/2N. ---	287
N. by E. 3/4E. ----	19 3/4	E. by S. 3/4S.-----	109 3/4	S. by W. 3/4W. ---	199 3/4	W. by N. 3/4N. ---	289 3/4
N.N.E. ------------	**22 1/2**	**E.S.E.**------------	**112 1/2**	**S.S.W.** ------------	**202 1/2**	**W.N.W.**-----------	**292 1/2**
N.E. by N. 3/4N.-	25 1/4	S.E. by E. 3/4E. --	115 1/4	S.W. by S. 3/4S.--	205 1/4	N.W. by W. 3/4W.	295 1/4
N.E. by N. 1/2N.-	28 1/4	S.E. by E. 1/2E. --	118 1/4	S.W. by S. 1/2S.--	208 1/4	N.W. by W. 1/2W.	298 1/4
N.E. by N. 1/4N.-	31	S.E. by E. 1/4E. --	121	S.W. by S. 1/4S.--	211	N.W. by W. 1/4W.	301
N.E. by N.--------	33 3/4	S.E. by E. --------	123 3/4	S.W. by S. -------	213 3/4	N.W. by W.-------	303 3/4
N.E. 3/4N. ---------	36 1/2	S.E. 3/4E. ---------	126 1/2	S.W. 3/4S.---------	216 1/2	N.W. 3/4W. -------	306 1/2
N.E. 1/2N. ---------	39 1/2	S.E. 1/2E. ---------	129 1/2	S.W. 1/2S.---------	219 1/2	N.W. 1/2W. -------	309 1/2
N.E. 1/4N. ---------	42 1/4	S.E. 1/4E. ---------	132 1/4	S.W. 1/4S.---------	222 1/4	N.W. 1/4W. -------	312 1/4
N.E. ---------------	**45**	**S.E.** ---------------	**135**	**S.W.**---------------	**225**	**N.W.** --------------	**315**
N.E. 1/4E.---------	47 3/4	S.E. 1/4S. ---------	137 3/4	S.W. 1/4W. --------	227 3/4	N.W. 1/4N.--------	317 3/4
N.E. 1/2E.---------	50 3/4	S.E. 1/2S. ---------	140 3/4	S.W. 1/2W.--------	230 3/4	N.W. 1/2N.--------	320 3/4
N.E. 3/4E.---------	53 1/2	S.E. 3/4S. ---------	143 1/2	S.W. 3/4W.--------	233 1/2	N.W. 3/4N.--------	323 1/2
N.E. by E. --------	56 1/4	S.E. by S.---------	146 1/4	S.W. by W. -------	236 1/4	N.W. by N.-------	326 1/4
N.E. by E. 1/4E.--	59	S.E. by S. 1/4S. --	149	S.W. by W. 1/4W.	239	N.W. by N. 1/4N.	329
N.E. by E. 1/2E.--	62	S.E. by S. 1/2S.--	152	S.W. by W. 1/2W.	242	N.W. by N. 1/2N.	332
N.E. by E. 3/4E.--	64 3/4	S.E. by S. 3/4S. --	154 3/4	S.W. by W. 3/4W.	244 3/4	N.W. by N. 3/4N.	334 3/4
E.N.E. ------------	**67 1/2**	**S.S.E.** ------------	**157 1/2**	**W.S.W.** -----------	**247 1/2**	**N.N.W.** -----------	**337 1/2**
E. by N. 3/4N.----	70 1/4	S. by E. 3/4E.-----	160 1/4	W. by S. 3/4S. ----	250 1/4	N. by W. 3/4W.---	340 1/4
E. by N. 1/2N.----	73 1/4	S. by E. 1/2E.-----	163 1/4	W. by S. 1/2S. ----	253 1/4	N. by W. 1/2W.---	343 1/4
E. by N. 1/4N.----	76	S. by E. 1/4E.-----	166	W. by S. 1/4S. ----	256	N. by W. 1/4W.---	346
E. by N.-----------	78 3/4	S. by E. -----------	168 3/4	W. by S. ----------	258 3/4	N. by W. ---------	348 3/4
E. 3/4N. -----------	81 1/2	S. 3/4E.------------	171 1/2	W. 3/4S. -----------	261 1/2	N. 3/4W. ----------	351 1/2
E. 1/2N. -----------	84 1/2	S. 1/2E.------------	174 1/2	W. 1/2S. -----------	264 1/2	N. 1/2W. ----------	354 1/2
E. 1/4N. -----------	87 1/4	S. 1/4E.------------	177 1/4	W. 1/4S. -----------	267 1/4	N. 1/4W. ----------	357 1/4
EAST-------------	**90**	**SOUTH** ----------	**180**	**WEST**------------	**270**	**NORTH**----------	**0**

2019 SUN'S RISING AND SETTING AT BOSTON – 42° 20'N   71°W
Daylight Saving Time is March 10 – November 3, transitions are noted with an *

Times shown in table are first tip of Sun at Sunrise and last tip at Sunset.

Day	JAN. Rise	JAN. Set	FEB. Rise	FEB. Set	MAR. Rise	MAR. Set	APR. Rise	APR. Set	MAY Rise	MAY Set	JUN. Rise	JUN. Set	Day
01	7:13	16:22	6:58	16:58	6:20	17:34	6:27	19:10	5:40	19:43	5:10	20:14	01
02	7:13	16:23	6:57	16:59	6:18	17:35	6:25	19:11	5:38	19:44	5:10	20:15	02
03	7:13	16:24	6:56	17:01	6:17	17:36	6:24	19:12	5:37	19:46	5:09	20:16	03
04	7:13	16:25	6:55	17:02	6:15	17:37	6:22	19:13	5:36	19:47	5:09	20:16	04
05	7:13	16:26	6:53	17:03	6:13	17:38	6:20	19:14	5:34	19:48	5:08	20:17	05
06	7:13	16:27	6:52	17:04	6:12	17:40	6:18	19:15	5:33	19:49	5:08	20:18	06
07	7:13	16:28	6:51	17:06	6:10	17:41	6:17	19:16	5:32	19:50	5:08	20:18	07
08	7:13	16:29	6:50	17:07	6:08	17:42	6:15	19:17	5:31	19:51	5:08	20:19	08
09	7:13	16:30	6:49	17:08	6:07	17:43	6:13	19:19	5:30	19:52	5:07	20:19	09
10	7:12	16:31	6:47	17:10	*7:05	18:44	6:12	19:20	5:28	19:53	5:07	20:20	10
11	7:12	16:32	6:46	17:11	7:03	18:46	6:10	19:21	5:27	19:54	5:07	20:21	11
12	7:12	16:33	6:45	17:12	7:02	18:47	6:08	19:22	5:26	19:55	5:07	20:21	12
13	7:11	16:34	6:43	17:14	7:00	18:48	6:07	19:23	5:25	19:56	5:07	20:22	13
14	7:11	16:35	6:42	17:15	6:58	18:49	6:05	19:24	5:24	19:57	5:07	20:22	14
15	7:11	16:37	6:41	17:16	6:56	18:50	6:04	19:25	5:23	19:58	5:07	20:22	15
16	7:10	16:38	6:39	17:17	6:55	18:51	6:02	19:26	5:22	19:59	5:07	20:23	16
17	7:10	16:39	6:38	17:19	6:53	18:53	6:00	19:28	5:21	20:00	5:07	20:23	17
18	7:09	16:40	6:37	17:20	6:51	18:54	5:59	19:29	5:20	20:01	5:07	20:23	18
19	7:08	16:41	6:35	17:21	6:50	18:55	5:57	19:30	5:19	20:02	5:07	20:24	19
20	7:08	16:43	6:34	17:22	6:48	18:56	5:56	19:31	5:18	20:03	5:07	20:24	20
21	7:07	16:44	6:32	17:24	6:46	18:57	5:54	19:32	5:17	20:04	5:07	20:24	21
22	7:06	16:45	6:31	17:25	6:44	18:58	5:53	19:33	5:17	20:05	5:08	20:24	22
23	7:06	16:46	6:29	17:26	6:43	18:59	5:51	19:34	5:16	20:06	5:08	20:25	23
24	7:05	16:48	6:28	17:27	6:41	19:01	5:50	19:35	5:15	20:07	5:08	20:25	24
25	7:04	16:49	6:26	17:29	6:39	19:02	5:48	19:37	5:14	20:08	5:08	20:25	25
26	7:03	16:50	6:24	17:30	6:37	19:03	5:47	19:38	5:14	20:09	5:09	20:25	26
27	7:02	16:51	6:23	17:31	6:36	19:04	5:45	19:39	5:13	20:10	5:09	20:25	27
28	7:02	16:53	6:21	17:32	6:34	19:05	5:44	19:40	5:12	20:11	5:10	20:25	28
29	7:01	16:54			6:32	19:06	5:42	19:41	5:12	20:12	5:10	20:25	29
30	7:00	16:55			6:30	19:07	5:41	19:42	5:11	20:12	5:10	20:25	30
31	6:59	16:57			6:29	19:08			5:11	20:13			31

Day	JUL. Rise	JUL. Set	AUG. Rise	AUG. Set	SEP. Rise	SEP. Set	OCT. Rise	OCT. Set	NOV. Rise	NOV. Set	DEC. Rise	DEC. Set	Day
01	5:11	20:25	5:36	20:04	6:09	19:18	6:41	18:26	7:17	17:38	6:53	16:13	01
02	5:12	20:24	5:37	20:02	6:10	19:17	6:42	18:24	7:18	17:36	6:54	16:12	02
03	5:12	20:24	5:38	20:01	6:11	19:15	6:43	18:22	*6:19	16:35	6:55	16:12	03
04	5:13	20:24	5:39	20:00	6:12	19:13	6:44	18:21	6:21	16:34	6:56	16:12	04
05	5:13	20:24	5:41	19:59	6:13	19:12	6:45	18:19	6:22	16:33	6:57	16:12	05
06	5:14	20:23	5:42	19:58	6:14	19:10	6:46	18:17	6:23	16:30	6:58	16:11	06
07	5:15	20:23	5:43	19:56	6:15	19:08	6:47	18:16	6:24	16:30	6:59	16:11	07
08	5:15	20:23	5:44	19:55	6:16	19:06	6:49	18:14	6:26	16:29	7:00	16:11	08
09	5:16	20:22	5:45	19:54	6:17	19:05	6:50	18:12	6:27	16:28	7:01	16:11	09
10	5:17	20:22	5:46	19:52	6:18	19:03	6:51	18:11	6:28	16:26	7:02	16:11	10
11	5:17	20:21	5:47	19:51	6:19	19:01	6:52	18:09	6:29	16:26	7:03	16:11	11
12	5:18	20:21	5:48	19:50	6:21	18:59	6:53	18:07	6:31	16:25	7:04	16:12	12
13	5:19	20:20	5:49	19:48	6:22	18:58	6:54	18:06	6:32	16:24	7:04	16:12	13
14	5:20	20:20	5:50	19:47	6:23	18:56	6:55	18:04	6:33	16:23	7:05	16:12	14
15	5:21	20:19	5:51	19:45	6:24	18:54	6:57	18:02	6:34	16:22	7:06	16:12	15
16	5:21	20:18	5:52	19:44	6:25	18:52	6:58	18:01	6:36	16:21	7:07	16:12	16
17	5:22	20:18	5:53	19:42	6:26	18:51	6:59	17:59	6:37	16:21	7:07	16:13	17
18	5:23	20:17	5:54	19:41	6:27	18:49	7:00	17:58	6:38	16:20	7:08	16:13	18
19	5:24	20:16	5:55	19:39	6:28	18:47	7:01	17:56	6:39	16:19	7:08	16:13	19
20	5:25	20:15	5:56	19:38	6:29	18:45	7:02	17:55	6:41	16:18	7:09	16:14	20
21	5:26	20:15	5:57	19:36	6:30	18:43	7:04	17:53	6:42	16:18	7:10	16:14	21
22	5:27	20:14	5:58	19:35	6:31	18:42	7:05	17:52	6:43	16:17	7:10	16:15	22
23	5:28	20:13	5:59	19:33	6:32	18:40	7:06	17:50	6:44	16:16	7:11	16:15	23
24	5:29	20:12	6:01	19:32	6:33	18:38	7:07	17:49	6:45	16:16	7:11	16:16	24
25	5:29	20:11	6:02	19:30	6:34	18:36	7:08	17:47	6:46	16:15	7:11	16:17	25
26	5:30	20:10	6:03	19:28	6:35	18:35	7:10	17:46	6:48	16:15	7:12	16:17	26
27	5:31	20:09	6:04	19:27	6:36	18:33	7:11	17:44	6:49	16:14	7:12	16:18	27
28	5:32	20:08	6:05	19:25	6:38	18:31	7:12	17:43	6:50	16:14	7:12	16:19	28
29	5:33	20:07	6:06	19:23	6:39	18:29	7:13	17:42	6:51	16:13	7:13	16:19	29
30	5:34	20:06	6:07	19:22	6:40	18:28	7:14	17:40	6:52	16:13	7:13	16:20	30
31	5:35	20:05	6:08	19:20			7:16	17:39			7:13	16:21	31

2019 SUN'S RISING AND SETTING AT NEW YORK – 40° 42'N 74°W

Daylight Saving Time is March 10 – November 3, transitions are noted with an *

Times shown in table are first tip of Sun at Sunrise and last tip at Sunset.

Day	JAN. Rise h m	Set h m	FEB. Rise h m	Set h m	MAR. Rise h m	Set h m	APR. Rise h m	Set h m	MAY Rise h m	Set h m	JUN. Rise h m	Set h m	Day
01	7:20	16:39	7:06	17:13	6:30	17:47	6:40	19:21	5:55	19:52	5:27	20:21	01
02	7:20	16:40	7:05	17:15	6:29	17:48	6:38	19:22	5:54	19:53	5:27	20:22	02
03	7:20	16:41	7:04	17:16	6:27	17:49	6:37	19:23	5:53	19:54	5:26	20:22	03
04	7:20	16:42	7:03	17:17	6:26	17:50	6:35	19:24	5:51	19:55	5:26	20:23	04
05	7:20	16:43	7:02	17:18	6:24	17:52	6:33	19:25	5:50	19:56	5:26	20:24	05
06	7:20	16:44	7:01	17:20	6:23	17:53	6:32	19:26	5:49	19:57	5:25	20:24	06
07	7:20	16:45	7:00	17:21	6:21	17:54	6:30	19:27	5:48	19:58	5:25	20:25	07
08	7:20	16:46	6:59	17:22	6:19	17:55	6:29	19:28	5:47	19:59	5:25	20:25	08
09	7:20	16:47	6:58	17:23	6:18	17:56	6:27	19:29	5:45	20:00	5:25	20:26	09
10	7:20	16:48	6:56	17:25	*7:16	18:57	6:25	19:30	5:44	20:01	5:25	20:27	10
11	7:19	16:49	6:55	17:26	7:15	18:58	6:24	19:31	5:43	20:02	5:25	20:27	11
12	7:19	16:50	6:54	17:27	7:13	18:59	6:22	19:32	5:42	20:03	5:24	20:28	12
13	7:19	16:51	6:53	17:28	7:11	19:00	6:21	19:33	5:41	20:04	5:24	20:28	13
14	7:18	16:52	6:51	17:29	7:10	19:01	6:19	19:34	5:40	20:05	5:24	20:28	14
15	7:18	16:53	6:50	17:31	7:08	19:03	6:18	19:35	5:39	20:06	5:24	20:29	15
16	7:18	16:54	6:49	17:32	7:06	19:04	6:16	19:36	5:38	20:07	5:24	20:29	16
17	7:17	16:55	6:48	17:33	7:05	19:05	6:15	19:37	5:37	20:08	5:24	20:30	17
18	7:17	16:57	6:46	17:34	7:03	19:06	6:13	19:38	5:37	20:09	5:25	20:30	18
19	7:16	16:58	6:45	17:35	7:01	19:07	6:12	19:39	5:36	20:10	5:25	20:30	19
20	7:15	16:59	6:43	17:37	7:00	19:08	6:10	19:40	5:35	20:11	5:25	20:30	20
21	7:15	17:00	6:42	17:38	6:58	19:09	6:09	19:41	5:34	20:12	5:25	20:31	21
22	7:14	17:01	6:41	17:39	6:57	19:10	6:07	19:43	5:33	20:13	5:25	20:31	22
23	7:14	17:02	6:39	17:40	6:55	19:11	6:06	19:44	5:33	20:13	5:25	20:31	23
24	7:13	17:04	6:38	17:41	6:53	19:12	6:04	19:45	5:32	20:14	5:26	20:31	24
25	7:12	17:05	6:36	17:42	6:52	19:13	6:03	19:46	5:31	20:15	5:26	20:31	25
26	7:11	17:06	6:35	17:44	6:50	19:14	6:02	19:47	5:30	20:16	5:26	20:31	26
27	7:11	17:07	6:33	17:45	6:48	19:15	6:00	19:48	5:30	20:17	5:27	20:31	27
28	7:10	17:09	6:32	17:46	6:47	19:16	5:59	19:49	5:29	20:18	5:27	20:31	28
29	7:09	17:10			6:45	19:17	5:58	19:50	5:29	20:18	5:28	20:31	29
30	7:08	17:11			6:43	19:18	5:56	19:51	5:28	20:19	5:28	20:31	30
31	7:07	17:12			6:42	19:19			5:28	20:20			31

Day	JUL. Rise h m	Set h m	AUG. Rise h m	Set h m	SEP. Rise h m	Set h m	OCT. Rise h m	Set h m	NOV. Rise h m	Set h m	DEC. Rise h m	Set h m	Day
01	5:29	20:31	5:53	20:12	6:23	19:29	6:52	18:38	7:26	17:53	7:00	16:29	01
02	5:29	20:31	5:53	20:10	6:24	19:27	6:53	18:37	7:27	17:51	7:01	16:29	02
03	5:30	20:31	5:54	20:09	6:25	19:25	6:54	18:35	*6:28	16:50	7:02	16:29	03
04	5:30	20:30	5:55	20:08	6:26	19:24	6:55	18:34	6:30	16:49	7:03	16:29	04
05	5:31	20:30	5:56	20:07	6:27	19:22	6:56	18:32	6:31	16:48	7:04	16:29	05
06	5:31	20:30	5:57	20:06	6:28	19:20	6:57	18:30	6:32	16:47	7:05	16:28	06
07	5:32	20:30	5:58	20:05	6:29	19:19	6:58	18:29	6:33	16:46	7:06	16:28	07
08	5:33	20:29	5:59	20:03	6:30	19:17	6:59	18:27	6:34	16:45	7:07	16:28	08
09	5:33	20:29	6:00	20:02	6:31	19:15	7:01	18:25	6:35	16:44	7:08	16:28	09
10	5:34	20:29	6:01	20:01	6:32	19:14	7:02	18:24	6:37	16:43	7:09	16:29	10
11	5:35	20:28	6:02	20:00	6:33	19:12	7:03	18:22	6:38	16:42	7:10	16:29	11
12	5:35	20:28	6:03	19:58	6:34	19:10	7:04	18:21	6:39	16:41	7:10	16:29	12
13	5:36	20:27	6:04	19:57	6:34	19:09	7:05	18:19	6:40	16:40	7:11	16:29	13
14	5:37	20:27	6:05	19:56	6:35	19:07	7:06	18:18	6:41	16:39	7:12	16:29	14
15	5:38	20:26	6:06	19:54	6:36	19:05	7:07	18:16	6:42	16:38	7:13	16:29	15
16	5:38	20:25	6:07	19:53	6:37	19:04	7:08	18:15	6:44	16:37	7:13	16:30	16
17	5:39	20:25	6:08	19:51	6:38	19:02	7:09	18:13	6:45	16:37	7:14	16:30	17
18	5:40	20:24	6:09	19:50	6:39	19:00	7:10	18:12	6:46	16:36	7:15	16:30	18
19	5:41	20:23	6:10	19:49	6:40	18:59	7:11	18:11	6:47	16:35	7:15	16:31	19
20	5:42	20:23	6:11	19:47	6:41	18:57	7:12	18:09	6:48	16:34	7:16	16:31	20
21	5:43	20:22	6:12	19:46	6:42	18:55	7:13	18:07	6:49	16:34	7:16	16:32	21
22	5:43	20:21	6:13	19:44	6:43	18:54	7:15	18:06	6:51	16:33	7:17	16:32	22
23	5:44	20:20	6:14	19:43	6:44	18:52	7:16	18:04	6:52	16:33	7:17	16:33	23
24	5:45	20:19	6:15	19:41	6:45	18:50	7:17	18:03	6:53	16:32	7:18	16:33	24
25	5:46	20:19	6:16	19:40	6:46	18:48	7:18	18:02	6:54	16:32	7:18	16:34	25
26	5:47	20:18	6:17	19:38	6:47	18:47	7:19	18:00	6:55	16:31	7:18	16:35	26
27	5:48	20:17	6:18	19:36	6:48	18:45	7:20	17:59	6:56	16:31	7:19	16:35	27
28	5:49	20:16	6:19	19:35	6:49	18:43	7:21	17:58	6:57	16:30	7:19	16:36	28
29	5:50	20:15	6:20	19:33	6:50	18:42	7:23	17:56	6:58	16:30	7:19	16:37	29
30	5:51	20:14	6:21	19:32	6:51	18:40	7:24	17:55	6:59	16:30	7:20	16:37	30
31	5:52	20:13	6:22	19:30			7:25	17:54			7:20	16:38	31

2019 SUN'S RISING AND SETTING AT JACKSONVILLE – 30° 20'N 81° 37'W
Daylight Saving Time is March 101 – November 3, transitions are noted with an *

Times shown in table are first tip of Sun at Sunrise and last tip at Sunset.

Day	JAN. Rise h m	Set h m	FEB. Rise h m	Set h m	MAR. Rise h m	Set h m	APR. Rise h m	Set h m	MAY Rise h m	Set h m	JUN. Rise h m	Set h m	Day
01	7:23	17:37	7:17	18:03	6:53	18:25	7:16	19:45	6:43	20:04	6:25	20:24	01
02	7:23	17:38	7:17	18:04	6:52	18:26	7:15	19:46	6:43	20:05	6:25	20:24	02
03	7:24	17:39	7:16	18:05	6:51	18:27	7:14	19:47	6:42	20:06	6:25	20:25	03
04	7:24	17:39	7:15	18:06	6:50	18:27	7:12	19:47	6:41	20:06	6:25	20:25	04
05	7:24	17:40	7:15	18:06	6:48	18:28	7:11	19:48	6:40	20:07	6:24	20:26	05
06	7:24	17:41	7:14	18:07	6:47	18:29	7:10	19:48	6:39	20:08	6:24	20:26	06
07	7:24	17:42	7:13	18:08	6:46	18:29	7:09	19:49	6:38	20:08	6:24	20:27	07
08	7:24	17:42	7:13	18:09	6:45	18:30	7:08	19:50	6:37	20:09	6:24	20:27	08
09	7:24	17:43	7:12	18:10	6:44	18:31	7:06	19:50	6:37	20:10	6:24	20:28	09
10	7:24	17:44	7:11	18:11	*7:43	19:31	7:05	19:51	6:36	20:10	6:24	20:28	10
11	7:24	17:45	7:10	18:12	7:41	19:32	7:04	19:51	6:35	20:11	6:24	20:28	11
12	7:24	17:46	7:09	18:12	7:40	19:33	7:03	19:52	6:35	20:11	6:24	20:29	12
13	7:24	17:47	7:09	18:13	7:39	19:33	7:02	19:53	6:34	20:12	6:24	20:29	13
14	7:24	17:47	7:08	18:14	7:38	19:34	7:01	19:53	6:33	20:13	6:24	20:29	14
15	7:24	17:48	7:07	18:15	7:37	19:35	7:00	19:54	6:33	20:13	6:24	20:30	15
16	7:24	17:49	7:06	18:16	7:35	19:35	6:59	19:55	6:32	20:14	6:24	20:30	16
17	7:23	17:50	7:05	18:16	7:34	19:36	6:57	19:55	6:31	20:15	6:24	20:30	17
18	7:23	17:51	7:04	18:17	7:33	19:37	6:56	19:56	6:31	20:15	6:25	20:31	18
19	7:23	17:52	7:03	18:18	7:32	19:37	6:55	19:56	6:30	20:16	6:25	20:31	19
20	7:23	17:53	7:02	18:19	7:31	19:38	6:54	19:57	6:30	20:17	6:25	20:31	20
21	7:22	17:53	7:01	18:19	7:29	19:38	6:53	19:58	6:29	20:17	6:25	20:31	21
22	7:22	17:54	7:00	18:20	7:28	19:39	6:52	19:58	6:29	20:18	6:25	20:32	22
23	7:22	17:55	6:59	18:21	7:27	19:40	6:51	19:59	6:28	20:18	6:26	20:32	23
24	7:21	17:56	6:58	18:22	7:26	19:40	6:50	20:00	6:28	20:19	6:26	20:32	24
25	7:21	17:57	6:57	18:22	7:24	19:41	6:49	20:00	6:27	20:20	6:26	20:32	25
26	7:21	17:58	6:56	18:23	7:23	19:42	6:48	20:01	6:27	20:20	6:26	20:32	26
27	7:20	17:59	6:55	18:24	7:22	19:42	6:47	20:02	6:27	20:21	6:27	20:32	27
28	7:20	18:00	6:54	18:25	7:21	19:43	6:46	20:02	6:26	20:21	6:27	20:32	28
29	7:19	18:00			7:20	19:43	6:45	20:03	6:26	20:22	6:27	20:32	29
30	7:19	18:01			7:18	19:44	6:44	20:04	6:26	20:23	6:28	20:32	30
31	7:18	18:02			7:17	19:45			6:25	20:23			31

Day	JUL. Rise h m	Set h m	AUG. Rise h m	Set h m	SEP. Rise h m	Set h m	OCT. Rise h m	Set h m	NOV. Rise h m	Set h m	DEC. Rise h m	Set h m	Day
01	6:28	20:32	6:45	20:20	7:03	19:49	7:20	19:12	7:41	18:39	7:05	17:26	01
02	6:29	20:32	6:45	20:20	7:04	19:48	7:20	19:11	7:41	18:38	7:06	17:25	02
03	6:29	20:32	6:46	20:19	7:04	19:10	7:21	19:10	*6:42	17:38	7:07	17:25	03
04	6:29	20:32	6:47	20:18	7:05	19:46	7:22	19:08	6:43	17:37	7:08	17:26	04
05	6:30	20:32	6:47	20:17	7:05	19:45	7:22	19:07	6:44	17:36	7:08	17:26	05
06	6:30	20:32	6:48	20:16	7:06	19:43	7:23	19:06	6:45	17:35	7:09	17:26	06
07	6:31	20:32	6:49	20:16	7:06	19:42	7:23	19:05	6:45	17:35	7:10	17:26	07
08	6:31	20:32	6:49	20:15	7:07	19:41	7:24	19:04	6:46	17:34	7:11	17:26	08
09	6:32	20:32	6:50	20:14	7:08	19:40	7:25	19:02	6:47	17:33	7:11	17:26	09
10	6:32	20:31	6:50	20:13	7:08	19:38	7:25	19:01	6:48	17:33	7:12	17:26	10
11	6:33	20:31	6:51	20:12	7:09	19:36	7:26	19:00	6:49	17:32	7:13	17:27	11
12	6:33	20:31	6:52	20:11	7:09	19:36	7:27	18:59	6:49	17:31	7:13	17:27	12
13	6:34	20:31	6:52	20:10	7:10	19:35	7:27	18:58	6:50	17:31	7:14	17:27	13
14	6:34	20:30	6:53	20:09	7:10	19:33	7:28	18:57	6:51	17:30	7:15	17:27	14
15	6:35	20:30	6:53	20:08	7:11	19:32	7:28	18:56	6:52	17:30	7:15	17:28	15
16	6:35	20:30	6:54	20:07	7:11	19:31	7:29	18:55	6:53	17:29	7:16	17:28	16
17	6:36	20:29	6:55	20:06	7:12	19:30	7:30	18:53	6:54	17:29	7:17	17:28	17
18	6:37	20:29	6:55	20:05	7:12	19:28	7:30	18:52	6:54	17:28	7:17	17:29	18
19	6:37	20:28	6:56	20:04	7:13	19:27	7:31	18:51	6:55	17:28	7:18	17:29	19
20	6:38	20:28	6:56	20:03	7:14	19:26	7:32	18:50	6:56	17:28	7:18	17:30	20
21	6:38	20:27	6:57	20:02	7:14	19:25	7:33	18:49	6:57	17:27	7:19	17:30	21
22	6:39	20:27	6:57	20:01	7:15	19:23	7:33	18:48	6:58	17:27	7:19	17:31	22
23	6:39	20:26	6:58	20:00	7:15	19:22	7:34	18:47	6:59	17:27	7:20	17:31	23
24	6:40	20:26	6:59	19:59	7:16	19:21	7:35	18:46	6:59	17:27	7:20	17:32	24
25	6:41	20:25	6:59	19:58	7:16	19:20	7:35	18:45	7:00	17:26	7:21	17:32	25
26	6:41	20:25	7:00	19:56	7:17	19:18	7:36	18:44	7:01	17:26	7:21	17:33	26
27	6:42	20:24	7:00	19:55	7:17	19:17	7:37	18:43	7:02	17:26	7:21	17:34	27
28	6:42	20:23	7:01	19:54	7:18	19:16	7:38	18:43	7:03	17:26	7:22	17:34	28
29	6:43	20:23	7:01	19:53	7:19	19:15	7:38	18:42	7:04	17:26	7:22	17:35	29
30	6:44	20:22	7:02	19:52	7:19	19:13	7:39	18:41	7:04	17:26	7:23	17:36	30
31	6:44	20:21	7:03	19:51			7:40	18:40			7:23	17:36	31

2019 SUN'S SETTING AT OTHER LOCATIONS FOR FLAG USE
Daylight Saving Time is March 10 – November 3

Times shown in tables p. 226-228 are first tip of Sun at Sunrise and last tip at Sunset.

Vernal Equinox: March 20th, 5:58 p.m. E.D.T.   Summer Solstice: June 21st, 11:54 a.m. E.D.T.
Autumnal Equinox: Sept. 23rd, 3:50 a.m. E.D.T.   Winter Solstice: Dec. 21st, 11:19 p.m. E.S.T.

Add to or subtract from the referenced table

	Jan	Feb	Mar	Apr	May	Jun	Jul	Aug	Sep	Oct	Nov	Dec
BOSTON p. 226												
New London, CT	+7	+6	+4	+2	0	-1	0	+1	+2	+5	+6	+7
Newport, RI	+4	+3	+1	-1	-2	-3	-2	-1	0	+2	+4	+5
New Bedford, MA	+3	+2	0	-1	-2	-3	-2	-1	0	+1	+2	+3
Vineyard Haven, MA	+1	-1	-2	-4	-5	-6	-5	-4	-3	-2	0	+1
Nantucket, MA	-1	-2	-4	-6	-7	-8	-7	-6	-5	-3	-2	-1
Portland, ME	-8	-6	-3	-1	+1	+2	+1	0	-2	-4	-6	-7
Rockland, ME	-14	-12	-8	-6	-4	-2	-4	-5	-7	-10	-12	-14
Bar Harbor, ME	-18	-15	-11	-8	-5	-3	-5	-7	-9	-13	-17	-18
NEW YORK p. 227												
Hampton Roads, VA	+18	+15	+9	+2	0	-1	-1	+2	+7	+13	+18	+20
Oxford, MD	+14	+12	+9	+5	+4	+3	+3	+5	+8	+11	+14	+15
Annapolis, MD	+14	+13	+10	+7	+6	+5	+5	+7	+9	+12	+14	+15
Cape May, NJ	+8	+7	+4	+1	0	-1	-1	+1	+3	+6	+8	+9
Atlantic City, NJ	+5	+4	+2	0	-1	-2	-2	0	+2	+4	+6	+6
Mannasquan, NJ	+2	+1	0	-1	-2	-2	-2	-1	0	+1	+2	+2
Port Jefferson, NY	-5	-4	-4	-3	-3	-3	-3	-3	-4	-4	-5	-5
Bridgeport, CT	-4	-4	-3	-2	-2	-1	-1	-2	-3	-4	-4	-5
New Haven, CT	-7	-6	-4	-3	-3	-3	-3	-3	-4	-5	-6	-7
JACKSONVILLE p. 228												
Morehead City, NC	-28	-24	-20	-14	-10	-7	-9	-13	-19	-24	-28	-29
Wilmington, NC	-22	-18	-14	-10	-5	-3	-5	-8	-14	-18	-22	-23
Myrtle Beach, SC	-16	-14	-10	-6	-3	-1	-3	-5	-7	-12	-17	-17
Charleston, SC	-11	-9	-6	-3	+1	0	-1	-3	-7	-9	-11	-12
Savannah. GA	-1	0	+2	+4	+6	+6	+5	+4	+3	0	-2	-2
Brunswick, GA	+1	-1	0	+1	+2	+2	+1	+1	-1	+1	+2	+2
Ponce Inlet, FL	+1	-1	-1	-2	-4	-5	-5	-4	-2	0	+1	+1
Melbourne, FL	+1	-2	-4	-5	-7	-9	-9	-8	-5	-1	0	+1
N. Palm Beach, FL	+2	-2	-6	-8	-11	-14	-14	-11	-7	-4	0	+2
Miami, FL	+6	0	-3	-8	-13	-15	-15	-11	-7	-2	+3	+5
Key West, FL	+13	+7	+2	-3	-8	-12	-12	-6	-1	+6	+11	+14

Swimmers Beware:
Undertow, Alongshore Currents and Rip Currents

Understanding the behavior of ocean water near the shore can help bathers enjoy swimming with greater confidence. There are three types of water movement which swimmers should understand.

Undertow

When a large wave approaches a beach, it breaks, rides up the beach, and then retreats. The retreating water is **undertow**. The water motion is circular: water moves toward the beach at the top of the wave, and away from the beach beneath the wave. The force of undertow increases with wave size and angle of the ocean bottom. Swimmers knocked down either by a breaking wave or by the undertow will not be dragged far to sea by the undertow, as the next wave reverses the process.

Alongshore Current

Water motion parallel to the beach is called **alongshore current**. Swimmers, especially children, should choose landmarks before entering the water to find their way back if an alongshore current has moved them along the beach. In the highest surf conditions, these currents can be strong enough to make standing difficult.

Rip Current

A third type is **rip current**, occasionally mislabeled "rip tide." This dangerous phenomenon is water moving seaward, away from the beach. It results from water finding an exit in a depression in the bottom between shoal areas, or from being deflected from the shore by sandbars, piers, and shoreline anomalies. To avoid this danger, study the water surface before going into the water. Rip currents might appear as wide breaks in the wave crests, or smooth-looking low spots in the approaching waves. The boundaries of the rip current might appear as lines of foam, debris, or swirling eddies. Be aware that rip currents can change locations in short periods of time as they create new channels.

What to Do

When caught in a rip current and being carried to sea, a swimmer should avoid swimming directly against the current toward land. Instead, escape the rip current by swimming perpendicular to the current and parallel to the shoreline. Once out of the stream, head for land.

We thank Dr. Ben J. Korgen for his contribution to this article.

TIME OF LOCAL APPARENT NOON (L.A.N.) 2019
FOR THE CENTRAL MERIDIAN OF ANY TIME ZONE

LOCAL APPARENT NOON 2019

	JAN.	FEB.	MAR.	APR.	MAY	JUN.	JUL.	AUG.	SEP.	OCT.	NOV.	DEC.
	h:m:s	h:m:s	h:m:s	h:m:s	h:m:s	h:m:s	h:m:s	h:m:s	h:m:s	h:m:s	h:m:s	h:m:s
1	12:03:32	12:13:34	12:12:21	12:03:54	11:57:07	11:57:51	12:03:53	12:06:21	12:00:01	11:49:40	11:43:34	11:48:59
2	12:04:00	12:13:41	12:12:09	12:03:36	11:57:00	11:58:00	12:04:04	12:06:17	11:59:42	11:49:21	11:43:33	11:49:22
3	12:04:28	12:13:48	12:11:56	12:03:19	11:56:54	11:58:10	12:04:15	12:06:13	11:59:23	11:49:02	11:43:33	11:49:45
4	12:04:56	12:13:54	12:11:44	12:03:01	11:56:48	11:58:20	12:04:26	12:06:07	11:59:03	11:48:44	11:43:33	11:50:09
5	12:05:23	12:13:59	12:11:30	12:02:44	11:56:43	11:58:31	12:04:37	12:06:01	11:58:43	11:48:25	11:43:35	11:50:33
6	12:05:49	12:14:04	12:11:17	12:02:27	11:56:39	11:58:42	12:04:47	12:05:55	11:58:23	11:48:07	11:43:37	11:50:59
7	12:06:15	12:14:07	12:11:03	12:02:10	11:56:34	11:58:53	12:04:57	12:05:48	11:58:02	11:47:50	11:43:40	11:51:24
8	12:06:41	12:14:10	12:10:48	12:01:54	11:56:31	11:59:04	12:05:06	12:05:40	11:57:42	11:47:33	11:43:43	11:51:50
9	12:07:06	12:14:12	12:10:33	12:01:37	11:56:28	11:59:16	12:05:15	12:05:32	11:57:21	11:47:16	11:43:48	11:52:17
10	12:07:31	12:14:13	12:10:18	12:01:21	11:56:26	11:59:28	12:05:24	12:05:23	11:57:00	11:47:00	11:43:53	11:52:44
11	12:07:55	12:14:14	12:10:03	12:01:05	11:56:24	11:59:40	12:05:32	12:05:14	11:56:39	11:46:44	11:43:59	11:53:11
12	12:08:18	12:14:13	12:09:47	12:00:50	11:56:23	11:59:52	12:05:40	12:05:04	11:56:17	11:46:29	11:44:07	11:53:39
13	12:08:41	12:14:12	12:09:30	12:00:34	11:56:22	12:00:05	12:05:47	12:04:53	11:55:56	11:46:14	11:44:15	11:54:07
14	12:09:03	12:14:10	12:09:14	12:00:19	11:56:22	12:00:17	12:05:54	12:04:42	11:55:34	11:46:00	11:44:23	11:54:35
15	12:09:24	12:14:07	12:08:57	12:00:05	11:56:22	12:00:30	12:06:00	12:04:30	11:55:13	11:45:46	11:44:33	11:55:04
16	12:09:45	12:14:04	12:08:40	11:59:50	11:56:23	12:00:43	12:06:05	12:04:18	11:54:51	11:45:33	11:44:43	11:55:33
17	12:10:05	12:14:00	12:08:23	11:59:36	11:56:25	12:00:56	12:06:11	12:04:05	11:54:30	11:45:21	11:44:55	11:56:02
18	12:10:24	12:13:55	12:08:06	11:59:22	11:56:27	12:01:08	12:06:15	12:03:52	11:54:08	11:45:09	11:45:07	11:56:31
19	12:10:43	12:13:49	12:07:48	11:59:09	11:56:29	12:01:21	12:06:19	12:03:38	11:53:47	11:44:57	11:45:20	11:57:01
20	12:11:00	12:13:43	12:07:30	11:58:56	11:56:32	12:01:34	12:06:23	12:03:24	11:53:26	11:44:47	11:45:34	11:57:31
21	12:11:17	12:13:36	12:07:12	11:58:44	11:56:36	12:01:47	12:06:26	12:03:09	11:53:04	11:44:37	11:45:49	11:58:01
22	12:11:34	12:13:29	12:06:54	11:58:32	11:56:40	12:02:00	12:06:28	12:02:54	11:52:43	11:44:27	11:46:04	11:58:31
23	12:11:49	12:13:21	12:06:36	11:58:21	11:56:45	12:02:13	12:06:30	12:02:38	11:52:22	11:44:19	11:46:21	11:59:00
24	12:12:04	12:13:12	12:06:18	11:58:10	11:56:50	12:02:26	12:06:31	12:02:22	11:52:01	11:44:11	11:46:38	11:59:30
25	12:12:18	12:13:03	12:06:00	11:57:59	11:56:56	12:02:39	12:06:32	12:02:06	11:51:40	11:44:04	11:46:56	12:00:00
26	12:12:31	12:12:53	12:05:42	11:57:49	11:57:03	12:02:52	12:06:32	12:01:49	11:51:20	11:43:57	11:47:15	12:00:30
27	12:12:44	12:12:43	12:05:24	11:57:40	11:57:09	12:03:04	12:06:32	12:01:32	11:50:59	11:43:51	11:47:34	12:01:00
28	12:12:55	12:12:32	12:05:06	11:57:31	11:57:17	12:03:17	12:06:31	12:01:15	11:50:39	11:43:46	11:47:54	12:01:29
29	12:13:06		12:04:48	11:57:22	11:57:25	12:03:29	12:06:29	12:00:57	11:50:19	11:43:42	11:48:15	12:01:59
30	12:13:16		12:04:30	11:57:14	11:57:33	12:03:41	12:06:27	12:00:39	11:50:00	11:43:39	11:48:37	12:02:28
31	12:13:25		12:04:12		11:57:41		12:06:24	12:00:20		11:43:36		12:02:57

Explanatory Notes: The noon sight and the Sun's Declination (p. 233) result in the vessel's parallel of latitude. It is taken at the time of the sun's meridian passage, when the sun is at maximum altitude.

The moment of meridian passage is called Local Apparent Noon (L.A.N.), and only rarely is it the same time as noon Standard Time or Local Mean Time. Instead, as this Table shows, the sun is either ahead of or behind its theoretical schedule.

Two corrections are involved. 1) To correct for your difference in longitude from the central meridian of your time zone (i.e. 75° for U.S. Atlantic Coast), either a) add 4 minutes of time for each degree West or b) subtract 4 minutes of time for each degree East. 2) If necessary, convert from Daylight Savings Time to Standard Time by subtracting 1 hour from your watch.

Thus for Boston, at 71° West longitude (or 4° East of 75°), L.A.N. occurs 16 minutes before the times listed in the Table.

For New York, at 74° West (1° East of 75°), L.A.N. occurs 4 minutes earlier than times shown.

Converting arc to time:

360° =	24	hours
15° =	1	hour
1° =	4	minutes
15' =	1	minute
1' =	4	seconds

Sun's True Bearing at Rising and Setting

To find compass deviation using the Sun.

Figures are correct for all Longitudes.

Sun's decl.	38°N		40°N		42°N		44°N		Sun's decl.
	Rise	Set	Rise	Set	Rise	Set	Rise	Set	
N 23°	60.3	299.7	59.3	300.7	58.3	301.7	57.1	302.9	N 23°
22	61.6	298.4	60.7	299.3	59.7	300.3	58.6	301.4	22
21	63.0	297.0	62.1	297.9	61.2	298.8	60.1	299.9	21
20	64.3	295.7	63.5	296.5	62.6	297.4	61.6	298.4	20
19	65.6	294.4	64.9	295.1	64.0	296.0	63.1	296.9	19
18	66.9	293.1	66.2	293.8	65.4	294.6	64.6	295.4	18
17	68.2	291.8	67.6	292.4	66.8	293.2	66.0	294.0	17
16	69.5	290.5	68.9	291.1	68.2	291.8	67.5	292.5	16
15	70.8	289.2	70.3	289.7	69.6	290.4	68.9	291.1	15
14	72.1	287.9	71.6	288.4	71.0	289.0	70.4	289.6	14
13	73.4	286.6	72.9	287.1	72.4	287.6	71.8	288.2	13
12	74.7	285.3	74.3	285.7	73.8	286.2	73.2	286.8	12
11	76.0	284.0	75.6	284.4	75.1	284.9	74.6	285.4	11
10	77.3	282.7	76.9	283.1	76.5	283.5	76.0	284.0	10
9	78.6	281.4	78.2	281.8	77.9	282.1	77.4	282.6	9
8	79.8	280.2	79.5	280.5	79.2	280.8	78.9	281.1	8
7	81.1	278.9	80.9	279.1	80.6	279.4	80.3	279.7	7
6	82.4	277.6	82.2	277.7	81.9	278.1	81.7	278.3	6
5	83.7	276.3	83.5	276.5	83.3	276.7	83.0	277.0	5
4	84.9	275.1	84.8	275.2	84.6	275.4	84.4	275.6	4
3	86.2	273.8	86.1	273.9	86.0	274.0	85.8	274.2	3
2	87.5	272.5	87.4	272.6	87.3	272.7	87.2	272.8	2
N 1°	88.7	271.3	88.7	271.3	88.7	271.3	88.6	271.4	N 1°
0	90.0	270.0	90.0	270.0	90.0	270.0	90.0	270.0	0
S 1°	91.3	268.7	91.3	268.7	91.3	268.7	91.4	268.6	S 1°
2	92.5	267.5	92.6	267.4	92.7	267.3	92.8	267.2	2
3	93.8	266.2	93.9	266.1	94.0	266.0	94.2	265.8	3
4	95.1	264.9	95.2	264.8	95.4	264.6	95.6	264.4	4
5	96.3	263.7	96.5	263.5	96.7	263.3	97.0	263.0	5
6	97.6	262.4	97.8	262.2	98.1	261.9	98.3	261.7	6
7	98.9	261.1	99.1	260.9	99.4	260.6	99.7	260.3	7
8	100.2	259.8	100.5	259.5	100.8	259.2	101.1	258.9	8
9	101.4	258.6	101.8	258.2	102.1	257.9	102.6	257.4	9
10	102.7	257.3	103.1	256.9	103.5	256.5	104.0	256.0	10
11	104.0	256.0	104.4	255.6	104.9	255.1	105.4	254.6	11
12	105.3	254.7	105.7	254.3	106.2	253.8	106.8	253.2	12
13	106.6	253.4	107.1	252.9	107.6	252.4	108.2	251.8	13
14	107.9	252.1	108.4	251.6	109.0	251.0	109.6	250.4	14
15	109.2	250.8	109.7	250.3	110.4	249.6	111.1	248.9	15
16	110.5	249.5	111.1	248.9	111.8	248.2	112.5	247.5	16
17	111.8	248.2	112.4	247.6	113.2	246.8	114.0	246.0	17
18	113.1	246.9	113.8	246.2	114.6	245.4	115.4	244.6	18
19	114.4	245.6	115.1	244.9	116.0	244.0	116.9	243.1	19
20	115.7	244.3	116.5	243.5	117.4	242.6	118.4	241.6	20
21	117.0	243.0	117.9	242.1	118.8	241.2	119.9	240.1	21
22	118.4	241.6	119.3	240.7	120.3	239.7	121.4	238.6	22
S 23°	119.7	240.3	120.7	239.3	121.7	238.3	122.9	237.1	S 23°

Instructions: (1) Knowing the date, find the Sun's Declination from the facing page. Find that Declination down the left column on this page. (2) Find the column with your Latitude, and choose either Rise or Set to determine the True Bearing. (3) Add the local Westerly Variation to the figure. (4) If you are a couple of minutes after sunrise or before sunset, the Sun's bearing changes about 1° each 6 minutes during the first hour after sunrise and before sunset. (5) The deviation found will be correct only for the heading you are on at that time.

232

The Sun's Declination 2019

For celestial navigators, the "noon sight" reading of the Sun's height above the horizon, together with the Sun's Declination from this table, determines latitude.

The Sun's Declination 2019

MEAN NOON – 75° MERIDIAN (1700 G.M.T.)

Day	JAN. South	FEB. South	MAR. South	APR. North	MAY North	JUN. North	JUL. North	AUG. North	SEP. North	OCT. South	NOV. South	DEC. South
1	-22 58	-16 58	-7 25	+4 43	+15 12	+22 07	+23 04	+17 54	+8 07	-3 21	-14 34	-21 52
2	-22 52	-16 41	-7 02	+5 06	+15 30	+22 14	+22 60	+17 39	+7 45	-3 45	-14 53	-22 01
3	-22 46	-16 23	-6 39	+5 29	+15 48	+22 22	+22 55	+17 23	+7 23	-4 08	-15 12	-22 09
4	-22 40	-16 05	-6 16	+5 51	+16 05	+22 29	+22 50	+17 07	+7 01	-4 31	-15 30	-22 17
5	-22 33	-15 47	-5 53	+6 14	+16 23	+22 35	+22 44	+16 51	+6 39	-4 54	-15 48	-22 25
6	-22 26	-15 29	-5 30	+6 37	+16 39	+22 42	+22 38	+16 34	+6 16	-5 17	-16 06	-22 32
7	-22 19	-15 10	-5 06	+6 59	+16 56	+22 47	+22 32	+16 18	+5 54	-5 40	-16 24	-22 39
8	-22 11	-14 51	-4 43	+7 22	+17 12	+22 53	+22 25	+16 01	+5 31	-6 03	-16 41	-22 45
9	-22 02	-14 32	-4 20	+7 44	+17 28	+22 58	+22 18	+15 43	+5 09	-6 26	-16 59	-22 51
10	-21 53	-14 12	-3 56	+8 06	+17 44	+23 02	+22 10	+15 26	+4 46	-6 48	-17 16	-22 57
11	-21 44	-13 53	-3 33	+8 28	+17 59	+23 07	+22 02	+15 08	+4 23	-7 11	-17 32	-23 02
12	-21 34	-13 33	-3 09	+8 50	+18 15	+23 10	+21 54	+14 50	+4 00	-7 34	-17 48	-23 06
13	-21 24	-13 12	-2 45	+9 12	+18 29	+23 14	+21 45	+14 32	+3 37	-7 56	-18 04	-23 10
14	-21 13	-12 52	-2 22	+9 34	+18 44	+23 17	+21 36	+14 13	+3 14	-8 18	-18 20	-23 14
15	-21 02	-12 31	-1 58	+9 55	+18 58	+23 19	+21 27	+13 54	+2 51	-8 41	-18 35	-23 17
16	-20 51	-12 11	-1 34	+10 17	+19 12	+23 22	+21 17	+13 36	+2 28	-9 03	-18 50	-23 20
17	-20 39	-11 50	-1 10	+10 38	+19 25	+23 23	+21 07	+13 16	+2 05	-9 25	-19 05	-23 22
18	-20 27	-11 28	-0 47	+10 59	+19 39	+23 25	+20 56	+12 57	+1 42	-9 46	-19 19	-23 24
19	-20 14	-11 07	-0 23	+11 19	+19 52	+23 26	+20 46	+12 37	+1 19	-10 08	-19 33	-23 25
20	-20 01	-10 46	+0 01	+11 40	+20 04	+23 26	+20 34	+12 18	+0 55	-10 30	-19 47	-23 26
21	-19 48	-10 24	+0 24	+12 00	+20 16	+23 26	+20 23	+11 58	+0 32	-10 51	-20 00	-23 26
22	-19 34	-10 02	+0 48	+12 21	+20 28	+23 26	+20 11	+11 38	+0 09	-11 12	-20 13	-23 26
23	-19 20	-9 40	+1 12	+12 41	+20 40	+23 25	+19 59	+11 17	-0 15	-11 33	-20 26	-23 25
24	-19 06	-9 18	+1 35	+13 00	+20 51	+23 24	+19 46	+10 57	-0 38	-11 54	-20 38	-23 24
25	-18 51	-8 56	+1 59	+13 20	+21 02	+23 22	+19 33	+10 36	-1 01	-12 15	-20 50	-23 23
26	-18 36	-8 33	+2 23	+13 39	+21 12	+23 20	+19 20	+10 15	-1 25	-12 35	-21 01	-23 21
27	-18 20	-8 11	+2 46	+13 58	+21 22	+23 18	+19 06	+9 54	-1 48	-12 55	-21 12	-23 18
28	-18 05	-7 48	+3 09	+14 17	+21 32	+23 15	+18 52	+9 33	-2 11	-13 16	-21 22	-23 15
29	-17 48		+3 33	+14 36	+21 41	+23 12	+18 38	+9 12	-2 35	-13 35	-21 33	-23 12
30	-17 32		+3 56	+14 54	+21 50	+23 08	+18 24	+8 50	-2 58	-13 55	-21 42	-23 08
31	-17 15		+4 19		+21 58		+18 09	+8 29		-14 15		-23 04

Vernal Equinox: March 20th, 4:58 p.m. E.S.T.
Summer Solstice: June 21st, 10:54 a.m. E.S.T.

Autumnal Equinox: September 23rd, 2:50 a.m. E.S.T.
Winter Solstice: December 21st, 11:19 p.m. E.S.T.

To find Sun's Declination in the Atlantic Time Zone (1 hour earlier than E.S.T.), take 1/24 of the difference between Day 1 and Day 2. Add or subtract this figure from Day 2 to find the Declination for Day 2.

If Declination is increasing (N. or S.), *subtract*.   If Declination is decreasing (N. or S.), *add*.

2019 MOON'S RISING AND SETTING AT BOSTON – 42° 20'N 71°W
Daylight Saving Time is March 10 – November 3, transitions are noted with an *

Day	JAN. Rise h m	JAN. Set h m	FEB. Rise h m	FEB. Set h m	MAR. Rise h m	MAR. Set h m	APR. Rise h m	APR. Set h m	MAY Rise h m	MAY Set h m	JUN. Rise h m	JUN. Set h m	Day
01	2:49	13:32	4:42	14:12	3:29	12:58	5:05	15:35	4:30	16:23	4:17	18:21	01
02	3:53	14:06	5:34	15:03	4:15	13:51	5:34	16:34	4:55	17:24	4:50	19:29	02
03	4:54	14:45	6:16	15:57	4:56	14:47	6:01	17:34	5:20	18:27	5:29	20:36	03
04	5:52	15:28	6:55	16:54	5:31	15:45	6:27	18:34	5:48	19:31	6:16	21:41	04
05	6:46	16:16	7:29	17:52	6:03	16:44	6:52	19:35	6:18	20:37	7:10	22:41	05
06	7:35	17:08	8:00	18:50	6:31	17:43	7:18	20:38	6:53	21:44	8:13	23:32	06
07	8:17	18:03	8:27	19:49	6:57	18:42	7:46	21:42	7:34	22:49	9:22	...	07
08	8:55	19:01	8:53	20:48	7:23	19:42	8:18	22:47	8:23	23:50	10:34	0:17	08
09	9:28	19:59	9:19	21:48	7:48	20:43	8:54	23:52	9:19	...	11:47	0:55	09
10	9:57	20:57	9:44	22:49	*9:15	22:45	9:37	...	10:23	0:45	12:59	1:28	10
11	10:24	21:56	10:12	23:52	9:44	23:48	10:27	0:55	11:32	1:34	14:09	1:58	11
12	10:50	22:56	10:42	...	10:17	...	11:26	1:54	12:44	2:15	15:19	2:27	12
13	11:15	23:57	11:18	0:57	10:55	0:53	12:32	2:47	13:56	2:51	16:29	2:56	13
14	11:42	...	11:59	2:03	11:40	1:57	13:43	3:33	15:08	3:24	17:37	3:27	14
15	12:11	1:00	12:50	3:09	12:34	3:00	14:56	4:14	16:20	3:54	18:44	4:01	15
16	12:45	2:05	13:50	4:13	13:37	3:58	16:11	4:50	17:31	4:24	19:48	4:39	16
17	13:24	3:13	14:59	5:11	14:47	4:51	17:25	5:22	18:42	4:54	20:48	5:22	17
18	14:12	4:22	16:14	6:02	16:02	5:37	18:39	5:54	19:52	5:27	21:40	6:11	18
19	15:09	5:30	17:31	6:47	17:19	6:17	19:51	6:25	20:59	6:03	22:26	7:04	19
20	16:15	6:33	18:48	7:25	18:35	6:53	21:03	6:57	22:02	6:44	23:05	8:01	20
21	17:28	7:29	20:04	8:00	19:50	7:26	22:11	7:32	22:58	7:30	23:39	9:00	21
22	18:45	8:16	21:17	8:31	21:04	7:57	23:16	8:10	23:48	8:21	...	9:59	22
23	20:01	8:57	22:27	9:02	22:15	8:29	...	8:53	...	9:16	0:08	10:59	23
24	21:15	9:32	23:35	9:34	23:24	9:03	0:15	9:41	0:30	10:13	0:35	11:58	24
25	22:26	10:04	...	10:07	...	9:39	1:08	10:33	1:07	11:12	1:00	12:57	25
26	23:35	10:34	0:40	10:44	0:29	10:18	1:53	11:28	1:38	12:11	1:24	13:57	26
27	...	11:04	1:41	11:24	1:30	11:03	2:33	12:26	2:07	13:11	1:49	14:59	27
28	0:41	11:35	2:38	12:09	2:25	11:51	3:07	13:24	2:32	14:10	2:16	16:03	28
29	1:46	12:08			3:13	12:44	3:37	14:24	2:57	15:10	2:47	17:09	29
30	2:48	12:45			3:56	13:39	4:04	15:23	3:22	16:12	3:22	18:17	30
31	3:47	13:26			4:33	14:37			3:49	17:16			31

Day	JUL. Rise h m	JUL. Set h m	AUG. Rise h m	AUG. Set h m	SEP. Rise h m	SEP. Set h m	OCT. Rise h m	OCT. Set h m	NOV. Rise h m	NOV. Set h m	DEC. Rise h m	DEC. Set h m	Day
01	4:05	19:24	5:56	20:48	8:38	21:01	9:57	20:34	12:05	21:21	11:17	21:02	01
02	4:57	20:28	7:13	21:27	9:53	21:32	11:09	21:11	12:57	22:17	11:51	22:03	02
03	5:58	21:24	8:30	22:02	11:06	22:04	12:17	21:53	*12:42	22:16	12:21	23:03	03
04	7:06	22:13	9:46	22:33	12:17	22:38	13:19	22:41	13:19	23:16	12:47	...	04
05	8:20	22:55	10:59	23:03	13:24	23:17	14:14	23:33	13:51	...	13:11	0:02	05
06	9:34	23:30	12:10	23:33	14:28	23:59	15:02	...	14:19	0:16	13:35	1:01	06
07	10:48	...	13:20	...	15:26	...	15:43	0:29	14:44	1:15	13:58	2:01	07
08	12:00	0:02	14:28	0:05	16:18	0:48	16:18	1:27	15:08	2:14	14:23	3:02	08
09	13:11	0:31	15:33	0:39	17:03	1:40	16:48	2:26	15:31	3:14	14:51	4:04	09
10	14:20	1:00	16:34	1:18	17:41	2:36	17:15	3:26	15:56	4:14	15:23	5:08	10
11	15:28	1:30	17:30	2:02	18:15	3:35	17:40	4:25	16:22	5:15	16:01	6:14	11
12	16:35	2:03	18:19	2:52	18:44	4:34	18:04	5:24	16:51	6:18	16:47	7:19	12
13	17:39	2:38	19:03	3:45	19:11	5:33	18:27	6:24	17:25	7:23	17:41	8:21	13
14	18:39	3:19	19:40	4:42	19:35	6:32	18:52	7:24	18:05	8:27	18:44	9:18	14
15	19:34	4:05	20:12	5:41	19:59	7:31	19:19	8:25	18:53	9:30	19:52	10:07	15
16	20:22	4:56	20:41	6:41	20:23	8:30	19:50	9:28	19:49	10:29	21:04	10:50	16
17	21:03	5:52	21:06	7:40	20:49	9:30	20:25	10:31	20:53	11:22	22:17	11:26	17
18	21:39	6:50	21:31	8:39	21:16	10:31	21:08	11:34	22:01	12:08	23:29	11:58	18
19	22:10	7:49	21:55	9:37	21:49	11:34	21:58	12:35	23:13	12:48	...	12:27	19
20	22:38	8:49	22:19	10:37	22:26	12:37	22:56	13:32	...	13:22	0:41	12:55	20
21	23:03	9:48	22:46	11:37	23:11	13:40	...	14:23	0:26	13:53	1:52	13:24	21
22	23:27	10:46	23:15	12:39	...	14:41	0:02	15:07	1:39	14:23	3:04	13:55	22
23	23:51	11:45	23:50	13:42	0:05	15:37	1:13	15:46	2:53	14:52	4:15	14:30	23
24	...	12:45	...	14:47	1:08	16:27	2:27	16:21	4:06	15:23	5:25	15:10	24
25	0:17	13:47	0:31	15:51	2:18	17:11	3:43	16:53	5:20	15:56	6:32	15:56	25
26	0:45	14:51	1:21	16:52	3:34	17:50	4:59	17:23	6:33	16:34	7:33	16:48	26
27	1:17	15:57	2:21	17:48	4:51	18:24	6:15	17:54	7:44	17:18	8:26	17:46	27
28	1:56	17:04	3:29	18:37	6:09	18:56	7:30	18:27	8:49	18:07	9:12	18:47	28
29	2:42	18:09	4:45	19:19	7:26	19:27	8:45	19:03	9:47	19:02	9:49	19:48	29
30	3:38	19:09	6:03	19:56	8:43	19:59	9:57	19:44	10:36	20:01	10:21	20:49	30
31	4:44	20:02	7:21	20:30			11:04	20:30			10:49	21:50	31

2019 MOON'S RISING AND SETTING AT NEW YORK – 40° 42'N 74°W
Daylight Saving Time is March 10 – November 3, transitions are noted with an *

	JAN. Rise	JAN. Set	FEB. Rise	FEB. Set	MAR. Rise	MAR. Set	APR. Rise	APR. Set	MAY Rise	MAY Set	JUN. Rise	JUN. Set	
Day	h m	h m	h m	h m	h m	h m	h m	h m	h m	h m	h m	h m	Day
01	2:59	13:47	4:49	14:30	3:37	13:16	5:14	15:51	4:41	16:36	4:32	18:31	01
02	4:02	14:23	5:39	15:20	4:23	14:08	5:44	16:49	5:07	17:36	5:06	19:37	02
03	5:02	15:02	6:24	16:14	5:04	15:04	6:12	17:48	5:34	18:38	5:46	20:44	03
04	6:00	15:45	7:03	17:10	5:40	16:01	6:38	18:47	6:02	19:41	6:33	21:49	04
05	6:54	16:33	7:38	18:07	6:12	16:59	7:04	19:47	6:34	20:46	7:28	22:48	05
06	7:42	17:25	8:09	19:05	6:41	17:57	7:32	20:49	7:09	21:52	8:31	23:40	06
07	8:25	18:20	8:38	20:03	7:08	18:55	8:01	21:51	7:51	22:56	9:39	...	07
08	9:03	19:17	9:05	21:01	7:35	19:54	8:33	22:55	8:40	23:57	10:50	0:25	08
09	9:37	20:14	9:31	22:00	8:01	20:54	9:11	23:59	9:37	...	12:02	1:04	09
10	10:07	21:12	9:58	23:00	*9:29	22:55	9:54	...	10:41	0:53	13:12	1:38	10
11	10:35	22:10	10:26	...	9:59	23:58	10:45	1:02	11:49	1:42	14:22	2:10	11
12	11:01	23:09	10:57	0:02	10:32	1:00	11:44	2:01	13:00	2:24	15:31	2:40	12
13	11:28	...	11:34	1:06	11:12	1:01	12:49	2:54	14:11	3:01	16:39	3:10	13
14	11:56	0:08	12:16	2:11	11:58	2:05	13:59	3:41	15:22	3:35	17:47	3:42	14
15	12:26	1:10	13:07	3:17	12:52	3:07	15:12	4:23	16:32	4:06	18:53	4:17	15
16	13:00	2:15	14:07	4:20	13:55	4:06	16:25	5:00	17:43	4:37	19:56	4:56	16
17	13:41	3:22	15:16	5:19	15:04	4:59	17:38	5:34	18:52	5:09	20:55	5:40	17
18	14:29	4:30	16:30	6:11	16:18	5:46	18:50	6:06	20:01	5:42	21:47	6:29	18
19	15:26	5:38	17:47	6:56	17:33	6:27	20:02	6:38	21:07	6:20	22:33	7:22	19
20	16:32	6:40	19:03	7:35	18:49	7:04	21:12	7:12	22:09	7:01	23:13	8:19	20
21	17:45	7:37	20:17	8:11	20:03	7:38	22:20	7:47	23:05	7:48	23:48	9:17	21
22	19:01	8:25	21:28	8:44	21:15	8:11	23:24	8:27	23:55	8:39	...	10:15	22
23	20:15	9:06	22:38	9:16	22:25	8:44	...	9:11	...	9:34	0:18	11:13	23
24	21:28	9:43	23:44	9:49	23:33	9:18	0:22	9:59	0:38	10:30	0:45	12:12	24
25	22:38	10:16		10:23	...	9:55	1:15	10:51	1:15	11:28	1:11	13:10	25
26	23:46	10:47	0:48	11:00	0:37	10:35	2:01	11:46	1:47	12:27	1:37	14:09	26
27	...	11:18	1:49	11:41	1:37	11:20	2:41	12:43	2:16	13:25	2:03	15:10	27
28	0:52	11:50	2:45	12:26	2:32	12:09	3:15	13:40	2:43	14:23	2:31	16:13	28
29	1:55	12:24			3:21	13:01	3:46	14:39	3:09	15:23	3:02	17:18	29
30	2:56	13:02			4:03	13:56	4:14	15:37	3:35	16:23	3:39	18:25	30
31	3:55	13:43			4:41	14:53			4:02	17:26			31

	JUL. Rise	JUL. Set	AUG. Rise	AUG. Set	SEP. Rise	SEP. Set	OCT. Rise	OCT. Set	NOV. Rise	NOV. Set	DEC. Rise	DEC. Set	
Day	h m	h m	h m	h m	h m	h m	h m	h m	h m	h m	h m	h m	Day
01	4:22	19:32	6:13	20:57	8:51	21:14	10:07	20:49	12:12	21:39	11:24	21:19	01
02	5:14	20:35	7:29	21:37	10:05	21:46	11:17	21:28	13:04	22:35	12:00	22:19	02
03	6:15	21:32	8:45	22:12	11:16	22:19	12:24	22:11	*12:49	22:33	12:30	23:18	03
04	7:24	22:21	9:59	22:45	12:26	22:54	13:26	22:59	13:27	23:32	12:57	...	04
05	8:36	23:04	11:11	23:16	13:33	23:34	14:21	23:51	14:00	...	13:22	0:16	05
06	9:50	23:40	12:22	23:47	14:36	...	15:09	...	14:28	0:31	13:47	1:15	06
07	11:03	...	13:30	...	15:33	0:17	15:50	0:46	14:55	1:30	14:11	2:13	07
08	12:14	0:13	14:37	0:20	16:25	1:05	16:26	1:44	15:19	2:28	14:37	3:13	08
09	13:23	0:44	15:41	0:56	17:10	1:58	16:57	2:42	15:44	3:26	15:06	4:14	09
10	14:31	1:14	16:41	1:35	17:49	2:54	17:25	3:41	16:09	4:25	15:39	5:17	10
11	15:38	1:45	17:37	2:20	18:23	3:51	17:51	4:39	16:36	5:26	16:18	6:22	11
12	16:44	2:18	18:27	3:09	18:54	4:50	18:15	5:37	17:07	6:28	17:04	7:26	12
13	17:47	2:55	19:10	4:03	19:21	5:48	18:40	6:36	17:42	7:31	17:59	8:28	13
14	18:47	3:36	19:48	5:00	19:46	6:46	19:06	7:35	18:23	8:35	19:01	9:25	14
15	19:41	4:23	20:21	5:58	20:11	7:44	19:34	8:35	19:11	9:37	20:09	10:15	15
16	20:29	5:14	20:50	6:56	20:36	8:42	20:06	9:37	20:07	10:36	21:20	10:58	16
17	21:11	6:09	21:17	7:54	21:03	9:41	20:42	10:39	21:10	11:29	22:32	11:35	17
18	21:48	7:07	21:42	8:52	21:32	10:41	21:25	11:42	22:18	12:16	23:43	12:08	18
19	22:19	8:05	22:07	9:50	22:05	11:43	22:16	12:42	23:29	12:56	...	12:38	19
20	22:48	9:04	22:33	10:48	22:43	12:45	23:14	13:39	...	13:32	0:53	13:08	20
21	23:14	10:02	23:00	11:47	23:29	13:47	...	14:30	0:41	14:04	2:03	13:38	21
22	23:39	11:00	23:31	12:48	...	14:48	0:19	15:15	1:53	14:35	3:14	14:10	22
23	...	11:58	...	13:51	0:23	15:44	1:29	15:55	3:05	15:05	4:24	14:46	23
24	0:04	12:57	0:06	14:55	1:26	16:35	2:42	16:31	4:17	15:37	5:33	15:27	24
25	0:31	13:57	0:48	15:58	2:35	17:20	3:57	17:04	5:30	16:12	6:39	16:14	25
26	1:00	15:00	1:39	16:59	3:50	17:59	5:11	17:36	6:42	16:51	7:40	17:06	26
27	1:33	16:05	2:39	17:55	5:06	18:35	6:26	18:08	7:51	17:35	8:33	18:04	27
28	2:12	17:11	3:47	18:45	6:23	19:08	7:41	18:42	8:56	18:25	9:19	19:04	28
29	2:59	18:16	5:01	19:29	7:39	19:41	8:54	19:19	9:53	19:20	9:57	20:05	29
30	3:56	19:16	6:18	20:07	8:53	20:14	10:05	20:01	10:43	20:19	10:30	21:05	30
31	5:01	20:10	7:35	20:41			11:12	20:48			10:59	22:04	31

PHASES OF THE MOON 2019 E.T.

Daylight Saving Time is March 10 – November 3, transitions are noted with an *

● New Moon, ◑ 1st Quarter, ○ Full Moon, ◐ Last Quarter, A in Apogee,
P in Perigee, N, S Moon farthest North or South of Equator, E on Equator

January	February	March	April	May	June
S 5 2PM	S 1 8PM	S 1 2AM	E 4 10PM	E 2 6AM	● 3 6AM
● 5 8PM	● 4 4PM	A 3 6AM	● 5 5AM	● 4 7PM	N 5 9AM
A 8 11PM	A 5 4AM	● 6 11AM	N 11 8PM	N 9 2AM	P 7 7PM
E 13 3AM	E 9 10AM	E 8 3PM	◑ 12 3PM	◑ 11 9PM	◑ 10 2AM
◑ 14 2AM	◑ 12 5PM	◑ 14 *6AM	P 16 6PM	P 13 6PM	E 11 6PM
N 19 7PM	N 16 5AM	N 15 2PM	E 18 3AM	E 15 11AM	○ 17 5AM
○ 21 12AM	P 19 4AM	P 19 4PM	○ 19 7AM	○ 18 5PM	S 18 12PM
P 21 3PM	○ 19 11AM	○ 20 10PM	S 24 6PM	S 22 3AM	A 23 4AM
E 25 8PM	E 22 5AM	E 21 4PM	◐ 26 6PM	A 26 9AM	◐ 25 6AM
◐ 27 4PM	◐ 26 6AM	◐ 28 12AM	A 28 2PM	◐ 26 1PM	E 26 12AM
		S 28 9AM		E 29 3PM	
		A 31 8PM			

July	August	September	October	November	December
● 2 3PM	P 2 3AM	E 1 2PM	◑ 5 1PM	S 1 9PM	◑ 4 2AM
N 2 6PM	E 5 6AM	◑ 5 11PM	S 5 1PM	◑ 4 *5AM	A 4 11PM
P 5 1AM	◑ 7 2PM	S 8 6AM	A 10 2PM	A 7 4AM	E 6 4PM
E 8 11PM	S 12 1AM	A 13 10AM	E 13 1AM	E 9 7AM	○ 12 12AM
◑ 9 7AM	○ 15 8AM	○ 14 1AM	○ 13 5PM	○ 12 9AM	N 13 4PM
S 15 7PM	A 17 7AM	E 15 7PM	N 20 4AM	N 16 9AM	P 18 3PM
○ 16 6PM	E 19 1PM	◐ 21 11PM	◐ 21 9AM	◐ 19 4PM	◐ 19 12AM
A 20 8PM	◐ 23 11AM	N 22 10PM	P 26 7AM	E 22 8PM	E 20 2AM
E 23 7AM	N 26 2PM	P 27 10PM	E 26 12PM	P 23 3AM	● 26 12AM
◐ 24 9PM	● 30 7AM	● 28 2PM	● 28 12AM	● 26 10AM	S 26 3PM
N 30 5AM	P 30 12PM	E 29 1AM		S 29 6AM	
● 31 11PM					

Midnight is the *beginning* of the day.

The Tides, The Moon and The Sun

Tides are created on the earth by the pull of gravity between the earth and moon, and to a lesser extent the sun. Since the moon's pull weakens with distance, its pull is stronger on water located on the near side of the earth than it is on the earth's center. This creates a bulge of water on the side facing the moon. Similarly, the moon's pull on the earth's center is stronger than it is on the water on the earth's far side. This tends to pull the earth away from the water, creating another bulge of water of equal size on the far side of the earth. High tides are where the bulges are. The two bulges can also be explained as the moon's gravity being dominant on the earth's near side, and centrifugal force being dominant on the earth's far side.

The earth rotates in the same direction as the moon orbits, but much more rapidly, with a period of 24 hours vs. 27.3 days. The earth thus spins rapidly under the slowly rotating bulges, which follow the moon. A given point on the earth thus takes 24 hours and 50 minutes to rotate from one tidal bulge around to the same bulge, so the tides occur 50 minutes later than the previous day. As there are usually two highs and two lows per day, highs and lows average about 6 hours 12 1/2 minutes apart. A handy fact for planners: in the course of 7 days, the tides are about the reverse of the previous week: if there is a low on Sunday at about noon, the following Sunday it will be about high at noon.

The time of high tide does not usually coincide exactly with the time the moon is overhead or underneath. The largest astronomical reason for this is the effect of the sun, which has its own tidal effect on the earth. Although the sun has a mass 27 million times that of the moon, it is the moon which dominates by being on average 390 times closer to earth. Since the sun's effect on the tides is about

Continued on p. 238

Billion Oyster Project
by Pete Malinowski

At Billion Oyster Project, we know that most cities grow and flourish at the expense of the natural environments that were integral to their initial success, and that New York City is no exception. New York's early growth was made possible by the abundance of animal protein that was easily accessible in the Hudson River Estuary. Central to that productivity were hundreds of thousands of acres of oyster reefs.

In New York Harbor oyster reefs supported the ecosystem by providing food and habitat to thousands of other species. Oysters filtered water, improved water clarity and their reefs stabilized the bottom of the Harbor, protecting shorelines for storms and waves. Without these reefs, most of the Harbor is flat and featureless leaving most of the animals in the Harbor with nowhere to live and nothing to eat.

Amazingly, it took only about 100 years for New Yorkers to harvest all the oysters and remove the reef habitat from the Harbor. In the three and a half centuries since, pollution, overharvesting, landfills, and dredging further destroyed what was left of this fragile ecosystem. But in the last fifty years, progressive environmental policies have mitigated many of these negative impacts, allowing the Harbor to begin to bounce back. Water quality is greatly improved, making the harbor swimmable and fishable most days of the year, according to EPA standards. Seahorses, mussels, seals, dolphin, seabirds, oyster and clams are all coming back to the Harbor. But without oysters, the Harbor's keystone species, the success of these new residents is limited. With this in mind, one of the main goals of Billion Oyster Project is to restore one billion oysters by 2035 to begin building back this lost habitat.

Billion Oyster Project is an effort to connect the two, often disparate efforts of ecosystem restoration and public education in an urban setting. We believe that students learn best when their lessons are relevant to the place that they live, and their work products have real value to an effort to restore the natural environment. Similarly, we believe that it is imperative to connect young people to the natural resources where they live in order to build and ensure the health of these ecosystems and gradually change the relationship between people and the resource. To achieve our goals we work with the New York Harbor School and one hundred other public schools throughout the city. Furthermore, we know that changing the perception of the city waterways is central to the work of restoring the Harbor. What is currently seen as a system of transportation and waste conveyance, could be understood as a great natural resource and invaluable open space. Therefore, for New York Harbor to thrive, it is essential that the ten million people who live near and benefit from this resource be invested in it. Considering this, we designed Billion Oyster Project to provide access points to people from all walks of life. In addition to our work with students, we operate a shell collection program at restaurants in Brooklyn and Manhattan which provides an opportunity for diners at the some of the finest restaurants in the city to play a role in restoring the Harbor and to learn more about our project.

Ultimately, if we are successful in New York City—with its 10 million people, 600 miles of coastline, and 1.1 million public school students—then we will have created a model that is replicable wherever high densities of people live on or near degraded natural systems.

Pete Malinowski is the Executive Director of Billion Oyster Project. Find out more about this project and how to become involved at www.billionoysterproject.org

The Tides, The Moon and The Sun

Continued from p. 236

one-half that of the moon, the sun can shift tidal times by up to one hour or more, depending on its position. Tidal times are also greatly affected by land masses that impede the current flows necessary to create the tides, the speeds of traveling ocean waves, and underwater topography.

How much the ocean tides rise and fall depends basically on three conditions. (See Phases of the Moon, p. 236.) First, when the sun and moon are in a line with the earth, their gravitational forces work together to produce a greater range of tide than usual. This occurs both at full moon, when the moon is opposite the earth from the sun, and at new moon, when the moon is between the earth and sun. These higher tides are called "spring tides." But when the moon and sun are at right angles to the earth (first and last quarter, or half moon), their forces are working against each other, and the result is a lower range of tide than usual. These are called "neap tides." As each year has about 13 "lunar" months, we have 26 spring tides and 26 neap tides in the year.

Second, the moon's orbit around the earth is elliptical, ranging from 252,000 miles at apogee (A) down to 221,000 miles at perigee (P), so the moon's effect on the earth is greater at "P" than at "A." Note again in the High and Low Water Tables how much higher the tide is when the Full Moon is at "P" than when the Full Moon is at "A." The position of the moon along its elliptical path is very important to the height of the tides.

Third, the moon's orbit about the earth is inclined to the plane of the earth's equator, varying from 18° to 28°. The moon therefore travels above and below the earth's equator, and sits directly above the equator only twice a month When it is over the equator, the day's two high tides will be about the same height. The rest of the time the moon is either above the northern hemisphere or the southern hemisphere, and the two high water marks on the same day will differ in height. This is known as "semidiurnal inequality." When the moon has northern declination, the highest part of the nearside bulge is located under the moon in the north, and the highest part of the farside bulge is opposite the moon in the south. When the U.S. at northern latitudes is on the moon side, it therefore experiences a very high tide, but when it rotates around to be on the far side, it will find itself north of the maximum bulge and will experience a lower tide.

The height of tides is influenced most by the moon's phase, with the highest tides at Full and New Moon; second by the moon's distance from earth in its elliptical orbit, tides being highest when the moon is closest, at perigee; and last by the moon's declination, north or south, which creates tides of different heights on the same day.

For a more exhaustive exploration of astronomical and physical forces acting on the tides, see NOAA's website at http://tidesandcurrents.noaa.gov/restles1.html

The Publishers thank Nelson Caldwell, of the Smithsonian Astrophysical Observatory, Cambridge, MA, and Hale Bradt, Department of Physics, M.I.T., for their valuable contributions to this article.

Visibility of Planets in Twilight

	Morning	Evening
VENUS	January 1 – July 8	September 20 – December 31
MARS	—	January 1 – July 18
	October 17 – December 31	—
JUPITER	January 1 – June 10	June 10 – December 15
SATURN	January 19 – July 9	July 9 – December 27

Visibility of the Planets 2019

MERCURY can only be seen low in the east before sunrise, or low in the west after sunset. It is visible in the mornings from January 1 to January 15, March 22 to May 14, July 30 to August 26 and November 18 to December 25. It is brighter at the end of each period. It is visible in the evenings from February 11 to March 8, May 29 to July 13 and September 15 to November 6. It is brighter at the beginning of each period.

VENUS is a brilliant object in the sky from the beginning of the year until the second week of July when it becomes too close to the Sun for observation. It reappears in the second half of September in the evening sky where it stays until the end of the year. Venus is in conjunction with Mercury on October 30, with Jupiter on January 22 and November 24 and with Saturn on February 18 and December 11.

MARS is visible as a reddish object in Pisces in the evening sky at the beginning of the year. Its eastward elongation decreases as it moves through Aries from mid-February, Taurus from late March (passing 7° N of Aldebaran on April 16), into Gemini from mid-May (passing 6° S of Pollux on June 23) and into Cancer in late June. It becomes too close to the Sun for observation in mid-July. It reappears in the morning sky during the third week of October in Virgo (passing 3° N of Spica on November 8) and then moves into Libra early in December, where it remains for the rest of the year. Mars is in conjunction with Mercury on June 18 and July 17.

JUPITER is visible in the morning sky in Ophiuchus at the beginning of the year. Its westward elongation increases and from mid-March it can be seen for more than half the night. It is at opposition on June 10 when it is visible throughout the night. By early September it can only be seen in the evening sky. It moves into Sagittarius in mid-November and from mid-December becomes too close to the Sun for observation. Jupiter is in conjunction with Venus on January 22 and November 24.

SATURN is too close to the sun for observation from the beginning of the year until the third week of January when it rises just before sunrise in Sagittarius, in which constellation it remains throughout the year. Its westward elongation increases and in mid-April it becomes visible for more than half the night. It is at opposition on July 9 when it can be seen throughout the night. From early October until late December it can only be seen in the evening sky and then becomes too close to the sun for observation for the remainder of the year. Saturn is in conjunction with Venus on February 18 and December 11.

Conjunction Conjunction occurs when a body has the same horizontal bearing from Earth as another. When Venus is in conjunction with Mercury on March 5, they appear one over the other, in the same sector of the sky.

Opposition occurs when a body, farther than Earth from the Sun, appears opposite the Sun. On a line drawn from the Sun through the Earth and beyond, the body lies on that extension. It is brightest at that time.

Elongation is apparent motion eastward (clockwise) or westward (counterclockwise) relative to the Sun across the sky. When a planet has 0° elongation, it lies on a line from Earth to the Sun, is in conjunction with the Sun and is not visible; when it has 90° elongation, it is in eastern quadrature; when it has 180° elongation, it is in opposition and has the best visibility; when it has 270° elongation, it is in western quadrature.

DIAL-A-BUOY Service
Sea-State & Weather Conditions By Telephone

If you are planning a coastwise voyage, you can rely on a number of sources for weather. A possible source is **Dial-A-Buoy**, offering reports of conditions at numerous coastal and offshore locations along the Atlantic Coast, as well as the coasts of the Gulf of Mexico, the Pacific, and the Great Lakes. In all there over 100 buoy and 60 Coastal-Marine Automated Network (C-MAN) stations. The system is operated by the National Data Buoy Center (NDBC), with headquarters at the Stennis Space Center in Mississippi. The NDBC is part of the National Weather Service (NWS).

The reports from offshore buoys include wind speed, gusts, and direction, wave heights and periods, water temperature, and barometric pressure as recorded within the last hour or so. Reports from land stations cover wind speed and direction, temperature and pressure; some land stations also add water temperature, visibility, and dew point.

The value of this information is apparent. Say someone in your boating party is susceptible to seasickness, and the Dial-A-Buoy report says wave heights are six feet with a period (interval) of eight seconds. Maybe that person would rather stay ashore and experience the gentler motion of a rocking chair. (Wave heights of six feet with a period of twenty seconds, on the other hand, might be tolerable.) Surfers, too, can benefit greatly from wave height reports. Likewise, since actual conditions frequently differ dramatically from forecasts, someone sailing offshore might be interested to know that a Data Buoy ahead is reporting squalls, giving time to shorten sail. And bathers and fishermen might gain from hearing the water temperature reports.

On the next page, we give the station or buoy identifier, location name, and lat/long in degrees and hundredths, as provided by the NWS. To find the station or buoy locations and identifiers using the Internet, you can see maps with station identifiers at www.ndbc.noaa.gov. To find locations by telephone, you can enter a latitude and longitude to receive the locations and identifiers of the closest stations.

To access Dial-A-Buoy using any touch-tone or cell phone, here are the steps:

1. Call 888-701-8992.
2. If you know the identifier of the station or buoy, press 1. Press 2 to get station locations by entering the approximate lat/long of the area you want.
3. Enter the five-digit (or character) station identifier. To enter a Character press the key containing the character.
4. If, after hearing the latest report, you wish to hear a forecast for that same location, press 2 then 1.
5. If you want to hear the report for another station, press 2 then 2.

NOTE: In some cases a buoy may become temporarily unavailable. You should try again later to see if it has come back online. Please be aware that stations that may be adrift and not at the stated location are not reported via the telephone feature. This information is only available on the website by typing in the station identifier at: www.ndbc.noaa.gov/dial.shtml

DIAL-A-BUOY and C-MAN STATION LOCATIONS

Station ID	Location Name	Latitude	Longitude
44027	JONESPORT, ME	44.28N	67.30W
MDRM1	MT DESERT ROCK, ME	43.97N	68.13W
MISM1	MATINICUS ROCK, ME	43.78N	68.86W
44007	PORTLAND, ME	43.53N	70.14W
44005	GULF OF MAINE	43.20N	69.13W
IOSN3	ISLE OF SHOALS, NH	42.97N	70.62W
44013	BOSTON, MA	42.35N	70.65W
BUZM3	BUZZARDS BAY, MA	41.40N	71.03W
44017	MONTAUK POINT, NY	40.69N	72.05W
44008	NANTUCKET, MA	40.50N	69.25W
44065	NEW YORK HARBOR ENT., NY	40.37N	73.70W
44025	LONG ISLAND, NY	40.25N	73.16W
TPLM2	THOMAS POINT, MD	38.90N	76.44W
44066	TEXAS TOWER #4, NJ	39.57N	72.59W
44009	DELAWARE BAY, NJ	38.46N	74.70W
44099	CAPE HENRY, VA	36.92N	75.72W
44014	VIRGINIA BEACH, VA	36.61N	74.84W
DUKN7	DUCK PIER, NC	36.18N	75.75W
41025	DIAMOND SHOALS	35.01N	75.40W
CLKN7	CAPE LOOKOUT, NC	34.62N	76.53W
41013	FRYING PAN SHOAL, NC	33.44N	77.74W
41004	EDISTO, SC	32.50N	79.10W
41002	S. HATTERAS, SC	31.76N	74.84W
41008	GRAYS REEF, GA	31.40N	80.87W
SAUF1	ST AUGUSTINE, FL	29.86N	81.27W
41010	CANAVERAL EAST, FL	28.88N	78.45W
41009	CANAVERAL, FL	28.50N	80.18W
LKWF1	LAKE WORTH, FL	26.61N	80.03W
FWYF1	FOWEY ROCKS, FL	25.59N	80.10W
MLRF1	MOLASSES REEF, FL	25.01N	80.38W
LONF1	LONG KEY, FL	24.84N	80.86W
SMKF1	SOMBRERO KEY, FL	24.63N	81.11W
SANF1	SAND KEY, FL	24.46N	81.88W

Most stations have added the ability to access information via RSS feed using your Internet browser. For information regarding how to use this feature please go to: www.ndbc.noaa.gov/rss_access.shtml

RADIO TELEPHONE INFORMATION – VHF SYSTEM

Calling Guidelines: Avoid excessive calling. Make calls as brief as possible. Give name of called vessel first, then "This is (name of your vessel)," your call sign (if you have a Station License), and the word "Over." If station does not answer, delay your repeat call for 2 minutes. At the end of your message, sign off with "This is (your vessel's name)," your call sign, and "Out."

Range and Power: Operation is essentially line-of-sight. Since the elevation of antennas at both communications points extends the "horizon," range may be 20 to 50 miles on a 24-hour basis between a boat and a land station. Effective range between boats will be less because of lower antenna heights. 25 watts is the maximum power permitted.

Interference factor: Most VHF-FM equipment has 6 or more channels, so it is possible to shift to a clear channel. Like the FM in your home radio, the system is practically immune to interference from ignition noise, static, etc., except under unusual conditions.

Channelization: A minimum of 3 channels is required by the FCC. Two are mandatory: Channel 16 (156.800 MHz), the International Distress frequency; and Channel 06 (156.300 MHz), the Intership Safety Frequency. The Coast Guard *strongly* recommends that you have Channel 22A as your third channel.

Note: designations for channels that previously ended with "A" have changed. To convert to the new format, prepend "10" and drop the "A" – e.g., 22A becomes 1022. The table below includes both new and old designations. Frequencies are not changing; older VHF radios will function as before the change.

Channel	Purpose and Comments
16 156.800 MHz **Vessels are required to maintain a watch on this channel.**	**Distress and Safety**: Ship to Shore and Intership. Guarded 24 hours by the Coast Guard. No routine messages allowed other than to establish the use of a working channel. See p. 243 for Distress calling procedure. **Calling**: Ship to Shore and Intership. Use Channel 16 to establish contact, then switch to a working channel (see below). Calling Channel: New England waters. Commercial and pleasure.
09 156.450 MHz	**Boater Calling:** Commercial and Non-Commercial
06 156.300 MHz	**Intership Safety:** No routine messages allowed. 06 is limited to talking with the Coast Guard and others at the scene of an emergency, and to information on the movement of vessels.
22A/1022 157.100 MHz (21 in Canada 161.65 MHz)	**Maritime Safety Information** channel. Not guarded by the CG, but after a vessel makes contact with the CG for non-distress calls on Channel 16, they will tell you to switch to and use *only* 22A for communicating. Also used for CG weather advisories and Notices to Mariners. *Times* of these broadcasts given on Channel 16.
12, 14, 20A/1020, 65A/1065, 66A/1066, 73, 74, 77	**Ship to Shore and Intership:** Port operations, harbormasters, etc. Your electronics dealer should have local frequencies.
08, 67, 88A/1088	**Commercial (intership only):** For ocean vessels, dredges, tugs, etc.
07A, 10, 11, 18A/1018, 19A/1019, 79A, 80A/1080	**Commercial only**
13 156.650 MHz	**Intership Navigation Safety:** (bridge to bridge). Ships > 20 m length maintain a listening watch on this channel in US waters.
68, 69, 71, 72, 78A/1078	**Ship to Shore and Intership, pleasure craft only:** Shore stations, marinas, etc. The best channels for general communication.
70 156.525 MHz	**Digital Selective Calling (DSC)**. Special equipment required. See p. 245 Marine Communications.
81A/1081 157.075 MHz 83A/1083 157.175 MHz	**Keyed Fog Signals**. See note on p.173 Lights, Fog Signals and Offshore Buoys.
AIS 1 161.975 MHz AIS 2 162.025 MHz	**Automatic Identification System** (AIS)

MARINE EMERGENCY AND DISTRESS CALLS

If you have DSC-equipped VHF radio, obtain an MMSI number and connect your radio to GPS. This setup will enable you to send a distress signal, vessel information, and location with the push of a button. See p. 245 for more information on DSC.

If you do <u>not</u> have a DSC-equipped radio, call out on VHF Ch. 16 (156.800 MHz.)

I. DISTRESS SIGNAL (top priority)

If you are in distress (i.e. when threatened by grave and imminent danger) transmit— MAYDAY MAYDAY MAYDAY, THIS IS your vessel's name repeated three times, followed by your call sign or registration said once.

IF CALLING FROM A VESSEL IN TROUBLE—give:
1. Who you are—repeat MAYDAY THIS IS your vessel's name once.
2. Where you are—your vessel's position in latitude/longitude, or bearing (specify true or magnetic) and distance in nautical miles from a known geographical point. State vessel movement: course, speed, and destination.
3. Nature of distress.
4. Kind of assistance desired.
5. Number of persons aboard, noting condition of any injured.
6. Present seaworthiness of your vessel.
7. Description of your vessel (i.e., length, type cabin, masts, power, color of hull, superstructure and trim.)
8. End transmission with OVER.

Repeat at intervals until the message is received. Stay by your radio if possible, so you can transmit a signal that responders can home.

If you receive no response and have an MF/HF radiotelephone, repeat your call on a HF frequency that is guarded by the USCG: 4125 kHz (2300-1100 UTC,) 6215 kHz (24 hours,) 8291 kHz (24 hours,) 12290 kHz (1100- 2300 UTC.)

IF CALLING WHILE OBSERVING ANOTHER VESSEL IN DIFFICULTY—give:
1. Your position and the bearing and distance of the vessel in difficulty.
2. Nature of distress or difficulty.
3. Description of the vessel in distress or difficulty, (i.e., length, type cabin, masts, power, color of hull, superstructure and trim.)
4. Your intentions, course and speed, etc.
5. Your radio call sign, name of your vessel, listening frequency and schedule.

If there is no immediate response, repeat appropriate messages above; if still no response, you may send on any other available frequency until you make contact.

IF YOU HEAR A MAYDAY CALL—If you hear a distress message from a vessel and it is not answered, then you must answer. If you are reasonably sure that the distressed vessel is not in your vicinity, you should wait a short time for others to acknowledge. Note details in your radio log right away. Do not make any transmission on this distress channel until MAYDAY condition is lifted by the Coast Guard, unless you are in a position to be of assistance.

II. URGENCY SIGNAL (second priority)

If you have an urgent message to send (threat to a vessel's safety or to someone on board, overboard or within sight), use the same procedure as above but say the word "PAN" three times. "PAN" (pronounced "PAWN") is also used as a warning signal that a Distress Signal may be sent out at a later stage. Morse Code signal is – (T) – (T) – (T)

III. SAFETY SIGNAL (third priority)

If you wish to report navigation or weather warnings (ice, derelicts, tropical storms, etc.) use the same procedure as above but say the word "SECURITY" (pronounced SAY-CUR-I-TAY) three times. Morse Code signal is – • • – (X) – • • – (X) – • • – (X)

How to Contact the U.S. Coast Guard

U.S. Coast Guard Rescue Coordination Centers (RCCs)
24-hour Regional Contacts for Emergencies

RCC Boston, MA – (617) 223-8555 Maine to Northern New Jersey
RCC Norfolk, VA – (757) 398-6231 New Jersey to border of N. Carolina and S. Carolina
RCC Miami, FL – (305) 415-6800 S. Carolina to Key West including much of Caribbean

USCG Navigation Information Service (NIS). Watchstander, (24/7): (703) 313-5900

USCG National Response Center (NRC): (800) 424-8802

USCG Marine Safety Center: (202) 795-6729

INTERNET: USCG - www.navcen.uscg.gov/ Canada - www.notmar.gc.ca/

U.S. Coast Guard Stations – (monitoring VHF Ch. 16)

1st District – Boston – (800) 848-3942

Eastport, ME (207) 853-2845
Jonesport, ME (207) 497-3404
Southwest Harbor, ME (207) 244-4270
Rockland, ME (207) 596-6667
Boothbay Hbr., ME (207) 633-2661
S. Portland, ME (207) 767-0363
Sector Northern New England (207) 767-0302
Portsmouth, NH (603) 436-4415
Merrimack-Newburyport, MA (978) 465-0731
Gloucester, MA (978) 283-0705
Boston, MA (617) 223-3224
Point Allerton-Hull, MA (781) 925-0165
  Scituate, MA (781) 545-3800
Cape Cod Canal-E. Entr. (508) 888-0020
Provincetown, MA (508) 487-0077
Chatham, MA (508) 945-3830
Brant Pt.-Nantucket, MA (508) 228-0388
Woods Hole, MA (508) 457-3211
Menemsha, MA (508) 645-2662
Castle Hill, Newport, RI (401) 846-3676
Point Judith, RI (401) 789-0444
New London, CT (860) 442-4471
New Haven, CT (203) 468-4498
Sector NY, NY (718) 354-4353
Fire Island, NY (631) 661-9100
Eatons Neck, NY (631) 261-6959
Kings Point, NY (516) 466-7136
Jones Beach, NY (516) 785-2995
Shinnecock, NY (631) 728-0078
Montauk, NY (631) 668-2773
Sandy Hook, NJ (732) 872-3429

5th District – Portsmouth, VA (757) 686-4002

Manasquan Inlet, NJ (732) 899-0887
  Shark River, NJ (732) 776-6730
Barnegat, NJ (609) 494-2661
Atlantic City, NJ (609) 344-6594
Cape May, NJ (609) 898-6995
Ocean City, NJ (609) 399-0144
Indian River Inlet, DE (302) 227-2440
Ocean City, MD (410) 289-1905
St. Inigoes, MD (301) 872-4344

5th District, cont.

Crisfield, MD (410) 968-0323
Annapolis, MD (410) 267-8108
Oxford, MD (410) 226-0581
Curtis Bay-Baltimore, MD (410) 576-2620
Stillpond, MD (410) 778-2201
Chincoteague, VA (757) 336-2874
Little Creek-Norfolk, VA (757) 464-9371
Wachapreague, VA (757) 787-9526
Portsmouth, VA (757) 483-8527
Cape Charles, VA (757) 331-2000
Milford Haven, VA (804) 725-3732
Oregon Inlet, NC (252) 441-6260
Hatteras Inlet, NC (252) 986-2176
Hobucken, NC (252) 745-3131
Fort Macon, NC (252) 732-4326
Elizabeth City, NC (252) 335-6086
Wrightsville Beach, NC (910) 256-4224
Emerald Isle, NC (252) 354-2719
Oak Island, NC (910) 278-1133

7th District – Miami, FL (305) 415-6800

Georgetown, SC (843) 546-2052
Charleston, SC (843) 724-7600
Tybee, GA (912) 786-5440
Brunswick, GA (912) 267-7999
Mayport, FL (904) 564-7500
Ponce de Leon Inlet, FL (386) 428-9084
Cape Canaveral, FL (321) 868-4200
Fort Pierce Inlet, FL (772) 464-6100
Lake Worth Inlet, FL (561) 840-8503
Ft. Lauderdale, FL (954) 927-1611
Miami Beach, FL (305) 535-4368
Islamorada, FL (305) 664-8077
Marathon, FL (305) 535-4565
Key West, FL (305) 292-8713

Canada-Nova Scotia

Canadian Coast Guard
Joint Rescue Coordination Center
Halifax, NS   (902) 427-8200

Marine Communications

Emergencies: The Coast Guard is required to monitor Channel 16; they are not required to answer the telephone. In an emergency, use your VHF radio to call the Coast Guard on Channel 16 (156.80 MHz). Digital Selective Calling (DSC) is on Channel 70 on your VHF. The Coast Guard urges, in the strongest terms possible, that you take the time to interconnect your GPS and DSC-equipped radio. Doing so may save your life in a distress situation!

DSC: As part of the Global Maritime Distress and Safety System (GMDSS), Rescue 21 is the Coast Guard system that provides the emergency response made possible by DSC-equipped VHF radios. It has been active for a while, and if you don't yet have a DSC-VHF radio, you need to know the significant advantages it offers.

Rescues initiated by DSC-equipped radios are far quicker and more successful. Why? With the push of one button, an automated digital distress alert is sent to other DSC-equipped vessels and rescue facilities. This transmission includes your vessel's unique, 9-digit MMSI (Marine Mobile Service Identity) number, which contains your vessel's description for easier identification by response teams. If connected to a compatible GPS, the signal will give your vessel's latitude and longitude for faster and more efficient assistance or rescue. For more information go to: http://www.navcen.uscg.gov. Domestic users (non-commercial) who do not travel outside of the US can be issued an MMSI number without applying for an FCC Station License. You can register for an MMSI online at http://www.boatus.com/mmsi/, or http://mmsiregister.seatow.com.

Non-emergency: Near shore (range will vary) a cell phone can be used successfully for non-emergency calls. The usable distance assumes line-of-sight, so an antenna which is higher may help communicate farther. That distance may be less where there are fewer cell towers.

Marine Weather Forecasts

VHF-FM, NOAA All-Hazards Weather Radio - Continuous broadcasts 24 hours a day are provided by the National Weather Service with taped messages repeated every 4-6 minutes. These are updated every 3-6 hours and include weather and radar summaries, wind observations, visibility, sea conditions and detailed local forecasts. NOAA VHF-FM broadcasts can be received 20-40 miles from transmitting site.

	MHz		MHz
WX-1	162.550	WX-5	162.450
WX-2	162.400	WX-6	162.500
WX-3	162.475	WX-7	162.525
WX-4	162.425		

Jonesboro, ME (5)	Philadelphia, PA (3)	New Bern, NC (2)	Fort Pierce, FL (4)
Ellsworth, ME (2)	Atlantic City, NJ (2)	Georgetown, SC (6)	Miami, FL (1)
Dresden, ME (3)	Lewes, DE (1)	Charleston, SC (1)	Key West, FL (2)
Gloucester, MA (4)	Baltimore, MD (2)	Beaufort, SC (5)	
Boston, MA (3)	Hagerstown, MD (3)	Brunswick, GA (4)	
Hyannis, MA (1)	Norfolk, VA (1)	Jacksonville, FL (1)	
Providence, RI (2)	Mamie, NC (4)	Daytona Bch., FL (2)	
Riverhead, NY (3)	Cape Hatteras, NC (3)	Melbourne, FL (1)	

Time Signals

Bureau of Standards Time Signals: WWV, Ft. Collins, Col., every min. on 2500, 5000, 10000, 15000, 20000, 25000 kHz. **Canadian Time Signals:** CHU, (frequently easier to get than WWV) 45° 17' 47" N, 75° 45' 22" W. Continuous transmission on 3330, 7850, and 14670 kHz. For more information on time, visit www.nist.gov/pml/time-and-frequency-division.

Omission of a tone indicates the 29th second of each minute. The new minute is marked by the full tone *immediately* following the voice announcement. Five sets of two short tones mark the first five seconds of the next minute. The hour is identified by a pulse of one full second followed by 12 seconds of silence.

HYPOTHERMIA
and Cold Water Immersion
What You Need To Know

It is not uncommon for a boater to fall off a boat or dock. Most are rescued immediately. However, when rescue is delayed and conditions are present which threaten survival, all who go boating should know what to do.

Hypothermia is a state of low body core temperature - specifically below 95° F. This loss of body heat may be caused by exposure to cold air or cold water. Since water conducts heat away 25 times more quickly than air, time is critical for rescue. There are many variables beyond water temperature that combine to determine survival time: whether a life jacket is on, body size and composition, type of clothing, movement in the water, etc. Wearing a Personal Flotation Device (PFD) greatly extends survival time by keeping your head above water and by allowing you to float without expending energy.

What a person in the water should do:
1. If at all possible, get out of the water, or at least grab hold of anything floating. If the boat is swamped, stay with it and crawl as far out of the water as possible.
2. Do not try to swim, unless a boat or floating object is very nearby and you are certain you can get to it.
3. Control heat loss by keeping clothing on as partial insulation. In particular, keep the head out of water. To protect the groin, sides, and chest from heat loss, use the H.E.L.P. (heat escape lessening position), a fetal position with hands clasped around the legs, which extends survival time.
4. Conserve energy by remaining as still as possible. Physical effort promotes heat loss. Swimming, or even treading water, reduces survival time.

The states of hypothermia:
1. Mild: victim feels cold, exhibits violent shivering, lethargy, slurred speech
2. Medium: loss of some muscle control, incoherence or combativeness, stupor, and exhaustion
3. Severe: unconsciousness, respiratory distress, possible cardiac arrest

What a rescuer should do:
1. Move the victim to a warm place, position on his/her back, and check breathing and heartbeat.
2. Start CPR (p. 247) if necessary.
3. Carefully remove wet clothing, cutting it away if necessary.
4. Take steps to raise the body temperature gradually: cover the victim with blankets or a sleeping bag, and apply warm moist towels to the neck, chest, and groin.
5. Provide warm oral fluids and sugar sources after uncontrolled shivering stops and the patient shows evidence of ability to swallow and of rewarming.

What NOT to do:
1. Do not give alcohol, coffee, tea, or nicotine. If the victim is not fully conscious, do not attempt to provide food or water.
2. Do not massage arms or legs or handle the patient roughly, as this could cause cold blood from the periphery to circulate to the body's core, which needs to be warm first.

Emergency First Aid

These are guidelines to be used only when professional help is not readily available.

Good Samaritan laws were enacted to encourage people to help others in emergency situations. Laws vary from state to state, but all require that the caregiver use common sense and a reasonable level of skill.

Before giving care to a conscious victim you must first get consent. If the victim does not give consent call 911. Consent may be implied if a victim is unconscious, confused, or seriously ill.

Prevent disease transmission by avoiding contact with bodily fluids, using protective equipment such as disposable gloves and thoroughly washing hands after giving care.

Primary Assessment —
Check for
1. Unresponsiveness
2. Breathing - Look, listen and feel.
3. Pulse (any movement or sign of life) - If pulse and breathing are present, check for and control any severe bleeding.

If no sign of life or breathing, call for help and then begin CPR. For children, do 2 minutes of CPR, then call for help while continuing CPR.

If pulse is present but no breathing, begin Rescue Breathing (p. 248).

If airway is obstructed, do Heimlich to clear airway. Do not use Heimlich if drowning is suspected; go to Rescue Breathing.

CPR - Cardiopulmonary Resuscitation* — Use only when there is no
sign of breathing and no sign of movement or life. First, call or get someone to call for help. CPR has two components: compressions and giving breaths. Pushing hard and fast on the chest is the most important part of CPR because you are pumping blood to the brain and heart.

Roll victim onto back as a unit, being careful to keep spine in alignment. Move clothing out of the way. Put the heel of 1 hand on the lower half of the breastbone. Put the heel of your other hand on top of the first hand. Push straight down at least 2 inches at a rate of at least 120 compressions a minute. After each compression, let the chest come back up to its normal position, but do not remove your hands. Giving compressions is tiring. If someone else is available, take turns being careful to make pauses in giving compressions as short as possible.

Compressions are the most important part of CPR. If you are also able to give breaths, you will help even more. To give breaths, tilt the head back while lifting the chin up unless neck or back injury is suspected; in that case, keep neck in alignment and open mouth by jutting the jaw forward. Pinch nose shut, seal your lips tight around victim's mouth, GIVE 2 FULL BREATHS for 1 to 1 ½ seconds each, checking for chest rise. Do not take more than 10 seconds away from compressions to give breaths or to move the patient. It is better to have two rescuers to do both compressions and breaths.

If you are unable or uncomfortable doing Rescue Breathing, the American Heart Association states that performing Chest Compressions alone can be effective in helping to circulate oxygenated blood through the body. Follow these two important steps: 1) first call 911 and 2) using both hands pump on center of chest between the nipples hard, fast and continuously.

* To perform CPR you should be trained. Courses are available through the American Red Cross and the American Heart Association. For in depth information about the science of CPR, see CPR on www.heart.org. For the new hands only technique, see www.handsonlycpr.org.

Continued on p. 248   **247**

Emergency First Aid
continued

Rescue Breathing, no obstruction — Call or get someone to call for help.

Pulse present, unresponsive, no breathing.

Roll victim onto back and open airway. Tilt head back and lift chin except where neck or back injury is suspected. Look, listen and feel for breath for 3-5 seconds.

If no breath, keep head tilted back, pinch nose shut, seal your lips tight around victim's mouth, GIVE 2 NORMAL FULL BREATHS for 1 to 1 ½ seconds each until chest rises. Feel for pulse at side of neck for 5-10 seconds.

If pulse present, continue Rescue Breathing for 1 minute. Keep head tilted back, pinch nose. Give 1 breath every 5 seconds. Look, listen and feel for breath between breaths.

RECHECK PULSE EVERY MINUTE. If victim has pulse but is not breathing, continue rescue breathing.

If victim has no sign of life or breath, go to CPR (p. 247.)

Obstructed Airway — If victim cannot cough, breathe, or speak, use HEIMLICH.

If drowning suspected, use Rescue Breathing.

Do not try to clear water from lungs. Roll to side if vomiting occurs so victim won't choke.

Heimlich — If victim is conscious, stand behind him. Wrap your arms around victim's waist. Place your fist (thumbside) against the victim's stomach in the midline, just above the navel and well below the rib margin. Grasp your fist with other hand. Press into stomach with a quick upward thrust.

If victim is unconscious, lay victim on back, do finger sweep on adult (on child only if you can see object). Attempt rescue breathing. If airway remains blocked, give 6-10 abdominal thrusts and repeat as necessary. If victim has no sign of life or pulse, commence CPR.

Bleeding — Apply pressure directly over wound with a dressing, until bleeding stops or until EMS rescuers arrive. If possible, press edges of a large wound together before using dressing and bandage.

If bleeding continues, apply additional bandages and continue to maintain pressure. ssure. If bleeding cannot be stopped to an extremity, use a tourniquet above the wound. If necessary, apply a second tourniquet above the first. Never remove a tourniquet once it is applied

If possible, elevate wounded area, apply ice wrapped in cloth to wound and keep the patient warm.

Burns, Scalds — No open blisters: Use cool water, then cover with a dry sterile dressing.

Open blisters - Heat: Cover with dry sterile dressing. Do not put water on burn or remove clothing sticking to burn. Treat for shock.

Open blisters - Chemical: Flush all chemical burns with water for 15 to 30 minutes. Remove all clothing on which chemical has spilled. Cover with dry sterile dressing and treat for shock. Eyes: Flush with cool water only for 45 minutes.

Shock — Confused behavior, rapid pulse and breathing, cool moist skin, blue tinge to lips and nailbeds, weakness, nausea and vomiting, etc.

Keep patient lying lying on their left side in "recovery postion" Remove wet clothing. Maintain normal body temperature. Do not give victim food or drink.

Emergency First Aid
continued

Fractures — Do not move victim or try to correct any deformity. Immobilize the area. If bone penetrates the skin use a sterile dressing and control bleeding before splinting.

Splint a broken arm to the trunk or a broken leg to the other leg. A padded board or pole can be used along the side, front or back of a broken limb. A pillow or a rolled blanket can be used around the arm or leg.

For an injured shoulder put a pillow between the arm and chest and bind arm to body.

For an injured hip, place pillow between legs and bind legs together.

Head, Neck, and Spine Injuries — Do not move victim or try to correct any deformity. Stabilize head, neck and torso as you found them.

Poisoning — Call for help immediately: Poison Control Center 800-222-1222.

Have poison container available. Antidotes listed on the label may be wrong.

Heat Prostration — Strip victim. Move to shaded area. Wrap in cool, wet sheet. Treat for shock. Reduce body temperature to normal and avoid causing shivering.

Exposure to Cold — Provide a warm dry bunk and warm drink, not coffee, tea or alcohol.

Frostbite: rewarm slowly, beginning with the body core rather than the extremities. Elevate and protect affected area. Do not rub frozen area, break blisters or use dry heat to thaw.

Treat for shock. See *Hypothermia and Cold Water Immersion* (p. 246.)

Sunburn — Treat heat prostration if present. Take the heat out of the skin by using a cool damp cloth laid over the area. Do not apply ice as this may damage the skin further.

Painkillers like acetaminophen (Tylenol) or ibuprofen may be used for pain. Use topical lotions to keep the skin moist and reduce dehydration. Those containing aloe work well.

If the skin is blistering, prevent secondary infection by keeping the area clean.

Victim should rest and keep hydrated. Seek medical help if area does not improve.

Seasickness — This form of motion sickness is characterized by headache, drowsiness, nausea and vomiting often brought on by sailing in rough or inconsistent seas. Seasickness can be difficult to control.

Preventive: Medications taken before you get on the boat: Dramamine® and Bonine® are the two most common over the counter seasickness remedies. Transderm Scop® Scopolamine patch is a common prescription medicine. Talk with your doctor or pharmacist about which approach might be right for you. Avoid strong odors, greasy, spicy, high-fat foods as well as alcohol and excessive sugars as they can make you queasy or light-headed. Avoid reading books and computer screens.

Coping with seasickness: Take ginger, chew gum, look at the horizon, stay on deck, get fresh air, try to sleep, stay as close to the center of the boat as possible. Anti-seasickness wristbands are also known to relieve symptoms. Keep hydrated.

Vessel Safety Check

The Vessel Safety Check (VSC) is a good option for boaters who wish to have a trained examiner inspect their boats, at no cost, to ensure they have all the equipment required by regulations.

VSC involves the U.S. Coast Guard Auxiliary and the U.S. Power Squadrons who provide free safety examination of recreational boats. Examiners are available to check boats for meeting federal and state equipment requirements. They also check for general safety conditions.

Owners of boats that meet the VSC requirements receive the VSC decal to indicate that their boat was examined and passed. If a boat does not meet all of the VSC requirements, the owner gets a listing of what is needed. No tickets are ever issued and no reports are made to law enforcement authorities.

If you are interested in having a VSC go to: http://safetyseal.net and enter your zipcode for the nearest examiner. You may email the examiner from the site to arrange for a VSC, or contact either of the following organizations:

U.S. Power Squadrons: http://www.usps.org

U.S. Coast Guard Auxiliary: http://www.cgaux.org

U.S. Coast Guard Boardings

The U.S. Coast Guard has the authority to enforce federal laws by making inquiries, examinations, inspections, searches, seizures, and arrests on the waters over which the United States has jurisdiction. Unlike law enforcement regulations ashore, the U.S. Coast Guard does not need probable cause to board your vessel.

The U.S. Coast Guard personnel are armed and may use necessary force to compel compliance. They are charged with the enforcement of laws dealing with safety, water pollution, drug smuggling, illegal immigration, and the 200-mile fishery conservation zone. In nearly half the boardings, they find some kind of non-compliance with regulations. A civil penalty may be imposed for failure to comply with equipment or numbering regulations, navigation rules, accident reporting procedures, etc.

A boat underway that is hailed by a U.S. Coast Guard vessel or patrol boat is required to follow the boarding officer's instructions, which may be to stop, to continue at reduced speed, or to maneuver in such a way as to permit boarding. Instructions will depend on sea conditions. The Coast Guard follows a standard procedure before boarding, and the boarding team will provide as explanation before the actual boarding. If the boarding party has full cooperation from you, the inspection will be completed quickly.

The editors wish to thank the U.S. Power Squadrons (USPS) for permission to reprint this article from their Seamanship Manual.

Weather Signs In the Sky

"When the rain before the wind, topsail sheets and halyards mind,
But when the wind before the rain, then you may set sail again."

Signs of Good Weather

- A gray sky in the morning or a "low dawn" – when the day breaks near the horizon, with the first streaks of light low in the sky – brings fair weather.
- "Rain before 7, clear before 11"
- Light, delicate tints with soft, undefined clouds accompany fine weather.
- Seabirds flying out early and far to sea suggest moderate wind, fair weather.
- A rosy sky at sunset, clear or cloudy: "Red sky at night, sailor's delight."
- High, wispy cirrus clouds, or even high cumulus, indicate immediate fair weather, with a possible change from a front within 24 hours.
- High contrails disappearing quickly show dry air aloft.
- Steady mild-to-moderate winds from the same direction indicate continuing fair weather.
- A low dew point relative to temperature means dry air. (See p. 261)

Signs of Bad Weather

- "Red sky at morning, sailor take warning." Poor weather, wind, maybe rain.
- A "high dawn" – when the first streaks of daylight appear above a bank of clouds – often precedes a turn for worse weather.
- Light scud clouds driving across higher, heavy clouds show wind and rain.
- Hard-edged, inky clouds foretell rain and strong wind.
- Seabirds hanging over the land or headed inland suggest wind and rain.
- Remarkable clearness of atmosphere near the horizon, when distant hills or vessels are raised by refraction, are signs of an Easterly wind and indicate coming wet weather.
- Long-lasting contrails indicate humid air aloft.
- Low-level clouds, and clouds at several heights
- Rising humidity, dewpoint close to temperature

Signs of Wind

- Soft-looking, delicate clouds indicate light to moderate wind.
- Stronger wind is suggested by hard-edged, oily-looking, ragged clouds, or a bright yellow sky at sunset.
- A change in wind is indicated by high clouds crossing the sky in a different direction from that of lower clouds.
- Increasing wind and possibly rain are preceded by greater than usual twinkling of stars, indistinctness of the moon's horns, "wind dogs" (fragments of rainbows) seen on detached clouds, and the rainbow.
- "First rise after very low, indicates a stronger blow."

Time Out

by Jay MacLaughlin

I grew up sailing wooden Snipe and Blue Jay class boats on Barnegat Bay in New Jersey. My mother and her brother were fiercely competitive sailors when they were racing, but patient teachers who knew enough to dial back the competitiveness when it came to time to teach my cousins and me the pleasures of small-boat handling.

The summer I was ten, my mother decided to spend real time on the water with me, hoping to give me the gift of her love of sailing. I was a slightly distracted pupil, a little mad to miss time on Little League diamonds in order to have to mess around in boats, but it was fun—lots to learn, nice surroundings, fresh air, the works. Our first time out, on a bluebird August day with light air from the southwest, my mother and I were poking around the bay, taking turns as skipper and crew while my mom showed me how to read the water to find a lift, then trim the sails to maximize the wind's shifting gifts. While we were out, the wind backed around to the northeast, commenced blowing steadily and hard. Then the bay got choppy enough that the rollers turned into whitecaps. Although we were in no deadly peril, to a ten-year-old in a 15-foot boat things were suddenly a little scary. My mother took the tiller, asked me quietly to do everything she asked with the sheets quickly and exactly, and we beat our way back to our mooring and tied up, cold and wet.

Back at the dock, shivering, not with cold but with excitement, I told my mother that that was the best time I'd ever had, that I'd never done anything "realer." I was hooked.

What does it mean to do something real these days? To restore a wooden boat or rebuild an outboard motor? To stand a 2- or 4-hour watch on a trans-oceanic boat race? For me it's to stand in the surf casting for stripers for a couple of hours on either side of a high tide. To be actively engaged, using your hands and heart as well as your head in some—any—activity that isn't mediated or delivered by electrons these days is rare and precious.

Anglers say time spent on the water doesn't count against the biblically ordained three score and ten. That's true of any pastime, domain, discipline, hobby--whatever you call it--that is so absorbing as to erase clock time. If we slow down, immerse ourselves, actively participate, we restore our spirits and refresh our minds.

And the mastery that comes from that immersion can be life-saving. The ability to read a map or a compass becomes critical if your cell phone dies while hiking in the Green Mountains. Reading the wind and weather along with the capacity to plot a course using charts, compass and one's wits has saved many a mariner from ending their voyage hard aground. Study, yes, but more so experience and time spent earn you a mastery of your chosen pursuit. This type of immersion is valuable for the soul, the spirit, and one's lifetime acumen.

Continued on p. 254

Beaufort Scale

Force	Knots	Wind Condition	Conditions at Sea	Conditions Ashore
0	0-1	Calm	Smooth, mirror-like sea	Calm, smoke rises vertically
1	1-3	Light Air	Scaly ripples, no foam crests	Smoke drifts at an angle, leaves move
2	4-6	Light Breeze	Small wavelets, crests glassy, not breaking	Leaves rustle, flags begin to move
3	7-10	Gentle Breeze	Large wavelets, some crests break, scattered whitecaps	Small branches move, light flags extended
4	11-16	Moderate Breeze	Small waves 1-4 ft. getting longer, numerous whitecaps	Leaves, loose paper lifted, larger flags flapping
5	17-21	Fresh Breeze	Moderate waves 4-8 ft., many whitecaps	Small trees in leaf begin to sway, flags extended
6	22-27	Strong Breeze	Larger waves 8-13 ft., more whitecaps, spray	Larger tree branches and small trees in motion
7	28-33	Near Gale	Sea heaps up, waves 13-20 ft., white foam streaks	Whole trees moving, resistance in walking
8	34-40	Gale	Waves 13-20 ft. of greater length, crests break, spindrift	Large trees in motion, small branches break
9	41-47	Strong Gale	High waves, 20+ ft., dense streaks of foam, spray reduces visibility	Slight structural damage, roof shingles may blow off, signs in motion
10	48-55	Storm	Very high waves, 20-30 ft., overhanging crests, lowered visibility, sea white with densely blown foam	Trees broken or uprooted, considerable structural damage, very high tides
11	56-63	Violent Storm	Exceptionally high waves, 30-45 ft., foam patches cover sea, visibility limited	Widespread damage, light structures in peril, coastal flooding
12	64+	Hurricane	Air filled with foam, waves 45+ ft., wind shrieks, sea white with spray, visibility poor	Storm surge at coast, serious beach erosion, extensive flooding, trees and wires down

NOTE: When the wind speed doubles, the pressure of the wind on an object *quadruples*. Example: the wind pressure at 40 kts.is *four times* what it is at 20 kts.

In many tidal waters wave heights are apt to increase considerably in a very short time, and conditions can be more dangerous near land than in the open sea.

Continued from p. 252

Before the seals, I used to fish Nantucket's Great Point for long stretches every fall, usually with only ordinary or even sub-par success. After learning the difference between tides, and the direction of water flow in the channel, it became clear when fishing would be optimum; subsequently my catch rate went up. That was information available only in the illustrations in this analog publication. No online searches could have answered the question, and only time on the water could confirm the hypothesis. Now I know it in my bones.

I suspect online gamers or Facebook or Twitter or Instagram adepts would say they can get into a "zone" as deep and profound as the person creating whole-body muscle memory. But I'd argue that the runner, the tennis player, the golfer, yes, even the skipper with his hand on a tiller feeling the push and pull of wind and tide or the angler feeling the elemental tug of a fish fighting the drag get a kind of sensory payback that no amount of time hunched over keys, screens, or joysticks can equal.

More than ever as the media technology giants admit to creating addictive algorithms, we owe it to ourselves to step away from the screens, breathe in some fresh, or better, salt air and do for our spirits the things that slow down time and are "realer."

Jay MacLaughlin is a surfcaster and flyfisherman. He fishes from boats and from shore in the waters of Cape Cod and the South Coast of Massachusetts. He is a writer and editor and the principal of his own marketing communications firm.

Forecasting
with Wind Direction and Barometric Pressure

Wind Dir.	Pressure	Trend	Likely Forecast
SW to **NW**	30.1-30.2	Steady	Fair, little temp. change
	30.1-30.2	Rising rapidly	Fair, perhaps warmer with rain
	30.2+	Steady	Fair, no temp. change
	30.2+	Falling	Fair, gradual rise in temp.
S to **SW**	30.0	Rising slowly	Clearing, then fair
S to **SE**	30.2	Falling rapidly	Increasing wind, rain to follow
S to **E**	29.8	Falling rapidly	Severe NE gale, heavy rain/snow
SE to **NE**	30.1-30.2	Falling slowly	Rain
	30.1-30.2	Falling rapidly	Increasing wind and rain
	30.0	Falling slowly	Rain continuing
	30.0	Falling rapidly	Rain, high wind, then clearing and cooler
E to **NE**	30.0+	Falling slowly	Rain with light winds
	30.1	Falling rapidly	Rain or snow, increasing wind
Shifting W	29.8	Rising rapidly	Clearing and cooler

Wind Chill Chart

Wind (mph)	Temperature (°F)																	
Calm	40	35	30	25	20	15	10	5	0	-5	-10	-15	-20	-25	-30	-35	-40	-45
5	36	31	25	19	13	7	1	-5	-11	-16	-22	-28	-34	-40	-46	-52	-57	-63
10	34	27	21	15	9	3	-4	-10	-16	-22	-28	-35	-41	-47	-53	-59	-66	-72
15	32	25	19	13	6	0	-7	-13	-19	-26	-32	-39	-45	-51	-58	-64	-71	-77
20	30	24	17	11	4	-2	-9	-15	-22	-29	-35	-42	-48	-55	-61	-68	-74	-81
25	29	23	16	9	3	-4	-11	-17	-24	-31	-37	-44	-51	-58	-64	-71	-78	-84
30	28	22	15	8	1	-5	-12	-19	-26	-33	-39	-46	-53	-60	-67	-73	-80	-87
35	28	21	14	7	0	-7	-14	-21	-27	-34	-41	-48	-55	-62	-69	-76	-82	-89
40	27	20	13	6	-1	-8	-15	-22	-29	-36	-43	-50	-57	-64	-71	-78	-84	-91
45	26	19	12	5	-2	-9	-16	-23	-30	-37	-44	-51	-58	-65	-72	-79	-86	-93
50	26	19	12	4	-3	-10	-17	-24	-31	-38	-45	-52	-60	-67	-74	-81	-88	-95
55	25	18	11	4	-3	-11	-18	-25	-32	-39	-46	-54	-61	-68	-75	-82	-89	-97
60	25	17	10	3	-4	-11	-19	-26	-33	-40	-48	-55	-62	-69	-76	-84	-91	-98

Frostbite Times: ☐ 30 minutes ☐ 10 minutes ☐ 5 minutes

Marine Fog

Common Types and Causes

GPS and radar can help, but that doesn't change the fact that mariners hate fog. Understanding the common types and causes may help mariners forecast its arrival, and better anticipate its departure.

Any discussion of fog begins with a basic understanding of *dew point*. Warm air holds more moisture than cool air. Dew point is the atmospheric temperature to which air must be cooled for it to reach a saturation point, resulting in fog, rain, or condensation. In other words, when warm air cools at night, dew on the deck (or grass) in the morning is the result. Fog dissipates when air warms above its dew point.

When warm, moist air blows over cool ocean water, *advection fog* forms. Under these conditions, the warm air is being cooled to its dew point, forming fog. Advection fog can be up to 2000 feet thick, and tends to persist until either the wind direction changes or wind speed increases, but it can remain over the water even with wind speeds of 30 knots.

A warm front approaching means that warm air aloft advances over cooler air below, and rain is often the result. As warm rain descends into cool air, the water vapor raises the dew point of the air and causes *precipitation* or *frontal fog*. This fog usually lasts until it stops raining or until there's a shift in wind direction.

In late fall, winter, or early spring, cold arctic air passes over cool but relatively warmer ocean water to create fog. *Steam fog* or *sea smoke* is created by water vapor rising from the surface, meeting much colder air just above it. As the vapor rises and cools, it meets its dew point and forms a smoky mist, with wisps or plumes of fog rising from the surface.

The Saffir-Simpson Hurricane Wind Scale

CATEGORY ONE: Winds 74-95 mph: Very dangerous winds will produce some damage. Falling or flying debris. Damage primarily to power lines, mobile homes, shopping center roofs, shrubbery, and trees. Also, some coastal road flooding and minor pier damage.

CATEGORY TWO: Winds 96-110 mph: Extremely dangerous winds will cause extensive damage. Some roofing material, door, and window damage to buildings. Considerable damage to vegetation, mobile homes, and piers. Small craft in unprotected areas break moorings. Near-total power outages. Some water systems fail.

CATEGORY THREE: Winds 111-130 mph: Devastating damage will occur. Some structural damage to small residences. Mobile homes destroyed. Many trees snapped or uprooted. Coastal flooding may extend inland, destroying smaller structures, damaging larger structures. Electricity and water may be unavailable for days or weeks.

CATEGORY FOUR: Winds 131-155 mph: Catastrophic damage will occur. More extensive failures including roofs on small residences. Major erosion of beach areas. Major damage to lower floors of structures near the shore. Power poles down. Terrain may be flooded well inland. Long-term water shortages.

CATEGORY FIVE: Winds greater than 155 mph: Catastrophic damage will occur. Complete roof failure on many residences and industrial buildings. Some complete building failures with small utility buildings destroyed. Major damage to most structures located near the shoreline. Massive evacuation of residential areas may be required. Most of the area will be uninhabitable for weeks or months.

Hurricanes

For their awesome power to wreak havoc by wind and water, hurricanes have always been fascinating. Early warnings have all but eliminated surprise, yet these storms often defy attempts to prepare. Always vulnerable, we must know what to expect.

Hurricanes affecting the East Coast are born as tropical depressions in the Atlantic west of Africa, move westward through the eastern Caribbean, and eventually veer northwest and then north and northeast up our coast. Counter-clockwise winds spiral inward and accelerate toward the eye, the center of lowest pressure. The sharper the drop in pressure, the more violent the winds. Hurricanes lose power as they move north out of the tropics because warm ocean water, the energy source which helped create them, turns cooler.

A hurricane's forward motion, which can vary from 5 to 50+ knots, means that the winds are stronger on the right side. Winds of 100 knots spiraling around the eye, when you add a forward speed of 25 knots, create a speed of 125 knots on the right side, but only 75 knots on the left side, a dramatic difference. Note: a doubling of wind speed means the force on an object is increased four times, so that a wind of 100 knots has four times the power it does at 50 knots.

If the eye is moving directly toward you, the wind direction will remain fairly constant and the velocity will increase until the eye arrives. When the eye passes, the velocity will suddenly increase, rather stronger than before, from the opposite direction. These factors make the vicinity of the eye most dangerous.

In our diagram the hurricane is approaching, and vessels A, B, and C are at positions A1, B1, and C1 relative to the storm. When the storm passes, these vessels will be at positions A2, B2, and C2. Each will have experienced very different wind speeds and directions:

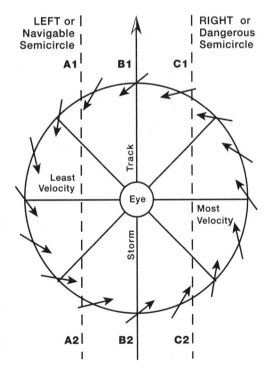

Vessel A, in the least dangerous semi-circle, will experience winds from the NE (at A1), backing to N (least velocity), NW, and finally W (at A2) as the storm passes.

Vessel B (at B1) will have ENE winds, increasing until the eye arrives. After the deceptive calm of the eye passes, the wind will rise, stronger than before, from the WSW (at B2), gradually decreasing.

Vessel C, in the most dangerous semi-circle, has the strongest winds, beginning (at C1) from the E, veering to SE, S (greatest velocity), and finally to SW (at C2).

If space and time permit, try to reduce your vulnerability by proceeding at right angles to the storm track. Which way to go depends on a number of factors, including how far away the storm is, its speed, the speed of the vessel, and sea conditions or sea room on either side of the expected storm path.

Hurricane Precautions Alongshore

Extremely high tides accompany hurricanes. If the storm arrives anywhere near the usual time of high water, low-lying areas will be flooded. Especially high tides will occur in all bays or V-mouth harbors if they are facing the wind direction. High water in all storm areas will remain a much longer time.

At or near the coastline, pull small craft well above the high water mark, dismast sailboats, remove outboard motors, and remove or lash down loose objects.

Seek the most protected anchorage possible, considering possible wind direction reversals, extreme tides, and other vessels. If on a mooring or at anchor, use maximum scope, allowing for room to swing clear of other boats. In a real blow it is easy to slack off, but not to shorten scope. Use as much chain in your anchor rode as possible. Another piece of chain or a weight, attached halfway along your mooring or anchor line, will help absorb sudden strains. Use chafing gear liberally at bits and bow chocks to minimize fraying of lines. Rig fenders to minimize damage from/to other boats.

Shut off gas, stove tanks, etc. Douse any fires in heating stoves. Secure all portholes, skylights, ventilators, hatch covers, companionways, etc. Pump the boat dry.

At a wharf or pier, use fenders liberally. If possible, rig one or more anchors abreast of the boat in the event the tide rises above pilings.

Boats are replaceable: don't wait for the last moment to get ashore!

Hurricane Precautions Offshore

Monitor storm reports on your radio. The U.S. Coast Guard warns all vessels offshore to seek shelter at least 72 hours ahead of a hurricane.

But, if caught offshore with no chance to reach shelter, watch the wind most carefully. First, note that if you face the wind, the eye is about 10 points or 112° to your right. If the wind "backs" (moves counter-clockwise), you are already on the less dangerous side of the storm track. If the wind "veers" (moves clockwise), you are on the right or more dangerous side. If the wind direction is constant, the hurricane's eye is headed directly at you, so make haste to get to the left side of the track.

Use your radiotelephone to advise the Coast Guard and other vessels of your position. Have a liferaft and safety equipment (flares, flashlights, EPIRB, etc.) ready. Put on life jackets. If it is impossible to hold your intended course, head your powerboat directly into the wind and sea, using only enough power to maintain steerageway. If power fails, rig a sea anchor or drogue to keep the bow to the wind.

Sailing vessels heaving to should consider doing so on the starboard tack (boom to port) in the more dangerous semicircle, or on the port tack (boom to starboard) in the less dangerous semicircle, to keep the wind drawing aft.

NOTE: This information is necessarily very general, the diagram (p. 257) is over-simplified, and the suggestions assume a straight storm track. If the storm track curves to the right, vessels A and B will have an easier time of it, but C may wind up on the track. The best advice: monitor weather reports continuously and seek shelter well ahead of time.

National Weather Service – www.weather.gov
National Hurricane Center – www.nhc.noaa.gov
NOAA Hurricane Research – www.aoml.noaa.gov/hrd

Weather Notes
From Maine to the Chesapeake

Sea Fog

There is always invisible moisture in the air, and the warmer the air, the more moisture it can contain invisibly. But when such a mass of moist air is cooled off, as it does when passing over a body of cooler water, the moisture often condenses into visible vapor, or fog. The fog clears when the air temperature rises, from the sun or a warm land mass, or by a warm, dry wind.

To predict fog accurately, you can use a "sling psychrometer." This instrument uses two thermometers side by side, one of which has a wick fastened to the bulb end. After wetting the wick on the "wet bulb" thermometer, the user swings the instrument in a circle for 60-90 seconds. This causes water to evaporate from the wet bulb thermometer, lowering its reading. The dry bulb thermometer simply tells air temperature. The difference in readings between the dry bulb and wet bulb thermometers determines the relative humidity of the air, and - especially valuable for determining the likelihood of fog - the dew point. The dew point is the (lower) temperature to which air must be cooled for condensation, or fog, to occur (see Marine Fog, p. 255; Dew Point Table, p. 261)

Eastport, Maine to Cape Cod

Cold water (48°-55°) off the northern New England coast often causes heavy fog conditions in the spring and summer, when a warm moist southwesterly flow of air passes over it. East of Portland to the Bay of Fundy, fog is not apt to occur when the dew point is under 55°, unless there is a very warm moist wind. The effect of the cold water on the warm air is reduced if the winds become brisk, as they are apt to do in the afternoon. Visibility should then improve.

Long Island Sound and the New Jersey Coast

Summertime warm water (in the 70s) in this area rarely cools down any warm air mass enough to produce fog. This is not the case farther offshore, where cooler water temperatures (in the 50s) can produce fog.

On the south coast of Long Island, when the southwest wind blows toward the shore at the same time as the ebb tide, inlets can become dangerous with short, steep seas. Also, offshore swells can become very high near the mouths of inlets.

On the New Jersey shore, prevailing winds in summer are southerly, increasing in mid-morning to rarely more than 20 knots and usually dying down at dusk. Occasional summer thunderstorms can be expected. Any brisk winds from the east, northeast, or southeast can produce dangerous conditions along this lee shore and at the mouths of inlets. When the wind is from offshore like this, inlets should be entered on a flood tide.

At the mouth of Delaware Bay, seas can build up to a hazardous degree when there is a southeast wind at the same time as an ebb current at the mouth of the Bay.

Chesapeake Bay

There is little chance of fog in this region because of the warmth of the water. The Bay has quirks of its own in weather and sea conditions. It is a narrow and fairly shallow body of water, and winds tend to blow up or down it. Sharp seas can result, depending on the direction of the current and the wind. Opposing forces make for rough water.

Prevailing winds in spring and summer are southerly, freshening in the afternoon after a morning of calm. Summer thunderstorms occur frequently in afternoon and early evening, usually from the west. In the fall, after a cold front passes through, the winds will shift into the north or northeast, usually for three days, and increase in velocity, causing seas to build up. Calm follows for a day or so until the wind shifts to the southwest.

Pinned

by Rusty Kransky

It's a good idea to always check the high and low tides!

Several years ago, a sailing trip with my boyfriend Jeff took us to Chatham, Massachusetts.

We tied up our dinghy to the cement dock and went into town where we strolled around and enjoyed a nice dinner out and made our way back to the dock. There the trouble began.

We had tied the dinghy up loosely to the dock. As the dock was cement it was not a floating dock. The tide had lowered, and our dinghy drifted under the dock, and then became pinned underneath as the tide rose. By the time we arrived the dinghy was firmly pinned under the dock, with no way to get it out.

Low tide was at 2 AM, and so we had no choice but to sit and wait for the tide in order to get the dinghy out. It was about 10 PM then, which meant a good long wait, which wasn't very thrilling. But we decided to sit on the dock and wait the tide out.

Erica M. Szuplat

We hadn't counted on the mosquitoes! They discovered fresh meat and swarmed down on us. We knew in a matter of minutes that we wouldn't be able to sit there for four hours.

Jeff decided the best thing to do was to go to the nearby hotel and ask if we could sit inside out of Mosquito Land. By now most restaurants and bars were closed, so that seemed our best bet. We made our way to the hotel, sweaty, itchy, covered with mosquitoes. I was really unhappy and no doubt extremely crabby.

Headed our way was a crowd of young boys, a Scout troop supervised by two older men. Suddenly the boys all started singing a song I'd never heard:

> I know a song that gets on everybody's nerves
> Everybody's nerves
> Everybody's nerves!
> I know a song that gets on everybody's nerves
> And this is how it goes…

There was a long pause and then the song resumed:

I know a song that gets on everybody's nerves...

Even in my foul mood, I couldn't help myself. I started cracking up, and then Jeff and I were laughing uncontrollably. As they passed, one of the men shrugged at us, grinned sheepishly and said, "Sorry!"

That song helped a lot, and when we explained to the hotel desk clerk what had happened with our dinghy, he stared at us and said, "You couldn't possibly be making THAT up. Sure, you can sit in our lobby, as long as you stay awake."

We sat in the lobby in uncomfortable chairs, reading. By 2 AM the tide had gone down enough for us to retrieve the flattened dinghy and head back to the boat. To this day, on every sailing trip that song is repeated whenever we head ashore... and we've never gotten stuck under a dock again.

Dew Point and Humidity Afloat

Relative humidity (RH) is the measure of the air's capacity to hold water vapor at a certain temperature. At higher temperatures the air can hold more moisture: a 50%RH at 60°F is pleasant, but 50%RH at 80°F is unpleasant because the air is holding far more moisture. High humidity makes fog more likely and tends to make everyone uncomfortable.

Dew point is slightly different. It is the temperature to which air must be cooled for suspended (invisible) water vapor to condense into (visible) water. Fog and rain are examples. Dew on the deck in the morning means the night temperatures were low enough that the air could no longer hold all its daytime moisture.

DEW POINT

Dry-bulb temp. F	Difference between dry-bulb and wet-bulb temperatures														Dry-bulb temp. F
	1°	2°	3°	4°	5°	6°	7°	8°	9°	10°	11°	12°	13°	14°	
+50	+48	+46	+44	+42	+40	+37	+35	+32	+29	+25	+21	+17	+12	+5	+50
52	50	48	46	44	42	40	37	35	32	29	25	21	17	11	52
54	52	50	49	47	44	42	40	37	35	32	28	25	21	16	54
56	54	53	51	49	47	45	42	40	37	35	32	28	25	21	56
58	56	55	53	51	49	47	45	43	40	38	35	32	28	25	58
+60	+58	+57	+55	+53	+51	+49	+47	+45	+43	+40	+38	+35	+32	+28	+60
62	60	59	57	55	54	52	50	48	45	43	41	38	35	32	62
64	62	61	59	57	56	54	52	50	48	46	43	41	38	35	64
66	64	63	61	60	58	56	54	52	50	48	46	44	41	39	66
68	67	65	63	62	60	58	57	55	53	51	49	46	44	42	68
+70	+69	+67	+66	+64	+62	+61	+59	+57	+55	+53	+51	+49	+47	+45	+70
72	71	69	68	66	64	63	61	59	58	56	54	52	50	47	72
74	73	71	70	68	67	65	63	62	60	58	56	54	52	50	74
76	75	73	72	70	69	67	66	64	62	61	59	57	55	53	76
78	77	75	74	72	71	69	68	66	65	63	61	59	57	55	78
+80	+79	+77	+76	+74	+73	+72	+70	+68	+67	+65	+64	+62	+60	+58	+80
82	81	79	78	77	75	74	72	71	69	67	66	64	62	61	82
84	83	81	80	79	77	76	74	73	71	70	67	65	63	84
86	85	83	82	81	79	78	76	75	74	72	70	69	67	66	86
88	87	85	84	83	81	80	79	77	76	74	73	71	70	68	88
+90	+89	+87	+86	+85	+84	+82	+81	+79	+78	+76	+75	+73	+72	+70	+90
92	91	89	88	87	86	84	83	82	80	79	77	76	74	73	92
94	93	92	90	89	88	86	85	84	82	81	79	78	76	75	94
96	95	94	92	91	90	88	87	86	84	83	82	80	79	77	96
98	97	96	94	93	92	91	89	88	87	85	84	82	81	80	98
+100	+99	+98	+96	+95	+94	+93	+91	+90	+89	+87	+86	+85	+83	+82	+100

ESSENTIALS

THOUSANDS OF KNOTS yet most sailors rely on only a few reliables. These are basics and the rest are useful variations. We encourage you to consult that venerable tome, *The Ashley Book of Knots* by C. W. Ashley to refine your cordage skills.

A ROUND TURN SAVED HER MAJESTY'S SHIP: this traditional caution is as true for Elizabeth II's sailors as for the seadogs of Elizabeth I. It's also a low-tech physics lesson: taking one full turn or, better, multiple turns around a piling or bollard multiplies the friction that resists tension. With this dictum the smallest member of the crew can, by keeping the turns tight with mild effort, hold a great vessel securely. Just as importantly, the line can be "slacked away," released in small adjustment amounts in a controlled, safe, calm manner. Like blocks, windlasses, and winches, round turns are a force multiplier giving mortal sailors heroic power.

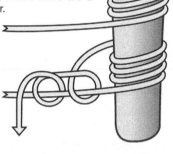

MOST OF MAKING FAST can be as simple as round turns and two half-hitches. There are dozens of hitches (see Ashley) for many special tasks but this basic combination is simple, reliable, familiar, quick. It can be done and undone in the dark. Take enough turns around your holdfast so that you can "slack away" after unlocking the turns from the security of the half-hitches.

CLEATING is closely related to round turns: the cleat is a two-horned friction device. There is no complex technique, only a couple of guidelines. *First*, the "standing part" of the line (coming from the object to be secured) is led under BOTH horns of the cleat, usually clockwise. *Second*, lay figure-8 passes over the cleat's center and under its diagonal opposite cleat to supply friction. Cleats are so efficient that two figure-eights are usually enough for a line diameter that matches the cleat. A dock line is **secured** by folding the last figure-8 under its standing part and tightening this half-hitch. But ask your skipper: some lines – like sheets controlling sails and a few other cleat functions – are never hitched so they're always ready to let go.

Big cleat, small line: take a round turn around the base and three, four , or more figure-8s.

JAN ADKINS for ELDRIDGE 2019

262

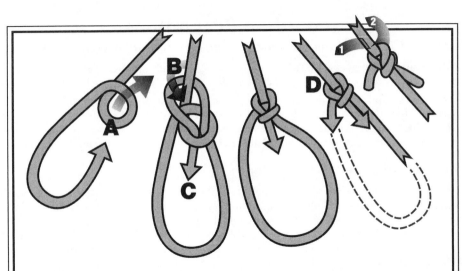

THE BOWLINE is so ingenious that it's the basis for two important nautical knots: it can be a secure loop at a line's end, or it can be a **SHEET BEND** to join two lines. Both are made in the same way. Flip over a circlet in the standing part, **A**, so pulling the standing end will tighten the circlet. Lead the line's end (called the "bitter end") up through the circlet and around the standing part, **B**, then back through the circlet so the bitter end remains inside the loop you've formed, **C**. Important: "fair" the bowline, push and pull it into good shape and tension before it's used. A **SHEET BEND** is tied exactly the same way using two bitter ends, **D**. A virtue of the bowline is that it can be easily undone even after it has been under major tension. It has a latch: push the standing part (upper, in this case), **1**, forward and then push the turn around the standing part, **2**, forward. The knot should now untie easily.

ALL LINES ARE NOT EQUAL. The **BECKET BEND** joins lines of unequal diameters. The smaller line, **A**, is led up through a bight (a U-curve of line) of the larger line, **B**, then around both legs of the large line's bight, **C**, under its own standing end, making several round turns, **D**. The more unequal the line diameters, the more round turns. Remember to *fair* the bend – shape and tension it – before it's used.

THE FIGURE-8 KNOT is a *stopper* or *button knot* used to prevent a line from slipping through an opening like a grommet, **A**. To stopper a line, the bitter end comes back and under its standing part, **B**, around it, **C**, then through the loop it's just formed, **D**. Fair before using this simple, effective, frequently useful knot.

Pollution Regulations

Simplified Regulations for Waste Disposal Outside Special Areas

Prohibited in all waters: The discharge of garbage including synthetic ropes, fishing gear, plastic bags, bottles, packing materials, cooking oil, metal, dunnage, and similar refuse.

Food waste: The discharge of any garbage or ground food waste is prohibited within 3 n.m. of land. Beyond 3 n.m., food waste may be discharged if ground to particles less than 1 inch. Unground food waste may be discharged if 12 n.m. or more from land. In any case, the vessel must be *en route* and discharge should be as far from land as practicable.

The Damage Caused by Pollution

Sewage is not just a repulsive visual pollutant. The microorganisms in sewage, including pathogens and bacteria, degrade water quality by introducing diseases like hepatitis, cholera, typhoid fever and gastroenteritis, which can contaminate shellfish beds. Shellfish are filter feeders that eat tiny food particles filtered through their gills into their stomachs, along with bacteria from sewage. Nearly all waterborne pathogens can be conveyed by shellfish to humans.

Marine Sanitation Devices (MSDs)

USCG-certified MSDs are required on all vessels with installed toilets. Vessels under 65' may install type I, II or III MSD. Vessels over 65' must install a type II or III MSD.

Type I MSDs are allowed only on vessels under 65'. They treat sewage with disinfectant chemicals before discharge. The discharge must not show any visible floating solids, and must have a fecal coliform bacterial count not greater than 1000 per 100 milliliters of water.

Type II MSDs are allowed on vessels of any length. They provide a higher level of treatment than Type I, using greater levels of chemicals to create effluent having less than 200 per 100 milliliters and suspended solids not greater than 150 milligrams per liter.

Type III MSDs are allowed on vessels of any length. They do not allow discharge of sewage, except through a Y-valve to discharge at a pumpout facility, or overboard when outside the 3 nautical miles. They include holding tanks, recirculating and incinerating units.

Portable toilets or "porta-potties" are not considered installed toilets and are not subject to MSD regulations. They are, however, subject to the disposal regulations which prohibit the disposal of raw sewage within the 3 nautical miles of shore.

No Discharge Zones (NDZs)

NDZs are water bodies where the Environmental Protection Agency (EPA) and local communities prohibit the discharge of all vessel sewage. Many States are adding NDZs. **It is the boater's responsibility to be aware of where those NDZs are.** For NDZs by state see https://www.epa.gov/vessels-marinas-and-ports/no-discharge-zones-ndzs-state. See p. 265 for Pumpout Information.

When operating vessel in NDZs, the operator must secure each Type I or Type II MSD in a manner which prevents discharge of treated or untreated sewage.

Type III MSDs, or holding tanks, must also be secured in a manner that prevents discharge of sewage. Acceptable methods of securing the device include: closing appropriate valves, removing the handle, padlocking each valve, or using a non-reusable wire-tie to hold each valve in a closed position. Sewage held in Type III MSDs can be removed by making arrangements with pumpout stations or pumpout boats. Call Harbormaster for details.

Pumpout Information — State Sources

Please be sure to call or radio in advance for rates and availability. While we have taken all possible care in compiling this list, changes may have occurred and we cannot guarantee accuracy. For more current information check the state website or call the agency listed. See also *Pollution Regulations* on opposing page.

Look for the pumpout symbol

For more information on the Clean Vessel Act (CVA), see http://wsfrprograms.fws.gov/Subpages/GrantPrograms/CVA/CVA.htm

Most major harbors now have a pumpout boat. Contact the local Harbormaster. Many monitor VHF channel 09.

MAINE: ME Dept. of Environ. Protection, 207-485-3038
www.maine.gov/dep/water/wd/vessel/pumpout/index.html

NEW HAMPSHIRE: NH Environ. Serv., CVA Coordinator, 603-271-8803
www.des.nh.gov/organization/divisions/water/wmb/cva/

MASSACHUSETTS: MA Coastal Zone Mgmt., 617-626-1624
www.mass.gov/service-details/boat-pumpout-facilities

RHODE ISLAND: RI Environmental Police, 401-222-3070
RI Environmental Mgmt., Marine Pumpout Coordinator, 401-222-4700
www.dem.ri.gov/maps/mapfile/pumpmap.pdf

CONNECTICUT: CT Energy and Environ. Protection, 860-447-4340
www.ct.gov/deep/pumpoutdirectory

NEW YORK: NY State Environmental Facilities Corp., 518-486-9267
www.efc.ny.gov/cvap (link to map at bottom of page)

NEW JERSEY: NJ Fish & Wildlife, 908-637-4125 ext. 116
NJBoating.org

DELAWARE: DE Division of Fish & Wildlife, 302-739-9910
www.dnrec.delaware.gov/p2/Pages/PumpoutStations.aspx

MARYLAND: MD Dept. of Natural Resources, 410-260-8772
dnr.maryland.gov/boating/pages/pumpout/locations.aspx

VIRGINIA: VA Dept. of Health, 804-864-7468
www.vdh.virginia.gov/environmental-health/marina-program/maps-marina/

NORTH CAROLINA: NC Div. of Coastal Management, 252-808-2808 ext. 228
deq.nc.gov/about/divisions/coastal-management/coastal-management-recognition/find-pumpout-stations

SOUTH CAROLINA: SC Dept. of Natural Resources, 843-953-9062
www.dnr.sc.gov/marine/vessel/stationmaps.html

GEORGIA: Georgia Dept. of Natural Resources, 912-264-7218
coastalgadnr.org/pumpout — contact local marinas

FLORIDA: FL Dept. of Environmental Protection, 850-488-5600
arcg.is/1quLP0

Got a Minute?
Angular and Linear Equivalents

Whether you are navigating purely by GPS or using a paper chart, it can be helpful to know how degrees, minutes, and seconds – or tenths or hundredths of a minute – translate into linear distance on the water. Knowing both is important because your GPS can display part of a coordinate as 41° 23′ 25″, or as 41° 23.42′, where each is correct, but one is more accurate.

First, the basics. Latitude is the angular distance north or south of the Equator, and the parallels are equidistant. The latitude scale appears on the vertical edges of your chart. (Longitude, measured east and west of Greenwich and appearing along the top and bottom edges of your chart, is never used for distance measurement.) For practical purposes, the distance between parallels of latitude which are one degree (1°) apart is 60 nautical miles (n.m.).

- 1° (degree) = 60 nautical miles (Ex: from 42° North to 43° North is 60 n.m.)
- 1′ (minute, or 1/60th of a degree) = 1 n.m., or 6076 feet)
- 1″ (second, or 1/60th of a minute) = 101.3 feet (acceptable for general purposes)

The U.S. Coast Guard gives positions of buoys, lights, and lighthouses in degrees, minutes, and seconds, or within roughly 100 feet. (See pp. 173-203).

Sometimes minutes are divided into tenths or hundredths instead of seconds.

- 1′ (minute) = 1 n.m., or 6076 feet
- 0.1′ (1/10th of a minute) = 608 feet (acceptable tolerance at sea; not so near shore)
- 0.01′ (1/100th of a minute) = 61 feet (acceptable for almost any purpose)

Use the Table below to convert seconds to tenths or hundredths of a minute.

Table for Converting Seconds to Decimals of a Minute

From many sources, including charts, Light Lists, and Notices to Mariners, positions are in degrees, minutes, and seconds. These are written either 34° 54′ 24″ or 34-54-24

However, for navigating with GPS, Loran, chart plotters, and celestial calculators, it can be useful to convert the last increment – seconds – to either tenths or hundredths of a minute. The numbers above become 34° 54.40′ or 34-54.4′

Secs.	Tenths	Hundredths	Secs.	Tenths	Hundredths	Secs.	Tenths	Hundredths
1	.0	.02	21	.4	.35	41	.7	.68
2	.0	.03	22	.4	.37	42	.7	.70
3	.1	.05	23	.4	.38	43	.7	.72
4	.1	.07	24	.4	.40	44	.7	.73
5	.1	.08	25	.4	.42	45	.8	.75
6	.1	.10	26	.4	.43	46	.8	.77
7	.1	.12	27	.5	.45	47	.8	.78
8	.1	.13	28	.5	.47	48	.8	.80
9	.2	.15	29	.5	.48	49	.8	.82
10	.2	.17	30	.5	.50	50	.8	.83
11	.2	.18	31	.5	.52	51	.9	.85
12	.2	.20	32	.5	.53	52	.9	.87
13	.2	.22	33	.6	.55	53	.9	.88
14	.2	.23	34	.6	.57	54	.9	.90
15	.3	.25	35	.6	.58	55	.9	.92
16	.3	.27	36	.6	.60	56	.9	.93
17	.3	.28	37	.6	.62	57	1.0	.95
18	.3	.30	38	.6	.63	58	1.0	.97
19	.3	.32	39	.7	.65	59	1.0	.98
20	.3	.33	40	.7	.67	60	1.0	1.00

Table of Equivalents
and other useful information

Length

English	Metric
1 inch	2.54 centimeters
1 foot	0.30 meters
1 fathom	1.61 meters
1 statute mile	1.61 kilometers
1 nautical mile	1.85 kilometers

Metric	English
1 meter	39.37 inches
"	3.28 feet
"	0.55 fathoms
1 kilometer	0.62 statute miles
"	0.54 nautical miles

Nautical	Terrestrial
1 fathom	6 feet
1 cable	608 feet
1 nautical mile	6076 feet
"	1.15 statute miles
1 knot	1.15 mph
7 knots	8 mph approx.

Capacity

English	Metric
1 quart	0.95 liters
1 gallon	3.78 liters

Metric	English
1 liter	1.06 quarts
"	0.26 US gallons

Weight

English	Metric
1 ounce	28.35 grams
1 pound	0.45 kilograms
1 US ton	0.907 metric tons
"	0.893 long tons

Metric	English
1 gram	0.035 ounces
1 kilogram	2.20 pounds
1 metric ton	2204.6 pounds

Weight of 1 US Gallon

Gasoline	6 pounds
Diesel fuel	7 pounds
Fresh water	8.3 pounds
Salt water	8.5 pounds

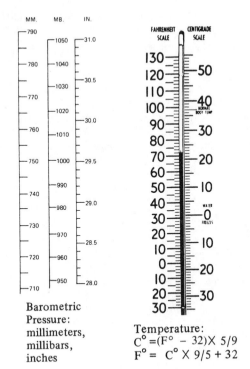

Barometric Pressure: millimeters, millibars, inches

Temperature:
$C° = (F° - 32) \times 5/9$
$F° = C° \times 9/5 + 32$

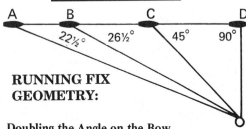

RUNNING FIX GEOMETRY:

Doubling the Angle on the Bow
1. Angle DCO = 45°; Angle CDO = 90°; True distance run (CD) = distance DO.
2. Angle DAO = 22½°; Angle DCO = 45°; True distance run (AC) = Distance CO.

Other Useful Bow Bearings
3. Angle DBO = 26½°; Angle DCO = 45°; True distance run (BC) = distance DO.
4. Example 3 also works with angles of 25° and 41°; 32° and 59°; 35° and 67°; 37° and 72° when distance run will be distance DO.

Nautical Charts

Desirable Cruising Charts From Cape Breton I. To Key West, FL.

Numbers listed to the left are general coastal charts. Indented numbers refer to harbor charts. Scale is included after chart name.

See local Notices to Mariners for critical chart updates!

Canada

4013	Halifax to Sydney 1:350
4279	Bras d'Or Lake 1:60
4447	Pomquet and Tracadie Harbours 1:25
4385	Chebucto Hd. to Betty Is. 1:39
4335	Strait of Canso and Approaches 1:75
4321	Cape Canso to Liscomb Is. 1:108.8
4227	Country Hbr. to Ship Hbr. 1:150
4320	Egg Is. to W. Ironbound Is. 1:145
4012	Yarmouth to Halifax 1:300
4386	St. Margaret's Bay 1:39.4
4381	Mahone Bay 1:38.9
4384	Pearl Is. to Cape LaHave 1:39
4211	Cape LaHave to Liverpool Bay 1:37.5
4230	Little Hope Is. to Cape St. Mary's 1:150
4240	Liverpool Hbr. to Lockeport Hbr. 1:60
4241	Lockeport to Cape Sable 1:60
4242	Cape Sable to Tusket Is. 1:60
4243	Tusket Is. to Cape St. Marys 1:60
4010	Bay of Fundy (inner portion) 1:200
4011	Approaches to Bay of Fundy 1:300
4118	St. Marys Bay 1:60
4396	Annapolis Basin 1:24
4116	Approaches to St. John 1:60
4340	Grand Manan 1:60

U.S. East Coast

13325	Quoddy Narrows to Petit Manan Is. 1:80
13312	Frenchman & Blue Hill Bays & apprs. 1:80
13315	Deer Is. Thoro. and Casco Pass. 1:20
13302	Penobscot Bay and apprs. 1:80
13308	Fox Islands Thorofare 1:15
13288	Monhegan Is. to Cape Elizabeth 1:80
13290	Casco Bay 1:40
13286	Cape Elizabeth to Portsmouth 1:80
13283	Cape Neddick Hbr. to Isles of Shoals 1:20, Portsmouth Hbr. 1:10
13278	Portsmouth to Cape Ann 1:80, Hampton Harbor 1:30
13281	Gloucester Hbr. and Annisquam R. 1:10
13267	Massachusetts Bay; North River 1:80
13275	Salem and Lynn Harbors 1:25, Manchester Harbor 1:10
13276	Salem, Marblehead & Beverly Hbrs. 1:10
13270	Boston Harbor 1:25
13246	Cape Cod Bay 1:80
13253	Plymouth, Kingston and Duxbury Hbrs; 1:20, Green Hbr. 1:10

13236	Cape Cod Canal and approaches 1:20
13237	Nantucket Sound and approaches 1:80
13241	Nantucket Island 1:40
13242	Nantucket Harbor 1:10
13218	Martha's Vineyard to Block Island 1:80
13230	Buzzards Bay 1:40, Quicks Hole 1:20
13233	Martha's Vineyard 1:40, Menemsha Pond 1:20
13221	Narragansett Bay 1:40
13219	Point Judith Harbor 1:15
13205	Block Island Sound and apprs. 1:80
13217	Block Island 1:15
13209	Block Is. Sd. & Gardiners Bay 1:40; Montauk Harbor 1:7.5
13214	Fishers Island Sound 1:20
13212	Approaches to New London Hbr. 1:20
13213	New London Harbor and Vicinity 1:10, Bailey Point to Smith Cove 1:5
13211	North Shore of Long Is. Sd.-Niantic Bay & Vicinity 1:20
12354	Long Island Sound - eastern part 1:80
12375	Connecticut R. -Long Is. Sd. to Deep R. 1:20
12374	Duck Island to Madison Reef 1:20
12373	Guilford Hbr to Farm R. 1:20
12371	New Haven Harbor 1:20
12370	Housatonic R. and Milford Hbr. 1:20
12362	Port Jefferson & Mt. Sinai Hbrs. 1:10
12363	Long Island Sound - western part 1:80
12369	Stratford to Sherwood Pt. 1:20
12368	Sherwood Pt. to Stamford Hbr. 1:20
12367	Greenwich Pt. to New Rochelle 1:20
12366	L.I. Sd. and East R., Hempstead Hbr. to Tallman Is. 1:20
12365	L.I. Sd. S. Shore, Oyster and Huntington Bays 1:20
12353	Shinnecock Light to Fire Island Light 1:80
12352	Shinnecock B. to E. Rockaway In. 1:20; 1:40
12339	East R. - Tallman I. to Queensboro Br. 1:10
12331	Raritan Bay and Southern Part of Arthur Kill 1:15

12327 New York Harbor 1:40

12335 Hudson & E. Rs. - Governors I. to
67 St. 1:10

12326 Appr. to N.Y., Fire I. to Sea Girt
1:80

12350 Jamaica Bay and Rockaway In.
1:20

12323 Sea Girt to Little Egg In. 1:80

12324 Sandy Hook to Little Egg Harbor
1:40

12318 Little Egg In. to Hereford In. 1:80,
Absecon In. 1:20

12316 Little Egg Harbor to Cape May
1:40, Atlantic City 1:20

12304 Delaware Bay 1:80

12311 Delaware R.- Smyrna R. to
Wilmington 1:40

12312 Wilmington to Philadelphia 1:40

12277 Chesapeake and Delaware Canal 1:20

12214 Cape May to Fenwick I. 1:80

12211 Fenwick I. to Chincoteague In.1:80,
Ocean City In. 1:20

12210 Chincoteague In. to Great Machipongo
In. 1:80, Chincoteague In. 1:20

12221 Chesapeake Bay Entrance 1:80

12222 Cape Charles to Norfolk Hbr. 1:40

12224 Cape Charles to Wolf Trap 1:40

12256 Chesapeake Bay-Thimble Shoal
Channel 1:20

12225 Wolf Trap to Smith Point 1:80

12228 Pocomoke and Tangier Sds. 1:40

12230 Smith Point to Cove Point 1:80

12231 Tangier Sd.-northern part 1:40

12233 Chesapeake Bay to Piney Pt. 1:40

12285 Potomac River, DC 1:80, DC 1:20

12286 Piney Pt. to Lower Cedar Pt. 1:40

12288 Lower Cedar Pt. to Mattawoman
Cr. 1:40

12289 Mattawoman Cr. to Georgetown
1:40; Washington Hbr. 1:20

12263 Cove Point to Sandy Point 1:80

12282 Severn and Magothy Rs. 1:25

12273 Sandy Point to Susquehanna River 1:80

12274 Head of Chesapeake Bay 1:40

12278 Appr. to Baltimore Harbor 1:40

12207 Cape Henry to Currituck Bch. Lt. 1:80

12253 Norfolk Hbr. and Elizabeth R. 1:20

12254 Cape Henry to Thimble Shoal
Lt. 1:20

12245 Hampton Roads 1:20

12205 Cape Henry to Pamlico Sd.
incl. Albemarle Sd. 1:40; 1:80

12204 Currituck Beach Lt. to Wimble
Shoals 1:80

11555 Cape Hatteras-Wimble Shoals to
Ocracoke In. 1:80

11548 Pamlico Sd.-western part 1:80

11550 Ocracoke In. and N. Core
Sd. 1:40

11544 Portsmouth I. to Beaufort
incl. Cape Lookout Shoals 1:80

11545 Beaufort In. and S. Core
Sd. 1:40, Lookout Bight 1:20

11543 Cape Lookout to New R. 1:80

11539 New R. In. to Cape Fear 1:80

11536 Appr. to Cape Fear R. 1:80

11535 Little R. In. to Winyah Bay Entr.1:80

11531 Winyah Bay to Bulls Bay 1:80

11532 Winyah Bay 1:40

11521 Charleston Hbr. & Appr. 1:80

11513 St. Helena Sd. to Savanna R. 1:80

11509 Tybee I. to Doboy Sd. 1:80

11502 Doboy Sd. to Fernandina 1:80

11488 Amelia I. to St. Augustine 1:80

11486 St. Augustine Lt. to Ponce
de Leon In. 1:80

11484 Ponce de Leon In. to Cape
Canaveral 1:80

11476 Cape Canaveral to Bethel
Shoal 1:80

11474 Bethel Shoal to Jupiter In. 1:80

11466 Jupiter In. to Fowey Rocks
1:80, Lake Worth In. 1:10

11469 Straits of FL.Fowey Rks., Hillsboro
Inlet to Bimini Is. Bahamas 1:100

11462 Fowey Rocks to Alligator
Reef 1:80

11452 Alligator Reef to Sombrero
Key 1:80

11442 Florida Keys - Sombrero Key to
Sand Key 1:80

11439 Sand Key to Rebecca Shoal 1:80

11438 Dry Tortugas 1:30

Note:

See NOAA's website, www.nauticalcharts.noaa.gov, for U.S. charts available for free in
multiple electronic formats, information on purchasing paper copies, and updates. To find
your nearest Canadian chart agent and updates, see www.charts.gc.ca.

Watch for updates in your local Notices to Mariners. Both sites listed above offer useful
tools to search for updates by chart number.

Fishing Fast-Moving Water
by Lou Tabory

Tide, wind and wave action affect how fish feed. Fish use water conditions to make their feeding easier. Baitfish are a primary food source for most active gamefish. In calm conditions it is much easier for baitfish to hide and avoid gamefish. But when you add in wave action along a beach or waves breaking over a bar the gamefish can feed more effectively. Any kind of flowing water makes it much easier for gamefish to feed.

Stripers are the kings of feeding along beaches when the surf is breaking. I have seen these fish feed when most other species could not swim. They will sometimes even swim up on the beach, grab bait and slide back into the trough. Along most ocean beaches there will be a trough, a deeper section of water created by rolling surf. In some cases, these pockets are formed from waves breaking onto the beach and will constantly keep moving and changing as the wave action changes. Some beaches might look different from one day to the next if wave direction or size changes. Other beaches however may require a big storm to alter the holes and structure along the beachfront. These pockets can hold baitfish that draw gamefish into the water along the beach. If the wave action is light, these pockets can attract bluefish, albacore, and bonito as well as stripers. But if the surf is big then stripers are usually the only New England gamefish that run the surf.

In surf, the best technique is to get your lure to swim in the flowing water along the beach. Watch the water flow and cast angling up current and swim the plug down the flow using enough retrieve to keep control of the lure. Once the lure is down current let it keep moving, getting the plug to swing with the flow. You can use this same technique with fly tackle as long as the waves are not too large. This simple retrieve and swing is very effective in many different surf conditions. For spin fishing the Rebel or Yo-zuri type lures are very effective. For fly fishing 5- to 6-inch-long streamer flies made with active materials will give the fly good action. If you plan to fish at night it's wise to fish in daylight first to learn how a lure acts and what it feels like when the lure flows, swings, and then turns up-current. And swimming plugs or flies are the best lures for fishing in the dark.

Another technique is to try fishing at different angles to the flow and varying the casting distances as well. This helps to place your offering into different locations along the beach. Remember, not all beaches with wave action are the same so plan to work each piece of water carefully, covering as much water as possible.

If you see the ocean speedsters feeding try to determine the bait type and match your lure or fly to its size and color. These fish can be very selective with both lure and fly size. It is often better to use a lure that is slightly smaller than the bait size.

When the surf is smaller there is less flow speed and less water movement so you must keep your lure moving which gives it more action in order to make up for the slower moving water. This is another time when fly tackle is very effective and a time when other species like albies and bonito might be feeding along the beach.

Bucktails and tins are also effective. A3-ounce Hopkins gives good casting distance. Smaller tins work well for albies and bonito and these fish move more quickly along the shore. Try different retrieve speeds and use the rod tip to add action to the tin. When fishing bucktails use the rod tip to make the lure hop. For most conditions I like a short, quick hop unless the water is rolling hard then use larger hops and a slower retrieve. Remember tins and bucktails are effective in many conditions.

Locations with moving water produce great fishing. Rips flowing over bars, water that moves around a point, or flowing water over a reef produce ideal feeding locations for gamefish. Often the flowing water will carry baitfish from one location to another and the moving water traps these small fish. Baitfish in a flow are often easy targets for gamefish. Stripers like to hold in the flowing water using a bar or structure to hide behind. As the bait approaches the stripers bolt out or up to feed. These are ideal feeding conditions because the bait is often pushed from shallow water into deep fast moving water.

Bluefish will sometimes hold in rips or swim slowly into the current. When bluefish feed in schools or large groups they attack the bait creating confusion. All gamefish that travel in schools will feed like this. And once the bait is scattered feeding becomes very easy for gamefish. This is a time when gamefish are easier to catch because they are feeding quickly and recklessly.

This is when surface lures like poppers or rabbits that hop quickly along the surface work well for bluefish. Lure speed is the key when bluefish are feeding in rips. The faster you can move the lure, skipping it along the surface, the more action you'll have. A rabbit style lure is just a block of wood tapered on both ends with weight in the tail. They give excellent casting distance and are easy to fish.

Erica M. Szuplat

When stripers are holding in flowing water, a big swimming plug like a JR Atom can be very effective. Swim the plug along the surface, making it splash by using a sharp pull with the rod tip. Often these plugs need to be fine-tuned by bending down the plug's eye or bending down the plug's lip. You'll know the plug is working properly when it swims just below the surface with the plug's tail leaving a wake. Cast at different angles to the flowing water getting it to swing then keep using the rod tip to pop and splash the plug every 10 to 15 feet. If there is structure get the plug to work just below it and make it splash right when it swings past the structure. Once you get a feel for working rips and surf you'll find that working fast moving water is one of the most productive ways to fish for many New England gamefish.

Lou Tabory has been an outdoor writer for over 40 years and is considered one of the early pioneers of Northeast fly fishing.

It helps to say, "I saw it in the **ELDRIDGE TIDE & PILOT BOOK.**"

INDEX TO ADVERTISERS

For more information about **ELDRIDGE** advertisers and links to their websites visit:
www.eldridgetide.com